Lecture Notes in Computer Science 13704

More information about this series at https://link.springer.com/bookseries/558

Tiziana Margaria · Bernhard Steffen (Eds.)

Leveraging Applications of Formal Methods, Verification and Validation

Practice

11th International Symposium, ISoLA 2022
Rhodes, Greece, October 22–30, 2022
Proceedings, Part IV

Springer

Editors
Tiziana Margaria
University of Limerick, CSIS and Lero
Limerick, Ireland

Bernhard Steffen
TU Dortmund
Dortmund, Germany

ISSN 0302-9743 ISSN 1611-3349 (electronic)
Lecture Notes in Computer Science
ISBN 978-3-031-19761-1 ISBN 978-3-031-19762-8 (eBook)
https://doi.org/10.1007/978-3-031-19762-8

This Springer imprint is published by the registered company Springer Nature Switzerland AG
The registered company address is: Gewerbestrasse 11, 6330 Cham, Switzerland

Introduction

As General and Program Chairs we would like to welcome you to the proceedings of ISoLA 2022, the 11th International Symposium on Leveraging Applications of Formal Methods, Verification and Validation held in Rhodes (Greece) during October 22–30, 2022, and endorsed by EASST, the European Association of Software Science and Technology.

Returning to the traditional in-person event, ISoLA 2022 provided a forum for developers, users, and researchers to discuss issues related to the adoption and use of rigorous tools and methods for the specification, analysis, verification, certification, construction, testing, and maintenance of systems from the point of view of their different application domains. Thus, since 2004 the ISoLA series of events has served the purpose of bridging the gap between designers and developers of rigorous tools on one side, and users in engineering and in other disciplines on the other side. It fosters and exploits synergetic relationships among scientists, engineers, software developers, decision makers, and other critical thinkers in companies and organizations. By providing a specific, dialogue-oriented venue for the discussion of common problems, requirements, algorithms, methodologies, and practices, ISoLA aims in particular at supporting researchers in their quest to improve the practicality, reliability, flexibility, and efficiency of tools for building systems, and users in their search for adequate solutions to their problems.

The program of ISoLA 2022 consisted of a collection of special tracks devoted to the following hot and emerging topics:

1. Rigorous Engineering of Collective Adaptive Systems
(Organizers: Rocco De Nicola, Stefan Jähnichen, Martin Wirsing)
2. Programming: What is Next?
(Organizers: Klaus Havelund, Bernhard Steffen)
3. X-by-Construction meets Runtime Verification
(Organizers: Maurice H. ter Beek, Loek Cleophas, Martin Leucker, Ina Schaefer)
4. Automated Software Re-Engineering
(Organizers: Serge Demeyer, Reiner Hähnle, Heiko Mantel)
5. Digital Twin Engineering
(Organizers: John Fitzgerald, Peter Gorm Larsen, Tiziana Margaria, Jim Woodcock, Claudio Gomes)
6. SpecifyThis - Bridging gaps between program specification paradigms
(Organizers: Wolfgang Ahrendt, Marieke Huisman, Mattias Ulbrich, Paula Herber)
7. Verification and Validation of Concurrent and Distributed Heterogeneous Systems
(Organizers: Marieke Huisman, Cristina Seceleanu)
8. Formal Methods Meet Machine Learning
(Organizers: Kim Larsen, Axel Legay, Bernhard Steffen, Marielle Stoelinga)
9. Formal methods for DIStributed COmputing in future RAILway systems
(Organizers: Alessandro Fantechi, Stefania Gnesi, Anne Haxthausen)

10. Automated Verification of Embedded Control Software
(Organizers: Dilian Gurov, Paula Herber, Ina Schaefer)
11. Digital Thread in Smart Manufacturing
(Organizers: Tiziana Margaria, Dirk Pesch, Alan McGibney)

It also included the following the embedded or co-located events:

- Doctoral Symposium and Poster Session (Sven Jörges, Salim Saay, Steven Smyth)
- Industrial Day (Axel Hessenkämper, Falk Howar, Hardi Hungar, Andreas Rausch)
- DIME Days 2022 (Tiziana Margaria, Bernhard Steffen)

Altogether, the proceedings of ISoLA 2022 comprises contributions collected in four volumes:

- Part 1: Verification Principles
- Part 2: Software Engineering
- Part 3: Adaptation and Learning
- Part 4: Practice

We thank the track organizers, the members of the program committee, and their reviewers for their effort in selecting the papers to be presented, the local Organization Chair, Petros Stratis, and the EasyConferences team for their continuous precious support during the entire period preceding the events, and the Springer for being, as usual, a very reliable partner for the proceedings production. Finally, we are grateful to Christos Therapontos for his continuous support for the Web site and the program, and to Steve Bosselmann for his help with the editorial system EquinOCS.

Special thanks are due to the following organizations for their endorsement: EASST (European Association of Software Science and Technology) and Lero - The Irish Software Research Centre, along with our own institutions - TU Dortmund and the University of Limerick.

We wish you, as an ISoLA participant, lively scientific discussions at this edition, and also later, when reading the proceedings, valuable new insights that contribute to your research and its uptake.

October 2022

Bernhard Steffen
Tiziana Margaria

Organization

Program Committee Chairs

Margaria, Tiziana	University of Limerick and Lero, Ireland
Steffen, Bernhard	TU Dortmund University, Germany

Program Committee

Ahrendt, Wolfgang	Chalmers University of Technology, Sweden
Cleophas, Loek	Eindhoven University of Technology (TU/e), The Netherlands
De Nicola, Rocco	IMT School for Advanced Studies, Italy
Demeyer, Serge	Universiteit Antwerpen, Belgium
Fantechi, Alessandro	Università di Firenze, Italy
Fitzgerald, John	Newcastle University, UK
Gnesi, Stefania	ISTI-CNR, Italy
Gomes, Claudio	Aarhus University, Denmark
Gurov, Dilian	KTH Royal Institute of Technology, Sweden
Havelund, Klaus	Jet Propulsion Laboratory, USA
Haxthausen, Anne	Technical University of Denmark, Denmark
Herber, Paula	University of Münster, Germany
Hessenkämper, Axel	Schulz Systemtechnik GmbH, Germany
Howar, Falk	TU Dortmund University, Germany
Huisman, Marieke	University of Twente, The Netherlands
Hungar, Hardi	German Aerospace Center, Germany
Hähnle, Reiner	TU Darmstadt, Germany
Jähnichen, Stefan	TU Berlin, Germany
Jörges, Sven	FH Dortmund, Germany
Lamprecht, Anna-Lena	University of Potsdam, Germany
Larsen, Kim	Aalborg University, Denmark
Larsen, Peter Gorm	Aarhus University, Denmark
Legay, Axel	UCLouvain, Belgium
Leucker, Martin	University of Lübeck, Germany
Mantel, Heiko	TU Darmstadt, Germany
Margaria, Tiziana	University of Limerick and Lero, Ireland
McGibney, Alan	Munster Technological University, Ireland
Pesch, Dirk	University College Cork, Ireland
Rausch, Andreas	Clausthal University of Technology, Germany

Saay, Salim	University of Limerick, Ireland
Schaefer, Ina	Karlsruhe Institute of Technology, Germany
Seceleanu, Cristina	Mälardalen University, Sweden
Smyth, Steven	TU Dortmund University, Germany
Steffen, Bernhard	TU Dortmund University, Germany
Stoelinga, Marielle	University of Twente, The Netherlands
Ulbrich, Mattias	Karlsruhe Institute of Technology, Germany
Wirsing, Martin	LMU Munich, Germany
Woodcock, Jim	University of York, UK
ter Beek, Maurice	ISTI-CNR, Italy

Additional Reviewers

Abbas, Houssam
Adelt, Julius
Alberts, Elvin
Arbab, Farhad
Bainczyk, Alexander
Barbanera, Franco
Beckert, Bernhard
Berducci, Luigi
Beringer, Lennart
Bettini, Lorenzo
Bhattacharyya, Anirban
Blanchard, Allan
Boerger, Egon
Bogomolov, Sergiy
Bonakdarpour, Borzoo
Bortolussi, Luca
Bourr, Khalid
Brandstätter, Andreas
Breslin, John
Broy, Manfred
Bubel, Richard
Bures, Tomas
Busch, Daniel
Chaudhary, Hafiz Ahmad Awais
Chiti, Francesco
Ciancia, Vincenzo
Cok, David
Cordy, Maxime
Damiani, Ferruccio
De Donato, Lorenzo
Demrozi, Florenc
Di Stefano, Luca
Dierl, Simon
Dubslaff, Clemens
Duchêne, Fabien
Eldh, Sigrid
Ernst, Gidon
Feng, Hao
Flammini, Francesco
Freitas, Leo
Gabor, Thomas
Gerastathopoulos, Ilias
Groote, Jan Friso
Grosu, Radu
Grunske, Lars
Hallerstede, Stefan
Hansen, Simon Thrane
Hartmanns, Arnd
Hatcliff, John
Heydari Tabar, Asmae
Hnetynka, Petr
Inverso, Omar
Jakobs, Marie-Christine
John, Jobish
Johnsen, Einar Broch
Jongmans, Sung-Shik
Kamburjan, Eduard
Katsaros, Panagiotis
Kittelmann, Alexander
Knapp, Alexander
Kosmatov, Nikolai
Kretinsky, Jan

Kuruppuarachchi, Pasindu
Köhl, Maximilan
König, Christoph
Könighofer, Bettina
Lee, Edward
Lluch Lafuente, Alberto
Loreti, Michele
Madsen, Ole Lehrmann
Massink, Mieke
Mauritz, Malte
Mazzanti, Franco
Merz, Stephan
Micucci, Daniela
Monica, Stefania
Monti, Raul
Morichetta, Andrea
Nardone, Roberto
Naujokat, Stefan
Nayak, Satya Prakash
Neider, Daniel
Niehage, Mathis
Nolte, Gerrit
Ölvecky, Peter
Pace, Gordon
Perez, Guillermo
Petrov, Tatjana
Phan, Thomy
Piterman, Nir
Pugliese, Rosario
Reisig, Wolfgang
Remke, Anne
Riganelli, Oliviero
Ritz, Fabian
Rocha, Henrique
Runge, Tobias
Santen, Thomas
Scaletta, Marco
Schallau, Till
Schiffl, Jonas
Schlatte, Rudolf
Schlüter, Maximilian
Schneider, Gerardo
Schürmann, Jonas
Seisenberger, Monika
Smyth, Steven
Soudjani, Sadegh
Spellini, Stefano
Stankaitis, Paulius
Stewing, Richard
Stolz, Volker
Tapia Tarifa, Silvia Lizeth
Tegeler, Tim
Tiezzi, Francesco
Trubiani, Catia
Tschaikowski, Max
Tuosto, Emilio
Valiani, Serenella
Van Bladel, Brent
van de Pol, Jaco
Vandin, Andrea
Vittorini, Valeria
Weber, Alexandra
Weigl, Alexander
Wright, Thomas
Zambonelli, Franco

Contents – Part IV

Digital Twin Engineering

Engineering of Digital Twins for Cyber-Physical Systems ... 3
John Fitzgerald, Peter Gorm Larsen, Tiziana Margaria, Jim Woodcock, and Cláudio Gomes

Towards Requirements Engineering for Digital Twins of Cyber-Physical Systems ... 9
Tao Yue, Shaukat Ali, Paolo Arcaini, and Fuyuki Ishikawa

Digital Twins for Organ Preservation Devices ... 22
Aaron John Buhagiar, Leo Freitas, William E. Scott III, and Peter Gorm Larsen

Using Digital Twins in the Development of Complex Dependable Real-Time Embedded Systems ... 37
Xiaotian Dai, Shuai Zhao, Benjamin Lesage, and Iain Bate

Towards Reactive Planning with Digital Twins and Model-Driven Optimization ... 54
Martin Eisenberg, Daniel Lehner, Radek Sindelar, and Manuel Wimmer

Digital Twin Reconfiguration Using Asset Models ... 71
Eduard Kamburjan, Vidar Norstein Klungre, Rudolf Schlatte, S. Lizeth Tapia Tarifa, David Cameron, and Einar Broch Johnsen

Formally Verified Self-adaptation of an Incubator Digital Twin ... 89
Thomas Wright, Cláudio Gomes, and Jim Woodcock

Adaptive Data-driven Predictor of Ship Maneuvering Motion Under Varying Ocean Environments ... 110
Tongtong Wang, Robert Skulstad, Motoyasu Kanazawa, Lars Ivar Hatledal, Guoyuan Li, and Houxiang Zhang

Robust Adaptive Back-Stepping Control Approach Using Quadratic Lyapunov Functions for MMC-Based HVDC Digital Twins ... 126
Le Liu, Aleksandra Lekić, and Marjan Popov

Data-Driven Reachability Analysis of Digital Twin FMI Models ... 139
Sergiy Bogomolov, John Fitzgerald, Sadegh Soudjani, and Paulius Stankaitis

Towards Secure Digital Twins 159
Tomas Kulik, Cláudio Gomes, Hugo Daniel Macedo, Stefan Hallerstede, and Peter Gorm Larsen

Digital Thread in Smart Manufacturing

Digital Thread in Smart Manufacturing 179
Tiziana Margaria, Dirk Pesch, and Alan McGibney

Integrating Wearable and Camera Based Monitoring in the Digital Twin for Safety Assessment in the Industry 4.0 Era 184
Michele Boldo, Nicola Bombieri, Stefano Centomo, Mirco De Marchi, Florenc Demrozi, Graziano Pravadelli, Davide Quaglia, and Cristian Turetta

Model-Driven Engineering in Digital Thread Platforms: A Practical Use Case and Future Challenges 195
Hafiz Ahmad Awais Chaudhary, Ivan Guevara, Jobish John, Amandeep Singh, Amrita Ghosal, Dirk Pesch, and Tiziana Margaria

Trust and Security Analyzer for Collaborative Digital Manufacturing Ecosystems 208
Pasindu Kuruppuarachchi, Susan Rea, and Alan McGibney

DISTiL: DIStributed Industrial Computing Environment for Trustworthy DigiTaL Workflows: A Design Perspective 219
Alan McGibney and Sourabh Bharti

Using Model Selection and Reduction to Develop an Empirical Model to Predict Energy Consumption of a CNC Machine 227
Liam Morris, Rose Clancy, Andriy Hryshchenko, Dominic O'Sullivan, and Ken Bruton

Crazy Nodes: Towards Ultimate Flexibility in Ubiquitous Big Data Stream Engineering, Visualisation, and Analytics, in Smart Factories 235
Mirco Soderi and John G. Breslin

Formal Methods for DIStributed COmputing in Future RAILway Systems

Formal Methods for Distributed Control Systems of Future Railways 243
Alessandro Fantechi, Stefania Gnesi, and Anne E. Haxthausen

Safe and Secure Future AI-Driven Railway Technologies: Challenges for Formal Methods in Railway 246
Monika Seisenberger, Maurice H. ter Beek, Xiuyi Fan, Alessio Ferrari, Anne E. Haxthausen, Phillip James, Andrew Lawrence, Bas Luttik, Jaco van de Pol, and Simon Wimmer

Future Train Control Systems: Challenges for Dependability Assessment 269
Alessandro Fantechi, Stefania Gnesi, and Gloria Gori

Standardisation Considerations for Autonomous Train Control 286
Jan Peleska, Anne E. Haxthausen, and Thierry Lecomte

Automatic Generation of Domain-Aware Control Plane Logic for Software Defined Railway Communication Networks 308
Roberto Canonico, Francesco Flammini, Stefano Marrone, Roberto Nardone, and Valeria Vittorini

Safe and Secure Architecture Using Diverse Formal Methods 321
Thierry Lecomte

Industrial Day

Formal Methods for a Digital Industry: Industrial Track at ISoLA 2022 337
Axel Hessenkämper, Falk Howar, Hardi Hungar, and Andreas Rausch

Domain-Specificity as Enabler for Global Organization aLignment and Decision 340
Barbara Steffen and Steve Boßelmann

Evolving Data Space Technologies: Lessons Learned from an IDS Connector Reference Implementation 366
Julia Pampus, Brian-Frederik Jahnke, and Ronja Quensel

Towards a Methodology for Formally Analyzing Federated Identity Management Systems 382
Katerina Ksystra, Maria Dimarogkona, Nikolaos Triantafyllou, Petros Stefaneas, and Petros Kavassalis

Model-Driven Edge Analytics: Practical Use Cases in Smart Manufacturing . 406
Ivan Guevara, Hafiz Ahmad Awais Chaudhary, and Tiziana Margaria

Author Index 423

Digital Twin Engineering

Engineering of Digital Twins for Cyber-Physical Systems

John Fitzgerald[1], Peter Gorm Larsen[2](✉), Tiziana Margaria[3], Jim Woodcock[2,4], and Cláudio Gomes[2]

[1] School of Computing, Newcastle University, Newcastle upon Tyne, UK
John.Fitzgerald@ncl.ac.uk
[2] DIGIT, Department of Electrical and Computer Engineering, Aarhus University, Aarhus, Denmark
{pgl,claudio.gomes}@ece.au.dk
[3] University of Limerick and Confirm, Limerick, Ireland
Tiziana.Margaria@ul.ie
[4] Department of Computer Science, University of York, York, UK
jim.woodcock@york.ac.uk

Abstract. Technologicaladvances in sensing, communications, and data analytics make it possible to construct virtual replicas of Cyber-Physical Systems (CPSs). Such replicas are known as digital twins. They can either make decisions on system updates during operation or provide input to decision-makers for system evolution. This short paper introduces the ISoLA 2022 series of papers on the technology and practice in engineering dependable digital twins for CPSs. The focus is on the relationship between model-based design, machine learning, digital twins and CPSs from different application domains.

1 Introduction

Ensuring the dependability of Cyber-Physical Systems (CPSs) poses challenges for model-based engineering. These stem from the semantic heterogeneity of the models of computational, physical, and human processes, and the range of stakeholders involved. Delivering such dependability requires the coordinated use of multi-disciplinary models. These include models developed during design and models derived from data gathered during system operation. These models form the basis of a learning *digital twin*, able to inform or conduct decision-making both in redesign and in operation.

There is extensive and diverse literature on digital twins and it is growing fast [7]. In 2018 digital twin technology was at the top of the hype cycle from the Gartner group[1] and in 2019 it was identified as one of the 10 strategically most important technologies, because of the many potential benefits of establishing digital twins[2]. In 2022 the Gartner group estimate that the market for digital twins is growing significantly[3]:

---

[1] See https://tinyurl.com/yc86c53v.
[2] See https://tinyurl.com/y5wkfewe.
[3] See www.gartner.com/en/documents/4011590.

T. Margaria and B. Steffen (Eds.): ISoLA 2022, LNCS 13704, pp. 3–8, 2022.
https://doi.org/10.1007/978-3-031-19762-8_1

> The digital twin market will cross the chasm in 2026 to reach $183 billion in revenue by 2031, with composite digital twins presenting the largest opportunity. Product leaders must build ecosystems and libraries of prebuilt function and vertical market templates to drive competitiveness.

The benefits claimed for digital twins include the ability to:

1. Reduce time to market;
2. Establish preventive maintenance possibilities;
3. Enable additional services for the users;
4. Visualise the physical twin;
5. Enable fault detection and possibly fault diagnosis;
6. Increase autonomy; and
7. Provide decision support capabilities.

Although there is great potential in digital twins, the technology poses many open research questions for both researchers and practitioners. For example, the inclusion of humans in the loop and the need for dependability so that decisions based on twins are sound. The foundations, processes, techniques, and tools for engineering digital twins have not so far been the subject of large-scale and systematic study. Important research questions for such a study must include:

- What foundations are needed for a dependable digital twin of a CPS?
- What are the key concepts to be captured in understanding the requirements for a digital twin?
- Where are the limits for a digital twin? When is it 'good enough'?
- What value can be expected from a digital twin and when it is worthwhile constructing one?

Although much research has been focussed on digital twins for mainly physical systems, the increasingly cyber-physical character of systems on which people, businesses and societies rely comes into play here also. The dependable operation of a CPS requires the ability to address the consequences of evolving system components. It also requires the ability to explore and identify optimal changes that do not unduly compromise overall dependability. This combination of prediction and response, alongside support for informed decision-making and redesign by humans, requires both the data derived from operations and the models developed in design. Tackling the challenges of CPS design thus requires a marriage of both descriptive multi-models developed in a design process and inductive models derived from data acquired during operation. This combination of models, cutting across formalisms as well as across design and operation, has the potential to form a learning digital twin for a CPS, enabling off-line and online decision-making. However, it also makes it imperative that a discipline of Digital Twin Engineering for dependable CPSs should be encouraged to emerge.

The goal of the track on the Engineering of Digital Twins for CPSs at ISoLA 2022 is to discuss the well-founded engineering of digital twins for dependability with autonomy. To make the benefits listed above a reality, there are important challenges to overcome. These include:

- The creation of a common basis for discourse in this multidisciplinary field;
- The creation of a design methodology to cope with the uncertainties that arise when computational process interact with the physical environment;
- Patterns for CPS architecture;
- Multi-model and operational verification and validation.

The papers selected for this track address some of these issues from the perspective of formal and model-based approaches. They exploit advances in modelling and verification to address the dependability of digital twins for CPSs. The 11 papers in this track fall into two broad categories. The first is where the focus is on different technological solutions and approaches for elements of the engineering of digital twins in a generic setting (typically, simple use-cases). The second category is where the focus is on the application domain. In all cases, there are safety-critical and/or security-critical aspects.

2 Contributions

The handling of requirements for digital twins is crucial for the success of the value they bring to the system operators. Yue et al. provide a comprehensive discussion of the context and realities of digital twin engineering [13]. Their paper focuses on how requirements engineering affects digital twins. They outline the subject, identify research questions, and provide many pointers to the patchy literature. They consider the evolution and uncertainties of digital twins from a requirements perspective.

Dai et al. [3] suggest using a digital twin for improving the timing analysis of complex real-time embedded systems compared with the traditional worst-case execution time approach. That is a novel use of digital twins but their framework may be more widely applicable. Their target is to improve the performance and resilience of multi-core embedded systems. They describe a method for analysing the temporal properties of digital twins. It is a challenge to construct models with suitable fidelity and abstraction that captures the properties of a real-time embedded system. Dai et al. address the challenge with their approach that decides if the model should be manually updated or not.

When a CPS is deployed it may have an initial plan for its optimal behaviour. More often, a new plan must be created for the initial operational conditions. Eisenberg et al. [4] introduce a reactive planning framework in a digital twin context applied to a simple case of a stack load-balancing system. As the calculation of re-planning takes time, the main issue here is how the system reacts with the re-planning time. Eisenberg et al. propose two re-planning strategies: idle-mode and on-the-fly-mode. Idle mode stops the system immediately and uses the current state of the runtime model to do the planning. On-the-fly-mode does not stop the system but runs a simulation. This requires the simulation to be fast enough. The simulation is used to predict the future states of the system, which are then used for planning.

Kamburjan et al. [8] consider how to support reconfiguration of a CPS in a digital twin context. They illustrate this with a language called SMOL (Semantic

Micro Object Language) focusing on structural changes. It does not currently work on real digital twins. Instead, it uses an abstraction based on asset models that are queried to detect allowed structural changes. It uses detected discrepancies to reconfigure the digital twin using an event handler. Kamburjan et al. propose a technology based on a simple motivating example of temperature control in a building.

Bogomolov et al. [1] present a novel simulation-based reachability method for black-box systems in the context of digital twins and FMI (Functional Markup Interface) models. Their approach uses robust convex optimisation and a method based on an extreme value theorem to approximate Lipschitz constants. They use these to compute the set of reachable states. They apply results on robust complex optimisation to determine the number of samples required to guarantee a given probabilistic confidence for the computed set. They evaluate randomly sampled linear systems to assess the accuracy of the approximate Lipschitz constants. They compare the computed sets to those from an existing model-based reachability tool. They also evaluate the computed sets for an example non-linear system.

If one dares to take the human operator out of the loop, then digital twins can help enable autonomy. Wright et al. [12] consider how to formally verify interesting properties of a digital twin in a safety-critical setting. Their case study is a simple incubator where the variation of the environment is limited [5]. Wright et al. propose a new method for the evaluation of discrepancies between digital and physical twins for continuous systems. They explore self-adaptation based on simulation runs to find new configuration parameters that fit the physical twin. Their techniques are based on STL (Signal Temporal Logic) property verification. They compute the envelope of potential behaviours for the system and check that the property is always satisfied.

As well as safety, security aspects are important for digital twins. Communication channels between a physical and a digital twin open up new attack vectors. Kulik et al. [9] systematically analyse different attacks and mitigations that counter them. A novel contribution here is a supporting notation for describing security properties of digital twins. This paper also using the incubator as a case study.

Four of the contributed papers examine the potential and the challenges of machine learning, model-based, and formal techniques in realising the potential of digital twins in specific industry sectors: healthcare, rail transportation, autonomous ships, and energy grids.

Buhagiar et al.'s contribution is from the healthcare sector [2]. Their work concerns transplanting organs between humans. The organ donor and its recipient may not be co-located, so it may be necessary to transport the organ from one place to another. Buhagiar et al. present a vision of how a digital twin can improve the current approach of ensuring the preservation and healthiness of the organs during transport. The heterogeneous models used in their approach are interdisciplinary. The uncertainties in the behaviour of organs from different people may make it impossible to use digital twins.

Transportation using ships has some extra challenges from the environment because of the uncertainties at sea with different weather conditions. Wang et al. [11] propose an adaptive, data-driven predictor for ship movements. Their approach copes with the ocean environment: wind, waves, and currents. They validate their approach using co-simulation and a Gaussian process predictor. This adaptive predictor provides future velocity forecasts with confidence intervals using an anomaly detector. Ship operations are co-simulated under dynamic environments to supply credible manoeuvring data. Some experimental results attest to the effectiveness of the proposed predictor.

Finally, Liu et al. [10] consider the use of digital twins in relation to energy grids, where uncertainties come from consumers. They present a new approach: Robust Adaptive Back-stepping Control, which secures vulnerable power-electronic equipment. The major advantage of the controller is a smooth transient response and accurate tracking abilities, which is superior to classical control methods. They demonstrate their approach on a power-system digital twin using a real-time digital simulator.

3 Concluding Remarks

The contributions in this track show that realising the considerable potential benefits of digital twins for CPSs presents many challenges and opportunities for research and innovation. It is not a matter of using heterogeneous design models and streaming data from a physical twin to identify discrepancies. The papers presented in this track tackle safety and security aspects. But many other factors have a significant impact on the interaction between the physical and digital twins. These must be considered before a digital twin's predictive functionality is sufficiently dependable. We look forward to the results of interdisciplinary research over the next decade, as digital twin technology delivers its promise in different application domains. We will learn lessons to include in a book about engineering digital twins currently in production [6].

Acknowledgment. We acknowledge the support of the Poul Due Jensen Foundation for research in the engineering of digital twins; the European Union's funding of HUBCAP (Grant Agreement 872698) and DIGITbrain (Grant Agreement 952071); the Innovation Foundation Denmark for funding MADE FAST; AgroRobottiFleet, ITEA3 for funding the UPSIM project (19006) and Confirm - Smart Manufacturing Ireland (Science Foundation Ireland grant 16/RC/3918).

References

1. Bogomolov, S., Fitzgerald, J., Soudjani, S., Stankaitis, P.: Data-driven reachability analysis of digital twin FMI models. In: Margaria, T., Steffen, B. (eds.) ISoLA 2022. LNCS, vol. 13704, pp. 139–158. Springer, Switzerland (2022). https://doi.org/10.1007/978-3-031-19762-8

2. Buhagiar, A.J., Freitas, L., Scott III, W.E., Larsen, P.G.: Digital twins for organ preservation devices. In: Margaria, T., Steffen, B. (eds.) ISoLA 2022. LNCS, vol. 13704, pp. 22–36. Springer, Switzerland (2022). https://doi.org/10.1007/978-3-031-19762-8
3. Dai, X., Zhao, S., Lesage, B., Bate, I.: Using digital twins in the development of complex dependable real-time embedded systems. In: Margaria, T., Steffen, B. (eds.) ISoLA 2022. LNCS, vol. 13704, pp. 37–53. Springer, Switzerland (2022). https://doi.org/10.1007/978-3-031-19762-8
4. Eisenberg, M., Lehner, D., Sindelar, R., Wimmer, M.: Towards reactive planning with digital twins and model-driven optimization. In: Margaria, T., Steffen, B. (eds.) ISoLA 2022. LNCS, vol. 13704, pp. 54–70. Springer, Switzerland (2022). https://doi.org/10.1007/978-3-031-19762-8
5. Feng, H., Gomes, C., Thule, C., Lausdahl, K., Sandberg, M., Larsen, P.G.: The incubator case study for digital twin engineering. Tech. rep., Aarhus University (2021). https://arxiv.org/abs/2102.10390
6. Fitzgerald, J., Larsen, P.G., Margaria, T., Woodcock, J.: Engineering of digital twins for cyber-physical systems. In: Margaria, T., Steffen, B. (eds.) ISoLA 2020. LNCS, vol. 12479, pp. 49–53. Springer, Cham (2021). https://doi.org/10.1007/978-3-030-83723-5_4
7. Jones, D., Snider, C., Nassehi, A., Yon, J., Hicks, B.: Characterising the digital twin: a systematic literature review. CIRP J. Manuf. Sci. Technol. **29**, 36–52 (2020)
8. Kamburjan, E., Klungre, V.N., Schlatte, R., Tarifa, S.L.T., Cameron, D., Johnsen, E.B.: Digital twin reconfiguration using asset models. In: Margaria, T., Steffen, B. (eds.) ISoLA 2022. LNCS, vol. 13704, pp. 71–88. Springer, Switzerland (2022). https://doi.org/10.1007/978-3-031-19762-8
9. Kulik, T., Gomes, C., Macedo, H.D., Hallerstede, S., Larsen, P.G.: Towards secure digital twins. In: Margaria, T., Steffen, B. (eds.) ISoLA 2022. LNCS, vol. 13704, pp. 159–176. Springer, Switzerland (2022). https://doi.org/10.1007/978-3-031-19762-8
10. Liu, L., Lekić, A., Popov, M.: Robust adaptive back-stepping control approach using quadratic Iyapunov functions for MMC-based HVDC digital twins. In: Margaria, T., Steffen, B. (eds.) ISoLA 2022. LNCS, vol. 13704, pp. 126–138. Springer, Switzerland (2022). https://doi.org/10.1007/978-3-031-19762-8
11. Wang, T., Skulstad, R., Kanazawa, M., Hatledal, L.I., Li, G., Zhang, H.: Adaptive data-driven predictor of ship maneuvering motion under varying ocean environments. In: Margaria, T., Steffen, B. (eds.) ISoLA 2022. LNCS, vol. 13704, pp. 110–125. Springer, Switzerland (2022). https://doi.org/10.1007/978-3-031-19762-8
12. Wright, T., Gomes, C., Woodcock, J.: Formally verified self-adaptation of an incubator digital twin. In: Margaria, T., Steffen, B. (eds.) ISoLA 2022. LNCS, vol. 13704, pp. 110–125. Springer, Switzerland (2022). https://doi.org/10.1007/978-3-031-19762-8
13. Yue, T., Ali, S., Arcaini, P., Ishikawa, F.: Towards requirements engineering for digital twins of cyber-physical systems. In: Margaria, T., Steffen, B. (eds.) ISoLA 2022. LNCS, vol. 13704, pp. 9–21. Springer, Switzerland (2022). https://doi.org/10.1007/978-3-031-19762-8

Towards Requirements Engineering for Digital Twins of Cyber-Physical Systems

Tao Yue[1], Shaukat Ali[1(✉)], Paolo Arcaini[2], and Fuyuki Ishikawa[2]

[1] Simula Research Laboratory, Oslo, Norway
{tao,shaukat}@simula.no
[2] National Institute of Informatics, Tokyo, Japan
{arcaini,f-ishikawa}@nii.ac.jp

Abstract. Digital twins (DTs) are promising to revolutionize the way future Cyber-Physical Systems (CPSs) – which are becoming increasingly complex every day– will be developed and operated. To deal with such increasing complexity and to enable CPSs to handle uncertain and unknown situations, DTs provide a viable solution, although they are themselves complicated to build. Thus, a fundamental question is how to engineer DTs for CPSs that are secure and trustworthy. When developing a DT, the first step is the engineering of its requirements to ensure that we are building a correct DT. In this paper, we present our ideas and a research agenda on how requirements engineering of various types of DTs for CPSs should be performed. We present research challenges that need to be addressed, open research questions, and discuss possible solutions.

Keywords: Cyber-physical systems · Digital twins · Requirements engineering

1 Introduction

Digital twins (DT) aim to transform, in a cost-effective and trustworthy manner, the way we currently develop and operate Cyber-Physical Systems (CPS) [4,18]. Many challenges exist to develop functionally correct DT that also ensure extra-functional requirements such as security. The challenges include: how to support the *entire lifecycle* of its corresponding long-lived CPS, how to interact with the CPS without disturbing its normal operation, and how to be secure at all time.

When developing a DT for a CPS, the first stage is to systematically collect, specify, and validate and verify (V&V) requirements of the DT, as both systems are complex. Given that the DT for a CPS can be built at any stage of the CPS

T. Yue and S. Ali are supported by the Co-tester (No. 314544) and WTT4Oslo (No. 309175) projects funded by the Research Council of Norway. P. Arcaini and F. Ishikawa are supported by MIRAI Engineerable AI Project (No. JPMJMI20B8), JST; and ERATO HASUO Metamathematics for Systems Design Project (No. JPMJER1603), JST, Funding Reference number: 10.13039/501100009024.

T. Margaria and B. Steffen (Eds.): ISoLA 2022, LNCS 13704, pp. 9–21, 2022.
https://doi.org/10.1007/978-3-031-19762-8_2

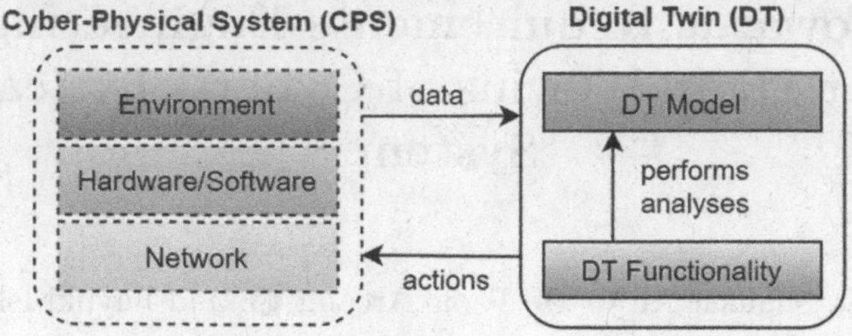

Fig. 1. Digital Twin for CPS.

lifecycle (e.g., development, operation), requirements engineering (RE) methodologies for the DT might vary. For example, when the CPS already exists, eliciting DT requirements can take CPS development artifacts (e.g., requirements, design models) into account. But this is impossible if the DT is developed before the CPS exists. Thus, it is needed to devise RE methodologies for DTs appearing at various stages of the CPS lifecycle.

This paper presents challenges, research questions, and our vision on developing RE methodologies for DTs at different stages of the *DT and CPS dual lifecycle*: developing the DT before the CPS exists, during its development, or after it exists. The outline of the paper is as follows: Sect. 2 provides the context of the work, Sect. 3 discusses RE for DTs, and Sect. 4 discusses common DT requirements. We present related work in Sect. 5, and conclusions in Sect. 6.

2 Context

In [7], a DT is defined as *"a digital replica of a living or non-living physical entity"*. As shown in Fig. 1, a DT is connected to its counterpart CPS, and receives continuous data from the CPS during its operation to synchronize the DT model with the latest state of the CPS. Besides, the DT can intervene with the operation of the CPS.

In our context, a DT consists of *DT Model* and *DT Functionality*. *DT Model* is a *digital* and *live* representation of various parts of the CPS, i.e., hardware, environment, software, and networks. By "live", we mean that the DT's state in the DT model is continuously synchronized with the state of its underlying CPS. Such synchronization can happen instantly when the state of the CPS changes, or it may take a while. Moreover, depending on the purpose of the DT, the abstraction level of the DT model varies. *DT Functionality* performs various activities on the DT model, and has two main features: 1) *Analysis*: it consists in performing, e.g., simulations and predictions about the CPS evolution; 2) *Management*: it consists in managing the CPS and recommending actions that vary from manual human actions to fully autonomous actions. Examples include performing acute maintenance of the CPS, or taking security measures.

A DT is expected to support the full lifecycle of a CPS, starting from its development to its decommissioning. This is also observed in [15], where the authors identified three stages: begin-of-life, mid-of-life, and end-of-life. Sometimes, the DT needs to exist even after the life of its counterpart CPS, to support the development and operation of similar CPSs or to provide new insights to design and operate novel CPSs. To support the CPS development and operation through a DT, a fundamental research question is: how to coordinate the lifecycle of the DT with the lifecycle of its counterpart CPS? Below, we list five such DT and CPS dual lifecycle options:

- **Option 1: CPS and DT do not exist**. This is the typical case when a very complex and safety-critical CPS (e.g., an entirely new smart hospital) needs to be built, and the usage of a DT is chosen to strengthen the safety and the performance of the CPS. Option 1 has three sub-options:
  - **Option 1.1**: Building a CPS and its DT together right from scratch;
  - **Option 1.2**: Starting with building a CPS, and, at a later point in time, starting the development of the DT and aligning its development with its CPS;
  - **Option 1.3**: Starting with building a DT for a CPS, and later introducing the development of the CPS, with the DT that has been (partially) developed as the basis.
- **Option 2: DT first**. It starts developing a CPS from an existing DT. This case could be considered as a typical design approach in which DT serves as a model from which a CPS is built. This case can also occur in product lines, i.e., a DT DT_1 has been developed in the past for a product p_1, and the DT DT_2 for another new product p_2 is derived by extending DT_1 (reasoning on the similarities and differences between p_1 and p_2).
- **Option 3: CPS first**. It builds a DT for an operational CPS to better support its operation and maintenance. This case happens when the CPS has been developed in the past, but further requirements on its operation have emerged. If its re-engineering is not feasible, the development of a DT can be a cost-effective solution. A specific application context of this case is when data from the operation is already available and shall be used to perform advanced analyses by learning from the past data such as anomaly detection in CPS through its digital twin [17].

Thus, the fundamental question to investigate is: how to perform RE for DTs in each of the previous lifecycle options, and what are the challenges of RE in these lifecycle options? This paper will discuss these research questions, and provide research directions and associated challenges.

3 Requirements Engineering for Digital Twins

We discuss RE for DTs by focusing on these three RE stages: requirements elicitation, requirements specification/modeling, and requirements verification and validation (V&V) for the five options (Sect. 2).

3.1 Requirements Elicitation

To systematically elicit DT requirements, well-established requirements elicitation methodologies (e.g., interviews, questionnaires, and brainstorming) can be applied. However, we need to at least take care of the following three aspects that are specific to the DT and CPS dual lifecycle development. First, if possible, activities of eliciting DT and CPS requirements should be coordinated, especially when developing the DT and the CPS together. Second, special effort is required to ensure the consistency between DT requirements with CPS requirements. Third, a special set of requirements are needed for capturing interactions between the CPS and its DT. For example, CPS requirements need to include one requirement on providing interfaces for the DT to get access to the CPS runtime status (Sect. 4.1). Below, we discuss requirements elicitation in the context of each of the five DT and CPS dual lifecycle options (Sect. 2).

CPS and DT Do Not Exist. For *Option 1*, there are three possible sub-options (see Sect. 2). For *Option 1.1*, naturally, activities of the DT and CPS requirements elicitation are inter-weaved and dedicated activities (e.g., brainstorming and requirements reviewing workshops) need to be carefully scheduled to ensure the consistency of their requirements.

It is highly possible that in *Option 1.2*, a CPS has completed its RE stages, it might or might not have completed its design and implementation, and has not yet been deployed. Hence, the input for eliciting DT requirements will include, at least, the CPS requirements. Depending on the progress of the CPS development, the input might include other artifacts such as CPS design models. Dedicated methods (with tool support) can be hence be applied to (semi-)automatically and partially derive DT model requirements (e.g., "the DT shall monitor and visualize (with 2D and 3D graphics) the vessel speed and the ocean current conditions") from existing CPS development artifacts (e.g., a SysML parameter diagram where parameters of vessel and ocean current speed and direction, and constraints among them and their values are specified, as part of the CPS design model). Traditional requirements elicitation methods (e.g., interviews) can still be applied to obtain requirements on DT functionality. To the best of our knowledge, there is no such a method in the literature.

For *Option 1.3*, DT requirements are elicited before CPS requirements and other CPS artifacts. Hence, traditional requirements elicitation methods can be applied. However, the elicitation process is most probably highly iterative and DT requirements need to be refined when knowing more about the CPS requirements and its development.

For all these three options, it is important to ensure the consistency of both the DT and CPS requirements, via dedicated requirements elicitation activities. Traditional requirements elicitation methods might also need to be specialized to accommodate the specialties mentioned earlier (e.g., interaction requirements). For instance, when designing a questionnaire for eliciting DT requirements, questions such as interactions with the CPS should be included in the questionnaire.

DT Exists. For *Option 2*, a DT for a CPS already exists and a new CPS (possibly a new version of the existing CPS, or a similar product of the same product line) must be implemented. Therefore, while doing requirements elicitation for the CPS, also the requirements for the DT need to be evolved/refined. After the requirements elicitation for the CPS has been performed, new requirements elicitation must be performed for the existing DT as well, to check whether the existing DT requirements conform with the CPS requirements and, if not, how they must be modified. Moreover, it could be that the CPS introduced new requirements that need to be considered also in the DT.

CPS Exists. *Option 3* is the most common among the five options, because a lot of CPSs have been developed in the past and now practitioners have started looking for cost-effective solutions of using DT to support the operation of CPSs. There are two scenarios for this option. First, the development team of the DT has no access to CPS development artifacts (e.g., requirements specifications and design models) and it has only access to either historical or live operational data of the CPS. Second, the DT development team has access to both the artifacts and the data.

For the first scenario, the DT model requirements can be partially extracted from operational data of the CPS, e.g., by analyzing the data to extract conceptual elements, which form the starting point to construct the DT model. One such approach has been proposed by Mazon and Trujillo [10]. Dedicated information extraction methods (e.g., using data analytic methods, AI methods) are needed. For the second scenario, in addition to deriving DT model requirements from operational data of the CPS, one might refer to CPS requirements to rationalize the elicitation of the DT requirements and ensure the consistency of the DT and CPS requirements.

For both scenarios, requirements for the DT functionality can still be elicited with traditional requirements elicitation methods. Considering that the CPS has already been built, a lot of design decisions have been made and the freedom of changing the CPS is very limited. Therefore, the DT requirements should explicitly take into account constraints that are enforced by the existing design, implementation, and even application contexts of the CPS. For example, if the CPS does not provide a convenient way to communicate with the DT, the DT functionality is rather limited, as it can only observe the external behavior of the CPS.

3.2 Requirements Specification and Modeling

Rigorous requirements specification and modeling are very necessary, because 1) a DT itself is a complex system and its interaction with the CPS is nontrivial, 2) rigorous DT requirements specifications/models (e.g., UML behavioral models) can be used to better facilitate requirements V&V (Sect. 3.3), and 3) formalized DT requirements (specifications and models) can be used to support other downstream activities of the DT development such as design and implementation.

As for a traditional system development lifecycle, DT requirements should be used as the input to develop requirements specifications and models. There exist a large number of requirements specification and modeling methods such as formal logic specifications, UML behavioral models, and/or modeling requirements with SysML, which can be applied for specifying and modeling DT requirements. However, when selecting such a methodology, one might want to consider using the same methodologies (including tool support) used for developing CPS requirements specifications and models. Doing so potentially eliminates the effort required to perform analyses across DT and CPS requirements specifications and models because, being these defined using the same notations/theories, their conformance can be checked more easily. To formalize requirements about interactions between the CPS and the DT, one might also need to tailor or specialize standard-based methods such as developing an extension to UML use cases for explicitly specifying interactions between the DT and the CPS, along with their properties such as the correctness of the synchronization. Early verification of such interactions is important for automated requirements V&V.

Depending on the option, specifying and modeling DT model requirements might also take CPS development artifacts –such as CPS requirements specifications and models, or CPS design models– as the input for DT requirements V&V (Sect. 3.3). This might lead to refining DT requirements (as discussed in Sect. 3.1) and, consequently, DT requirements specifications and models should be refined as well.

3.3 Requirements Verification and Validation

Requirements V&V are about ensuring that a right DT is being built in terms of satisfying stakeholders' goals and requirements (validation), and that the DT is being built right (verification) by checking that downstream artifacts (e.g., design and tests) are consistent to the DT requirements.

More specifically, requirements on DT functionality need to be validated to ensure that they satisfy what stakeholders want. Traditional requirements V&V methods such as reviews, inspections, prototyping, and model-based (formal) V&V methods can be used for this purpose.

As discussed in Sect. 3.1, DT requirements can be partially derived from CPS development artifacts (CPS requirement specifications and models) if available. If the derivation is done manually, traditional requirement V&V methods (e.g., checklist-based requirements inspection) should be applied to verify the correctness of the manually derived DT requirements. Otherwise, if the derivation was done with an automated solution, systematic methods (e.g., testing, formal verification methods) are recommended to ensure that the automated derivation solution produces correct DT requirements from existing CPS development artifacts.

As discussed in Sect. 3.1, AI can be used to extract information for DT model requirements. So, it is important to check the AI solutions from at least these aspects: 1) training data correspond to real data, 2) sufficient data is available for these solutions, and 2) used data is of high quality (in terms of, e.g., completeness, consistency). Other aspects such as freeing AI solutions from discrimination might also need to be checked when relevant. More discussions on this topic are provided in Vogelsang and Borg's work [16], which nicely discussed RE for ML from the perspective of data scientists.

Regarding Option 1, we recommend to coordinate requirements V&V activities of the DT and CPS so that consistent DT and CPS requirements are developed. Dedicated methods are needed to cost-effectively conduct and align the two activities.

4 Common DT Requirements

We discuss common requirements across different CPS domains that shall be considered when developing DTs.

4.1 Data Synchronization Between DT and CPS

One of the main DT functionalities is to maintain an up-to-date representation of the CPS (i.e., the DT model), over which to perform various kinds of analyses [5]. Hence, a *connection* must be established between the DT and the CPS. In this way, the CPS state can be observed and reflected in the DT state.

So, specific requirements should be specified for describing this connection. Depending on the option, different types of connection (with different strengths) are possible. Each type allows to obtain different views of the CPS, from very detailed ones to more coarse-grained ones. If the CPS and the DT have been developed together (*Option 1.1*), ideally requirements can be specified (without many constraints) to observe the CPS at various levels of detail. Specifically, if a DT functionality is only related to the CPS environment (e.g., temperature), simple IoT sensors can be deployed to sufficiently fit the purpose. On the other hand, if a DT functionality requires to observe the CPS internal state, the CPS will then need to have suitable interfaces allowing the DT to read the state. Note that this is possible because the CPS and the DT are developed together. Similarly, when a DT is developed before the CPS (*Option 1.3*), DT requirements can specify connections having various types of detail, and when the CPS is developed, the type of interface required by the "connection" requirements can then be implemented. On the other hand, if the DT is developed after the CPS exists (*Option 3*), the DT requirements that can be specified regarding the connection are limited, which is dependent on how the CPS has been developed. Specifically, if the CPS did not originally provide suitable interfaces to observe its internal state, the only type of connection is based on external sensors, because these are usually easy to install even for black-box CPSs.

4.2 Modeling Paradigms and Model Fidelity of DT Models

As described in Sect. 2, the DT model is a live representation of the CPS and it is the basis to perform various DT functionalities. So, requirements on DT models should include: how to enable the DT functionalities, being at the right level abstraction (i.e., suitable fidelity), requiring realistic modeling effort, conforming to modeling standards, and having good tool support. With these requirements in mind, we are convinced that Model-Based System Engineering (MBSE) can provide a viable solution to develop DT models [9]. Examples of such models include creating system models with Modelica (https://www.modelica.org/), and physical environment models as mathematical models (e.g., differential equations).

Consequently, the models created with MBSE can be used for supporting DT functionalities. An important requirement to be considered is the *abstraction level* of a DT model. If it is too detailed, there is the risk that it becomes a replica of the real CPS, and it becomes unusable for any real-time prediction activity, as the simulation is too slow to be timely [8]. Moreover, in certain contexts, it is impossible to create high fidelity models due to, for instance, the complexity of the CPS itself, unavailability of qualified modelers, unrealistic modeling efforts required, and/or insufficient knowledge about the CPS, especially for the options that the CPS is still under development (i.e., *Option 1* and *Option 2*).

Note that creating DT models can easily end up introducing unexpected accidental complexity. On the other hand, if a DT model is too abstract, it will not serve as a backbone of DT functionalities. Thus, models at different levels of abstraction could be used for different purposes. More abstract models can be used for a coarse-grained (and fast) analysis, while more concrete models can be used, on request, for performing more detailed (and slower) analyses. As also reported in [5], the fidelity of a DT model is one of the highly considered DT requirements. We believe that carefully designed guidelines (e.g., telling which DT functionality requires modeling which part of the CPS to which level of details) are needed to effectively determine the fidelity of a DT model. If a CPS design model is available when developing the DT model, the CPS design model may be reused as the starting point.

4.3 Extra-functional Requirements

Security and trustworthiness. As described in Sect. 4.1, at runtime, the DT must read data from the CPS to get a faithful representation to be used for different analyses. Sometimes, information read from the CPS may be sensitive and hence particular care should be taken to guarantee its protection. For example, if the DT is modeling a human body (or part of it), a breach in the security of the DT may reveal sensitive information about the patient. As another example, the DT of a building may have access to logs of accesses to apartments, which could be used by attackers to know occupants' habits. Hence, security requirements should be imposed on the DT on the basis of the sensitivity of the managed information.

Regarding the adopted dual lifecycle model, there should be no difference in security requirements. However, more attention to security requirements should be taken when the DT has access to internal states of the CPS (typical of *Option 1.1*, but possibly of also other options).

Note that, while here we have considered the cases that the DT may weaken the security of the CPS, there are some specific application scenarios [6] in which the DT is used to actually increase the security of the CPS (e.g., see discussion of [6] in Sect. 5).

DT performance. DT can provide different functionalities, ranging from runtime monitoring of the CPS to performing predictions. In order to perform such activities, specific non-functional requirements must be imposed on the performance of the DT. For example, if the DT is used for runtime monitoring, it must be fast enough to check at runtime if the CPS is reaching some dangerous state and, eventually, take suitable action. This imposes some requirements on the hardware running the DT, and on the speed of connection between the DT and the CPS. Even if the DT is used for prediction, the complexity of the DT may require particular requirements of the computational power provided by the DT. Consider, for example, the DT for a vessel. The physical models required to represent the environment in which the vessel is operating could be very complex, and so require substantial computational power [14].

4.4 DT Evolution

DTs are expected to live for a long time since their underlying CPSs often stay operational for long time. A DT may even live after its CPS's decommissioning to serve as the DT for other CPSs. Thus, managing the evolution of DTs over time is important. Situations of triggering the evolution of a DT of a CPS include: 1) the CPS evolves as a result of a software update or replacement of a hardware component, etc.; 2) the DT needs to be evolved to accommodate a new requirement (e.g., a new functionality) or refine the DT model when more data from the CPS becomes available. Such requirements need to be systematically elicited, specified/modeled, validated, and verified before they are implemented as part of the evolved DT. Methodologies are therefore expected to facilitate DT evolution by, e.g., clearly telling when it is an appropriate time to trigger the elicitation of new requirements with data. Automatically eliciting and implementing a new DT functionality is very hard (if possible at all) to achieve. But eliciting requirements with operational data of the CPS can be done automatically, as discussed in Sect. 3.1. Therefore, as the initial step, we classify DT evolution into two categories: *static*, e.g., requiring manual update of the DT, and *dynamic*, e.g., autonomous update of DT model with live operational data. Specific methodologies for handling dynamic DT evolution are one of the challenges of the field.

4.5 RE for Dealing with Uncertainty

Uncertainty is gaining notice because of the increasing complexity (in terms of scales, network communications, and/or deployed AI algorithms, etc.) of software systems (e.g., CPSs) and their ever-changing operating environment. DT functionalities are hence needed to elegantly deal with inherent uncertainties of the DT itself, the CPS, and its environment. Consequently, the DT model needs to explicitly specify known uncertainties such that a DT functionality can be implemented to discover unknowns with data from the CPS, through simulations or model execution. Therefore, RE methodologies for handling uncertainty upfront are needed.

There are RE approaches proposed in the context of dynamically adaptive systems in the presence of environmental uncertainty (e.g., [3]) for specifying and analyzing uncertainty in requirements models (e.g., [19]). These approaches are the starting point for specifying and analyzing DT requirements with uncertainty. However, it still lacks RE methodologies that can systematically elicit uncertainty information in requirements, and specify/model such information, based on which discover and analyze unknowns. Moreover, existing requirements V&V methods need to be extended for covering uncertainty information contained in RE artifacts of DTs.

4.6 Requirements Engineering for AI for DT

AI techniques allow for dealing with non-structural data such as images, and predicting future states from time-series data. Such AI advances can enhance both the features of analysis and management in DT. However, the use of AI introduces additional challenges (e.g., ensuring data quality) on RE as discussed in [16], for instance. These challenges are also valid for RE activities of developing AI-supported DTs.

Therefore, requirements of DTs that employ AI should include AI-specific requirements. One of such requirements is about the quality of training data and input data used by AI for realizing DT functionalities. Vogelsang and Borg discussed in [16] that data quality requirements should include data completeness (e.g., about ranges of data), correctness (e.g., on data collections), and consistency (e.g., regarding data formats). Such data requirements should be systematically elicited, specified, modeled, verified and validated as for other DT requirements with proper RE methodologies. The literature, however, does not have dedicated RE solutions for AI applications. Especially for DTs, we also need to consider the performance requirements of employed AI techniques as part of the overall performance of the DT functionalities (Sect. 4.3). The performance of AI is sensitive to several factors, such as the changes in statistical properties of input data over time, i.e., *concept drift* that needs to be explicitly considered. Requirements should also be carefully aligned for continuous monitoring and performance evaluation. Training with runtime data allows the inference model to follow the up-to-date data trend. However, since re-training can change the AI behavior in an unpredictable way, the requirements for automated validation of the updated model become very challenging. Moreover, security requirements should be enhanced to defend against unique attacks such as data poisoning that changes the data trend and thus the AI behavior.

4.7 AI for RE for DT

In some options of the DT and CPS dual lifecycle (Sect. 2) and to support DT evolution (Sect. 4.4), DT requirements can be elicited from the CPS operational data. In such cases, AI techniques (e.g., reinforcement learning, neural networks) can be used for automatically eliciting, verifying, and evolving DT requirements. If they are specified in natural language, Natural Language Processing (NLP) techniques can be used for (semi-)automatically evolving them or generating executable test cases to validate them. Evolutionary computation methods (e.g., search algorithms) can also be applied to prioritize DT requirements, so to facilitate cost-effective requirements review. We hence see a lot of opportunities to enhance RE activities for DT with AI.

Using AI to support RE is not new. It has been recognized decades ago [13] and technologies (e.g., NLP, ML, Neural Networks, Game Theory, and Evolutionary Computation) have been applied to support various RE activities (e.g., [1] and [11]). Especially NLP has been applied to help exploit information in natural language and facilitate various automation (e.g., [12]), and check consistency and completeness of NL artifacts (e.g., [2]). Though there exist a number of AI applications in RE which can be borrowed to support RE activities for DTs, we are not aware of any systematic applications of AI techniques for supporting the full-fledged RE activities for developing DTs. We therefore call for defining a very first road map on this topic. Challenges include how to use AI techniques to improve the cost-effectiveness of (automatically) aligning DT requirements with CPS requirements to ensure their consistency during the long lifecycles of the DT and CPS, and how to wisely use historical and live data of the DT and CPS to refine existing requirements artifacts (e.g., specifications, models, traceability links).

5 State of the Art

A literature review and industry interview on DT requirements in Industry 4.0 is reported in [5]. Motivated by the fact that DT definition and requirements are not well-established, the authors tried to synthesize DT requirements from the literature with industry's understanding of DTs. Results of the review show that DT requirements that most frequently appear in the literature are *real-time data*, *integration*, and *fidelity*. Results of the interview with 7 interviewees show that most of them consider DTs as simulation models, and their main challenge is how to robustly equip DTs with real-time data for enabling actual real-time control of a manufacturing system.

In [6], the authors discuss developing DT requirements as possible use cases across three CPS lifecycle stages (i.e., engineering, operation, and end-of-life), such as security design of a CPS at the engineering stage, detecting hardware and software misconfigurations of the CPS at the engineering and operation stages, secure decommissioning at the end-of-life stage, and intrusion detection during the operation of the CPS. A DT implementing such use cases can be used to potentially enhance the security of a CPS throughout its entire lifecycle.

The paper also presents a list of research directions, and particularly mentions three practical aspects that are generic (i.e., not specific to information security) and across all the three stages of the CPS lifecycle: 1) limited understanding of the required fidelity for use cases, 2) unknown accuracy and performance requirements for use cases, and 3) requiring evaluation in a real-world setting.

To the best of our knowledge, apart from the works discussed above, there is no other work on RE for DT, or discussing DT requirements. This clearly indicates that it is definitely the time to set up a research agenda on RE for DT.

6 Conclusion

Digital Twins (DTs) are recognized as an effective solution to improve the safety, performance, and security of Cyber-Physical Systems (CPSs). A DT monitors at runtime the corresponding CPS, performs analyses (e.g., simulations/predictions) about the CPS evolution, and eventually interacts with the CPS to suggest or perform recovery actions. A DT is a software system whose development can start at different phases of the CPS lifecycle (i.e., options): the CPS and the DT are developed together, the DT is developed before the CPS, or the DT is developed for an operational CPS. In this paper, we discussed how to perform requirements engineering (elicitation, specification and modeling, and verification and validation) for the different options and the common requirements (e.g., data synchronization between DT and CPS, extra-functional requirements) that need to be consider for DTs. Moreover, we provided research challenges.

References

1. Alami, D., Dalpiaz, F.: A gamified tutorial for learning about security requirements engineering. In: 2017 IEEE 25th International Requirements Engineering Conference (RE), pp. 418–423 (2017). https://doi.org/10.1109/RE.2017.67
2. Arora, C., Sabetzadeh, M., Briand, L.C.: An empirical study on the potential usefulness of domain models for completeness checking of requirements. Empirical Softw. Engg. **24**(4), 2509–2539 (2019). https://doi.org/10.1007/s10664-019-09693-x
3. Cheng, B.H.C., Sawyer, P., Bencomo, N., Whittle, J.: A goal-based modeling approach to develop requirements of an adaptive system with environmental uncertainty. In: Schürr, A., Selic, B. (eds.) MODELS 2009. LNCS, vol. 5795, pp. 468–483. Springer, Heidelberg (2009). https://doi.org/10.1007/978-3-642-04425-0_36
4. Costello, K., Omale, G.: Gartner survey reveals digital twins are entering mainstream use. https://www.gartner.com/en/newsroom/press-releases/2019-02-20-gartner-survey-reveals-digital-twins-are-entering-mai (2019). Accessed 21 Sept 22
5. Durão, L.F.C.S., Haag, S., Anderl, R., Schützer, K., Zancul, E.: Digital twin requirements in the context of industry 4.0. In: Chiabert, P., Bouras, A., Noël, F., Ríos, J. (eds.) PLM 2018. IAICT, vol. 540, pp. 204–214. Springer, Cham (2018). https://doi.org/10.1007/978-3-030-01614-2_19
6. Eckhart, M., Ekelhart, A.: Digital twins for cyber-physical systems security: state of the art and outlook. In: Security and Quality in Cyber-Physical Systems Engineering, pp. 383–412. Springer, Cham (2019). https://doi.org/10.1007/978-3-030-25312-7_14

7. El-Saddik, A.: Digital twins: The convergence of multimedia technologies. IEEE Multimedia **25**(2), 87–92 (2018). https://doi.org/10.1109/MMUL.2018.023121167
8. Fitzgerald, J., Larsen, P.G., Pierce, K.: Multi-modelling and co-simulation in the engineering of cyber-physical systems: towards the digital twin. In: ter Beek, M.H., Fantechi, A., Semini, L. (eds.) From Software Engineering to Formal Methods and Tools, and Back. LNCS, vol. 11865, pp. 40–55. Springer, Cham (2019). https://doi.org/10.1007/978-3-030-30985-5_4
9. Madni, A.M., Madni, C.C., Lucero, S.D.: Leveraging digital twin technology in model-based systems engineering. Systems **7**(1), 7 (2019). https://doi.org/10.3390/systems7010007
10. Mazón, J.-N., Trujillo, J.: A model driven modernization approach for automatically deriving multidimensional models in data warehouses. In: Parent, C., Schewe, K.-D., Storey, V.C., Thalheim, B. (eds.) ER 2007. LNCS, vol. 4801, pp. 56–71. Springer, Heidelberg (2007). https://doi.org/10.1007/978-3-540-75563-0_6
11. Palacio, D.N., McCrystal, D., Moran, K., Bernal-Cárdenas, C., Poshyvanyk, D., Shenefiel, C.: Learning to identify security-related issues using convolutional neural networks. In: 2019 IEEE International Conference on Software Maintenance and Evolution (ICSME), pp. 140–144. IEEE (2019)
12. Rosadini, B., et al.: Using NLP to detect requirements defects: an industrial experience in the railway domain. In: Grünbacher, P., Perini, A. (eds.) REFSQ 2017. LNCS, vol. 10153, pp. 344–360. Springer, Cham (2017). https://doi.org/10.1007/978-3-319-54045-0_24
13. Ryan, K.: The röle of AI in requirements engineering. Position paper for the dagstuhl seminar on system requirements: analysis, management and exploitation (1994)
14. Sadjina, S., et al.: Seismic RTDT: real-time digital twin for boosting performance of seismic operations. In: ASME 2019 38th International Conference on Ocean, Offshore and Arctic Engineering. American Society of Mechanical Engineers Digital Collection (2019)
15. Stark, R., Fresemann, C., Lindow, K.: Development and operation of digital twins for technical systems and services. CIRP Ann. **68**(1), 129–132 (2019). https://doi.org/10.1016/j.cirp.2019.04.024
16. Vogelsang, A., Borg, M.: Requirements engineering for machine learning: perspectives from data scientists. In: 2019 IEEE 27th International Requirements Engineering Conference Workshops (REW), pp. 245–251 (2019). https://doi.org/10.1109/REW.2019.00050
17. Xu, Q., Ali, S., Yue, T.: Digital twin-based anomaly detection in cyber-physical systems. In: 2021 14th IEEE Conference on Software Testing, Verification and Validation (ICST), pp. 205–216 (2021). https://doi.org/10.1109/ICST49551.2021.00031
18. Yue, T., Arcaini, P., Ali, S.: Understanding digital twins for cyber-physical systems: a conceptual model. In: Margaria, T., Steffen, B. (eds.) ISoLA 2020. LNCS, vol. 12479, pp. 54–71. Springer, Cham (2021). https://doi.org/10.1007/978-3-030-83723-5_5
19. Zhang, M., et al.: Specifying uncertainty in use case models. J. Syst. Softw. **144**, 573–603 (2018). https://doi.org/10.1016/j.jss.2018.06.075

Digital Twins for Organ Preservation Devices

Aaron John Buhagiar[1(✉)], Leo Freitas[2], William E. Scott III[1], and Peter Gorm Larsen[3]

[1] Translational and Clinical Research Institute, Newcastle University, Newcastle-upon-Tyne, UK
{a.j.buhagiar2,bill.scott3}@newcastle.ac.uk

[2] School of Computing, Newcastle University, Newcastle-upon-Tyne, UK
leo.freitas@newcastle.ac.uk

[3] DIGIT, Department of Electrical and Computer Engineering, Aarhus University, Finlandsgade 22, 8200 Aarhus, Denmark
pgl@ece.au.dk

Abstract. Digital Twins (DTs) are a promising technology for integrating device monitoring and data consumption to improve performance. This technology has seen utilisation in various industries that use cyber-physical systems. An unexpected area is medical devices. In this paper, we explore DTs use for an organ preservation device, which, helps improve transplantation outcomes by actively managing the organ during transport to prevent biological degradation.

Whilst reducing the burden on specialists. Digital twinning offers an exciting direction of development for medical devices to improve transplantation outcomes.

Keywords: Digital twins · Medical device · Organ preservation

1 Introduction

Physical processes can be integrated with a digital aspect to improve their performance. These cyber-physical systems are experiencing widespread adoption, as they generate data to iteratively improve them [39]. In safety-critical cyber-physical systems failure is considered disastrous, as it can be financially costly or lead to severe injury or death.

In safety-critical systems it is often difficult to have access to physical scenarios to gather data. This is more so in medical devices, as clinical trials can be difficult, costly and time-sensitive (as running trials requires additional hospital and clinician time). Moreover, changes to the device may lead to the designation that it is a "new" device hence restarting the certification process.

These issues necessitate strict pre-clinical testing requirements from regulatory bodies prior to reaching trials. Any issues detected during clinical-trials

Supported by ScubaTx™ Ltd. https://www.scubatx.com.

T. Margaria and B. Steffen (Eds.): ISoLA 2022, LNCS 13704, pp. 22–36, 2022.
https://doi.org/10.1007/978-3-031-19762-8_3

halts the process and requires it to restart after being resolved, which can become very costly in terms of time, money and reputation. Trials are also limited in size and scope, making exposing all relevant scenarios unlikely. We argue that, having the ability to digitally emulate the physical system to better test and improve devices before going to trials, can be greatly beneficial. Some organ preservation devices provide a unique challenge: they operate not only during organ retrieval, but also during organ transport. This necessitates that they are accompanied by specialists to set up, monitor and, operate them during transit by adjusting internal parameters and catering for changes in the operating environment. Furthermore, this enables the simulation of a greater number of scenarios than what would be physically possible (due to research-organ availability), hence possibly minimizing failure points before the device reaches the market.

Moreover, currently up to 75% of expert clinician time is spent on ordinary diagnostic and therapeutic tasks [35]. This is the result of numerous time-sensitive complex data that has to be interrogated by trainee doctors and reported to senior consultants thus increasing delay and introducing more chances for human error. Improved monitoring and Visualization technology will help automate this process thus reducing reliance on human interaction that simultaneously decreases delays and incidences of human error. However, in aberrant cases, direct human intervention may still be necessary.

Digital twins (DTs) offer an exciting avenue for dealing with these issues. Through the use of mathematical models, DTs present the possibility of reproducing the physical system digitally. This facilitates the possibility of asking questions about such physical systems without requiring actual physical access. Moreover, DTs can operate in a closed loop system (*i.e.* no external interaction) with the physical device to further improve performance, enabling advanced monitoring and control options during runtime.

In this paper, we explore the use of DTs within medical devices and processes, specifically within organ preservation. First, a brief background about DTs is given in Sect. 2. Next, Sect. 3 provides an overview of medical devices and organ preservation. We use the ScubaTx^{TM} device as a case study in Sect. 4, where we discuss the specifics of what is involved in creating a DT, such as the underlying models and communications required, whilst also looking into the challenges that it presents. We go further by looking into how such a technology might be viewed from the regulatory processes' perspectives. Finally, we discuss the possibility of using DTs for other medical devices and processes, both for organ preservation and beyond in Sect. 5.

2 Digital Twins

A DT is a digital replica of physical assets, processes, people, places, systems or devices, created and maintained in order to answer questions about its physical counterpart [16]. We will denote the latter as the Physical Twin (PT). Coupled with new sensor technology, such replicas can provide a new layer of engineering insight, which will be valuable in optimising product performance, and providing a seed for the next generation of products. The conceptual idea of using a "twin" in an engineering setting dates back to NASAs Apollo program in the 1970s s and it was taken up in a manufacturing setting in 2002 [19].

The concept of Model-Based Design (MBD) covers different types of digital models based on different kinds of mathematics. With the definition given above, one can also potentially see models without connection to physical devices. However, in order to be a DT, the communication between the PT and the DT has to be automated in both directions. An important simplified DT, where there is only automated communication from the PT, but not the other way around, is called a Digital Shadow (DS).

2.1 Aims and Benefits

DTs aim to enhance the value and dependability of the corresponding PTs in different ways. The potential benefits of DTs can be categorized in different areas:

Visualization: when 3D models of the PT exists and data is continuously fed to the DT, PT performance visualization is enabled.

Safety Monitoring: when the PT can cause damage to its surroundings it may be worthwhile letting the DT monitor if there are any potential risks for hazardous situations, such that interventions can be instigated in order to ensure safety for the PT and its surroundings.

Predictive Maintenance: as an alternative to periodic maintenance, it may be possible to use data from the PT to determine when maintenance is required.

Fault Diagnosis: in case a fault of a PT has been detected, it is possible for the DT to be able to diagnose the root cause of the fault and report that to the human operators or to a supervisory control system.

Support for Decision-making: DTs may be able to support human operators for optimal decisions to be taken. For example, be by enabling what-if analysis, such that the operator can try to investigate the potential consequences of different inputs before actually giving the input to the PT.

Re-configuration, Robustness, and Optimisation: DTs may have the capability to re-configure the PT, in order to optimize its performance, increasing robustness. However, before moving to this stage, one needs to have a significant amount of trust in the state of the DT and the ability to handle the situation autonomously in a dependable manner (e.g. through formal modelling).

2.2 Challenges

The main DT challenge is that its models will never be 100% aligned with the state of the PT. Thus, it is necessary to define for any given case when the difference is tolerable. When it is no longer tolerable, it may be necessary to re-calibrate the DT to achieve autonomy [15]. Another challenge that always requires attention is that the state of the PT is never a 100% identical to the DT state because there will always be a time delay in the communication. The DT model(s) can either be based on first principles or models that are based on data using different kinds of machine learning techniques [26].

Functional Mockup Interfaces (FMI), are the de-facto industry standard that enable various important simulations [5] Generally they act as black-boxes to the users so Intellectual Property (IP) can be protected [34].

2.3 Medical Applications

DTs have seen some usage in healthcare. Whilst not specifically used for medical devices or organ preservation, there are some studies on personal and precision healthcare [6,25,38].

Through data aggregation, DTs are used to enable a public data-driven precision environment to gain new knowledge through experiments "*in silico*" [6]. This further enables the possibility of developing personalized medicine. Similarly, public health data can be used with DTs for other applications, such as modelling viral infections or improving individualized disease management [25,38].

3 Medical Devices

Medical devices provide significant benefit in monitoring, diagnostics, prevention and treatment [24]. The utilisation of software within these devices has increased as a means to improve the quality of therapy provided [2]. This is proving to be more costly and difficult to regulate due to its complex and opaque nature [24].

As medical devices evolve to address more challenging and complex scenarios, certain tasks and decision making can be delegated to the devices. Due to the increase in responsibility, ensuring that these devices and their software follow proper medical procedure and regulations becomes a priority, to minimise errors that may occur and ensure that no harm is caused.

The development of medical devices, and their software, is heavily regulated by multiple agencies around the globe. Each regulatory body uses different standards for certification, however, they all share a similar approach to regulate the software development life-cycle and the trail of documents required [13,22].

Due to the strict review process needed for certification and their safety-critical nature, medical device failures are costly during clinical trials. Early failures may cause retesting, increasing timelines; while later failures may cost lives and could put an entire programme or even company's existence at jeopardy [2].

3.1 Challenges

Innovation in the medical device software space is challenging because of trials and regulatory processes. It is common in most industries for software to be released and updated, as it evolves; improving performance over time. Existing medical device regulations make this process difficult [21]. Updating software can often be a costly process, as new versions must go through the regulatory process once again before they are certified for release. This creates a situation where, updates might not be rolled out due to how costly and time-consuming undergoing regulation might become [4].

Emerging technologies in the software space are outpacing the regulatory bodies' standards for certification in our experience. This creates an issue with applying for certification for software that uses new, innovative techniques that have not been considered beforehand [18]. One example of this is the use of Artificial Intelligence (AI), where the US Food and Drug Administration (FDA) restricts regulation to "locked" algorithms; software that do not evolve over time and do not adapt based on new data [12]. This can negate the effects of using techniques, such as AI, where the core benefit of the technology is to learn, adapt, and evolve over time based on improved datasets.

Certification for medical devices is clinical trial-based versus dependability-based approaches applied in avionics and other safety-critical fields. Software dependability is not easily determined through trials, as it is within hardware [17]. However, existing techniques standard to other safety-critical domains are not typically applied in medicine. This is a shortcoming that regulators and guidelines have yet to properly address.

Designing medical devices intended for use in high-pressure situations is a challenging task. It is important to ensure that the device can convey crucial information and alert the users when needed without contributing to additional stresses. One example is "alarm fatigue" (*i.e.*, where the user might unsafely ignore important alarms due to their overly frequent recurrence).

These issues disincentivise innovation in medical software and create update-averse atmospheres. This, prevents innovation and the benefits they provide. We see DSs and DTs as a technological mechanism to unlock such legal and innovation limitations.

3.2 Organ Preservation

One sector that has seen an increase in medical device development is organ preservation. The current standard of human organ preservation is "Static Cold Storage" (SCS), which is a simple and cost-effective method (due to its passive nature), however, it provides preservation for a short period of time and is unsuitable to use on organs of lower quality [28]. This often leads to additional time constraints that necessitate transplantations to be done out of hours, and requiring the usage of costly private planes to get the organ transported in time.

To deal with ever-expanding demand for transplantation, the boundaries of the criteria for organ donation is constantly being pushed to allow for usage of extended criteria donor organs (i.e. organs that would have previously been rejected due to poor quality) [1,29]. Worst, some legal frameworks impose limits on geographical basis [11].

Unlike passive techniques like SCS, where the therapy delivered to the organ is through a static process, active techniques adjust function according to the circumstances. These present their own challenges, as these devices often require the need to be accompanied by experienced operators; adding significant costs and logistical issues. This necessitates hospitals to employ specialised staff to operate the device 24/7. Beyond this, the cost of these devices is substantial and often requires the purchase of consumables per use (*e.g.*, 35–40K£). Known Organ preservation techniques are classified as:

Static Cold Storage (SCS): a passive technique that works by cooling down organs to hypothermic temperatures (*i.e.*, 4–8 °C) to reduce the metabolic rate of the cells and the oxygen required to keep them alive [23]. The lack of active oxygenation increases the risks with extended preservation periods. Additionally, when this method is used on organs of lower quality, such as those donated after cardiac death, the organs have to be discarded, as usage is considered too high risk. Commercially, there are many available solutions that rely on insulation to keep the organ at the desired temperature, with some products offering more advanced features, such as real-time monitoring.

Hypothermic Machine Perfusion (HMP): a popular active preservation technique, clinically and commercially. This method uses a device to cool down the organ to hypothermic temperatures and perfuse it with an preservation fluid to extend its preservation capability [10]. In some cases, the preservation solution may be oxygenated; however, being an aqueous medium, the oxygen payload is only a fraction of the blood [31]. Commercially, the method has seen use for kidney and liver preservation.

Persufflation (PSF): uses humidified oxygen as the perfusate, instead of a preservation solution. One issue with these preservation solutions is that they can only provide a fraction of the oxygen needed to maintain proper whole organ oxygenation. Humidified oxygen is a mixture oxygen and other inert gases that can aptly deliver the necessary oxygenation payload without drying the vasculature of the organ. The organ is maintained at hypothermic temperatures similar to HMP. This technique caters for multiple organs including the kidney, liver, heart, pancreas and composite tissues [8]. This is the technology used by ScubaTx^{TM}, particularly as the only available device for pancreas preservation [33].

Normothermic Machine Perfusion (NMP): perfuses a liquid into the organ at ~37 °C temperatures. Keeping the organ close to normal physiological temperatures allows for real-time functional monitoring, which neither of the three previous methods provide. It also enables the use of more advanced perfusates that better emulate blood [20]. This technique has seen some use commercially for liver, heart and kidney preservation.

4 Case Study: ScubaTx^{TM} Organ Preservation Device

In order to investigate the usage of DTs for medical devices, specifically ones used for organ preservation, a case study on such a device from ScubaTx^{TM} is presented (www.scubatx.com) as the PT. This case study highlights what the deployment of DTs will look like as a medical device, with accompanying description of models needed, expected benefits, and identified technological challenges.

This case study is based on an active ongoing commercial project owned by ScubaTx^{TM} Given the commercial sensitivity of the device and its software, details not relevant to this case study and the resultant models were intentionally obfuscated. As part of separate project, an overview of the device software in question exists publicly as part of the HUBCAP project on applying MBD in novel industry applications [36,37].

4.1 The Device

The ScubaTx^{TM} device (see Fig. 1) is a closed-loop automated control system used to preserve multiple organ types (kidney, pancreas, heart, liver and composite tissue) by actively providing oxygen using PSF. This is to both extend organ preservation times and to improve the quality of preservation provided. It consists of a software controller that automatically maintaining target parameters for a given organ preservation and also auditing all events that occur in the device for later reporting to the transplant surgeons. This automation process is what will be analysed and optimized by the use of DT technology.

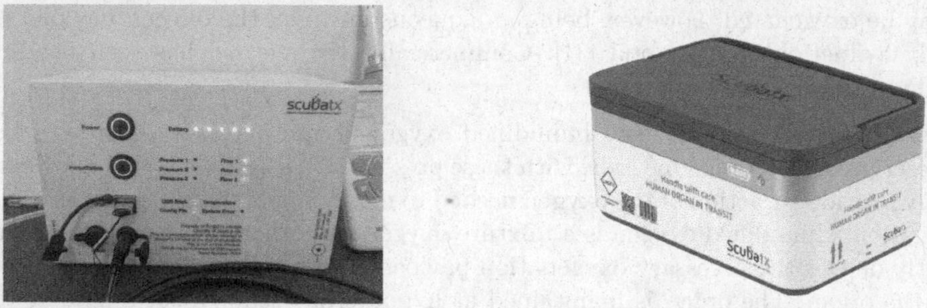

(a) Current Prototype (b) Final Product Render

Fig. 1. ScubaTx^{TM} organ preservation device

The "active" part of the device is the method of oxygen supply. The device uses a flow rate target as the means of achieving its goal of maintaining organ function. The onboard controller measures the flow rate of the gas through the organ and adjusts the oxygen pressure to increase or decrease flow. The control of the pressure is carefully maintained to ensure that accidental overshoots of key target parameters do not occur, as it could damage the organs' vasculature thus compromising their status.

Apart from recording the temperature, flow, and pressure, the onboard controller also logs events of interest, which occur once the device is turned on. These events include when PSF begins and ends, as well as error states and other key events which are hard to acquire given the nature and expense of clinical trials. Due to the device's portable nature, other information may be logged, such as tracking and movement data. Alarms are triggered when certain events occur to alert the user of key changes or aspects that could be addressed.

The onboard controller directly deals with flow/pressure regulation; however, it also communicates to an external software (mobile app) to produce data Visualization. This app reads the device's data and offers monitoring functionality [7].

The device is currently in prototype phase. It has successfully undergone human organ testing (Aug 2019), where a live human organ was preserved for over 26 hours. A number of prototype bench devices have been produced (Mar 2022) and are being placed at different clinical research centre partners around the world. Due to commercial sensitivity, we cannot give further details.

4.2 The Software

This controller collects and stores data in memory. Through a security protocol, it can transfer this data in real-time, wirelessly to a mobile application called Smart Audits [3,27]. The architecture and communications described here can be seen in Fig. 2.

This mobile app serves as the DT in this case. The application handles the data processing and visualization capabilities. The models created of the PT are at the centre of this app's algorithm [7].

Given the complex nature of the preservation process, multiple models are used to model as many aspects of the PT as possible. Whilst some of these models are used to provide feedback back to the controller to optimise performance, other models are used solely for visualization. The nature of the model depends on the related controller's function and its ability to effect the particular aspect that the model is describing.

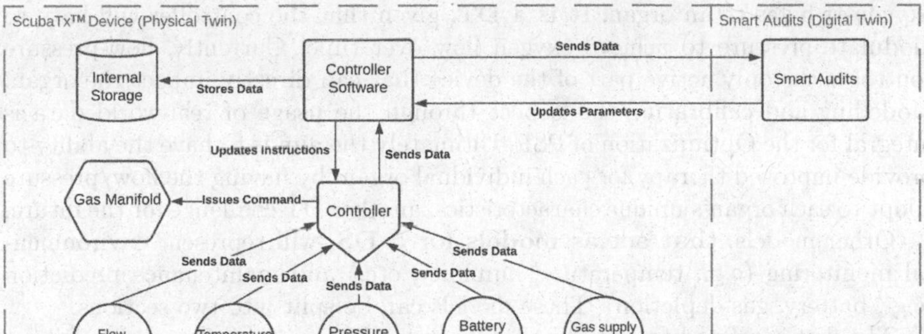

Fig. 2. Overview of the DT schematic for the ScubaTx^{TM} device

Data Communication is an integral part of a DT system: the enabling of communication channels between the PT and DT models through the data being transmitted. The PT sends the logged data to DT for processing, whilst the DT responds by sending information back to the PT based on the results the DT's models have obtained. **This represents the backbone of the reconfigurability offered by a DT system, as the PT can adapt and improve based on the DT's response.**

For the ScubaTx^{TM} device, this response includes data to update the controller's operating parameters to improve performance or optimise battery usage. Other responses include the activation of alarms based on predicted outcomes.

Furthermore, we consider a medical device not only a safety-critical system, but a system where security concerns have to be taken into account. Otherwise, patient data or medical conditions could be vulnerable to attack or misuse [9,27]. Thus, we use security protocols for data exchange at every step, where data is transferred between the physical plant, controller and twin through cryptographic primitives. This ensures that communication is kept secret, and only authenticated parties can participate. Yet, if the protocol is incomplete (i.e. unforeseen attacks take place), this creates an opportunity for another twinning functionality: if data security or authenticity is breached in any way, the twin can alarm the user (and log the the interference for future reference/audit), akin to the well known two-factor authentication mechanisms.

Models are key aspect associated with digital twinning is the identification of models that can replicate the relevant behaviours, as well as the interaction modes involved. That is, a DT is expected to influence the control and physical device, whereas a DS is expected to monitor its processes. Nevertheless, this could create certification challenges.

The primary model the device is concerned with is the flow-pressure model. This corresponds to a PID-controller operating over different channels delivering oxygen-rich gas to an organ. **It is a DT**, given that the controller will have to modulate pressure to achieve oxygen flow over time. Currently, flow-pressure control is the only active part of the device that can directly impact the organ. Modelling and calibrating this aspect through the usage of real-world data is integral for the Optimization of PSF. Ultimately the aim is to have the ability to provide improved therapy for each individual organ, by having the flow/pressure adapt to each organ's unique characteristics, another DT challenge for the future.

Other models, **that act as models for a DS**, will represent environmental monitoring (e.g., temperature, humidity, etc.) and maintenance prediction (e.g., battery, gas depletion). These models can be split into two sections.

The first is related to providing feedback to the users to take actions. Whilst they cannot reconfigure the device themselves, they can influence the decision making of operators. An example of this is the battery model, which can be used to predict how long the device has to operate before it runs out of power. In this case, the operators may be prompted to provide external power. Battery depletion is dependent on the flow-pressure model, as gas manifolds actuation, which is used to regulate the flow, uses power. Similarly, the temperature model can be used to predict when the device's temperature is going beyond desired hypothermic conditions. Using temperature formulae and multiple readings from inside and outside the device (as evidenced in other DS applications [14]) , it is possible to detect when the cooling packs need to be changed, for example.

Other models are used specifically for maintenance and diagnostics **as DSs**. Information gathered from these cannot be used in real-time during the device's operation. The reason being is that it might compromise the integrity of the preservation process by breaking the sterile field or interrupting the PSF (e.g. leaky channel that cannot be reattached to the organ). However, they may provide valuable maintenance and diagnostic data. Gas supply sensors are an example of this. Whilst these cannot be hot-swapped during device operation, it is important to be aware when the gas bottle needs to be replaced, to ensure that there is enough supply for a full preservation period.

Moreover, we are considering models for organ's behaviours, whilst under preservation. To accurately replicate the PT digitally, understanding and modelling the organ is key and challenging. Using the models mentioned above, we envisage an organ model can be created based on their physiological resistance to flow. This would provide insight into the physiology of the specific organ being preserved. This resistance model would help establish pressure thresholds that help guide (and refine) practice in an iterative manner. Given the nature of PSF and the regulation of flow/pressure, establishing a "relaxation time" constant[1] would greatly improve the monitoring and visualization by sanitising the data shown. Nevertheless, such models will be hard to calibrate in general, given the human physiology has many unknown-unknowns. Yet, we predict that it will be possible to represent organs' behaviours relevant to the twinning process.

If that experiment works, this will entail considerable change in how organ preservation technologies and DT research can work together, given research will not be completely dependent on research-organ availability, a crucial and limited resource. Presuming that DTs would produce sufficient evidence, this might positively impact future care decisions, given fewer organs would be necessary to reach improved care outcomes.

Visualization and Outcomes can be enhanced by using DTs. Beyond the desired aim of tailoring the preservation process to each organ, DTs also provide the possibility for improved visualisations. This may contain predictive visualization for device component wear or data directly pertaining to the process.

Medical device regulations complicates the usage of DTs due to its adaptive qualities. We still see potential applications of twinning that would not compromise certification. As mentioned in a battery-powered system, where the twinning process predicts that battery will run out before the end of treatment, an alarm may be triggered on the device. Even though such alarming for predictive scenarios will interact with the medical device, it will not interfere with the actual treatment (or regulatory process), for example.

[1] This is a time constant that describes how long it would take for the oxygen flow to stabilise.

4.3 Challenges

Known-unknown and unknown-unknown conditions create a key challenge when designing organ preservation models for DTs. The efficacy of these models hinges on the accuracy of their design and the unknown conditions present an obstacle that must be overcome to properly cater for all possible scenarios specifically relevant for organ preservation (i.e. not all aspects of the organs need to be precisely characterized, only those important for improved preservation through the DT process). This is particularly problematic for the organ-under-preservation models. The physiology of the organs can vary and the effects of this variance can often have an unknown effect on how the organ may react to PSF.

External forces that are out of the control of the device, such as the environment during transportation (e.g. airplane or ambulance turbulence), will have an effect. These are difficult to model as the device is designed to be transported using a variety of methods and under varying conditions. Some external factors impact the efficacy of the PSF and should be considered by the DT, to better replicate their effects in our device. Given the myriad of environmental factor combinations possible, accurately conveying them in the DT is a challenge.

The models used require careful calibration based on existing data. Gathering this data prior to deployment is difficult in the case of organ preservation devices, as this requires the usage of real organs. Given the wide range of organs available and the matching of donors and recipients plus additional data like cancer status, it is difficult to define the quality of an organ a prior. In general, research organs will be less optimal when compared to clinical ones. Obtaining clinical data to calibrate ScubaTx's device presents a large number of challenges including issues of consent, logistics, and assurance that this will not negatively impact on care. Without careful calibration, the DTs will be unable to properly emulate the PT.

Given the different medical certification processes [12,22], digital twinning influencing the device during runtime might create room for the argument that this is a novel device (different from the one being certified). This creates a technical (and regulatory) challenge for the digital twins community!

Currently, these medical device regulations stipulate that there is a design freeze when the device is submitted for approval. This enforces that the software deployed with the device is static and final, as changes would require the certification process to restart, which is time-consuming and costly. Given the nature of DTs, it would be classified as an "adaptive" software, since it can effect the operating parameters during runtime. Current regulation frameworks [12,22] frown upon the usage of such software, as it is no longer static and can prove hard to certify or show safety during clinical trials, yet another pressing challenge.

5 Discussion

DTs present a new approach to software engineering for cyber-physical systems. Through closed-loop automated data communication, DTs can replicate a PT and allow for advanced visualisations and optimisation of data and processes. We envisage this technology as being greatly beneficial in the medical device space.

Owing to the key benefits provided by DTs, several challenges faced by medical devices can be alleviated. Improved visualization helps declutter the information received by the operators allowing them to better understand the data and reduce misinterpretations [16]. Improved safety monitoring and diagnostics helps maintain the device in operational conditions and reduce faults, which in medical devices, can be disastrous. Furthermore, DTs can lead to improved quality of care by providing the necessary tools to support the decisions taken by the devices' operators through the use of simulated scenarios, before ever reaching patients. Treatment provided by the device is further improved by the automated ability to optimise its function during treatment time.

These benefits can be seen in our case-study, where the visualisations and annotated output of the devices software is supported by the DT's models. These models, further assist in notifying the users when action needs to be taken to resolve issues, such as low gas supply or low battery. Detailed models of how the different organ behave under preservation helps provide useful feedback to the controller of how to best regulate the oxygen for optimal organ quality.

As previously discussed, medical devices can be very complex in their design and operations, which makes finding the right models to replicate the PT, a challenge. Taking for example the ScubaTx^{TM} device discussed in Sect. 4, it requires several models, describing a wide variety of aspects to accurately emulate the system. Beyond this, many of the models involved will not be trivial.

Furthermore, medical regulatory pathways can make the introduction of DT technology difficult [12,22]. The certification process' nature limits the use of adaptive/dynamic software in favour of static code. Thus, it is expected that once submitted for certification, the device and its software do not change. This goes contrary to DTs, as reconfigurability and optimisations are a key benefit of the technology. So, DS presents an easier route for certification, as it does not directly affect the operating parameters of the device.

Additionally, DT technology can be coupled with other techniques, such as formal methods [30]. The certification process prefers static software due to the ease of testing in clinical trials. Given the dynamic nature of DTs, using formal methodologies to help prove correctness might alleviate some of the concerns from the regulatory bodies [17]. Whilst not required, there are examples of formal methods in medicine showing a beneficial impact on the final product [17]. DT and formal methods complement each other well, with one providing improved efficacy and the other ensuring correctness. This ultimately helps build trust in DT technologies for use in healthcare.

The benefits and challenges extend beyond the organ preservation device case studied in Sect. 4. We believe that DT can greatly increase the efficacy of certain medical devices and medical manufacturing equipment by enabling more automated approaches to healthcare, whilst also providing the operators and device manufacturers improved diagnostics and visualization tools as well as assurances to certifiers.

The systems' ability to automatically reconfigure cannot be understated in its potential to lead to better outcomes. This however comes at the cost of going against the grain of current regulatory standards, which might complicate certification processes.

5.1 Beyond Organ Preservation

Whilst the discussed case study deals solely with an organ preservation device, these ideas can be applied at large to a whole eco-system. For example, in islet manufacturing (Fig. 3)[2], pancreas preservation is only a single step of the process. Applying DT technology to the whole process can yield additional benefits by utilising the synergistic effects of the DT used at each step.

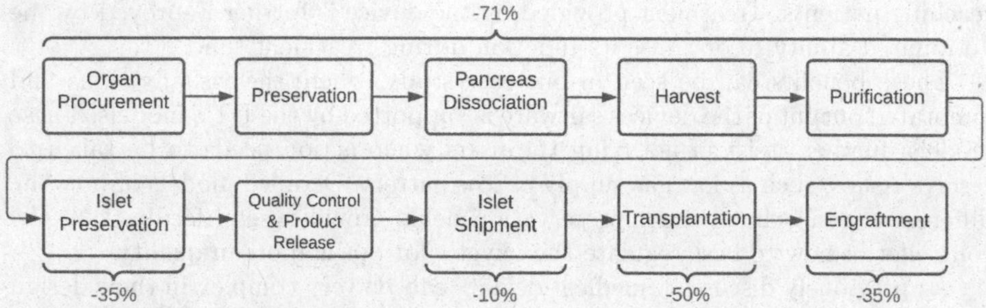

Fig. 3. Islet manufacturing process and yield loss

DTs have shown to be beneficial for manufacturing processes [32]. This can apply to medicine. For islet manufacturing, the current yield is very low, requiring several organs per patient to achieve a desired result. Beyond this, the current process is only semi automated. This presents an opportunity for DTs to be used to holistically improve the process, by optimising each step and providing better automation possibilities. This process is a very delicate balancing act between ensuring proper islet yield and function. Negative effects at any point can cascade downwards through the process, leading to very poor islet transplantation outcomes, a known limiting factor on why pancreas preservation is so challenging. As such, DTs can be used to improve the efficacy of the whole system by optimising each step, hence negating issues that might compromise islet quality.

Furthermore, by understanding an individual care journey, a bespoke approach may be possible improving case by case efficiency, due to treating the individual rather than the population. The benefits of twinning this process as a whole is that calibration done to models in one step can inform others down the line, ensuring synchronization. We believe this methodology can be transferred to other medical processes, such as cell-therapies manufacturing and regenerative medicine, which we predict will yield similar benefits.

Acknowledgements. We are grateful to the Poul Due Jensen Foundation, which has supported the establishment of a new Centre for Digital Twin Technology at Aarhus University. Also, for EU industrial PhD bursary (IIIP), and for ScubaTx^{TM} for access to their device, which UK MRC funded the first prototype.

[2] The post process of a preserved pancreata to make its islets viable for transplantation.

References

1. OPTN/SRTR 2018 annual data report. Am. J. Transp. 20(s1), 1–10 (2020). https://doi.org/10.1111/ajt.15670
2. Alemzadeh, H., et al.: Analysis of safety-critical computer failures in medical devices. IEEE Secur. Priv. **11**(4), 14–26 (2013)
3. Aluko, S.: Development of a Mobile Monitoring Application for a Persufflation Device. Master's thesis, School of Computing, Newcastle University, UK (2022)
4. Babic, B., et al.: Algorithms on regulatory lockdown in medicine. Science **366**(6470), 1202–1204 (2019). https://doi.org/10.1126/science.aay9547
5. Blochwitz, T., et al.: The functional mockup interface 2.0: the standard for tool independent exchange of simulation models. In: Proceedings of the 9th International Modelica Conference. Munich, Germany (2012)
6. Boulos, M.N.K., et al.: Digital twins: fFrom personalised medicine to precision public health. J. Personalized Med. (2021). https://doi.org/10.3390/jpm11080745
7. Buhagiar, A.J.: Automated organ transplant preservation smart audit. Master's thesis, School of Computing, Newcastle University, UK (2020)
8. Buhagiar, A.J., Freitas, L., Scott, W.E.: Persufflation—current state of play. Transplantology (2021). https://doi.org/10.3390/transplantology2030035
9. Clifford, H.: Modelling data extraction protocols for an organ preservation machine. Bachelor's thesis, School of Computing, Newcastle University, UK (2022)
10. De Deken, J., et al.: Hypothermic machine perfusion in kidney transplantation. Curr. Opin. Organ Transplant. **21**(3), 294–300 (2016)
11. Department of health and human services, centers for medicare & medicaid services: organ procurement organizations (OPOs) (CMS-3380) (2020). https://www.cms.gov/files/document/112020-opo-final-rule-cms-3380-f.pdf
12. FDA: Proposed regulatory framework for modifications to artificial intelligence/machine learning based software as a medical device (SaMD) (2019)
13. General principles of software validation: standard. International Organization for Standardization, USA (2002)
14. Feng, H., et al.: The incubator case study for digital twin engineering. Tech. rep., Aarhus University (2021). https://arxiv.org/abs/2102.10390
15. Feng, H., et al.: Integration of the Mape-K loop in digital twins. In: Submitted to IEEE Modelling and Simulation. IEEE (2022)
16. Fitzgerald, J., Larsen, P.G., Pierce, K.: Multi-modelling and co-simulation in the engineering of cyber-physical systems: towards the digital twin. In: ter Beek, M.H., Fantechi, A., Semini, L. (eds.) From Software Engineering to Formal Methods and Tools, and Back. LNCS, vol. 11865, pp. 40–55. Springer, Cham (2019). https://doi.org/10.1007/978-3-030-30985-5_4
17. Freitas, L., et al.: Medicine-by-wire: practical considerations on formal techniques for dependable medical systems. Sci. Comput. Prog. (2020). https://doi.org/10.1016/j.scico.2020.102545
18. Gerke, S., et al.: The need for a system view to regulate artificial intelligence/machine learning based software as medical device. NPJ Digit. Med. **3**(1), 53 (2020). https://doi.org/10.1038/s41746-020-0262-2
19. Grieves, M., Vickers, J.: Digital twin: mitigating unpredictable, undesirable emergent behavior in complex systems. In: Kahlen, F.-J., Flumerfelt, S., Alves, A. (eds.) Transdisciplinary Perspectives on Complex Systems, pp. 85–113. Springer, Cham (2017). https://doi.org/10.1007/978-3-319-38756-7_4

20. Hosgood, S.A., et al.: Reducing proinflammatory signaling and enhancing insulin secretion with the application of oxygen persufflation in human pancreata. Transplantation **103**(1), 13–14 (2019)
21. Hrgarek, N.: Certification and regulatory challenges in medical device software development. In: 2012 4th International Workshop on Software Engineering in Health Care (SEHC), pp. 40–43 (2012). https://doi.org/10.1109/SEHC.2012.6227011
22. Medical device software - Software life cycle processes. Geneva, CH (2006)
23. Taylor, M.J., et al.: Current state of hypothermic machine perfusion preservation of organs: the clinical perspective. Cryobiology **60**(3), S20–S35 (2010). https://doi.org/10.1016/j.cryobiol.2009.10.006
24. Kuca, K., et al.: The potential of medical device industry in technological and economical context. Therapeutics Clin. Risk Manag., 1505 (2015). https://doi.org/10.2147/tcrm.s88574
25. Laubenbacher, R., et al.: Using digital twins in viral infection. Science **371**(6534), 1105–1106 (2021). https://doi.org/10.1126/science.abf3370
26. Legaard, C.M., et al.: Constructing neural network-based models for simulating dynamical systems (2021)
27. Miller, J.: Using formal methods to design, model, and verify the goals of a communication protocol between a perfusion machine and its consumable components. Bachelor's thesis, School of Computing, Newcastle University, UK (2020)
28. Minor, T., et al.: Rewarming injury after cold preservation. Int. J. Mol. Sci. **20**(9), 2059 (2019). https://doi.org/10.3390/ijms20092059
29. NHSBT: organ donation and transplantation activity report 2019/20 (2020). www.odt.nhs.uk/statistics-and-reports/annual-activity-report/
30. Nipkow, T., Wenzel, M., Paulson, L.C. (eds.): Isabelle/HOL. LNCS, vol. 2283. Springer, Heidelberg (2002). https://doi.org/10.1007/3-540-45949-9
31. Patrono, D., et al.: Hypothermic oxygenated machine perfusion of liver grafts from brain-dead donors. Sci. Rep. (2019). https://doi.org/10.1038/s41598-019-45843-3
32. Tao, F., et al.: Digital twin in industry: state-of-the-art. IEEE Trans. Ind. Inform. **15**(4), 2405–2415 (2019). https://doi.org/10.1109/TII.2018.2873186
33. Tempelman, L.A., et al.: Perfusing an organ with an in situ generated gas (9 Oct 2018). US Patent 10091985
34. Thule, C., et al.: Maestro: The INTO-CPS co-simulation framework. Simul. Model. Pract. Theor. **92**, 46–61 (2019). https://doi.org/10.1016/j.simpat.2018.12.005
35. Topol, E.: The Topol Review: preparing the healthcare workforce to deliver the digital future. Technical Report, Health Education England (2019)
36. Tudor, N., et al.: ScubaDIVE: D1 - Sprint 1 Report. HUBCAP (2021)
37. Tudor, N., et al.: ScubaDIVE: D2 - Sprint 2 Report. HUBCAP (2021)
38. Voigt, I., et al.: Digital twins for multiple sclerosis. Frontiers in Immunology 12 (2021). https://doi.org/10.3389/fimmu.2021.669811
39. Zeng, J., et al.: A survey: cyber-physical-social systems and their system-level design methodology. Future Gener. Comput. Syst. **105**, 1028–1042 (2020). https://doi.org/10.1016/j.future.2016.06.034

Using Digital Twins in the Development of Complex Dependable Real-Time Embedded Systems

Xiaotian Dai(✉), Shuai Zhao, Benjamin Lesage, and Iain Bate

Department of Computer Science, University of York, York, UK
{xiaotian.dai,shuai.zhao,benjamin.lesage,iain.bate}@york.ac.uk

Abstract. Modelling execution times in complex real-time embedded systems is vital for understanding and predicting tasks' temporal behaviour, and to improve the system scheduling performance. Previous research mainly relied on worst-case execution time estimations based on formal static analyses that are often pessimistic. The models that resulted are hard to maintain and even harder to validate. In this work, the novel use of Digital Twins provides opportunities to improve this issue and beyond for dependable real-time systems. We aim to establish and contribute to three questions: (i) how to easily model execution times with an adequate level of abstraction, and how to evaluate the quality of that model; (ii) how to identify errors in the models and how to evaluate the impact of errors; and (iii) how to make decisions as to when and how to improve the models. In this paper, we proposed a Digital Twin-based adaptation framework, and demonstrated its use for modelling and refining execution time profiles. Key decisions concerning the quality of the model and its impact on performance are evaluated. Finally, some challenges and key research questions for the formal method community are proposed.

Keywords: Digital twin · Real-time embedded systems · Execution time model · Error modelling · Error refinement · System adaptation

1 Introduction

For complex real-time embedded systems (RTES), modelling of the execution times is essential as it helps to understand and predict a system's temporal behaviour, validating the timing requirements, and to improve the system performance. In RTES, the execution times can be largely affected by a number of factors, to name a few: the program execution path, which is based on the current inputs; the interference and blocking from other sources, *e.g.*, co-running tasks, and contentions due to accessing shared resources; the underlying hardware and architectural features on which the program is executed; and the current system mode, and in some contexts is subjected to operational scenarios, *etc.*.

In the real-time systems community, the widely applied practice is to derive the worst-case execution time (WCET) of a program to understand its

T. Margaria and B. Steffen (Eds.): ISoLA 2022, LNCS 13704, pp. 37–53, 2022.
https://doi.org/10.1007/978-3-031-19762-8_4

worst-case performance, with static analyses applied based on the control flow graph and the hardware and memory model [19]. However, this formal approach is pessimistic and lacks the ability to adapt to changes and to mitigate faults when there exists model inaccuracy due to partial information or change of system, *etc.*. The models that resulted are hard to maintain and even harder to validate. As the WCET fits in with a larger, more complex problems including worst-case response time and task scheduling and allocation, consequently the methods based on the WCET model can be both too pessimistic that produce low resource utilisation, and being fragile to uncertainties or violation of any assumptions that are used to derive the model.

In recent years, there is an increasing trend to apply Digital Twins (DT) in automotive, aerospace, manufacturing, transportation and healthcare systems. The idea of a DT is to establish a digital representative of the target system that is largely based on models and simulations. We recognise the potential of DTs in the design and development of real-time embedded systems.

In this paper, we apply Digital Twin as a first step towards improving the adaptiveness, accuracy and dependability in RTES. We are interested in applying it to both critical systems, *e.g.,* avionics (HiClass[1]), and more conventional systems, *e.g.,* telecoms (MOCHA[2]). Our DT work continues the success of model-based design for embedded systems where previously it was largely based on off-line simulations and verification, while lacking the ability of on-line adaptation. In our case, the Digital Twin is running in parallel with the physical entity at the same time while the target system is in operation. Data carrying the information of the target system and decision from the Digital Twin exchanges between the physical system and the digital counterpart in real-time. The novel use of Digital Twin in this work provides opportunities to be adapted to multi-core real-time systems from the following aspects:

- to correct timing models in which inaccuracies exist that could reduce performance or invalidate dependability;
- to suggest improvements to scheduling policies based on evidence obtained through observation;
- to make on-line decisions relevant to scheduling (*e.g.,* admit new tasks to schedule or allow more events to be processed);
- to support off-line assurance decisions through large-scale simulations.

Without losing generality, we focus on the timing aspects as it is recognised as the most critical factor in RTES. Specifically, we started from an execution time model based on task-level cache reuse, the cache recency profile (CRP), as an alternative to the WCET. The CRP describes the benefit in terms of execution time speedup a task can have based on a warmed cache from previous executed job instances. It is a sensitivity model of execution times in terms of how many cache lines have been accessed since the task of interest was last executed.

However, like other models, the CRP is sensitive to the current workload and operational context. Thus, it can be inaccurate if the context is shifted from the

[1] https://www.cs.york.ac.uk/news-events/news/2020/hi-class/.
[2] https://www.cs.york.ac.uk/rts/mocha/.

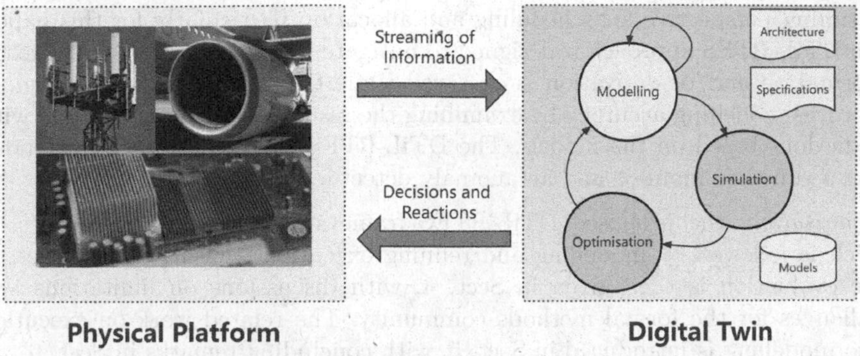

Fig. 1. The DTiL-RTES framework for complex real-time embedded systems

context in which the model was originally produced. The task scheduling and allocation algorithm is then based on this CRP. Associated with the CRP is an error model which represents the differences between the real system and the simulated part of the Digital Twin. The error model indicates the misalignment of models and supports analysis to understand robustness or resilience of the task scheduling and allocation of the system.

In this paper two key challenges are exploited: what should the components and models in the Digital Twin feature (*e.g.,* level of abstraction and key features that exist) and how the key models (*e.g.,* the parameters associated with the model and the model itself) are refined based on decisions made with them. In this paper, this modelling paradigm with Digital Twin and key decisions concerning the modelling accuracy and its impact are evaluated.

Contributions: In this work, we formulate a model-based Digital Twin framework for multi-core embedded systems to improve the system performance and resilience. We aim to establish and contribute to the following key research questions (RQs):

- RQ. 1. How to easily model execution times with an adequate level of abstraction, and how to evaluate the quality of that model against observations.
- RQ. 2. How to identify errors in the models and how to evaluate the impact of errors on key performance indices.
- RQ. 3. How to make decisions as to when and how to improve the models, supported by evidence collected from the real system and/or a simulator.

We propose the concept of *Digital Twin in-the-Loop design for real-time embedded systems* (DTiL-RTES), as shown in Fig. 1. The idea is to extend the use of Digital Twin for real-time and embedded systems beyond the design process, and exploit its usage at operational time by formulating an observation-decision loop. The DTiL-RTES performs both static and dynamic profiling, while making predictions from simulation and based on models of the system. Although there are many potentials of applying Digital Twin in multi-core systems, we focus on timing perspective for scheduling and allocation particularly for this paper. The DTiL-RTES approach is designed to mitigate model inaccuracy given extra information and/or derivation is observed while the system is in operation. It improves modelling accuracy by examining the results of the actual system with predictions based on the models. The DTiL-RTES can also be easily extended with a run-time monitor and an anomaly detector.

Organisation: the proposed DTiL-RTES framework is introduced in Sect. 2, which is followed by modelling and refining execution time models in Sect. 3. The evaluation is then given in Sect. 4, with discussions on limitations and challenges for the formal methods community. The related work on execution time modelling is introduced in Sect. 5, with concluding remarks in Sect. 6.

2 The DTiL-RTES Framework

In this section, we introduce the proposed DTiL-RTES framework, including its design intuition and components. We will then give more details in Sect. 3 on the execution time model and error refinement.

2.1 Design Philosophy

A Digital Twin is defined as a digital replica of a target physical system (*i.e.*, the system of interest) [5]. It can run independently and/or in parallel with the target system to facilitate making predictions and/or decisions. From a modelling perspective, the Digital Twin combines models, and methods based on the models to simulate, predict, analyse, and evaluate. The Digital Twin is normally running on a more capable machine (*i.e.*, the host) other than the target system. It is normally built based on existing services that are already established between the system and the host.

Efforts of using a DT in real-time systems for run-time WCET modelling and parameter adaptation were early discussed in [3,4]. The requirements and open challenges of adapting DT to the context of multi-core real-time systems have been discussed in [5]. Different to a cycle-accurate simulator, a Digital Twin often focuses on a higher level of abstraction where the key characteristics are identified. In general, the proposed DT is designed to meet the following required purposes: (1) answering what-ifs (decision making and optimisation) [7]; (2) support continuous modelling [3]; (3) understanding outliers and detecting anomalies. In addition, abnormal behaviours can be observed, which provides useful information to, for example, studying online and offline scheduling and allocation policy in embedded real-time systems. It is recognised that these concepts in Digital Twin provide a foundation and form a general background of this work, as well as the design and modelling philosophy.

2.2 DTiL-RTES Overview and Components

An overview of the DTiL-RTES framework proposed in this work is shown in Fig. 2. Key functions of the DT are: (a) decision support at both design-time and

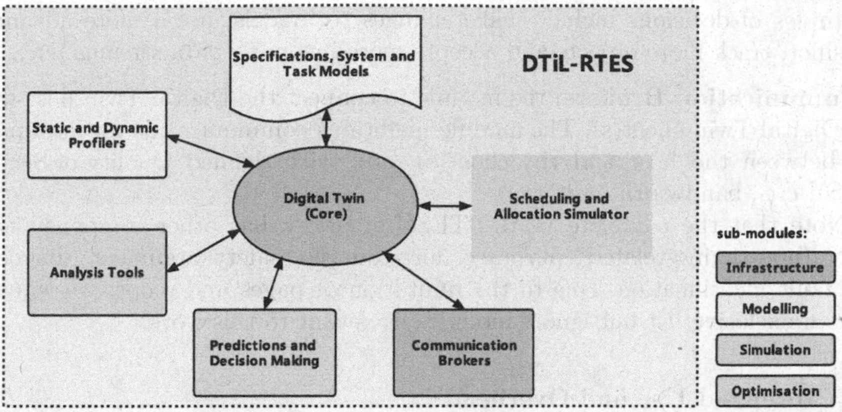

Fig. 2. An overview of the Digital Twin in-the-loop design conceptAn overview of the Digital Twin in-the-loop design concept

run-time; (b) anomaly detection to indicate inadequacy of the model; (c) tuning models based on new/novel observations. The DTiL-RTES consists a number of components. We introduce the key components of the proposed DT as follows.

Specification, System and Task Models: the specification and models are provided as database files to be used by the DT. Specifications include: (i) system-level requirements, *e.g.,* deadline miss rate requirement; and (ii) task-level requirements, *e.g.,* response time and jitter requirements. The models include: (i) system model, *i.e.,* processor and memory model, including processor grouping, frequencies, memory hierarchy, *etc.*; (ii) task model, provide properties of the task set, including inter-task dependencies, period, deadline and the worst-case execution time of the tasks; (iii) Execution Time Models: models to predict the execution times of tasks given system input states. There is also an associated error model to include factors that are not included in the execution time model.

Scheduling and Allocation Simulator: simulates the behaviour of the scheduler, by interpreting the processor, task and execution time models into a high-level simulator. The key is to understand what is the impact that a change in the model has on the scheduling decisions and performance.

Analysis Tools: accesses data from the system, streaming data to a local or remote database, and then applies statistical analysis upon the observations. For strictly hard real-time tasks, a formal schedulability test has to be checked against deadline constraints, for example, using response time analysis. As part of the DTiL-RTES, if it is established that a change is needed to a task's execution time model then the impact of this change is also checked.

Predictions and Decision Making: the decision making process applies changes to the model based on results from the scheduling simulator and, optionally, schedulability analysis. The decision process can either be offline or online.

Examples of decisions include make changes to models, use a more advanced classifier, track more objects and accepts more incoming data streams, *etc.*.

Communication Brokers: the module to connect the Digital Twin host with the Digital Twin client(s). The module maintains communication for data passing between the host and the client(s), and with defined Quality-of-Service (QoS), *e.g.*, bandwidth limitation.

Note that the complete DTiL-RTES framework has other components for other (non-timing-related) purposes, for example, safety argument, diagnosis and fault identification. Due to the limitation of pages and scope, we will not give an exclusive list but ignore modules irrelevant to this work.

2.3 Intended Use and Overhead

The position of the DT in this work focuses on building and refining a predictive timing model, named as Execution Time Model (ETM). To be more specific, an ETM is used to produce predictions of the execution time of a program, given inputs including the system states, data inputs, system modes, *etc.*

The ETM advances the WCET model in the way that it produce run-time predictions in addition to the worst-case single estimation of the execution time, thus the scheduler can make better use of the CPU resources without being too pessimistic from the overly assumed worst-case scenario. The ETM model can be built offline with data from running the system in a test environment. However, it is notable that there are many factors that will make the original ETM (*i.e.*, the model built offline) imprecise. Examples of these factors include insufficient information of the system, dynamically changing environment, contentions from dynamic workload, self-adaptation of system software and hardware. The idea of DTiL-RTES is to overcome these by collecting evidence from observations of the system, change the model where it deems it necessary. The decision of whether changing the model is based on outcomes from an internal simulator that evaluates the impact of errors.

In terms of the overhead of this approach, DTiL-RTES has profiling, communication, and memory (for data buffering) overhead. However, most of the heavy computation is offloaded on the Digital Twin host, thus has limited impact on the performance of the client.

3 ETM Modelling and Refinement

We motivated that the ETM is subjected to changes and the DT has the capability to accommodate the issue. However, a number of research questions remain: (1) when it is necessary to change the model; (2) how to change the model; (3) how to evaluate the change to the model is safe. Based on the introduced framework, we aim to provide solutions to (1) and (2), and provides some insights on the third question in this work.

To refine the model at run-time, we introduce a process for ETM error modelling. With a statistical learning process, the error is decomposed and analysed

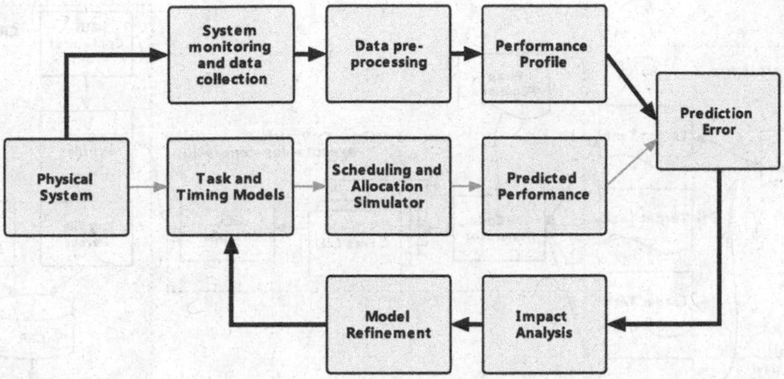

Fig. 3. Workflow of DTiL-RTES for model refinement (bold lines: feedback loop)

to understand the sufficiency of the relevant model and if the model can be further improved. For troublesome cases, the system would then take a snapshot, record it into a database, before it is further analysed with statistical or machine learning based techniques, for example, with *Principal Component Analysis* (PCA).

The workflow of the approach is shown in Fig. 3. From the figure, the general structure and the flow of the DTiL-RTES approach can be seen in more detail. The basic idea of this approach is to compare the results from simulation using models based on predictions against the models using real observation with an impact analysis.

3.1 Execution Time Model

The Execution Time Model (ETM) is a predictive model that produces execution time estimations based on given inputs. In this work, we apply a model known as cache recency profile (CRP) as it represents a good abstraction of the system. The CRP is a sensitivity model that represents the reduction in WCET against a stress metric, the recency distance, which is the distance measured by cache line accesses between the current job execution and its last instance. This is based on the understanding that execution time is largely dependent on cache reuse. We note that the choice of this model as ETM is just an example use case and we envisage our Digital Twin framework is adaptable to similar predictive timing models, for example, using recurrent neural networks. A full ETM can consist of a combination of models, but in this work we focus on the CRP to illustrate the idea, and use the term ETM and CRP interchangeably.

To clarify, there is a few assumptions of applying this model: (i) application tasks are modelled as functions with a single entry point; (ii) level of task abstraction: each task represents the minimal schedulable entity. Within a node there is no multi-threading. However, the level of abstraction in itself is a research question; (iii) the system has turned off *dynamic voltage and frequency scaling* (DVFS). DVFS adds significant interference to timing and adds unnecessary

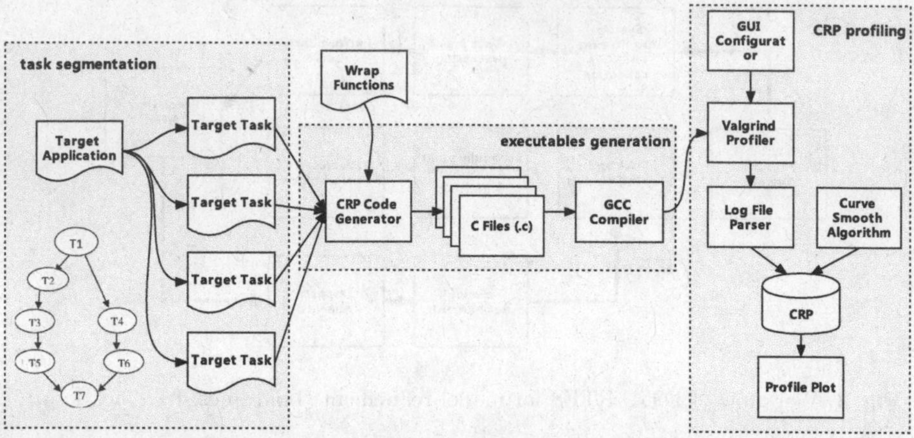

Fig. 4. The offline CRP profiling process

dynamics that is not favoured against predictability; and (iv) the system uses non-preemptive scheduling, for example, standard Linux OS without RT-patch or any other *commercial off-the-shelf* (COTS) OS. These assumptions form a very common setup of industrial real-time embedded systems.

The CRP is a simple yet effective abstraction of the temporal behaviour of a task. For the current implementation of CRP, the following factors are considered implicitly even if not being directly modelled: (i) prior-condition of tasks execution, (ii) data dependency between tasks, and (iii) instruction dependency through shared libraries.

3.2 Offline Profiling of CRP Model

The initial CRP model is produced offline with the support of a cache analysis tool (Valgrind[3]). Alternatively, it can be generated with static program analysis with control flow graph. The offline profiling tool stretches the independent variable (*i.e.*, the recency distance; defined in Sect. 3.1), and estimates the corresponding dependent variable (*i.e.*, the ET w.r.t. the percentage of WCET). The process is shown in Fig. 4.

However, the model produced in this way is limited by the prior-assumptions of the system, and the capability of the tool used. For example, the tool has limited support of multi-core, thus is not able to capture multi-core effects. The model will hardly be right, as we motivated earlier. The lack of run-time information, the exact impact factors to the execution time, cannot be fully known until the system is in an operating state. The initial model has to be either pessimistic or optimistic, or partially pessimistic for some parts but optimistic for the others.

[3] https://valgrind.org/.

3.3 Prediction Error

It is expected that the offline profiled model is not capable of fully capturing all the features related to task timing, and thus prediction errors are inevitable. A prediction error in this context is defined as the difference between the prediction and the real observation, *i.e.*, $e_i = \hat{y}_i - y_i$. Errors are inevitable in the modelling process and it is important to identify the existence of errors and its impact to the performance. The prediction error can be evaluated using either squared error, $e_i^2 = (\hat{y}_i - y_i)^2$, or root mean squared error (RMSE), $RMSE = \sqrt{\sum (\hat{y}_i - y_i)^2 / n}$.

Generally, there are common sources of errors in the context of a multi-core real-time embedded systems. To list a few:

- Data and instruction dependency across the tasks.
- New tasks arriving and old tasks finishes execution/terminates.
- Change of system modes due to switch of environment.
- Bus interference due to, *e.g.*, memory and I/O access.
- Operating system interference (*e.g.*, Linux services).

These are known unknowns, *i.e.*, we know their existence but do not know when and how they will have impact. Note these interferences will not be considered explicitly but implicitly in the error modelling. While the rest that is not categorised here would be considered as unknown unknowns, *i.e.*, we do not know their existence and do not know when and how they will have impact, and be considered as contributions to the errors.

3.4 Continuous Refinement Through Naive Feedback

The model can be improved incrementally through a feedback-based process. In this naive approach, the CRP model is improved through a feedback loop, and we introduce a parameter (L) as the feedback gain. Assuming the current active CRP model to be $CRP = \{c_0, c_1, ..., c_n\}$ where c_i is a model parameter and n is the total number of model parameters (*i.e.*, degree of freedom, or DoF), and the candidate model to be $CRP^c = \{c_0^c, c_1^c, ..., c_n^c\}$. We define a new operator, $\otimes$, as element-wise adaptation. We also define a function, $g(X_1, X_2)$, to extract modelling errors between models represented by parameters X_1 and X_2, respectively. The feedback model update process is defined as:

$$\begin{bmatrix} c_0' \\ c_1' \\ \cdots \\ c_n' \end{bmatrix} = L \otimes g\left(\begin{bmatrix} c_0 \\ c_1 \\ \cdots \\ c_n \end{bmatrix}, \begin{bmatrix} c_0^c \\ c_1^c \\ \cdots \\ c_n^c \end{bmatrix} \right) + \begin{bmatrix} c_0 \\ c_1 \\ \cdots \\ c_n \end{bmatrix} \tag{1}$$

where $L \in [0, 1]$ is the gain, which can be understood as a 'learning rate' and it controls the speed of the adaptation process. The new parameters are the result of the original parameters plus an error matrix that is extracted from the candidate model against the original model. This adaptation method does enable timely changes – depending on the adaptation frequency, a change in the model can take place every few hours or even a few minutes. However, we note this naive approach lacks guarantee on stability. The continuous change could invalid the safety properties if applied without any constraints, and may lead to unnecessary changes and may also be too frequent.

3.5 Model Refinement Through Condition-Based Model Rebuilding

To overcome the drawbacks of the naive approach, an alternative way of refining the model is through a more controlled process that rebuilds the model based on significance of observations. The idea is that the action needs to pass through an impact identification phase, before the new model can be applied to the system. The intuition behind this strategy is that an error is relevant only when it has an impact on system performance. Any decision that is made to refine the model should come with the expectation that the refinement would lead to improvement of the system.

The whole process is shown in Fig. 5. The input data is firstly collected and cleaned with anomalies being removed. The challenge to do so is to distinguish anomalies from outliers, as outliers may contain information that is important to the modelling process, but anomalies will negatively impact the accuracy thus lead to a unusable model. As an example, we remove anomalies based on statistics of every 200 samples, where any data point that is outside the range of $\mu \pm 3 \times \sigma$ is removed. The anomaly removal can be much more complicated.

The candidate models are then built after a resampling and classification process. The identification of the error impact is through a statistical test against simulated result based on the new and the original timing models. The scenario database (*SCN_DB*) is the database to save identified representative/difficult scenarios which helps to train the model in the future. When testing, the process will also go through the test cases in the scenario database. This overcomes the problem of limited sampling window and avoid considering all historical data.

To fit the CRP model, a piece-wise linear regression (PWLR) model is applied for each task:

$$y(x) = \begin{cases} \eta_1 + \beta_1 (x - b_1), & b_1 < x \leqslant b_2 \\ \eta_2 + \beta_2 (x - b_2), & b_2 < x \leqslant b_3 \\ \ldots & \\ \eta_n + \beta_n (x - b_{n-1}), & b_{n-1} < x \leqslant b_n \end{cases} \tag{2}$$

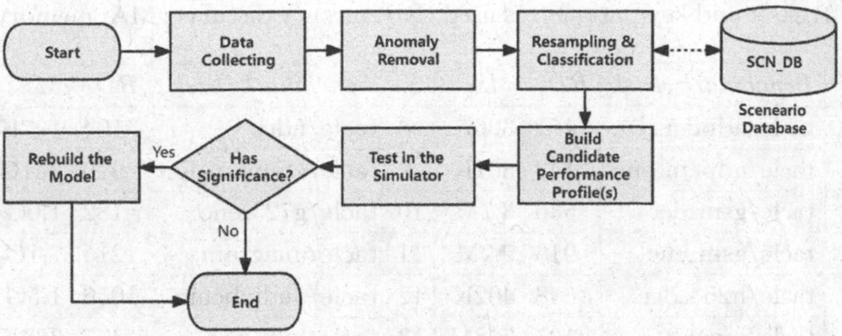

Fig. 5. Flow chart of ETM error modelling

where the parameters of the model (η_x, β_x, b_x) are found using least square estimation that minimised the RMSE. When building the PWLR model, the resampling processing can choose to favour the rare cases more, or average cases more. This is depending on the requirement of the scheduling algorithm. After the CRP model is obtained, there is an associated error evaluation process, in which it can indicate the model is not adequate and thus it needs to be changed (for example, by using a different level of abstraction). This is supported by an internal simulator that simulates scheduling and allocation where it utilises the ETM to estimate the system timing performance.

In DTiL-RTES, there are two levels of assessments, and consequent actions. One level is tuning the parameters of the model (this paper) and the other is to redesign the model (future work). When tuning the parameters, an automatic process is introduced that can adjust the model parameters to fit the observations and thus reduce the error. However in some cases, the tuning would be inadequate and the model may need to be re-designed. We thus compensate this by making humans in the loop, and introduce a testing phase which indicates the existence of such scenarios. Finally, a decision on rebuilding the model is made based on the impact analysis, where statistical test is performed based on the performance evaluated in the high-level simulator.

4 Evaluation

In this section, we evaluate the proposed method with respect to modelling accuracy and improvement in system performance with respect to scheduling results. The evaluation has two main objectives: the first objective is to demonstrate the modelling and error modelling process (in Sect. 4.2); the second objective is to show the impact on the system and how the decision can be made based on the observations (in Sect. 4.3).

Table 1. Taskset and key parameters used (RD: recency distance; MA: memory access)

#	*Benchmark Task*	*RD*	*MA*	#	*Benchmark Task*	*RD*	*MA*
1	tacle/adpcm_dec	151	306K	8	tacle/ndes	194	127K
2	tacle/adpcm_enc	148	307K	9	tacle/ammunition	970	261G
3	tacle/gsm_dec	536	3.7M	10	tacle/g723_enc	182	1.0G
4	tacle/gsm_enc	916	9.9M	11	tacle/anagram	1215	7.1G
5	tacle/h264_dec	648	402K	12	tacle/audiobeam	1056	1.5G
6	tacle/mpeg2	4105	568M	13	tacle/huff_dec	477	368K
7	tacle/statemate	97	60.6K	14	tacle/huff_enc	840	1.6G

4.1 Evaluation Setup

The testbed environment uses an Intel Core i5 quad-core processor running at 800 MHz with 16 GB of RAM. Three of the four cores (core 1–3) are used as worker cores to run application tasks, and one core (core 0) is used to run the global scheduler and the Digital Twin client. The dynamic voltage and frequency scaling (DVFS) is disabled. The data was profiled on the client then transferred in chunks to a desktop PC that serves as the Digital Twin host. The client schedules jobs with a global non-preemptive task scheduler, *i.e.*, a job will not be preempted by another job on the same core once it is executed.

The taskset we used is from a well-established benchmark in real-time embedded systems, the *TACLe Benchmarks* [6]. We modelled the taskset with an offline modelling tool. The main parameters of the tasks are shown in Table 1. The tasks were released randomly, and the system scheduler randomly chose one task to run. The execution time of each task (the dependent variable) and the accumulated recency distance since its last run (the independent variable) was recorded into a light-weight SQL database (SQLite[4]).

4.2 Modelling and Residual Error Evaluation

First, we evaluated the effectiveness of the modelling method and the modelling accuracy. The observation is organised into a (*Recency Distance*, *Execution Time*) pair. We select one of the tasks, *tacle/ndes*, for further analysis. There are overall 24868 valid data points after removal of anomalies, of which 80% is used for training and 20% is used for testing. A piece-wise regression model was then fitted onto the data using least square estimation as described earlier.

The residual error is then evaluated with the prediction from the testing data against the number of model parameters n (shown in Fig. 6) to understand the trade-off between model complexity and sum of squared error. By scaling n from 2 to 12, the error drops significantly for the first iterations but then stops after $n = 7$. This indicates that a more complex model would not always produce a

[4] https://www.sqlite.org.

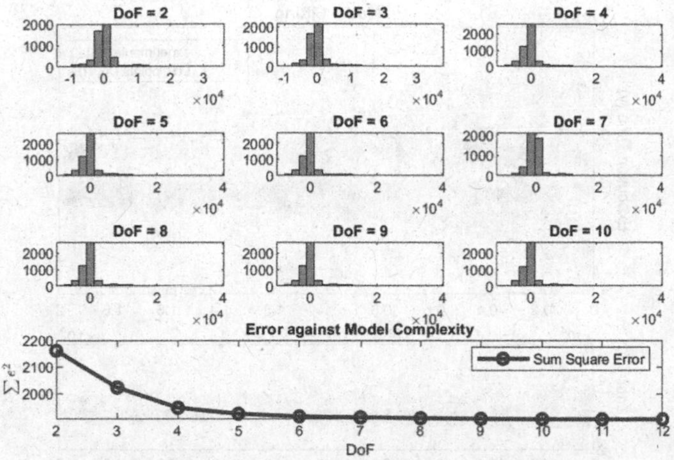

Fig. 6. ETM model DoF against associated error

better result, and thus there is clearly an optimal model complexity in the sense that it produces accurate results but at a reasonable low computational and memory cost. The other observation is that from the histograms on the top of the diagram, it can be seen that the error does not follow a normal distribution. There are two modals of the distribution, one at 0 and another at 1. The message it deliveries is that the error pattern indicates the model has accurately captured the main characteristics, however there could be another factor that is missed from the model.

To further investigate, by making $n = 10$, we evaluated the sum of squared residual error, $\sum(y_i - \hat{y}_i)^2$ where y_i is from the observation and $\hat{y}_i$ is the estimation based on the predictive model. The error is plotted out against the recency distance. The result is shown in Fig. 7. From the figure, it can be seen that the model fits well with the data in general. However, as can be seen, there is a large number of outliers that lie in the range of 5 - 10 $\times$ 10^4. For dependable systems, these outliers can be more important than the normal data that is successfully captured by the model and should be recorded into the scenario database for further analysis.

4.3 Evaluation of Model Refinement and Performance Improvement

To see how our Digital Twin can be used in decision making and model refinement, we compared the system performance using old (based on offline synthetic model) and new CRPs (based on observations from the real system). The evaluation metric of performance is the total execution time of 100 randomised job instances. The result is shown in Fig. 8. Two pairs of statistical tests were done with a non-parametric test (*Kolmogorov-Smirnov test*, or *K-S test* [11]) applied, with the null hypothesis H_0 being the two datasets are from the same distribution. The system made a decision to apply the new model based on the first

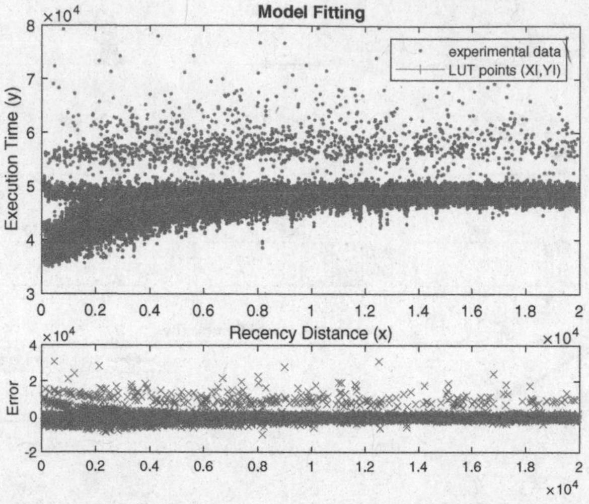

Fig. 7. Model fitting and residual error

test as there exists statistically difference. The decision is further evaluated by applying the new model to the system and re-measured the performance.

The second test between the sim and the real data gave a more positive result, with null hypothesis not being rejected and p-value $= 0.307$. This shows the predictions from the Digital Twin are broadly similar to the real data. However, this is not a strong accept, and by cross-comparing the data distribution, there are still significant differences and some could affect dependability.

4.4 Discussion on Safety Challenges

As demonstrated in the evaluation, although benefits can be gained, we note safety is important to construct a dependable system. Systems such as communication base stations can be more open for adaptation while the other systems such as those in avionics are less adaptable and more sensitive to risks. The involvement of decision making in mission-critical or safety-critical systems makes it vital to argue the system integrity. The current statistical test lacks richness with respect to safety guarantees, and it requires formal methods and formal verification during the decision making process [18], where model checking tools including *UPPAAL*[5] and *PRISM*[6] can be applied. Concepts such as *Models@runtime* [16] can also be utilised, as well as converting the current safety case from *Goal Structuring Notation* (GSN) [9] to a model-based safety argument, *e.g.*, using *Structured Assurance Case Metamodel* (SACM) [17]. However, as revealed in the evaluation, the outliers and misaligned data distribution, which

[5] https://uppaal.org/.
[6] https://www.prismmodelchecker.org/.

are keys to safety, could make formal methods much more challenging. Again, this is related to how the model is built and what level of abstraction is sufficient.

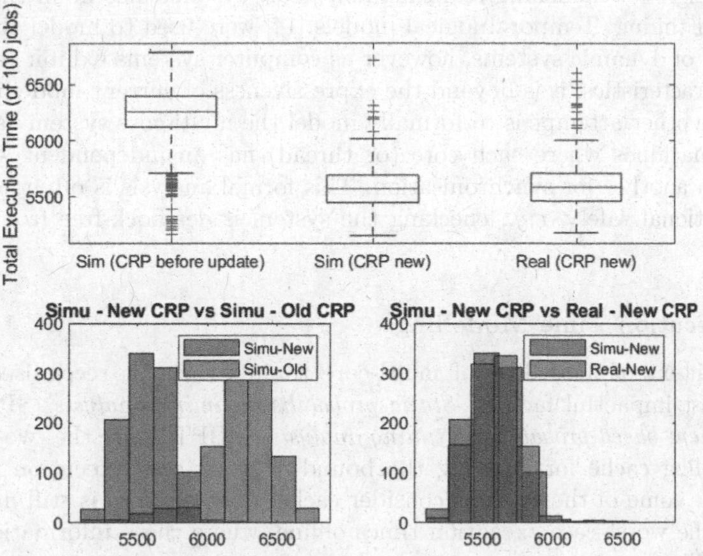

Fig. 8. Comparison of estimation from DTiL-RTES v.s. real observation

A further challenge is also motivated. That is, when it is safe to change the model being used and how to make transition between models. For this challenge, it will be key that rely-guarantee style contracts [2,15] are specified and proven to uphold the essential safety properties of the system. The proof that these are met will be needed both offline for the mechanisms and online for the specific changes applied.

5 Related Work

In this section, we introduce related work from two facets: timing prediction in multi-cores, and execution time modelling for real-time and embedded systems.

5.1 Timing Prediction for Multi-core Real-Time Embedded Systems

Traditionally, when modelling multi-core systems, the integrated timing behaviour is represented by the composition of a number of independent modelled factors including bus interconnection, cache reuse, memory contention, context switches, operating system (OS) interference and so on. However, for COTS systems, it is hard to consider some individual factors – in terms of hardware, some processor specifications are vague, inaccurate and even incorrect; and with respect to software, some binary code and dynamics libraries are closed-source, and even worse when the application is running on an operating systems that is not initially designed for real-time, *e.g.,* Linux, where the characteristics of the timing due to OS is difficult if not impossible to model accurately [12].

Challenges for modelling real-time multi-core systems also lie in the expressiveness of timing. Temporal logical models [14] were used to model the timing behaviour of dynamic systems, however as computer systems exhibit more non-linear characteristics, it is beyond the expressiveness of current modelling capability. The other attempt is to formally model the multi-core system as a group of state machines where each core (or thread) has an independent state diagram with another for synchronisation. This formal analysis is often associated with functional safety, *e.g.,* checking the system is deadlock-free from sharing resources.

5.2 Execution Time Modelling

In the context of modelling of multi-core timing, cache is recognised as one of the most impactful factors. *Static probabilistic timing analysis* (SPTA) and *measurement-based probabilistic timing analysis* (MBPTA) are the two methods for modelling cache for deriving the bound of worst-case execution times [1] [10]. While some of these works consider cache, their purpose is still mainly for deriving the worst-case execution times offline, where these information is not further utilised.

Recent work including analytical cache model with data-driven learning methods provides another direction for execution time modelling, which including *Deep Neural Network* (DNN) and *Recurrent Neural Network* (RNN) including *Long Short-Term Memory* (LSTM). A survey of using some of those models for computer architecture design is given in [13]. There is also work that focuses on inter-core cache effects, *e.g.,* cache interference prediction in multi-cores [8]. Also with high prediction accuracy, those models either does not support run-time use, or has significant overheads for online scheduling and model re-training.

6 Conclusion

In this work, we introduced the DTiL-RTES approach that aims to improve the timing models at run-time to enhance adaptiveness, resilience and robustness of the system. DTiL-RTES makes decisions based on data observed from the system in operation. We first introduced the DTiL-RTES framework, including its key functions and components. We then demonstrated the performance and introduce further challenges. Future work includes how to use this framework to improve scheduling and allocation, apply formal analysis on this framework, and extend the framework with a run-time monitor and anomaly detector.

References

1. Bernat, G., Colin, A., Petters, S.: pWCET: a tool for probabilistic worst-case execution time analysis of real-time systems. University of York (2003)

2. Burns, A., Jones, C.: An approach to formally specifying the behaviour of mixed-criticality systems. In: Euromicro Conference on Real-Time Systems. ACM (2022)
3. Dai, X., Burns, A.: Predicting worst-case execution time trends in long-lived real-time systems. In: Ada-Europe International Conference on Reliable Software Technologies, pp. 87–101. Springer (2017)
4. Dai, X., Burns, A.: Period adaptation of real-time control tasks with fixed-priority scheduling in cyber-physical systems. J. Syst. Archit. **103**, 101691 (2020)
5. Dai, X., Zhao, S., Bate, I.J., Burns, A., Guo, X., Chang, W.: Brief industry paper: digital twin for dependable multi-core real-time systems–requirements and open challenges. In: Real-Time and Embedded Technology and Applications Symposium. IEEE (2021)
6. Falk, H., et al.: Taclebench: a benchmark collection to support worst-case execution time research. In: 16th International Workshop on Worst-Case Execution Time Analysis (2016)
7. Feng, H., Gomes, C., Thule, C., Lausdahl, K., Iosifidis, A., Larsen, P.G.: Introduction to digital twin engineering. In: 2021 Annual Modeling and Simulation Conference (ANNSIM), pp. 1–12. IEEE (2021)
8. Griffin, D., Lesage, B., Bate, I., Soboczenski, F., Davis, R.I.: Forecast-based interference: modelling multicore interference from observable factors. In: Proceedings of International Conference on Real-Time Networks and Systems (2017)
9. Kelly, T., Weaver, R.: The goal structuring notation-a safety argument notation. In: Proceedings of the Dependable Systems and Networks 2004 Workshop on Assurance Cases, p. 6 (2004)
10. Lesage, B., Griffin, D., Soboczenski, F., Bate, I., Davis, R.I.: A framework for the evaluation of measurement-based timing analyses. In: Proceedings of International Conference on Real Time and Networks Systems (2015)
11. Massey, F.J., Jr.: The kolmogorov-smirnov test for goodness of fit. J. Am. Stat. Assoc. **253**, 68–78 (1951)
12. de Oliveira, D.B., Casini, D., de Oliveira, R.S., Cucinotta, T.: Demystifying the real-time linux scheduling latency. In: 32nd Euromicro Conference on Real-Time Systems (ECRTS 2020). Schloss Dagstuhl-Leibniz-Zentrum für Informatik (2020)
13. Penney, D.D., Chen, L.: A survey of machine learning applied to computer architecture design. arXiv preprint (2019)
14. Pnueli, A., Harel, E.: Applications of temporal logic to the specification of real time systems. In: Joseph, M. (ed.) FTRTFT 1988. LNCS, vol. 331, pp. 84–98. Springer, Heidelberg (1988). https://doi.org/10.1007/3-540-50302-1_4
15. Sangiovanni-Vincentelli, A., Damm, W., Passerone, R.: Taming Dr. Frankenstein: contract-based design for cyber-physical systems. Euro. J. Control **18**(3), 217–238 (2012)
16. Szvetits, M., Zdun, U.: Systematic literature review of the objectives, techniques, kinds, and architectures of models at runtime. Softw. Syst. Model. **15**(1), 31–69 (2016)
17. Wei, R., Kelly, T.P., Dai, X., Zhao, S., Hawkins, R.: Model based system assurance using the structured assurance case metamodel. J. Syst. Softw. **154**, 211–233 (2019)
18. Weyns, D., Iftikhar, M.U., De La Iglesia, D.G., Ahmad, T.: A survey of formal methods in self-adaptive systems. In: Proceedings of the Fifth International C* Conference on Computer Science and Software Engineering, pp. 67–79 (2012)
19. Yan, J., Zhang, W.: WCET analysis for multi-core processors with shared L2 instruction caches. In: Real-Time and Embedded Technology and Applications Symposium, pp. 80–89. IEEE (2008)

Towards Reactive Planning with Digital Twins and Model-Driven Optimization

Martin Eisenberg(✉), Daniel Lehner, Radek Sindelar, and Manuel Wimmer

CDL-MINT Institute of Business Informatics - Software Engineering,
Johannes Kepler University Linz, Linz, Austria
{martin.eisenberg,daniel.lehner,radek.sindelar,
manuel.wimmer}@jku.at

Abstract. Digital Twins are emerging in several domains. They allow to connect various models with running systems based on bi-directional data exchange. Thus, design models can be extended with runtime views which also opens the door for many additional techniques such as identifying unexpected system changes during runtime. However, dedicated reactions to these unexpected changes, such as adapting an existing plan which has been computed in advance and may no longer be seen beneficial, are still often neglected in Digital Twins.

To tackle this shortcoming, we propose so-called reactive planning that integrates Digital Twins with planning approaches to react to unforeseen changes during plan execution. In particular, we introduce an extended Digital Twin architecture which allows to integrate existing model-driven optimization frameworks. Based on this integration, we present different strategies how the replanning can be performed by utilizing the information and services available in Digital Twins. We evaluate our approach for a stack allocation case study. This evaluation yields promising results on how to effectively improve existing plans during runtime, but also allows to identify future lines of research in this area.

Keywords: Digital twin · Planning · Models@Runtime · Optimization

1 Introduction

According to Kritzinger et al. [24], a Digital Twin (DT) is a digital object representing a physical object, with an automated data flow from the physical to the digital object, and vice versa. This bi-directional data flow can be used to gain insights into the running system and foster decision-making through visualization and prediction, or eventually achieve autonomous decision-making through self-adaptation [15].

Automated planning can be used to achieve such self-adaptation [18]. Automated planning approaches [17] calculate a set of actions, i.e., a plan, that can be executed to shift a system from an initial state to a desired goal state. Usually, such approaches separate the planning which happens offline and the execution of a plan which happens online while the system is running. This however neglects the online uncertainty of changes that might happen in the system in parallel to the realization of the plan [14]. As a result of these changes, (i) parts of the plan may not be executable any more, or

T. Margaria and B. Steffen (Eds.): ISoLA 2022, LNCS 13704, pp. 54–70, 2022.
https://doi.org/10.1007/978-3-031-19762-8_5

(*ii*) realizing the initial plan leads to an inferior quality in the goal state of the system. In both cases, the old plan does not leverage its initial potential in the running system.

The reactive planning framework proposed in this paper accounts for these unexpected changes during plan execution by providing capabilities for DTs (*i*) to identify deviations in the running system, and (*ii*) to enable online replanning to react to these deviations. In particular, we make use of an existing model-driven optimization (MDO) framework [8]. The MDO framework can be leveraged to reason about the runtime states, and take into account the continuous evaluation of the quality of a plan, considering unforeseen changes in the system. To achieve this technical integration of MDO with DTs, we propose the infrastructure for this integration, i.e., the actual runtime model and the expected runtime model of the system at a specific point in time, a conformance checker component that identifies unexpected system changes by comparing the expected runtime model with the actual runtime model, and a decision maker component that decides how to react to these changes. This infrastructure supports three different reactive planning strategies: (*i*) repairing the old plan by skipping non-executable actions, (*ii*) stopping the system to calculate a new plan using its current state, with the option to use the old plan as a starting point, and (*iii*) calculating a new plan in parallel to executing the repaired plan on the system. We investigate the efficiency of these reactive planning strategies using a stack allocation case study. To sum up, the contribution of this work is (*i*) a reactive planning framework that integrates DTs with MDO, and (*ii*) an experimental investigation of the three strategies to react to unforeseen changes.

The remainder of the paper is structured as follows. Section 2 introduces a running example and outlines the necessary background. Section 3 presents the proposed reactive planning framework by investigating its architecture and realization. In Sect. 4, we describe the experimental evaluation of this framework. Section 5 discusses related work, while Sect. 6 concludes by giving an outlook to future work.

2 Background and Running Example

To make our work more tangible, we use a Stack Load Balancing use case which has been used in previous work on MDO [8] as the running example for this paper. The involved domain concepts are captured in a domain meta-model that is depicted in Fig. 1a. In this use case, a cyber-physical system encompasses several `Stacks` of items. In the context of a production system, these stacks can be thought of as circularly connected machines, each containing a specific quantity of goods, the `load`, to be processed. To simplify this example, we assume that each machine in the system can be treated equally, independently, and processes the same kind of item. The overall productivity depends on the distribution of workload amongst these machines. Therefore, one goal should be to distribute the items as equally as possible between available stacks, i.e., the standard deviation of the item load per stack should be minimized. To achieve this goal, items can be relocated between stacks by shifting them from its original stack to the `left` or `right` neighbour stack. As the transfer can take some time, shorter relocation plans are generally preferred.

To provide an abstract system representation, the design-time and runtime aspects of such a system are represented using models expressed in a domain-specific modeling language [10]. In a `domain metamodel` (cf. Fig. 1a), the available static concepts

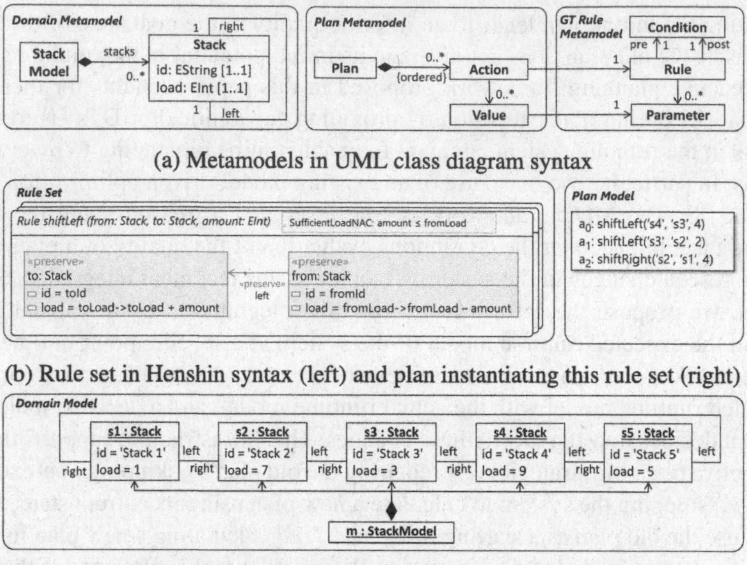

(c) Example Domain Model in UML object diagram syntax

Fig. 1. Artefacts of the running example.

(i.e., stacks), their attributes (id, initial load) and relationships (left and right neighbours) are described. Specific operations (e.g., shiftLeft and shiftRight) of a stack can be specified using graph transformation rules [21] (cf. Fig. 1b). These graph transformations use the graph-based structure of domain models (cf. Fig. 1c) to define rules on this graph structure (based on the `GT rule metamodel` (cf. Fig. 1a)). These rules can be executed to change the model accordingly. Henshin [5] is one prominent graph-based transformation framework that supports their specification and execution. In particular, the rules specify pre- and postconditions for their application and effects, respectively, as well as allow for parameters to be bound for a particular rule application. For our running example, Fig. 1b shows the `shiftLeft` rule with parameters `from`, `to`, and `amount` to declare source and target stacks as well as the shifted load.

The `domain model` (cf. Fig. 1c) is an instantiation of the domain metamodel representing specific items and their attribute values. This model can be used for offline planning, but also for online representation of the runtime state of the system [7]. Specific operations of the system (e.g., shifting stacks) can be simulated on such a domain model by applying the respective graph transformations that change the model accordingly (e.g., change the loads of stacks to simulate the shifting of items).

2.1 Automated Planning and Model-Driven Optimization

Automated planning [17] creates a `Plan` (cf. Fig. 1a—`plan metamodel`) which consists of an ordered list of `Actions`. In our setting, actions are represented as executions of graph transformation rules. They are executed to transfer a system from an initial state to a desired goal state (cf. Fig. 1b). For instance, a plan evolves the system from the state in Fig. 1c into a balanced state with equal item distribution between the available stacks by executing a sequential list of actions. These actions are chosen from the action types (represented as graph transformations rules in our setting) that are offered by the system which executes the plan (cf. Fig. 1b).

Such a plan can be found, e.g., by optimization techniques, to reach the goal state in the most efficient way. However, creating such an optimal plan usually requires to evaluate a large number of potential action sequences for which exhaustive approaches are infeasible. Domain-specific knowledge can facilitate efficient navigation in the solution space, although beneficial heuristics may not be available for the task at hand, or their development poses a challenging endeavour. Accordingly, meta-heuristics such as local search or Genetic Algorithms (GAs) [31] depict a problem-independent and therefore widely adopted alternative. The latter are based on natural selection within a population, i.e., the solution candidates, whose individuals are crossed and mutated while retaining only the fittest subset. In the case of our running example, each candidate resembles a plan consisting of a list of actions (i.e., individuals). The fitness of each plan is calculated based on a predefined fitness function that resembles the optimization goal (e.g., minimize standard deviation in the system, and minimize the number of actions of a plan to reduce its execution time). Presuming a suitable encoding, GAs are known to produce fit individuals fast. Their performance is influenced by the following parameters: (i) the population size, i.e., the number of individuals maintained over generations, (ii) the alteration probabilities concerning crossover and mutation, (iii) the selection operator, and (iv) the number of generations.

In MDO [22], the abstraction capabilities of Model-Driven Engineering [10] are leveraged to provide problem-agnostic frameworks for optimization tasks, e.g., [1, 8, 11]. In the context of automated planning, these frameworks use a model representation of the initial system state (cf. Fig. 1a for our running example), a list of action types represented as graph transformation rules, and produce a plan containing an ordered list of applications of these graph transformation rules (cf. Fig. 1b). This plan is produced by applying an optimization algorithm such as GA.

One MDO tool is MOMoT [8] which bridges the Eclipse Modeling Framework (EMF)[1] for domain modeling with the MOEA Framework[2] as a library for multi-objective search algorithms such as the Non-Dominated Sorting Genetic Algorithm II (NSGA-II) [13], and Henshin [5] for specifying and executing graph transformations. MDO tools such as MOMoT are however intended for offline optimization. The created plans are simulated on the initial model using respective graph transformations to evaluate their effectiveness, but not on the physical systems that are represented by the model. This execution of the plan requires dedicated components, which decouples the execution from the actual planning. If a plan proves to not be beneficial any more during execution on the system level, there is no opportunity to perform online replanning as this would require runtime models which are derived directly from the systems [7]. DTs are intended to integrate the design-time and runtime phases of a system [30], thus they seem promising to solve this challenge of online replanning by reusing MDO tools.

[1] https://www.eclipse.org/modeling/emf.
[2] http://moeaframework.org.

2.2 Digital Twins

As mentioned before, DTs enable a bi-directional data flow between a physical system and its virtual representation [24], requiring different software components to enable this communication [33]. DT platforms [25] offer tool support for the creation of DTs, and their connection to value-adding services that make use of the collected data, e.g., for simulation, visualization, or prediction. One aspect of these platforms is the modeling language used to represent the digital objects [32,38]. In particular, these languages consider design-time aspects (cf. Fig. 1a) and runtime aspects (cf. Fig. 1c), a view that is also supported, e.g., by [30].

Besides connecting the design-time model to the running system to get the runtime model representing the current system state, simulation [16,19] also enables to create several alternative versions of the actual system (referred to as Experimentable Digital Twins (EDTs) [36]). In this work, EDTs can be used to provide an expected runtime model, simulating how the system would look like at a certain point in time when the created plan is executed as expected. However, even if the capabilities of such EDTs are used, the following challenges for achieving reactive planning are still to be tackled:

- **Challenge 1:** How to identify deviations between expected and actual runtime models? The different models need to be compared to identify unexpected changes in the running system which may trigger replanning.
- **Challenge 2:** How to react to unexpected changes in the running system? If such changes are detected, the DT should react to these deviations to achieve a high potential of the system.
- **Challenge 3:** How to avoid stopping the system while planning during runtime? Replanning should be performed efficiently, if possible in parallel to running the system, as stopping the system might be expensive, e.g., just-in-time production.

3 Reactive Planning Framework

In this section, we present an extended DT architecture and strategies for reactive planning which tackle the three challenges presented in the previous section.

3.1 Reactive Planning Architecture

We propose the reactive planning architecture for DTs as depicted in Fig. 2 which follows the general idea of MAPE-K [3,41]. In this architecture, the `Planner` calculates a `Plan Model` to achieve the goal specified in the `Goal Model` starting from the system state represented in the `Initial Model`, using the action types available in the system as functions. This part is the standard MDO processes as it is realized for instance in MOMoT.

The computed plan model is then sent to the `Digital Twin` (cf. Fig. 2), where the `Plan Execution Engine` extracts the ordered list of `Actions` from this plan model. For each Action a_i, the plan execution engine passes a_i to (i) the `Effector` to execute it on the actual system, and (ii) the `Simulator`, in our case Henshin, to calculate the `Expected Runtime Model` after a_i is executed on the system.

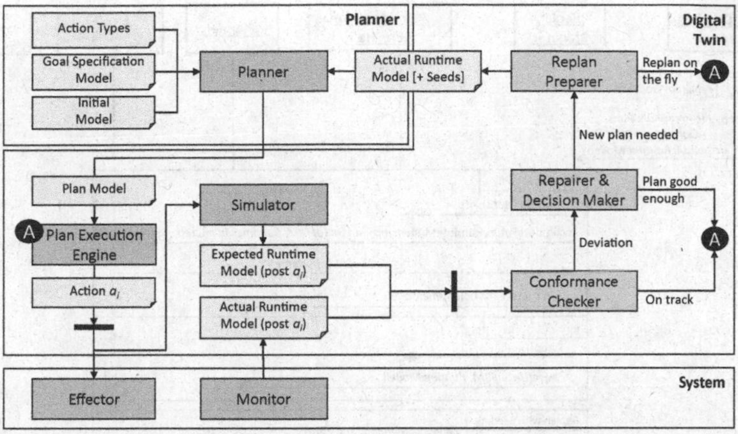

Fig. 2. Reactive planning architecture (components in green are newly introduced). (Color figure online)

The expected runtime model is then passed to the `Conformance Checker` (cf. Fig. 2) together with the `Actual Runtime Model` that is collected from the `Monitor` after a_i is actually executed on the system. If the conformance checker cannot identify any deviation between the actual and expected runtime model, the plan execution engine continues to execute the next action in the plan (i.e., a_{i+1}) in the system and in the simulator. In the opposite case, i.e., a deviation is found, the `DecisionMaker` is invoked to judge the impact of the unforeseen change in the runtime model on the quality of the overall system. If this impact does not require a new plan, the old plan is simply repaired by deleting all actions that are not executable on the new runtime model any more (i.e., the precondition of the respective action type cannot be satisfied). If replanning is required, the `Replan Preparer` is invoked to perform the respective replanning using the planner component. The output of the planner component is the new plan that is then executed on the system by the plan execution engine.

3.2 Reactive Planning Strategies

If the repairer & decision maker component from Fig. 2 identifies that a new plan is necessary, two replanning strategies are provided by our framework (cf. Fig. 3):

- **On-the-fly Mode**: A predefined number of actions of the initial plan is still executed on the system in parallel to the replanning. Therefore, the `proceed` method of the plan execution engine (cf. Fig. 3) is called with the specified number of executed actions. Only after these actions are performed, the system is stopped (just in case that the replan process is not finished by then). The simulator is used to predict the expected runtime model after the execution of the steps, i.e., after execution of a_{a+i}, if `i` steps are executed in parallel to the planning. This runtime model can be injected into the planner as initial model for the replanning.

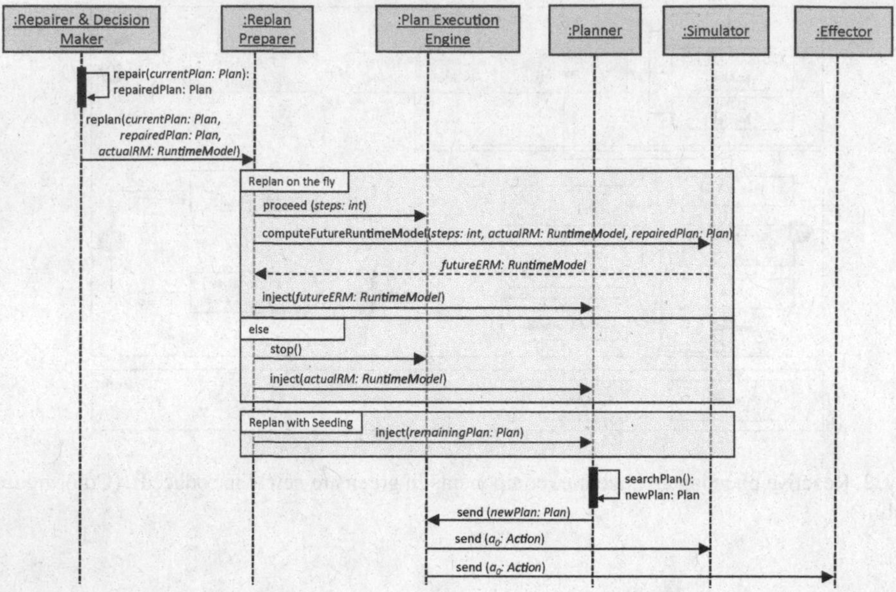

Fig. 3. Replanning options in UML sequence diagram syntax.

– **Idle Mode**: The execution of the old plan is stopped immediately, and the current actual runtime model (after a_i) is injected into the planner as the initial model.

In both strategies, the remaining actions of the old plan can be used as a seed for the replan by injecting them into the planner (cf. Fig. 3). This seed can be used as a starting point for the optimization algorithm as also proposed in previous studies [23, 34], e.g., as individual of the initial population of the GA, in contrast to using a full random starting point that does not take the previous plan into account. After this preparation of the replanning, the planner searches for a new plan, using the injected runtime model, the injected repaired plan in case that seeding is chosen, the initial goal specification model, as well as the action types available in the system. After this plan is created, it is executed on the system using the plan execution engine.

3.3 Prototypical Implementation

To demonstrate our proposed architecture and its capabilities, we provide a prototypical implementation on Github [12]. In this prototype, the MOMoT framework [8] is used as planner. The plan execution engine uses the interpreter engine from Henshin as simulator for the execution of actions and as a stub of the system. To mimic unexpected changes that occur during the execution on the actual system, the monitor reports the expected result by using the Henshin interpreter to produce the next model version and randomly introduces changes in this resulting model. The components that are newly introduced in this paper are all implemented in Java.

3.4 Demonstration Using the Stack Example

In the following, our reactive planning framework is demonstrated by using the running example introduced in Sect. 2. Therefore, we assume Fig. 1c to be the initial model based on which the initial plan (cf. Fig. 1b) is created. After execution of action a_0 however, unexpected changes in the system may happen, which require one of the replanning strategies under consideration.

One such change may be that stack 2 (`s2`) breaks down, leading to its exclusion from the system along with the items residing on it. Following this, intermediate neighbours are rewired to maintain the continuous circular connection intact. Possible causes could be malfunction, or intentional shutdown for maintenance or safety reasons. Once this deviation (`s2` is not available in the actual runtime any more) is identified by the conformance checker, the decision maker repairs the remaining plan (i.e., deletes actions a_1 and a_2, as they involve the removed `s2`), and judges whether a replan is necessary. As the standard deviation (2.2) is significantly higher than the value expected by the original plan (0), a replan is triggered. Since none of the planned actions remain from repair, execution is stopped, and a new plan is calculated.

In an alternative change, a new empty (`load` = 0) stack (`s6`) is added to the system, and connected to the respective neighbours depending on the inserted location (to the right of `s5`). This may occur during reintegration after temporary exclusion to perform maintenance, or to increase throughput in a production context. In this case, although not directly affected by this change, the planned actions are no longer optimal. Thus, replanning would be appropriate. In this case, besides the idle replanning option, also on-the-fly replanning is possible. In the on-the-fly mode, a_1 and a_2 are executed during replanning. The initial model for the parallel replanning is the expected runtime model resulting from these two actions.

4 Evaluation

4.1 Case Study Setup

To evaluate the effectiveness of the proposed reactive planning approach, we perform a case study [35]. The aim is to answer the following research questions:

RQ1: What is the potential of a replanning approach to mitigate runtime deviations compared to naive repair?

RQ2: To which extent does the quality/execution time of replanning solutions change if parts of the initial plan are used as a seed for the replanning algorithm?

RQ3: What is the difference with respect to execution time between calculating the new plan in parallel to running the system, or stopping the system during replanning?

Experimental Setting. We perform the case study on two different systems, i.e., instances, of the stack example. Both systems comprise 50 stacks initially, which are more sparsely and extensively loaded, respectively. More precisely, in the first system, each stack holds between 1 and 10 items with an overall load amount of 250, whereas in the second system, each stack holds between 1 and 100 items with a total of 2500 items. In both cases, loads are fairly unequal distributed with a standard deviation of 27.359 and 3.181, respectively. Plans are calculated using NSGA-II (MOMoT encoding) until an improvement of 50% is achieved with respect to our primary planning objective, i.e., decreasing the standard deviation. We assume actions take time to execute, hence shorter plans are of interest besides equal distribution. Therefore, we face a multi-objective planning task which also takes into account the plan size. We initialize NSGA-II with the population size set to 100 individuals, each reflecting a plan with up to 200 actions. Descendants of a generation are subject to one-point crossover, effectively exchanging parts of two "parent" plans at the same position, with a probability $p = 0.8$. For mutation within plans, three operators are used to remove ($p = 0.1$) or add ($p = 0.2$) actions, or vary ($p = 0.2$) the actions' shifting amounts. The value range for the shift amount is set to 5 and 50, respectively, for the lesser and more loaded instance. Execution of a plan is disturbed by changes introduced to the running system at partly random points in time. With this setting, we perform the following three experiments.

Experiment 1. For RQ1 and RQ2, we investigate the objective value reached with (i) a **naive repair** treatment, i.e., skipping the now unfeasible steps in our original plan, to (ii) a replanning treatment in which we execute the GA for 200 generations to plan with the disturbed runtime model. For this, we distinguish between a traditional **replanning** (denoted replan) setting in which the initial population consists of randomly synthesized plans, and a **replanning with seed** (denoted $\text{replan}_{10\%}$) approach, in which 10% of the population is initialized with the remaining actions of the initial plan. In this regard, initial experiments showed that 10% was most beneficial for the seeding factor, as increasing the proportion further degraded the GAs performance. Excessive embedding of action sequences appears to lead to an overwhelming preference for them, putting the GA on a suboptimal path from the start and affecting population diversity.

Experiment 2. To continue with the results of Experiment 1 for achieving a 50% improvement in the target value, we perform another experiment in which we run replan against $\text{replan}_{10\%}$. This time, however, the GA runs until a plan is found that matches the improvement threshold, rather than over a fixed number of generations.

Experiment 3. We leverage the DT's simulation capabilities for on-the-fly replanning, where the planner is requested to find a plan for the runtime model after projecting it to a future time step. This makes it possible to execute the original (repaired) plan during replanning to avoid stopping the system. We examine on-the-fly replanning for 1 up to 10 prediction steps and compare it to idle replanning, where no further execution on the system during replanning is performed. In all settings, the planner searches until a solution is found that satisfies the 50% improvement over the initial model.

All three experiments are performed under different conditions, varying in the type of perturbation and the time of its occurrence. Recall the two types of perturbation introduced in Sect. 3.4. Accordingly, five stacks are either added or removed from the environment. The locations are chosen randomly but evenly from parts of the stack configuration, i.e., the first stack is inserted/removed somewhere between the first ten consecutive stacks, the second between the next ten, and so on. In each case, it is ensured that

Table 1. Experiment 1: 50 stacks with 1–100 items per stack. First three rows report median values for deviation of adding 5 stacks. Rows 4–6 report values for removing 5 stacks. Results are replicable for the system with 1–10 items per stack.

Error occurence	Initial plan	Naive repair		Replan		Replan with seed	
	Median value	Median value	Diff to initial plan	Median value	Diff to naive repair	Median value	Diff to no seed
First 10%	13.602	22.176	63.0%	13.583	–38.8%	14.971	10.2%
Middle 10%	13.636	20.063	47.1%	12.317	–38.6%	14.544	18.1%
Last 10%	13.603	19.384	42.5%	11.688	–39.7%	17.905	53.1%
First 10%	13.650	17.068	25.0%	11.737	–31.2%	12.536	6.8%
Middle 10%	13.585	15.752	16.0%	10.751	–31.8%	13.038	21.3%
Last 10%	13.574	13.760	1.4%	9.771	–29.0%	13.108	34.2%

the remaining stacks are connected in such a way that the circular connection remains intact. In terms of timing, the disruption occurs (i) in the first 10%, (ii) in the middle 10%, or (iii) in the last 10% of scheduled actions. That is, for a delegated plan with 200 actions, a deviation for the particular case occurs during one of actions 1–20, 90–110, or 180–200, in the latter case guaranteed before the scheduled plan is completed. Each experiment is run 30 times for each setting, except for Experiment 3. On occasion, perturbation in the last 10% of planned actions obstruct forecasting considering that simulation steps may exceed the remaining planned actions. Therefore, this setting is excluded from this experiment.

Evaluation Metrics. In Experiment 1, we measure the objective value of the system (i) after the deviation, (ii) after executing the naive repair approach, (iii) after replan, and (iv) after replan$_{10\%}$. Also, to gain more insights into the GAs performance over time, we plot the lowest objective value resulting from the current best available plan in each generation for both replan and replan$_{10\%}$. In Experiment 2, we measure the time required to achieve the desired 50% improvement as an indicator of the execution time of the replanning variants. Note that this is not achievable by merely removing infeasible actions, thus the naive repair approach is omitted here. In Experiment 3, the execution time is measured. It corresponds to the sum of (i) the time needed to find the new plan and (ii) the time needed to execute the tasks of the new plan (assuming an execution time of 10 s per task).

Regarding results, we report on the median values after recording 30 runs to deal with the stochastic nature concerning deviation settings and the GA. In addition, we conduct statistical tests [4] to identify whether our observations are significant. We perform a Mann-Whitney U test [29] with a significance level $\alpha = 0.01$, and opt for a two-sided test where appropriate. It is a non-parametric test that enables comparison of two random variables without the premise on having a normally distributed sample. If the p-value is less than or equal to α, the null hypothesis (H0) is rejected and we assume a true difference; if the p-value is greater than α, H0 is accepted. All data and scripts are available in the Github repository [12].

4.2 Case Study Results

Experiment 1: A first result is the impact of the deviations (i.e., adding and removing stacks) on the standard deviation in the system. Conducting tests comparing the standard deviation in the system before and after deviation shows that adding five (empty) stacks has a significant impact on the objective value of the system ($p < .001$, in all settings), whereas removing five does not ($.641 < p < .739$, in all settings).

Table 1 reports the objective values expected from the initial plan prior deviation, and those resulting from plans after naive repair/replan/replan$_{10\%}$ post deviation for previously described add/remove scenarios. Albeit removing stacks does not necessarily lead to a more or less balanced item allocation, in the first or middle 10% of planned execution, continuing with the repaired plan results in a much worse setting than executing the initial plan on the system would have, provided that no deviation has occurred ($p = 5.07e^{-10}$ and $p = 1.31e^{-08}$). Only when removing stacks after 90% plan execution, the difference between executing the repaired plan and the expectation from initial planning turns out insignificant ($p = 0.091$). For the removing case with 1–100 items per stack, results indicate that replan performs better than naive repair and replan$_{10\%}$ with a deviation at the beginning (replan vs. naive repair, $p < 1.51e^{-11}$, and replan vs. replan$_{10\%}$, $p = 3.178e^{-05}$), in the middle (replan vs. naive repair, $p < 1.509e^{-11}$, and replan vs. replan$_{10\%}$, $p = 1.431e^{-05}$), and towards the end of execution (replan vs. naive repair, $p < 1.51e^{-11}$, and replan vs. replan$_{10\%}$, $p = 1.51e^{-11}$). These results can also be replicated for the smaller model with 1–10 items per stack.

Looking at the target evolution over several generations (cf. Fig. 4 for the add case), replan$_{10\%}$ performs better than replan with its random initial population in the first generations. In fact, the random initialization performs so poorly initially that the plans produced are also inferior to the naive repair solution. After about 25 generations, however, replan generally outperforms the naive repair solution, and between 25 and 75 generations, it also outperforms the replan$_{10\%}$. It can also be seen that the more advanced the execution of the plan, the less advantageous reseeding is and the less different the result is from a naive repair. The remove cases show a similar pattern, as do these cases in regard to the less loaded system.

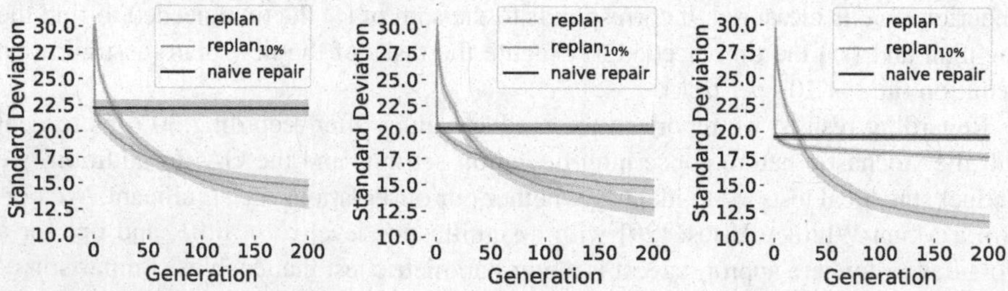

(a) After 0-10% execution (b) After 45-55% execution (c) After 90-100% execution

Fig. 4. Development of objective value over 200 generations for the add stack deviation.

Experiment 2: In Experiment 1, we found that the performance of replanning options varies with the number of generations developed by the GA. Clearly, more generations are required in general to find a new plan that satisfies higher target requirements. The progressions in Fig. 4 nevertheless indicate that choosing the right option depends on the desired target value. Therefore, in Experiment 2, we compare the generations required to achieve the initial goal value (i.e., 50% reduction of standard deviation in the system). Inspection of the median execution times for replan and $\text{replan}_{10\%}$ reveals both to be a beneficial choice dependent on the application context: when introducing new stacks, the bias in the initial population leads to substantially longer execution times to find a plan conformant with the improvement requirement, compared to its unbiased counterpart ($\text{replan}_{10\%}$ vs. replan, $1.505e^{-11} < p < .002$, in all cases). In contrast, after removing stacks from the environment, the search time is significantly reduced when considering the outdated plan with $\text{replan}_{10\%}$, given a deviation at the beginning or towards the end ($p = 8.0e^{-06}$ and $p = 2.93e^{-04}$).

Experiment 3: In Fig. 5, the median over 30 runs is shown for the relative decrease in execution time when planning from states the system will enter during the next 10 actions. A trend towards lower overall execution times is observable in all cases although seemingly more substantial for later deviations w.r.t. completion of the initial plan. Hence the further we can anticipate the system situation, the more efficient planning seems to become while plans still comply with the 50% improvement condition, but seemingly facilitate faster system operation at the same time. Table 2 contains the p-values to establish significance between on-the-fly planning for up to 10 upcoming plan steps, and disruptive planning where the system is idle. Following the trend of Fig. 5, planning from states further down the line leads to increasingly more efficient system operation. Evidently, parallel replanning outperforms idle replanning from seven anticipated steps onwards, in 3 of 4 cases, with exception of the system being augmented soon after execution start. Planning 10 steps in advance turns out superior in any case.

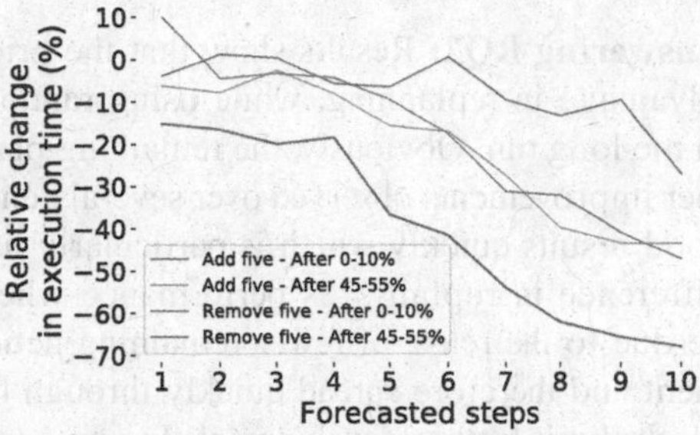

Fig. 5. Results of Experiment 3.

Table 2. Test statistic (p-value) comparing idle replanning vs. replanning on-the-fly. Results are reported for the system with 1–100 items per stack, but express the same tendency for the system with 1–10 items per stack. Significant results are highlighted.

Case		Forecasted steps									
		1	2	3	4	5	6	7	8	9	10
Add	0–10%	.45	.754	.685	.404	.305	.679	.069	.015	.3	**.001**
	45–55%	.255	.163	.562	.228	.058	.015	**$1.06e^{-04}$**	$7.4e^{-07}$	$7.4e^{-07}$	**$2.110e^{-09}$**
Remove	0–10%	.929	.178	.573	.63	.26	.031	**$1.340e^{-04}$**	**$2.804e^{-05}$**	**$1.127e^{-04}$**	**$7.733e^{-10}$**
	45–55%	**.007**	**.004**	**.001**	.019	**$1.0e^{-06}$**	**$1.1e^{-05}$**	**$1.505e^{-07}$**	**$3.56e^{-09}$**	**$2.039e^{-11}$**	**$4.533e^{-11}$**

4.3 Discussion

Answering RQ1: As one would expect, accepting downtime to raise a new plan that is dedicated to the current state is superior to enforcing a partly obsolete and broken plan. This holds true for both augmentation and reduction in the system, and regardless of the deviation occurring sooner or later in the execution span. Nonetheless, late-occurring perturbations naturally carry a lower potential for degeneration, where few actions remain in the plan, which should be taken into account to consider replanning worthwhile. It is also worth noting that our case may not be affected by disruption to the extent that would be observed in other cases. Indeed, actions that do not involve added or removed stacks remain unaffected. Thus, simply omitting infeasible actions is more detrimental when the actions are causally interdependent, so it is expected that a plan with the naive repair approach becomes infeasible in many parts.

Answering RQ2: Results show that the prior plan in the GA population provides an advantage in replanning, while using randomly synthesized plans is more beneficial in the long run. Obviously, the remaining plan provides a good starting point, with further improvements observed over several generations. Therefore replan$_{10\%}$ can provide good results quickly which is particularly useful for urgent scenarios. The noticeable difference in replan$_{10\%}$'s performance when perturbations tend to occur later could be due to the reuse of fewer remaining actions, which still provide a small improvement and therefore spread quickly through the rest of the population, but also significantly limit further development. In contrast, the exclusive randomness present in the replan option allows for better solutions overall, with the advantage of replan$_{10\%}$ disappearing over time. Moreover, results show that it makes sense to use one or the other option depending on the situation. If the goal is to reach a certain quality threshold, the seed option is preferable when stacks are disconnected from the system. In this case, replan$_{10\%}$ provides such a solution much faster. However, if the quality of the plan is paramount or if additional stacks are introduced, random initialization is recommended. In this context, the bias associated with the seed variant seems counter-intuitive when the updated runtime model indicates severe impairments of the system, but works well to counteract minor impairments of the system. Similar to naive repair, which is highly dependent on how functional the remaining plan part is, this likely also affects building on previous planning solutions, as is the case with replan$_{10\%}$, and requires further investigation.

Answering RQ3: Results of Experiment 3 suggest that execution times can be reduced by anticipating future system states and coordinating the planning effort with the running system, assuming things go as planned. To this end, on-the-fly replanning outperformed the "stop and replanning" treatment, i.e., idle replanning, in 3/4 of the cases where execution of at least seven more steps was granted. It should be noted that the execution times are calculated assuming that an action takes 10 s. Remarkably, on-the-fly replanning is favored the longer the actions take, leaving more time for the planner to search for better quality and shorter plans, which in turn leads to faster execution overall. In addition, more time for planning also increases the likelihood of finding a plan that meets the requirements with fewer steps executed in parallel, which can reduce the risk of further disruptions in the meantime.

4.4 Threats to Validity

The presented study builds on assumptions and decisions regarding their design, employed tools, and methods used that can affect its validity.

Internal Validity. As elaborated in Sect. 2.1, we use MOMoT as MDO tool for planning, thereby employing NSGA-II to derive the plan models on request of the DT. For plan evaluation we consider an objective dedicated to the task we investigated, minimizing the plan size. Reproducibility is threatened as the Henshin engine proposes actions during planning in a non-deterministic way which affects NSGA-II's initialization. Moreover, GAs are of stochastic nature and performance relies on several parameter settings whereby we adhere to commonly reported values. We counteract by repeating experiments for 30 times and conducting statistical tests to establish significance. Finally, the possibility of obtaining better results with a seeding factor other than 10% can not be ruled out and is left to further work.

External Validity. MOMoT uses Henshin to execute graph transformations on models and the MOEA framework to encode rule applications. Therefore action types have to be defined as graph transformation rules, and the runtime model of the DT has to be conformant with EMF. To demonstrate our DT integration we used a Stack Load Balancing case with two different configurations. Although suitable to clarify our contributions in this work, it is unclear whether our observations convey to other, possibly more complex domains and may be subject to more severe restrictions. For this reason, applicability needs to be shown also for other use cases, e.g., to envisage further deviation and action types. In this regard, assuming 10 s per action in Experiment 3 poses a strong limitation for the on-the-fly approach and is essential for our results. Moreover, we deal with several circumstances that may not be present elsewhere, including (i) enough feasible steps to enable forecasting post disruption, (ii) no system deviations during parallel replanning, and (iii) estimations for action execution times, all of which can suffer from variations and uncertainties in the environment, making adoption in other contexts challenging.

5 Related Work

Two threads of related work are discussed: (i) DT architectures and (ii) previous efforts to leverage prior planning information to tackle unforeseen changes.

DT Architectures. Different architectures have been proposed to exchange and handle data in DT systems in a unified, expandable way (e.g., see [28]). Whereas these architectures give a conceptual overview on how a DT can be used together with a CPS and value-adding services, there is also work that discusses specific key elements of a DT, e.g., Talkhestani et al. [37] mention synchronization with the physical asset, data acquisition, and simulation as key requirements and emphasize the importance of intelligence in DTs to enable autonomous CPS, e.g., to enrich them with predictive and learning capabilities, and also propose an architecture for AI-assisted decision making. An alternative to this AI-based solution is to employ case-based reasoning [9].

In comparison, our framework supports targeted adaptation in response to perturbation. Instead of acting on predefined patterns, the planner in our architecture is triggered by a separate checker component, e.g., when a critical quality threshold is reached. A new plan is then calculated, possibly reusing the outdated plan, to reach a desired system state. Furthermore, we use simulation to investigate the implications of planning in anticipation of future system states (i.e., on-the-fly replanning). This mitigates downtime and decreases execution time, and thus, may become a valuable property for DTs. Such a forecasting module has already been considered, e.g., for iterative plan refinement parallel to execution [40], but without considering uncertainty in plan execution.

Automated Planning and Adaptation. Initialization of GAs was investigated to improve adaptation in case-based reasoning [20], also using a memory to be leveraged on similar problems [27]. There is already work on considering reactions to runtime changes after an initial plan is calculated, e.g., using rule-based rewriting and local search [2], contemplating negative impacts for upcoming actions during execution to find a more robust alternative plan [6], an iterative procedure of plan simulation and adjustment upon detection of error-prone actions [26], and reasoning from past decisions and outcomes [39]. In [34], the authors even use a GA, similar to our work, and in order to strive for quick adaption to newly emerging tasks in a real-time mission replanning case. Therefore, the GA is initialized with previously computed task assignments (comparable to the seeding in our work). This improved initialization of a GA is also investigated by Kinneer et al. [23], but they face substantial evaluation overhead after embedding previous plans into the population. However, in our approach randomly generated plans demand more evaluation effort than solutions from prior planning as they exhaust the maximum solution length, hence we observe speedups after reseeding the obsolete plan, in contrast to the result from [23]. In general, their work focuses on handling uncertainty in a non-reactive manner whereas the planning layer in our framework couples disturbance detection with subsequent treatment. The MDO engine integrated into our architecture potentially also supports adaptation to unforeseen scenarios such as changing action types, goals, or system developments.

To sum up, our work is the first approach to use an MDO framework for replanning, also utilizing DT features to realize on-the-fly replanning. Seeding and initializing GA for replanning has been already used in the past, but our results provide interesting insights in case time critical replanning is required for CPS.

6 Conclusion and Future Work

In this paper, we have connected MDO with DTs and utilized the resulting overall framework for reactive planning. As the initial results are promising, the framework is also considered as a testbed for future experiments on reactive planning as all components are published as open source solutions.

For future work, we see the following lines of research. First, additional scenarios have to be explored to further validate the different replanning strategies and integration with running systems. Moreover, learning-based methods seem beneficial to be integrated in our framework to reach predictive planning. Finally, dedicated repair mechanisms may be a valuable extension as an alternative to replanning, e.g., if replanning is costly or only a few actions need to be repaired.

Acknowledgements. Work partially funded by the Austrian Science Fund (P 30525-N31) and by the Austrian Federal Ministry for Digital and Economic Affairs and the National Foundation for Research, Technology and Development (CDG).

References

1. Abdeen, H., et al.: Multi-objective optimization in rule-based design space exploration. In: ASE (2014)
2. Ambite, J.L., Knoblock, C.A.: Planning by rewriting. In: JAIR (2001)
3. Arcaini, P., Riccobene, E., Scandurra, P.: Modeling and analyzing MAPE-K feedback loops for self-adaptation. In: SEAMS (2015)
4. Arcuri, A., Briand, L.C.: A practical guide for using statistical tests to assess randomized algorithms in software engineering. In: ICSE (2011)
5. Arendt, T., Biermann, E., Jurack, S., Krause, C., Taentzer, G.: Henshin: Advanced concepts and tools for in-place EMF model transformations. In: MODELS (2010)
6. Beetz, M., McDermott, D.V.: Improving robot plans during their execution. In: AIPS (1994)
7. Bencomo, N., Götz, S., Song, H.: Models@run.time: a guided tour of the state of the art and research challenges. In: SoSyM (2019)
8. Bill, R., Fleck, M., Troya, J., Mayerhofer, T., Wimmer, M.: A local and global tour on MOMoT. In: SoSyM (2019)
9. Bolender, T., Bürvenich, G., Dalibor, M., Rumpe, B., Wortmann, A.: Self-adaptive manufacturing with digital twins. In: SEAMS (2021)
10. Brambilla, M., Cabot, J., Wimmer, M.: Model-Driven Software Engineering in Practice, 2nd edn. Morgan & Claypool Publishers, San Rafael (2017)
11. Burdusel, A., Zschaler, S.: Towards scalable search-based model engineering with MDEOptimiser scale. In: MODELS-C (2019)
12. CDL-MINT: ReactiveMOMoT (2022). https://github.com/cdl-mint/momot-reactive
13. Deb, K., Agrawal, S., Pratap, A., Meyarivan, T.: A fast and elitist multiobjective genetic algorithm: NSGA-II. In: TEC (2002)
14. Esterle, L., Porter, B., Woodcock, J.: Verification and uncertainties in self-integrating system. In: ACSOS-C (2021)
15. Feng, H., Gomes, C., Thule, C., Lausdahl, K., Iosifidis, A., Larsen, P.G.: Introduction to digital twin engineering. In: ANNSIM (2021)
16. Fitzgerald, J.S., Larsen, P.G., Pierce, K.G.: Multi-modelling and co-simulation in the engineering of cyber-physical systems: towards the digital twin. In: From Software Engineering to Formal Methods and Tools, and Back (2019)
17. Ghallab, M., Nau, D., Traverso, P.: Automated Planning: Theory and Practice. Elsevier, Amsterdam (2004)
18. Gil, R.: Automated planning for self-adaptive systems. In: ICSE (2015)
19. Gomes, C., Thule, C., Broman, D., Larsen, P.G., Vangheluwe, H.: Co-simulation: a survey. In: CSUR (2018)
20. Grech, A., Main, J.: Case-base injection schemes to case adaptation using genetic algorithms. In: ECCBR (2004)
21. Heckel, R., Taentzer, G.: Graph Transformation for Software Engineers. Springer, Cham (2020). https://doi.org/10.1007/978-3-030-43916-3

22. John, S., et al.: Searching for optimal models: comparing two encoding approaches. In: JOT (2019)
23. Kinneer, C., Garlan, D., Goues, C.L.: Information reuse and stochastic search: managing uncertainty in self* systems. In: TAAS (2021)
24. Kritzinger, W., Karner, M., Traar, G., Henjes, J., Sihn, W.: Digital twin in manufacturing: a categorical literature review and classification. In: IFAC (2018)
25. Lehner, D., et al.: Digital twin platforms: requirements, capabilities, and future prospects. IEEE Softw. **39**(2), 53–61 (2022)
26. Lesh, N., Martin, N.G., Allen, J.F.: Improving big plans. In: AAAI/IAAI (1998)
27. Louis, S.J., McDonnell, J.R.: Learning with case-injected genetic algorithms. In: TEC (2004)
28. Malakuti, S., Schmitt, J., Platenius-Mohr, M., Grüner, S., Gitzel, R., Bihani, P.: A four-layer architecture pattern for constructing and managing digital twins. In: ECSA (2019)
29. Mann, H.B., Whitney, D.R.: On a test of whether one of two random variables is stochastically larger than the other. Ann. Stat. **18**(1), 50–60 (1947)
30. Margaria, T., Schieweck, A.: Towards engineering digital twins by active behaviour mining. In: Olderog, E.-R., Steffen, B., Yi, W. (eds.) Model Checking, Synthesis, and Learning. LNCS, vol. 13030, pp. 138–163. Springer, Cham (2021). https://doi.org/10.1007/978-3-030-91384-7_8
31. Mitchell, M.: An Introduction to Genetic Algorithms. MIT Press, Cambridge (1998)
32. Pfeiffer, J., Lehner, D., Wortmann, A., Wimmer, M.: Modeling capabilities of digital twin platforms - old wine in new bottles? In: ECMFA (2022)
33. Qi, Q., Tao, F., Hu, T., Anwer, N., Liu, A., Wei, Y., Wang, L., Nee, A.: Enabling technologies and tools for digital twin. J. Manuf. Syst. **58**, 3–21 (2021)
34. Ramirez-Atencia, C., Bello-Orgaz, G., R-Moreno, M.D., Camacho, D.: MOGAMR: a multi-objective genetic algorithm for real-time mission replanning. In: SSCI (2016)
35. Runeson, P., Höst, M.: Guidelines for conducting and reporting case study research in software engineering. In: EMSE (2009)
36. Schluse, M., Priggemeyer, M., Atorf, L., Rossmann, J.: Experimentable digital twins - streamlining simulation-based systems engineering for industry 4.0. In: TII (2018)
37. Talkhestani, B.A., et al.: An architecture of an intelligent digital twin in a cyber-physical production system. at-Automatisierungstechnik (2019)
38. Tao, F., Zhang, H., Liu, A., Nee, A.Y.C.: Digital twin in industry: state-of-the-art. In: TII (2019)
39. Veloso, M.M.: Flexible strategy learning: analogical replay of problem solving episodes. In: AAAI (1994)
40. Wally, B., et al.: Leveraging iterative plan refinement for reactive smart manufacturing systems. In: TASE (2021)
41. Weyns, D., Iftikhar, M.U., de la Iglesia, D.G., Ahmad, T.: A survey of formal methods in self-adaptive systems. In: C3S2E (2012)

Digital Twin Reconfiguration Using Asset Models

Eduard Kamburjan(✉), Vidar Norstein Klungre, Rudolf Schlatte, S. Lizeth Tapia Tarifa, David Cameron, and Einar Broch Johnsen

Department of Informatics, University of Oslo, Oslo, Norway
{eduard,vidarkl,rudi,sltarifa,davidbc,einarj}@ifi.uio.no

Abstract. Digital twins need to adapt to changes in the physical system they reflect. In this paper, we propose a solution to dynamically reconfigure simulators in a digital twin that exploits formalized asset models for this purpose. The proposed solution uses (1) semantic reflection in the programs orchestrating the simulators of the digital twin, and (2) semantic web technologies to formalize domain constraints and integrate asset models into the digital twin, as well as to validate semantically reflected digital twin configurations against these domain constraints on the fly. We provide an open-source proof-of-concept implementation of the proposed solution.

1 Introduction

Digital twins are model-centric applications in which some asset—typically a physical system—is mirrored in near real-time, or *twinned*, by a digital artefact in order to understand, predict or control the behaviour of the asset (e.g., [15,36]). We envision a digital artefact, the so-called *digital twin* (DT), that contain components that compare the behaviour of the targeted asset, the so-called *physical twin* (PT), with expected behaviour based on a model, optimize the behaviour of the asset and prototype new designs. A typical example of such a component in the digital twin is a simulation model to explore the expected behaviour of the physical system.

The digital and physical twins are *coupled*: Data concerning the physical twin, such as live sensor data obtained by monitoring the physical system, are transmitted to the digital twin. Decisions made by the digital twin by analysing this data in the context of its model of the physical system, are communicated back. The connection between the digital twin and the physical system, and the integration of new observations of the physical system (such as live sensor data) into the digital twin's model of the physical system, are realized by the application itself; in this work, we refer to this architectural layer of the digital twin as the *Digital Twin Infrastructure (DTI)*; The DTI is not only responsible

This work was supported by the Research Council of Norway through the projects SIRIUS (237898) and PeTWIN (294600).

T. Margaria and B. Steffen (Eds.): ISoLA 2022, LNCS 13704, pp. 71–88, 2022.
https://doi.org/10.1007/978-3-031-19762-8_6

for communication between the components of the DT but also of its evolution through the dynamic reconfiguration of simulation models.

As the physical system evolves over time, we may experience that the digital twin and the physical twin drift apart. This leads to a precision loss in the digital twin's ability to reflect the behaviour of the physical system. For example, the physical system may change through maintenance operations or unexpected events (such as failures). The simulation model may also drift due to uncertainty in parameters or noise in the sensor data it receives from the physical system.

This paper considers how digital twins can be *dynamically reconfigured* in response to changes in the physical twin. There are two categories of reconfiguration. The first category is *behavioural reconfiguration*, where the behaviour of the digital twin must be adapted but the structure of the physical system remains intact. For example, if simulated behaviour drifts away from the sensor data from the physical system, the corresponding simulator must be recalibrated with different parameters to match the real behaviour [8]. The second category is *structural reconfiguration*, where the structure of the physical system changes and the digital twin must perform some adaptation that goes beyond adjusting a single component. For example, reconstruction work or reorganisation in a factory may affect its entire production pipeline. The main focus of this paper is on the structural reconfiguration of digital twins.

To accommodate such reconfigurations, we here consider the use of *semantic web* technologies to connect the configuration of the digital twins to formalized *asset models.* Semantic web technologies are logic-based techniques to formalize knowledge and data, as well as to query and reason over the formalized knowledge represented as a *knowledge graph.* Semantic web technologies have been recognized as one of the potential pillars in symbolic AI for digital twins. Asset models are descriptions of the composition and properties of some physical asset, which is essential to represent the structure of the physical system not only for digital twins, but also for other engineering and maintenance applications [32,41].

In short, the main contributions of this paper are:

- a solution for structural reconfiguration of digital twins using formalized asset models, and
- a proof-of-concept realization of a digital twin infrastructure which orchestrates and configures simulation models, integrated with asset models.

We use the *Semantic Micro Object Language (SMOL)* [21] for our implementation. SMOL is a small, experimental and formally defined programming language with explicit primitives both to integrate simulation units, namely for the Functional Mock-Up Interface [4], and to integrate semantic web technologies that operate directly on the program state of the SMOL program itself. SMOL is open source and available from http://smolang.org.

Related Work. The connection of digital twins and knowledge bases so far is mostly limited to data integration to handle the numerous heterogeneous data sources in a digital twin. For example, Yan et al. [43] use knowledge bases to integrate data in manufacturing equipment and enable the user to query this

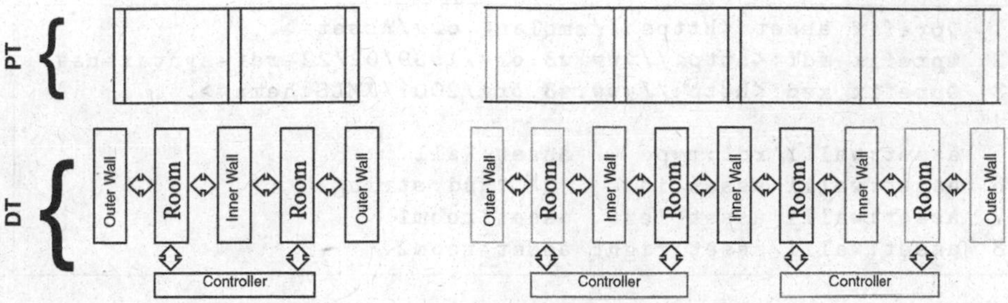

Fig. 1. A house (left top), its digital twin (left bottom), an extension of the house (right top) and the corresponding structural reconfiguration of the digital twin (right bottom). In the reconfigured digital twin, gray components are new and blue components need to be adapted. (Color figure online)

information more easily. Banerjee et al. [2] use a similar approach to interact with data from IoT sensors in industrial production lines, and Oakes et al. [28] for drivetrains. Going one step further, Wascak et al. [40] aim to use asset models as part of this integration in their abstract digital twin architecture. More abstractly, Kharlamov et al. [22] have investigated the use of KBs for data integration in the context of the energy industry, and used this integrated data to enable machine learning on data streams [45]. Lietaert et al. [25] use KBs similarly to integrate data for machine learning approaches. To the best of our knowledge, the use of KBs to influence the structure of the digital twin after its initial construction is hitherto unexplored. We discuss related work for asset models in Sect. 3.

Structure. Section 2 explains the problem of digital twin reconfiguration in terms of a motivating example and Sect. 3 introduces preliminaries. We use the motivating example to discuss the interplay of asset models, semantic web technologies, simulation units and programming in Sect. 4 and structural reconfiguration in Sect. 5. Section 6 concludes the paper.

2 Motivating Example

Let us consider the digital twin of a small house, which should retain some targeted temperature (inspired by an example developed by OSP [34]). The physical system consists of two rooms, each with an outer wall and a heater, separated by an inner wall. The physical system is depicted in Fig. 1 (top left). The corresponding DT has five simulators modelling the rooms with their heaters, the inner wall and the outer walls, respectively. In addition, the DT includes a controller that decides how to regulate the heaters of the two adjacent rooms, based on the input data. The DT is depicted in Fig. 1 (bottom left). In our example, the controller's restriction to two adjacent rooms is inherent to the available controller software.

```
@prefix asset:<https://smolang.org/Asset#>.
@prefix rdf:<http://www.w3.org/1999/02/22-rdf-syntax-ns#>.
@prefix xsd:<http://www.w3.org/2001/XMLSchema#>.

asset:wall1 rdf:type    asset:Wall.
asset:wall1 asset:id    "2"^^xsd:string.
asset:wall1 asset:left  asset:room1.
asset:wall1 asset:right asset:room2.
```

Fig. 2. Example RDF graph with four statements.

A *behavioural reconfiguration* of the digital twin could be triggered by the following scenario: One of the heaters breaks down and is replaced with a different model which heats the room faster than the previous heater. The digital twin needs to reconfigure itself to adjust the parameters of its corresponding simulation model to reflect that heating in one of the rooms now works faster.

A *structural reconfiguration* of the digital twin could be triggered by the following scenario: The house is extended with two new rooms, one to the left and the other to the right of the existing rooms. The resulting physical system is depicted in Fig. 1 (top right), where the blue walls depict the former outer walls of the house, which have now become inner walls. This change in the physical system would require a complete reconfiguration of the digital twin. A solution, depicted in Fig. 1 (bottom right), would be to add four new simulators which capture the new rooms and new outer walls of the physical system (gray color in the figure), to change two of the existing simulators to reflect the change from outer walls to inner walls (blue color in the figure), and to replace the old controller by two new controllers (blue color in the figure). For example, the old controller could be removed and two new controllers added to reflect the constraint that only two adjacent rooms can be controlled by one controller.

3 Preliminaries

This section covers technical background for the proposed digital twin infrastructure: Knowledge bases and semantic web technologies, asset models and simulation units.

3.1 Knowledge Bases

Knowledge bases are a triple-based data representation of domain knowledge and other axioms. We here ignore their theoretical properties as description logic models, and briefly introduce four essential semantic web technologies: RDF, OWL, SPARQL and SHACL. All these technologies are W3C recommendations.

The *Resource Description Framework* (RDF) [38] is the framework and data model on which all other Semantic Technologies are built. RDF is used to describe entities (called resources) and their relation to other resources and

```
1 asset:Room rdf:type owl:Class ;
2   rdfs:subClassOf [ rdf:type owl:Restriction ;
3                     owl:onProperty asset:next ;
4                     owl:cardinality 2 ].
5 asset:next rdf:type owl:ObjectProperty.
6 asset:next rdfs:domain asset:Room.
7 asset:next rdfs:range asset:Wall.
8
9 asset:room1 asset:next asset:wall5
```

Fig. 3. Example OWL ontology.

data values (called literals). Each such relationship can be represented as a link between a subject and an object via a given predicate. In RDF, triples of the form (*subject*, *predicate*, *object*) are called statements, and multiple statements constitute a knowledge graph. Each RDF resource is represented by a Uniform Resource Identifier (URI), a unique identifier which makes it possible to refer to the same resource in different RDF graphs.

Figure 2 shows an example RDF graph using Turtle[1] syntax. The first three lines are all prefix declarations (aliases) while each of the lines 5–8 corresponds to a single triple.The statement in line 5 expresses that an entity `asset:wall1` exists and that it is a wall. The statement consists of a subject that is a resource with the URI https://smolang.org/Asset#wall1, which has been simplified to `asset:wall1` by using the prefix in line 1, a predicate that is a resource with URI `rdf:type` that expresses type membership, and an object `asset:Wall`, which is an OWL class.[2] The next line gives an identifier to the wall (`asset:id`), in this case the value "2" of type `xsd:string`. The last two lines express that the wall is between the two rooms `asset:room1` and `asset:room2`.

OWL [37] is an extension to RDF that makes it possible to develop complex models (called ontologies) of any application domain. OWL provides a vocabulary to declare which classes and properties exist, and the rules to which each such class and property must adhere. Figure 3 shows how OWL can be used to make a small ontology for the house example from Sect. 2.The statements in lines 1–4 declare an OWL class `asset:Room`, that has exactly two things stored using the `asset:next` Property. OWL has the open world assumption, at this point we know there are 2 things next to a room, but we may not have them explicit in our KB. The property `asset:next` itself is defined in lines 5–7 and relates `asset:Room` instances to `asset:Wall` instances. In line 9, we increase the KB and said that one of the things next to a `room1` is `wall5`.

OWL gives precise and formal semantics to RDF, which allows automated reasoners to detect inconsistencies in RDF graphs and to infer implicit facts.

[1] https://www.w3.org/TR/turtle/.

[2] OWL classes and individuals are declared when they occur in a triple, not in a separate construct. We can derive that `asset:Wall` is a class, because it is a subject of a triple with predicate `rdf:type`. One can add a triple `asset:Wall a owl:Class` to make this explicit.

For example, by considering the range and domain of the property `asset:next`, a reasoner can infer that the individual `asset:room1` in line 9 is an `asset:Room` and the individual `asset:wall1` is a `asset:Wall`. Subproperties can be defined in OWL; for example, we can declare property `asset:left` to be a subproperty of `asset:next`, in the sense that all `Room` resources that are `left` of a `Wall` resource are also `next` to that `Wall` resource.

SPARQL [30] is the prevailing language for querying and manipulating RDF graphs. It resembles languages such as SQL, but the way it specifies which data to return is specially suited for RDF graphs. In SPARQL, a basic `SELECT` query contains a `WHERE` clause with a graph pattern, which is an RDF graph where parts of the pattern are replaced with variables. The answers to this query are all subgraphs of the RDF knowledge graph that match this pattern, as given by the values from the RDF knowledge graph that were assigned to the variables in the matched pattern. This is demonstrated in the following query, which asks for all walls and their id.

```
SELECT ?a ?i WHERE{?a rdf:type asset:Wall. ?a asset:id ?i}
```

Here, `?a` and `?i` are both variables. When this query is posed over the RDF graph in Fig. 2 it returns only one result: `?a = asset:wall1, ?i = "2"`. SPARQL queries can access derived information by means of a logical consequence relation (technically, an *entailment regime*) [11,12,23].

In contrast to SPARQL, *SHACL* [39] ignores information that is not explicit in the knowledge base. SHACL is not used to check consistency of the knowledge base with respect to the ontology, but to ensure basic validity conditions on the concrete data.

3.2 Asset Modelling

An asset model is an organized description of the composition and properties of an asset (e.g., [16,32,41]). It is common practice in engineering to build asset models to support, e.g., maintenance operations on an asset. Asset models are useful in a digital twin context because they can provide the twin with static configuration data for the twin's simulation model [6]. In industrial applications, the asset model is often spread across several databases such as an asset management system, a engineering database and computer-aided design systems. Asset models may be directly formalized as knowledge bases (e.g., READI [9]), connected to them [26], or treated as such by means of ontology-based data access [29,33] which enable data integration across multiple databases. We can conceptually distinguish two kinds of asset models: top-down and bottom-up.[3]

Top-down asset models start with modelling the desired functionality of the cyber-physical system as a whole, and then decomposing the system into functional sub-systems. There is a tight coupling between functional sub-systems

[3] Standard semantic data for both top-down and bottom-up asset models is the subject of current research projects (e.g., DEXPI [42], CFIHOS [18] and READI [9]).

and simulation components in the digital twin setting [27,35]. This approach, which relates to model-driven engineering [3], is supported by modelling tools and languages such as SysML (e.g., [27]). A top-down model provides a scalable framework for tracking requirements along a system decomposition and linking requirements to individual components to higher-level system requirements [7,10]. However, the semantics of top-down models can be less well defined than for bottom-up models; for example, the Reference Designation System for ISO/IEC81346 [17,31] provides a taxonomy of functional systems for engineering, energy and construction, but is not so far supported by an ontology.

Bottom-up asset models can be given a well-defined semantics since they are organized around the actual physical components of the asset. Depending on the domain, the semantics and data models are provided by standards like ISO15926 [24] for the process industries, ISO10303 for manufacturing and aerospace [1] and BIM [5,44] for the built environment. The common feature of these models is their focus on physical artefacts. The functional behaviour that we want to simulate, is modelled by functional objects that correspond to the physical object. This tight linkage to the physical artefact means these models do not scale well for managing information about system behaviour and requirements, even though they are effective in organizing detailed information regarding individual components.

For the purposes of this paper, we work with a bottom-up asset model. We do this because, for this simple example, there is a tight correspondence between physical artefacts and systems. We do not commit to any specific standard and instead use an RDF based representation and our own ontology. This corresponds to the abstraction layer one would typically use after ontology-based data integration of the different databases that make up a complex asset model. Aspects typically associated with top-down asset models, such as the connection to the functionality, are here realized by the digital twin infrastructure.

3.3 Simulation Units

Simulation units are simulator prototypes that can be instantiated as simulation instances to perform some computation. Simulation units have inputs (to influence the computation) and outputs (to access results) and perform the computation step-wise, where the step size is determined by the driver that uses the simulation instance.

Formally, simulation units [13] are hextuples $(S, U, Y, \texttt{set}, \texttt{get}, \texttt{doStep})$, where S is the internal state space, U the set of input variables, Y the set of output variables, $\texttt{set} : S \times U \times \mathcal{V} \rightarrow S$ the function to set the values of the input variables to some values of domain $\mathcal{V}$, $\texttt{get} : S \times Y \rightarrow \mathcal{V}$ the function to get the results and $\texttt{doStep} : \texttt{S} \times \mathbb{R}^+ \rightarrow \texttt{S}$ the function to perform the simulation for a given amount of time.

We work with a special form of simulation units, namely *functional mock-up units* (FMUs) [14], as defined by the functional mock-up interface (FMI) [4]. The FMI defines additional structures for simulation units, such as types or parameter variables, which cannot be reset, and additional information on the correct usage, e.g., the order of calls needed to initialize an FMU. Most importantly, it defines the *model description*, an XML formatted description of input and output variables, and further information about the FMU.

4 Semantically Lifted Co-simulation

Semantically lifted programs can interpret their runtime state as a knowledge base, and access this knowledge base *describing their own current state* by means of language primitives at runtime [21]. This *semantic reflection* operates on a knowledge base which connects the representation of the runtime state with further ontologies, most importantly static domain knowledge and, in our case here, asset models.

Semantic lifting is supported by the Semantic Micro Object Language (`SMOL`), a Java-like object-oriented programming language. Semantic reflection in `SMOL` is realized through dedicated language primitives, such as an **access** expression, which loads the result of a SPARQL query, evaluated over a lifted enriched ontology under a logical consequence relation (see Sect. 3.1), into a list of objects in the runtime state.

Beyond semantic lifting, `SMOL` supports *Functional Mock-Up Objects*, a transparent layer that tightly integrates FMUs directly into the object model [19]. We here introduce `SMOL` by presenting a minimal digital twin infrastructure for the first scenario of Sect. 2 (see Fig. 1 left) and highlight its distinctive features as we proceed.

Digital Twin. Let us now consider a digital twin of the house from the motivating example in Sect. 2. The overall structure of the digital twin consists of objects of the classes `Wall` and `Room` that mirror the structure of the physical house, and objects of the additional classes `House`, that manages the overall DTI of a single house, `Outside`, to provide the context for the house, and class `Controller`, to make decisions about the heating behaviour.

Figure 4 shows the classes `Dynamic` and `Wall` (the class `Room` is analogous to `Wall`). In the figure, the class `Dynamic` defines two methods that are used for co-simulation (`propagate` and `advance`) to propagate values and uniformly advance time throughout the system, and a getter (`getHeat`) to access the output heat of a simulator. The class `Wall` defines a wrapper for the simulation unit of a wall, it has the following four fields:

- The field `fmo` contains an FMO, i.e., a wrapped FMU. Its type `Cont` wraps descriptions of the ports to the FMU: there are two input variables (`T_room1` and `T_room2`), preceded by the modifier **in**, and one output variable (`h_wall`), preceded by the modified **out**.
- The fields `left` and `right` point to the areas to the left and the right of the wall (an area is either a room or the outside).
- The field `id` is the identifier in the asset model for the physical wall that this object is mirroring (see Fig. 2).

```
1 abstract class Dynamic()
2   abstract Int propagate()
3   abstract Int advance(Double db)
4 end
5
6 class Wall extends Dynamic(
7   Cont[in Double T_room1, in Double T_room2, out Double h_wall] fmo,
8   Area left, Area right, Int id)
9
10  override Int propagate()
11    this.fmo.T_room1   = this.left.getHeat();
12    this.fmo.T_room2   = this.right.getHeat();
13    return 0;
14  end
15  override Int advance(Double db)
16    this.fmo.tick(db); return 0;
17  end
18  Double getHeat() return this.fmo.h_wall; end
19 end
```

Fig. 4. SMOL class for the digital twin of a wall.

The methods realize the propagation of values into the FMU, time advance and the reading of the current temperature of the wall. In SMOL, the FMO is treated as a standard object with a method for time advance (l. 16) and the variables of its type are treated as fields (e.g., l. 11).

We next discuss how to instantiate a wall according to an asset model. Before introducing the asset model for our example in full detail in Sect. 5, we consider a restricted form here: There are OWL classes `asset : Wall` and `asset : Room` that model physical walls and rooms, with a property `asset : id` for their id and two properties `asset : left` and `asset : right` that connects a room to the wall left and right of it. Additionally, there is an OWL subclass `asset : Outer` of `asset : Wall` for the outermost walls.

The code in Fig. 5 shows how `Wall` instances for the outermost walls are created by exploiting the semantic reflection. This requires both access to the semantically lifted program state (to query over the ids of existing objects) and an external knowledge base with an asset model (to query over the ids of existing walls). First, a SPARQL query is executed on the knowledge base (l. 3), using the **access** statement, to select all the ids of outermost walls from the physical asset, from this list we retain the ids of outermost walls which are not stored in the `id` field of any existing `Wall` object (l. 4). Then, a new FMO is loaded for each id, using the **simulate** statement which takes the filepath to an FMU file (l. 7). The type of the FMO is then checked against the variable description given in the model description of the FMU file. Finally, the `Wall` object itself is created and stored in the list of all outermost walls.

```
List<Wall> walls = null;
List<Int> outer
  = access("SELECT ?id WHERE {?a asset:id ?id. ?a a asset:Outer.
               FILTER NOT EXISTS { ?o prog:wall_id ?id}}");
for Int i in outer do
   Cont[in Double T_room1, in Double T_room2, out Double h_wall] fmo
     = simulate("outerWall.fmu");
   walls = this.add(walls, new Wall(fmo, null, null, i));
end
```

Fig. 5. Prettified SMOL code loading walls from the asset model into the digital twin.

Note that the connection of the `outerWall.fmu` FMU and the `asset : Outer` OWL class is established by the digital twin infrastructure, i.e., the code creating the object instances, as we assume a bottom-up asset model. Furthermore, communication to the physical system happens through the `Room` objects, which encapsulate some interface to push and pull values to (resp. from) the physical system. The actual control of the actuators for the heaters in the `Room` objects is not detailed in this paper.

Behavioural Reconfiguration. Reconfiguration can be either structural or behavioural. A behavioural reconfiguration does not change the structure of the DT or DTI, but reacts to changes in the data stream from the PT, such as detected model/sensor drift. To do so, parameters of the existing twinned structure must be set again. Similarly, newly created DTs must be configured as part of their initialization. In the example above, where an outer wall is loaded, it does not suffice to simply create an FMU, if the FMU is used for simulation and not only as an interface to the PT.[4]

Consider an FMU `outerSim` and the case where the outer wall FMU has an additional parameter `in Double p`, which may be set to some value in the interval $[-1, 1]$, and a starting point `in Double init`. To estimate this parameter, one may collect some additional data and perform a model search, for example by recording the n data points coming from the PT, and then testing which value for `p` generates the best fit for these data points. Figure 6 shows a simple linear search for this case [19].

In case an FMU is replaced, the state of the old FMU, which may not be fully exposed, may contain additional information required for the simulation. To handle this, either the FMUs must expose enough information about their inner state to allow such operations, or the parameters of the new FMU, if there are any, must be determined.

Behavioural reconfiguration must be part of structural reconfiguration as the sensor streams, simulators and eventual feedback communication units are all

[4] If it is used as an interface, the identifier of connection to the PT must be given to the FMU (this is elided here).

```
Cont[...] reconfigure(Double last, List<Double> sysVal, Int n)
 Double step = -1;
 List<Double> sim = null;
 while step <= 1 do
  Cont[...] wall = simulate("outerSim.fmu", init=last, p=step);
  for( 0 <= i <= n ) do
   wall.tick(1.0);
   sim = Cons(shadow.h_wall, sim);
  end
  Double d = compare(sim, sysVal); //some error measurement
  if(d <= threshold) then return wall; end //new parameter
  step = step + 0.1;
 end
 return null; //no parameter found
end
```

Fig. 6. Model search for behavioural reconfiguration.

affected by changes in the asset, but as the mechanisms for it are orthogonal to asset models, we refrain from discussing it in more detail.

5 Structural Reconfiguration in SMOL

In this section, we consider the structural reconfiguration of the digital twins, focusing on its simulation component. For the digital twin infrastructure to structurally reconfigure its simulation component, we must (1) detect that the Digital Twin and Physical Twin have structurally drifted apart, as well as the exact kind of change that has occurred, (2) amend the relation between DT and PT, and (3) repair the Digital Twin Infrastructure. We continue with our house example to illustrate how semantic reflection is used to detect structural drift and monitor basic properties after repair. In this paper, we consider a domain-specific approach to the problem of structural reconfiguration in which the reconfiguration of the DT mimics the changes that occur in the PT.

Recall from Sect. 2 that a house must have an even number of rooms to be twinnable. For the sake of the example, we thus assume that the only structural changes that can occur to the asset is adding two rooms to the left of the existing rooms, adding two rooms to the right of the existing rooms, or adding one new room to the left and one to the right of the existing rooms in the house.

Detecting Structural Drift. Every n simulation steps, the DTI runs a query to retrieve all IDs of rooms and walls that are in the asset model but not in the DT. If the number of such IDs is neither 0 (no change) or 2 (valid change), then the change is rejected – it is expressing an update that is not possible to twin because it violates our assumptions about the asset model and its changes. The relevant query is given in Fig. 7. It constructs `RoomAssert` instances, each

```
class RoomAssert(String room, String wallLeft, String wallRight) end
....
List<RoomAssert> newRooms =
  construct("
  SELECT ?room ?wallLeft ?wallRight WHERE
  { ?x a asset:Room;
       asset:right [asset:Wall_id ?wallRight];
       asset:left [asset:Wall_id ?wallLeft]; asset:Room_id ?room.
    FILTER NOT EXISTS {?y a prog:Room; prog:Room_id ?room.} }");
if newRooms != null then // if newRooms == null then no update is needed
  Int nrRooms = newRooms.length();
  if nrRooms != 2 then /* report error */ end
  RoomAssert n1 = newRooms.content;
  RoomAssert n2 = newRooms.next.content;
  ...// (continued in Fig. 8)
end
```

Fig. 7. Detecting structural drift using semantic reflection.

containing the room id of the room in the asset model, as well as the ids of the walls to the left and the right of the room. The query itself is analogous to the example described in Fig. 5. Afterwards, the number of retrieved rooms is used to detect whether a change has happened and, if so, whether the resulting house is still twinnable. The new house is twinnable if there are two new rooms that satisfy our criteria (see above).

Next, the position of the new rooms with respect to the existing structures needs to be detected. To this aim, we determine whether the two new rooms are adjacent to each other, their spatial relation to each other, and their relation to the left-most (resp. right-most) existing room. This is shown in Fig. 8: the first case is that the first retrieved room (`r1`) is right of the second room (`r2`) and left of the existing structure. The second case is that the first retrieved room (`r1`) is left of the second room (`r2`) and right of the existing structure. The last two cases are when the two new rooms are not adjacent and the remaining cases are omitted for readability.

Structural Reconfiguration. Having detected the kind of structural drift, the structure of the DT can be updated in two steps. First, we create the new simulation elements and insert them into the structure. Second, we update the DTI and repair possible virtual elements that are not reflecting elements in the asset (such as the controllers in our example). Figure 9 shows the resulting method which implements the addition of one new room to each side of the existing model. First, the rooms are created using `addOneLeft` and `addOneRight`, then the controller structure is rebuilt in `rebuildCtrl`, before we finally use SHACL to validate that the structural constraints hold for the new model configuration.

```
if n1.wallLeft == n2.wallRight &
  n1.wallRight == house.firstRoom.wallLeft.id then
  house.addTwoRight(n1.wallLeft, n1.room, n2.wallLeft, n2.room);
else
...
if n1.wallRight == n2.wallLeft &
  n1.wallLeft == house.firstRoom.wallRight.id then
  house.addTwoLeft(n1.wallRight, n1.room, n2.wallRight, n2.room);
else
...
if house.firstRoom.wallLeft.id == n1.wallRight then
  house.addLeftRight(n1.wallLeft, n1.room, n2.wallRight, n2.room);
else
  house.addLeftRight(n2.wallLeft, n2.room, n1.wallRight, n1.room);
end
...
```

Fig. 8. Determining the kind of structural drift.

```
Unit addLeftRight(String iw1, String ir1, String iw2, String ir2)
  this.addOneLeft(iw1, ir1); this.addOneRight(iw2, ir2);
  this.firstRoom.rebuildCtrl();
  Boolean valid = validate("examples/House/shape.ttl");
  if !valid then /* report error */ end
end
```

Fig. 9. Adding two rooms and reconstructing the controller structure.

Figure 10 details the addition of a single room. Object creation is straightforward, the interesting change is at its end where the old outer wall becomes an inner wall and the method reloads the FMU. An (omitted) method `calibrate` can adjust the behavioural configuration of the newly loaded FMU, if needed. If the FMU is only an interface that receives data from the PT, then this method may not perform any action. The method `addOneRight` has no counterpart in sole operations on the PT (i.e., addition of a single room is not supported), thus is does not validate the structure at its end.

Figure 11 details the code to completely rebuild the controller structure. It is called on the left-most room and creates a new controller, connects it to the currently considered room and its neighbour, deletes the old controller and continues with the next room with an old controller. A particular detail of semantic lifting is that it requires manual memory management: objects are retrievable by queries even if no pointer to them exists and can, thus, not be garbage collected.

Validation. We can use the knowledge base also to validate consistency constraints. This can be done either using the underlying logic, e.g., by checking

```
Unit addOneRight(String idw, String idr)
  //create new wall and room
  Cont[...] new_outer = simulate("examples/DummyFMUs/OuterWall.fmu");
  Wall new_wall  = new Wall(idw, new_outer, null, null);
  Cont[...] new_room_fmu = simulate("examples/DummyFMUs/Room.fmu");
  Room new_room =
    new Room(idr, new_room_fmu, null, null, null, False, null);
  new_wall.areaLeft = new_room; //link
  ...
  //repair old outer wall
  Cont[...] new_inner = simulate("examples/DummyFMUs/InnerWall.fmu");
  new_room.wallLeft.fmuSim = new_inner;
end
```

Fig. 10. Adding one room and adjusting the wall simulator.

```
Unit rebuildCtrl()
  Cont[...] ctrl = simulate("examples/DummyFMUs/Controller.fmu");
  Controller control = new Controller(ctrl, this, this.nextRoom);
  if this.ctrl != null then destroy(this.ctrl); end
  this.ctrl = control;
  this.nextRoom.ctrl = control;
  if this.nextRoom.nextRoom != null then
    this.nextRoom.nextRoom.rebuildCtrl();
  end
end
```

Fig. 11. Rebuilding the controller structure.

that the knowledge base must is consistent. One can also use queries, by giving special SPARQL queries or OWL classes that must be empty or return an empty answer set. The approach sketched above can be seen as a variation of this idea: the query detecting structural drift formulates the constraint that the DT and the PT are consistent with each other. Such queries can also be used without a following repair.

Alternatively, one can perform data validation using SHACL, which is a more lightweight approach as it does not involve reasoning. For example, to validate the DTI we can formulate that the room that is stored in the `House.firstRoom` field is indeed the first one from the left, as the following SHACL shape.

```
schema:FirstShape a sh:NodeShape ;
  sh:targetClass prog:House ;
  sh:property [
    sh:path
      (prog:House_firstRoom prog:Room_wallLeft prog:Wall_areaLeft);
    sh:class prog:Outside;
  ].
```

It expresses that for every node that is of `prog:House` class, following the path `prog:House_firstRoom prog:Room_wallLeft prog:Wall_areaLeft` ends in an object of type `prog:Outside` . I.e., the area to the left of the left wall of the first room must be outside.

Removal of Assets. To remove objects that are no longer part of the asset model, we run a similar query as before, but must consider that an asset that is removed from the physical system is not removed from the KB, but instead marked as removed. An example for such a query, which directly returns all the `Room` instances to be removed is the following. We refrain from giving the repair methods, which are analogous to adding assets.

```
SELECT ?y WHERE { ?x asset:Room_id ?id;
                     a asset:removed.
                  ?y a prog:Room; prog:Room_id ?id. }
```

6 Conclusion

We have presented an approach to reconfiguring digital twin infrastructure according to structural changes. The approach integrates a knowledge base with a digital twin infrastructure. The knowledge base includes an asset model, which formalises our knowledge of the physical twin, with a similar representation of the runtime state of the digital twin. We provide a proof of concept implementation of the approach in SMOL, a programming language which allows the runtime state of programs to be lifted into a knowledge base and queried from within the running program (so-called semantic reflection). We implement the DTI as a SMOL program and view the physical twin through an asset model. Both DTI and asset models are integrated into a knowledge base, so that the DTI can perform semantic reflection and perform queries on itself and the asset model to detect discrepancies and guide the reconfiguration. The very same integrated knowledge base is also used to validate domain specific constraints on the DTI and the relation of the DTI to asset model.

Our proof of concept implementation in SMOL has assumed a one-to-one relation between the components of the asset model and those of the simulation system. In future work, we will explore other relations between the structure of the asset and the structure of the digital twin. Furthermore, we aim to automatically generate the digital twin infrastructure from a top-down asset model, including automatic detection of structural drift and repair, using the more advanced RDF loading mechanism recently developed for SMOL [20]. Our work so far does not incorporate data streams from the asset into the knowledge base. We expect that this integration can be handled similar to the semantic lifting of the runtime state into the knowledge base's static structure of the digital twin, but this remains to be done. Whereas the knowledge base is well suited to store and query information, solving constraints is not directly supported (e.g., for parameter optimisation). We believe that this apparent limitation of the approach can be naturally overcome by using the knowledge base to collect constraints, to be solved by an external solver.

References

1. Anderl, R., Haag, S., Schützer, K., Zancul, E.: Digital twin technology - an approach for Industrie 4.0 vertical and horizontal lifecycle integration. IT Inf. Technol. **60**(3), 125–132 (2018)
2. Banerjee, A., Dalal, R., Mittal, S., Joshi, K.P.: Generating digital twin models using knowledge graphs for industrial production lines. In: Proceedings Web Science Conference (WebSci 2017), pp. 425–430. ACM (2017)
3. Bickford, J., Van Bossuyt, D.L., Beery, P., Pollman, A.: Operationalizing digital twins through model-based systems engineering methods. Syst. Eng. **23**(6), 724–750 (2020)
4. Blochwitz, T.: Functional mockup interface 2.0: the standard for tool independent exchange of simulation models. In: Modelica Conference, pp. 173–184. The Modelica Association (2012)
5. Bolpagni, M.: Building information modelling and information management. In: Bolpagni, M., Gavina, R., Ribeiro, D. (eds.) Industry 4.0 for the Built Environment. SI, vol. 20, pp. 29–54. Springer, Cham (2022). https://doi.org/10.1007/978-3-030-82430-3_2
6. Cameron, D.B., Waaler, A., Komulainen, T.M.: Oil and gas digital twins after twenty years. How can they be made sustainable, maintainable and useful? In: Proceedings 59th Conference on Simulation and Modelling (SIMS 59), pp. 9–16. Linköping University Electronic Press (2018)
7. Delgoshaei, P., Austin, M.A., Veronica, D.A.: A semantic platform infrastructure for requirements traceability and system assessment. In: Ninth International Conference on Systems (ICONS 2014). IARIA, February 2014
8. Feng, H., Gomes, C., Thule, C., Lausdahl, K., Iosifidis, A., Larsen, P.G.: Introduction to digital twin engineering. In: Martin, C.R., Blas, M.J., Inostrosa-Psijas, A. (eds.) Annual Modeling and Simulation Conference, ANNSIM 2021, Virtual Event/Fairfax, VA, USA, 19–22 July 2021, pp. 1–12. IEEE (2021)
9. Fjøsna, E., Waaler, A.: READI Information modelling framework (IMF). Asset Information Modelling Framework. Technical report, READI Joint Industry Project (2021)
10. Fraga, A., Llorens, J., Alonso, L., Fuentes, J.M.: Ontology-assisted systems engineering process with focus in the requirements engineering process. In: Boulanger, F., Krob, D., Morel, G., Roussel, J.-C. (eds.) Complex Systems Design & Management, pp. 149–161. Springer, Cham (2015). https://doi.org/10.1007/978-3-319-11617-4_11

11. Glimm, B., Krötzsch, M.: SPARQL beyond subgraph matching. In: Patel-Schneider, P.F., et al. (eds.) ISWC 2010. LNCS, vol. 6496, pp. 241–256. Springer, Heidelberg (2010). https://doi.org/10.1007/978-3-642-17746-0_16
12. Glimm, B., Ogbuji, C.: SPARQL 1.1 entailment regimes. W3C Recommendation (2013). http://www.w3.org/TR/sparql11-entailment/
13. Gomes, C., Lúcio, L., Vangheluwe, H.: Semantics of co-simulation algorithms with simulator contracts. In: MoDELS (Companion), pp. 784–789. IEEE (2019)
14. Gomes, C., Thule, C., Broman, D., Larsen, P.G., Vangheluwe, H.: Co-simulation: a survey. ACM Comput. Surv. **51**(3), 49:1–49:33 (2018)
15. Grieves, M., Vickers, J.: Digital twin: mitigating unpredictable, undesirable emergent behavior in complex systems. In: Kahlen, F.-J., Flumerfelt, S., Alves, A. (eds.) Transdisciplinary Perspectives on Complex Systems, pp. 85–113. Springer, Cham (2017). https://doi.org/10.1007/978-3-319-38756-7_4
16. Heaton, J., Parlikad, A.K.: Asset information model to support the adoption of a digital twin: west Cambridge case study. IFAC-PapersOnLine **53**(3), 366–371 (2020). 4th IFAC Workshop on Advanced Maintenance Engineering, Services and Technologies - AMEST 2020
17. IEC TC3. IEC 81346–1 Structuring principles and reference designations - Part 1 Basic rules. International Standard IEC 81346–1 Ed. 1, IEC, July 2009
18. IOGP Jip 36: CFIHOS Standards. https://www.jip36-cfihos.org/cfihos-standards/. Accessed 12 Dec 2021
19. Kamburjan, E., Johnsen, E.B.: Knowledge structures over simulation units. In: Proceedings SCS Annual Modeling and Simulation Conference (ANNSIM 2022) (2022, in press)
20. Kamburjan, E., Klungre, V.N., Giese, M.: Never mind the semantic gap: modular, lazy and safe loading of RDF data. In: Proceedings 19th International Conference on the Semantic Web (ESWC 2022), vol. 13261. Lecture Notes in Computer Science, pp. 200–216. Springer (2022). https://doi.org/10.1007/978-3-031-06981-9_12
21. Kamburjan, E., Klungre, V.N., Schlatte, R., Johnsen, E.B., Giese, M.: Programming and debugging with semantically lifted states. In: Verborgh, R., et al. (eds.) ESWC 2021. LNCS, vol. 12731, pp. 126–142. Springer, Cham (2021). https://doi.org/10.1007/978-3-030-77385-4_8
22. Kharlamov, E., Martín-Recuerda, F., Perry, B., Cameron, D., Fjellheim, R., Waaler, A.: Towards semantically enhanced digital twins. In: IEEE BigData, pp. 4189–4193. IEEE (2018)
23. Kostylev, E.V., Grau, B.C.: On the semantics of SPARQL queries with optional matching under entailment regimes. In: ISWC, pp. 374–389 (2014)
24. Leal, D.: ISO 15926 "Life Cycle Data for Process Plant": an Overview. Oil Gas Sci. Technol. **60**(4), 629–637 (2005)
25. Lietaert, P., Meyers, B., Van Noten, J., Sips, J., Gadeyne, K.: Knowledge graphs in digital twins for AI in production. In: Dolgui, A., Bernard, A., Lemoine, D., von Cieminski, G., Romero, D. (eds.) APMS 2021. IAICT, vol. 630, pp. 249–257. Springer, Cham (2021). https://doi.org/10.1007/978-3-030-85874-2_26
26. Mehmandarov, R., Waaler, A., Cameron, D., Fjellheim, R., Pettersen, T.B.: A semantic approach to identifier management in engineering systems. In: Proceedings International Conference on Big Data (Big Data), pp. 4613–4616. IEEE (2021)
27. Nigischer, C., Bougain, S., Riegler, R., Stanek, H.P., Grafinger, M.: Multi-domain simulation utilizing SysML: state of the art and future perspectives. Procedia CIRP **100**, 319–324 (2021)

28. Oakes, B.J., Meyers, B., Janssens, D., Vangheluwe, H.: Structuring and accessing knowledge for historical and streaming digital twins. In: Tiddi, I., Maleshkova, M., Pellegrini, T., de Boer, V. (eds.) Joint Proceedings of the Semantics Co-located Events: Poster & Demo Track and Workshop on Ontology-Driven Conceptual Modelling of Digital Twins, vol. 2941. CEUR Workshop Proceedings. CEUR-WS.org (2021)
29. Poggi, A., Lembo, D., Calvanese, D., Giacomo, G.D., Lenzerini, M., Rosati, R.: Linking data to ontologies. J. Data Semant. **10**, 133–173 (2008)
30. Prud'hommeaux, E., Seaborne, A.: SPARQL query language for RDF. W3C Recommendation (2008). http://www.w3.org/TR/rdf-sparql-query/
31. READI: Reference Designation System for Oil and Gas - READI (2020)
32. Rotondi, M., Cominelli, A., Di Giorgio, C., Rossi, R., Vignati, E., Carati, B.: The benefits of integrated asset modelling: lessons learned from field cases. In: Europec/EAGE Conference and Exhibition, OnePetro (2008)
33. Skjæveland, M.G., Giese, M., Hovland, D., Lian, E.H., Waaler, A.: Engineering ontology-based access to real-world data sources. J. Web Semant. **33**, 112–140 (2015)
34. Smogeli, Ø.R., et al.: Open simulation platform - an open-source project for maritime system co-simulation. In: COMPIT, Technische Universität Hamburg-Harburg (2020)
35. Sohier, H., Lamothe, P., Guermazi, S., Yagoubi, M., Menegazzi, P., Maddaloni, A.: Improving simulation specification with MBSE for better simulation validation and reuse. Syst. Eng. **24**(6), 425–438 (2021)
36. Tao, F., Zhang, H., Liu, A., Nee, A.Y.C.: Digital twin in industry: state-of-the-art. IEEE Trans. Ind. Informatics **15**(4), 2405–2415 (2019)
37. W3C, OWL Working Group. Web ontology language. https://www.w3.org/OWL
38. W3C, RDF Working Group. Resource description framework. https://www.w3.org/RDF
39. W3C, SHACL Working Group. Shapes constraint language. https://www.w3.org/TR/shacl/
40. Waszak, M., Lam, A.N., Hoffmann, V., Elvesæter, B., Mogos, M.F., Roman, D.: Let the asset decide: digital twins with knowledge graphs. In: 19th IEEE International Conference on Software Architecture (ICSA 2022). IEEE (2022)
41. Wei, K., Sun, J.Z., Liu, R.J.: A review of asset administration shell. In: 2019 IEEE International Conference on Industrial Engineering and Engineering Management (IEEM), pp. 1460–1465 (2019)
42. Wiedau, M., von Wedel, L., Temmen, H., Welke, R., Papakonstantinou, N.: ENPRO data integration: extending DEXPI towards the asset lifecycle. Chem. Ing. Tec. **91**(3), 240–255 (2019)
43. Yan, H., Yang, J., Wan, J.: KnowIME: a system to construct a knowledge graph for intelligent manufacturing equipment. IEEE Access **8**, 41805–41813 (2020)
44. Zhang, J., Luo, H., Xu, J.: Towards fully BIM-enabled building automation and robotics: a perspective of lifecycle information flow. Comput. Ind. **135**, 103570 (2022)
45. Zhou, B., et al.: SemML: facilitating development of ML models for condition monitoring with semantics. J. Web Semant. **71**, 100664 (2021)

Formally Verified Self-adaptation of an Incubator Digital Twin

Thomas Wright[1(✉)], Cláudio Gomes[2], and Jim Woodcock[1,2]

[1] Department of Computer Science, University of York, Heslington, UK
{thomas.d.wright,jim}@york.ac.uk
[2] DIGIT, Department of Engineering, Aarhus University, Aarhus, Denmark
claudio.gomes@ece.au.dk

Abstract. The performance and reliability of Cyber-Physical Systems are increasingly aided through the use of digital twins, which mirror the static and dynamic behaviour of a Cyber-Physical System (CPS) in software. Digital twins enable the development of self-adaptive CPSs which reconfigure their behaviour in response to novel environments. It is crucial that these self-adaptations are formally verified at runtime, to avoid expensive re-certification of the reconfigured CPS. In this paper, we demonstrate formally verified self-adaptation in a digital twinning system, by constructing a non-deterministic model which captures the uncertainties in the system behaviour after a self-adaptation. We use Signal Temporal Logic to specify the safety requirements the system must satisfy after reconfiguration and employ formal methods based on verified monitoring over Flow* flowpipes to check these properties at runtime. This gives us a framework to predictively detect and mitigate unsafe self-adaptations before they can lead to unsafe states in the physical system.

Keywords: Digital twin · Self-adaptation · Reachability analysis · Signal temporal logic · Optimization · Cyber-physical system

1 Introduction

A Cyber-Physical System (CPS) consists of a digital component controlling a physical asset within some operating environment. Cyber-Physical Systems design poses significant engineering challenges, whilst scalably verifying that CPSs meet their requirements has long been a central problem in formal methods research [2,5,29,51]. Moreover, a CPS must cope with significant uncertainty and change during its operations. This motivates the need for *self adaptive* cyber-physical systems which dynamically reconfigure their behaviour in response to anomalous situations. However, the dynamic nature of these reconfigurations induces significant additional design and verification challenges, demanding new methods for engineering safe self-adaptive CPSs.

One approach to the challenges of CPS engineering comes through the use of digital twins. A *digital twin* is a computational replica of a CPS, which we refer to

T. Margaria and B. Steffen (Eds.): ISoLA 2022, LNCS 13704, pp. 89–109, 2022.
https://doi.org/10.1007/978-3-031-19762-8_7

as the *physical twin*. The digital twin is constructed from heterogeneous models of the physical system, including its hardware components, control software, and physical environment. The digital twin synchronises with the physical twin by monitoring its behaviour in order to update the state of these models.

Whilst a digital twin for a simple CPS can be implemented directly based on sensory data, it is difficult to get a comprehensive view of the state of a more complex CPS. This requires a combination of state estimators, data-fusion algorithms, and numerical simulation, which may still leave discrepancies between the digital and physical twins. Such discrepancies can also arise due to unexpected shifts in the CPS's operating environment, causing the model parameters of the digital twin to become out of date. Hence, we must continually monitor the conformance of the physical twin behaviour to the models in the digital twin to detect these anomalies and recalibrate the digital twin parameters based on the data from the physical twin. The digital twin may also be used to alter the behaviour of the CPS when conformance is violated (see Kritzinger et al. [33] and Tao et al. [54]).

Because the digital twin changes the behaviour of the physical twin, it is crucial that these changes are formally verified to be safe. This challenge has been well discussed in [57] and [28] where the application of formal methods is surveyed in the context of self-adaptive systems. This is relevant since a digital twin enables self-adaptation of its physical twin. However, digital twins place a higher emphasis on physical systems, which means that traditional formal methods must be adapted. Indeed, in practical systems, self-adaptation cannot be deployed, since each system reconfiguration requires re-certification of the equipment, leading to long potential downtimes. Nevertheless, it is our vision that re-certification can be sped up with the application of formal methods.

We will explore many of these challenges through a model incubator system [25] in which a digital controller regulates the temperature inside an incubator box by controlling a heat-bed inside the box. A digital twin of the incubator can measure the temperature within the box through digital temperature sensors placed at different locations within the box; these temperature readings can be used to calibrate the parameters of the digital twin models. If effectively calibrated, these models can be used to predict the future values of the box temperature or to synthesise optimal control policies for the heat-bed. However, we must handle discrepancies in these predictions arising from a number of uncertainties inherent in the calibration process: (i) temperature sensors at different locations in the box may give inconsistent readings; (ii) the sensor data represents delayed discrete samples of the system; (iii) sensors have noisy readings and actuators are inaccurate; (iv) the digital twin models only approximate the physical twin; (v) there are processing delays in the digital twin; (vi) the incubator's operating environment is uncertain and changeable.

Contribution. In this paper, we demonstrate formally verified self-adaptation in the context of an incubator digital twin system. To this end, we construct a second non-deterministic model that predicts the behaviour of the physical twin after a self-adaptation whilst we perform *uncertainty calibration* to measure and account for the uncertainties introduced during the self-adaptation process. This enables us to apply exact formal verification, leveraging Flow* verified integration [13] to perform verified monitoring [59] of the non-deterministic model against high-level safety requirements specified in the Signal Temporal Logic (STL) [39]. Verification is performed inside the self-adaptive loop to predict future violations after each self-adaptation. This is in contrast with most (offline or online) STL monitoring approaches that use data from the physical system to detect violations which have already occurred. Thus we may perform online monitoring of self-adaptations, which predictively identifies unsafe self-adaptations, or active enforcement, enabling the system to take evasive action to avert unsafety.

Related Work. Woodcock et al. [58] demonstrated how safety violations of CPSs in uncertain environments may be detected based on statistical analysis of digital twin cosimulations. Formally verified self-adaptation can be seen as an alternative approach to handling environmental uncertainty, with the non-deterministic model assuring that safety is maintained.

A variety of works have considered formal verification of self-adaptive software systems. Of these, our approach is particularly related to [8,9,21] which develop predictive monitoring of non-functional requirements expressed in the QCTL [4] temporal logic. It should also be compared to SimCA* [52] which is able to give formal guarantees for control-theoretic requirements under environmental uncertainties. On the other hand, most of the work on self-adaptive CPSs has focused on self-adaptation at the architectural or software levels [41]. These also include applications of concurrency-theoretic formalisms [7,55] to verify self-adaptations which reconfigure the network topology of a CPS. However, none of this work has considered formal verification of the controlled continuous dynamics of the system, which is the main focus of this paper. These challenges are related to Fault Detection, Isolation, and Reconfiguration (FDIR) problems [30], which have been considered in the control theory community, although the focus of these works is quite different than our temporal-logic based approach.

Another distinctive feature of our approach is the application of predictive STL model checking at runtime. Outside of the context of self-adaptive systems, this is related to the Clairvoyant monitoring approach of Qin and Deshmukh [44] which fits statistical models to traces in order to predict the probability that a STL property will be satisfied by future extension of the trace and to the approach of Ma et al. [37] which makes predictions based on Bayesian Recurrent Neural Networks with calibrated uncertainty estimation. In contrast, our approach expands a system's digital twin into an uncertain dynamical system model, which is used to predict its future behaviour. This is worth comparing to the model-bounded monitoring approaches of Waga, André, and Hasuo [56] and of Ghosh and André [27] which both use uncertain linear dynamical systems to interpolate between sparsely sampled time series data. Also relevant is the closely related problem of model predictive synthesis of controllers satisfying STL specifications [20,22,43,45,46,48–50] including the recent reachability-based methods [11,16,53].

A number of works [1,15,17,35,60] have also applied reachability analysis to predict future safety violations at runtime. Zhang et al. [62] have also demonstrated online repair based on control synthesis. However, the only one of these methods which moves beyond reach-avoidance properties to a full range of STL properties is that of Yu et al. [61], which targets discrete rather than continuous time dynamical systems.

2 Background

In this section we introduce some background material on the incubator system and on our verified monitoring approach for STL specifications.

2.1 Notation

Firstly, we introduce some mathematical notation which we will use throughout the paper. We will frequently work with the real numbers $\mathbb{R}$, including the space of non-negative real numbers $\mathbb{R}_{\geq 0} = [0, \infty)$ and the space of n-dimensional real vectors $\mathbb{R}^n$. We use boldface to distinguish the names of vectors $\mathbf{x}$ from scalars x, and write a specific n-dimensional vector with real entries $x_1, \ldots, x_n \in \mathbb{R}$ as $\mathbf{x} = (x_1, \ldots, x_n) \in \mathbb{R}^n$. We rely upon interval arithmetic [40], which represents uncertain quantities as closed real intervals $I = [a, b] \in \mathbb{IR}$ and defines over-approximate arithmetic operations based on the endpoints of intervals so that, for example, $[a, b] + [c, d] = [a + c, b + d]$. We also work with interval vectors $\mathbf{I} = (I_1, \ldots, I_n) \in \mathbb{IR}^n$ which consist of interval entries $I_1, \ldots, I_n \in \mathbb{IR}$ and support all of the standard vector operations. We define the interval vector $[\mathbf{x}, \mathbf{y}] = ([x_1, y_1], \ldots, [x_n, y_n])$ ranging between two real vectors $\mathbf{x} = (x_1, \ldots, x_n)$ and $\mathbf{y} = (y_1, \ldots, y_n)$ (assuming $x_i \leq y_i$ for all i). Finally, we define the width of an interval $[a, b]$, $\text{width}([a, b]) = b - a$, and the distance of a point x from an interval $[a, b]$,

$$\text{dist}(x, [a, b]) \triangleq \begin{cases} x - b & \text{if } x > b \\ a - x & \text{if } x < a \\ 0 & \text{otherwise} \end{cases}.$$

2.2 Incubator

The incubator system, detailed in [25], consists of a styrofoam box and a digital controller. An overview of the incubator and its control logic is shown in Fig. 1. It consists of a heat-bed (that radiates heat when turned on) and a fan (that ensures uniform temperature distribution inside the box). The temperature can be sensed and sent to the controller from two different spots inside the box, and a spot outside the box. The duty cycle of the controller regulates the steady state temperature inside the box. In this paper we will consider an open-loop controller (shown in Fig. 1b) which operates independently of the temperature measurements, but is periodically reconfigured based on the temperature measurements and a digital twin of the incubator system.

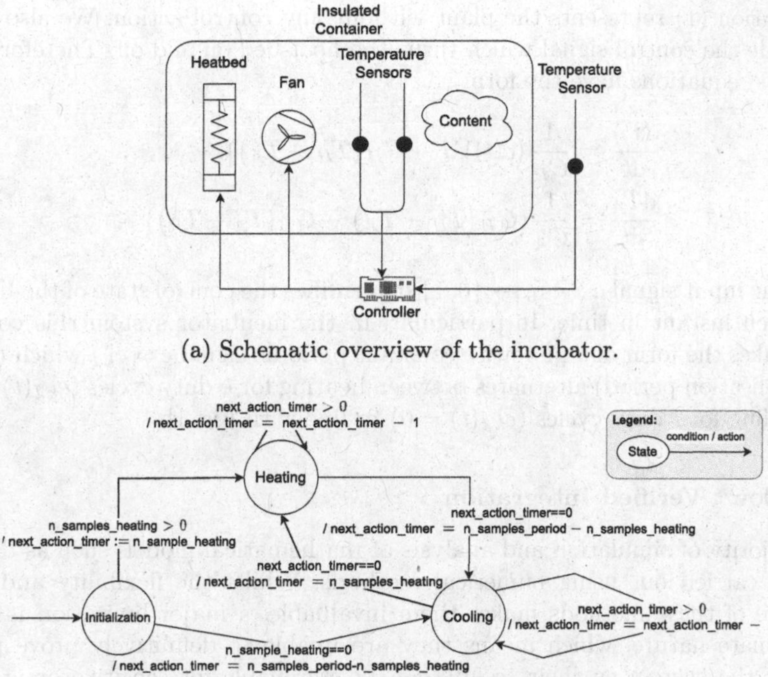

(a) Schematic overview of the incubator.

(b) Statechart of the open-loop controller.

Fig. 1. Overview of the incubator system.

As shown in [25, Section 3], we can model the incubator using the following system of equations which describe the evolution of the temperature of the air inside the box T_A and of the heat-bed T_H, in degrees Celsius:

$$\begin{aligned}\frac{\mathrm{d}T_H}{\mathrm{d}t} &= \frac{1}{C_H}(VI - G_H(T_H - T_A))\\ \frac{\mathrm{d}T_A}{\mathrm{d}t} &= \frac{1}{C_A}(G_H(T_H - T_A) - G_B(T_A - T_R))\end{aligned} \tag{1}$$

where:

- V and I denote voltage and current, respectively, and the product VI represents power (rate of energy produced at the heat-bed);
- G_H represents the rate of energy transfer between the surface of the heat-bed and the surrounding air;
- C_H encapsulates both the heat capacity of the heat-bed as well as its mass;
- C_A encapsulates the heat capacity and mass of the air inside the box;
- G_B represents the rate of energy transfer between the air inside the box and the air outside the box (e.g. the lid being opened is equivalent to increasing this value by an order of magnitude).

Equation (1) represents the plant without any control action. We also need to include the control signal which turns the heat-bed on and off. Therefore the controlled equations have the form

$$\begin{aligned}\frac{\mathrm{d}T_H}{\mathrm{d}t} &= \frac{1}{C_H}(c(t)VI - G_H(T_H - T_A)) \\ \frac{\mathrm{d}T_A}{\mathrm{d}t} &= \frac{1}{C_A}(G_H(T_H - T_A) - G_B(T_A - T_R))\end{aligned} \tag{2}$$

where the input signal $c : \mathbb{R}_{\geq 0} \to \{0, 1\}$ determines the control state of the heater at a given instant in time. In particular, in the incubator system this control signal takes the form of a piecewise constant periodic signal $c = c_{k,l}$ which (after an initialisation period) alternates between heating for k duty cycles ($c_{k,l}(t) = 1$) and cooling for l duty cycles ($c_{k,l}(t) = 0$) in line with Fig. 1b.

2.3 Flow* Verified Integration

The majority of simulation and analysis of mathematical models such as digital twins is carried out using numerical methods. Whilst the flexibility and performance of these methods makes them invaluable, a major limitation is their approximate nature, which means they are unable to definitively prove properties of the system as their results can be unreliable for sensitive or chaotic systems [10]. An even larger practical limitation is their inability to represent and account for uncertainties in the system, preventing us from providing verification results which are robust to noise or mismatches between a digital twin and a physical system.

Verified integration applies exact formal methods in order to move beyond the approximate simulation results produced by classical numerical methods, to computing a verified enclosure of all possible trajectories of a system over time. One leading such method is the Flow* verified integrator [14] which applies a variety of Taylor model-based [6] methods to tightly enclose the dynamics of continuous and hybrid dynamical systems featuring complex non-linear dynamics and large uncertainties in initial conditions and model parameters.

In particular, Flow* verified integration is able to handle uncertain parametric continuous systems of form,

$$\frac{\mathrm{d}\mathbf{x}}{\mathrm{d}t} = \mathbf{f}(\mathbf{x}, \mathbf{p}, \mathbf{c}(t), t) \tag{3}$$

whose dynamics are specified by a Lipschitz continuous function $\mathbf{f} : \mathbb{R}^n \times \mathbb{R}^m \times \mathbb{R}^q \times \mathbb{R}_{\geq 0} \to \mathbb{R}^n$ (i.e. a vector of n coupled non-linear ODEs) subject to a vector $\mathbf{p}$ of system parameters and a predetermined open-loop control policy $\mathbf{c} : \mathbb{R}_{\geq 0} \to \mathbb{R}^m$ which we assume to be a piecewise constant. We are able to introduce uncertainties in this class of models both through an interval initial value constraint $\mathbf{x}(0) \in \mathbf{I}$ which states that the system must start inside the n-dimensional box $\mathbf{I} \in \mathbb{IR}^n$ of initial conditions and the interval parameter constraint $\mathbf{p} \in \mathbf{U}$ which constrains the parameters of the system to the

m-dimensional box $\mathbf{U} \in \mathbb{IR}^m$. These uncertain parameters are assumed to be *time-invariant* (so that they have fixed real values; we just do not know what they are); whilst such uncertain parameters have been tackled explicitly by verified-integration methods such that of Lin and Stadtherr [36], we handle them by implicitly re-encoding them as uncertain initial conditions for additional derivative-zero variables of the model[1]. We denote an uncertain parametric system of the above form as $\mathcal{M}(\mathbf{I}, \mathbf{U}, \mathbf{c})$ where $\mathbf{I}$ and $\mathbf{U}$ record the interval initial condition and parameter constraints of the system and $\mathbf{c}$ records the control policy.

In order to enclose all possible behaviours of the system under uncertainty, Flow* moves from approximating a single trajectory $\mathbf{x} : \mathbb{R}_{\geq 0} \to \mathbb{R}^n$ of the system, to computing a *flowpipe* enclosing all possible trajectories of the system. Whilst internally Flow* uses a complex symbolic flowpipe representation based on preconditioned Taylor models [38] to give the tightest possible bounds on system dynamics, we can view these flowpipes as interval vector functions $\mathbf{g} : \mathbb{IR} \to \mathbb{IR}^n$ which map interval regions $T \in \mathbb{IR}$ of the time domain to n-dimensional regions $\mathbf{g}(T) \in \mathbb{IR}^n$ of the system state space. These flowpipes are then guaranteed to form an *interval extension* of every possible trajectory of the underlying system in the sense that, for every trajectory $\mathbf{x} : \mathbb{R}_{\geq 0} \to \mathbb{R}^n$, every time point $t \in \mathbb{R}_{\geq 0}$, and every time interval $T \in \mathbb{IR}$ such that $t \in T$ we are guaranteed that $\mathbf{x}(t) \in \mathbf{g}(T)$. This means a Flow* flowpipe computed for a given uncertain model, which we henceforth denote flowpipe($\mathcal{M}(\mathbf{I}, \mathbf{U}, \mathbf{c})$), is guaranteed to soundly enclose all possible behaviours of a system regardless of any uncertainties in the initial conditions $\mathbf{I}$ or parameters $\mathbf{U}$ of the system.

Example 1. We can view the incubator model Eq. (1) as an uncertain model of form Eq. (3) if we assume uncertain knowledge of the initial state of the system, given by the interval initial value constraints,

$$T_A(0) \in I_A = [25.0, 25.1], \qquad T_H(0) \in I_H = [20.59, 21.60],$$

uncertain knowledge of the system parameters C_A, G_B given by the interval constraints,

$$C_A \in U_A = [68.20, 68.71], \qquad C_H \in U_H = [0.73, 0.79],$$

and the following fixed values of the remaining system parameters,

$$V = 12.00, \qquad I = 10.45, \qquad T_R = 21.25, \qquad G_H = 0.87095429.$$

Following the notation of the previous section, we denote the overall uncertain incubator model as $\mathcal{M}((I_A, I_H), (U_A, U_H), c)$.

If we apply a constant control policy $c_{\text{off}}(t) \equiv 0$ in which the heater is always off, then applying Flow* gives the flowpipes shown in Fig. 2a. This demonstrates

[1] Flow* also has native support for time-varying interval uncertain parameters [12, Section 3.5], which may vary throughout the simulation leading to much greater uncertainty in the overall behaviour of the system over time.

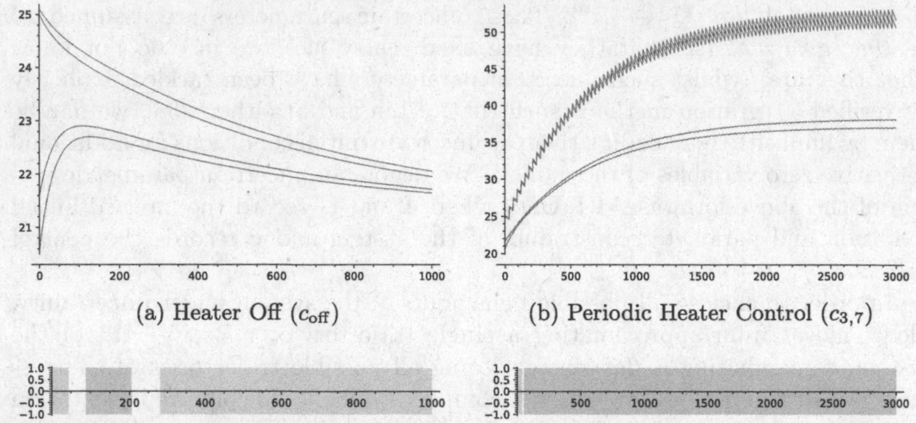

(a) Heater Off (c_{off}) (b) Periodic Heater Control ($c_{3,7}$)

(c) Signal for $T_A > 22.6$ under c_{off} (d) Signal for $T_A > 22.6$ under $c_{3,7}$

Fig. 2. Verified integration and monitoring results for the incubator under uncertainty.

that the system absorbs the uncertainties introduced by the uncertain initial conditions and hence the long-term behaviour of the system is robust under these variations, as demonstrated in [26].

We can also apply a periodic open-loop control policy $c_{3,7}(t)$ in which the heater alternates between switching on for periods of 3 duty cycles and cooling down for periods of 7 duty cycles. This results in the flowpipes shown in Fig. 2, which demonstrates that this control policy results in an initial rise of the box and heater temperature before eventual stabilisation.

2.4 Verified Monitoring

Whilst models and simulation techniques provide a powerful way to analyse the behaviour of systems, their application typically depends on human insight to interpret the results and determine whether it is consistent with the expected safe behaviour of the system. Since self-adaptive systems are designed to operate without human intervention, we propose the use of specification languages such as temporal logics to capture the safety requirements of the system, and offline or online monitoring techniques to check whether a given system behaviour is consistent with these requirements.

Signal Temporal Logic (STL) [39] has emerged as a popular specification language for the behaviour of Cyber-Physical Systems [5]. STL formulae are defined according to the following grammar,

$$\phi, \psi ::= \rho \mid \phi \wedge \psi \mid \phi \vee \psi \mid \neg \phi \mid \mathcal{F}_{[a,b]}\, \phi \mid \mathcal{G}_{[a,b]}\, \phi \mid \phi\, \mathcal{U}_{[a,b]}\, \psi\,,$$

and incorporate as atomic propositions inequalities $\rho \triangleq f(\mathbf{x}) \geq 0$ featuring functions $f(\mathbf{x})$ of the system variables alongside complex propositions with the logical operators *not* $\neg\phi$, *and* $\phi \wedge \psi$, and *or* $\phi \vee \psi$, as well as the temporal operators $\mathcal{F}_{[a,b]}\,\phi$ or *eventually* ϕ (which states that the STL property ϕ should hold at *some* time point between a and b time units in the future), $\mathcal{G}_{[a,b]}\,\phi$ or *globally* ϕ (which states that the STL property ϕ should hold at *all* time points between a and b time units in the future); as well as the *until operator* $\phi\ \mathcal{U}_{[a,b]}\ \psi$ (which states that there is some time point t between a and b time units in the future such that ψ is true at t and that ϕ is true at every time point t' between now and then).

STL monitoring has traditionally been applied to a single *numerical signal* $\mathbf{x} : \mathbb{K} \rightarrow \mathbb{R}^n$ (with either bounded real-time domain $\mathbb{K} = [0, T]$ or discrete time domain $\mathbb{K} = \{t_1, \ldots, t_N\} \subseteq [0, T]$ based on time-sampling points $t_1 < t_2 < \ldots < t_N$) either from a running system or a numerical simulation of its behaviour using bottom-up monitoring algorithms [39] that recursively compute *Boolean signals* $s : [0, T] \rightarrow \{\text{True}, \text{False}\}$ which record the truth of a STL given property at each time point $t \in [0, T]$. In contrast, verified methods such as Flow* have traditionally focused on *reachability analysis* to enclose all possible behaviours of the system without supporting the rich timed specifications which STL allows. However, recently a number of methods [11,31,34,47,59] have emerged applying verified reachability analysis as a basis for *verified monitoring* of STL properties. In particular we apply the method of Wright and Stark [59] which implements verified monitoring of STL properties over Flow* flowpipes by computing three-valued signals $s : \mathbb{R}_{\geq 0} \rightarrow \{\text{True}, \text{Unknown}, \text{False}\}$ which uses a third truth value, Unknown, to record when the uncertainty in the flowpipe is too great to either verify or refute a property at a given time point $t \in \mathbb{R}_{\geq 0}$. Thus, the signal produced by verified monitoring of a STL property over a flowpipe $\mathcal{M}(\mathbf{I}, \mathbf{U}, \mathbf{c})$ for a given uncertain model gives formal guarantees, with True and False values guaranteeing the truth or falsehood of the property for all possible initial conditions $\mathbf{x} \in \mathbf{I}$ and parameters $\mathbf{p} \in \mathbf{U}$ of the model. We are therefore able to apply verified STL monitoring in order to capture many interesting properties of the incubator system.

Example 2. As a simple example, we can monitor properties of system state variables such as $T_A \geq 22.6$ which asserts that the air temperature within the incubator is at least 22.6 °C. A three-valued signal for this property when the heater is off is shown in Fig. 2c illustrating that the property is true at both ends of the time period of truth at the peak of the temperature graph and periods of uncertainty in between. Similarly, a three-valued signal for the same property with a periodic heater control policy $c_{3,7}$ is shown in Fig. 2d.

We are also able to apply the full monitoring algorithm to verify properties of the overall timed behaviour of the incubator. For example, under the periodic control policy $c_{3,7}$ we are able to verify the STL property

$$\mathcal{F}_{[0,2000]}\,\mathcal{G}_{[0,100]}(T_A \geq 33 \wedge T_A \leq 36)$$

which states that the air temperature eventually (within 2000 seconds) reaches and (for at least 100 seconds) remains within the interval range [33, 36]. This corresponds to the control-theoretic requirement that the air temperature stabilises close to 34.5 °C, however, the use of STL allows us to strengthen this to require that the temperature stabilises within a timely manner (within 2000 s).

3 Formally Verified Self-Adaptation

This section lays out our approach for introducing formally verified self-adaptation into an incubator digital twin system, through the use of a self-adaptation loop, and formal verification of a non-deterministic model capturing the behaviour of the incubator after each self-adaptation.

3.1 Incubator Self-Adaptation Loop

The digital twin of the incubator, originally introduced in [24], has been extended with a self-adaptation loop in [23], that reconfigures the duty cycle of the open loop controller whenever an external disturbance undermines the predictive power of the model in Eq. (1). The most common example disturbance is when the lid of the incubator is opened.

A disturbance is detected by comparing the output from a Kalman filter (that uses Eq. (1)) with the actual temperature measurements. After some time, the disturbance is confirmed, and the following steps, based on the MAPE-K loop [32], are taken:

Gather Data —The system is left to operate normally for some more time steps, in order to gather sufficient data for the next step.

Recalibrate Model —The data gathered since the time the anomaly was detected is used to re-estimate a real-valued vector $\mathbf{p}^* = (C_A^*, G_H^*)$ of parameters for the incubator model in Eq. (1) by repeatedly running simulations and comparing them to the data, while adjusting the parameters to make the simulation match the data (we use a non-linear optimisation package which is part of SciPy[2]).

Recompute Control Policy —Use the newly found parameters to inform an optimisation problem where the new controller parameters are derived to determine an updated control policy c^*. Repeated simulations of the controlled incubator equations (Eq. (2)) are performed with different control duty cycles, to find the optimal one.

Update Control Parameter Finally, the new parameters are uploaded to the controller.

For more details on this self-adaptation loop, we refer the reader to [23].

[2] https://docs.scipy.org/doc/scipy/index.html.

Figure 3a shows an example of self adaptation of the incubator. Initially the duty cycle of the controller has been optimised to keep the temperature at 41 °C. After the lid is opened, an anomaly is detected (shown by the discrepancy between the orange signal and the blue line, at time 500 s). Shortly after, the duty cycle is changed to maximum power, to try to compensate for the loss of energy in the system. The same process happens in reverse when the lid is closed.

3.2 Verified Monitoring Architecture for Safe Self-Adaptation

Whilst self-adaptation through the use of a numerical digital twin such as that described in the previous section provides an effective way of detecting and responding to anomalies, one can question whether the resulting adaptive control policies lead to long-term safe behaviour for the overall system. Indeed, the deployment of such a self-adaptive loop in a safety-critical setting typically requires both offline verification that a safe configuration exists and that the self-adaptive procedure is able to identify it. This is often not possible in practice given the uncertain and unpredicatable system contexts which self-adaptation seeks to address.

We propose an alternative approach in which verified monitoring is deployed online in order to verify the safety of the system after self-adaptation. To this end, we propose to modify the self-adaptation loop architecture introduced in the previous section so that after each anomaly we construct a non-deterministic model of the system denoted as $\mathcal{M}(\mathbf{I}^*, \mathbf{U}, \mathbf{c}^*)$ which aims to over-approximate all possible behaviours of the physical twin after the anomaly, based on the data collected during the **Gather Data** phase. We can then apply verified STL monitoring to $\mathcal{M}(\mathbf{I}^*, \mathbf{U}, \mathbf{c}^*)$ in order to verify a set $\mathcal{S}$ of STL properties representing the safety requirements of the system. Thus, whilst we cannot guarentee that self-adaptation will always succeed, we can use the verified STL monitoring results to guarentee that any unsafe self-adaptations can be detected, enabling the safety of the deployed system to be ensured by other means (such as human intervention or an automated safe-shutdown procedure).

3.3 Uncertainty Calibration

A key stage of the verified monitoring procedure proposed in the previous section is constructing $\mathcal{M}(\mathbf{I}^*, \mathbf{U}, \mathbf{c}^*)$ which attempts to over-approximate the behaviour of the physical incubator system after the anomaly based on the data gathered during the **Gather Data** stage.

To accomplish this we propose to perform an *uncertainty calibration* process in which we start off with a model $\mathcal{M}(\mathbf{x}^*, \mathbf{p}^*, \mathbf{c}) = \mathcal{M}((T_A^*, T_H^*), (C_A^*, G_H^*), c)$ based on the digital twin state $\mathbf{x}^* = (T_A^*, T_H^*)$ at the start of the calibration period, the vector $\mathbf{p}^* = (C_A^*, G_H^*)$ of real-valued parameters determined in the **Recalibrate Model** stage, and the old control policy $\mathbf{c}$. We then expand these real parameters into interval parameters achieving a minimal enclosure of the plant data signal $\mathbf{y} : \{t_1, \ldots, t_N\} \to \mathbb{R}^n$ over the calibration period. To this end we first define the *inflated model*

$$\mathcal{M}_\delta^\varepsilon(\mathbf{x}^*, \mathbf{p}^*, \mathbf{c}) \triangleq \mathcal{M}\Big(\mathbf{x}^* + [-\varepsilon, \varepsilon], \mathbf{p}^* + [-\delta, \delta], \mathbf{c}\Big)$$

of the model $\mathcal{M}(\mathbf{x}^*, \mathbf{p}^*, \mathbf{c})$ by the inflation parameter vectors $\boldsymbol{\varepsilon} = (\varepsilon_A, \varepsilon_H)$ and $\boldsymbol{\delta} = (\delta_A, \delta_H)$. This inflated model encloses each initial condition $\mathbf{x}_i^*$ or parameter $\mathbf{p}_i^*$ of the calibrated digital twin in a radius ε_i or δ_i interval of uncertainty respectively. In order to fit these intervals of uncertainty to the plant data, we define the *non-conformity*[3] of a plant signal $\mathbf{y}$ to a flowpipe $\mathbf{g}$ as

$$\text{non-conformity}(\mathbf{y}, \mathbf{g}) = \sum_{i=1}^{N} \sqrt{\sum_{j=1}^{m} \text{dist}(\mathbf{y}(t_i)_j, \mathbf{g}(t_i)_j)^2}$$

and the *uncertainty* of a n-dimensional interval vector $\mathbf{I} \in \mathbb{IR}^n$ as

$$\text{uncertainty}(\mathbf{I}) = \sqrt{\sum_{i=1}^{n} \text{width}(I_i)^2}.$$

Then suitable inflation parameters $\boldsymbol{\varepsilon}^* = (\varepsilon_A^*, \varepsilon_H^*)$ and $\boldsymbol{\delta} = (\delta_A^*, \delta_H^*)$ are found by applying an optimisation process to minimize,

$$K \,\text{non-conformity}\left(\mathbf{y}, \text{flowpipe}(\mathcal{M}_{\boldsymbol{\delta}}^{\boldsymbol{\varepsilon}}(\mathbf{x}^*, \mathbf{p}^*, \mathbf{c}))\right) + \text{uncertainty}\left(\text{flowpipe}(\mathcal{M}_{\boldsymbol{\delta}}^{\boldsymbol{\varepsilon}}(\mathbf{x}^*, \mathbf{p}^*, \mathbf{c}))(t_N)\right)$$

thus jointly minimising the non-conformity of the plant signal to the flowpipe and the uncertainty of the flowpipe at the end of the calibration period (since this gives a measure of how strongly the overall uncertainty in the parameters feeds into the long term behaviour of the system). Here we use the weight parameter $K \gg 1$ to prioritise enclosure of the plant data over minimising the uncertainty in the parameters.

Provided we can find a solution with zero non-conformity, this then provides a non-deterministic model $\mathcal{M}(\mathbf{I}, \mathbf{U}, \mathbf{c}) = \mathcal{M}_{\boldsymbol{\delta}}^{\boldsymbol{\varepsilon}}(\mathbf{x}^*, \mathbf{p}^*, \mathbf{c})$ for the system over the calibration period. To predict the plant behaviour after the anomaly and calibration period have passed, we use a flowpipe from the non-deterministic model to predict the possible system state $\mathbf{I}^* = \text{flowpipe}\big(\mathcal{M}_{\boldsymbol{\delta}^*}^{\boldsymbol{\varepsilon}^*}(\mathbf{x}^*, \mathbf{p}^*, \mathbf{c})\big)(t_N)$ at the end of the calibration period. We can then obtain and utilize the non-deterministic model $\mathcal{M}(\mathbf{I}^*, \mathbf{U}, \mathbf{c}^*)$ where $\mathbf{c}^*$ is the new control policy produced by self-adaptation, as detailed next.

3.4 Self-adaptation Monitoring and Enforcement

We propose that the verified self-adaptation loop may use the non-deterministic model in two ways. Firstly, it may be used in a *monitoring mode* in which we apply verified STL monitoring to the uncertainty-calibrated non-deterministic model after each self-adaptation in order to validate the self-adaptation process itself against the safety requirements $\mathcal{S}$ of the system. Thus, the monitoring mode

[3] This notion is worth comparing this to notions of conformance between continuous and hybrid systems traces such as [19] and [3].

will report the durations of each self-adaptation period, alongside the calibrated intervals of uncertain model parameters for the non-deterministic model after the anomaly, and a record of whether each safety requirement is satisfied or violated after the anomaly. Secondly, it may be used in an *enforcing mode* in which the violation of a safety property blocked the application of the new control policy (deemed unsafe) and instead triggers a safe shutdown of the system, preventing potential harm when self-adaptation is insufficient to ensure safety. Whilst enforcement is necessary to ensure overall safety, in cases where it is not practical, we argue that monitoring provides an invaluable tool to identify design flaws in self-adaptation loops and alert human supervisors to potential issues when safe self-adaptation is not possible.

4 Incubator Self-adaptation Verification Results

In this section we examine some example executions of our formally verified self-adaptation loop for the incubator system in order to explore how the use of verified monitoring allows us to identify unsafe self-adaptations and to correct design flaws in the self-adaptation loop.

4.1 System Setup

We consider an instantiation of the incubator self-adaptation loop which simulates the full digital twinning setup *in silico* based on experimental data and the use another numerical model of the incubator in place of the physical twin. We configure the plant with an initial open-loop control policy $\mathbf{c} = c_{10,30}$ whilst the physical and digital twins are both initially configured with parameters $C_A \approx 177.63$, $G_B \approx 0.77$, $C_H \approx 239.61$, and $G_H \approx 2.32$, and the self-adaptation process is configured to optimize the control policy based on a desired incubator temperature of 41 ° C, a data gathering period of 12 seconds, and a minimum period of 20 seconds between anomalies.

In order to simulate a situation requiring self-adaptation, we introduce discontinuous jumps which change the parameter G_B to 10 times its original value after $500s$ and then again after $1500s$. This simulates the box lid being opened at time 500 and closed again at time 1500. We have validated this procedure with the real system, to certify that our simulation results are representative of the real opening of the lid [23].

4.2 Safety Properties

We capture the desired safety properties for controller in the set $\mathcal{S} = \{\phi_1, \phi_2\}$ consisting of the two STL properties:

- $\phi_1 \triangleq \mathcal{F}_{[0,1000]}\,\mathcal{G}_{[0,100]}(T_A \geq 36 \wedge T_A \leq 46)$: the incubator air temperature should stabilise between 36 °C and 46 °C within 1000 seconds;
- $\phi_2 \triangleq \mathcal{G}_{[0,1000]}(T_A \leq 60)$: the incubator air temperature should never exceed 60 °C.

Of these we note that ϕ_2 is the most critical, given the potential for excessive air temperatures inside the box to rapidly harm its contents.

4.3 Self-adaptation Results

Figure 3a demonstrates the behaviour of the incubator self-adaptation loop as it adapts to the opening and closing of the box lid. The self-adaptation loop detects and responds to two anomalies: and anomaly a_1 when the incubator box lid is opened and an anomaly a_2 once the box lid is closed again.

We were able to apply our verified monitoring procedure to check the properties ϕ_1 and ϕ_2 after each self-adaptation. Uncertainty calibration produced non-deterministic models which tightly over-approximated the plant behaviour after reconfiguration; for example, the non-deterministic model flowpipe after a_2 is shown in Fig. 4. This allowed us to generate the monitoring results for each property, producing the results shown in Fig. 3d. From these we can see that ϕ_1 is true after a_1 showing that the system finds a control policy which achieves the desired temperature once the lid is opened. On the other hand, we get a monitoring result of False for ϕ_1 after a_2: whilst the control policy is eventually returning the air temperature to the desired range, it is not able to do so within the time limit stipulated in ϕ_1 (see Fig. 4). More seriously, the crucial property ϕ_2 fails after a_2. We can see that in trying to keep the box close to the desired temperature when the lid is open, the heat-bed temperature has risen to over 70 °C, placing the system in a state where overheating is unavoidable once the lid is closed again and the accumulated energy in the heat-bed dissipates to the air in the box.

4.4 Repairing the Loop

We can also use verified monitoring as a means to understand and mitigate the potential for unsafe self-adaptations. The failure of ϕ_2 after the box lid was closed again demonstrates the danger of allowing unrestricted heater temperatures, motivating us to introduce an additional safety requirement

$$\phi_3 \triangleq \mathcal{G}_{[0,1000]}(T_H \leq 70)$$

which requires the heater temperature to be kept below 70 °C for at least 1000 seconds after every self-adaptation. From Fig. 3d this property was violated after each of the two anomalies a_1, a_2 demonstrating the ability of the verified monitor to predict future failures after a self-adaptation. This could allow us to notify a human supervisor or to use the verified monitor in enforcing mode, initiating a safe-shutdown by turning off the heater before an unsafe self-adaptation can lead to directly detectable damage (as shown in Fig. 3b).

We are also able to use our new understanding of this potential hazard to improve the design of the underlying self-adaptation loop. For example, we can limit the overall heater temperature by modifying the **Recompute Control Policy** stage to select control policies which prevent the heater temperature from

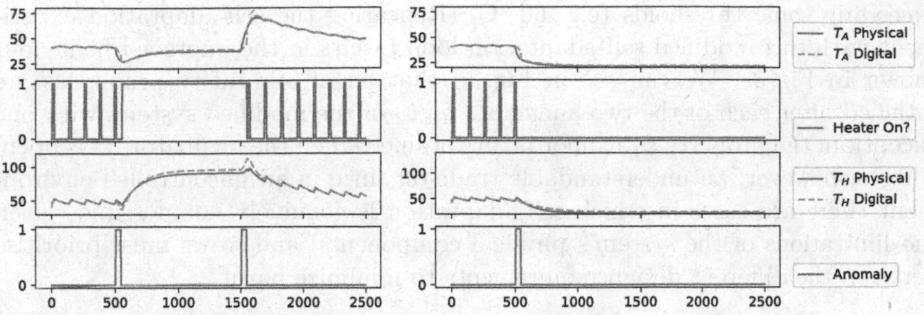

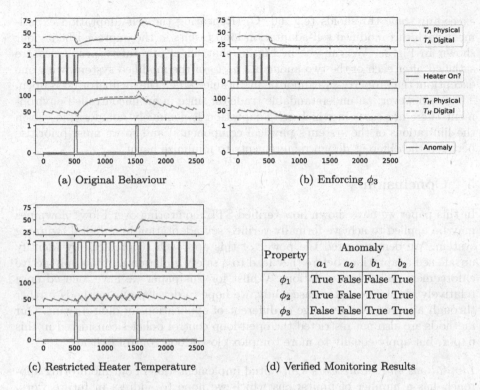

(a) Original Behaviour

(b) Enforcing ϕ_3

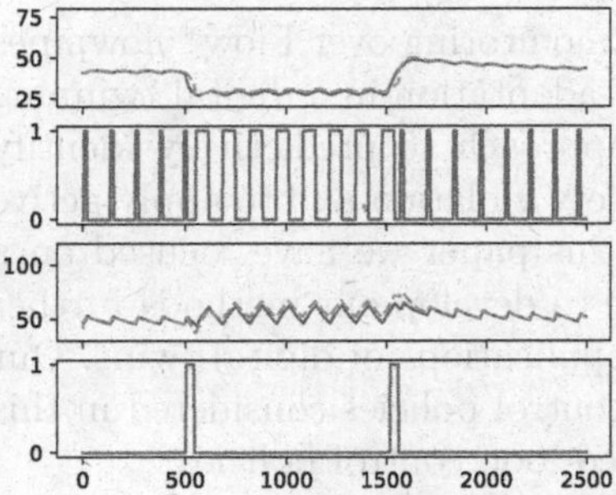

(c) Restricted Heater Temperature

Property	Anomaly			
	a_1	a_2	b_1	b_2
ϕ_1	True	False	False	True
ϕ_2	True	False	True	True
ϕ_3	False	False	True	True

(d) Verified Monitoring Results

Fig. 3. Self-adaptation experiment results.

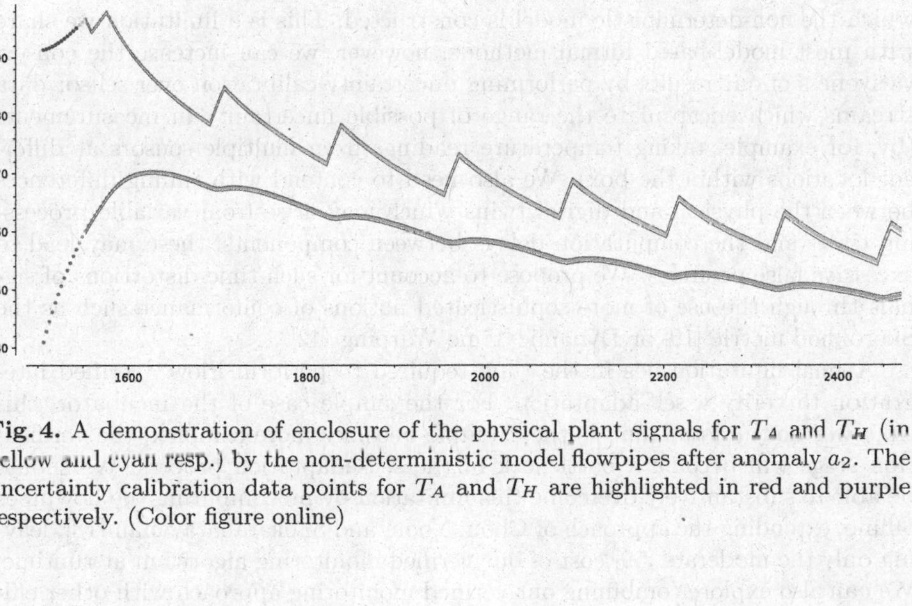

Fig. 4. A demonstration of enclosure of the physical plant signals for T_A and T_H (in yellow and cyan resp.) by the non-deterministic model flowpipes after anomaly a_2. The uncertainty calibration data points for T_A and T_H are highlighted in red and purple respectively. (Color figure online)

exceeding some thresholds (e.g. 60 °C). Repeating the self-adaptation experiment with this modified self-adaptation loop results in the improved behaviour shown in Fig. 3c. We can see in Fig. 3d that all of our safety properties are satisfied after each of the two anomalies b_1, b_2 of the modified system, with one exception: the property ϕ_1 cannot be maintained when the incubator lid is open. This is, however, an understandable trade-off since in an uncontrolled environment there are cases in which self-adaptation is genuinely not possible (given the limitations of the system's physical components) and so we must prioritise between the different design requirements to minimize harm.

5 Conclusion

In this paper we have shown how verified STL monitoring over Flow* flowpipes may be applied to achieve formally-verified self-adaptation in a digital twinning system. We demonstrated the power of this approach to predictively identify unsafe self-adaptations before they lead to a safety violation and to apply active enforcement to prevent violations. Whilst for this paper we have focused on a relatively simple incubator case study, we hope to develop our methods further through a representative range of different of applications of digital twins. Our methods are also not restricted the open-loop control policies considered in this paper, but apply equally to more complex closed-loop control policies.

Limitations and Future work Our initial implementation of our monitoring approach has a number of limitations which we hope to address in future work. Firstly, the accuracy of our predictions is ultimately determined by the representitativeness of the digital twin and the sampled physical twin data from which the non-deterministic model is constructed. This is a limitation we share with most model-based formal methods, however, we can increase the conservativeness of our results by performing uncertainty calibration over sensor data streams which encapsulate the range of possible uncertainty in measurements (by, for example, taking temperature readings from multiple sensors at different locations within the box). We also need to contend with timing differences between the physical and digital twins which may arise from variable processing times and the computation delays between components; these may lead to excessive false positives. We propose to account for such time distortions of signals through the use of more sophisticated notions of conformance such as the Skorokhod metric [19] or Dynamic Time Warping [42].

A final limitation lies in the time required to perform Flow* verified integration to verify a self-adaptation. For the simple case of the incubator, this time was not an issue, but as the example becomes more complex, the verification stage will become a bottleneck in the self-adaptation process. We should be able to substantively overcome this limitation by precomputing the flowpipes offline, extending the approach of Chou, Yoon, and Sankaranarayanan [18], leaving only the moderate [59] cost of our verified monitoring algorithm at runtime. We can also explore combining our verified monitoring approach with other efficient online flowpipe computation methods [15]. Additionally, whilst our focus thus far has been on control over relatively short timespans, it would also be worth exploring the applicability of our verified monitoring approach to different application domains for digital twins such as infrastructure, civil engineering, and biomedical engineering which feature control over much longer timespans. Whilst we expect our core approach should be equally applicable to models in these domains, the longer timespans of control offer scope for more extensive applications of formal verification inside of the control cycle.

Acknowledgements. Cláudio Gomes and Jim Woodcock are grateful to the Poul Due Jensen Foundation, which has supported the establishment of a new Centre for Digital Twin Technology at Aarhus University. Thomas Wright and Jim Woodcock gratefully acknowledge the support of the UK EPSRC for grant EP/V026801/1, UKRI Trustworthy Autonomous Systems Node in Verifiability. We also thank Jos Gibbons and Juliet Cooke for their feedback and suggestions on drafts of this paper as well as our anonymous reviewers for all of their valuable feedback which fed into the final version of the paper.

References

1. Althoff, M., Dolan, J.M.: Online verification of automated road vehicles using reachability analysis. IEEE Trans. Robot. **30**(4), 903–918 (2014)
2. Althoff, M., et al.: ARCH-COMP18 category report: continuous and hybrid systems with linear continuous dynamics. In: Frehse, G. (ed). ARCH18. 5th International Workshop on Applied Verification of Continuous and Hybrid Systems, vol. 54 of EPiC Series in Computing EasyChair, pp. 23–52 (2018)
3. Araujo, H., et al.: Sound conformance testing for cyber-physical systems: theory and implementation. Sci. Comput. Program. **162**, 35–54 (2018)
4. Aziz, A., Singhal, V., Balarin, F., Brayton, R.K., Sangiovanni-Vincentelli, A.L.: It usually works: the temporal logic of stochastic systems. In: Wolper, P. (ed.) CAV 1995. LNCS, vol. 939, pp. 155–165. Springer, Heidelberg (1995). https://doi.org/10.1007/3-540-60045-0_48
5. Bartocci, E., et al.: Specification-based monitoring of cyber-physical systems: a survey on theory, tools and applications. In: Bartocci, E., Falcone, Y. (eds.) Lectures on Runtime Verification. LNCS, vol. 10457, pp. 135–175. Springer, Cham (2018). https://doi.org/10.1007/978-3-319-75632-5_5
6. Berz, M., Makino, K.: Verified integration of odes and flows using differential algebraic methods on high-order taylor models. Reliab. Comput. **4**(4), 361–369 (1998)
7. Borda, A., Pasquale, L., Koutavas, V., Nuseibeh, B.: Compositional verification of self-adaptive cyber-physical systems. In: 2018 IEEE/ACM 13th International Symposium on Software Engineering for Adaptive and Self-Managing Systems (SEAMS), pp. 1–11. IEEE (2018)
8. Calinescu, R., Rafiq, Y., Johnson, K., Bakır, M.E.: Adaptive model learning for continual verification of non-functional properties. In: Proceedings of the 5th ACM/SPEC International Conference on Performance Engineering, pp. 87–98 (2014)
9. Calinescu, R., Ghezzi, C., Kwiatkowska, M., Mirandola, R.: Self-adaptive software needs quantitative verification at runtime. Commun. ACM **55**(9), 69–77 (2012)
10. Cellier, F.E., Kofman, E.: Continuous System Simulation. Springer, New York (2006). https://doi.org/10.1007/0-387-30260-3

11. Chen, M., Tam, Q., Livingston, S.C., Pavone, M.: Signal temporal logic meets reachability: connections and applications. In: Morales, M., Tapia, L., Sánchez-Ante, G., Hutchinson, S. (eds.) WAFR 2018. SPAR, vol. 14, pp. 581–601. Springer, Cham (2020). https://doi.org/10.1007/978-3-030-44051-0_34
12. Chen, X.: Reachability Analysis of Non-Linear Hybrid Systems Using Taylor Models. PhD thesis, Fachgruppe Informatik, RWTH Aachen University (2015)
13. Chen, X., Abraham, E., Sankaranarayanan, S.: Taylor model flowpipe construction for non-linear hybrid systems. In: 2012 IEEE 33rd Real-Time Systems Symposium, pp. 183–192. IEEE (2012)
14. Chen, X., Ábrahám, E., Sankaranarayanan, S.: Flow*: an analyzer for non-linear hybrid systems. In: Sharygina, N., Veith, H. (eds.) CAV 2013. LNCS, vol. 8044, pp. 258–263. Springer, Heidelberg (2013). https://doi.org/10.1007/978-3-642-39799-8_18
15. Chen, X., Sankaranarayanan, S.: Model predictive real-time monitoring of linear systems. In: 2017 IEEE Real-Time Systems Symposium (RTSS), pp. 297–306. IEEE (2017)
16. Chen, Y., Anderson, J., Kalsi, K., Ames, A.D., Low, S.H.: Safety-critical control synthesis for network systems with control barrier functions and assume-guarantee contracts. IEEE Trans. Control Netw. Syst. **8**(1), 487–499 (2021)
17. Chou, Y., Yoon, H., Sankaranarayanan, S.: Predictive runtime monitoring of vehicle models using bayesian estimation and reachability analysis. In: 2020 IEEE/RSJ International Conference on Intelligent Robots and Systems (IROS), pp. 2111–2118, October 2020. ISSN: 2153–0866
18. Chou, Y., Yoon, H., Sankaranarayanan, S.: Predictive runtime monitoring of vehicle models using bayesian estimation and reachability analysis. In: 2020 IEEE/RSJ International Conference on Intelligent Robots and Systems (IROS), pp. 2111–2118. IEEE (2020)
19. Deshmukh, J.V., Majumdar, R., Prabhu, V.S.: Quantifying conformance using the skorokhod metric. Formal Methods in Sys. Des. 168–206 (2017). https://doi.org/10.1007/s10703-016-0261-8
20. Donzé, A., Raman, V., Frehse, G., Althoff, M.: BluSTL: controller synthesis from signal temporal logic specifications. ARCH@ CPSWeek **34**, 160–168 (2015)
21. Fang, X., et al.: Fast parametric model checking through model fragmentation. In: 2021 IEEE/ACM 43rd International Conference on Software Engineering (ICSE), pp. 835–846. IEEE (2021)
22. Farahani, S.S., et al.: Formal controller synthesis for wastewater systems with signal temporal logic constraints: the Barcelona case study. J. Process Control **69**, 179–191 (2018)
23. Feng, H., et al.: Integration of the MAPE-K loop in digital twins. In: 2022 Annual Modeling and Simulation Conference (ANNSIM), San Diego, California, USA, IEEE (2022)
24. Feng, H., et al.: Introduction to digital twin engineering. In: 2021 Annual Modeling and Simulation Conference (ANNSIM), Fairfax, VA, USA, pp. 1–12. IEEE, July 2021
25. Feng, H., et al. The incubator case study for digital twin engineering. arXiv:2102.10390 [cs; eess], February 2021
26. Feng, H., Gomes, C., Sandberg, M., Macedo, H.D., Larsen, P.G.: Under what conditions does a digital shadow track a periodic linear physical system?. In Software Engineering and Formal Methods. SEFM 2021 Collocated Workshops. SEFM 2021. Lecture Notes in Computer Science, vol. 13230. Springer, Cham (2022). https://doi.org/10.1007/978-3-031-12429-7_11

27. Ghosh, B., Étienne, A.: Offline and online monitoring of scattered uncertain logs using uncertain linear dynamical systems. Technical Report. arXiv:2204.11505. [cs, eess] April 2022
28. Hachicha, M., Halima, R.B., Kacem, A.H.: Formal verification approaches of self-adaptive systems: a survey. Procedia Comput. Sci. **159**, 1853–1862 (2019)
29. Henzinger, T.A., Ho, P.-H., Wong-Toi, H.: HyTech: a model checker for hybrid systems. In: Grumberg, O. (ed.) CAV 1997. LNCS, vol. 1254, pp. 460–463. Springer, Heidelberg (1997). https://doi.org/10.1007/3-540-63166-6_48
30. Hwang, I., et al.: A survey of fault detection, isolation, and reconfiguration methods. In: IEEE Transactions on Control Systems Technology, Conference Name: IEEE Transactions on Control Systems Technology, vol. 18 no. 3, pp. 636–653, May 2010
31. Ishii, D., Yonezaki, N., Goldsztejn, A.: Monitoring temporal properties using interval analysis. IEICE Trans. Fund. Electron. Commun. Comput. Sci. **99**(2), 442–453 (2016)
32. Kephart, J.O., Chess, D.M.: The vision of autonomic computing. Computer **36**(1), 41–50 (2003)
33. Kritzinger, W., et al.: Digital Twin in manufacturing: a categorical literature review and classification. IFAC-PapersOnLine **51**, 1016–1022 (2018)
34. Lee, J., Yu, G., Bae, K.: Efficient SMT-based model checking for signal temporal logic. In: 2021 36th IEEE/ACM International Conference on Automated Software Engineering (ASE), pp. 343–354. IEEE (2021)
35. Lin, Q., et al.: Reachflow: an online safety assurance framework for waypoint-following of self-driving cars. In: 2020 IEEE/RSJ International Conference on Intelligent Robots and Systems (IROS), pp. 6627–6632 (2020)
36. Lin, Y., Stadtherr, M.A.: Validated solutions of initial value problems for parametric odes. Appl. Numer. Math. **57**(10), 1145–1162 (2007)
37. Meiyi, M., et al.: Predictive monitoring with logic-calibrated uncertainty for cyber-physical systems. ACM Trans. Embed. Comput. Syst. **20**(5s), 101:1–101:25 (2021)
38. Makino, K., Berz, M.: Suppression of the wrapping effect by taylor model-based verified integrators: long-term stabilization by preconditioning. Int. J. Diff. Equat. Appl. **10**(4), 353–384 (2011)
39. Maler, O., Nickovic, D.: Monitoring temporal properties of continuous signals. In: Lakhnech, Y., Yovine, S. (eds.) FORMATS/FTRTFT -2004. LNCS, vol. 3253, pp. 152–166. Springer, Heidelberg (2004). https://doi.org/10.1007/978-3-540-30206-3_12
40. Moore, R.E., Kearfott, R.B., Cloud, M.J.: Introduction to Interval Analysis, vol. 110. Siam, Philadelphia (2009)
41. Muccini, H., Sharaf, M., Weyns, D.: Self-adaptation for cyber-physical systems: a systematic literature review. In: Proceedings of the 11th International Symposium on Software Engineering for Adaptive and Self-Managing Systems, SEAMS 2016, New York, pp. 75–81. Association for Computing Machinery, May 2016
42. Warping, D.T.: In: Meinard, M. (ed.), Information Retrieval for Music and Motion, pp. 69–84. Springer, Berlin (2007). https://doi.org/10.1007/978-3-540-74048-3_4
43. Pant, Y.V., Abbas, H., Mangharam, R.: Smooth operator: control using the smooth robustness of temporal logic. In: 2017 IEEE Conference on Control Technology and Applications (CCTA), pp. 1235–1240, August 2017
44. Qin, X., Deshmukh, J.V.: Clairvoyant monitoring for signal temporal logic. In: Bertrand, N., Jansen, N. (eds.) FORMATS 2020. LNCS, vol. 12288, pp. 178–195. Springer, Cham (2020). https://doi.org/10.1007/978-3-030-57628-8_11

45. Raman, V., et al.: Model predictive control with signal temporal logic specifications. In: 53rd IEEE Conference on Decision and Control, pp. 81–87, December 2014. ISSN: 0191–2216
46. Raman, V., et al.: Reactive synthesis from signal temporal logic specifications. In: Proceedings of the 18th International Conference on Hybrid Systems: Computation and Control, HSCC 2015, New York, pp. 239–248. Association for Computing Machinery, April 2015
47. Roehm, H., Oehlerking, J., Heinz, T., Althoff, M.: STL model checking of continuous and hybrid systems. In: Artho, C., Legay, A., Peled, D. (eds.) ATVA 2016. LNCS, vol. 9938, pp. 412–427. Springer, Cham (2016). https://doi.org/10.1007/978-3-319-46520-3_26
48. Sadigh, D., Ashish, K.: Safe control under uncertainty. Technical Report, arXiv:1510.07313 [cs] type: article, arXiv, October 2015
49. Sadraddini, S., Belta, C.: Model predictive control of urban traffic networks with temporal logic constraints. In: 2016 American Control Conference (ACC), pp. 881–881, July 2016. ISSN: 2378–5861
50. Sahin, Y.E., Quirynen, R., Di Cairano, S.: Autonomous vehicle decision-making and monitoring based on signal temporal logic and mixed-integer programming. In: 2020 American Control Conference (ACC), pp. 454–459, July 2020. ISSN: 2378–5861
51. Sanwal, M.U., Hasan, O.: Formal verification of cyber-physical systems: coping with continuous elements. In: Murgante, B., et al. (eds.) ICCSA 2013. LNCS, vol. 7971, pp. 358–371. Springer, Heidelberg (2013). https://doi.org/10.1007/978-3-642-39637-3_29
52. Shevtsov, S., Weyns, D., Maggio, M.: Simca*: a control-theoretic approach to handle uncertainty in self-adaptive systems with guarantees. ACM Trans. Auton. Adapt. Syst. **13**(4), 1–34 (2019)
53. da Silva, R.R., Kurtz, V., Lin, H.: Symbolic control of hybrid systems from signal temporal logic specifications. Guidance Navig. Control **01**(02), 2150008 (2021)
54. Tao, F., et al.: Digital twin in industry: state-of-the-art. IEEE Trans. Ind. Inf. **15**(4), 2405–2415 (2019)
55. Tsigkanos, C., et al.: On the interplay between cyber and physical spaces for adaptive security. IEEE Trans. Dependable Secur. Comput. **15**(3), 466–480 (2016)
56. Waga, M., et al.: Model-bounded monitoring of hybrid systems. In: Proceedings of the ACM/IEEE 12th International Conference on Cyber-Physical Systems, pp. 21–32. Association for Computing Machinery, New York, May 2021
57. Weyns, D., et al.: A survey of formal methods in self-adaptive systems. In: Proceedings of the Fifth International C* Conference on Computer Science and Software Engineering - C3S2E 2012, Montreal, Quebec, Canada, pp. 67–79. ACM Press (2012)
58. Woodcock, J., Gomes, C., Macedo, H.D., Larsen, P.G.: Uncertainty quantification and runtime monitoring using environment-aware digital twins. In: Margaria, T., Steffen, B. (eds.) ISoLA 2020. LNCS, vol. 12479, pp. 72–87. Springer, Cham (2021). https://doi.org/10.1007/978-3-030-83723-5_6
59. Wright, T., Stark, I.: Property-directed verified monitoring of signal temporal logic. In: Deshmukh, J., Ničković, D. (eds.) RV 2020. LNCS, vol. 12399, pp. 339–358. Springer, Cham (2020). https://doi.org/10.1007/978-3-030-60508-7_19
60. Yoon, H., Chou, Y., Chen, X., Frew, E., Sankaranarayanan, S.: Predictive runtime monitoring for linear stochastic systems and applications to geofence enforcement for UAVs. In: Finkbeiner, B., Mariani, L. (eds.) RV 2019. LNCS, vol. 11757, pp. 349–367. Springer, Cham (2019). https://doi.org/10.1007/978-3-030-32079-9_20

61. Yu, X., et al.: Online monitoring of dynamic systems for signal temporal logic specifications with model information. Technical Report. arXiv:2203.16267 [cs, eess] type: article, arXiv, March 2022
62. Zhang, L., Chen, X., Kong, F., Cardenas, A.A.: Real-time attack-recovery for cyber-physical systems using linear approximations. In: 2020 IEEE Real-Time Systems Symposium (RTSS), pp. 205–217, December 2020. ISSN: 2576-3172

Adaptive Data-driven Predictor of Ship Maneuvering Motion Under Varying Ocean Environments

Tongtong Wang[1(✉)], Robert Skulstad[1], Motoyasu Kanazawa[1], Lars Ivar Hatledal[2], Guoyuan Li[1], and Houxiang Zhang[1]

[1] Department of Ocean Operations and Civil Engineering, Faculty of Engineering, Norwegian University of Science and Technology (NTNU), Trondheim, Norway
{tongtong.wang,robert.skulstad,motoyasu.kanazawa,guoyuan.li,hozh}@ntnu.no
[2] Department of ICT and Natural Sciences, Faculty of Information Technology and Electrical Engineering, Norwegian University of Science and Technology (NTNU), Trondheim, Norway
laht@ntnu.no

Abstract. Modern marine vessels operate increasingly autonomously, enabled by the strong interaction between data acquisition and analysis. The data-driven technology has been widely applied and significantly benefits maritime clusters by providing real-time predictions, optimizations, monitoring, controlling, improved decision-making, etc. While offshore engineering applications are usually operating in highly dynamic environments, which is an unavoidable obstacle when developing motion predictors. To this end, we propose an adaptive data-driven predictor aiming to supply decision support for vessels under varying ocean status. The predictor based on the Gaussian Process can decide whether and when to update itself from the assessment of external situations. By optimizing the ancient model with new observations, the adaptive model better fits the current situation, and efforts of re-training from scratch could be saved. Co-simulation, as an enabling tool, is utilized to simulate the dynamic ocean environments and ship maneuvers. Experimental results have demonstrated the effectiveness of the adaptive predictor, especially when unseen weather is encountered.

Keywords: Ship motion prediction · Adaptive · Gaussian process · Co-simulation

1 Introduction

The maritime industrial clusters are experiencing a digital revolution. The advances in digital technology are continuously pushing the boundaries of ship

This work was supported by a grant from the Research Council of Norway through the Knowledge-Building Project for industry “Digital Twins for Vessel Life Cycle Service” (Project no: 270803).

T. Margaria and B. Steffen (Eds.): ISoLA 2022, LNCS 13704, pp. 110–125, 2022.
https://doi.org/10.1007/978-3-031-19762-8_8

technology towards intelligence more in line with the demanding marine operations. It is seen that modern marine vessels operate increasingly autonomously through strongly interacting subsystems, which are dedicated to a specific, primary objective of the vessel or may be part of the general ship operations. Between subsystems, they exchange data and make coordinated operational decisions, ideally without any user interaction. Designing, operating, and life cycle service supporting such vessels is a complex and intricate engineering task requiring an efficient development approach to accommodate the mutual interaction between subsystems and the inherent uncertainties. Traditional simulation approaches are too inflexible, too costly, and too inefficient to be applied in complex maritime systems [21]. Compared to more conventional monolithic simulations, co-simulation encourages re-usability, model sharing, and fusion of simulation domains. Therefore, the idea of using co-simulation to simulate maritime vessels and auxiliary equipment seems promising.

With the increasing interest in developing autonomous vehicles and ensuring ship navigation safety, a higher requirement for ship motion forecasting technology is put forward. Predicting ship motion in the near future can give the operator (autonomous ship operating system or human) ample time to respond and avoid dangerous operations. Therefore, modeling and predicting the behavior of ships have been pursued extensively to support state estimation and motion control. Vessels operating on the surface of the ocean are exposed to an array of uncertainties, such as the external perturbations produced by wind, waves, sea currents, etc. Moreover, the nonlinear time-varying ship dynamics and the coupling effects with also time-varying environments increase the difficulty of deriving an accurate predictor. A solution that relies on data sampled from vessels becomes promising owing to the fast advancement in instrumentation and data analysis techniques. These data-driven models learn the experience included in the training data and represent the dependency relationships between input and output variables in an implicit way. Thereby, the data-driven predictors always present excellent performance.

While in maritime scenarios, the general data-driven techniques are applied with difficulties. Due to the complexity and uncertainties introduced by the time-varying external disturbances such as wind, waves, currents, etc., and navigation conditions, for instance, loading and speeds, it is hard to obtain a proper prediction model by a static machine learning structure. Traditional machine learning models require all the samples to be available at training time. While in many practical applications, the acquisition of representative training data is expensive and time-consuming. Consequently, it is not common for such data to be well-prepared over a period of time. In such situations, updating an existing model in an incremental way to accommodate new information is a popular option.

In literature, online ship motion predictions are achieved in various manners. For instance, Yin et al. [30] applied radial basis function (RBF) neural networks to predict ship roll motion, where the structure and parameters of the RBF network were adjusted at each step via a sequential learning algorithm. Wavelet networks are also frequently applied to predict nonlinear ship motion in various forms, such as by adjusting structure and parameters through coarse and fine tuning [10], taking in the time-delayed information [32], or decomposing the time-series data into few frequency-related sub-series [29]. Besides, as a particular form of single-hidden-layer feedforward networks, the extreme learning machine (ELM) is improved from batch learning (offline) to sequential learning for online purpose [12]. An online sequential extreme learning machine (OS-ELM) has the input weights and hidden nodes randomly settled, and the output weights analytically determined. Yu et al. [31] applied the OS-ELM to forecast ship roll motion facilitated by the temporal difference learning technique. To address the anomalies and change points that might occur in the unseen future data, Guo et al. [5] proposed an adaptive gradient learning approach for recurrent neural networks to forecast streaming time series. A support vector machine (SVM), as a novel and powerful machine learning tool, is also found to be widely applied for time-series prediction and has been reported to perform well by promising results. Generally, the online SVM is implemented on incremental learning and decremental pruning algorithms with the data number in the training set kept constant [14,23,26,27].

These attempts make the online prediction task a success in capturing the changes in time-varying ship dynamics. Nevertheless, it is found that except for the ship dynamics, ocean environmental changes are not accounted for in these examples. In fact, the anticipated weather conditions could vary a lot along the voyage. As learned, the weather characteristics not only vary with season [13] but also change from place to place along the path [18]. Even though weather forecast mechanisms such as full-spectral third-generation wind-wave model NOAA WAVEWATCH III (NWW3 hereinafter) [24] and the Ocean Surface Currents Analysis - Real time (OSCAR) [11] are getting more developed, the estimation uncertainties and subsequent influence on the ship motion predictions cannot be eliminated. To this end, we propose an online learning short-term ship motion predictor which is designed exclusively to fit the time-varying ocean environments. A Gaussian Process-based time series prediction model is developed to provide future velocity forecasts with confidence intervals. When the ship is exposed to new environmental scenarios, the preceding optimal model may be different from the succeeding one influenced by the latest data. Therefore, modifying and updating the model is needed for adequate prediction performance. Given that the weather is firmly serially correlated [1], incorporating information about what has happened in the past to update the model is promising. Gaussian processes are a natural way of specifying prior distributions over functions of one or more input variables [17], and it appears the best conceivable approach for model upgrades. In this work, ship maneuver tests at varying ocean conditions are carried out. A co-simulation platform developed by our team—Vico, is utilized to simulate the environment.

The rest of the paper is organized as follows. Related works on incremental learning and transfer learning are presented in Sect. 2. The following Sect. 3 presents the proposed adaptive data-driven ship motion predictor under changing immediate environments. Details of the modeling process are also explained. Maneuver experiments of a real ship in a co-simulation platform are executed to validate the efficiency of the proposed method in Sect. 4. Conclusions and future work are delivered in Sect. 5.

2 Related Work

Online or incremental learning will be favored in assimilating new information and evolving the model to the latest data.

2.1 Incremental Learning

Incremental learning (IL) refers to a learning system that continuously learns new knowledge from new samples and maintains most of the previously learned knowledge [16]. It is separated from machine learning by continuously learning and memorizing and plays increasingly essential roles in intelligent robots, autonomous driving, unmanned vehicles, etc. However, one long-standing challenge in applying incremental learning is known as catastrophic forgetting (CF). Adjusting the network's weights to fit the newly available data unavoidably leads to a decreased performance on the previously learned knowledge. Learning new information without forgetting previously acquired knowledge raises the stability-plasticity dilemma [4], one of the fundamental challenges that have to be tackled with concern. Another issue arises in real-life applications where the data distribution of already learned classes may change in unforeseen ways, which are related to concept drift [19]. When concept drift happens, regardless of the effort put into retraining the old classes' knowledge, degradation in performance is inevitable [8].

In seeking solutions to facilitate incremental learning, efforts are devoted to traditional approaches and deep learning ways [2]. Initial methods for incremental learning targeted the SVM classifier by exploiting the support vectors and Karush-Kuhn-Tucker conditions [3,20]. To maintain the previously learned information and keep the sample pool as concise as possible, support vectors whose number is typically smaller than that of the training examples are selected to represent the past [14,23]. In deep learning architectures, knowledge distillation is more recently used to preserve the memories of the old tasks [2]. Actually, distillation is originally applied in transfer learning between networks [9]. Although different proposed algorithms, the core is to compress the already learned knowledge and reduce forgetting as the new data comes in.

2.2 Transfer Learning

In contrast with incremental learning, which requires the model to retain performance on the old task after learning a new job, transfer learning (TL) only utilizes ancient knowledge to discover new knowledge. When learning is completed, the new representations are more concerned, and the old knowledge is no longer considered. Historically, transfer learning is inspired by the capabilities of human beings of re-suing the knowledge from experienced tasks without learning new tasks from scratch. Thus, it is natural to be applied for knowledge migration, either from proceeding to succeeding or domain to domain.

Various algorithms suggested in the literature are used in cross-domain cases. Due to practical difficulties such as data sparsity or the different distributions of training and test data, traditional machine learning (ML) is sometimes limited to generating promising results. While with TL, the restrictions can be lifted a little bit [22]. A typical application relates to fault diagnosis scenarios where labeled fault data acquisition is always an obstacle, and identical distributed features are rare in real-world applications. To handle the task challenging to traditional ML, TL is an excellent choice to offer an alternative solution [28,33].

3 Methodology

The methodology of developing ship motion predictors based on data-driven approaches that adapt to the immediate ocean environments is presented.

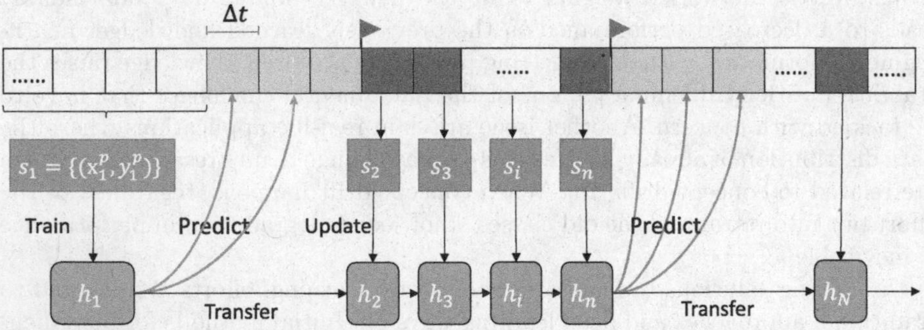

Fig. 1. Online ship motion prediction. A sequence of models is generated using each new data block with block size p, where $(\mathbf{x}_i^p, y_i^p)$ indicates the i-th new data for the p-th block.

As shown in Fig. 1, the base model h_1 is initially trained on the original data set $s_1 = (x_1^p, y_1^p)$, where p refers to the data chunk size. Being trained with sufficient data that fully reflects the past experience, the model h_1 should be qualified to predict the future states of the ship. When a new observation arrives, anomaly detection is performed to determine whether it works well with the current model. If so, the model is kept unchanged; otherwise, it will be updated to fit the current scenario better. A sequence of model $h_1, h_2, ..., h_n$ are generated on the sequential data chunks $s_1, s_2, ..., s_n$ until the updated model gets representative of the new profile. In this transition process, the model h_i is updated from h_{i-1} by using block of new data s_i. Because the successive optimal model is obtained based on the preceding optimal model, only one computing step is needed to determine the optimal kernel corresponding to the minimum of an optimization problem.

Distinct from traditional offline learning, the complete data is unavailable during training. We need to detect and update the model when the immediate environment changes to make it dynamically fit the scenarios experienced so far. So there are two phases to go before the model is adapted to the new scenarios: predictive anomaly detection and online model learning.

Regarding time series anomaly detection, an autonomous detection mechanism based on the prediction metrics is proposed. An assumption is introduced here that the external environmental change is the only factor that leads to the passive ship motion deviation during ship maneuvering instead of the active control changes. This way, when the predictor is determined anomaly, one can tell that the anticipated weather varies and a new model is in call to fit the current sailing conditions. Motivated by the fact that the weather conditions are generally sequentially correlated and the desire to learn from previous experience, Gaussian process regression is applied to construct the data-driven predictor. By transferring the knowledge from the last data chunk into the learning process of the future data chunks, the Gaussian Process (GP) is able to adapt to new scenarios by incorporating new data and discarding out-of-date information. The proposed algorithm yields a sparse approximation and online implementation of the incremental GP for time-varying dynamics. The online prediction process is shown in Fig. 2. The two key step—online model learning and predictive anomaly detection will be explained in detail.

3.1 Gaussian Process Regression

Gaussian Process can be viewed as a collection of random variables with a joint Gaussian distribution for any finite subject. It is specified by a mean function $m(\mathbf{x})$ and a covariance function $k(\mathbf{x}, \mathbf{x}')$, as:

$$m(\mathbf{x}) = E[f(\mathbf{x})] \tag{1}$$

$$k(\mathbf{x}, \mathbf{x}') = E[(f(\mathbf{x}) - m(\mathbf{x}))(f(\mathbf{x}') - m(\mathbf{x}'))] \tag{2}$$

where E denotes the expectation operator and $k(\mathbf{x}, \mathbf{x}')$ is the covariance function describing the information coupling between two independent variables $\mathbf{x}$ and $\mathbf{x}'$. Given a data set $\mathcal{D}$ with N observations $\mathcal{D} = \{(\mathbf{x}_i, y_i), i = 1, \ldots, N\}$, where $\mathbf{x}$ denotes an input vector of dimension D, and y denotes a scalar output. GP regression approximates a function $f(x)$ mapping a multiple dimensional input $\mathbf{x}_i$ to a scalar output y_i.

The regular GP defines a prior on the function values,

$$p(f \mid \mathbf{x}) \sim \mathcal{N}(m(\mathbf{x}), k(\mathbf{x}, \mathbf{x}')) \tag{3}$$

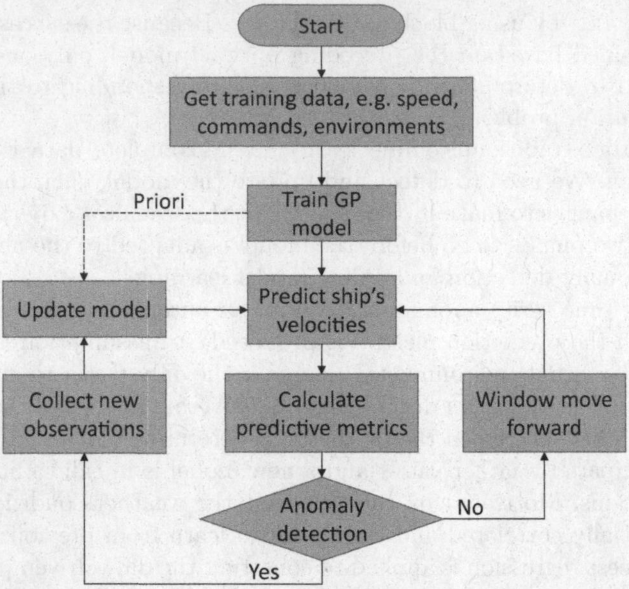

Fig. 2. A flowchart showing the online prediction process.

The likelihood function is obtained as,

$$p(y \mid f, \mathbf{x}) = \prod_{i=1}^{N} \mathcal{N}(y_i; f_i, \sigma_y^2) \tag{4}$$

With the prior Eq. (3) and likelihood Eq. (4) functions in place, the posterior probability distribution and prediction the function value f^* at a whole set of test points $\mathbf{x}^*$ are derived as,

$$\begin{bmatrix} f^* \\ f \end{bmatrix} \sim \mathcal{N}(\begin{bmatrix} m(\mathbf{x}^*) \\ m(\mathbf{x}) \end{bmatrix}, \begin{bmatrix} K(\mathbf{x}^*, \mathbf{x}^*) & K(\mathbf{x}^*, \mathbf{x}) \\ K(\mathbf{x}, \mathbf{x}^*) & K(\mathbf{x}, \mathbf{x}) \end{bmatrix}) \tag{5}$$

which leads to the predictive equations,

$$p(f^* \mid \mathcal{D}, x^*) = \mathcal{N}(m, s) \tag{6}$$

where

$$m = m(\mathbf{x}^*) + K(\mathbf{x}^*, \mathbf{x})K(\mathbf{x}, \mathbf{x})^{-1}(y - m(\mathbf{x})) \tag{7}$$

$$s = K(\mathbf{x}^*, \mathbf{x}^*) - K(\mathbf{x}^*, \mathbf{x})K(\mathbf{x}, \mathbf{x})^{-1}K(\mathbf{x}, \mathbf{x}^*) \tag{8}$$

Typically, the hyperparameters are learned by the maximum log-likelihood method, which is given as:

$$
\begin{aligned}
-\log p(y \mid \mathbf{x}, \theta) = \frac{1}{2}(y - m(\mathbf{x}))^T (K(\mathbf{x}, \mathbf{x}) + \sigma_y^2 I)^{-1} (y - m(\mathbf{x})) \\
+ \frac{1}{2} \log \left| K(\mathbf{x}, \mathbf{x}) + \sigma_y^2 I \right| + \frac{N}{2} \log 2\pi
\end{aligned} \tag{9}
$$

According to Eq. (6), the prediction value f^* can be estimated by evaluating the mean and covariance matrix. A new measurement $(\mathbf{x}_{n+1}, y_{n+1})$ can be incorporated into the training GP through a matrix update by Eq. (6), leading to an online GP update law.

Ensuring scalar output variables, three GP predictors are separately trained on the initial data set s_1 with the input and output specified as:

- I(t) = $[u_t, v_t, r_t, n_{p_t}, \delta_{p_t}, n_{s_t}, \delta_{s_t}, V_{w_t}, \beta_{w_t}, V_{c_t}, \beta_{c_t}, H_t, T_{p_t}, \beta_{wa_t}]$
- O(t) = u_{t+1} for surge direction
- O(t) = v_{t+1} for sway direction
- O(t) = r_{t+1} for yaw direction

where u, v, r are the velocities in the surge, sway, and yaw direction. n and δ refer to the shaft speeds in revolution-per-minute and the orientations of both stern thrusters. The subscripts p and s represent the port side and starboard side. The environmental features unfold as:

- Wind measurements: speed V_w and direction β_w
- Current measurements: speed V_c and direction β_c
- Wave measurements: significant height H, wave period T_p, and wave direction β_{wa}

In each GP, the squared exponential covariance function (10) is adopted.

$$
k(\mathbf{x}_i, \mathbf{x}_j) = \sigma_f \exp\left(-\frac{\|\mathbf{x}_i - \mathbf{x}_j\|}{2\ell}\right) \tag{10}
$$

where σ_f and ℓ are hyperparameters, representing the amplitude and length scale, respectively. $\|\cdot\|$ is the Euclidean distance between two vectors.

To avoid the situation that the future weather conditions are located far from the training spectrum, the environment-related variables are scaled by their reasonable maximum value according to the Beaufort scale before normalization. For example, the global angles are scaled by 180°C to [0, 1], and the wind speed is scaled by 12 m/s, etc. The mean value and covariance function are randomly initialized for h_1 learning. With the time window moving forward, the posterior mean and covariance of h_i are used as the prior mean and covariance for h_{i+1} learning. During training, the training set evaluated the performance by minimizing the mean square error (MSE) metric between desired and regressed values. The proposed regressor is implemented by using Scikit-learn in Python.

3.2 Predictive Anomaly Detection

Generally, the divergence between the GP model predictions and the new measurements is used to assign a measure of abnormality. Thus, the square residual (SR) (11) is calculated between the actual observation y^* and the mean prediction at each time interval.

$$\mathrm{SR} = (y^* - \bar{f}(\mathbf{x}^*))^2 \tag{11}$$

The abnormality decision is usually made by comparing the error metrics with a settled threshold ϵ. If $SR > \epsilon + \lambda\sigma$, then an anomaly is detected; otherwise, the model is running as expected, where σ is defined as the confidence interval, and λ is a scaling factor. The rule works based on the human experience, and the threshold value affects the detection efficiency. A lower threshold leads to a sensitive alarm, while a higher threshold is more likely to ignore an anomaly. In order to improve the detection accuracy and release the reliance on human expertise, one other metric assessing the prediction uncertainty is introduced as the predictive log-likelihood (12) to get a local anomaly score [15].

$$\text{score} = -\log p(y^* \mid \mathcal{D}, \mathbf{x}^*) = \frac{1}{2}\log(2\pi\sigma_*^2) + \frac{(y^* - \bar{f}(\mathbf{x}^*))^2}{2\sigma_*^2} \tag{12}$$

where predictive variance is registered as σ_*^2. A high score will be obtained if σ_*^2 has a large value which occurs when the model is uncertain about prediction.

When the anticipated environment varies slightly, the effects on the generated mean predictions may not be as sensitive as the prediction uncertainty. Thus, taking the predictive log-likelihood measures to detect surrounding neighbors provides a more confident decision. The rule is defined as: if the average score of the succeeding time window is larger than the proceeding value, then detection is activated.

4 Experiment Results

In this section, the experiments of ship motion prediction under varying ocean environments are implemented using co-simulation tools.

4.1 Experiment Setup

Ship maneuvering experiments under varying ocean environments are simulated in the co-simulation platform Vico. It is a generic co-simulation framework based on the Entity-Component-System software architecture that supports the Functional Mock-up Interface (FMI) as well as the System Structure and Parameterization (SSP) standards [7]. The user may manipulate the wind, waves, and ocean currents to mimic environmental conditions. The ship maneuvering simulation is set up as Fig. 3 shows. Each block represents an Functional Mock-up

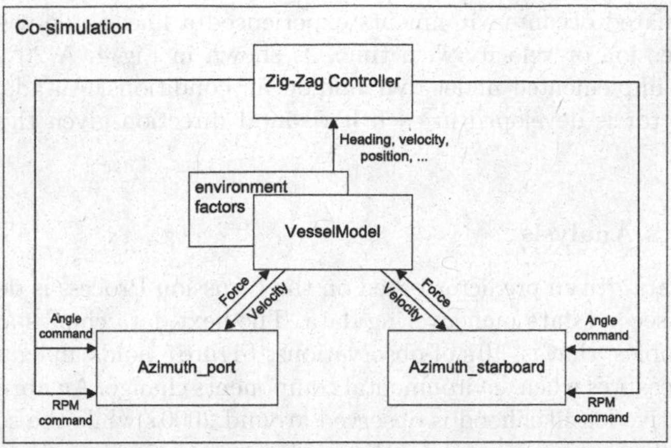

Fig. 3. Diagram showing the relationship of components in co-simulation of executing zigzag maneuver.

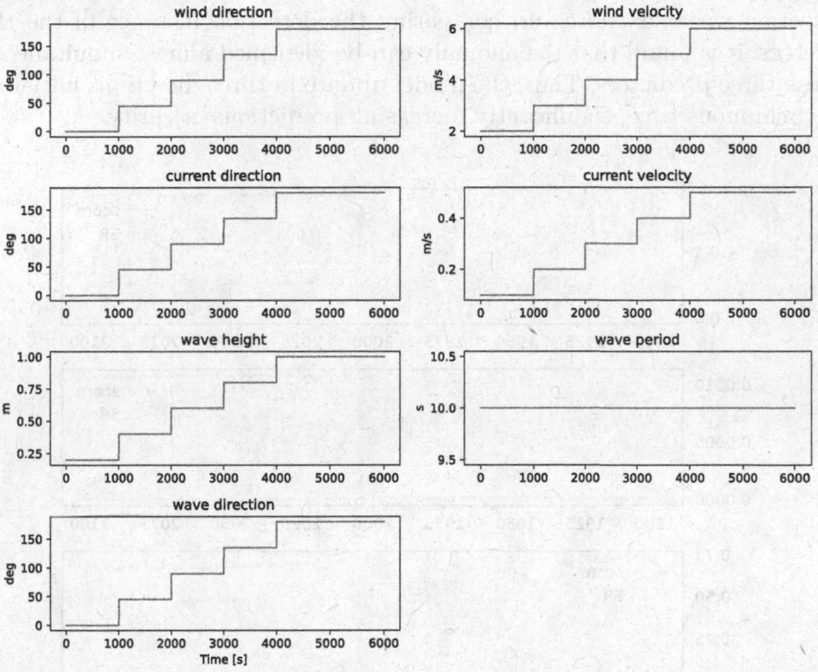

Fig. 4. The environmental components change with time during ship maneuvering.

Unit (FMU) of which the input and output variables are declared. The sampling frequency in the simulation 10 Hz. Details regarding each FMU can be found in [6,25].

The simulated ocean environments experienced a linear step-wise variation in either direction or velocity with time, as shown in Fig. 4. A 20°/20° zigzag maneuver is implemented under dynamic ocean conditions. An adaptive data-driven predictor is developed in each horizontal direction given the sequential ship data.

4.2 Results Analysis

The initial data-driven predictor based on the Gaussian Process is developed on the first 100-second data maneuvering data. The next data chunks are obtained with 100 samples, that is, 10 s of observations. Figure 5 holds an example of the predictive measures when environmental components change. An abrupt increase in the predictive log-likelihood is observed around 2000 s while the square residuals are not fluctuating as much as the local score, especially in the sway direction. It suggests that even though acceptable mean predictions are possible, the risk that the misbehavior will result in future failure increases when an accident happens. This finding evidenced the application of uncertainty metrics as a detection variable. Moreover, comparing the detection instance of the three predictors, it is found that the anomaly can be identified almost simultaneously in these three predictors. Thus, the model update in three directions initiates at the synchronous time, significantly increasing predictions' security.

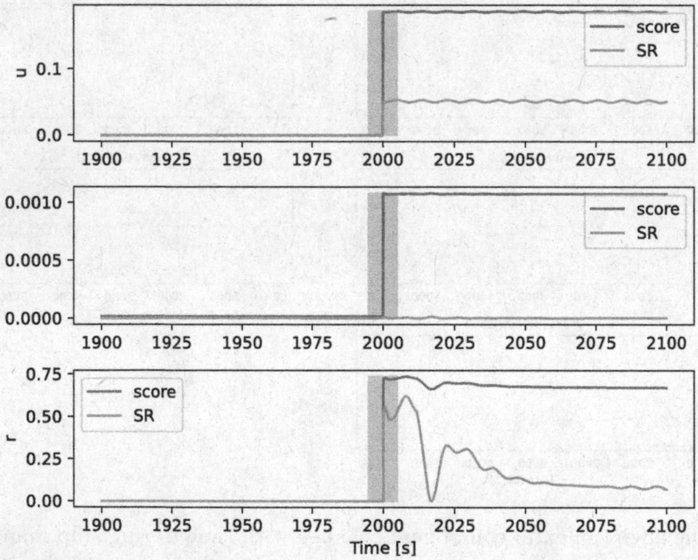

Fig. 5. An illustration of predictive anomaly detection.

Figure 5 shows an example of anomaly identification if the previously trained model is used to predict the future ship velocities subject to different sea states.

In the proposed adaptive predictor, the model will be asked to update once an abnormality is observed, as shown in Fig. 6. In this phase, the data chunk length has an impact. Supposing a chunk with length $p = 100$, the surge predictive model updates three times from h_1 to h_4 until the renewed model fits to the new ocean profile indicated in Fig. 6. The base model h_1 is applied to predict future ship velocities until an abnormality is identified at data chunk s_2 referred to as the first shaded area. Consequently, s_2 is collected as new training data to update the posterior mean and covariance functions of h_1 yielding model h_2. It is found that predictions made by h_2 is still unreliable, thus new chunk s_3 is working to upgrade h_2 to h_3. The process continues unless the predictive score meets the requirement. It is noticed that there is a time lag to collect new operation data that cannot be ignored. During the transition period, the predictive anomaly score decreases gradually, along with the model renewing. Similar results are observed in sway and yaw directions in Fig. 7 and Fig. 8.

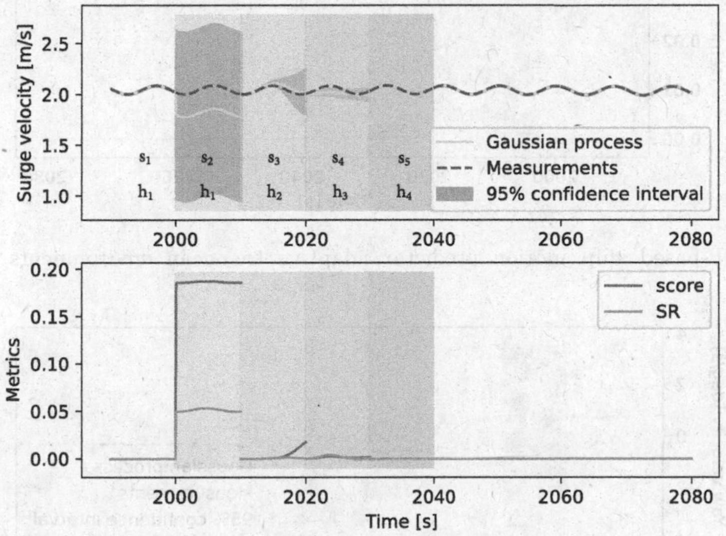

Fig. 6. GP-based ship motion predictor adaptive to ocean environments in surge direction.

Looking into the transition period in these three predictors, we can see that the consequent model of the first upgrade h_2 behaves less stable than succeeding and proceeding. The new data sparsity reason could explain it because its performance gets more stable with more samples getting learned. Given that the model is updated chunk by chunk, it is worth finding the optimal chunk size to minimize the transition period. In seeking a solution to that question, we implemented model revision in three chunk sizes, and the transition time is compared and visualized as Fig. 9 shows. Results suggest that a smaller chunk size could detect the variation more precisely, but its performance will be less stable in the near future time. Controversially, the larger block size may respond too slowly to alert timely to external perturbations. Although only twice model upgrades occur before it reaches stable performance, it costs the longest time. When the block size is set as $p = 100$, a most satisfying performance is generated in terms of stability and efficiency.

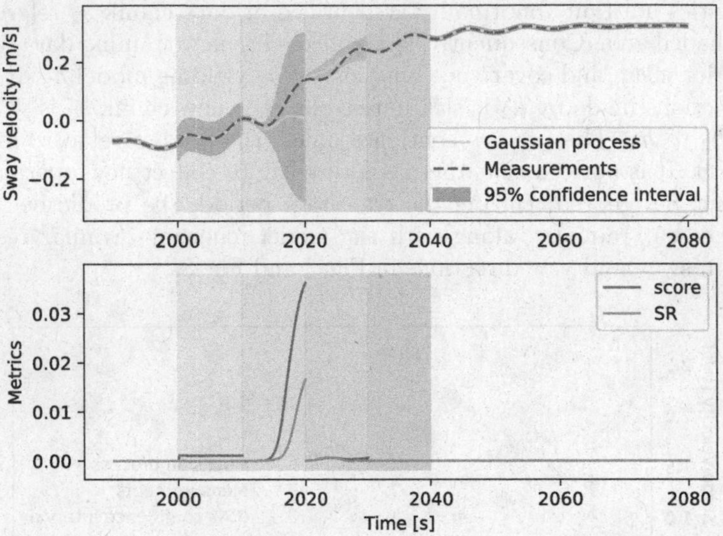

Fig. 7. GP-based ship motion predictor adaptive to ocean environments in sway direction.

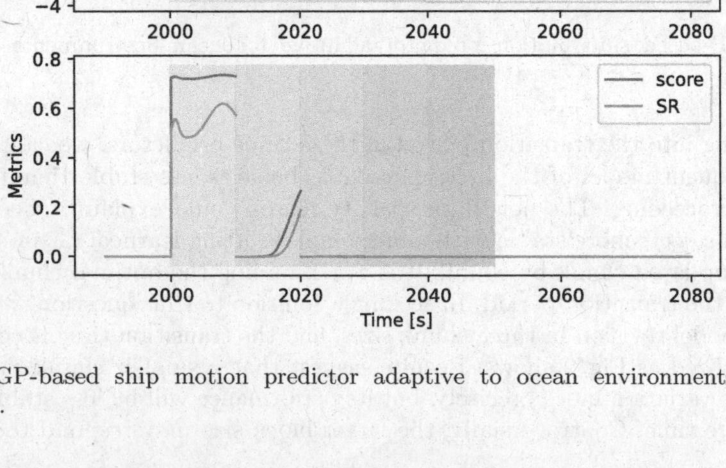

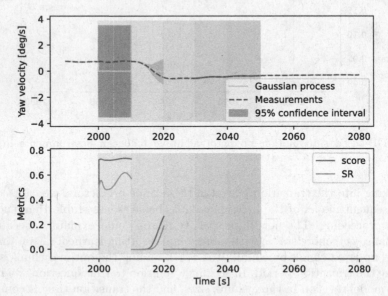

Fig. 8. GP-based ship motion predictor adaptive to ocean environments in yaw direction.

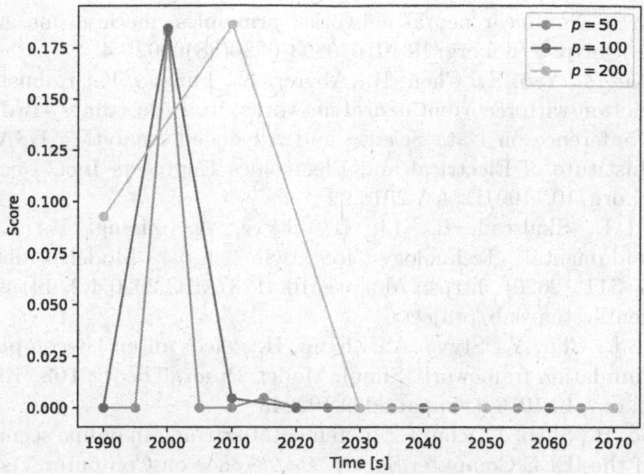

Fig. 9. The model predictive score changes with time at different data block sizes.

5 Conclusion

This paper proposes an adaptive data-driven predictor for ship maneuvering motion under varying ocean environments and validates the approach by co-simulation technique. The predictor based on the Gaussian Process can detect and update itself based on whether the current encountering is experienced. A predictive anomaly detection mechanism is introduced to facilitate this procedure. Benefiting from the prior knowledge learned from historical data upon which the succeeding model is optimized, the adaptive model better fits the current situation and efforts could be saved compared to retraining from scratch. Furthermore, the data block size deciding the model renew frequency is optimized to get the shortest transition time before the upgraded model entirely fits the new ocean scenario. Co-simulation, as an enabling tool, is utilized to simulate ship operations under dynamic environments and supply credible maneuvering data. Results have evidenced the effectiveness of the proposed predictor.

References

1. Allsop, T., Mason, A.J., Philpott, A.: Optimal sailing routes with uncertain weather. In: 35th Annual Conference of the Operations Research Society of New Zealand, pp. 65–74 (2000)
2. Castro, F.M., Marín-Jiménez, M.J., Guil, N., Schmid, C., Alahari, K.: End-to-end incremental learning. In: Ferrari, V., Hebert, M., Sminchisescu, C., Weiss, Y. (eds.) ECCV 2018. LNCS, vol. 11216, pp. 241–257. Springer, Cham (2018). https://doi.org/10.1007/978-3-030-01258-8_15
3. Cortes, C., Vapnik, V.: Support-vector networks. Mach. Learn. **20**(3), 273–297 (1995). https://doi.org/10.1007/bf00994018

4. Grossberg, S.: Nonlinear neural networks: principles, mechanisms, and architectures (1988). https://doi.org/10.1016/0893-6080(88)90021-4
5. Guo, T., Xu, Z., Yao, X., Chen, H., Aberer, K., Funaya, K.: Robust online time series prediction with recurrent neural networks. In: Proceedings - 3rd IEEE International Conference on Data Science and Advanced Analytics, DSAA 2016, pp. 816–825. Institute of Electrical and Electronics Engineers Inc., December 2016. https://doi.org/10.1109/DSAA.2016.92
6. Hatledal, L.I., Skulstad, R., Li, G., Styve, A., Zhang, H.: Co-simulation as a Fundamental Technology for twin ships. Model. Ident. Control **41**(4), 297–311 (2020), https://doi.org/10.4173/MIC.2020.4.2, https://org.ntnu.no/intelligentsystemslab/project/
7. Hatledal, L.I., Chu, Y., Styve, A., Zhang, H.: Vico: an entity-component-system based co-simulation framework. Simul. Model. Pract. Theory **108**, 102243 (2021). https://doi.org/10.1016/j.simpat.2020.102243
8. He, J., Mao, R., Shao, Z., Zhu, F.: Incremental learning in online scenario. In: Proceedings of the IEEE Computer Society Conference on Computer Vision and Pattern Recognition, pp. 13923–13932 (2020). https://doi.org/10.1109/CVPR42600.2020.01394
9. Hinton, G., Vinyals, O., Dean, J.: Distilling the knowledge in a neural network, March 2015. https://doi.org/10.48550/arxiv.1503.02531, arXiv:1503.02531v1
10. Huang, B.G., Zou, Z.J., Ding, W.W.: Online prediction of ship roll motion based on a coarse and fine tuning fixed grid wavelet network. Ocean Eng. **160**, 425–437 (2018). https://doi.org/10.1016/j.oceaneng.2018.04.065
11. Lagerloef, G., Mitchum, G., Bonjean, F., Cheney, R.: OSCAR (Ocean surface currents analysis - real time): an operational resource for various maritime applications and El Niño monitoring in the tropical pacific using jason-1 data. In: AGU Fall Meeting Abstracts. vol. 2002, pp. OS51C-12 (2002). https://ui.adsabs.harvard.edu/abs/2002AGUFMOS51C..12L/abstract
12. Liang, N.Y., Huang, G.B., Saratchandran, P., Sundararajan, N.: A fast and accurate online sequential learning algorithm for feedforward networks. IEEE Trans. Neural Networks **17**(6), 1411–1423 (2006). https://doi.org/10.1109/TNN.2006.880583
13. Lin, Y.H.: The simulation of east-bound transoceanic voyages according to ocean-current sailing based on particle swarm optimization in the weather routing system. Mar. Struct. **59**, 219–236 (2018). https://doi.org/10.1016/j.marstruc.2018.02.001
14. Liu, J., Shi, G., Zhu, K.: Online multiple outputs least-squares support vector regression model of ship trajectory prediction based on automatic information system data and selection mechanism. IEEE Access **8**, 154727–154745 (2020). https://doi.org/10.1109/ACCESS.2020.3018749
15. Loy, C.C., Xiang, T., Gong, S.: Modelling multi-object activity by Gaussian processes. In: British Machine Vision Conference, BMVC 2009 - Proceedings, pp. 1–11 (2009). https://doi.org/10.5244/C.23.13
16. Luo, Y., Yin, L., Bai, W., Mao, K.: An appraisal of incremental learning methods, October 2020. https://doi.org/10.3390/e22111190, https://www.mdpi.com/1099-4300/22/11/1190/htm
17. Neal, R.M.: Regression and classification using gaussian process priors. Bayesian Stat. **6**, 475–501 (1998). http://www.cs.utoronto.ca/radford/.Gaussianprocesses
18. Nishida, T., Waseda, T., Katori, M., Ohuchi, K.: Optimization of integrated weather routing systems for sailing cargo ships, June 2011

19. Royer, A., Lampert, C.H.: Classifier adaptation at prediction time. In: Proceedings of the IEEE Computer Society Conference on Computer Vision and Pattern Recognition, vol. 07–12-June, pp. 1401–1409. IEEE Computer Society, October 2015. https://doi.org/10.1109/CVPR.2015.7298746
20. Rüping, S.: Incremental learning with support vector machines. In: Proceedings - IEEE International Conference on Data Mining, ICDM, pp. 641–642 (2001). https://doi.org/10.1109/icdm.2001.989589
21. Sadjina, S., Kyllingstad, L.T., Rindarøy, M., Skjong, S., Esøy, V., Pedersen, E.: Distributed co-simulation of maritime systems and operations. J. Offshore Mech. Arctic Eng. **141**(1) (2019). https://doi.org/10.1115/1.4040473
22. Tan, C., Sun, F., Kong, T., Zhang, W., Yang, C., Liu, C.: A survey on deep transfer learning. In: Kůrková, V., Manolopoulos, Y., Hammer, B., Iliadis, L., Maglogiannis, I. (eds.) ICANN 2018. LNCS, vol. 11141, pp. 270–279. Springer, Cham (2018). https://doi.org/10.1007/978-3-030-01424-7_27
23. Tang, H.S., Xue, S.T., Chen, R., Sato, T.: Online weighted LS-SVM for hysteretic structural system identification. Eng. Struct. **28**(12), 1728–1735 (2006). https://doi.org/10.1016/j.engstruct.2006.03.008
24. Twumasi, Y.A., Merem, E.C.: User manual and system documentation of WAVEWATCH III. Int. J. Environ. Res. Public Health **3**(1), 98–106 (2006)
25. Wang, T., Li, G., Hatledal, L.I., Skulstad, R., Aesoy, V., Zhang, H.: Incorporating approximate dynamics into data-driven calibrator: a representative model for ship maneuvering prediction. IEEE Trans. Ind. Inf. **18**(3), 1781–1789 (2022). https://doi.org/10.1109/TII.2021.3088404
26. Wang, W., Men, C., Lu, W.: Online prediction model based on support vector machine. Neurocomputing **71**(4–6), 550–558 (2008). https://doi.org/10.1016/j.neucom.2007.07.020
27. Xu, C.Z., Zou, Z.J.: online prediction of ship roll motion in waves based on auto-moving gird search-least square support vector machine. Math. Probl. Eng. **2021** (2021). https://doi.org/10.1155/2021/2760517
28. Yan, R., Shen, F., Sun, C., Chen, X.: Knowledge transfer for rotary machine fault diagnosis. IEEE Sens. J. **20**(15), 8374–8393 (2020). https://doi.org/10.1109/JSEN.2019.2949057
29. Yin, J.C., Perakis, A.N., Wang, N.: A real-time ship roll motion prediction using wavelet transform and variable RBF network. Ocean Eng. **160**, 10–19 (2018). https://doi.org/10.1016/j.oceaneng.2018.04.058
30. Yin, J.C., Zou, Z.J., Xu, F.: On-line prediction of ship roll motion during maneuvering using sequential learning RBF neuralnetworks. Ocean Eng. **61**, 139–147 (2013)
31. Yu, C., Yin, J., Hu, J., Zhang, A.: Online ship rolling prediction using an improved OS-ELM, September 2014
32. Zhang, W., Liu, Z.: Real-time ship motion prediction based on time delay wavelet neural network. J. Appl. Math. **2014** (2014). https://doi.org/10.1155/2014/176297
33. Zheng, H., et al.: Cross-domain fault diagnosis using knowledge transfer strategy: a review. IEEE Access **7**, 129260–129290 (2019). https://doi.org/10.1109/ACCESS.2019.2939876

Robust Adaptive Back-Stepping Control Approach Using Quadratic Lyapunov Functions for MMC-Based HVDC Digital Twins

Le Liu(✉), Aleksandra Lekić, and Marjan Popov

Delft University of Technology, Delft 2628 CD, The Netherlands
{L.liu-7,A.Lekic,M.Popov}@tudelft.nl

Abstract. Due to its excellent performance, VSC-based high voltage direct current (HVDC) power systems draw significant attention. They are being heavily used in modern industrial applications, such as onshore and offshore wind farms, and for interconnection between asynchronous networks. However, the traditional proportional-integral (PI) control method is not robust enough to track the reference signal quickly and accurately during significant system disturbances. This paper proposes a robust adaptive back-stepping control (BSC) method that secures vulnerable power-electronic equipment. The adaptive BSC controller regulates the sum of capacitor energy, and the AC grid current through decoupled and closed control-loop design. The major advantage of the proposed control approach is the smooth transient response and accurate tracking ability, which is superior to classical control methods. In addition, the proposed methods have the merits of systematic and recursive design methodology and demand a low processing burden for *Lyapunov* functions and control laws. Moreover, the implementation particularities of the proposed approach are illustrated and verified for a power system digital twin using real-time digital simulator (RTDS).

Keywords: MMC · Energy controller · Nonlinear robust control · Adaptive back-stepping control · *Lyapunov* stability · HVDC grids · RTDS · Digital twins

1 Introduction

The Modular Multilevel Converters (MMC) have high reliability, modular structure, high efficiency, and adequate redundancy. Due to the technical excellence of flexibility and reliability, the MMC-based HVDC power system is attracting significant attention in modern industrial applications. It has been increasingly utilized as the solution for wind farms, STATCOMs, HVDC, and energy storage systems [2].

The most pressing technical challenge of MMC is the simultaneous control of state variables, including the AC/DC voltage, sum capacitor voltages, and circulating currents [3]. MMC, being a switching power converter, features a variety of state variables and complex dynamics, which present nonlinear behaviors [4]. Therefore, to accelerate the feasibility of the MMC-based HVDC system, MMCs are supposed to utilize advanced and robust control methods.

T. Margaria and B. Steffen (Eds.): ISoLA 2022, LNCS 13704, pp. 126–138, 2022.
https://doi.org/10.1007/978-3-031-19762-8_9

These control approaches can be divided into linear and nonlinear controllers. Currently, the HVDC system generally adopts a centralized dispatch approach for power management [5]. The active and reactive power control is usually achieved by implementing the cascaded PI controllers, which can track the set-points without steady-state errors. The structure is simple and easy to employ. However, the linear-based PI controller always encounters complex cascade or parallel structures, and decoupling assumptions between control variables. The transient response is generally attained after 100 ms, which is very slow regarding the fast nature of electrical transients in power systems. Additionally, the selection of proportional and integral gain values is complicated.

Hence, there are many open research topics of advanced nonlinear control strategies, which can control multiple variables, within allowable safe boundaries and constraints. One promising approach for nonlinear control of power electronic converters is the Back-Stepping Control (BSC) method. The BSC has the merits of systematic and recursive design methodology. Some approaches are outlined in [6, 7]. A dual-layer back-stepping control method is reported in [6], where the energy controller delivers the set-point to the lower layer controller. However, the controller is configured as STATCOM, and the feasibility of the method in a point-to-point HVDC system is not proven yet. The authors of [7] designed the BSC method based on the simplified transmission model, and the interaction of wind farms is also considered. However, due to the imprecision of the model, the effectiveness of the control needs to be further verified.

This paper proposes an adaptive back-stepping controller for the MMC-based HVDC system to overcome the challenges mentioned above. The BSC is used to control ac gird *d-q* frame currents. The capacitor energy stored in MMC's sub-modules is used as the upper layer control that generates the corresponding set-point for the *d*-axis grid current. The reactive grid side power is used to deliver the desired value to the *q*-axis current. Additional adaptive terms are introduced for each controlling loop to ensure resiliency to the influence of the angular frequency and minimize the steady-state variation. With proper construction of *Lyapunov* functions and control laws, the system stability is guaranteed. The RTDS device is used as the testing environment, and the simulation results present the robustness and effectiveness of the proposed controller.

The outline of this paper is as follows. Section 2 briefly introduces the state variables of the MMC system. Section 3 presents a detailed design approach of the adaptive BSC. Section 4 introduces the studied digital twin in the RTDS environment. Section 5 presents the results of the transient case studies. Finally, meaningful conclusions are provided in Sect. 6.

2 System Description of MMC

As a basis for the MMC model, the classical MMC configuration is briefly recalled in Fig. 1, and the stationary reference frame using $\Sigma - \Delta$ vector representation is introduced. For the adaptive BSC method design, this section aims at obtaining the MMC state variables through simplified steady-state analysis.

In Fig. 1 with N is denoted the number of H-bridge submodules (SMs) in one arm, the equivalent losses are represented as series inductance L_{arm} and resistance R_{arm} forming the connection between DC-terminals and AC-side output. Two identical arms are connected to the upper (denoted as U) and lower (denoted as L) DC-terminals, forming one leg of each phase $j \in \{a, b, c\}$. The AC-side interface is assumed as an equivalent resistance and inductance, denoted as R_r and L_r, respectively. Each H-bridge SM consists of four semiconductor switches (S_1, S_2, D_1 and D_2) with the antiparallel connected capacitor. The voltage across the capacitor of each SM is recorded as $v_{Cj}^{U,L}$, where items U and L stand for upper and lower, respectively.

Combined with the switching status, each SM can be controlled in three working modes: inserted, bypassed, and blocked. With proper control of switching conditions of all SMs at each phase, one can obtain the multi-level output voltage. In general, the more inserted SMs, the higher the arm-voltage level.

Sub-modules are considered with their average equivalents, and thus, the modulated currents $i_{Mj}^{U,L}$ and voltages $v_{Mj}^{U,L}$, of the upper and lower arm of a generic phase j, are here given by the following equations,

$$v_{Mj}^{U,L} = m_j^{U,L} \cdot v_{Cj}^{U,L},\ i_j^{U,L} = m_j^{U,L} \cdot i_{Cj}^{U,L}, \tag{1}$$

where $m_j^{U,L}$ are called the modulation indices of the upper and lower arms for all three phases. Values $v_{Cj}^{U,L}$ and $i_{Cj}^{U,L}$ are the voltages and currents of the upper and lower arm equivalent capacitances.

As mentioned before, the state-space modeling adopted in this work uses the $\Sigma - \Delta$ representation instead of commonly used *Upper-Lower* (*U-L*) form. More precisely, under the $\Sigma - \Delta$ nomenclature, it is possible to propose four state- and four control variables for the presented MMC topology. It is worthwhile mentioning that the Δ variables are associated with the fundamental angular frequency ω, and the third harmonic 3ω components. In comparison, the $\sum$ variables are associated with -2ω harmonics and contain a DC component.

For this converter's model, the aforementioned $\Sigma - \Delta$ variables in the upper and lower arms can be represented as follows [8],

$$\begin{aligned} &v_{Cj}^{\Delta} = (v_{Cj}^{U} - v_{Cj}^{L})/2,\ v_{Cj}^{\Sigma} = (v_{Cj}^{U} + v_{Cj}^{L})/2, \\ &m_j^{\Delta} = m_j^{U} - m_j^{L},\ m_j^{\Sigma} = m_j^{U} + m_j^{L}, \\ &v_{Mj}^{\Delta} = (-v_{Mj}^{U} + v_{Mj}^{L})/2 = -(m_j^{\Delta} v_{Cj}^{\Sigma} + m_j^{\Sigma} v_{Cj}^{\Delta})/2, \\ &v_{Mj}^{\Sigma} = (v_{Mj}^{U} + v_{Mj}^{L})/2 = (m_j^{\Sigma} v_{Cj}^{\Sigma} + m_j^{\Delta} v_{Cj}^{\Delta})/2. \end{aligned} \tag{2}$$

For the MMC configuration in Fig. 1, we define the AC-gird currents dynamics i_j^{Δ} and circulating currents dynamics i_j^{Σ} for three-phase as:

$$i_j^{\Delta} = i_j^{U} - i_j^{L},\ i_j^{\Sigma} = (i_j^{U} + i_j^{L})/2. \tag{3}$$

Applying the Kirchhoff voltage law (KVL) to the MMC equivalent circuit depicted in Fig. 1, we immediately obtain the grid currents and circulating currents dynamics as:

$$\begin{aligned} &L_{eq}^{ac} \tfrac{d}{dt}(\vec{i}_j^{\Delta}) = \vec{v}_{Mj}^{\Delta} - R_{eq}^{ac} \vec{i}_j^{\Delta} - \vec{v}_j^{G}, \\ &L_{arm} \tfrac{d}{dt}(\vec{i}_j^{\Sigma}) = \tfrac{v_{dc}}{2} - \vec{v}_{Mj}^{\Sigma} - R_{arm} \vec{i}_j^{\Sigma}, \end{aligned} \tag{4}$$

where, L_{eq}^{ac} and R_{eq}^{ac} are the equivalent inductor and resistor in the AC control loop, which can be expressed as $L_{eq}^{ac} = L_{arm}/2 + L_r$ and $R_{eq}^{ac} = R_{arm}/2 + R_r$, respectively. $\vec{v}_{Mj}^{\Delta}$ is the modulated voltage at the interfacing point between MMC and AC-grid side, and $\vec{v}_j^G$ are the balanced AC-grid voltages.

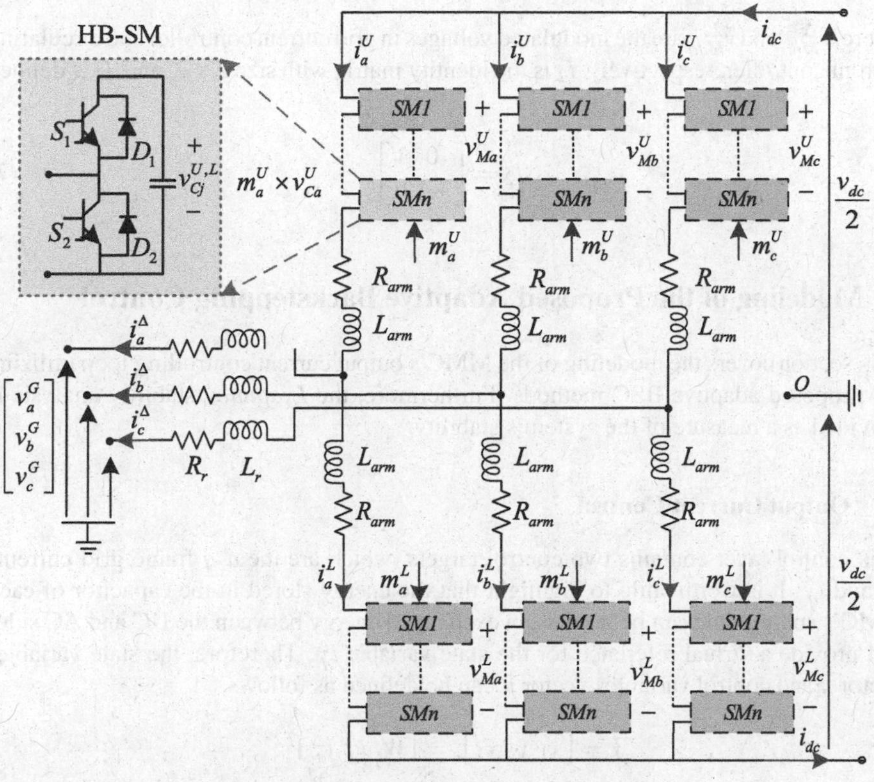

Fig. 1. Schematic diagram of MMC topology.

The Park's transformation and the inverse Park's transformation at ω angular frequency are applied to determine the dynamics of the state variables in *d-q* frame, which are given with formula as,

$$
\begin{aligned}
P_{n\omega}(t) &= \frac{2}{3}\begin{bmatrix} \cos(n\omega t) & \cos(n\omega t - 2\pi/3) & \cos(n\omega t - 4\pi/3) \\ \sin(n\omega t) & \sin(n\omega t - 2\pi/3) & \sin(n\omega t - 4\pi/3) \\ \frac{1}{2} & \frac{1}{2} & \frac{1}{2} \end{bmatrix}, \\
P_{n\omega}^{-1}(t) &= \frac{3}{2}P_{n\omega}^{T}(t) + \frac{1}{2}\begin{bmatrix} 0 & 0 & 1 \\ 0 & 0 & 1 \\ 0 & 0 & 1 \end{bmatrix},
\end{aligned}
\quad (5)
$$

where $n = 1$ for the "Δ" variables, whereas $n = 2$ for the "$\sum$" variables.

By Park's transformation, one can obtain the dynamics of grid current $\vec{i}_{dq}^{\Delta}$ and circulating currents:

$$\begin{aligned} \frac{d}{dt}(\vec{i}_{dq}^{\Delta}) &= \frac{1}{L_{eq}^{ac}}(\vec{v}_{Mdq}^{\Delta} - (\omega L_{eq}^{ac} J_2 + R_{eq}^{ac} I_2)\vec{i}_{dq}^{\Delta} - \vec{v}_{dq}^{G}), \\ \frac{d}{dt}(\vec{i}_{dq}^{\Sigma}) &= -\frac{1}{L_{arm}}(\vec{v}_{Mdq}^{\Sigma} + (R_{arm} I_2 - 2\omega L_{arm} J_2)\vec{i}_{dq}^{\Sigma}), \end{aligned} \tag{6}$$

where, $\vec{v}_{Mdq}^{\Delta}$ and $\vec{v}_{Mdq}^{\Sigma}$ are the modulated voltages in grid current controller and circulating current controller, respectively. I_2 is the identity matrix with size 2×2, and J_2 is defined as:

$$J_2 = \begin{bmatrix} 0 & 1 \\ -1 & 0 \end{bmatrix}. \tag{7}$$

3 Modeling of the Proposed Adaptive Backstepping Control

This section covers the modeling of the MMC's output current controlling loop utilizing the proposed adaptive BSC methods. Furthermore, the *Lyapunov* stability analysis is provided as a measure of the system's stability.

3.1 Output Current Control

This control layer contains two control targets, which are the *d-q* frame grid currents i_d^{Δ} and i_q^{Δ}. It is worthwhile to highlight that the energy stored in the capacitor of each MMC's sub-module can be used as an exchanged energy between the DC and AC sides and provide a virtual reference for the state variable i_d^{Δ}. Therefore, the state variables vector $\vec{x}$ and control variables vector $\vec{u}$ can be defined as follows,

$$\begin{aligned} \vec{x} &= \begin{bmatrix} x_1 \; x_2 \; x_3 \end{bmatrix}^T = [\,W_z \; i_d^{\Delta} \; i_q^{\Delta}\,]^T, \\ \vec{u} &= \begin{bmatrix} u_1 \; u_2 \end{bmatrix}^T = \begin{bmatrix} v_{Md}^{\Delta} \; v_{Mq}^{\Delta} \end{bmatrix}^T, \end{aligned} \tag{8}$$

where W_z represents the sum of the stored energy in SMs and can be calculated as $W_z = 3C(V_{dc})^2 / N$, and C is the capacitance of each sub-module.

Then, the MMC's dynamics described in Sect. 2 can be presented as,

$$\begin{aligned} \dot{x}_1 &= P_{ac} - P_{dc} = \tfrac{3}{2} u_d^G i_d^{\Delta} - P_{dc}, \\ \dot{x}_2 &= \tfrac{1}{L_{eq}^{ac}}(v_{Md}^{\Delta} - R_{eq}^{ac} i_d^{\Delta} - \omega L_{eq}^{ac} i_q^{\Delta} - v_d^G), \\ \dot{x}_3 &= \tfrac{1}{L_{eq}^{ac}}(v_{Mq}^{\Delta} - R_{eq}^{ac} i_q^{\Delta} + \omega L_{eq}^{ac} i_d^{\Delta} - v_q^G). \end{aligned} \tag{9}$$

To analyze the system *Lyapunov* stability, the error variables $\boldsymbol{e}$ and their time derivatives are defined as follows,

$$\begin{aligned} \boldsymbol{e} &= \begin{bmatrix} e_1 \; e_2 \; e_3 \end{bmatrix}^T = \begin{bmatrix} W_{zref} - W_z \; e_v - x_2 \; e_3 - x_3 \end{bmatrix}^T, \\ \dot{\boldsymbol{e}} &= \begin{bmatrix} \dot{e}_1 \; \dot{e}_2 \; \dot{e}_3 \end{bmatrix}^T = \begin{bmatrix} \dot{W}_{zref} - \dot{W} \; \dot{e}_v - \dot{x}_2 \; \dot{e}_3 - \dot{x}_3 \end{bmatrix}^T, \end{aligned} \tag{10}$$

where e_v is the virtual control variable, which corresponds to the desired value of the state variable x_2.

Now let us define the following *Lyapunov* function:

$$\mathrm{V}(x) = \frac{1}{2}e_1^2 + \frac{1}{2}e_2^2 + \frac{1}{2}e_3^2. \tag{11}$$

It is straightforward to conclude that $\mathrm{V}(x)$ is positive for all $e_1,\ e_2,\ e_3 \neq 0$, and $\mathrm{V}(x) = 0$ is met only in the condition that $e_1,\ e_2,\ e_3 = 0$, which means that the system is operating in a steady-state. According to Lyapunov's direct method [10], the transient stability analysis is used to determine whether the *Lyapunov* function is decreasing along the system's trajectories. Given that the constructed *Lyapunov* function is differentiable everywhere, we need to prove that the time derivative of *Lyapunov* function is negative everywhere except in the origin (steady-state) where it is zero.

The negative derivatibe $\dot{\mathrm{V}}(x)$ can be expressed as follows,

$$\dot{\mathrm{V}}(x) = e_1\dot{e}_1 + e_2\dot{e}_2 + e_3\dot{e}_3. \tag{12}$$

Let us first consider the item $e_1\dot{e}_1$. The $\dot{e}_1$ can be expressed as $\dot{e}_1 = \dot{W}_{zref} - 3v_d^G i_d^\Delta \big/ 2 + P_{dc}$ according to Eq. (9). Notice that the W_{zref} is a constant, which gives its derivative $\dot{W}_{zref}$ being 0. To ensure $e_1\dot{e}_1$ is strictly negative, we can define the item $\dot{e}_1$ as $-k_1 e_1$. Thus, the desired value of i_d^Δ, which refers to the variable e_v, should be:

$$e_v = 2(k_1 e_1 + P_{dc}) \Big/ 3v_d^G. \tag{13}$$

Therefore, $e_1\dot{e}_1$ is always negative and can be expressed as $-k_1 e_1^2$ for $k_1 > 0$, where one can obtain:

$$\begin{aligned} \dot{\mathrm{V}}(x) &= e_1(-3v_d^G(e_v - e_2) \Big/ 2 + P_{dc}) + e_2\dot{e}_2 + e_3\dot{e}_3 \\ &= -k_1 e_1^2 + e_2(\dot{e}_2 - 3e_1 v_d^G \Big/ 2) + e_3(\dot{i}_{qref}^\Delta - (v_{Mq}^\Delta - R_{eq}^{ac} i_q^\Delta + \omega L_{eq}^{ac} i_d^\Delta - v_q^G) \Big/ L_{eq}^{ac}) \end{aligned} \tag{14}$$

If the following conditions are satisfied and we guarantee that $k_2, k_3 > 0$, then $\dot{\mathrm{V}}(x) < 0$ if:

$$\begin{aligned} &\dot{e}_2 - 3e_1 v_d^G \big/ 2 = -k_2 e_2, \\ &\dot{i}_{qref}^\Delta - (v_{Mq}^\Delta - R_{eq}^{ac} i_q^\Delta + \omega L_{eq}^{ac} i_d^\Delta - v_q^G) \Big/ L_{eq}^{ac} = -k_3 e_3. \end{aligned} \tag{15}$$

Up to this point, we have proved the time derivative of *Lyapunov* function is strictly negative everywhere, which can be expressed as: $\dot{\mathrm{V}}(x) = -k_1 e_1^2 - k_2 e_2^2 - k_3 e_3^2 < 0$. The control variables v_{Md}^Δ and v_{Mq}^Δ are then:

$$\begin{aligned} v_{Md}^\Delta &= L_{eq}^{ac}(\dot{i}_{dref}^\Delta + k_2 e_2 - 3e_1 v_d^G \big/ 2) + R_{eq}^{ac} i_d^\Delta + \omega L_{eq}^{ac} i_q^\Delta + v_d^G, \\ v_{Mq}^\Delta &= (\dot{i}_{qref}^\Delta + k_3 e_3) L_{eq}^{ac} + R_{eq}^{ac} i_q^\Delta - \omega L_{eq}^{ac} i_d^\Delta + v_q^G. \end{aligned} \tag{16}$$

However, when the system is subjected to AC/DC faults or sudden changes of active/reactive power, the angular frequency ω of the AC system will be affected to some extent, which affects the accuracy of the *Lyapunov* function and affects the tracking ability of the BSC controller. Therefore, adaptive control is introduced in our work. We can use the estimated value $\hat{\omega}_{dq}$ as the adaptive rate of the system frequency to replace ω. The corresponding tracking errors of the frequency ω can be defined as:

$$e_{\omega dq} = \omega - \hat{\omega}_{dq},\ \dot{e}_{\omega dq} = \dot{\omega} - \dot{\hat{\omega}}_{dq}, \tag{17}$$

where $\dot{\omega}$ is considered 0 in this paper. This gives the new condition for v^{Δ}_{Md} and v^{Δ}_{Mq}:

$$\begin{aligned} v^{\Delta}_{Md} &= L^{ac}_{eq}(\dot{i}^{\Delta}_{dref} + k_2 e_2 - 3e_1 v^G_d/2) + R^{ac}_{eq} i^{\Delta}_d + \hat{\omega} L^{ac}_{eq} i^{\Delta}_q + v^G_d, \\ v^{\Delta}_{Mq} &= (\dot{i}^{\Delta}_{qref} + k_3 e_3) L^{ac}_{eq} + R^{ac}_{eq} i^{\Delta}_q - \hat{\omega} L^{ac}_{eq} i^{\Delta}_d + v^G_q. \end{aligned} \tag{18}$$

Then, the time derivative of the updated *Lyapunov* function can be expressed as,

$$\begin{aligned} \dot{V}(x) =& e_1\dot{e}_1 + e_2\dot{e}_2 + e_3\dot{e}_3 + e_{\omega d}\dot{e}_{\omega d} + e_{\omega q}\dot{e}_{\omega q} \\ =& -k_1 e_1^2 - k_2 e_2^2 - k_3 e_3^2 + e_2(\hat{\omega}_d - \omega) L^{ac}_{eq} i^{\Delta}_q + e_{\omega d}\dot{e}_{\omega_d} + e_3(\hat{\omega}_q + \omega) L^{ac}_{eq} i^{\Delta}_d + e_{\omega q}\dot{e}_{\omega_q} \\ =& -k_1 e_1^2 - k_2 e_2^2 - k_3 e_3^2 - e_{\omega}(\dot{\hat{\omega}}_d + e_2 L^{ac}_{eq} i^{\Delta}_q) - e_{\omega}(\dot{\hat{\omega}}_q - e_3 L^{ac}_{eq} i^{\Delta}_d). \end{aligned} \tag{19}$$

In this case, we can make sure that the items $\dot{\hat{\omega}}_d + e_2 L^{ac}_{eq} i^{\Delta}_q$ and $\dot{\hat{\omega}}_q - e_3 L^{ac}_{eq} i^{\Delta}_d$ are zero. Thus, the derivative $\dot{V}(x)$ is negative semi-definte (NSD), which is $\dot{V}(x) \le 0$, where one can obtain that:

$$\hat{\omega}_d = -\int e_2 L^{ac}_{eq} i^{\Delta}_q dt,\ \hat{\omega}_q = \int e_3 L^{ac}_{eq} i^{\Delta}_d dt. \tag{20}$$

Up to this point, the instability brought by the transient frequency of the system ω has been eliminated. To further eliminate the steady-state errors, additional adaptive terms θ_d and θ_q are considered [1], which can be expressed as,

$$\theta_d = -k_{di} \int e_2 dt,\ \theta_q = -k_{qi} \int e_3 dt, \tag{21}$$

where the k_{di} and k_{qi} are the control gains of the adaptive terms. It is noted that all adaptive terms would be zero in the steady-state.

With the adaptive terms, the BSC method can bring the system to a new steady-state with fewer overshoots and undershoots. Therefore, the control variables v^{Δ}_{Md} and v^{Δ}_{Mq} with the proposed adaptive BSC method are obtained:

$$\begin{aligned} v^{\Delta}_{Md} &= L^{ac}_{eq}(\dot{i}^{\Delta}_{dref} + k_2 e_2 - 3e_1 v^G_d/2) + R^{ac}_{eq} i^{\Delta}_d - L^{ac}_{eq} i^{\Delta}_q (\textstyle\int e_2 L^{ac}_{eq} i^{\Delta}_q dt) + v^G_d \theta_d - k_{di} \textstyle\int e_2 dt, \\ v^{\Delta}_{Mq} &= (\dot{i}^{\Delta}_{qref} + k_3 e_3) L^{ac}_{eq} + R^{ac}_{eq} i^{\Delta}_q - L^{ac}_{eq} i^{\Delta}_d (\textstyle\int e_3 L^{ac}_{eq} i^{\Delta}_d dt) + v^G_q - k_{qi} \textstyle\int e_3 dt. \end{aligned} \tag{22}$$

The OCC is carefully designed and its design guarantees stability because the time derivative of *Lyapunov* function $\dot{V}(x)$ is strictly negative.

3.2 Other Controlling Loops

Since the BSC method is more suitable for higher-order systems, the circulating current suppression controller (CCSC) in this paper implements traditional PI control. The CCSC is constructed to set the circulating current to its reference, which is assumed to be $\vec{i}^{\Sigma}_{dq,ref} = [0\,0]^T$. The specific equations of CCSC adopted in this paper are presented as follows [6],

$$\begin{aligned} \dot{\vec{\xi}}^{\Sigma}_{dq} &= \vec{i}^{\Sigma}_{dq,ref} - \vec{i}^{\Sigma}_{dq}, \\ \vec{v}^{\Sigma}_{Mdq,ref} &= -K^{\Sigma}_{I}\vec{\xi}^{\Sigma}_{dq} - K^{\Sigma}_{P}(\vec{i}^{\Sigma}_{dq,ref} - \vec{i}^{\Sigma}_{dq}) + 2\omega L_{arm} J_2 \vec{i}^{\Sigma}_{dq}, \end{aligned} \tag{23}$$

where the proportional gain K_P is set to 0.8 p.u., the integral gain K_I is set to 0.0125 p.u. [6] in this paper.

The reference value $i^{\Delta}_{q,ref}$ for the q-axis grid current is provided by variation of the reactive power Q_{ac} of AC gird. The reactive power control can be designed using the equations as follows,

$$\begin{aligned} \dot{\xi}_Q &= Q_{ac,ref} - Q_{ac}, \\ i^{\Delta}_{q,ref} &= -K_{P,Q}(Q_{ac,ref} - Q_{ac}) + K_{I,Q}\xi_Q, \end{aligned} \tag{24}$$

where the K_P and K_I are the control gain of the reactive power controller.

Up to this point, the overall control scheme for the MMC is described in Fig. 2.

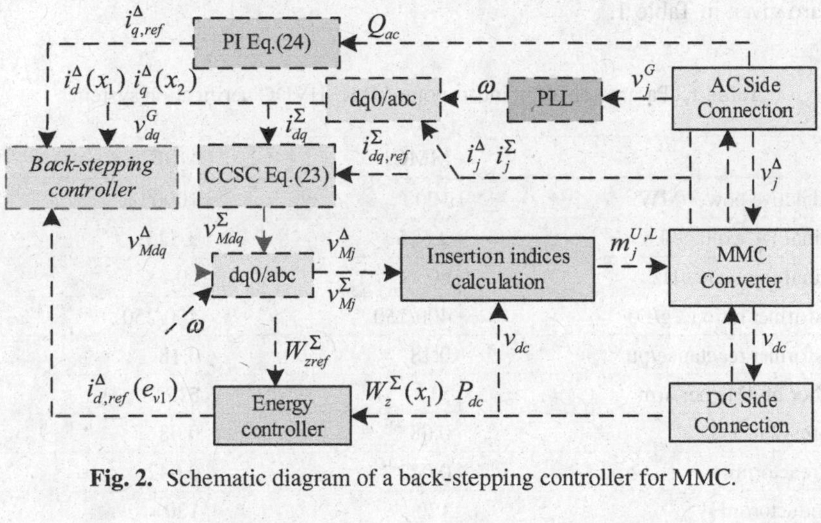

Fig. 2. Schematic diagram of a back-stepping controller for MMC.

4 Studied HVDC Digital Twin

To demonstrate the capabilities of the proposed adaptive BSC method, a point-to-point ±525 kV HVDC system is modeled in the RTDS test platform as a digital twin. The configuration of the system is given in Fig. 3.

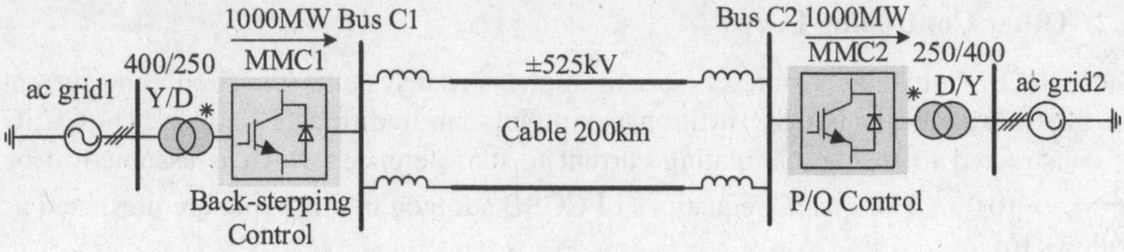

Fig. 3. Topology of the HVDC digital twin

Among the different models provided in RSCAD, the "rtds_vsc_MMC5" model is specified to evaluate the proposed controller in this paper. The chosen MMC RSCAD model is the Average Arm Model (AAM) with H-bridge configuration [9]. The specified model is suitable for testing outer control strategies [5]. The model consists of the automatic balancing algorithm for submodule capacitor voltages, which runs a small time-step between 1.2–1.5 μs.

The AC grid is linked with the MMC through a star/delta transformer, where the AC grid1 is working as sending end with nominal active power of 1000 MVA and AC grid2 as the receiving end. The AC transformer's star point is solidly grounded. The parameter rating of the transformer can be seen in Table 1. The series current limiting inductors are positioned at the outlets of DC cable lines, with the same inductance of 120 mH. The sampling frequency is standardized as 96 kHz following the recommendation of IEC 61869-9 1 [1]. The detailed parameters and nominal values of the studied HVDC digital twin are given in Table 1.

Table 1. Parameters of point-to-point MMC-HVDC verification system

Item	MMC1	MMC2
Rated active power/MW	1000	1000
Nominal DC voltage/kV	±525	±525
Nominal frequency/Hz	60	60
Transformer ratio (Yg/D)	400/250	400/250
Transformer reactance/pu	0.18	0.18
Number of SMs per arm	512	512
Arm resistance/Ω	0.08	0.08
Arm reactor/mH	0.042	0.042
DC inductor/mH	120	120

In this paper, only MMC1 is simulated with the proposed BSC method and taken as the studied converter in the analysis. The MMC2 is regulated using classical PI controllers with an active/reactive power control strategy. The control modes of each MMC converter and control gains of the studied system are presented in Table 2.

Table 2. Control mode and parameters of converters

Converter	Control mode	Parameters
MMC1	Adaptive back-stepping control (p.u.)	$K_1 = 13$
		$K_2 = 10$ $K_{di} = 0.01$
		$K_3 = 5$ $K_{qi} = 0.125$
	Q-control (p.u.)	$K_P = 2.0$ $K_I = 0.3$
MMC2	P-control (p.u.)	$K_P = 2.0$ $K_I = 0.15$
	Q-control (p.u.)	$K_P = 2.0$ $K_I = 0.3$

5 Effectiveness of the Proposed Control Method

In this section, we present the simulation results when the proposed BSC method is applied for the control of MMC. In addition, we compare the transient response of the proposed adaptive BSC with the classical PI methods to illustrate the major contribution of this paper. For a typical application of the HVDC system, active and reactive power reference signals are requested to be constant in a steady state. The test case carried out in the RTDS environment is the step change in active power from 0 p.u. to 0.5 p.u. at t_0 = 0.2 s and increases to 0.7 p.u. at t_1 = 1.2 s.

The detailed results are presented in Figs. 4 and 5. Figure 4(a) provides the results of energy controller. The capacitor energy W_z initials at 0.9 p.u. since the active power equals zero at this time instance. At the instant $t = t_0$, the active power reference experiences a step increase to 0.5 p.u., the SM capacitors of MMC1 start to charge, and the energy W_z gradually increases to the rated value. During the two-step changes, W_z is always comprised near the reference value, and hence, no energy overshoots are noticeable, which demonstrates the desired ability of the energy controller of delivering a precise reference signal to the *d*-axis gird current. Figure 4(b) is a good illustration of the tracking performance of i_d^Δ and its virtual reference signal e_{v1}. It is concluded that the current i_d^Δ and error e_{v1} are well controlled during these transients at the time instances t_0 and t_1, which completely overlap with each other without perceptible undershoots or overshoots. This constitutes the strength of the proposed BSC method, as the fast response is ensured for the grid currents. The entire transient process of each step changes only last for 10 ms. According to Fig. 4(b), the results strongly confirm the BSC method's superiority over the PI controller in control accuracy and tracking speed. Figure 4(c) provides the results of the *q*-axis current i_q^Δ and its reference signal i_{qref}^Δ. Due to the decoupling control design, the step changes in active power will not cause a significant impact on i_q^Δ, and after a short transient process, i_q^Δ is tuned in alignment with its rated value. Since the reference signal for the *q*-axis current is provided by the upper reactive power controller, the BSC method has similar results with the PI control. The simulation results of control variables can be observed in Fig. 4(d). The active power step-changes at the time instants t_0 and t_1 will not cause noticeable changes in voltages v_{Md}^Δ and v_{Mq}^Δ, and their values are equal to rated values.

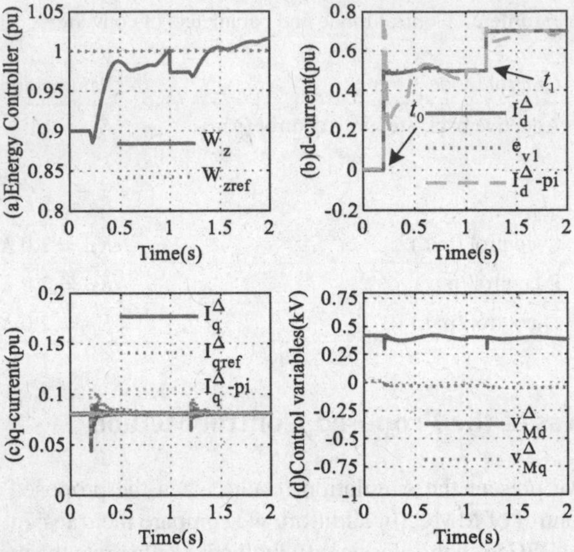

Fig. 4. Simulation results. (a) Energy controller (b) *d*-axis current (c) *q*-axis current (d) Control variables.

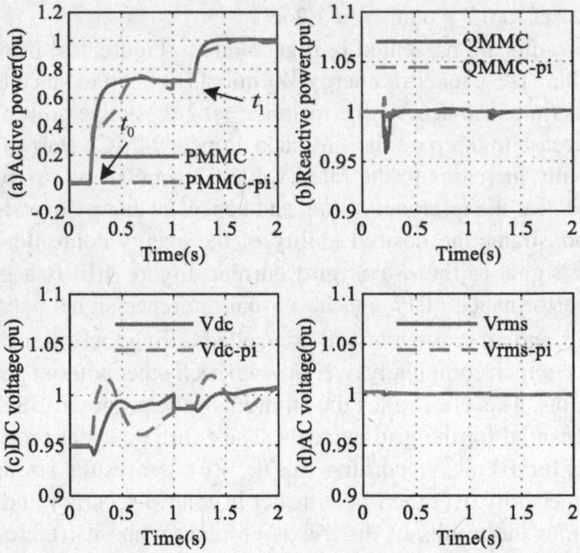

Fig. 5. Simulation results. (a) Active power (b) Reactive power (c) DC side voltage (d) AC grid voltage.

Figure 5(a) provides the active power on the AC grid, which has initial value 0 p.u and increases smoothly to the new steady-state without the phenomenon of oscillations and overshoots. However, it is obvious that the transient response of active power controlled by PI is slower and contains noticeable oscillations, which is caused by the inaccurate control of i_d^{Δ} presented in Fig. 5(b). The reactive power presented in Fig. 5(b) only exhibits a small decay at the instant of step-change and restores to 1 p.u. promptly. It is also marked that the DC voltage in Fig. 5(c) is aligned with the trends of active power, the value is always around the 1 p.u., and the BSC method causes smaller fluctuations. The Root-Mean-Square (RMS) value of AC gird observed in Fig. 5(d) is less affected by the step changes of active power, and hence, no saturation effects are evident.

In Fig. 6, the steady state operation during time interval 1.8 s–1.85 s is presented. It is observed that all the values of errors variables and *Lyapunov* function are clearly very small during the operation in steady state, which shows the accuracy of the designed controller.

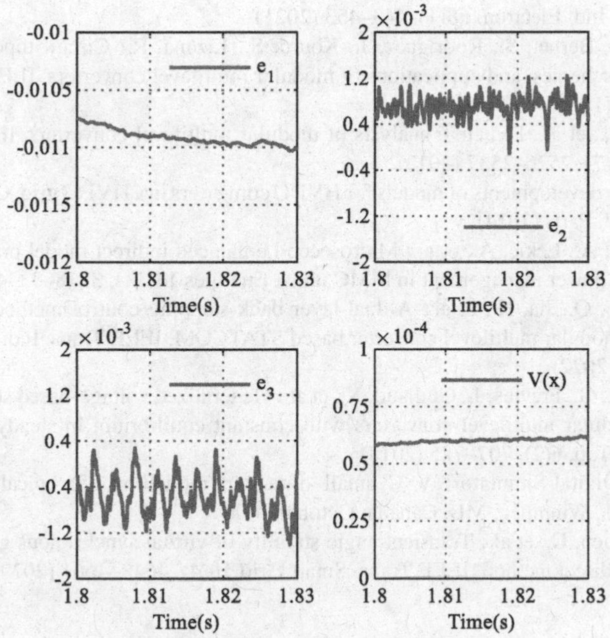

Fig. 6. Simulation results. (a) Error e_1 (b) Error e_2 (c) Error e_3 (d) *Lyapunov* function.

6 Conclusion

In this article, a non-linear control strategy relying on an adaptive BSC method was proposed. The *Lyapunov* theory is applied to stabilize the MMC's operation with several strict-feedback structures. These feedback structures include DC voltage, reactive power, and MMC arm capacitor energy controllers. To simplify the controller designing, the *abc* frame is transformed into decoupled *d*-*q* representation, which simplifies the proposed approach. A virtual control parameter is designed as the reference signal for the *d*-axis grid current, which is provided by the upper layer energy controller. Numerous simulations are carried out in the RTDS simulation environment for determining the control laws. The proposed adaptive BSC method is comprehensively evaluated for a classic point-to-point HVDC power system digital twin. In addition, the robustness of the proposed BSC method was precisely evaluated through a specific transient case. The results strongly support the superiority of the control strategy in stabilizing the MMC operation during transients.

References

1. Zhao, X., Li, K.: Adaptive backstepping droop controller design for multi-terminal high-voltage direct current systems. IET Gener. Transm. Distrib. **9**(10), 975–983 (2015)
2. Ahmadijokani, M., et al.: A back-stepping control method for modular multilevel converters. IEEE Trans. Ind. Electron. **68**(1), 443–453 (2021)
3. Perez, M.A., Bernet, S., Rodriguez, J., Kouro, S., Lizana, R.: Circuit topologies, modeling, control schemes, and applications of modular multilevel converters. IEEE Trans. Power Electron. **30**(1), 4–17 (2015)
4. Harnefors, L., et al.: Dynamic analysis of modular multilevel converters. IEEE Trans. Ind. Electron. **60**(7), 2526–2537 (2013)
5. Guide for the developments of models for HVDC converters in a HVDC grid. CIGRÉ Working Group B4.57, Paris (2014)
6. Shetgaonkar, A., Lekić, A., et al.: Microsecond enhanced indirect model predictive control for dynamic power management in MMC units. Energies **14**(11), 3318–3344 (2021)
7. Jin, Y., Xiao, Q., Jia, H., et al.: A dual-layer back-stepping control method for Lyapunov stability in modular multilevel converter based STATCOM. IEEE Trans. Ind. Electron **69**(3), 2166–2179 (2022)
8. Bergna-Diaz, G., Freytes, J., Guillaud, X., et al.: Generalized voltage-based state-space modeling of modular multilevel converters with constant equilibrium in steady state. IEEE J. Emerg. Sel. Top. **6**(2), 707–725 (2018)
9. Real-Time-Digital-Simulator: VSC small time-step modelling. Technical report, RTDS Technologies, Winnipeg, MB, Canada, October 2006
10. Shuai, Z., Shen, C., et al.: Transient angle stability of virtual synchronous generators using Lyapunov's direct method. IEEE Trans. Smart Grid **10**(4), 4648–4661 (2019)

Data-Driven Reachability Analysis of Digital Twin FMI Models

Sergiy Bogomolov, John Fitzgerald, Sadegh Soudjani, and Paulius Stankaitis(✉)

School of Computing, Newcastle University, Newcastle upon Tyne, UK
{sergiy.bogomolov,john.fitzgerald,sadegh.soudjani, paulius.stankaitis}@ncl.ac.uk

Abstract. Digital Twins are an emerging technology which makes it possible to couple cyber-physical assets with their virtual representation in real-time. The technology is applicable to a variety of domains and facilitates a more intelligent and dependable system design and operation. In this paper, we address the challenge of analysing Digital Twins by proposing a simulation-based reachability analysis of models based on the Functional Mock-Up Interface standard. The analysis approach uses simulations to obtain the Lipschitz constant of the model which is then used to compute reachable states of the system. The approach also provides probabilistic guarantees on the accuracy of the computed reachable sets that are based on simulations of the system from random initial states.

Keywords: Digital twin · Functional mock-up interface · Reachability analysis · Sampling-based methods

1 Introduction

Digital Twin is a technology that facilitates a real-time coupling of a cyber-physical system and its virtual representation. This promising technology can provide a more intelligent system design and operation [37]. In particular, techniques like reachability analysis of the virtual digital twin asset in real-time can be used for online validation and analysis of the physical asset. However, computing reachable states of the system requires in general knowing a model of the system, which for complex cyber-physical systems can be hard to obtain or even unavailable, e.g., in the case of IP protected Functional Mock-up Interface (FMI) multi-models [28]. Reachability analysis of black-box models based on simulation-driven approaches has been proposed in the literature [12,14,19].

This paper considers the problem of computing a reachable set of the virtual asset of the digital twin which is represented by a black-box FMI multi-model. The core of reachable set computation techniques is the computation of a bound on the sensitivity of the model's state with respect to its initial state. This bound is called the *Lipschitz constant* of the model. We propose to use simulations of the digital twin virtual model to estimate the Lipschitz constant of the model

T. Margaria and B. Steffen (Eds.): ISoLA 2022, LNCS 13704, pp. 139–158, 2022.
https://doi.org/10.1007/978-3-031-19762-8_10

which would then be used for computing a reachable set from the given initial region. However, since the *true* Lipschitz constant of the black-box model cannot be obtained with a finite number of simulations, we describe an approach that provides probabilistic approximation guarantees associated with a finite number of simulations.

The foremost contribution of this paper is a simulation-based approach for computing reachable states of the virtual digital twin model. The computation is generally applicable to any black-box system and can be used for a formal verification of black-box FMI models. The approach also provides probabilistic guarantees on the estimation of the Lipschitz constant given the complexity on sampling has been satisfied. The paper evaluates the proposed approach by (1) comparing the true Lipschitz value and the one obtained by the sampling approach on linear system; and by (2) comparing reachable sets produced by our approach against sets produced with the standard model-based reachability analysis tool – JuliaReach [5].

The paper is structured as follows. Section 2 provides preliminaries and problem statement of the paper. Section 3 provides theoretical results on solving robust convex optimisations using sampled datasets with associated bounds on the size of the dataset. In Sect. 4, we describe the sampling-based approach for estimating Lipschitz constant of the model and algorithm for simulation-based reachability analysis. Section 5 evaluates our proposed approach by computing Lipschitz value and reachable sets. In Sect. 6 we summarise our work and discuss directions for future work.

Related Work. A number of approaches have been proposed to facilitate FMI and Digital Twin model development and their co-simulation [20]. Formal verification of such models has remained a challenge to date due to their black-box nature. Thule et al. [40] have described a data brokering approach for FMI-enabled co-simulation of Digital Twins. Authors formally specified their data broker system and proved its timing properties by using TLA+ model checker [27]. Other approaches (e.g., [7,23]) proposed to integrate the state-of-the-art modelling and verification tools, which could be used for performing statistical model checking.

The model-based reachability analysis uses a mathematical model of the system to compute reachable states from a given set of possible initial states. Over the years, several reachability tools have been developed, for example, SpaceEx [4,6,16], JuliaReach [5], XSpeed [33] or Flow* [8], just to name a few. Alternative data-driven reachability analysis techniques have also been proposed for scenarios when a model of the system is unavailable or too complex. The data-driven methods generally use simulations of the system to estimate a *scaling* factor based on systems' sensitivity to perturbed initial values. In works by Donzé et al. [11,12] authors introduced a simulation-driven verification method which is based on a numerical sensitivity analysis. The numerically obtained sensitivity matrix is used to construct a so-called expansion function which specifies the closeness of neighbouring trajectories over time. Similar approaches, which are based on trajectory bi-similarity or sensitivity, have also been presented [14,19,24]. A number of verification tools have been developed C2E2 [13], DryVR [14], S-Taliro [32]. The data-driven reachability analysis has also been applied for a reachability analysis and verification of neural networks which are generally considered as black-box models [21,22]. In [41] authors proposed a data-driven approach based on the extreme value theorem to obtain Lipschitz constant of the neural network.

Data-driven approaches have also been developed recently for formal verification and synthesis of systems under uncertainty. The papers [34,35] check safety of a stochastic system using respectively multi-level methods and barrier certificates. The papers [25,26,29] provide data-driven methods for designing control actions to satisfy safety and other requirements on the system.

In summary, the main novelty of this work is the application of data-driven techniques for computation of reachability sets of black-box FMI and Digital Twin models. Our approach encodes the underlying inequalities needed for the computation of the reachable sets as a robust convex optimisation and provide sampling approaches to find an approximate solution. We connect the approximate solution to the actual solution by providing sample complexity results with guaranteed error bounds for a given probabilistic confidence.

2 Preliminaries and Problem Statement

Continuous-Time Systems. A continuous-time system is a tuple $\Sigma = (X, x_{\mathsf{in}}, f)$, where $X \subset \mathbb{R}^n$ is the state space and $x_{\mathsf{in}} \in X$ is the initial state. The vector field $f : X \to X$ is such that $f(\cdot)$ is locally Lipschitz, i.e., any small changes in x results in bounded changes in $f(x)$. The evolution of the state of Σ is characterised by the differential equation

$$\dot{x}(t) = f(x(t)), \quad x(0) = x_{\mathsf{in}}. \tag{1}$$

The assumption of f being locally Lipschitz guarantees the existence and uniqueness of a solution for every initial condition.

Given a sampling time $\tau > 0$ and an initial state $x_0 \in X$, define the *continuous-time trajectory* ζ_{x_0} of the system on the time interval $[0, \tau]$ as an absolutely continuous function $\zeta_{x_0} : [0, \tau] \to X$ such that $\zeta_{x_0}(0) = x_0$, and ζ_{x_0} satisfies the differential equation $\dot{\zeta}_{x_0}(t) = f(\zeta_{x_0}(t))$ for almost all $t \in [0, \tau]$. The solution of (1) from x_0 for all $t \geq 0$ is called the *nominal trajectory* of the system. For a fixed τ, we define the operator

$$\varphi(x) := \zeta_x(\tau) \quad \text{and} \quad \Phi(A) := \{\varphi(x) \mid x \in A\}$$

respectively for the trajectory at time τ and the set of such trajectories starting from A.

2.1 Reachability Analysis and JuliaReach

Reachability analysis is a technique for computing the set of all reachable states of a dynamical system from a set of initial states. The reachable set of $\mathcal{R}_t$ at time t can be defined formally as:

$$\mathcal{R}_t(\mathcal{X}_0) = \{\varsigma(t, x_0) \mid x_0 \in \mathcal{X}_0\} \tag{2}$$

where $\mathcal{X}_0 \subseteq \mathbb{R}^n$ represents the set of initial states and $\varsigma(t, x_0)$ is the unique solution of the ODE describing the system's dynamics, $\dot{x}(t) = f(x(t))$. More generally, reachability analysis methods aim to construct *conservative* flowpipes of the form

$$\mathcal{R}_{[0,T]}(\mathcal{X}_0) = \bigcup_{t \in [0,T]} \mathcal{R}_t(\mathcal{X}_0) \tag{3}$$

that encompass all the possible reachable sets of the system over a time horizon $[0, T]$.

Computing reachable states of a hybrid automaton requires computing *runs* of the hybrid system where a hybrid automaton run is an alternating N size sequence of trajectories and location jumps (see Sect. 5.2 in [1]). The reachability methods have been widely used in applications which range from a formal system verification to their synthesis [1]. Over the years, several reachability tools have been developed, for example, SpacEx [16], Checkmate [9] or Flow* [8] just to name a few. Furthermore, to efficiently and accurately over-approximate reachable sets different convex and nonconvex set representations have been developed.

The JuliaReach toolbox [5] is a set of Julia[1] programming language [2] libraries developed for an efficient prototyping of set-based reachability algorithms. A particular advantage of JuliaReach is its Julia language implementation providing high-performance computation with an adequate compilation time [18]. The Reachability package of the toolbox contains algorithms for performing reachability analysis of continuous and hybrid systems, while LazySets library contains algorithms for operation with convex sets. JuliaReach supports nonconvex set representations (e.g., Taylor models) which are required for a more conservative approximation of nonlinear systems.

2.2 Co-simulation and Functional Mock-Up Interface

Co-simulation is an approach to orchestrate a simulation of a multi-model system in which individual sub-models have been developed by different modelling and simulation tools [15,20]. Each sub-model is generally considered a black-box model and has an associated simulator which can produce an output of the sub-model given some inputs. The main objective of the co-simulation engine is to facilitate a correct exchange of outputs between different sub-models at each discrete output exchange step.

Functional Mock-up Interface (FMI) [3] is an open source and a tool independent co-simulation and model exchange framework which is widely used in academia and the industry. In a FMI-based co-simulation environment a master algorithm orchestrates discrete data exchanges between different sub-models (Functional Mock-up Units (FMUs)) which are simulated with their innate solvers. An individual FMU is made of a description file, which declares visible state variables and other model information, and proprietary solver. Over the years a number of well-known modelling and simulation tools have been

[1] Julia programming language website - https://julialang.org/.

upgraded (e.g., Simulink, OpenModelica [17,39]) or developed (INTO-CPS tool [28]) to support FMI standard.

2.3 Problem Statement

In this paper, we address the problem of computing reachable states of Digital Twin virtual models as formally defined in Problem 1.

Problem 1. Given a black-box Digital Twin model of a system Σ, initial set $\mathcal{X}_0$, and time bound T, compute an approximation of the reachable set $\bar{\mathcal{R}}_{[0,T]}(X_0)$ using a finite number of randomly simulated trajectories of Σ. Provide the sample complexity of the computation, *i.e.*, the required number of trajectories for achieving a certain level of approximation with a probabilistic confidence.

In the following sections, we describe how reachability computations can be connected to robust convex programs and chance-constrained optimisations, and provide the related computational methods with sample complexities to solve Problem 1.

3 Robust Convex Programs

In this section, we describe robust convex programs (RCPs) and data-driven approximations of their solution. In Sect. 4, we show how such an approximation can be used for providing a data-driven approach for reachability analysis with sample complexity results.

Let $T \subset \mathbb{R}^q$ be a compact convex set for some $q \in \mathbb{N}$ and $c \in \mathbb{R}^q$ be a constant vector. Let $\mathcal{D}$ be the space of *uncertainty* with $(\mathcal{D}, \mathscr{B}, \mathbb{P})$ denoting the uncertainty probability space and $g\colon T \times \mathcal{D} \to \mathbb{R}$ be a measurable function, which is convex in the first argument for each $d \in \mathcal{D}$, and bounded in the second argument for each $\theta \in T$.

The robust convex program (RCP) is defined as

$$\text{RCP:} \begin{cases} \min_\theta c^\top \theta \\ s.t.\ \theta \in T \text{ and } \ g(\theta, d) \leq 0 \quad \forall d \in \mathcal{D}. \end{cases} \tag{4}$$

Computationally tractable approximations of the optimal solution of the RCP (4) can be obtained using *scenario convex programs* (SCPs) that only require gathering finitely many samples from the uncertainty space [31].

Let $(d_i)_{i=1}^N$ be N independent and identically distributed (i.i.d.) samples drawn according to the probability measure $\mathbb{P}$. The SCP corresponding to the RCP (4) strengthened with $\gamma \geq 0$ is defined as

$$SCP_\gamma\colon \begin{cases} \min_\theta c^\top \theta \\ s.t.\ \theta \in T, \text{ and } \ g(\theta, d_i) + \gamma \leq 0 \ \forall i \in \{1, 2, \ldots, N\}. \end{cases} \tag{5}$$

We denote the optimal solution of RCP (4) as θ^*_{RCP} and the optimal solution of SCP_γ (5) as θ^*_{SCP}. Note that θ^*_{RCP} is a single deterministic quantity but θ^*_{SCP} is a random quantity that depends on the i.i.d. samples $(d_i)_{i=1}^N$ drawn according to $\mathbb{P}$. The RCP (4) is a challenging optimisation problem since the cardinality of $\mathcal{D}$ is infinite and the optimisation has infinite number of constraints. In contrast, the SCP (5) is a convex optimisation with finite number of constraints for which efficient optimisation techniques are available. The following two theorems provide sample complexity results for connecting the optimal solutions of the SCP_γ to that of the RCP.

Theorem 1 ([38]). *Let $\beta \in (0,1)$ be a confidence value and $\epsilon \in (0,1)$. Select N according to*

$$N \geq \frac{1}{\epsilon}\left(\frac{e}{e-1}\right)\log\left(\frac{1}{\delta}+q\right) \tag{6}$$

where e is Euler number and q is the dimension of the decision vector $\theta \in T$. Then the solution of (5) with $\gamma = 0$ computed by taking N i.i.d. samples $(d_i)_{i=1}^N$ from $\mathbb{P}$ is a feasible solution for the constraint

$$\mathbb{P}(g(\theta, d) \leq 0) \geq 1 - \epsilon \tag{7}$$

with confidence $(1-\beta)$.

The above theorem states that if we take the number of samples appropriately, we can guarantee that the solution satisfies the robust constraint in (4) on all the domain $d \in \mathcal{D}$ except for a small subset that has measure at most ϵ.

Theorem 2 ([31]). *Assume that the mapping $d \mapsto g(\theta, d)$ in (4) is Lipschitz continuous uniformly in $\theta \in T$ with Lipschitz constant L_d and let $h\colon [0,1] \to \mathbb{R}_{\geq 0}$ be a strictly increasing function such that*

$$\mathbb{P}(\Omega_\varepsilon(d)) \geq h(\varepsilon), \tag{8}$$

for every $d \in \mathcal{D}$ and $\varepsilon \in [0,1]$. Let θ^*_{RCP} be the optimal solution of the RCP (4) and θ^*_{SCP} the optimal solution of SCP_γ (5) with

$$\gamma = L_d h^{-1}(\varepsilon) \tag{9}$$

computed by taking N i.i.d. samples $(d_i)_{i=1}^N$ from $\mathbb{P}$. Then θ^*_{SCP} is a feasible solution for the RCP with confidence $(1-\beta)$ if the number of samples $N \geq N(\varepsilon, \beta)$, where

$$N(\varepsilon,\beta) := min\left\{N \in \mathbb{N} \,\middle|\, \sum_{i=0}^{q-1}\binom{N}{i}\varepsilon^i(1-\varepsilon)^{N-i} \leq \beta\right\}, \tag{10}$$

with q being the dimension of the decision vector $\theta \in T$.

The above theorem is stronger than Theorem 1 in guaranteeing that the solution will be feasible for the RCP (4) on the whole domain $d \in \mathcal{D}$. This is at the cost of requiring the knowledge of an upper bound on the Lipschitz constant of the function g and also being more conservative in the required number of samples. The confidence $(1-\beta)$ is a common feature of these two theorems and is due to the nature of the solution that depends on the sampled dataset $(d_i)_{i=1}^N$.

4 Simulation-Based Reachability Algorithm

This section describes the simulation-based algorithm for computing reachable states of a black-box model. First of all, we describe the overall algorithm and then we provide more detail on estimating Lipschitz constant of the system, namely, an estimation method based on the Extreme Value Theorem.

4.1 Reachable Set Computation

For computing the reachable set from a set of initial states $\mathcal{X}_0$, a common approach is to partition the set $\mathcal{X}_0$ into a union of hyper-rectangles $\{\mathcal{X}_j,\ j = 1,2,\ldots,m\}$ of size $\boldsymbol{\eta} = [\eta_1, \eta_2, \ldots, \eta_n]$ by gridding the state space. Then for each $\mathcal{X}_j$, we find a vector $L_j(t) \in \mathbb{R}^n$ such that

$$|\varsigma(t,x_0) - \varsigma(t,x_0')| \leq L_j(t)\,\|x_0 - x_0'\|, \quad \forall x_0, x_0' \in \mathcal{X}_j,\ t \geq 0, \tag{11}$$

where $\varsigma(t,x_0)$ and $\varsigma(t,x_0')$ are the state trajectories of the system at time t started from $x_0, x_0' \in \mathcal{X}_j$, and $|\cdot|$ denotes the element-wise absolute value. In the next step, the reachable set from each $\mathcal{X}_j$ is computed as the hyper-rectangle $\mathcal{Y}_j$ with edges

$$\varsigma(t,x_{cj}) \pm L_j(t)\cdot\boldsymbol{\eta}/2, \tag{12}$$

which gives a hyper-rectangle with centre $\varsigma(t,x_{cj})$ and size $L_j(t)\cdot\boldsymbol{\eta}$. The state x_{cj} is the centre of the initial hyper-rectangle $\mathcal{X}_j$. The union of all $\mathcal{Y}_j$, $j = 1,2,\ldots,m$ gives an over-approximation of the reachable set from $\mathcal{X}_0$.

The implementation of the above procedure requires computing $\varsigma(t,x_{cj})$, which is possible using a black-box model of the system. In the following, we discuss the computation of $L_j(t)$ using a sampling based approach and the results of Sect. 3.

RCP Formulation and Sampling. The inequality (11) used in the reachability analysis can written as the robust convex program

$$\text{RCP:}\ \begin{cases} \min c^\top L_j(t) \\ s.t.\ c = [1;1;\ldots;1],\ \ L_j(t) \geq 0,\ \text{ and} \\ \qquad |\varsigma(t,x_0) - \varsigma(t,x_{cj})| - L_j(t)\,\|x_0 - x_{cj}\| \leq 0, \quad \forall x_0 \in \mathcal{X}_j. \end{cases} \tag{13}$$

We can define the associated SCP_γ

$$SCP_\gamma:\begin{cases} \min c^\top L_j(t) \\ s.t.\ c = [1;1;\ldots;1],\ \ L_j(t) \geq 0,\ \text{ and for all } i \in \{1,2,\ldots,N\}, \\ \qquad |\varsigma(t,x_{0i}) - \varsigma(t,x_{cj})| - L_j(t)\,\|x_{0i} - x_{cj}\| + \gamma \leq 0, \end{cases} \tag{14}$$

where $x_{0i} \in \mathcal{X}_j$ are taken randomly from a probability distribution $\mathbb{P}$.

Once the SCP_γ (14) is solved, the sampling-based reachable set from $\mathcal{X}_j$ is computed as the hyper-rectangle $\tilde{\mathcal{Y}}_j$ with edges $\varsigma(t,x_{cj}) \pm L_j(t)\cdot\boldsymbol{\eta}/2$, where $L_j(t)$ is obtained by solving (14). The next theorem uses the results of Sect. 3 for picking the number of samples N to connect $\tilde{\mathcal{Y}}_j$ with the true reachable set.

Theorem 3. *If $\tilde{\mathcal{Y}}_j$ is computed using the solution of* (14) *with $\gamma = 0$ and N selected according to* (6), *then with confidence* $(1-\beta)$, *the set $\tilde{\mathcal{Y}}_j$ covers the whole true reachable set except for a small set with probability measure at most ϵ.*

If $\tilde{\mathcal{Y}}_j$ is computed using the solution of (14) *with N selected according to* (10), *then with confidence* $(1-\beta)$, *the set $\tilde{\mathcal{Y}}_j$ covers the whole true reachable set.*

The full algorithm for our sampling-based reachability analysis is presented in Algorithm 1.

Algorithm 1: Sampling-based reach set computation

Inputs: System as a black box, time instance t, initial set $\mathcal{X}_0 \subset \mathbb{R}^n$
Select discretisation $\boldsymbol{\eta} = [\eta_1, \eta_2, \ldots, \eta_n]$ with $\eta_i > 0$
Partition $\mathcal{X}_0$ into hyper-rectangles $\mathcal{X}_j$, $j = 1, 2, \ldots, m$, of size $\boldsymbol{\eta}$ with centre x_{cj}
for $j = 1, 2, \ldots, m$ **do**
  Select N according to (6) or (10)
  Take N samples x_{0i} uniformly from $\mathcal{X}_j$
  Obtain trajectories $\varsigma(t, x_{0i})$ and $\varsigma(t, x_{cj})$ from the black box model
  Solve the SCP$_\gamma$ in (14) to find $L_j(t)$
  Define $\tilde{\mathcal{Y}}_j$ as a hyper-rectangle with centre $\varsigma(t, x_{cj})$ and size $L_j(t) \cdot \boldsymbol{\eta}$.
end
Output: Sampling-based reach set $\tilde{\mathcal{Y}} := \cup_j \tilde{\mathcal{Y}}_j$

Exercising the second part of Theorem 3 for computing the number of samples requires knowing a (conservative) upper bound for the Lipschitz constant of the system. Computation of this bound is discussed in the next subsection.

4.2 Lipschitz Constant Estimation via Extreme Value Theorem

For estimating L_d in Theorem 2 and use it in Theorem 3, we should estimate an upper bound for that fraction

$$\Delta(x, x') := \frac{\|\varsigma(t, x) - \varsigma(t, x')\|}{\|x - x'\|} \tag{15}$$

that holds for all $x, x' \in \mathcal{X}_j$. We follow the line of reasoning in [41,42] and use Extreme Value Theorem for the estimation.

Let us fix a $\delta > 0$ and assign uniform distribution to the pair (x, x') over the domain $\{x, x' \in \mathcal{X}_j, \|x - x'\| \leq \delta\}$. Then $\Delta(x, x')$ is a random variable with an unknown cumulative distribution function (CDF). Based on the assumption of Lipschitz continuity of the system, the support of the distribution of $\Delta(x, x')$ is bounded from above, and we want to estimate an upper bound for its support. We take $\mathfrak{n}$ samples from (x, x') and compute $\mathfrak{n}$ samples $\Delta_1, \Delta_2, \ldots, \Delta_{\mathfrak{n}}$ for $\Delta(x, x')$. The CDF of $\max\{\Delta_1, \Delta_2, \ldots, \Delta_{\mathfrak{n}}\}$ is called the limit distribution of $\Delta(x, x')$. The Fisher-Tippett-Gnedenko theorem says that if the limit distribution exists, it can only belong to one of the three families of extreme value distributions - the Gumbel class, the Fréchet class and the Reverse Weibull class. These CDF's have the following forms:

$$\text{Gumbel class (Type I):} \qquad G(s) = \exp\left(-\exp\left(\frac{s-a}{b}\right)\right), \quad s \in \mathbb{R}$$

$$\text{Fréchet class (Type II):} \qquad G(s) = \begin{cases} 0 & \text{if } s < a \\ \exp\left(-(\frac{s-a}{b})^{-c}\right) & \text{if } s \leq a \end{cases}$$

$$\text{Reverse Weibull class (Type III):} \qquad G(s) = \begin{cases} \exp\left(-(\frac{a-s}{b})^{c}\right) & \text{if } s < a \\ 1 & \text{if } s \leq a \end{cases}$$

where $a \in \mathbb{R}, b > 0, c > 0$ are respectively the location, scale and shape parameters.

Among the above three distributions, only the Reverse Weibull class has a support bounded from above. Therefore, the limit distribution of $\Delta(x, x')$ will be from this class and the location parameter a is such an upper bound. As a result, we can estimate the location parameter of the limit distribution of $\Delta(x, x')$ to get an estimation of the Lipschitz constant.

A procedure for estimating the Lipschitz constant is presented in Algorithm 2. This uses obtained Lipschitz constants to compute approximate reachable sets. For each state of the system a single Lipschitz constant value is obtained from a previously sampled set. In this work we considered two operations for obtaining a final $L_s(x, t)$: a maximum value and value produced via curve-fitting and Extreme Value Theorem [10]. The algorithm then computes a central trajectory of the model by simulating it from the set of initial values which are midway between the lower and upper limits of the initial set.

Algorithm 2: Lipschitz constant estimation using Reverse Weibull distribution

---

Inputs: System as a black box, time instance t, initial set $\mathcal{X}_j \subset \mathbb{R}^n$
Parameters: $\delta > 0$, number of samples $\mathfrak{n}, \mathfrak{m}$
for $k = 1, 2, \ldots, \mathfrak{m}$ **do**
  Take $\mathfrak{n}$ samples (x_i, x_i') uniformly from the set $\{x, x' \in \mathcal{X}_j, \|x - x'\| \leq \delta\}$
  Compute $\{\Delta(x_i, x_i'), i = 1, 2, \ldots, \mathfrak{n}\}$ using (15) and trajectories from the black box model
  Define $\mathcal{L}_k = \max_i \Delta(x_i, x_i')$
end
Fit a Reverse Weibull distribution to the dataset $\{\mathcal{L}_1, \mathcal{L}_2, \ldots, \mathcal{L}_\mathfrak{m}\}$
Get the location, scale and shape parameters of the fitted distribution
Output: Estimated Lipschitz constant as the location parameter of the fitted distribution

---

Remark 1. The estimated Lipschitz constant from Algorithm 2 can also be used directly for estimating the reachable sets. Unfortunately, this quantity is just an estimation and will converge to the true Lipschitz constant in the limit. When it is computed with a finite number of samples, it is not attached with a quantitative closeness guarantee. In contrast, using the vector $L_j(t)$ for reachability computations is more likely to give a less conservative reach sets with formal probabilistic closeness guarantees.

4.3 Extension to Other Modelling Formalisms

Hybrid modelling frameworks have received significant attention recently due to their rich features in capturing the interaction between discrete elements and continuous variables (see e.g., the book [36] and the survey [30]). Our approach can in general be applied to hybrid models as it requires only the sample trajectories of the system. To get the guaranteed closeness bounds, we only need to assume the trajectories are continuous functions of the initial state, otherwise the Lipschitz constant of the system will not be bounded.

The work described so far only requires sample trajectories. We anticipate that these can be gathered from co-simulations of FMI-conformant co-models forming a digital twin of a system of interest. Alternatively, we envision that simulated trajectories could be replaced by trajectories gathered from the physical Digital Twin system, and thus, addressing issues related to accuracy of the virtual Digital Twin FMI co-model. However, these remain tasks for future work to confirm this (see Sect. 6).

5 Validation Exercises

In this section, we present three exercises for implementing and validating our simulation-based approach on multiple models. The first part of the section compares the Lipschitz constant of linear systems obtained using a sampling-based method and compared against the *true* Lipschitz constant obtained analytically. The second part of the section compares the reachable sets computed by our approach with the ones produced by the JuliaReach tool (to compare our *simulation-based* method with the *model-based* method implemented in JuliaReach). Finally, we compare the reachable set computed by our approach with the *true* reachable set on a nonlinear system.

5.1 Sampling-Based Lipschitz Constant Estimation

For a linear system in the form of $\frac{d}{dt}x(t) = \mathbf{A}x(t)$ with state matrix $\mathbf{A} \in \mathbb{R}^{n\times n}$, the true Lipschitz constant of the system is $L(t) = \left\|e^{\mathbf{A}\cdot t}\right\|_2$:

$$\|\varsigma(t, x_0) - \varsigma(t, x_0')\|_2 = \|e^{\mathbf{A}\cdot t}x_0 - e^{\mathbf{A}\cdot t}x_0'\|_2 \le \left\|e^{\mathbf{A}\cdot t}\right\|_2 \|x_0 - x_0'\|_2 .$$

For the sake of easier comparison, we consider a Lipschitz constant $L(t)$ instead of the more general vector form in (11) with only one partition set. We randomly generate $\mathsf{N} = 1000$ linear systems for each dimension $n \in \{2, 3, \ldots, 8\}$ and for each category of stable systems (i.e., all eigenvalues of $\mathbf{A}$ having negative real parts) and unstable systems (i.e., an eigenvalue with positive real part). The implementations compute the relative average error between the true and sampled Lipschitz constants for these randomly generated systems at time points t using either the average absolute error $\mathrm{Err}_a(t)$ or the average relative error $\mathrm{Err}_r(t)$ defined as

$$\mathrm{Err}_a(t) := \frac{1}{\mathsf{N}}\sum_{i=1}^{\mathsf{N}} \left|L^i(t) - L_s^i(t)\right|, \quad \mathrm{Err}_r(t) := \frac{1}{\mathsf{N}}\sum_{i=1}^{\mathsf{N}} \left|\frac{L^i(t) - L_s^i(t)}{L^i(t)}\right| \times 100, \quad (16)$$

where $L^i(t)$ and $L_s^i(t)$ are respectively the true and sampled Lipschitz constants of system i. We use $\mathrm{Err}_a(t)$ to compute the error for stable systems and $\mathrm{Err}_r(t)$ for unstable systems. The results are reported in Fig. 1 for the time interval $t \in [0.1, 1]$ and for 4 categories of the generated systems (2D and 8D, stable and unstable). The results are obtained for different number of samples, and as the figures show, the accuracy improves by increasing the number of samples. The rest of the results for other categories are reported in Table 1 of the appendix.

5.2 Reachable Set Computation for Linear Systems

We use Algorithm 1 to compute the sampling-based reach set $\mathcal{R}_S(t)$ at time t and compare it with the reach set produced by JuliaReach $\mathcal{R}_J(t)$. We use a stable linear system with $\mathbf{A} = [-1\ 0; 1\ -2]$, an unstable linear system with $\mathbf{A} = [2\ \ -1;\ 2\ 0]$, and a linear system with $\mathbf{A} = [0\ \ -1;\ 1\ 0]$ that shows oscillatory behaviour. The set of initial states is considered as $[0, 0.1] \times [0, 0.1]$. We use hyper-rectangles to approximate reachable sets of systems in JuliaReach. We run Algorithm 1 with $N = 1000$ samples to compute the sampled Lipschitz constant and get the reachable set. Figure 2 visualises the results (left figures for the first state and right figures for the second state of the systems).

We asses the accuracy using relative volumes of sets:

$$\mathrm{Acc}(t) = \frac{\mathcal{V}ol(\mathcal{R}_S(t) \cap \mathcal{R}_J(t))}{\mathcal{V}ol(\mathcal{R}_J(t))} \times 100 \quad (17)$$

where $\mathcal{V}ol(\cdot)$ is the volume of the set. The accuracy averaged over discrete time points in the interval $T = [0, 3]$ is 79.8% and 58.0% respectively for the stable and unstable system. The range of accuracy over time is $[78.1, 97.9]$ and $[49.2, 97.0]$ for these two systems. The accuracy for the oscillatory system has the average 62.7% over time interval $T = [0, 10]$ and belongs to the interval $[49.0, 98.0]$.

The main goal of this exercise was a relative comparison of our simulation-based approach with the model-based approach implemented in JuliaReach. The $\mathrm{Acc}(t)$ is the relative portion of the outcome of JuliaReach covered by the outcome of our approach. Since JuliaReach by itself gives an over-approximation of the *true* reachable set, $\mathrm{Acc}(t)$ is not sufficient for validating our theoretical results. Next we compare our approach with the true reachable set on a nonlinear model.

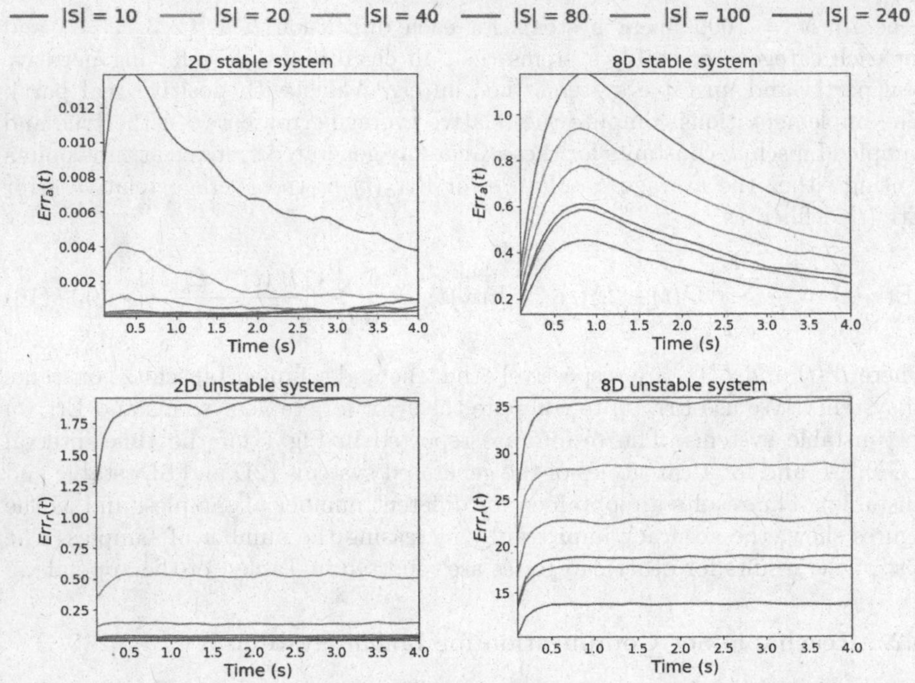

Fig. 1. Average relative error between the true and sampled Lipschitz constants for different number of samples. **Left top:** 2D stable, **Left bottom:** 2D unstable, **Right top:** 8D stable, **Right bottom:** 8D unstable. The error decreases by increasing the number of samples.

5.3 Reachable Set Computation for a Nonlinear System

Consider the 2D nonlinear pendulum system

$$\begin{cases} \dot{\theta}(t) = \omega(t) \\ \dot{\omega}(t) = -b \cdot \omega(t) - c \cdot \sin\theta(t) \end{cases} \tag{18}$$

with constants $b = 0.25$ and $c = 5.0$. Figure 3 compares the reachable set for the initial set $[0, 0.1] \times [0, 0.1]$ computed using our approach of Theorem 1 and JuliaReach. We obtain $L_j(t)$ using Algorithm 2 that is based on fitting a Reverse Weibull distribution. Figure 4 visualises the results for obtaining $L_j(t)$ at time $t = 0.7$.

We also consider comparing our approach with the true reach set of the system. Reachable sets of the pendulum system for the initial set $[0, 0.1] \times [0, 0.1]$ produced by our approach against randomly simulated trajectories is shown in Fig. 5. The random trajectories form a green area in all the plots of Fig. 5. The top plots include the blue area that is the reachable set computed using Theorem 1 with sample complexity $N = 10^3$, $\delta = 10^{-5}$, $\epsilon = 0.008$ and $q = 2$. The bottom plots include the red area obtained from Theorem 2 with sample complexity

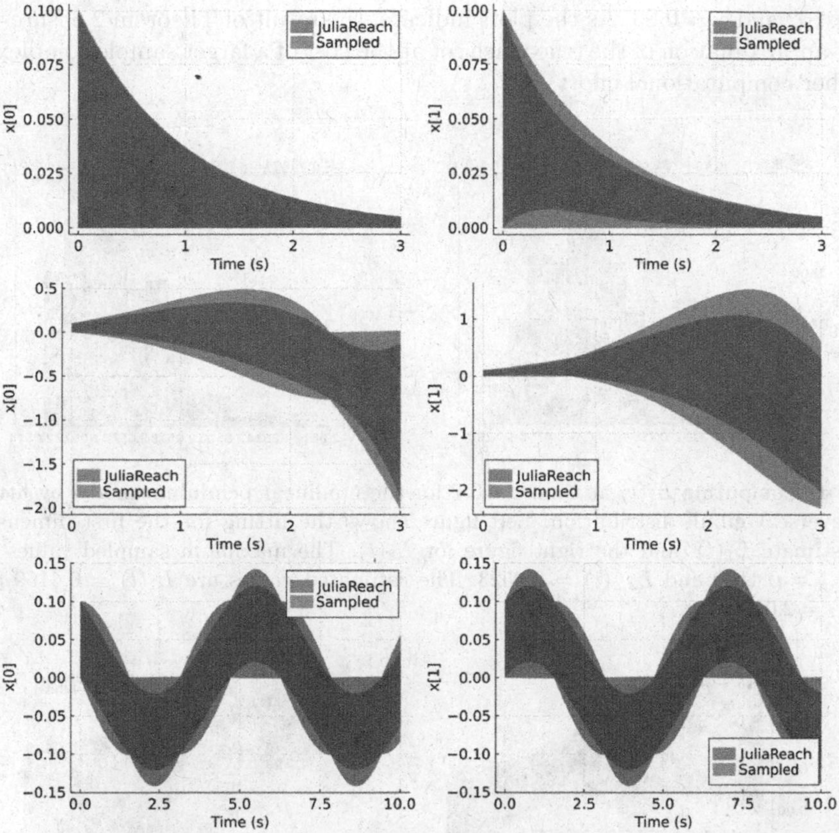

Fig. 2. Reachable set comparison of a stable linear system (top row), an unstable linear system (middle row), and a system with oscillatory behaviour. The systems are two dimensional: the figures in the left shows the reach set of the first state and the figures in the right shows it for the second state. The set of initial states is $[0, 0.1] \times [0, 0.1]$.

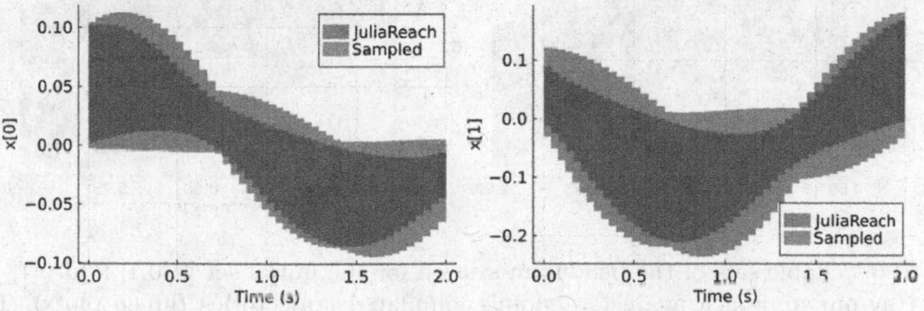

Fig. 3. Reachable set comparison of the nonlinear pendulum system for the initial set $[0, 0.1] \times [0, 0.1]$.

$N = 10^6$ and $\gamma = 0.03$. As the plots indicate, the result of Theorem 2 ensures an over-approximation of the true reach set at the cost of a larger sample complexity (higher computational effort).

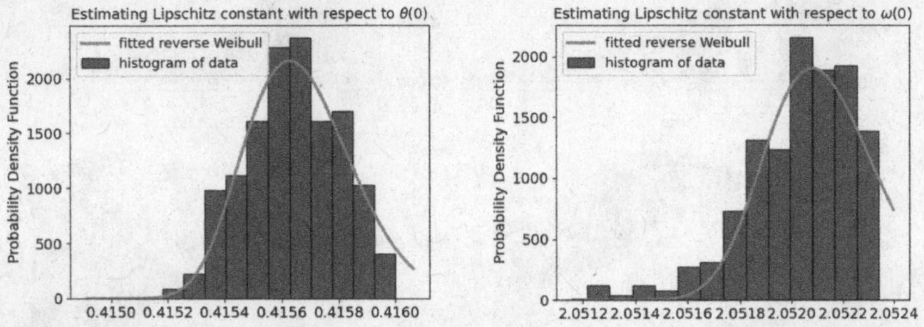

Fig. 4. Computing $L_j(t)$ at time $t = 0.7$ for the nonlinear pendulum model by fitting a Reverse Weibull distribution. Left figure shows the fitting for the first dimension to estimate $L_1(t)$, and the right figure for $L_2(t)$. The maximum sampled values are $L_{1s}(t) = 0.4160$ and $L_{2,s}(t) = 2.0523$. The estimated values are $L_1(t) = 0.4169$ and $L_2(t) = 2.0530$.

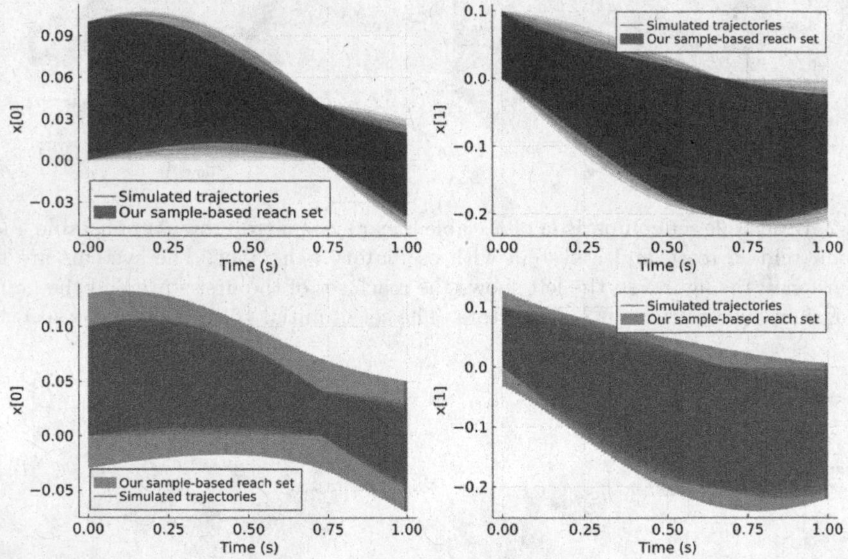

Fig. 5. Reachable sets of the pendulum system for the initial set $[0, 0.1] \times [0, 0.1]$ produced by our approach against randomly simulated trajectories (green plots). **Top**: sample complexity $N = 10^3$ based on Theorem 1 with $\delta = 10^{-5}$, $\epsilon = 0.008$ and $q = 2$; **Bottom**: sample complexity $N = 10^6$ based on Theorem 2 with $\gamma = 0.03$. (Color figure online)

Discussion. Our implementations have demonstrated that Algorithm 1 produces accurate reachable sets of linear and non-linear systems. The results are more accurate for stable systems, smaller time intervals, and lower-dimensional systems. However, the difference between actual and computed reachable sets increases for large time horizons and high-dimensional systems. The accuracy can be improved by utilising Algorithm 2 and increasing the number of samples.

6 Conclusions and Future Work

In this paper, we have presented an approach for computing reachable sets of black-box Digital Twin models. The proposed approach uses simulations of the system model to estimate an approximate Lipschitz constant which is then used to compute reachable states of the system. Our evaluation has demonstrated the accuracy of reachable sets computed with a simulation-based approach by comparing them against reachable sets produced by a model-based reachability tool - JuliaReach.

Our work is motivated by the desire to provide methods and tools that get the most value from Digital Twins of cyber-physical systems, particularly in relation to ensuring dependability, and this motivates our interest in reachability. In the Digital Twin context, systems of interest may have at least some IP-protected elements belonging to multiple stakeholders, and this suggests that we require to use simulations as a basis for computing reachability. In our future work, we aim to explore the integration of our proposed method into FMI-based co-simulation, for instance using the INTO-CPS tool chain [28] with its extensions for real-time physical and virtual assets [40].

Acknowledgements. We would like to thank Thomas Helyer for his contributions in the early stages of this research. This work was partially supported by the Air Force Office of Scientific Research under award no. FA2386-17-1-4065. Any opinions, findings, and conclusions or recommendations expressed in this material are those of the authors and do not necessarily reflect the views of the United States Air Force.

Appendix A

See Fig. 6.

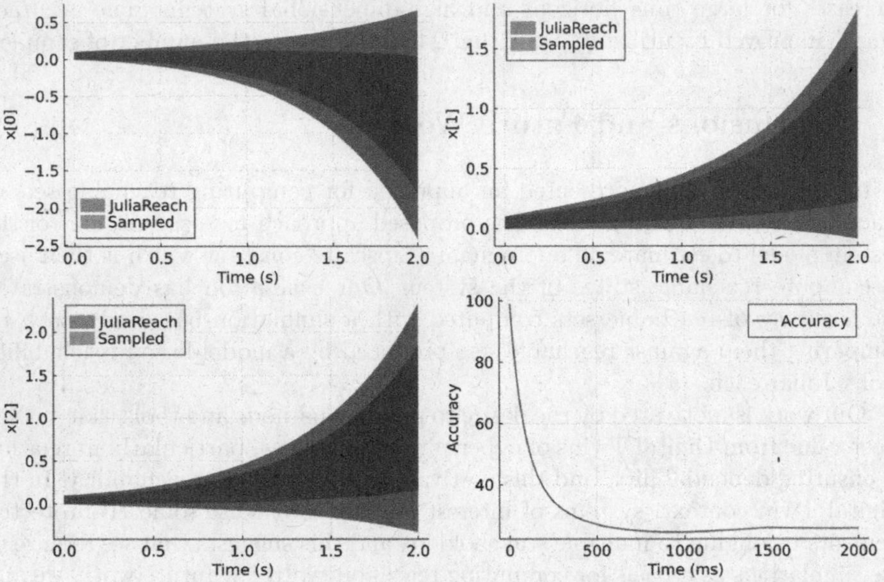

Fig. 6. Reachable set comparison of the 3D linear system $\mathbf{A} = [1\ -1\ 0;\ 1\ -1\ 3;\ -1\ 2\ -1]$ with initial region $[0, 0.1] \times [0, 0.1] \times [0, 0.1]$: (a, b, c) 1000 samples and maximum function, (d) accuracy plot over time

Table 1. The summary of results from Subsect. 5.1: variation of the average error between a true and sampled Lipschitz constant values over time for stable and unstable linear system.

D	No. Samples	$error(L)$				
		0.2	**0.4**	**0.6**	**0.8**	**1.0**
3D (stable)	10	0.08	0.095	0.092	0.085	0.078
	20	0.039	0.048	0.049	0.047	0.042
	40	0.021	0.026	0.026	0.024	0.022
	80	0.012	0.014	0.014	0.013	0.012
	100	0.009	0.011	0.011	0.011	0.01
	240	0.004	0.005	0.005	0.004	0.004
3D (uns.)	10	8.0	8.8	8.9	8.9	8.7
	20	4.0	4.4	4.4	4.4	4.5
	40	2.2	2.4	2.4	2.4	2.4
	80	1.2	1.3	1.3	1.2	1.2
	100	0.9	0.9	1.0	1.0	1.0
	240	0.4	0.4	0.5	0.4	0.4

(continued)

Table 1. (*continued*)

D	No. Samples	$error(L)$				
		0.2	**0.4**	**0.6**	**0.8**	**1.0**
4D (stable)	10	0.17	0.22	0.24	0.23	0.21
	20	0.11	0.15	0.15	0.15	0.13
	40	0.07	0.10	0.10	0.09	0.09
	80	0.05	0.06	0.06	0.06	0.06
	100	0.04	0.05	0.05	0.05	0.05
	240	0.02	0.03	0.03	0.03	0.03
4D (uns.)	10	14.1	15.9	16.1	16.0	15.8
	20	9.1	10.1	10.4	10.3	10.1
	40	5.7	6.4	6.4	6.3	6.3
	80	3.7	4.0	4.1	4.2	4.2
	100	3.2	3.7	3.8	3.7	3.7
	240	1.9	2.1	2.1	2.1	2.1
4D (uns.)	10	14.1	15.9	16.1	16.0	15.8
	20	9.1	10.1	10.4	10.3	10.1
	40	5.7	6.4	6.4	6.3	6.3
	80	3.7	4.0	4.1	4.2	4.2
	100	3.2	3.7	3.8	3.7	3.7
	240	1.9	2.1	2.1	2.1	2.1
5D (stable)	10	0.3	0.4	0.4	0.4	0.4
	20	0.2	0.3	0.3	0.3	0.3
	40	0.1	0.2	0.2	0.2	0.2
	80	0.1	0.1	0.2	0.1	0.1
	100	0.1	0.1	0.1	0.1	0.1
	240	0.1	0.1	0.1	0.1	0.1
5D (uns.)	10	19.5	21.80	22.1	21.9	22.0
	20	13.5	14.90	15.2	15.3	15.4
	40	9.90	11.00	11.2	11.1	11.0
	80	7.00	7.60	7.70	7.70	7.60
	100	6.40	6.90	6.90	6.90	7.00
	240	4.10	4.50	4.60	4.50	4.50
6D (stable)	10	0.4	0.6	0.6	0.6	0.6
	20	0.3	0.4	0.5	0.5	0.4
	40	0.2	0.3	0.4	0.4	0.3
	80	0.2	0.2	0.3	0.3	0.2
	100	0.2	0.2	0.3	0.2	0.2
	240	0.1	0.2	0.2	0.2	0.2
6D (uns.)	10	24.3	26.7	27.2	27.2	27.4
	20	18.4	20.2	20.5	20.5	20.7
	40	13.9	15.2	15.3	15.3	15.2
	80	10.5	11.5	11.6	11.4	11.5
	100	9.70	10.7	10.9	10.7	10.7
	240	6.80	7.50	7.60	7.50	7.60

References

1. Althoff, M., Frehse, G., Girard, A.: Set propagation techniques for reachability analysis. Annu. Rev. Control Rob. Auton. Syst. **4**(1), 369–395 (2021)
2. Bezanson, J., Edelman, A., Karpinski, S., Shah, V.B.: Julia: a fresh approach to numerical computing. SIAM Rev. **59**(1), 65–98 (2017)
3. Blochwitz, T., et al.: The functional mockup interface for tool independent exchange of simulation models. In: Proceedings of the 8th International Modelica Conference, pp. 105–114 (2011)
4. Bogomolov, S., et al.: Guided search for hybrid systems based on coarse-grained space abstractions. Int. J. Softw. Tools Technol. Transfer **18**(4), 449–467 (2016)
5. Bogomolov, S., Forets, M., Frehse, G., Potomkin, K., Schilling, C.: JuliaReach: a toolbox for set-based reachability. In: Proceedings of the 22nd ACM International Conference on Hybrid Systems: Computation and Control, HSCC 2019, pp. 39–44. Association for Computing Machinery, New York (2019)
6. Bogomolov, S., et al.: Assume-guarantee abstraction refinement meets hybrid systems. In: Yahav, E. (ed.) HVC 2014. LNCS, vol. 8855, pp. 116–131. Springer, Cham (2014). https://doi.org/10.1007/978-3-319-13338-6_10
7. Bogomolov, S., et al.: Co-simulation of hybrid systems with SpaceEx and Uppaal. In: 11th International Modelica Conference (Modelica 2015), Linköping Electronic Conference Proceedings, pp. 159–169. Linköping University Electronic Press, Linköpings universitet (2015)
8. Chen, X., Ábrahám, E., Sankaranarayanan, S.: Flow*: an analyzer for non-linear hybrid systems. In: Sharygina, N., Veith, H. (eds.) CAV 2013. LNCS, vol. 8044, pp. 258–263. Springer, Heidelberg (2013). https://doi.org/10.1007/978-3-642-39799-8_18
9. Chutinan, A., Krogh, B.H.: Verification of polyhedral-invariant hybrid automata using polygonal flow pipe approximations. In: Vaandrager, F.W., van Schuppen, J.H. (eds.) HSCC 1999. LNCS, vol. 1569, pp. 76–90. Springer, Heidelberg (1999). https://doi.org/10.1007/3-540-48983-5_10
10. De Haan, L., Ferreira, A., Ferreira, A.: Extreme Value Theory: An Introduction, vol. 21. Springer, New York (2006). https://doi.org/10.1007/0-387-34471-3
11. Donzé, A.: Breach, a toolbox for verification and parameter synthesis of hybrid systems. In: Touili, T., Cook, B., Jackson, P. (eds.) CAV 2010. LNCS, vol. 6174, pp. 167–170. Springer, Heidelberg (2010). https://doi.org/10.1007/978-3-642-14295-6_17
12. Donzé, A., Maler, O.: Systematic simulation using sensitivity analysis. In: Bemporad, A., Bicchi, A., Buttazzo, G. (eds.) HSCC 2007. LNCS, vol. 4416, pp. 174–189. Springer, Heidelberg (2007). https://doi.org/10.1007/978-3-540-71493-4_16
13. Duggirala, P.S., Mitra, S., Viswanathan, M., Potok, M.: C2E2: a verification tool for Stateflow models. In: Baier, C., Tinelli, C. (eds.) TACAS 2015. LNCS, vol. 9035, pp. 68–82. Springer, Heidelberg (2015). https://doi.org/10.1007/978-3-662-46681-0_5
14. Fan, C., Qi, B., Mitra, S., Viswanathan, M.: DryVR: data-driven verification and compositional reasoning for automotive systems. In: Majumdar, R., Kunčak, V. (eds.) CAV 2017. LNCS, vol. 10426, pp. 441–461. Springer, Cham (2017). https://doi.org/10.1007/978-3-319-63387-9_22
15. Fitzgerald, J., Larsen, P.G., Verhoef, M.: Collaborative Design for Embedded Systems. Academic Press (2014). **10**, 978-3

16. Frehse, G., et al.: SpaceEx: scalable verification of hybrid systems. In: Gopalakrishnan, G., Qadeer, S. (eds.) CAV 2011. LNCS, vol. 6806, pp. 379–395. Springer, Heidelberg (2011). https://doi.org/10.1007/978-3-642-22110-1_30
17. Fritzson, P., et al.: OpenModelica - a free open-source environment for system modeling, simulation, and teaching. In: 2006 IEEE Conference on Computer Aided Control System Design, pp. 1588–1595 (2006)
18. Geretti, L., et al.: ARCH-COMP20 category report: continuous and hybrid systems with nonlinear dynamics. In: Frehse, G., Althoff, M. (eds.) ARCH20, 7th International Workshop on Applied Verification of Continuous and Hybrid Systems (ARCH20). EPiC Series in Computing, vol. 74, pp. 49–75. EasyChair (2020)
19. Girard, A., Pappas, G.: Approximate bisimulations for nonlinear dynamical systems. In: Proceedings of the 44th IEEE Conference on Decision and Control, pp. 684–689 (2005)
20. Gomes, C., Thule, C., Broman, D., Larsen, P.G., Vangheluwe, H.: Co-simulation: a survey. ACM Comput. Surv. **51**(3) (2018)
21. Hu, H., Fazlyab, M., Morari, M., Pappas, G.J.: Reach-SDP: reachability analysis of closed-loop systems with neural network controllers via semidefinite programming (2020)
22. Huang, C., Fan, J., Li, W., Chen, X., Zhu, Q.: ReachNN: reachability analysis of neural-network controlled systems (2019)
23. Jensen, P.G., Larsen, K.G., Legay, A., Nyman, U.: Integrating tools: co-simulation in UPPAAL using FMI-FMU. In: 2017 22nd International Conference on Engineering of Complex Computer Systems (ICECCS), pp. 11–19 (2017)
24. Kapinski, J., Krogh, B.H., Maler, O., Stursberg, O.: On systematic simulation of open continuous systems. In: Maler, O., Pnueli, A. (eds.) HSCC 2003. LNCS, vol. 2623, pp. 283–297. Springer, Heidelberg (2003). https://doi.org/10.1007/3-540-36580-X_22
25. Kazemi, M., Perez, M., Somenzi, F., Soudjani, S., Trivedi, A., Velasquez, A.: Translating omega-regular specifications to average objectives for model-free reinforcement learning. In: Proceedings of the 21st International Conference on Autonomous Agents and Multiagent Systems, pp. 732–741 (2022)
26. Kazemi, M., Soudjani, S.: Formal policy synthesis for continuous-state systems via reinforcement learning. In: Dongol, B., Troubitsyna, E. (eds.) IFM 2020. LNCS, vol. 12546, pp. 3–21. Springer, Cham (2020). https://doi.org/10.1007/978-3-030-63461-2_1
27. Lamport, L.: Specifying Systems: The TLA+ Language and Tools for Hardware and Software Engineers. Addison-Wesley Longman Publishing Co., Inc., Boston (2002)
28. Larsen, P.G., et al.: Integrated tool chain for model-based design of cyber-physical systems: the INTO-CPS project. In: 2nd International Workshop on Modelling, Analysis, and Control of Complex CPS (CPS Data), pp. 1–6 (2016)
29. Lavaei, A., Somenzi, F., Soudjani, S., Trivedi, A., Zamani, M.: Formal controller synthesis for continuous-space MDPs via model-free reinforcement learning. In: 2020 ACM/IEEE 11th International Conference on Cyber-Physical Systems (ICCPS), pp. 98–107. IEEE (2020)
30. Lavaei, A., Soudjani, S., Abate, A., Zamani, M.: Automated verification and synthesis of stochastic hybrid systems: a survey. arXiv preprint arXiv:2101.07491 (2021)
31. Mohajerin Esfahani, P., Sutter, T., Lygeros, J.: Performance bounds for the scenario approach and an extension to a class of non-convex programs. IEEE Trans. Autom. Control **60**(1), 46–58 (2015)

32. Nghiem, T., Sankaranarayanan, S., Fainekos, G., Ivancić, F., Gupta, A., Pappas, G.J.: Monte-Carlo techniques for falsification of temporal properties of non-linear hybrid systems. In: Proceedings of the 13th ACM International Conference on Hybrid Systems: Computation and Control, HSCC 2010, pp. 211–220. Association for Computing Machinery, New York (2010)
33. Ray, R., Gurung, A., Das, B., Bartocci, E., Bogomolov, S., Grosu, R.: XSpeed: accelerating reachability analysis on multi-core processors. In: Piterman, N. (ed.) HVC 2015. LNCS, vol. 9434, pp. 3–18. Springer, Cham (2015). https://doi.org/10.1007/978-3-319-26287-1_1
34. Salamati, A., Lavaei, A., Soudjani, S., Zamani, M.: Data-driven safety verification of stochastic systems via barrier certificates. In: Proceedings of the 7th IFAC Conference on Analysis and Design of Hybrid Systems (ADHS), vol. 54, no. 5, pp. 7–12 (2021)
35. Esmaeil Zadeh Soudjani, S., Majumdar, R., Nagapetyan, T.: Multilevel Monte Carlo method for statistical model checking of hybrid systems. In: Bertrand, N., Bortolussi, L. (eds.) QEST 2017. LNCS, vol. 10503, pp. 351–367. Springer, Cham (2017). https://doi.org/10.1007/978-3-319-66335-7_24
36. Tabuada, P.: Verification and Control of Hybrid Systems: A Symbolic Approach. Springer, New York (2009). https://doi.org/10.1007/978-1-4419-0224-5
37. Tao, F., Zhang, H., Liu, A., Nee, A.Y.C.: Digital twin in industry: state-of-the-art. IEEE Trans. Industr. Inf. **15**(4), 2405–2415 (2019)
38. Tempo, R., Calafiore, G., Dabbene, F.: Randomized Algorithms for Analysis and Control of Uncertain Systems: with Applications. Springer, London (2012). https://doi.org/10.1007/b137802
39. The MathWorks: Simulink User's Guide (2021)
40. Thule, C., Gomes, C., Lausdahl, K.G.: Formally verified FMI enabled external data broker: RabbitMQ FMU. In: Proceedings of the 2020 Summer Simulation Conference. SummerSim 2020. Society for Computer Simulation International, San Diego (2020)
41. Weng, T.W., et al.: Evaluating the robustness of neural networks: an extreme value theory approach. In: International Conference on Learning Representations (2018)
42. Wood, G., Zhang, B.: Estimation of the Lipschitz constant of a function. J. Global Optim. **8**(1), 91–103 (1996)

Towards Secure Digital Twins

Tomas Kulik[1](✉), Cláudio Gomes[2], Hugo Daniel Macedo[2], Stefan Hallerstede[2], and Peter Gorm Larsen[2]

[1] Sweet Geeks, Innovations Allé 3, 7100 Vejle, Denmark
tomaskulik@icloud.com

[2] DIGIT, Department of Electrical and Computer Engineering, Aarhus University, Finlandsgade 22, 8200 Aarhus, Denmark

Abstract. Advanced digital technology is finding its way into industrial production and control systems. This led to development of further concepts such as digital shadow and digital twin. In the former an accurate model of the cyber-physical system (CPS) is used to monitor it virtually, while the latter provides a possibility to adapt the CPS's behavior. These developments are often welcome from the operators perspective, however they also pose new challenges in terms of cyber security: an operator could be led to believe the system is operating correctly due to the represented digital image while the CPS is under a cyber attack. In this paper we investigate several cyber security challenges of the digital twin technology and discuss potential mitigations for these challenges based on well established practices within the area of industrial control systems. We further describe the potential cyber attacks and mitigations using a semi-formal notation based on problem frames, we suggest in order to simplify the communication about cyber security challenges of digital twins between different stakeholders. This is shown within a context of a small case study. Finally we outline areas of research for the development of secure digital twin technology.

Keywords: Digital twins · Cyber security · Security model

1 Introduction

Digital twin technology is finding its way into different aspects of the modern society, especially within the industrial domain following the concepts of Industry 4.0 [27]. The access to digital representation of physical objects brings many benefits. For example, in manufacturing different configuration changes could be applied to the digital twin before being passed on to the physical system [11]. It is furthermore possible to provide a comprehensive overview of a system to a system operator, since the digital twin responds to the data provided from the physical device a similar way as the physical device itself. This could provide simplified troubleshooting employing a simple visual representation of the state of the physical devices.

This approach also poses several challenges. One of them is that the digital model needs to represent the physical object at a high degree of accuracy;

T. Margaria and B. Steffen (Eds.): ISoLA 2022, LNCS 13704, pp. 159–176, 2022.
https://doi.org/10.1007/978-3-031-19762-8_11

another challenge is that in some cases the data exchanged between the physical object and the digital twin must be close to real-time. Last but not least, is the need for cyber security assurances within the systems employing the digital twin technology, which is the focus of this paper. This aspect of digital twins is especially important for industrial use of digital twins because compromised security could lead to potentially harmful situations including unstable operation of the CPS with resulting physical and economic damage or even accidents leading to injury or death. To this end we perceive the digital twin as a prime target for potential attackers, similar to SCADA systems [20,22].

The practical difference between a digital twin and a SCADA system is the integration of the close to reality digital model of the CPS within the digital twin. In comparison the SCADA system mostly provides industrial connectivity modules to exchange data with the controlled plant via a user interface that enables the operator to interact with the system. It is important to note that in some cases digital twins have been proposed to be a potential solution to security challenges of large connected CPS [1]. However, even in this case the digital twin must be secure by itself in order not to provide a false sense of security for the operators and designers of the CPS.

Recently, an increase in attack surfaces within the industrial control systems has been observed [15]. This is mainly due to the additional connectivity being added to these systems. Utilizing a digital twin further increases the attack surface because the model underlying the digital twin might become an attack vector. Several ways of preventing attacks at industrial and specifically cyber physical systems have been proposed, such as among others, use of formal methods to create secure architectures [19], integration of different security controls [18] or the use of state estimators [16], where attack resilient state estimators have been proposed [21]. Securing digital twins consequently requires not only considering access control, network security and transmitted data integrity but also integrity of the model itself. One might also consider the question of how the digital twin is being used. For example, it could be shared by several entities and as such could be deployed within the cloud environment, creating security constraints for this environment, such as isolation of different users.

Contribution. While several cyber security challenges of digital twins have been pondered before [12] and a notion of digital twin trustworthiness has been presented [24], in this paper we explore potential security challenges of digital twins based on concrete types of attacks. We also describe potential mitigations for these attacks in the context of digital twins. Within the presented attacks we introduce multiple attack vectors against a digital twin. We further provide a supporting notation that could be used to describe security concerns of digital twins. We consider this is currently lacking and could provide benefits to the wider digital twin research and development community. We also present a case study based on a digital twin of our own design for an incubator system by means of which we discuss the listed security challenges. Finally, we present several open problems in regard to secure digital twins that pose interesting topics to be addressed by future research.

Structure. The rest of the paper is organized as follows: Section 2 presents work concerning security of digital twins with a focus on their industrial use and how they compare to our work. Section 3 introduces several cyber attacks against digital twins (possible attack vectors) as well as introduce a notation for describing these cyber attacks in a digital twin setting. Section 4 provides an overview of different mitigations that could be applied towards the attacks introduced before and discusses how these mitigations differ from their use within standard industrial control systems when applied to a digital twin setting. Section 5 describes the incubator system, considering the CPS and the digital twin including a potential cyber security challenge and mitigation within this setting. Section 6 presents several open problems that might be addressed by future research. Finally, Sect. 7 closes with concluding remarks.

2 Related Work

The majority of research works cover the security aspects of digital twin technology as yet another aspect to take into account while developing such systems, yet there are other works that focus on the security aspect itself or the usage of the digital twin as another security tool.

In [25], the authors models attacks on digital twins, and present a study on the abuse cases of digital twins. Compared to our technical descriptions of attacks and mitigations, the authors focus on the different attackers' strategies and the outcomes of attacks at specific phases of the lifecycle.

As examples of a digital twin as a security tool we have [4,7] both proposing using the digital twins assets in the design of the security aspects and attach modelling and mitigation. In [7], the authors propose a framework to generate digital twins from specifications for SCADA systems. The specifications may include specific security properties that shall hold within the system. As a proof of concept the authors propose a mitigation for man in the middle attacks such as the paradigmatic Stuxnet attack. In addition to being a security tool, the work of [4] proposes to use the digital twin in training and simulation, testing exercises for the security engineers.

Another aspect that has not been massively covered in publications with a technical aspect, but of importance and covered in philosophically oriented works like the one in [6] is the privacy impacts of a technology creating massive amounts of data and digital models of physical assets in the real world, which are used and tied to its users, who have the right to be protected from potential surveillance and discrimination.

3 Security Challenges

Digital twins face different kinds of security challenges. In this paper we introduce four security challenges with various levels of complexity and impact. In the first three cases we consider that the digital twin needs to be connected with the CPS via a network. But we also show that even an isolated digital twin can face potential security challenges. The four attack types we consider are *bandwidth sniffing*, *data injection*, *data delay* and *model corruption*. We describe the attacks in natural language followed by graphical a notation describing these attacks in a more succinct manner. We further introduce a notion of *direct* and *indirect* attack. In the case of a direct attack, the attacker interacts actively with components of the system, while in the case of an indirect attack the attacker utilizes methods such as side channel attacks where the attacker does not need to interact actively with the deployed system.

Attack Description Syntax. Textual descriptions of the different attacks are difficult to comprehend and explain, in particular, to the many non-expert –in security– stakeholders in a digital twin setting. We use context diagrams from the problem frames approach [14] to complement the textual descriptions semi-formally introducing the main concepts and how they are related. This is sufficient to understand how the different attacks and mitigations work. Context diagrams are composed of domains that describe the key aspects and participants. They do not describe an architecture. In fact, they only contain one machine domain representing "the software" or "the computer". In our diagrams it is always called *Digital Twin*. Some domains can be controlled like the *CPS* (whose behavior is predictable and therefore called *causal* and marked with a C). It is the objective of the Digital Twin to re-configure or augment the CPS, of course. The behavior of the *Attacker*, whose domain is called *biddable* and marked with a B, is not predictable in causal terms. Another relevant kind of domain is called *lexical*: they represent some form of data. Domains that are *designed* (by us) are marked with one vertical bar on the left and machine domains with two vertical bars. Domains that interact in some way are connected by edges that are annotated with the phenomena they share. Phenomena are abstractions of concepts from the real world that can be observed or measured (for a more thorough discussion see [13,14]). In order to emphasize the role of the network, we draw all edges connecting to it by "double bars". Attacks are described in oval dashed ellipses that are linked to the interactions that they manipulate.

3.1 Bandwidth Sniffing

This attack utilizes information gained about communication between the connected digital twin and the CPS as basis for further targeted attacks. The attacker does not acquire any confidential data that is being transmitted within the communication network connecting the digital twin and the CPS. In addition, the attacker does not try to inject malicious payload to the communication. However the attacker can learn some specific information by simply listening to the different communication channels without decoding the underlying traffic. The attacker can potentially discover which component of the CPS is currently active or even determine the activity within the CPS [28] based on the bandwidth used between the CPS and the digital twin. See Fig. 1 for a graphical description of the latter kind of attack. For the former kind of attack the domain "Activity" would need to be replaced by a domain "Component".

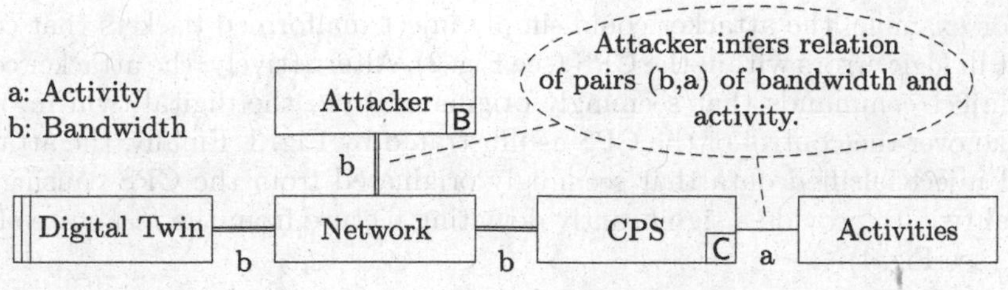

Fig. 1. Context diagram for bandwidth sniffing.

This information could in turn be used to execute cyber or physical attacks against the CPS in question. In many situations such information will be considered confidential and the system operator needs to be able to prevent the attacker from obtaining the information. While this attack is applicable to any connected system, the connected digital twin setup is uniquely well positioned for such attacks because a significant amount of data needs to be transmitted for processing by the digital twin model in order to keep the digital twin and the typically complex CPS in synchrony. This attack is an indirect side channel attack, where indirect information is used to gain knowledge.

3.2 Data Injection

Similarly to bandwidth sniffing, this kind of attack is mainly aimed at the system with connected digital twin. The attacker utilizes a network breach or a compromised entity within the network to inject malicious payload to the network.

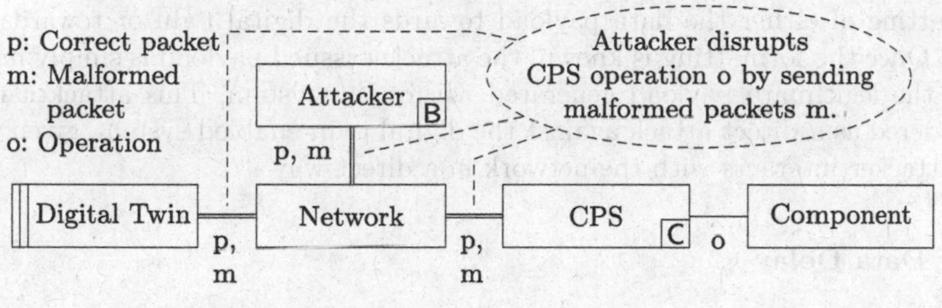

Fig. 2. Context diagram for data injection.

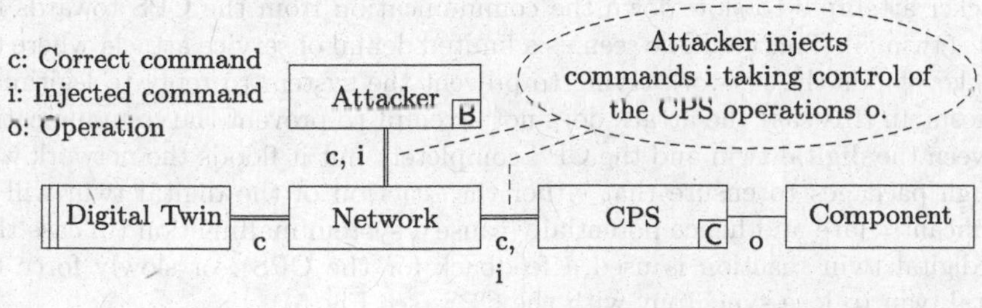

Fig. 3. Context diagram for data injection (variant 1).

For example, the attacker could simply inject malformed packets that could result in logic errors within the CPS (see Fig. 2). Alternatively, the attacker could also inject commands that seemingly originated from the digital twin in order to take over the control of the CPS as illustrated by Fig. 3. Finally, the attacker could inject falsified data that seemingly originated from the CPS causing the digital twin to provide a significantly deviating picture from the real state of the CPS (see Fig. 4).

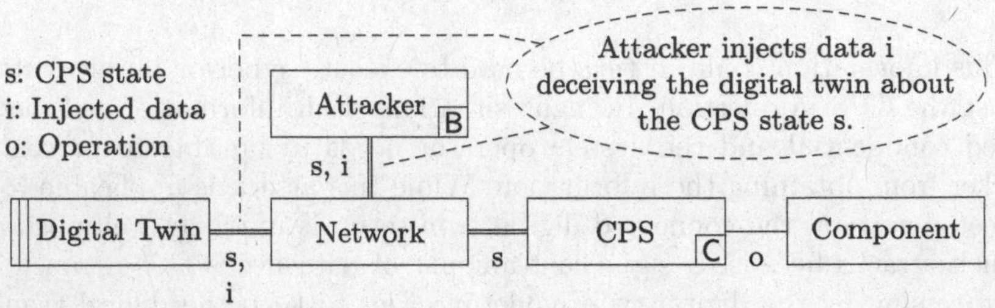

Fig. 4. Context diagram for data injection (variant 2).

Similar attacks have been also executed against industrial control systems with limited network connectivity [26], impacting the control network and subsequently causing catastrophic failure of the CPS.

We consider this one of the prime attacks that could be applied towards a digital twin given its data dependent nature. This class of attacks requires the attacker to be able to compromise the network and determine the correct formatting of either the data payload towards the digital twin or towards the CPS. Once the formatting is known, the attacker issued payload is simply mixed with the legitimate payload generated within the system. This attack can be considered as a direct attack against the digital twin enabled system, given that the attacker interacts with the network in a direct way.

3.3 Data Delay

This kind of attack is aimed at a system with a connected digital twin with real-time characteristics, a typical case as discussed in the introduction. The attacker attempts to slow down the communication from the CPS towards the digital twin [5]. This could be seen as a limited denial of service attack, where the attacker floods the network trying to prevent the system to reply to legitimate requests. In this case the attack does not attempt to prevent the communication between the digital twin and the CPS completely but it floods the network with enough packages to ensure that either the reaction of the digital twin will be significantly late and hence potentially cause a system malfunction (in case that the digital twin reaction is used a feedback for the CPS); or slowly force the digital twin to lose synchrony with the CPS (see Fig. 5).

In case that the digital twin needs to exchange data close to real-time, this type of attack could cause the digital twin to miss tight, crucial deadlines. In order to carry out such an attack the attacker needs to be present within the network and have an understanding of the specific network. Since the goal is to cause time delays in processing between the digital twin and the CPS, it is important for the attacker to send only as many packets as the network can handle, enabling the (cautious) attacker to avoid immediate detection. This attack can also be considered a direct attack where the attacker needs to have sufficient knowledge of the data being processed by the digital twin.

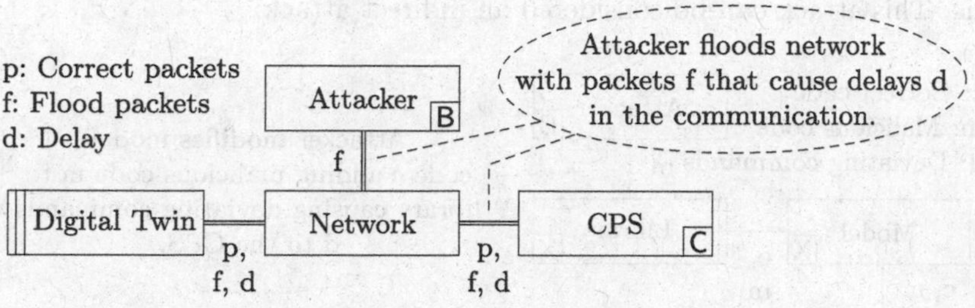

Fig. 5. Context diagram for data delay.

3.4 Model Corruption

This kind of attack aims at corrupting the model that the digital twin uses to represent the physical system. The models are often developed by multiple parties involving multiple developers or even multiple organizations; they are often stored in shared repositories that are used for version control. In this case the attacker would aim to attack the model at rest within the shared repository. The attack is based on injecting malicious code directly to the model causing the digital twin to either not represent the physical device truthfully, or provide malicious data payload to the physical device (see Fig. 6 for a description of the latter).

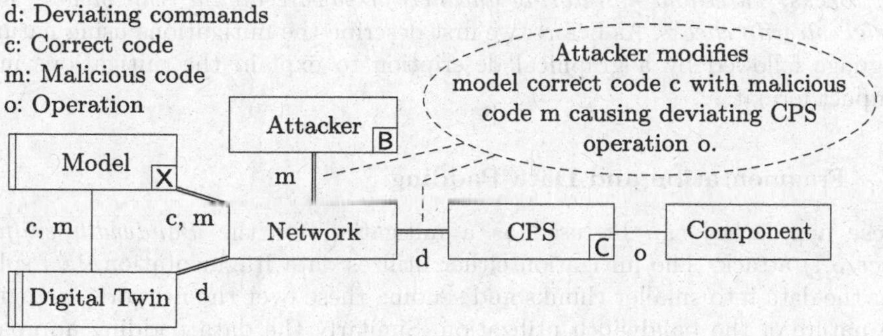

Fig. 6. Context diagram for model corruption (network).

Similar attacks have been proposed as a possible attack vectors to PLCs [30], impacting the control loop of a physical system and potentially leading to unsafe situations. In order to carry out this attack, potential attackers would need to gain access to the shared repository where they could inject the code. This attack is also well suited for insider attackers where a legitimate entity turns malicious. Another option is injection of malicious code to third party libraries used by the model (see Fig. 7). Similarly to the above, in this case the attacker would need to gain access to the storage of the library code and ensure that the malicious code will be included in the library when it gets deployed. However, it cannot be directly detected on the observed network unless all used libraries are included in this. This attack can be considered an indirect attack.

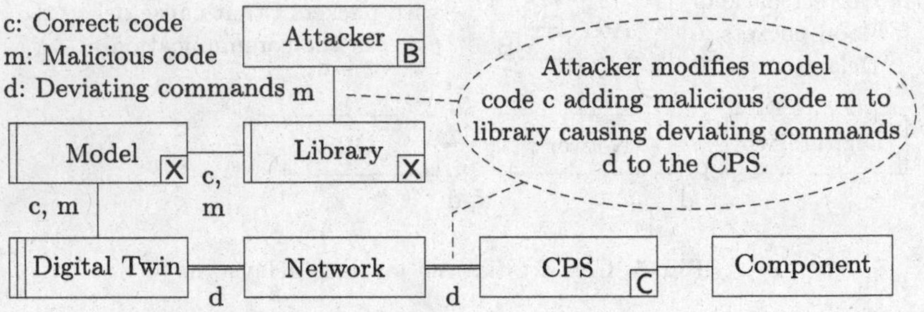

Fig. 7. Context diagram for model corruption (library).

4 Mitigations

In this section we propose specific mitigations that could be applied against the cyber attacks presented in the preceding section. The mitigations are based on approaches used in security of industrial control systems, and have been applied against similar attacks. We present similarities and differences between security needs of industrial control systems operating with and without digital twins. The approaches we present are: *Fragmentation and data padding*; *Signatures and tokens*; *Threshold monitoring and network-aware digital twin models*; and *Model integrity checks.* As before, we first describe the mitigations using natural language followed by a graphical description to explain the mitigations in a compact format.

4.1 Fragmentation and Data Padding

These approaches can be used as a mitigation for the *Bandwidth sniffing* (Sect. 3.1) attack. The mitigation either utilizes data fragmentation, i.e., splitting the data into smaller chunks and sending these over the network, changing the nature of the bandwidth utilization. Similarly the data padding approach changes the nature of the bandwidth utilization by adding more data to the original payload in order to keep the bandwidth utilization steady [29]. Once these techniques are employed it becomes difficult for the attacker to gather information about different targets simply by observing the bandwidth utilization (see Fig. 8).

It is important to note that this mitigation might directly conflict with some optimization strategies for the system, especially if network traffic shall be optimized to minimize the bandwidth utilization. It is however an effective mitigation that has been proposed for use within industrial control systems. One aspect of this mitigation that needs to be considered when incorporating a digital twin within a system is the need for the model and communication interfaces to be able to handle either the fragmented or padded data. This needs to be considered bidirectionally. As such, the digital twin needs to remove padding or fragmentation from incoming data payloads, as well as add these to the outgoing data payloads to ensure that the bandwidth stays protected from bandwidth sniffing attacks.

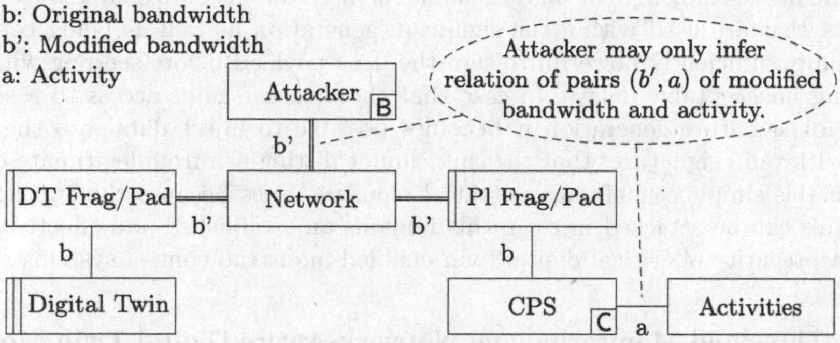

Fig. 8. Context diagram for bandwidth sniffing mitigation.

4.2 Signatures and Tokens

A mitigation scheme that can be applied towards the *Data injection* attack (Sect. 3.2) is the addition of digital signatures to the data transferred between legitimate entities [23]. This scheme has been utilized within different kinds of systems in order to ensure data integrity. One of the benefits of this mitigation is that it does not require use of more complicated schemes such as state estimators. It may be added to the majority of communication protocols because the signature or cryptographic token becomes a part of the regular data payload. See Fig. 9 for a graphical description of this mitigation. Two lexical domains DT Sign and PL Sign have been added to sign payload from the digital twin and the CPS, respectively. The protection mechanism relies on the data sources ability to cryptographically sign the generated data. The signature is subsequently validated at the data sink and any invalid signature is rejected and may be considered a potential intrusion.

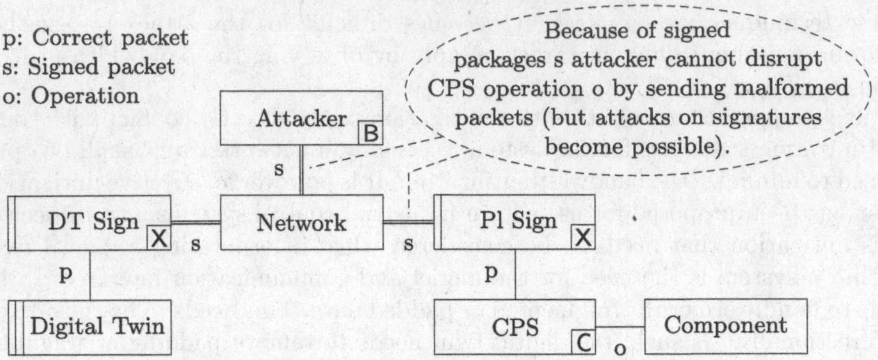

Fig. 9. Context diagram for data injection mitigation.

One of the challenges of this scheme is the need for the data source to protect secrets that are used within the signature generation as well as being computationally sufficiently powerful to sign the data payload before sending without causing unacceptable delays. In case that the attacker gains access to a secret used for signature generation it becomes possible to inject data into the system with valid signatures that the sink cannot distinguish from legitimate data. While this simple scheme has potential security issues because the two lexical domains can be attacked in turn, this remains an established and effective way achieve security of critical digital twin enabled industrial control systems.

4.3 Threshold Monitoring and Network-Aware Digital Twin Models

This layered mitigation is aimed at detecting and limiting the impact of the *Data delay* attack (Sect. 3.3). The mitigation is based on monitoring of network activity and determining whether different threshold parameters have been reached, e.g., a certain amount of data packets or network latency. Data delay attacks are especially difficult to detect in low rate attack scenarios. To this end several threshold based analysis mechanisms have been considered for different types of systems [3]. Within a digital twin enabled system the threshold analysis could be integrated directly into the model. As such, the digital twin is aware of the network performance under normal circumstances as well as what it considers a data delay attack (see Fig. 10). This requires the digital twin designers to have domain knowledge about the system at hand (not only from the functionality perspective but also concerning the network setup) and expected data load. If a data delay attack is detected, the digital twin could utilize its understanding of the network to limit the effect of the attack. Possible counter measures include locking the source addresses from the network communication or limiting its own communication with the system to provide more bandwidth for legitimate data packets. More advanced schemes could be utilized if the system employs additional DDoS protection mechanisms such as resource scaling. However, this often requires external components, i.e., cloud resource orchestration and is not practical in resource constrained environments.

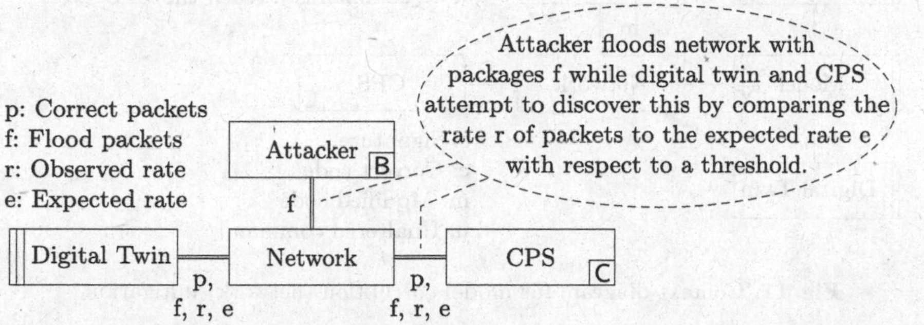

Fig. 10. Context diagram for data delay mitigation.

4.4 Model Integrity Checks

This mitigation ensures that the model utilized within the digital twin does not integrate malicious code and applies to the *Model corruption* attack (Sect. 3.4). This requires stringent access controls towards the repository that stores the model. Furthermore, the model itself must be validated before it is loaded onto the digital twin. To do this, only a model that is digitally signed by the authors must be allowed to be loaded. See Fig. 11 for a description of this mitigation. The additional lexical domain "Auth" is required to keep the authentication data for the signing keys. Furthermore, all of the potential libraries should be checked against provided hashes to ensure that the library has not been modified. In case that the hashes are not provided by the authors of the libraries, these must be created upon induction of the libraries to the code base of the model, where the induction process shall involve a thorough review of these libraries. This approach is a well known scheme [2] that is nowadays proposed to be used with additional schemes such as watermarking (embedding specific cryptographic elements in the code), dynamic whitelisting (dynamically determining which libraries are allowed to be loaded based on their signatures) or even formal analysis (analyzing the model against specific properties on the implementation level). While digital signing by itself would not protect the model from insider attacks and requires secure access to the signing keys, it provides a first level of guarantee that a genuine model is present within the digital twin. It should be mentioned that more advanced methods for integrity checks could be utilized. This approach has a very low impact on performance and other design constraints of digital twins, hence model signing is widely applicable even for models of digital twins that are not necessarily considered security critical.

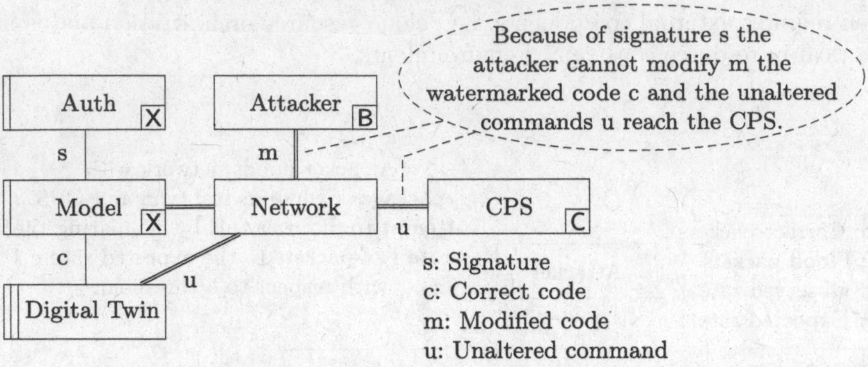

Fig. 11. Context diagram for model corruption (network) mitigation.

5 Case Study

This section introduces an example of a digital twin that is open and simple enough to be easily understood my most researchers and practitioners. The physical twin details are described in [10] and the digital twin is detailed in [8,9]. The content for this section is adapted from [8], with a focus on the communication architecture.

5.1 Physical Twin

The incubator system is a traditional control system, comprised of a controller and a plant. The plant is composed of a styrofoam box, a fan, three temperature sensors, and a heating device called a heatbed. Due to the room temperature always being smaller than the desired temperature inside the incubator, whenever the heatbed is off, the temperature inside the box drops. Therefore the controller can regulate the temperature by turning the heatbed on or off. The fan is usually always on to ensure air circulation and therefore avoid exceedingly hot spots inside the box.

The controller communicates with the driver of the plant using a RabbitMQ server, and the driver of the plant communicates with the relays that activate the heatbed and fans using a library. This is summarized in Fig. 12.

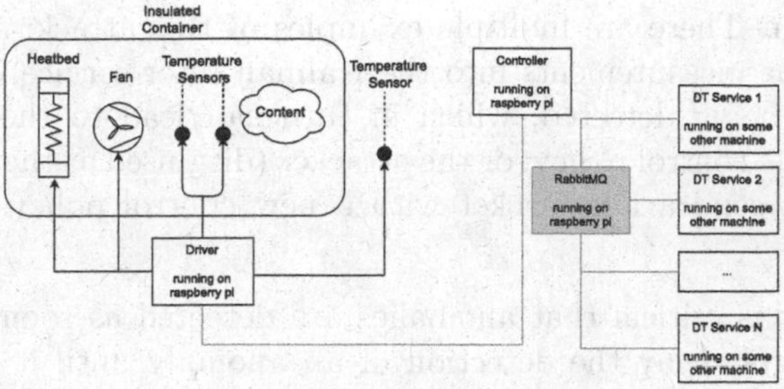

Fig. 12. Diagram of the communication among different digital twin services.

5.2 Digital Twin

The Digital Twin (DT), in the context of the incubator case study (see [8,9]), consists of a number of services that communicate via RabbitMQ messages, as illustrated in Fig. 12, each with one of the following goals:

Data Storage. We use InfluxDB to store the time series data and model parameters.

Visualization. We use InfluxDB's web application to create dashboards for querying relevant data streams;

State Estimation. We use a Kalman Filter (which uses the model parameters stored in the InfluxDB) to estimate the hidden state of the system (hidden state means variables that are part of the model but are not directly measurable from the plant)

What-if Simulation. We use a simulator that can be asked to run hypothetical simulations on past or future extrapolated data.

Self-adaptation Manager. The responsibility of this service is to implement a MAPE-K loop [17] that enables optimization of the control parameters whenever something in the environment of the incubator changes (more details in [8]). For example, when the lid is opened, the self adaptation manager will use the Kalman filter to detect an anomaly, and then carry out a number of simulations that attempt to find new parameters for the model. Finally, a new control policy is synthesized based on the newly found model parameters. A control policy refers to the optimal parameters of the controller, according to some cost function.

5.3 Example Security Challenges

In this subsection, we give concrete examples of the challenges introduced in Fig. 3 in the context of the incubator.

Bandwidth Sniffing. An attacker could use bandwidth sniffing to identify which service are involved in the implementation of the MAPE-K loop, because there is a burst of network activity when an anomaly is detected.

Data Injection. There are multiple examples of this attack: an attacker can inject fake sensor measurements into the Kalman filter service, which can lead to an anomaly being detected, which in turn can lead to the synthesis of a potentially unsafe control policy; or the attacker (disguised as the self-adaptation manager) might send a fake packet with a new control policy directly to the controller.

Data Delay. It is critical that anomalies are detected as soon as they occur. An attacker might delay the detection of an anomaly until it is too late. An example of this is if the lid of the incubator is open, the control loop is typical on an high power control policy, because of the excessive heat dissipation. If a person closes the lid, the self-adaptation manager typically reacts quickly to change the control policy to a low power mode, to avoid excessive warming in the incubator. Any extra seconds in this process might lead to unsafe temperatures in the incubator.

Model Corruption. Models are used almost in all DT services (state estimation, anomaly detection, what-if simulation, and self-adaptation), and the incubator digital twin uses controller models, plant models, and CPS (controller and plant combined) models. Any model manipulation leads to these DT services malfunctioning. For example, an incorrect model causes false anomalies to be detected, and in turn may cause incorrect control policies to be synthesized.

6 Open Problems

In this section we use the presented attacks, mitigations and the case study as a basis to discuss open research and engineering topics within digital twin security. The list presented within this section is not exhaustive as we merely aim at pointing at topics that could be acted upon with respect to the current state of the art of the digital twin area. We believe these are good starting points for further contributions to digital twin security.

The attacks presented in this paper are not only applicable to digital twins, but can be applied to wide variety of industrial control systems. In order to provide more targeted solutions for attack mitigation it is important that a clear taxonomy and definitions are created in order to be able to clearly categorize the system as a digital twin enabled or not. Clear informal and formal definitions of different digital twin enabled systems are required. We believe that the increased understanding and clarity will lead to an easier exchange of ideas with security researchers and engineers in the area of digital twins.

Another aspect is the design and development of security-aware protocols specifically for digital twins. We see digital twins as an area where models could be aware of the underlying security, including the data transfer protocol. As such it could provide continuous runtime analysis of the communication between the digital twin and the physical system. Specific challenges that need to be addressed within this topic are the minimization of the overhead such analysis would incur as well as simplicity of the design of such protocols. This approach would provide good security assurances for a data heavy digital twin system connected via an untrusted or a semi-trusted network.

We further see the need for development of a clear generalized notation for reasoning about security challenges of digital twins. In this aspect we have provided several examples in this paper, however we suggest that more work is done in this area and a possible catalogue of cyber attacks and respective mitigations is created. This could be in turn be utilized by the engineering teams developing digital twin enabled systems to semi-formally, yet clearly communicate the security aspects of the systems they create. We think, that such notation would provide a clear way of communication during the engineering of digital twin systems.

We would also suggest utilization of formal methods for analysis of different aspects of security of digital twin systems. Different attacks and mitigations could be expressed formally and applied to the formal model of the digital twin system. This could contribute to the development of a catalogue providing formal models in the area of digital twins where suitable. As security attacks are very broad and need to consider, e.g., aspects of physical materials used or social aspects about people involved, formal models will only cover some aspects of the overall security concerns.

Finally an investigation into the complementary nature of security methods based on anomaly detection and state estimation and traditional security protocols that could be utilized within the digital twin area is necessary. As we have discussed earlier, the large amount of communication required for operating digital twins means that the overhead must be kept low. Providing new options for combining these complementary methods will help to reduce the overhead.

7 Concluding Remarks

In this paper we have discussed security challenges and possible mitigations for digital twin enabled systems. We have described four specific kinds of challenges that such systems face and introduced mitigations for these challenges. To address these challenges in a way acceptable in practice, the defining characteristics of digital twin enabled systems need to be taken into consideration. Otherwise, implemented security measures might render a digital twin system inoperable. We have outlined several open problems, answers to which, will provide functioning security for digital twin systems. Besides gaining a better understanding about what comprises digital twin system, what different kinds of such systems must be considered, a catalogue of relevant security challenges and mitigations is needed. The four challenges that we have discussed can be a starting point for this, focusing on specific needs for digital twins. In the presentation of the challenges we have used semi-formal notation to state the challenges more clearly and help to communicate them with stakeholders of digital twin systems with diverse (engineering) backgrounds. Such a notation can serve to document the challenge in such way that they can easily be communicated widely.

Acknowledgements. We are grateful to the Poul Due Jensen Foundation, which has supported the establishment of a new Centre for Digital Twin Technology at Aarhus University.

References

1. Atalay, M., Angin, P.: A digital twins approach to smart grid security testing and standardization. In: 2020 IEEE International Workshop on Metrology for Industry 4.0 IoT, pp. 435–440 (2020). https://doi.org/10.1109/MetroInd4.0IoT48571.2020.9138264
2. Badhwar, R.: The case for code signing and dynamic white-listing. In: The CISO's Next Frontier, pp. 259–264. Springer, Cham (2021). https://doi.org/10.1007/978-3-030-75354-2_32
3. Baskar, M., Jayaraman, R., Karthikeyan, C., Anbarasu, V., Balaji, A., Arulananth, T.: Low rate DDoS mitigation using real-time multi threshold traffic monitoring system. J. Ambient Intell. Humanized Comput., 1–9 (2021). https://doi.org/10.1007/s12652-020-02744-y
4. Becue, A., et al.: Cyberfactory# 1-securing the industry 4.0 with cyber-ranges and digital twins. In: 2018 14th IEEE International Workshop on Factory Communication Systems (WFCS), pp. 1–4. IEEE (2018)
5. Bianchin, G., Pasqualetti, F.: Time-delay attacks in network systems. In: Koç, Ç.K. (ed.) Cyber-Physical Systems Security, pp. 157–174. Springer, Cham (2018). https://doi.org/10.1007/978-3-319-98935-8_8
6. Bruynseels, K., Santoni de Sio, F., van den Hoven, J.: Digital twins in health care: ethical implications of an emerging engineering paradigm. Front. Genet. **9** (2018). www.frontiersin.org/article/10.3389/fgene.2018.00031. https://doi.org/10.3389/fgene.2018.00031
7. Eckhart, M., Ekelhart, A.: Towards security-aware virtual environments for digital twins. In: Proceedings of the 4th ACM Workshop on Cyber-Physical System Security, CPSS 2018, pp. 61–72. Association for Computing Machinery, New York (2018). https://doi.org/10.1145/3198458.3198464
8. Feng, H., Gomes, C., Gil, S., Mikkelsen, P.H., Tola, D., Larsen, P.G.: Integration of the MAPE-K loop in digital twins. In: 2022 Annual Modeling and Simulation Conference (ANNSIM). IEEE, San Diego, July 2022
9. Feng, H., Gomes, C., Thule, C., Lausdahl, K., Iosifidis, A., Larsen, P.G.: Introduction to digital twin engineering. In: 2021 Annual Modeling and Simulation Conference (ANNSIM), pp. 1–12. IEEE, Fairfax, July 2021. https://doi.org/10.23919/ANNSIM52504.2021.9552135
10. Feng, H., Gomes, C., Thule, C., Lausdahl, K., Sandberg, M., Larsen, P.G.: The incubator case study for digital twin engineering. arXiv:2102.10390 [cs, eess], February 2021
11. Golovina, T., Polyanin, A., Adamenko, A., Khegay, E., Schepinin, V.: Digital twins as a new paradigm of an industrial enterprise. Int. J. Technol. **11**(6), 1115 (2020). https://doi.org/10.14716/ijtech.v11i6.4427
12. Holmes, D., Papathanasaki, M., Maglaras, L., Ferrag, M.A., Nepal, S., Janicke, H.: Digital twins and cyber security - solution or challenge? In: 2021 6th South-East Europe Design Automation, Computer Engineering, Computer Networks and Social Media Conference (SEEDA-CECNSM), pp. 1–8 (2021). https://doi.org/10.1109/SEEDA-CECNSM53056.2021.9566277

13. Jackson, M.: Software Requirements and Specification: A Lexicon of Practice, Principles and Prejudices. Addison-Wesley (1995)
14. Jackson, M.: Problem Frames. ACM Press (2001)
15. Kayan, H., Nunes, M., Rana, O., Burnap, P., Perera, C.: Cybersecurity of industrial cyber-physical systems: a review. ACM Comput. Surv. (2022). https://doi.org/10.1145/3510410
16. Kazemi, Z., Safavi, A.A., Naseri, F., Urbas, L., Setoodeh, P.: A secure hybrid dynamic-state estimation approach for power systems under false data injection attacks. IEEE Trans. Industr. Inf. **16**(12), 7275–7286 (2020). https://doi.org/10.1109/TII.2020.2972809
17. Kephart, J., Chess, D.: The vision of autonomic computing. Computer **36**(1), 41–50 (2003). https://doi.org/10.1109/MC.2003.1160055
18. Krutz, R.L.: Securing SCADA Systems. John Wiley & Sons (2005)
19. Kulik, T., Boudjadar, J., Tran-Jørgensen, P.: Security verification of industrial control systems using partial model checking. In: Proceedings of the 8th International Conference on Formal Methods in Software Engineering, FormaliSE 2020, pp. 98–108. Association for Computing Machinery, United States (2020). 8th International Conference on Formal Methods in Software Engineering; Conference date: 07 October 2020 Through 08 October 2020. https://doi.org/10.1145/3372020.3391558
20. Mo, Y., Chabukswar, R., Sinopoli, B.: Detecting integrity attacks on SCADA systems. IEEE Trans. Control Syst. Technol. **22**(4), 1396–1407 (2013)
21. Pajic, M., et al.: Robustness of attack-resilient state estimators. In: 2014 ACM/IEEE International Conference on Cyber-Physical Systems (ICCPS), pp. 163–174. IEEE, Berlin, April 2014. https://doi.org/10.1109/ICCPS.2014.6843720
22. Paridari, K., O'Mahony, N., El-Din Mady, A., Chabukswar, R., Boubekeur, M., Sandberg, H.: A framework for attack-resilient industrial control systems: attack detection and controller reconfiguration. Proc. IEEE **106**(1), 113–128 (2018). https://doi.org/10.1109/JPROC.2017.2725482
23. Pöhls, H.C.: JSON sensor signatures (JSS): end-to-end integrity protection from constrained device to IoT application. In: 2015 9th International Conference on Innovative Mobile and Internet Services in Ubiquitous Computing, pp. 306–312 (2015). https://doi.org/10.1109/IMIS.2015.48
24. Suhail, S., Hussain, R., Jurdak, R., Hong, C.S.: Trustworthy digital twins in the industrial internet of things with blockchain. IEEE Internet Comput. (2021)
25. Suhail, S., Zeadally, S., Jurdak, R., Hussain, R., Matulevičius, R., Svetinovic, D.: Security attacks and solutions for digital twins. arXiv preprint arXiv:2202.12501 (2022)
26. Tian, J., Tan, R., Guan, X., Xu, Z., Liu, T.: Moving target defense approach to detecting Stuxnet-like attacks. IEEE Trans. Smart Grid **11**(1), 291–300 (2020). https://doi.org/10.1109/TSG.2019.2921245
27. Uhlemann, T.H.J., Lehmann, C., Steinhilper, R.: The digital twin: realizing the cyber-physical production system for industry 4.0. Procedia CIRP **61**, 335–340 (2017). https://doi.org/10.1016/j.procir.2016.11.152. www.sciencedirect.com/science/article/pii/S2212827116313129. The 24th CIRP Conference on Life Cycle Engineering
28. Xiong, S., Sarwate, A.D., Mandayam, N.B.: Defending against packet-size side-channel attacks in IoT networks. In: 2018 IEEE International Conference on Acoustics, Speech and Signal Processing (ICASSP), pp. 2027–2031 (2018). https://doi.org/10.1109/ICASSP.2018.8461330

29. Yan, W., Hou, E., Ansari, N.: Defending against traffic analysis attacks with link padding for bursty traffics. In: Proceedings from the Fifth Annual IEEE SMC Information Assurance Workshop, pp. 46–51 (2004). IEEE (2004)
30. Zonouz, S., Rrushi, J., McLaughlin, S.: Detecting industrial control malware using automated plc code analytics. IEEE Secur. Priv. **12**(6), 40–47 (2014). https://doi.org/10.1109/MSP.2014.113

Digital Thread in Smart Manufacturing

Digital Thread in Smart Manufacturing

Tiziana Margaria[1,4(✉)], Dirk Pesch[2,4], and Alan McGibney[3,4]

[1] University of Limerick, Limerick, Ireland
Tiziana.Margaria@ul.ie
[2] University College Cork, Cork, Ireland
dirk.pesch@ucc.ie
[3] Munster Technological University, Cork, Ireland
alan.mcgibney@mtu.ie
[4] Confirm, the SFI Research Centre on Smart Manufacturing, Ireland
www.confirm.ie

Abstract. The concept of digital twins has emerged from the smart manufacturing space and is now gaining adoption in many other industries beyond manufacturing. A digital twin is a virtual replica of a cyber-physical system that is used to capture the state of the system and to allow reason and decision-making on that state. While there has been much research on this topic, there is less work on the overall lifecycle ecosystem that supports the smooth interoperation of a physical facility (like a machine, a factory or even a supply chain) and its digital components (like data, processes and digital twins), which is called the Digital Thread. The aim of the Digital Thread is the creation of a digital lifecycle ecosystem that links together the data generated throughout a product's lifecycle and represents the data, processes and communication platform that supports a product and its production at any instance of time.

1 Motivation and Goals

In order to realise the concept of a Digital Thread, a range of functions need to work together to allow for the integration and interoperability of physical and virtual representations of a product or process through the Digital Thread [7]. This takes the form of a "digital mesh" and/or open data spaces, that need to be managed, connected, protected, and shared. The research and innovation aspects around and within the digital thread span interdisciplinary topics including Internet of Things and Cyber-Physical System technologies, decentralised and edge computing architectures, Distributed Ledger Technologies (DLT), model driven development, low-code/no-code approaches, cybersecurity, trust and data management strategies.

Important in realising a Digital Thread in any organisation are testbeds and practical experience in collecting, processing and managing data, the integration of models and systems across heterogeneous technologies and paradigms [2,3,9], as well as the associated application development throughout a product lifecycle. In addition, novel mechanisms are required to enable the dynamic creation and adaptation of digital workflows [11] that leverage techniques such as containerisation and modular architectures that facilitate a secure and trustworthy Digital Thread for manufacturing applications [5,8].

T. Margaria and B. Steffen (Eds.): ISoLA 2022, LNCS 13704, pp. 179–183, 2022.
https://doi.org/10.1007/978-3-031-19762-8_12

The **Digital Thread in Smart Manufacturing** track originates from the collaboration of the organizers within the Confirm SFI Centre for Smart manufacturing[1]. It focuses on tools and methodologies that can drive the creation of a digital ecosystem that can form an integrated, open test and demonstration environment for industry and the broader research community.

The large scale adoption of Industry 4.0 has made modern manufacturing sites a rich source of data that can be leveraged to inform and improve decision-making at all levels in a complex manufacturing process. This data needs to be collected, processed and analysed to generate real-time insight that can be utilised to optimise operations, ensure efficiency, minimise costs and improve resilience of a manufacturing site. Despite the advantages of leveraging this data, often attempts to maximise the potential value can fall short due to additional constraints, such as complexity of integration, interoperability, privacy, security concerns and distributed data silos that are difficult to access and share. A recent white paper produced by PTC[2] conducted a survey with industry to analyse the current state of digital thread in industrial sectors. A number of pain points were highlighted, mainly oriented around the challenge with silo'd enterprise systems. These include (but not limited too) the inability of employees across different roles to leverage product data that can deliver value for customers; a disconnect between work streams and roles (e.g. planning, operations) that hinders collaboration and difficulty in getting access to data that can influence more effective decision-making to trigger improvements.

While Digital Thread aims to offer a solution to address these pain points, there remains some open research questions that demand further attention from the community:

1. **Application and infrastructure heterogeneity**: new methods that facilitate interoperability, portability, and integration across heterogeneous platforms and systems are required [4,6]. No code, low code development tools that combine formal model driven approaches are needed.
2. **Scalability**: the boundary between the physical and digital worlds is becoming increasingly blurred, solutions must be able to scale from low-end sensors to large data centres forming systems of systems with limited impact on performance.
3. **Orchestration and adaptation**: systems and services, particularly across heterogeneous compute infrastructure, are essential. Applications and platforms need to be easily re-configurable and have the capability to reside at the different tiers of IT infrastructures (edge-cloud continuum) [1].
4. **Testing and maintenance**: complex distributed systems require novel methods of testing, assurance and maintenance.
5. **Cyber-security and Privacy**: the convergence of IT and OT operations in manufacturing has raised many concerns surrounding the impact on the security of systems. The application and evaluation of emerging concepts

[1] See the Confirm website at https://confirm.ie.

[2] https://www.cimdata.com/images/PLMRoadMap/The-State-of-Digital-Thread-0721.pdf.

such as Zero Trust to address this is required. Scalable privacy preserving techniques are also required.

6. **Organizational Boundaries**: collaboration across industry sectors is viewed as a key component of smart and resilient manufacturing. As such, new mechanisms are required that provides incentives and trust assurance across independently operating entities and ecosystems [10] (e.g. embedding of governance policies in automated interactions and digital workflows).

The track presents a selection of papers that addresses aspects of the open research topics as discussed above. They include new architectures, models, techniques, and tools for the implementation of the Digital Thread. Particular emphasis is placed on the constraints, challenges and impact of achieving a digital thread in the smart manufacturing domain.

The included contributions provide a broad perspective on the current state-of-the-art in both Digital Thread and its role in the manufacturing domain. The research works propose solutions to address difficult problems relating to integration, interoperability, cyber-security, trust management, data-driven application development and systems modelling. The track offers an opportunity to discuss new ways in which we can leverage digital thread to tackle challenges of scalability, heterogeneity and interoperability in order to accelerate the development of adaptive, flexible and robust digital applications that are to become the digital fabric that binds the physical and virtual in factories of the future.

2 Overview of Contributions

In *Integrating Wearable and Camera based Monitoring in the Digital Twin for Safety Assessment in the Industry 4.0 Era* [2], the authors Michele Boldo, Nicola Bombieri, Stefano Centomo, Mirco De Marchi, Florenc Demrozi, Graziano Pravadelli, Davide Quaglia and Cristian Turetta propose an automatic system for monitoring individuals operating in an industrial environment. This information is utilised for mapping human actions to both the safety procedures and the behaviours of robotic systems that operate autonomously in the same environment. The authors leveraged federated Kafka instances as digital thread to integrate an edge based monitoring system with tools that create digital twins for risk assessment and prevention deployed on the cloud.

In *Model-driven Engineering in Digital Thread Platforms: A practical use case and future challenges* [3], the authors Hafiz Ahmad Awais Chaudhary, Ivan Guevara, Jobish John, Amandeep Singh, Amrita Ghosal, Dirk Pesch and Tiziana Margaria present a model-driven approach to the engineering of integrated Industrial Internet of Things (IIoT) applications covering a middleware for data acquisition from heterogeneous sensors, low-code platforms for analytics, process modelling and application development. The approach provides an abstraction layer for rapid prototyping and enable non-expert programmers to responsibly (through appropriate security measures) and directly participate in the software development cycle. The paper provides a practical use case in the context of Smart Manufacturing to demonstrate how a more efficient system construction and interoperability can be achieved using the proposed model-driven engineering approach.

In *Trust and Security Analyzer for Collaborative Digital Manufacturing Ecosystems* [5], the authors Pasindu Kuruppuarachchi, Susan Rea and Alan McGibney propose the development of a trust and security analyzer that can be utilised to provide assessment and assurance for integrating multiple digital twins that form a collaborative digital ecosystem in a smart manufacturing context. The focus is on providing a reference architecture to enable a holistic representation of trustworthiness across independently operated digital twins. By bootstrapping the digital thread with such an analyser aids in evaluating the security, resilience, reliability, uncertainty, dependability, and goal analysis of a collaborative ecosystem. A description of the initial implementation addressing security analysis of application programming interfaces (API) as data exchange end-points for digital twin integration is provided.

In *DISTiL: DIStributed Industrial Computing Environment for Trustworthy digiTaL workflows: A Design Perspective* [8], the authors Alan McGibney and Sourabh Bharti presents an initial analysis of the system requirements, architectural considerations, and challenges that need to be overcome to realise distributed and trusted digital workflows with a focus on use cases in the domain of smart manufacturing. The architecture outlines three tiers that constitute intelligent software agents that operate as Decentralised Autonomous Organisations (DOA) providing i) a distributed data layer, ii) trust overlay and ii) resource orchestration and provisioning.

In *Using Model Selection and Reduction to develop an empirical model to predict energy consumption of a CNC machine* [9], the authors Liam Morris, Andriy Hryshchenko, Rose Clancy, Dominic O'Sullivan and Ken Bruton provide an approach that leverages digital thread to feed a model development lifecyle to build an empirical energy consumption model of a CNC machine to predict energy consumption based on only product throughput in the absence of other features. An initial exploratory use case is provided which demonstrates a high accuracy of predictability that can be applied across other CNC machines or machining assets.

In *Crazy Nodes: Towards Ultimate Flexibility in Ubiquitous Big Data Stream Engineering, Visualisation, and Analytics, in Smart Factories* [11], the authors Mirco Soderi and John Breslin present a software framework, which allows users to remotely deploy, (re)configure, run, and monitor the most diverse software across all the three layers of the Smart Factory (edge, fog, Cloud) via API calls. This involves the integration of various software technologies, frameworks, and programming languages, including Node-RED, MQTT, Scala, Apache Spark, and Kafka. A proof-of-concept is provided where user interfaces and distributed systems are created from scratch via API calls to implement AI-based alerting systems and Big Data services (e.g. stream filtering and transformation, AI model training, visualization).

Acknowledgement. This project received funding from Science Foundation Ireland (SFI) under Grant Number 16/RC/3918 (CONFIRM Centre).

Finally, we would like to express our deep gratitude to the ISoLA organizers for their tenacious work to provide the infrastructure for our and other tracks, which allows engaging and creative discussions among researchers and practitioners across different communities, leading to new insights and perspectives of the techniques and foundations of design, analysis, implementation and testing for innovative and emerging applications.

References

1. Bharti, S., McGibney, A., O'Gorman, T.: Edge-enabled federated learning for vision based product quality inspection. In: 2022 33rd Irish Signals and Systems Conference (ISSC), pp. 1–6 (2022)
2. Boldo, M.: Integrating wearable and camera based monitoring in the digital twin for safety assessment in the industry 4.0 era. In: Margaria, T., Steffen, B. (eds.) ISoLA 2022, LNCS 13704, pp. 184–194 (2022)
3. Chaudhary, H.A.A., et al.: Model-driven engineering in digital thread platforms: a practical use case and future challenges. In: Margaria, T., Steffen, B. (eds.) ISoLA 2022, LNCS 13704, pp. 219–226 (2022)
4. John, J., Ghosal, A., Margaria, T., Pesch, D.: DSLs for model driven development of secure interoperable automation systems with EdgeX foundry. In: 2021 Forum on Specification & Design Languages (FDL), pp. 1–8. IEEE (2021)
5. Kuruppuarachchi, P., Rea, S., McGibney, A.: Trust and security analyzer for collaborative digital manufacturing ecosystems. In: Margaria, T., Steffen, B. (eds.) ISoLA 2022, LNCS 13704, pp. 208–218 (2022)
6. Margaria, T., Chaudhary, H.A.A., Guevara, I., Ryan, S., Schieweck, A.: The interoperability challenge: building a model-driven digital thread platform for CPS. In: Margaria, T., Steffen, B. (eds.) ISoLA 2021. LNCS, vol. 13036, pp. 393–413. Springer, Cham (2021). https://doi.org/10.1007/978-3-030-89159-6_25
7. Margaria, T., Schieweck, A.: The digital thread in industry 4.0. In: Ahrendt, W., Tapia Tarifa, S.L. (eds.) IFM 2019. LNCS, vol. 11918, pp. 3–24. Springer, Cham (2019). https://doi.org/10.1007/978-3-030-34968-4_1
8. McGibney, A., Bharti, S.: DISTiL: DIStributed industrial computing environment for trustworthy digital workflows: a design perspective. In: Margaria, T., Steffen, B. (eds.) ISoLA 2022, LNCS 13704, pp. 219–226 (2022)
9. Morris, L., Hryshchenko, A., Clancy, R., O'Sullivan, D., Bruton, K.: Using model selection and reduction to develop an empirical model to predict energy consumption of a CNC machine. In: Margaria, T., Steffen, B. (eds.) ISoLA 2022, LNCS 13704, pp. 227–234 (2022)
10. Ranathunga, T., McGibney, A., Rea, S.: The convergence of blockchain and machine learning for decentralized trust management in IoT ecosystems. In: Proceedings of the 19th ACM Conference on Embedded Networked Sensor Systems, SenSys 2021, pp. 499–504. Association for Computing Machinery, New York (2021)
11. Soderi, M., Breslin, J.: Crazy nodes: towards ultimate flexibility in ubiquitous big data stream engineering, visualisation, and analytics, in smart factories. In: Margaria, T., Steffen, B. (eds.) ISoLA 2022, LNCS 13704, pp. 235–240 (2022)

Integrating Wearable and Camera Based Monitoring in the Digital Twin for Safety Assessment in the Industry 4.0 Era

Michele Boldo, Nicola Bombieri, Stefano Centomo, Mirco De Marchi, Florenc Demrozi, Graziano Pravadelli(✉), Davide Quaglia, and Cristian Turetta

Department of Computer Science, University of Verona, 37134 Verona, Italy
{Michele.Boldo,Nicola.Bombieri,Stefano.Centomo,Mirco.Marchi, Florenc.Demrozi,Graziano.Pravadelli,Davide.Quaglia, Cristian.Turetta}@univr.it

Abstract. The occurrence of human errors in work processes reduces the quality of results, increases the costs due to compensatory actions, and may have heavy repercussions on the workers' safety. The definition of rules and procedures that workers have to respect has shown to be not enough to guarantee their safety, as negligence and opportunistic behaviours can unfortunately lead to catastrophic consequences. In the Industry 4.0 era, with the advent of the digital twin in smart factories, advanced systems can be exploited for automatic risk prediction and avoidance. By leveraging the new opportunities provided by the digital twin and, in particular, the introduction of wearable sensors and computer vision, we propose an automatic system for monitoring human behaviours in a smart factory in real time. The final goal is to feed cloud-based safety assessment tools that evaluate human errors and raise consequent alerts when required.

1 Introduction

Despite decades of industrial automation, the presence of humans in work processes cannot be avoided and is even becoming the indication of a new industrial era in which humans and robots collaborate to create high-quality products. While machines are programmed and there is vast literature about capturing program errors and faults, human behavior is unpredictable regarding both errors and operation timing, impacting the quality of results and safety. Likely, the advent of Internet of Things (IoT) and Industry 4.0 has introduced many technologies in working environments that can be exploited for coupling safety procedures with automatic monitoring mechanisms for risk prediction and avoidance. More and more, indeed, production lines are paired with a digital twin, i.e., a real-time virtual representation of what actually happens in the smart factory. This is created thanks to the integration among sensors, communication networks, cloud services and artificial intelligence (AI)-based algorithms, which

T. Margaria and B. Steffen (Eds.): ISoLA 2022, LNCS 13704, pp. 184–194, 2022.
https://doi.org/10.1007/978-3-031-19762-8_13

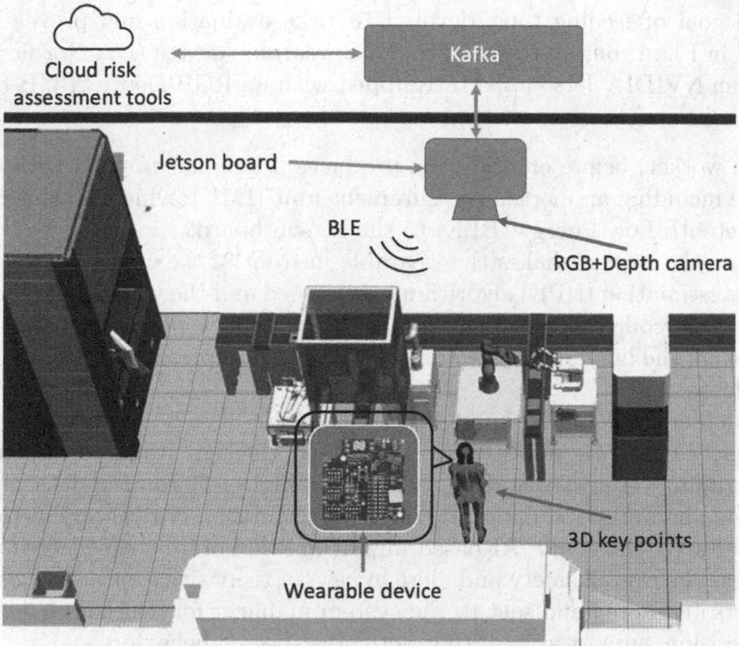

Fig. 1. Assessing risks in a smart factory through wearables and video-surveillance devices.

collect and elaborate real-time data from the production line to update its digital model [1]. Such a model is then mainly used for predictive maintenance, performance evaluation, failure detection and analysis.

In addition, as data related to human behaviours can be also collected by means, for example, of applications running on their smartwatches/smartphones, dedicated wearables [2], and camera-based video-surveillance systems [3], workers can be included in the digital twin as well. Therefore the digital twin can be exploited also for assessing safety and preventing risks related to human errors.

However, it is now known that the information collected by the digital twin cannot be effectively understood and used without knowledge of the work process that generated it. Although the formal models of work processes are the basis of their rationalization, the effort for their manual construction has so far discouraged their use. There is the need for an automatic method of extracting the properties of a work process starting from the observation of the data flows it generates, and the extension of formal techniques for the efficient modeling of human errors.

To contribute in this direction, this paper presents an automatic system for monitoring individuals in an industrial scenario. This is intended as a mandatory step for relating human actions to both the safety procedures and the behaviors of robotic systems, which autonomously operate in the same environment, with the final goal of feeding tools devoted to risks evaluation and prevention. As depicted in Fig. 1, our system consists of a wearable device (i.e., Nordic Thingy 52) and an NVIDIA Jetson board equipped with an RGB-Depth (RGB-D) camera. It works as follows:

(i) The worker, before entering the production line, is equipped with a wearable including an inertial measurement unit (IMU), which is connected via Bluetooth Low Energy (BLE) to the Jetson board.
(ii) When the worker shakes the wearable in front of the camera, a 3D human pose estimation (HPE) algorithm is activated and the wearable unique identification code is associated with a set of 3D key points representing the joints of the human body, actually recreating a representation of the human skeleton.
(iii) Both inertial data and human pose, which are linked together by the same identity code, are published in the Cloud through Kafka, an open-source distributed event streaming platform for high-performance data pipelines, streaming analytics, data integration, and mission-critical applications[1].
(iv) Finally, on the cloud, AI-based algorithms elaborate the collected data to assess the overall safety and alert in case of risky situations. The generated alerts are stored and sent to the system manager for decision-making or to a decision support system that activates specific behaviors.

In the Jetson board the software controlling the wearable and the one estimating the human pose from camera data have been dockerized to simplify deployment and support orchestration by using tools like Kubernetes[2].

While the description of the cloud-based safety assessment tools is out of the scope of this paper, this work deals with the architectural overview of the system and the description of the data collection flow. In particular, the paper is organized as follows. Section 2 summarizes the state of the art in the context of working safety. Section 3 presents the architecture we propose for data collection and integration to implement the safety assessment in working environments. Section 4 describes an industrial scenarios where the system has been applied. Finally, Sect. 5 draws some conclusions.

2 Related Work

Several solutions can be found in the literature to address safety in human-robot interaction and, in particular, to manage collisions. In [4], the authors propose a motion planning method to keep a robot body from colliding with objects while preserving the robot's original task. One of the most practical limitations is that cameras are required to be very close to the floor (i.e., at 1.38 m in the analysis), which is difficult to apply in a real industrial scenario. In [5], the authors present a real-time speed alteration strategy that relies on a danger index and a genetic algorithm. Only the upper part of the body is considered and only one camera is used

1 https://kafka.apache.org.
2 https://kubernetes.io/.

without addressing occlusions. In [6], the authors developed a trajectory planner, which formally guarantees the safety of humans. Markers are used to track bodies. In [7] formal and automatic verification techniques are used without details on the execution platform and time. In [8] a novel kinematic control strategy enforces safety, while maintaining the maximum level of productivity of the robot. Readers can find other examples of collision management techniques in [9–11].

With respect to such literature, our contributions are:

- a uniform and scalable data collection infrastructure based on publish/subscribe paradigm supported by Kafka;
- integration of inertial data from a wearable device with 3D HPE provided by a distributed set of smart cameras in real time.

In addition, the proposed system is more generic with respect to those found in literature since it opens to a wider set of safety assessing tools running on the cloud using a large and heterogeneous set of data to investigate human behaviours and related errors in a wider context.

3 Architecture Overview

Figure 2 shows the architecture of the proposed system. It relies on two main functions: sensing from wearable devices (one per worker) and a HPE system based on a set of distributed RGB-D cameras. Data coming from the wearable sensors and the HPE system are integrated, temporally aligned and published on the cloud through Kafka, where tools for risk prediction and avoidance implement automatic safety procedures.

Kafka implements a publish/subscribe paradigm of topic-labeled messages. Topics are represented by colors in Fig. 2. Blu arrows represent data related to wearable devices; green arrows represent human pose information related to each camera; NVIDIA Jetson boards act as both data publishers. Risk assessment tools run in the cloud and act as data subscribers from the shop floor. HPE data from each camera are not used directly. Instead, an aggregator service subscribes to them, merges single-view information to compensate for occlusions, and generates better HPE information (violet arrows), as detailed in Sect. 3.2.

Kafka creates a modular architecture for data distribution in which new sources can be easily added when the manufacturing infrastructure grows. Furthermore, new intermediate services that process data can be introduced later without changing the data distribution infrastructure but just touching topic subscriptions. Kafka itself implements specific mechanisms that increase scalability, such as the chance to deploy multiple instances of the broker running on different machines.

Figure 2 also reports the shop floor network (aka., dedicated network) that allows the connection of various machines of the manufacturing plant and to deliver information from the various sensors to the cloud, which can host heavy data processing tasks.

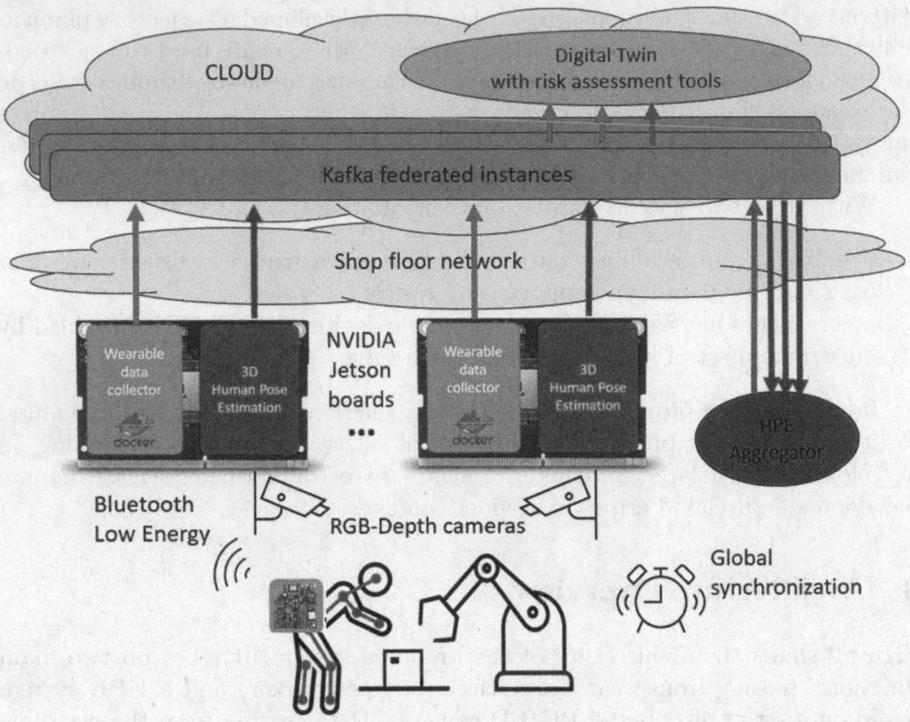

Fig. 2. Overview of the system architecture.

3.1 Wearable Node

The wearable device is based on the nRF52832 chip, by Nordic Semiconductor (i.e., we use the Nordic Thingy 52 IoT Sensors kit shown in Fig. 3). Such a node supports several communication protocols, e.g. Bluetooth 5, BLE, ANT and ZigBee and it guarantees a low-energy consumption thanks to a sophisticated

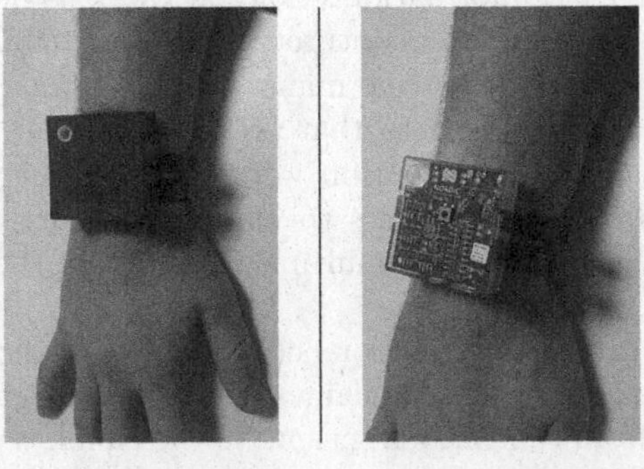

Fig. 3. Wearable node Nordic Thingy 52 (5 cm × 5 cm × 1.5 cm, 47 g, 37 $).

on-chip power management system. It is equipped with 3-axis accelerometer, gyroscope, compass, magnetometer whose sampling frequency can be configured 5 Hz 200 Hz and furthermore it computes directly onboard some motion-related information such as step count, rotation matrix, quaternion, pitch, roll and yaw. The wearable node is located on the human body as shown in Fig. 3. In such position, the proposed architecture can recognize the number of performed steps, its orientation, and specific activities such as falls, handshaking, or arm shaking. Other positions can be exploited based on the necessity of the overall architecture and activity to be recognized.

The wearable node is connected via BLE to a data collector running on an NVIDIA Jetson board, which is also connected to the RGB-D camera.

The role of the data collector consists of coordinating and synchronizing the data gathering from all the wearable nodes in the network, which means it has full control over them to: (i) set their sampling frequency; (ii) decide the data transmission mode (continuous or event-based); (iii) disconnect/connect each of them, (iv) running data analysis algorithms to immediately detect interesting events (e.g., wearable shaking, human falls). In addition, the data collector is responsible for sending the synchronized data from sensors to the Kafka system.

The data collector node supports two modes of data transmission: continuous and event-based. In the *continuous mode*, the collector forward the data coming from the connected wearables to the network in real time. For example, if there are three sensors connected to the collector node, and each sensor sample 32 Hz, every second the collector node will publish 96 messages. In large scale, this may cause network congestion. In the *event-based mode*, the collector locally analyses the data it received from the wearable device to keep track of its current status (e.g. the cardinal direction pointed by the sensor), and to identify interesting events (e.g., node shacking, worker falls). If the state change or a monitored event is recognized, the collector publishes this information on a specific Kafka topic. This mode reduces dramatically the network traffic and the workload of the Kafka broker.

3.2 HPE Subsystem

The human behaviour is also captured by a system of distributed 3D HPE edge devices and a centralized aggregation unit connected by the shop floor communication network. It aims at supporting both single and multi-person pose estimation in real-time.

Each edge device consists of an RGB-D camera and a heterogeneous embedded board running an inference application for single-view real-time 3D HPE. It is implemented as a set of communicating and concurrent ROS2 nodes[3] that build a pipeline of computer vision primitives and inference-based applications. The pipeline allows for an efficient processing of the video stream received in input from the RGB-D camera on the heterogeneous computing elements (i.e., CPU and GPU) of an NVIDIA Jetson device. The result is a set of *3D keypoints*

[3] https://ros.org.

representing the joints of the human body. The infrastructure has been made compliant to the standard ROS2 to allow for the integration of post-processing modules such as keypoints elaboration and monitoring in the embedded device or, through the network, on mobile phones, tablets or laptops.

On the basis of data collected by the edge devices, a centralized aggregation unit implements data merge through a combination of filtering, clustering, fusion, and association algorithms. Data are synchronized both spatially and temporally to guarantee common references for their aggregation. Local HPE information with timestamps is sent over the network through a standard communication protocol towards the centralized aggregation unit. Communication and synchronization of data flows rely on Kafka and the Network Time Protocol. The aggregator aims at generating one and only one 3D skeleton for each person present in the scene. To do that, it merges, in real time, the information coming from the different edge devices. The information consists of a sequence of macro-messages, where each macro-message contains the set of keypoints representing different scenarios like single person-single view, single person-multiple views, multiple people-single view, etc. For each macro-message, the aggregator first applies a *clustering* algorithm to associate skeletons belonging to the same person seen from different views. This allows the system to understand whether multiple sets of keypoints in the macro-message belong to a single subject or different subjects. The result is a number of clusters, one per human subject identified in the scene. The aggregator implements a *fusion* step to merge the keypoints of each cluster. This allows generating one single 3D skeleton per person. Then, the aggregator implements an algorithm of temporal *association* to guarantee consistency in the association of skeletons to people, from one frame to the next. This aims at avoiding switches between skeleton-person associations due to the dynamism in the scene in case of the presence of more than one person, which does not maintain the order of people identification along the frames. Finally, the identified 3D skeletons undergo a filtering step to reduce estimation errors in the detection of keypoints introduced by the neural network or by the depth estimation.

The HPE processes each RGB-D frame at 22–24 FPS (44 ms), it allocates about 3.3 Gbytes of RAM memory, most of which is occupied by the inference model, and the process uses an average of 22% CPU and 37% GPU. The communication bandwidth used, in a 4 cameras setup, is approximately 440 Kbps. The aggregation phase, which takes place on a server, minimally impacts on the computational resources.

4 Application Scenario

The proposed systems has been implemented in the Industrial Computer Engineering (ICE) Laboratory[4]: a research facility of the University of Verona, equipped with a complete smart manufacturing line [12] as depicted in Fig. 4.

[4] https://www.icelab.di.univr.it.

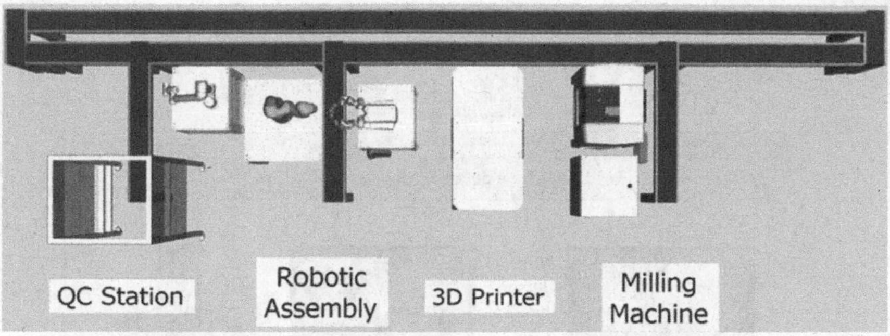

Fig. 4. The ICE laboratory working environment.

The line consists of several work cells connected by multiple conveyor belts: two 3D printers, a quality control cell, a collaborative robotic cell, a CNC cell, and a vertical warehouse.

The nodes implement a service-oriented manufacturing paradigm through the OPC UA protocol and the overall system is controlled by a commercial manufacturing execution system (MES) which orchestrates the execution of the different processes. A Kubernetes-based cloud architecture completes the set up. The transportation system is made by a closed-loop main conveyor belt. Other conveyor bays are linked to the main one to move the materials from the transportation system to each machine and back. The passage of material between the main belt and each bay is managed by a switching mechanism that is guided by sensors detecting and identifying the minipallets moving around the production system. Two Robotnik RB-Kairos mobile robots move the components to be assembled from the data warehouse to the main belt and place the final products back. The mobile robot consists of a skid-steering platform equipped with an Universal Robots UR5 manipulator and a Schunk WSG50 end-effector for grasping. Production orders are manually executed by operators.

The architecture proposed in this paper has been exploited to provide wearable and 3D HPE data to a risk prediction and avoidance tool running on the cloud in the previous working environment [13]. In this scenario, one human operator shares a workbench with a robot manipulator that performs pick-and-place operations. The safety tool correctly identified collision risks between humans and the robot with almost 100% accuracy. However, some false negative occurrences, which are under investigation in our current and future work, are generated from the inaccuracy of the 3D HPE software. Since such a system runs at the edge of resource-constrained devices, the challenge is to reach enough accuracy while guaranteeing the results in real time.

The management of such a large amount of data requires special precautions from the point of view of the privacy of the workers. The proposed integrated architecture stimulated the creation of a solution [14]. In such solution, the concept of privacy was associated with the concept of contextual integrity, that is the adequacy of an information flow within a specific context. Context is

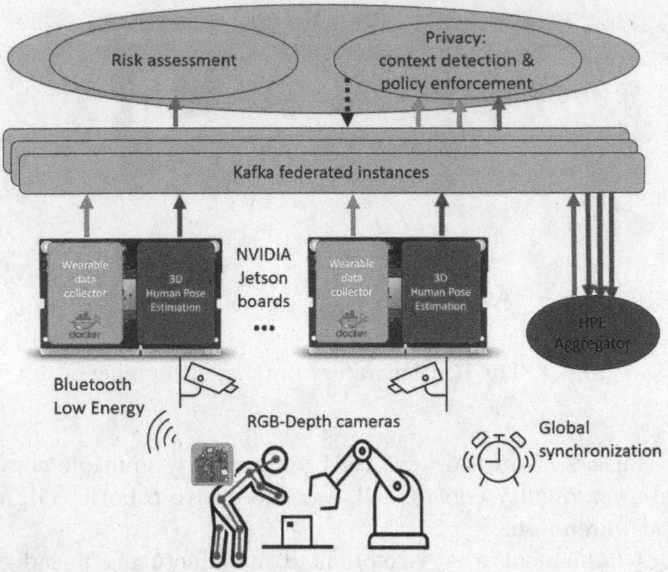

Fig. 5. An example of service for privacy management based on the proposed architecture.

defined as the formal description of a situation, e.g., "Approaching a dangerous machine", "work shift X", "work break", "fire emergency". Adequacy is defined as compliance with a formally expressed policy on the data that passes through. Each context corresponds to a different policy. The privacy policy changes in passing from one context to another. The policies and contexts ensure that the processing of workers' personal data complies with the privacy policy issued to workers. The privacy management system shown in Fig. 5 acts as a filter on the visibility of the collected data: all data is read by the Privacy Manager which uses it to determine its context.

Context knowledge is used by the Privacy Manager to set visibility rights on topics in the broker (black dotted arrow). The other risk assessment tools, as any external application that consumes data, can only read what the Privacy Manager allows them to read (gray arrow).

The number and placement of HPE cameras heavily depends on the environment to be monitored. Using a multi-view system allows us to monitor points that would be occluded by a single perspective. As the number of cameras increases, the percentage of keypoints detected increases. As for the standard procedures for multi-cameras, the system requires a geometrical synchronization phase to select the optimal positions.

Finally, Table 1 shows the performance results of each edge node. The total latency introduced by the system is the sum of the execution of the edge-side CNN model, the transmission of packets containing keypoints over the Ethernet network channel to the centralized aggregator, and the execution of the view fusion algorithms. Considering the whole pipelined procedure, in total the latency remains around 65 ms per frame and never exceeds 100 ms for real time guarantees.

Table 1. Analysis of accuracy and scalability with camera resolution 2K (15 FPS) and optimal network conditions

Setup	Edge: performance per node			Network		Centralized compute unit: performance			Accuracy
Cam (#)	Workload %CPU;%GPU	Mem. (MB)	Max rate (FPS)	Used BW (Kbps)	Frames/KPs lost due to time sync	HPE+Aggr. Workload %CPU;%GPU	HPE+Aggr. Mem. (MB)	HPE+Aggr. time(ms), (max FPS)	%Avg detected KPS
1	22.5;37.4	3,349	24	108	0/448 (0.0%)	16.2;0.0	85	4.2 (233 FPS)	93.5
2	22.7;37.4	3,312	22	214	1/896 (0.1%)	17.2;0.0	85	5.0 (197 FPS)	99.2
3	20.9;37.4	3,051	23	333	2/1,340 (0.1%)	16.9;0.0	85	4.9 (200 FPS)	99.5
4	22.5;37.4	3,310	22	442	1/1,788 (0.0%)	17.2;0.0	83	5.6 (176 FPS)	99.5

5 Conclusions

We have presented a Kafka-based architecture that integrates inertial data collected from wearable devices and human poses obtained through inference from RGB-Depth cameras, to feed cloud-based tools for safety assessment in a working environment. The wearable provides measurements about the acceleration, orientation and recognized events, while a human pose estimation software, elaborating the video frames from the RGB-Depth cameras, provides 3D key points representing the joints of the human body. The work shows that the joint consideration of both data types enables a more effective analysis, but in that case the synchronization among the various data flows becomes crucial. The adoption of the Kafka-based publish/subscribe paradigm provides a great flexibility in adding new input flows and modifying the pipeline at the core of the analysis tools.

References

1. Dall'Ora, N., Alamin, K., Fraccaroli, E., Poncino, M., Quaglia, D., Vinco, S.: Digital transformation of a production line: network design, online data collection and energy monitoring. IEEE Trans. Emerg. Top. Comput. **10**(01), 46–59 (2022)
2. Demrozi, F., Pravadelli, G., Bihorac, A., Rashidi, P.: Human activity recognition using inertial, physiological and environmental sensors: a comprehensive survey. IEEE Access **8**, 210 816–210 836 (2020)
3. Gorecky, D., Schmitt, M., Loskyll, M., Zühlke, D.: Human-machine-interaction in the industry 4.0 era. In: 12th IEEE International Conference on Industrial Informatics (INDIN). IEEE **2014**, 289–294 (2014)
4. Chen, J.-H., Song, K.-T.: Collision-free motion planning for human-robot collaborative safety under cartesian constraint. In: 2018 IEEE International Conference on Robotics and Automation (ICRA), pp. 4348–4354, May 2018
5. Chan, C.-C., Tsai, C.-C.: Collision-free speed alteration strategy for human safety in human-robot coexistence environments. IEEE Access **8**, 80 120–80 133 (2020)

6. Beckert, D., Pereira, A., Althoff, M.: Online verification of multiple safety criteria for a robot trajectory. In: 2017 IEEE 56th Annual Conference on Decision and Control (CDC), pp. 6454–6461, December 2017
7. Vicentini, F., Askarpour, M., Rossi, M., Mandrioli, D.: Safety assessment of collaborative robotics through automated formal verification. IEEE Trans. Rob. **36**(1), 42–61 (2020)
8. Zanchettin, A., et al.: Safety in human-robot collaborative manufacturing environments: metrics and control. IEEE Trans. Autom. Sci. Eng. **13**(2), 882–893 (2016)
9. Nascimento, H., Mujica, M., Benoussaad, M.: Collision avoidance in human-robot interaction using Kinect vision system combined with robot's model and data. In: IEEE International Conference on Intelligent Robots and Systems, pp. 10293–10298 (2020)
10. Lim, J., et al.: Designing path of collision avoidance for mobile manipulator in worker safety monitoring system using reinforcement learning. In: ISR 2021–2021 IEEE International Conference on Intelligence and Safety for Robotics, pp. 94–97 (2021)
11. Robla-Gómez, S., et al.: Working together: a review on safe human-robot collaboration in industrial environments. IEEE Access **5**, 26 754–26 773 (2017)
12. Spellini, S., Chirico, R., Panato, M., Lora, M., Fummi, F.: Virtual prototyping a production line using assume-guarantee contracts. IEEE Trans. Industr. Inf. **17**(9), 6294–6302 (2021)
13. Boldo, M., Bombieri, N., De Marchi, M., Geretti, L., Germiniani, S., Pravadelli, G.: Risk assessment and prediction in human-robot interaction through assertion mining and pose estimation. In: Proceedings of IEEE Latin-American Test Symposium (LATS) (2022)
14. Centomo, S., Paci, F., Quintarelli, E.: Context-aware privacy in industry 4.0. Internal report, University of Verona (2022)

Model-Driven Engineering in Digital Thread Platforms: A Practical Use Case and Future Challenges

Hafiz Ahmad Awais Chaudhary[1,4](✉), Ivan Guevara[1,4], Jobish John[2,4], Amandeep Singh[1,5], Amrita Ghosal[1,4], Dirk Pesch[2,4], and Tiziana Margaria[1,3,4,5]

[1] University of Limerick, Limerick, Ireland
{ahmad.chaudhary,ivan.guevara,amandeep.singh,amrita.ghosal, tiziana.margaria}@ul.ie
[2] University College Cork, Cork, Ireland
{j.john,d.pesch}@cs.ucc.ie
[3] Lero - The SFI Software Research Centre, Limerick, Ireland
[4] Confirm - Centre for Smart Manufacturing, Castletroy, Ireland
[5] Centre for Research Training in Artificial Intelligence (CRT AI), Cork, Ireland

Abstract. The increasing complexity delivered by the heterogeneity of the cyber-physical systems is being addressed and decoded by edge technologies, IoT development, robotics, digital twin engineering, and AI. Nevertheless, tackling the orchestration of these complex ecosystems has become a challenging problem. Specially the inherent entanglement of the different emerging technologies makes it hard to maintain and scale such ecosystems. In this context, the usage of model-driven engineering as a more abstract form of glue-code, replacing the boilerplate fashion, has improved the software development lifecycle, democratising the access to and use of the aforementioned technologies. In this paper, we present a practical use case in the context of Smart Manufacturing, where we use several platforms as providers of a high-level abstraction layer, as well as security measures, allowing a more efficient system construction and interoperability.

Keywords: Edge computing · Smart Manufacturing · Digital Thread · Model driven engineering

1 Introduction

In the actual data-centric era, where the shift towards distributed and ubiquitous architectures demands increasing computing capabilities, cloud-based processing represents a bottleneck. This is due to the increasing amount of devices taking part in the systems, which are often systems of systems. According to the Cisco Annual Report 2018–2023 [16], IoT devices will account for 50% (14.7 billion)

T. Margaria and B. Steffen (Eds.): ISoLA 2022, LNCS 13704, pp. 195–207, 2022.
https://doi.org/10.1007/978-3-031-19762-8_14

of all global networked devices by 2023, having an impact in the workload processing and forcing companies and organizations to look for more cost-effective and efficient alternatives. In this context, since the data is generated at the edge of the network, i.e., by the IoT devices, it would be more efficient if the processing of the data also happens at the edge. This is called Edge computing [29]. Edge computing plays a significant role in the Industrial IoT (IIoT) sector, lowering the cost of data transport, decreasing latency and improving the overall efficiency of the architecture [32]. This does not mean that cloud and edge computing are incompatible, rather they complement each other, allowing us to have more tools to confront these issues and be able to improve the overall performance in a balanced and customized way.

Based on physical configurations and functional requirements in the context of smart manufacturing, there are many standard architectures for the implementation of IoT based systems. ISA-95[IEC 62264-1:2013] [21] is one of the international standard for enterprise control system integration that defines both physical arrangements and functional hierarchies from device to device communication to functional management at different granular levels. FIWARE [27] platform is an EU initiative towards the development of smart applications in manufacturing with a set of standardized APIs. Similarly EdgeX Foundry [17] is an open source standardized interoperability framework for IIoT Edge computing and Gaia-X [13] is a European standard for the development of next generation of data oriented infrastructures.

Shifting massive amounts of data towards the edge has also a downside: it requires to reconfigure the computation architecture in order to leverage computations on the edge components, and, as a consequence, also the ability to orchestrate the different heterogeneous responses from each SDK brought in by devices of the ecosystem. This is a massive ask to the ability to integrate not just data, but processes whose bits and pieces are often buried in the SDKs. Another challenging task is the integration of the edge intelligence [20], where the cost of delivering such solutions could be high if the advantages and limitations of this technology are not taken into account.

Model driven development (MDD) is one of the key approaches to develop heterogeneous systems from the conceptual modelling design to automated model-to-code transformations [25]. The main goal [28] of MDD is to develop rapid applications, that are flexible and adaptive to continuously changing requirements. The goal of this case study is to rely on model-driven capabilities as far as it is possible and convenient, i.e., without forcing the entire ecosystem to be integrated in a single platform. We use here the EdgeX Foundry platform as a middleware for IIoT components for data acquisition from heterogeneous sensors. Additionally, we use three low-code platforms for the development of functional pipelines: Tines for notifications among systems, Pyrus for data analytics and the DIME platform for process modeling and data reporting, empowering prototype-driven application development. All three follow to different extents the XMDD paradigm [24], where the technical details of the communication with a component or subsystem are encapsulated in high-level models, and this abstraction is useful in order to rapidly bootstrap a workflow and enable non-expert programmers to responsibly and directly participate in the software development cycle.

In the following, Sect. 2, discusses the industrial use-case with its system architecture, Sect. 3 covers the secure access policies and encryption techniques, followed by our conclusions and reflections in Sect. 4.

2 Industrial Use-Case: Safe Operation of Machines

In this section, we detail an industrial use case associated with the safe operation of a machine. Most manufacturing industries are equipped with complex machines on their shop floor, such as computer numerical control (CNC), coordinate measuring machines (CMM), 3D printers, etc. They are monitored and controlled through an industrial automation network in addition to the human-machine interface. A safe, healthy operating environment is essential in such factory and laboratory areas. The machine operators are expected to comply with several health and safety measures, such as wearing gloves, glasses, boots, aprons and hats where opportune. For example, in certain areas on the production floor protection measures such as boots and glasses are mandatory.

The machine operators however may not always comply and follow all the safety measures, incurring higher safety risks. This is a recognized occupational hazard, and companies and organizations have high interest in minimizing such risks and hazards. In this direction, an automatic system [11] consists of a wearable devices and an NVIDIA Jetson board is proposed in an industrial scenario for monitoring activities of personals and the behaviors of robotic systems.

One way to address non-compliance is by monitoring the production floor with cameras that continuously monitor these areas for proper behaviour along health and safety guidance, and also for assistance in case of need. Several of these machines have inbuilt sensors that measure various parameters such as vibrations, temperature, pressure etc. In many cases, these parameters can be used as a marker to identify the health of machines and tools. Several industries follow additional digitization strategies by employing additional IIoT sensing modules. The machine/tool health status inferred from these sensor data, combined with the camera-based monitoring, can then ensure that proper health and safety measures for both machines and operators are followed on an industrial workyard. Security measures have to be taken as well, here we concentrate on attribute-based cryptography as a means to ensure that there are no leaks of business or privacy sensitive data.

2.1 Architecture of the Use Case

Figure 1 shows the system architecture of the case study. Several different sensors installed in critical locations across the factory workyard monitor the working conditions on the floor of the Industrial Setup, on the left. Cameras are also installed to visually supervise the safety of the workers. When the workers

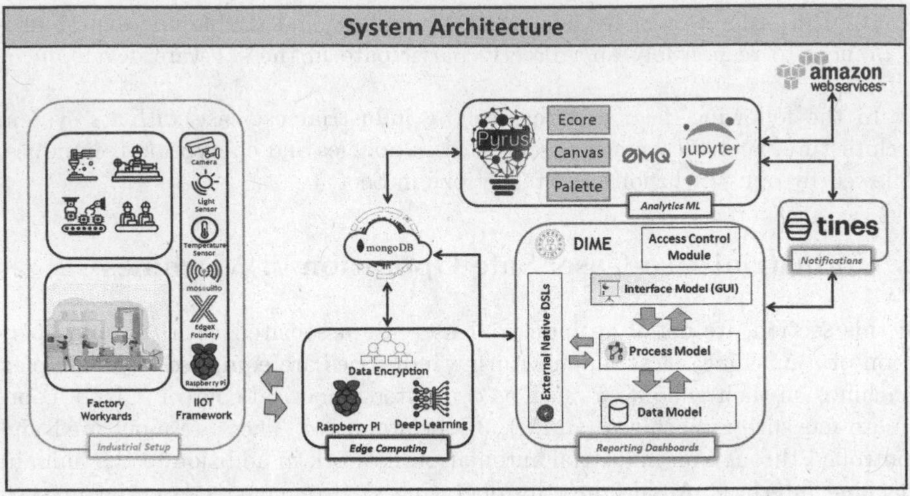

Fig. 1. System architecture of the case study

are working with critical equipment, the machine and environmental parameters/conditions, e.g. vibrations, temperature, light, etc. are recorded using the deployed sensors, belonging to the IIoT Framework. In addition, the camera feed is also used to record the workyard at random time intervals (Factory Workyard). These sensors and cameras are connected by an Edge-controlling device, here a Raspberry Pi, which securely sends the collected data to another Raspberry Pi that acts as an Edge-computing and collection node for all the devices across the factory workyard. This computing/collection node is responsible for communication with all the data nodes and for sending this data to a reliable database, in our case a MongoDB Atlas instance. It also performs deep learning-based computations at the edge (the Edge Computing system). Since the computing/collection node is a Raspberry Pi, its computing capacity is limited and is only used for computations that require an extra layer of privacy, accountability and scrutability. We consider here the facial recognition of the workers for an attendance call, or the identification of workers present in the workyard.

From MongoDB, the data is accessed by the Analytics/ML system. There, Pyrus is responsible for periodically running ML pipelines at fixed intervals by communicating with the Amazon Rekognition API to detect the PPE/safety equipment as shown in Fig. 2. The results from these pipelines are a number of reports on whether all workers are satisfying the safety requirements of their respective tasks. They are sent to the MongoDB Atlas database for remote secure access by workyard supervisors. When the results are stored on MongoDB, a notification about this event is sent via the Tines automation pipeline as shown in Fig. 3. Triggered by the Tines web-hook notification, a web application implemented in DIME fetches the data from MongoDB and generates reporting dashboards that can be viewed by the supervisors to make critical

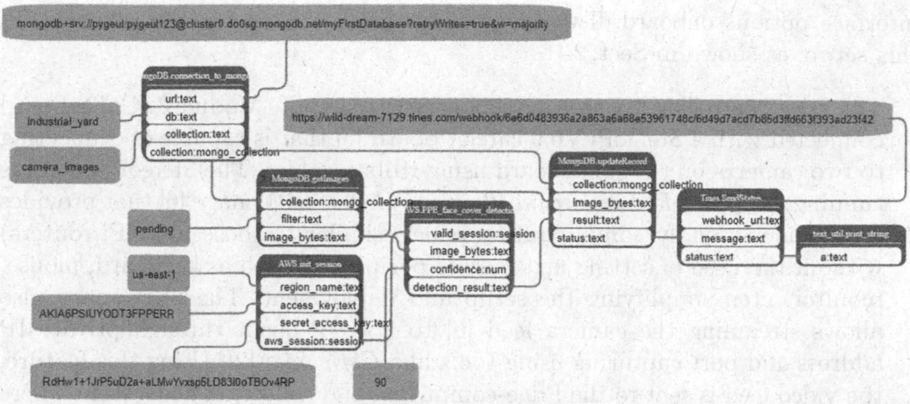

Fig. 2. Pyrus PPE detection pipeline

decisions, creating adequate Reporting Dashboards. The Access Control Module implements an attribute-based mechanism that abstracts from individuals and specific entities, basing the access through specific cryptography on attributes, that can be roles or other elements of a profile.

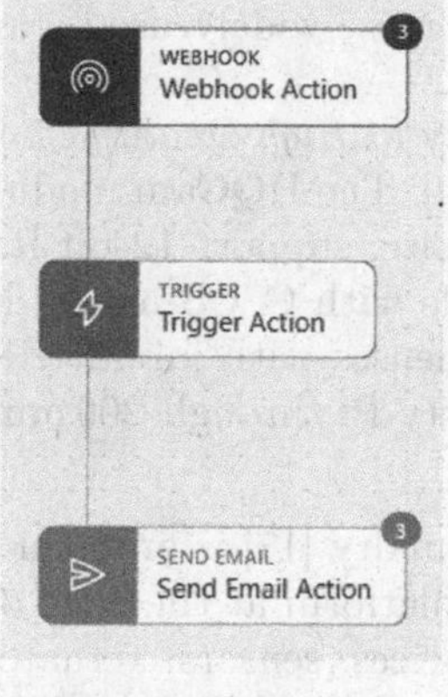

Fig. 3. Tines automation pipeline

2.2 The IT Ecosystem: Tools and Technologies

In this section, we briefly discuss the individual tools and technologies that form the heterogeneous ecosystem involved in this case study.

Raspberry Pi. The devices chosen for collection, computation and sharing of data in this research were Raspberry Pis due to their cost effectiveness, support for all devices used, support for Python and Linux, and availability of many interface options onboard. Two types of Raspberry Pis cover the two roles in this setup, as shown in Sect. 2.1:

- The Edge-controlling device is a Raspberry Pi Compute Module 3 (CM3) board connected with a StereoPi V0.9 carrier board [5] that is capable of connecting to two cameras on the same board using ribbon cables. The StereoPi device is running the *StereoPi Livestream Playground* v2 (SLP) image [6] that provides a consumer-friendly administration panel (similar to those in WiFi routers) without the need of setting up separate peripherals such as keyboard, mouse, monitor, etc., simplifying the setup and deployment. The SLP image also allows streaming the camera feed [6] to a UDP client through private IP address and port capturing using tools like *Gstreamer* [2]. Using this feature, the video feed is sent to the Edge-computing and collection node, from where it can be processed/stored according to the needs.
- The Edge-computing and collection device is a Raspberry Pi 4, model B with 4 GB RAM. It is the latest series in the Raspberry Pi series of single board computers with a high-performance 64-bit quad-core processor.

Sensors and Devices. The most commonly used sensors for the machine or tool maintenance are vibration and temperature sensors. *EPH-V11, EPH-V17, EPH-V18, EPH-T20* [18] are some of the widely used sensors that provide vibration and temperature data over wireless communication. They report data over ModBus, which is one of the most widely used standard for industrial communication.

The cameras are Raspberry Pi *High Quality Camera* (HQCam) Modules with CGL interchangeable lenses [4]. The HQCam modules have 12.3 megapixel cameras, 7.9 mm diagonal image size, support 12-bit RAW footage, have adjustable back focus and are compatible with C/CS mount lenses. The CGL lenses are 3 megapixel 6 mm HD CCTV lenses with inbuilt IR filter. The camera modules are connected to the Raspberry Pi through 200 mm ribbon cables.

Edgex Foundry. EdgeX Foundry [17] is an open source, vendor neutral, flexible, inter-operable, software platform at the edge of the network, that interacts with the physical world of devices, sensors, actuators, and other IoT objects. It is used as a middleware integration and virtualization platform, as it directly connects with the IoT devices and exposes high-level services through a REST API. We have described the EdgeX integration in DIME in [14,19].

DIME. The DIME [12] integrated modelling environment is a development environment to easily design, develop and deploy Web Applications in a low-code/no-code manner. It supports different model types (GUI, process and data models) that address different aspects of a Web Application. Built-in checks are supported both at the model and the project level for the purpose of debugging, as well as one-click code generation and deployment. Its *External Native DSL* layer, described in detail in [15], provides the flexibility to extend the platform capabilities with external services and platforms. This is the capability that we exploit for the integration of external devices, tools and platforms. We have not integrated everything in DIME for a number of reasons. First of all, DIME database and front-end components do not support the complex data types like video streams. In addition, we wanted to show the interoperability among the different heterogeneous tools and technologies.

Pyrus. The Pyrus [33] web-based no-code collaborative platform for data analytics provides the support of basic data manipulation and analytics operations in a model-driven fashion. It represents the individual capabilities as a collection of taxonomically grouped SIBs (Service-Independent Building blocks) in its Ecore (name of SIBs palette) section. On the backend, Pyrus communicates over the ZeroMQ protocol [8] with the connected Jupyter Hub, initially for functions discovery of the available SIBs, then at runtime to call and execute the advanced Python programs that the SIBs represent as proxies. Technically, the Pyrus workflows are data-flow orchestrations of SIBs.

Tines. The Tines [7] story board is a no-code automation tool that was initially built for automating workflows (called stories) in the domain of security. It also works in a low-code approach, with seven 'actions', i.e. generic components that are similar to highly parametric SIB templates in the world of DIME and Pyrus. Its webhook actions are here used as triggers, and its notification capabilities are domain-independent, so we use here a small story that implements an automation workflow for notifications.

Amazon Rekognition. The Amazon Rekognition [1] pre-trained deep learning API provides the capabilities of images and video analytics. Its models are trained by Amazon on billions of public photos from Amazon Prime and optimised for specific use-cases such as face detection, PPE detection, etc. We use this API in our Pyrus pipelines for the detection of safety-equipment among staff working in the factory workyard. The advantage of using Amazon Rekognition API in our Pyrus pipelines is that it does not require any additional setup and it worked out-of-the-box.

MongoDB. The MongoDB Atlas [3] is a cloud-based NoSQL database service that is used for high-volume data storage of semi-structured or unstructured data. In contrast to the structured records and tables used by relational databases, Atlas stores the data in the form of documents and collections which support the flexibility of different non-structured data types. The Atlas database is also scalable for Big Data storage with support for clusters that can store millions of documents. We use it here to store all the observational and processed data from different sensors, edge devices and compute systems. Atlas is pre-integrated in Tines, which provides no-code SIBs called 'actions' for easy communication with Atlas instances.

3 Access Control Using Attribute Based Encryption

To facilitate a fine-grained access control in the smart factory to which the workyard belongs, we utilize a public-key encryption, Ciphertext-Policy Attribute-Based Encryption (CP-ABE) [10] for this particular use-case. The CP-ABE algorithm allows for identification of the ciphertexts with access structures and the private keys with attributes. Whenever a message is encrypted using CP-ABE, it generates a ciphertext based on the condition that only a single user who is the owner of the specific attributes and satisfies the access structure will be able to produce the private key, and thereby decrypt the message. One of the highlights of CP-ABE is that it permits the definition of top-level policies, and is particularly suitable in scenarios where an individual wants to restrict the access to a specific information only to a subset of users within the same broadcast domain [9]. Another aspect of CP-ABE is that it is robust by design against collusion attacks [30]. A CP-ABE scheme consists of the following four basic algorithms:

- SETUP(). This algorithm generates the public key pk_c and master key mk_c.
- KEYGEN(mk_c, $Attr_c$). This algorithm takes mk_c and the user attribute list $Attr_c$ as input and returns a private key pv_c of user C.
- $\text{ABE}_{pk_c,w}(m)$. The encryption algorithm takes pk_c, an access policy w over the pool of attributes, and sensor reading m as input. It returns a ciphertext that can only be decrypted by a user that possesses a set of attributes $Attr_c$ such that $Attr_c$ satisfies w.
- $\text{ABD}_{pv_c}(\mathcal{C})$. The decryption algorithm takes pk_c, pv_c of user C and the ciphertext $\mathcal{C}$ as input. It outputs the plaintext m if and only if the user $Attr_c$ satisfies w.

For our industrial use case, we define a secure access policy along the lines of CP-ABE as follows: we consider three attributes in our use case scenario: *Sensor Examiner* (SE), *Video Analyst* (VA) and *Decision Manager* (DM) for three departments in our industrial use-case setting. The main characteristics of the three departments are described as follows:

- We first consider the Technical Fault Monitoring Department (TFMD). The primary task of TFMD is to monitor the readings of the three sensors (temperature, pressure, vibration) and it has access to the data collected by these three sensors. We assign SE attribute to TFMD.
- We then consider the Safety Surveillance Department (SSD). The main responsibility of SSD is to analyse the videos captured by the video camera. Thereby, the SSD has access to the readings of the video camera. We assign VA attribute to SSD.
- Finally, we consider the Operation Management Department (OMD). OMD takes the final call for the need of generating an alarm if any emergency occurs. Emergencies are reflected through the readings of the corresponding sensors and/or the videos. We assign DM attribute to OMD.

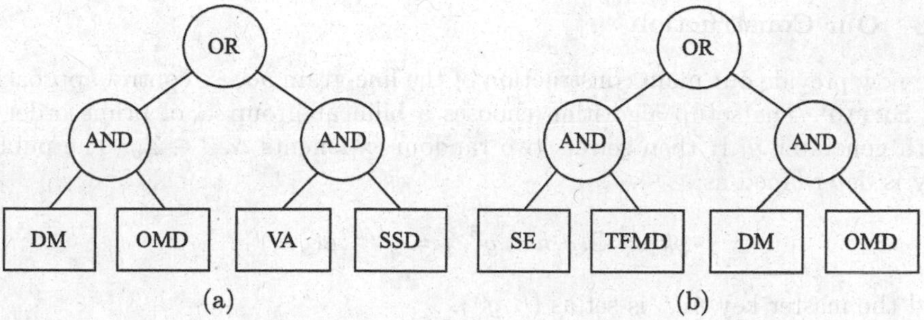

Fig. 4. Structure of access policies for our scheme: (a) Video surveillance, (b) Sensor reading.

3.1 Bilinear Map

Our CP-ABE is based on a bilinear map. Let $\mathbb{G}$ and $\mathbb{G}_T$ be two multiplicative cyclic groups of prime order p. Let g be a generator of $\mathbb{G}$ and e be a bilinear map, $e : \mathbb{G} \times \mathbb{G} \rightarrow \mathbb{G}_T$. The bilinear map e has the following properties:

- Bilinearity: for all $u, v \in \mathbb{G}$ and $a, b \in \mathbb{Z}_p$, we have $e(u^a, v^b) = e(u, v)^{ab}$.
- Non-degenerate: $e(g, g) \neq 1$.

Here, $\mathbb{G}$ is a bilinear group if the group operation in $\mathbb{G}$ and the bilinear map $e : \mathbb{G} \times \mathbb{G} \rightarrow \mathbb{G}_T$ are both efficiently computable. It is worth noting that the map e is symmetric as $e(g^a, g^b) = e(g, g)^{ab} = e(g^b, g^a)$.

3.2 Decision Tree

Let $\mathcal{T}$ be a decision tree representing an access structure. Figure 4 illustrates the simple decision trees that are generated from the access policies defined using the specific attributes and their entities. The access policies define which entities have access to specific data generated by the devices. As mentioned previously, we intend to allow fine-grained secure access control based on attributes, and for this we leverage public-key encryption, i.e., CP-ABE. In our case, the policies define that in a normal context, the Video Surveillance access policy is that either a DM belonging to the OMD department or a VA belonging to the SSD department can have access. Similarly, the Sensor reading policy is that either a SE belonging to the TFMD department or a DM belonging to the OMD department can have access.

As we complete the use case with the access to other elements of the ecosystem, the set of policies will become more complex, as different entities will be added, with typically partially overlapping rights. Only the individuals with the specific attributes will be able to access the data and/or perform operations.

3.3 Our Construction

We now provide our main construction of the fine-grain access control approach.

Setup. The setup algorithm chooses a bilinear group $\mathbb{G}$ of prime order p with generator g. It then selects two random exponents $\alpha, \beta \in \mathbb{Z}_p$. The public key is determined as:

$$pk_c = \mathbb{G}, g, h = g^{\beta}, f = g^{1/\beta}, e(g,g)^{\alpha}$$

and the master key mk_c is set as (β, g^{α}).

Keygen$(mk_c, Attr_c)$. Our key generation algorithm takes the master key mk_c and a set of attributes $S = \{SE, VA, DM\}$ associated with the department as inputs and provide a private key that identifies with that set. This algorithm initially chooses a random $r \in \mathbb{Z}_p$, and next random $r_j \in \mathbb{Z}_p$ for each attribute $j \in S$. In our algorithm, the private key is generated as follows:

$$pv_c = (D = g^{(\alpha+r)/\beta}, \forall j \in S : D_j = g^r \cdot H(j)^{r_j}, D'_j = g^{r_j}),$$

where H is a hash function, $H : \{0,1\}^* \rightarrow \mathbb{G}$.

ABE$_{pk_c,w}(m)$. Our encryption algorithm encrypts a message m under the decision tree structure $\mathcal{T}$. Beginning with the root node N, our algorithm chooses a random $\delta \in \mathbb{Z}_p$. Let L be the set of leaf nodes in $\mathcal{T}$. The ciphertext is generated by giving the decision tree $\mathcal{T}$ and determining:

$$\mathcal{C} = (\mathcal{T}, \tilde{C} = me(g,g)^{\alpha s}, C = h^s, \forall y \in Y : C_y = g^{q_y(0)}, C_{yp} = H(att(y))^{q_y(0)}),$$

where the function $att(x)$ signifies the attribute associated with the leaf node x in the decision tree $\mathcal{T}$. In the above equation, our algorithm generates random value s to calculate the shared value $q_y(0)$ for each attribute in the decision tree $\mathcal{T}$ using linear secret sharing. In CP-ABE, as private keys are generated randomly using the decision tree $\mathcal{T}$, it thus prevents collusion attack.

ABD$_{pv_c}(\mathcal{C})$. Our decryption algorithm executes recursively. Here, we present the simplest form of our decryption algorithm. If x is a leaf node, we let $i = att(x)$. If $i \in S$, our algorithm computes message m from the ciphertext $\mathcal{C}$ using pv_c as follows:

$$m = \frac{e(D_i, C_x)}{e(D'_i, C'_x)}.$$

We refer the reader to [10] for further details about the above computations.

4 Conclusions and Reflections

In terms of the Digital Thread [23], work on the overall lifecycle ecosystem that supports the smooth interoperation of a physical facility (like a machine, a factory or even a supply chain) and its direct or derived digital components (data and capabilities, but also processes, decisions, security) are still topic of ongoing research and are under-development. The integration is often done ad hoc, and successful platform attempts are domain and layer-specific, like EdgeX for IoT middleware. In this case study we have decided not to integrate everything in DIME, for a number of reasons.

First of all, we wanted to leverage the different integrations that already exist (like the IoT sensors in EdgeX, MongoDB in Tines, AWS in Pyrus) and preexisting communication routes (like EdgeX and MongoDB) and some of the workflows, and see how these islands of integration could be further brought together to a complex scenario. The experience is that there is still a considerable need of adaptation and testing, as for example the networks and protocols (which depend on configurations) and the specific software versions do matter.

We also decided against a full integration in DIME as for example the current DIME data types do not support video streams, therefore a direct integration of camera output would not be feasible at present. In this sense, we play to the individual strengths of the different platforms and integration and abstraction/virtualization approaches.

We wanted to show how a quite complex system of systems can come together in quasi-realistic settings. We also showed that it allows a piece-wise integration using four different platforms, three of whom using models and low code approaches (Tines, Pyrus and DIME). Of those, Pyrus and DIME are Cinco-products [26] and XMDD [24] approaches, whereby Pyrus is a web-based dataflow specialized tool for data analytics, while DIME is a much more complex and general-purpose tool with complex interdependent model types. Taken together, this is a step towards enabling a heterogeneous analysis and verification for distributed systems, as in [31], and the possibly hierarchical organization of reusable portions of logic in terms of features [22].

The inclusion of security is at the moment still simple: it is based on attributes that are roles. In this sense it is de facto similar to Role Based Access Control, but the use of attributes and their connection to the encryption make it more flexible (as one could also consider more attributes that are context-dependent), and more secure.

Acknowledgements. This project received funding from the European Union's Horizon 2020 research and innovation programme under the Marie Skłodowska-Curie Smart 4.0 Co-Fund, grant agreement No. 847577; research grants from Science Foundation Ireland (SFI) under Grant Number 16/RC/3918 (CONFIRM Centre), 2094-1 (Lero, the Software Research Centre) and 18/CRT/6223 (CRT-AI). We are also thankful to Dr. Kevin Moerman (National University of Ireland, Galway) for providing us the equipment and support for the StereoPi and cameras setup.

References

1. Amazon Rekognition | automate your image and video analysis with machine learning. https://aws.amazon.com/rekognition/. Accessed May 2022
2. GStreamer | Open Source Multimedia Framework. https://gstreamer.freedesktop.org/. Accessed May 2022
3. MongoDB Atlas Database | Multi-Cloud Database Service. https://www.mongodb.com/atlas/database. Accessed May 2022

4. Raspberry Pi High Quality Camera. https://www.raspberrypi.com/products/raspberry-pi-high-quality-camera/. Accessed May 2022
5. StereoPi - DIY stereoscopic camera based on Raspberry Pi. https://stereopi.com/. Accessed May 2022
6. StereoPi Wiki Main Page. https://wiki.stereopi.com/. Accessed May 2022
7. Tines | no-code automation for security teams. https://www.tines.com/lessons/storyboard/. Accessed May 2022
8. Zeromq | an open-source universal messaging library. https://zeromq.org/. Accessed May 2022
9. Ambrosin, M., Busold, C., Conti, M., Sadeghi, A.-R., Schunter, M.: Updaticator: updating billions of devices by an efficient, scalable and secure software update distribution over untrusted cache-enabled networks. In: Kutyłowski, M., Vaidya, J. (eds.) ESORICS 2014. LNCS, vol. 8712, pp. 76–93. Springer, Cham (2014). https://doi.org/10.1007/978-3-319-11203-9_5
10. Bethencourt, J., Sahai, A., Waters, B.: Ciphertext-policy attribute-based encryption. In: 2007 IEEE Symposium on Security and Privacy (SP 2007), pp. 321–334. IEEE (2007)
11. Boldo, M., et al.: Integrating wearable and camera based monitoring in the digital twin for safety assessment in the industry 4.0 era. In: Margaria, T., Steffen, B. (eds.) ISoLA 2022, LNCS 13704, pp. 184–194. Springer, Heidelberg (2022). https://doi.org/10.1007/978-3-031-19762-8_13
12. Boßelmann, S., et al.: DIME: a programming-less modeling environment for web applications. In: Margaria, T., Steffen, B. (eds.) ISoLA 2016. LNCS, vol. 9953, pp. 809–832. Springer, Cham (2016). https://doi.org/10.1007/978-3-319-47169-3_60
13. Braud, A., Fromentoux, G., Radier, B., Le Grand, O.: The road to European digital sovereignty with GAIA-x and IDSA. IEEE Network **35**(2), 4–5 (2021). https://doi.org/10.1109/MNET.2021.9387709
14. Chaudhary, H.A.A., Guevara, I., John, J., Singh, A., Margaria, T., Pesch, D.: Low-code internet of things application development for edge analytics. In: Camarinha-Matos, L. M., et al. (eds.) Internet of Things. IoT through a Multi-disciplinary Perspective, IFIPIoT 2022, IFIP AICT 665, pp. 1–20 (2022). https://doi.org/10.1007/978-3-031-18872-5_17
15. Chaudhary, H.A.A., Margaria, T.: DSL-based interoperability and integration in the smart manufacturing digital thread. Electron. Commun. EASST **80** (2022)
16. Cisco: Cisco, March 2022. https://www.cisco.com/c/en/us/solutions/collateral/executive-perspectives/annual-internet-report/white-paper-c11-741490.html
17. EdgeX Foundry: The preferred edge IoT plug and play ecosystem - eabled open source software platform. https://www.edgexfoundry.org/. Accessed May 2022
18. Erbessd instruments: Condition monitoring & industrial automation. https://www.erbessd-instruments.com/wireless-vibration-sensors/. Accessed May 2022
19. Guevara, I., Chaudhary, H.A.A., Margaria, T.: A low-code proposal for a rule-based engine integration in a digital thread platform context. In: International Manufacturing Conference IMC, vol. 38 (2022)
20. Guevara, I., Chaudhary, H.A.A., Margaria, T.: Model-driven edge analytics: practical use cases in smart manufacturing. In: Margaria, T., Steffen, B. (eds.) ISoLA 2022, LNCS 13704, pp. 406–421. Springer, Heidelberg (2022). https://doi.org/10.1007/978-3-031-19762-8_29
21. Enterprise-control system integration. Standard, International Organization for Standardization, May 2013

22. Karusseit, M., Margaria, T.: Feature-based modelling of a complex, online-reconfigurable decision support service. Electron. Notes Theor. Comput. Sci. **157**(2), 101–118 (2006)
23. Margaria, T., Schieweck, A.: The digital thread in industry 4.0. In: Ahrendt, W., Tapia Tarifa, S.L. (eds.) IFM 2019. LNCS, vol. 11918, pp. 3–24. Springer, Cham (2019). https://doi.org/10.1007/978-3-030-34968-4_1
24. Margaria, T., Steffen, B.: Service-orientation: conquering complexity with XMDD. In: Hinchey, M., Coyle, L. (eds.) Conquering Complexity, pp. 217–236. Springer (2012). https://doi.org/10.1007/978-1-4471-2297-5_10
25. Mellor, S.J., Clark, T., Futagami, T.: Model-driven development: guest editors' introduction. IEEE Softw. **20**(5), 14–18 (2003). ISSN 0740–7459
26. Naujokat, S., Lybecait, M., Kopetzki, D., Steffen, B.: CINCO: a simplicity-driven approach to full generation of domain-specific graphical modeling tools. Int. J. Softw. Tools Technol. Transfer **20**, 1–28 (2018). https://doi.org/10.1007/s10009-017-0453-6
27. Salhofer, P., Joanneum, F.: Evaluating the FIWARE platform: a case-study on implementing smart application with FIWARE. In: Proceedings of the 51st Hawaii International Conference on System Sciences. vol. 9, pp. 5797–5805 (2018)
28. Sanchis, R., García-Perales, Ó., Fraile, F., Poler, R.: Low-code as enabler of digital transformation in manufacturing industry. Appl. Sci. **10**(1), 12 (2020)
29. Shi, W., Cao, J., Zhang, Q., Li, Y., Xu, L.: Edge computing: vision and challenges. IEEE Internet Things J. **3**(5), 637–646 (2016). https://doi.org/10.1109/JIOT.2016.2579198
30. Song, H., Yin, F., Han, X., Luo, T., Li, J.: MPDS-RCA: multi-level privacy-preserving data sharing for resisting collusion attacks based on an integration of CP-ABE and LDP. Comput. Secur. **112**, 102523 (2022)
31. Steffen, B., Margaria, T., Claßen, A., et al.: Heterogeneous analysis and verification for distributed systems. Softw. Concepts Tools **17**, 13–25 (1996)
32. Wang, X., Han, Y., Leung, V.C., Niyato, D., Yan, X., Chen, X.: Convergence of edge computing and deep learning: a comprehensive survey. IEEE Commun. Surv. Tutorials **22**(2), 869–904 (2020)
33. Zweihoff, P., Steffen, B.: Pyrus: an online modeling environment for no-code data-analytics service composition. In: Margaria, T., Steffen, B. (eds.) ISoLA 2021. LNCS, vol. 13036, pp. 18–40. Springer, Cham (2021). https://doi.org/10.1007/978-3-030-89159-6_2

Trust and Security Analyzer for Collaborative Digital Manufacturing Ecosystems

Pasindu Kuruppuarachchi(✉), Susan Rea, and Alan McGibney

Munster Technological University, Cork, Ireland
p.kuruppuarachchi@mycit.ie, {susan.rea,alan.mcgibney}@mtu.ie
https://www.mtu.ie/

Abstract. To ensure competitiveness and to meet current market demands, the manufacturing industry continues to evolve into a more agile and integrated operating environment. Digital thread provides vital technology enablers to support this and drive the digitalization of the manufacturing sector to improve product quality, reduce time to market, support customization, etc. Digital thread capabilities provide the foundation for manufacturers to create digital twins; a virtual replica of a physical process, system, or asset supporting data-driven analysis and optimization. Connecting multiple digital twins distributed across owners, networks, and domains will create collaborative ecosystems. Since various systems need to connect to facilitate this ecosystem, trust and security are significant concerns. This paper proposes a trust and security analyzer that will aid in evaluating the trustworthiness of individual digital twins. Security, resilience, reliability, uncertainty, dependability, and goal analysis are the primary evaluation criteria for the proposed analyzer. When the trustworthiness of an individual digital twin increases, so too does the overall collaborative ecosystem.

Keywords: Digital thread · Digital twin · Trust · Smart manufacturing · Collaborative ecosystem

1 Introduction

Advanced and integrated digital technologies are required to connect all assets, systems, and decision-makers in a collaborative manufacturing ecosystem [15]. For example, considering that a product's life cycle requires connectivity across all systems, sub-systems, and processes involved, from the design of an asset right through to its decommissioning. As such, there is a need for a robust communication framework, such as a digital thread, to create such integration

This research work is supported by Science Foundation Ireland Centre for Research Training focused on Future Networks and the Internet of Things (AdvanceCRT), under Grant number 18/CRT/6222.

T. Margaria and B. Steffen (Eds.): ISoLA 2022, LNCS 13704, pp. 208–218, 2022.
https://doi.org/10.1007/978-3-031-19762-8_15

across multiple and heterogeneous connection points. The digital thread has emerged as a key enabler that can be used to connect various data flows and create an integrated view of an asset's life cycle [1,2,12,13,21,24]. Others have leveraged digital thread as a mechanism to digitally verify product origin and enhance visibility across a manufacturing process [13].

An article [1] indicates that the digital thread can be used not only for Product Lifecycle Management (PLM) but also can connect with Enterprise Resource Planning (ERP) and Asset Lifecycle Management (ALM). It also provides the perspective of digital thread being used to connect multiple digital twins across these chains and business processes [15].

A Digital Twin (DT) is a digital replica of an asset or a process in the physical domain. The main objective of having a DT is to enhance the capabilities of an asset, reduce interruptions, and operate efficiently. Leveraging this concept, a digital thread can also be utilized to connect multiple digital twins and create a collaborative DT ecosystem. For example, consider the scenario shown in the Fig. 1. Here, two kinds of digital twins are identified: a product DT and asset base DT.

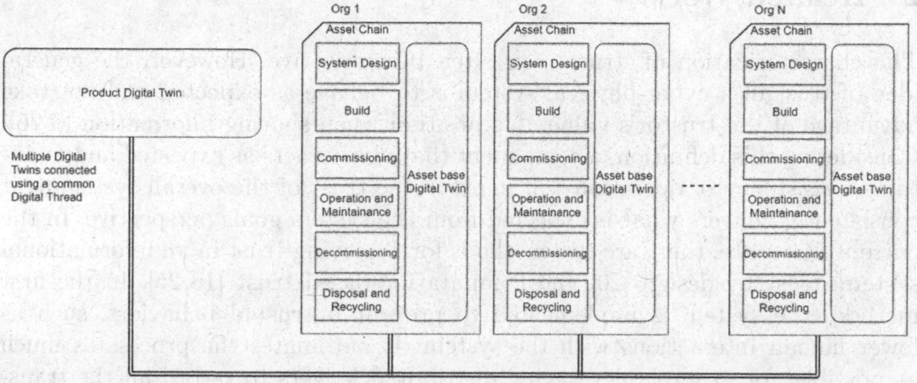

Fig. 1. Connecting multiple digital twins to create a collaborative ecosystem using the digital thread

For example, in this context, an Original Equipment Manufacturer (OEM) can produce a robotic arm that will be deployed as part of a manufacturing process. It can build a DT of this robotic arm based on the design and manufacturing of the device. In this case, a robotic arm DT is linked to the product of the OEM. The organization purchasing that robotic arm views this as an asset. It has the potential to leverage the existing (or part of) OEM DT or build a new DT that aligns with the context of the use of the robotic arm to manage and optimize the asset.

Leveraging these standpoint differences, asset-based DT learning can be used to improve the robotic arm's capabilities. This creates a collaborative situation that benefits both OEM and purchasing organizations. The OEM can produce improved versions of robotic arms, while purchasing organizations can improve the capabilities of their on-site robotic arms via OEM updates and modifications. Furthermore, as this scales (i.e., multiple robotic arms used in multiple organizations), it creates a scenario where rich data sets can be generated and utilized in different ways by the parties involved (e.g., fault detection, optimization, operating efficiencies).

A digital thread facilitates the connectivity and integration of these DT instances. As it will connect multiple systems and digital twins from different organizations, trust and security are essential considerations for the implementation. Un-trusted behaviors may considerably impact the entire ecosystem, such as incorrect data on the system, security vulnerabilities, conflicts between organizations, supply chain issues, etc. To address these challenges and to reduce the associated risk, this paper will present a trust and security analyzer to evaluate and represent the trustworthiness of connecting systems. This aims to improve a digital ecosystem's overall trust and security posture and create a robust information sharing platform.

2 Related Work

The characterization of "trust" can often be subjective. However, the general idea of trust in a cyber-physical system is to behave as expected and not take advantage of the trustor's vulnerable position when sharing information [6,26]. Considering this definition, a component that always acts as expected and maintains consistency of operation will improve the trust of the overall system as it consistently delivers what is expected from the system goals perspective. In the current literature, there are two methods for achieving trust in an informational system: trust by design [20] and computation-based trust [18,25]. In the first method, the system is implemented to prevent untrusted behaviors, such as fewer human interactions with the system. It automates the process as much as possible, for example, leveraging distributed ledgers to record all the transactions to keep everyone accountable for their actions, etc.[9,10,17,19,22]. This way, the system eliminates most of the possible trust-related vulnerabilities in the design and implementation phases. However, no system will be perfectly secured. Computation based trust systems are also implemented to strengthen trust and security. Computation based trust means analyzing system participants' behaviors and checking for anomalies in their actions. This is a continuous process; eventually, systems can develop the reputation of being trustworthy, which propagates to the overall system's trust posture. The most common computation based trust evaluations is Quality of Service (QoS) base analysis [7,8,14,16,25], ranking, and reputation information about their past behaviors [3,8,20,23,25]. QoS based trust evaluates if the system is providing a high-quality service for other participants in the system. If this is the case, it indicates that the entity is less likely to be an attacker, as providing continuous QoS requires a significant investment in the service infrastructure. Considering digital thread operations, it is essential to implement both trusts by design and computational trust methods to strengthen the trust and security posture of the manufacturing ecosystem.

The IIC defines trust based on five categories: safety, security, privacy, reliability, and resilience [11]. Some of these traits, such as safety and privacy, are strictly regulated by government agencies to ensure that all firms adhere to appropriate norms. For example, the European GDPR[1] (General Data Protection Regulation) enforces data protection and privacy in the European Union and the European Economic Area. Although IIC trust characteristics are largely common to various industrial applications, trust has an industry-specific perspective. Fatima et al. conducted an interview-based study to determine the most important criteria for multi-stakeholder trust [5]. According to this study, several factors, such as industry, prior experiences, and perception, will determine trust between two stakeholders. The most typical concerns about trust are operational responsibility, partnership goals, and long-term relationship emphasis. Operational responsibility, on the other hand, may be achieved by methodical execution. However, partnership goals and long-term emphasis are extremely subjective. When it comes to operational responsibility utilizing architectural components to ensure that all participating digital twins and systems behave as planned is required. However, the use case will determine the collaboration goals and long-term operational vision.

A DT is a system that consists of various parts, the physical system, communications, software tools, and services that create the digital version of that physical system. Their digital form makes them vulnerable to cyber security threats. In the manufacturing domain, physical devices and systems are typically secured from an IT perspective, and access to the outside world is typically limited. However, to maximize the potential of DT, it sometimes makes sense to have them exposed to the external world to leverage data (third party), other services (e.g., Industrial IoT), and users (e.g., third-party providers) using the internet over (potentially unsecured) networks. This additional network of processes increases the attack surface and the risk associated with the system's security posture. If a DT is not adequately secured, it can be exploited by attackers that can potentially access all the physical asset information and the DT predictions and insights and even send harmful commands to the physical counterpart.

Modern information systems use Application Programming Interfaces (API) to expose capabilities and data sharing outside organizational boundaries. This approach supports breaking down monolithic systems into microservices. It provides more modular and flexible software systems that help application developers to reuse and adapt faster to changing requirements. Unfortunately, APIs can also suffer from attacks for web applications such as cross-site scripting (XSS), SQL injection, cross-site request forgery (CSRF), etc. A shared secret key is one of the common techniques used to authenticate users, called an API key. This is an easy solution for authentication, but it is vulnerable to credential theft and compromise attacks, injections, and man-in-the-middle attacks [4]. The following solutions are typically implemented to mitigate API security issues [4].

1. Use of API Gateway to authenticate API key.

[1] https://gdpr-info.eu/.

2. Hash-based Message Authentication (HMAC) can be used to verify the integrity of the key. Before creating HMAC using the API key, additional data will be added that only legitimate users can access. This will prevent API key forgeries.
3. SSL and TLS certificates to prevent man-in-the-middle attacks.
4. Separate API keys and shortened life span of a key.
5. Conditional access tokens combine with API keys to add multiple layers of access validations.
6. Multi-factor authentication.

Considering the current literature concerning trust analysis, there are no DT specific trust analyzers. Some analyzers focus on one aspect, such as reliability, rather than considering all the ecosystem possibilities. Furthermore, some concepts consider multiple categories, such as IIC [11] resilience, privacy, security, and reliability. However, it is a general concept. The DT-based collaborative ecosystem's needs are somewhat different from other systems because it is a multiple data points aggregating system from different domains, owners, application domains, etc.

As mentioned above, there are ways to mitigate security-related concerns in the operational environment. However, security must be evaluated when connecting with other systems, such as a DT connecting to a digital thread. The work presented in this paper will focus on developing a trust and security analyzer to evaluate individual DTs and systems that will connect through a digital thread. Hence, this study proposes to bootstrap a digital thread connector with an analyzer to evaluate individual trustworthiness that can be utilized to facilitate robust data sharing among disparate and independent DT.

3 Architecture of Digital Thread Connector

The proposed architecture aims to support digital twins and systems involved in the manufacturing life cycle. The core of the architecture is the digital thread connector to facilitate this secure, trusted connection with other ecosystem participants. The Fig. 2 presents an ecosystem of organizations that host a connector to link internally operating DTs and systems via the digital thread. Providing a bridge via this connector allows the operator an abstraction from underlying operational functions and implements and enforces additional security measures before connecting with other external systems. Where appropriate, these can also be utilized to isolate threats without compromising traditional operations.

The Fig. 3, shows the five support services encapsulated within the digital thread connector. Communication monitoring services, intrusion detection, and prevention services are used to monitor the communication between connectors and notify if there are any unusual behaviors in the data traffic.

The data endpoint manager and translation service will support multiple domains and data models to be exchanged between stakeholders. A digital thread connector will store all the data locally, while all the operational and data transactions will also be recorded in a distributed ledger as activity events. This will

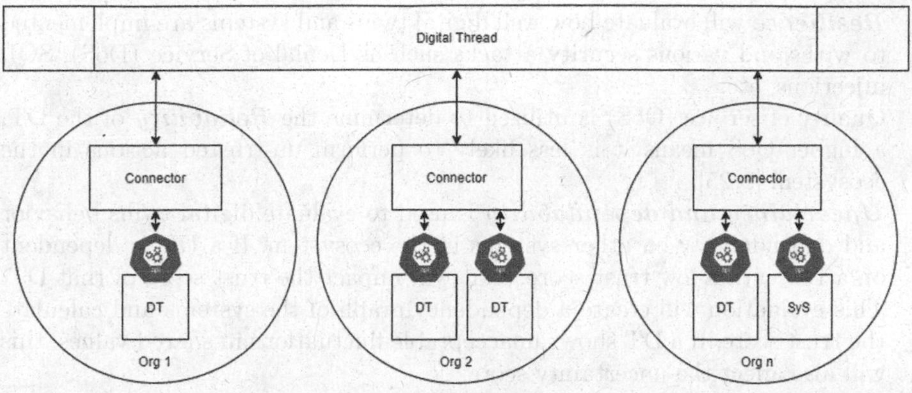

Fig. 2. Enhanced digital thread utilizing a mediator (connector) architectural pattern

provide an immutable record of activities between participants that can be used to ensure they are accountable for their actions and support conflict resolution. However, using a distributed ledger may introduce additional performance overhead, as such, the choice of technology, consensus mechanism, and data model are critical design considerations that must be taken into account with care.

If it is a mission critical system, it is envisaged that all transactions will be recorded in a distributed ledger, while less important transactions can be kept local data store.

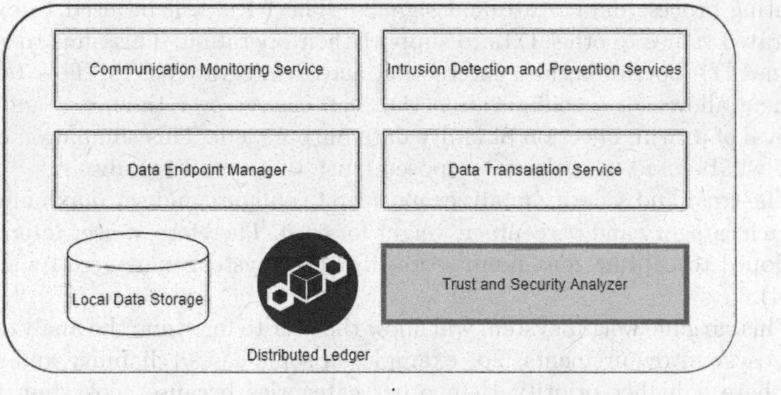

Fig. 3. Connector services for managed interactions across digital thread

The main focus of this paper is on the trust and security analyzer that encapsulates five categories of trust:

- ***Security*** related concerns such as API and system vulnerabilities, encryption techniques, etc., will be analyzed. Based on these features, overall security will be evaluated for connecting digital twins and systems.

- ***Resilience*** will evaluate how well digital twins and systems are implemented to withstand various security attacks such as Denial of Service (DoS), SQL injections, etc.
- Quality of service (QoS) is utilized to determine the ***Reliability*** of the DT, a higher QoS means it is less likely to perform un-trusted actions in the ecosystem [8,25].
- ***Uncertainty and dependability*** is used to evaluate digital twins behavior and dependability on other systems in the ecosystem. If a DT is dependent on a DT with a low trust score, that will impact the trust score of that DT. This evaluation will create a dependency graph of the systems and calculate the trust score. If a DT shows unacceptable fluctuations in shared values, this will also affect the uncertainty score.
- When multiple stakeholders connect to create a collaborative ecosystem, there will be a set of goals to achieve from this ecosystem. The ***Goal analysis*** module will monitor how well individual digital twins achieve these goals. If digital twins are trustworthy, they will operate to achieve these shared goals rather than their individual disruption goals.

4 Initial Implementation

The initial implementation tests involve the invocation of multiple DTs that represent a collaborative manufacturing process. Each DT has an associated set of API functions that enable DTs to communicate with each other to share data. Each twin incorporates a mathematical function that equates data values (representing process data, state and signals). The APIs will be used to exchange generated values to other DTs to support their operation. This aims to simulate internal DT operation, and interaction across integrated DTs. This test environment allows for a configuration that can change over time, e.g. addition or removal of a twin, injection of faulty data outputs, etc. This simulation environment will be used to evaluate proposed trust and security analyzer.

The trust and security analyzer must first configure and set maximum scores for each category and percentage weight for each. Therefore, a user interface was developed to capture maximum scores from the system manager (As shown in Fig. 4).

This variable weight system will allow the user to fine-tune the analyzer based on ecosystem requirements. For example, in some cases reliability and security may have a higher priority than other categories because ecosystem need to have high availability. To reflect customization on the ecosystem, weights can be increased on specific categories and reduced from others.

Current implementation of the connector is focused on the security analysis of DT API endpoints. The analyzer is capable of identifying and evaluating 22 known API vulnerabilities as mentioned below. These vulnerabilities are further categorized into three groups based on severity. As shown in Eq. 1, the weighted average of all three severity groups will be considered for the final API vulnerability value (A). A weight for each severity level is represented using (w_i), and

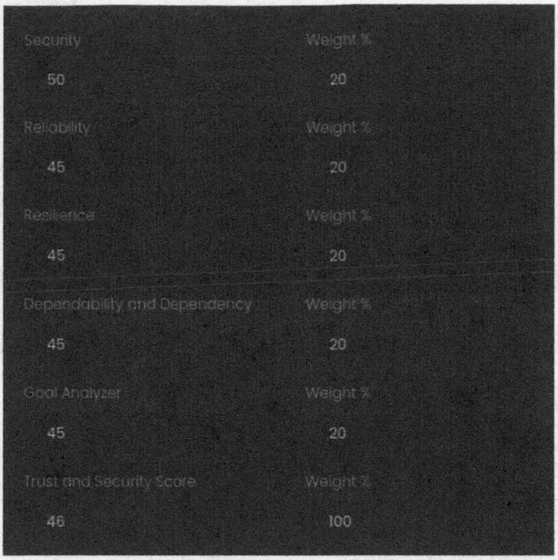

Fig. 4. Trust and security analyzer configuration panel

(x_i) will represent the number of vulnerabilities detected in each category. Initial weights are set to 6, 3, and 1 for high, mid, and low severity, these values are still subject to further evaluation through simulation and user tests.

$$A = \frac{\sum_{i=1}^{n} w_i . x_i}{\sum_{i=1}^{n} w_i} \tag{1}$$

The following tests are the main security evaluations out of 22 vulnerability tests.

1. CORS (Cross-Origin Resource Sharing) misconfiguration
2. Authentication and session management
3. CSRF (Cross-site Request Forgery)
4. Brute force attack limits
5. Token validations
6. SQL injections
7. Cross-site scripting
8. Request header manipulation
9. Response information

The API security analyzer utilizes an open source REST API penetration testing tool known as Astra[2]. This was extended to include additional security tests to align with the needs of DTs, such as data outliers, anomalies (based on application use case), and the use of encryption techniques to prevent leaking sensitive information.

[2] https://github.com/flipkart-incubator/Astra.

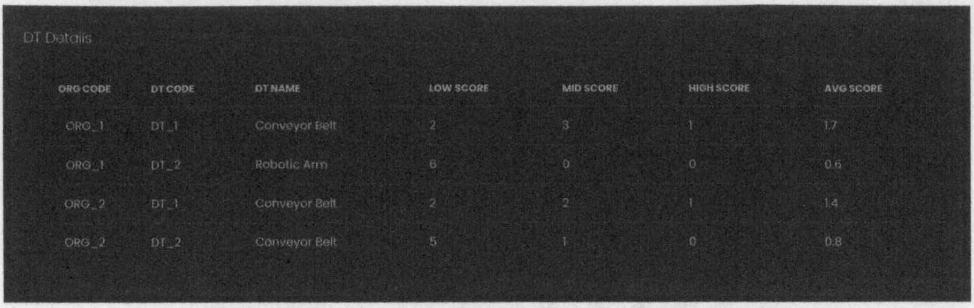

DT Details

ORG CODE	DT CODE	DT NAME	LOW SCORE	MID SCORE	HIGH SCORE	AVG SCORE
ORG_1	DT_1	Conveyor Belt	2	3	1	1.7
ORG_1	DT_2	Robotic Arm	6	0	0	0.6
ORG_2	DT_1	Conveyor Belt	2	2	1	1.4
ORG_2	DT_2	Conveyor Belt	5	1	0	0.8

Fig. 5. Sample trust and security analyzer, API vulnerability results

The trust and security analyzer agent runs continuously as part of the digital thread connector to proactively analyze individual digital twins and evaluate and report the trust scores for individual DT. The Fig. 5 shows an example setup showing results obtained from the trust and security analyzer. A higher average score means that the DT or system is having more security problems. Based on these metrics, other participants can decide whether to accept or reject connectivity and/or data from that particular DT or system.

5 Conclusion

The mainly digital thread is an interoperable layer between multiple product life cycle phases. However, a digital thread can also use to connect multiple digital twins to create a collaboration ecosystem. In this case, trust and security are vital concerns. This paper proposes a trust and security analyzer to evaluate individual digital twins and systems that will connect using a digital thread. Trust and security analyzer consists of five evaluation categories (security, resilience, reliability, dependability and uncertainty, and goal analysis) representing operational and management aspects of the life cycle phases and digital twins. The initial ongoing implementation is focused on realizing the trust and security analyzer's functionality, including API analysis and setup process. The next phase is to complete the analyzer and evaluate its performance in a real-world scenario.

References

1. IIoT for Smart Manufacturing part 2 - Digital Thread and Digital Twin. https://www.arcweb.com/blog/iiot-smart-manufacturing-part-2-digital-thread-and-digital-twin. (Accessed 09 Aug 2022)
2. Global horizons final report united states air force global science and technology vision (2013). https://www.hsdl.org/?abstract&did=741377
3. Albuquerque, R.D.O., Cohen, F.F., Mota, J.L.T., Sousa, R.T.D.: Analysis of a trust and reputation model applied to a computational grid using software agents. In: Proceedings - 2008 International Conference on Convergence and Hybrid Information Technology, ICHIT 2008, pp. 196–203 (2008). https://doi.org/10.1109/ICHIT.2008.182

4. Badhwar, R.: Intro to api security - issues and some solutions! The CISO's Next Frontier, pp. 239–244 (2021). https://doi.org/10.1007/978-3-030-75354-2_29
5. Barrane, F.Z., Ndubisi, N.O., Kamble, S., Karuranga, G.E., Poulin, D.: Building trust in multi-stakeholder collaborations for new product development in the digital transformation era. Benchmarking: Int. J. **28**(1), 205–228 (2021). https://doi.org/10.1108/BIJ-04-2020-0164
6. Cioroaica, E., et al.: Towards creation of automated prediction systems for trust and dependability evaluation. In: 2020 28th International Conference on Software, Telecommunications and Computer Networks, SoftCOM 2020 (2020). https://doi.org/10.23919/SoftCOM50211.2020.9238329
7. Cioroaica, E., Chren, S., Buhnova, B., Kuhn, T., DImitrov, D.: Reference architecture for trust-Based digital Ecosystems. In: Proceedings - 2020 IEEE International Conference on Software Architecture Companion, ICSA-C 2020, pp. 266–273 (2020). https://doi.org/10.1109/ICSA-C50368.2020.00051
8. Dessì, N., Pes, B., Fugini, M.G.: A distributed trust and reputation framework for scientific grids. In: Proceedings of the 2009 3rd International Conference on Research Challenges in Information Science, RCIS 2009, pp. 265–274 (2009). https://doi.org/10.1109/RCIS.2009.5089290
9. Dietz, M., Putz, B., Pernul, G.: A distributed ledger approach to digital twin secure data sharing. In: Foley, S.N. (ed.) DBSec 2019. LNCS, vol. 11559, pp. 281–300. Springer, Cham (2019). https://doi.org/10.1007/978-3-030-22479-0_15
10. Hasan, H.R., et al.: A blockchain-based approach for the creation of digital twins. IEEE Access **8**, 34113–34126 (2020). https://doi.org/10.1109/ACCESS.2020.2974810
11. Industrial Internet Consortium: The Industrial Internet of Things: Managing and Assessing Trustworthiness for IIoT in Practice, pp. 1–40 (2019)
12. Kraft, E.M.: Hpcmp create^{TM}-av and the air force digital thread. In: 53rd AIAA Aerospace Sciences Meeting (2015). https://doi.org/10.2514/6.2015-0042
13. Kurfess, T.R., Grimes, H.D.: cyberphysical passports. The Bridge (NAE) **51**(1), 1–6 (2020). https://www.ornl.gov/publication/role-digital-thread-security-resilience-and-adaptability-manufacturing
14. Ma, W., Wang, X., Hu, M., Zhou, Q.: Machine learning empowered trust evaluation method for IoT devices. IEEE Access **9**, 65066–65077 (2021). https://doi.org/10.1109/ACCESS.2021.3076118
15. Margaria, T., Schieweck, A.: The digital thread in industry 4.0. In: Ahrendt, W., Tapia Tarifa, S.L. (eds.) IFM 2019. LNCS, vol. 11918, pp. 3–24. Springer, Cham (2019). https://doi.org/10.1007/978-3-030-34968-4_1
16. Mayoral, A., et al.: Control orchestration protocol: Unified transport api for distributed cloud and network orchestration. J. Opt. Commun. Netw. **9**, A216–A222 (2017). https://doi.org/10.1364/JOCN.9.00A216
17. Putz, B., Dietz, M., Empl, P., Pernul, G.: EtherTwin: blockchain-based secure digital Twin information management. Inf. Process. Manage. **58**(1), 102425 (2021). https://doi.org/10.1016/j.ipm.2020.102425
18. Qureshi, B., Min, G., Kouvatsos, D.: Collusion detection and prevention with fire+ trust and reputation model. Proceedings - 10th IEEE International Conference on Computer and Information Technology, CIT-2010, 7th IEEE International Conference on Embedded Software and Systems, ICESS-2010, ScalCom-2010 pp. 2548–2555 (2010). https://doi.org/10.1109/CIT.2010.433
19. Sahal, R., Alsamhi, S.H., Brown, K.N., O'shea, D., McCarthy, C., Guizani, M.: Blockchain-empowered digital twins collaboration: smart transportation use case. Machines **9**(9), 1–33 (2021). https://doi.org/10.3390/machines9090193

20. Serov, I., Leitner, M.: An experimental approach to reputation in e-participation. In: Proceedings - 2016 International Conference on Software Security and Assurance, ICSSA 2016, pp. 37–42 (2017). https://doi.org/10.1109/ICSSA.2016.14
21. Singh, V., Willcox, K.E.: Decision-making under uncertainty for a digital thread-enabled design process. J. Mech. Design Trans. ASME **143**(9), 1–12 (2021). https://doi.org/10.1115/1.4050108
22. Suhail, S., Hussain, R., Jurdak, R., Hong, C.S.: Trustworthy digital twins in the industrial Internet of Things with blockchain. IEEE Internet Comput. **7801**(c), 1–8 (2021). https://doi.org/10.1109/MIC.2021.3059320
23. Sun, W., Xu, N., Wang, L., Zhang, H., Zhang, Y.: Dynamic Digital Twin and Federated Learning with Incentives for Air-Ground Networks. IEEE Trans. Netw. Sci. Eng. **4697**(c), 1–13 (2020). https://doi.org/10.1109/TNSE.2020.3048137
24. West, T.D., Pyster, A.: Untangling the digital thread: the challenge and promise of model-based engineering in defense acquisition. INSIGHT **18**, 45–55 (8 2015). https://doi.org/10.1002/INST.12022, https://onlinelibrary.wiley.com/doi/full/10.1002/inst.12022
25. Zong, B., Xu, F., Jiao, J., Lv, J.: A broker-assisting trust and reputation system based on artificial neural network. In: Conference Proceedings - IEEE International Conference on Systems, Man and Cybernetics, pp. 4710–4715 (2009). https://doi.org/10.1109/ICSMC.2009.5346098
26. Özalp Özer, Zheng, Y., Ren, Y.: Trust, trustworthiness, and information sharing in supply chains bridging china and the u.s. SSRN Elect. J. **60**, 2435–2460 (2014). https://doi.org/10.2139/SSRN.1961774, https://papers.ssrn.com/abstract=1961774

DISTiL: DIStributed Industrial Computing Environment for Trustworthy DigiTaL Workflows: A Design Perspective

Alan McGibney(✉) and Sourabh Bharti

Munster Technological University, Bishopstown, Cork, Ireland

alan.mcgibney@mtu.ie

Abstract. Digitalisation is continuing to play an essential role in modernising Europe's industrial capabilities, allowing companies to be well positioned for global competitiveness and sustainability. Data is viewed as an essential resource for economic growth, competitiveness, innovation, job creation and societal progress. As such, EU industry needs to develop highly integrated digital networks that can underpin the creation of innovative digital services. While the convergence of novel digital technologies are viewed as key enablers, their inherent complexity, heterogeneity and dynamicity create challenges for managing workflows and trust at scale. As a result valuable data assets are disparate sitting in silos across systems, roles and business functions and go unutilised. In addition, large volumes of data sit across organisations that can provide a rich cross-pollination of experience to identify common patterns, opportunities, and train robust models to support innovative data-driven services. The work presented here outlines an initial analysis of the system requirements, architectural considerations, and challenges that need to be overcome to realise distributed and trusted digital workflows with a focus on use cases in the domain of smart manufacturing.

Keywords: Distributed computing · Digital manufacturing · Architecture design

1 Introduction

1.1 Motivation

The convergence of industrial computing infrastructure (e.g. IIoT, 5G, and AI) and its integration within a holistic digital strategy enables smart manufacturers to improve forecasting, operate with extreme flexibility and accelerate the pathway towards hyper-connectivity through agile ecosystem of suppliers, customers and talent, with resilience and sustainability at the core. To achieve this, there is a need to provide secure, robust and trusted digital thread that can instill assurance and protection when integrating advanced digital technologies into existing processes. The aim is to create standardised, secure and

This publication has emanated from research conducted with the financial support of Science Foundation Ireland under Grant Number SFI/16/RC/3918 (Confirm).

T. Margaria and B. Steffen (Eds.): ISoLA 2022, LNCS 13704, pp. 219–226, 2022.
https://doi.org/10.1007/978-3-031-19762-8_16

intelligent digital frameworks that accelerate digital transformation through connectivity and a collaborative data management approach to create agile, resilient and sustainable factories of the future.

The challenge however is to provide the tools, mechanisms and knowledge that can address two key design considerations:

1. What architectures and management approaches are required to support the distribution of intelligence from cloud to edge supporting resource aware (energy, compute, network) data driven services?
2. What approaches are required to bring cross-sectoral organizations together to collaborate in a shared learning process while protecting their commercially sensitive data.

To achieve, it is proposed to utilize an open distributed industrial computing environment that delivers trusted digital workflows while maintaining data sovereignty and privacy as core design features.

1.2 Impact for Smart Manufacturing

In the short-term, to support manufacturers there is a need to advance research capacity focused on the technological areas of industrial data spaces, data privacy, distributed ledger technology, machine learning, and edge computing. At the practical level, this needs to provide important new knowledge for systems integrators, data and business analysts, factory managers and research community. This will advance industrial capability by providing key building blocks for next-generation industrial systems, building on advanced digital technologies such as Blockchain and machine learning methods and data security. The adoption of such technologies has the potential to increase the competitiveness and resilience of industry across evolving manufacturing value-chains. Considering the longer term impact, such systems will facilitate the transition to Industry 5.0 (I5.0). Smart factories of the future will be driven by a collaborative model where man and machine are closely interlinked, where robots do the mechanical production work, but humans acting as the creative architects, enabling personalized products and ensuring the factory runs smoothly and sustainably. This concept takes advantage of Industry 4.0 (digitalization), big data and artificial intelligence to address new and emerging requirements in the industrial, societal and environmental landscape. This means exploiting data to increase production flexibility, reliability and quality while creating robust industrial value chains; it requires deploying technology that adapts to the worker, rather than the other way around.

The work presented is focused on exploring the design considerations to create a DIStributed Industrial Computing Environment for Trustworthy digiTaL workflows known as DISTiL to accelerate the development of data-orientated decision making solutions. The framework will allow users to extract value from the vast quantities of data being collected in manufacturing environments and will assist in making factories more efficient and sustainable through collaborative decision making and information sharing.

2 DISTiL Design Requirements and Features

An initial analysis of system requirements were carried out based on a review of the current literature, systems and use case scenarios in the manufacturing sector. Three key design objectives (DO) have been identified, the following presents each and provides reference to the current state of the art:

DO 1: A reference architecture is required to support the creation of federated data exchange among independent entities. The International Data Spaces Association (IDSA) [1] and GAIA-X [2] initiatives target the provision of a reference architecture to deploy and operate federated, secure, sovereign systems of data exchange. The objective is to provide a standardised approach to deliver new services and business workflows that operate across industries in which all participants can realize the full value of their data (including meta models, specification for connectors, certification etc.). The European strategy for data outlines the ambition to creating a single market for data, key to this is the development of common European data spaces. The design intent is to ensure data owners (companies, state bodies, individuals) maintain in control (data sovereignty) while supporting the availability of this data for use in the economy and society. Data spaces will underpin data driven applications that can benefit both citizens and businesses in many ways, such as generating new products and services, reducing costs, improving sustainability and energy efficiency. While the references approaches provide guidelines for implementation of such open data spaces, concrete architectural implementations are still in progress.

DO 2: Auditability and transparency of interactions, transactions and communications between participating entities is critical to ensure operational trust. Distributed Ledger Technology (DLT) and Blockchain can play a key role in improving the provenance, traceability and auditability of trusted interactions across complex ICT systems. The technology is already being applied in sectors to address challenges such as identity, product traceability and provenance, safety and status monitoring in logistics, trust, billing and payment processes. Blockchain technology increases transparency across systems involving dynamic, complex interactions, thus providing assurances of provenance [3]. Blockchain technology also offers solutions for the traceability of interactions and connected objects/artefacts by adopting transparent and auditable methodologies, data sources, and design procedure. Finally, Blockchain based solutions for auditability provides features that allow for their interrogation and access to information at each stage of a product or process lifecycle to determine compliance with policy, standards, or regulations.

DO 3: Enable the distribution and operation of intelligent software agents across the cloud computing continuum. The EU data strategy contends that by 2025 there will be a paradigm shift towards more decentralized intelligence and data processing at the edge [5]. Edge and cloud computing represent key technologies to bridge between physical world through field devices (sensors, actuators) and the concept of a digital services and data analytics [4]. It is essential to reach a high level of convergence between both to eliminate the risk of data silos and enable the development of intelligent algorithms, models and adaptive approaches for process monitoring and optimization. The scale and volume of data to be extracted suggests that cloud-centric approaches provide the most appropriate architectural pattern to support processing large quantities of data. However, there are some associated challenges including: the cost of network bandwidth along with the potential connectivity and reliability issues that can occur in communication systems [6] impact scalability of the transferred data, security and availability of services [7]. An alternative is to use edge or on-premises solutions (i.e. deploy data processing capabilities to devices in the field); this would enable real-time (or near real-time) data analysis, reduced network traffic and lower operating costs and dependency on cloud services and data centers. However, appropriate mechanisms to leverage edge-cloud resources and edge analytics efficiently (on resource constrained devices) is currently limited in its application in real-world settings and requires further research. The convergence of a large number of nodes at the Industrial Internet of Things (IIoT) edge along with multiple service providers and network operators exposes data owners and resource providers to potential threats. To address cloud-edge risks, decentralized management of resources is needed. Novel approaches for managing cross-layer intelligent computation tasks that take into account resource utilization as well as quality of service are required.

3 Architecture Design

The following section provides an overview of the main architecture components to facilitate the design objectives as outlined in Sect. 2. The architecture, as presented in Fig. 1 is composed of a set of intelligent software agents that operate as Decentralized Autonomous Organizations (DAOs). These DAOs work as part of a broader ecosystem for a specific application scenario but can be deployed locally within on-premise servers or hosted in the cloud. The local agent is composed of three functional layers, i) Distributed Data Layer, ii) Trust overlay iii) Resource Orchestration and Provisioning.

3.1 Distributed Data Layer

The data layer provides decentralized trusted and secure data sharing across different organizations and industrial domains. This includes the provision of a federated data space that can encapsulate new operation and business models that maximize the value of industrial data (single digital market): DISTiL defines a secure edge connector (data broker) to coordinate participation in a broader manufacturing data space. From an implementation perspective existing architectures such as the IDS-RAM, GAIA-X and IIC OpenFog will be leveraged to specify common building blocks for managing the interaction of entities participating in the collaborative industrial data space. This includes registration and management of local data sets, facilitate data privacy techniques to ensure sensitive data is protected. A DISTiL node will facilitate the deployment of edge analytic services and in addition any insights generated based on data shared (e.g. local model training) will be distributed to all participants to ensure there are incentives and mutual benefits of participation. This requires the specification of a common information model to capture outcomes and meta-data. Communication between DISTiL nodes is facilitated by the use of secure open API, this allows for extensibility and flexibility of service deployment across infrastructure and network tiers.

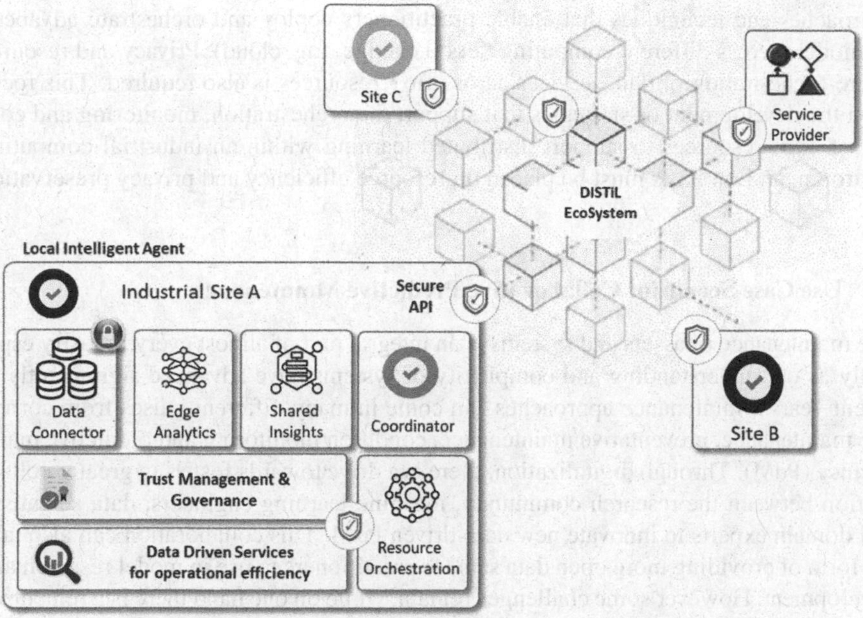

Fig. 1. DISTiL Distributed EcoSystem

3.2 Trust-Overlay

The architecture includes functionality to manage trust, security and policy governance when participating in the DISTiL ecosystem. The provision of a trust-overlay will incentivise participation in distributed data ecosystems by providing assurances and transparency of interactions and activities. The use of DLT will be leveraged to support provenance, traceability and immutability of data transactions within the DISTiL ecosystem. Tokenisation of digital assets and smart contracts encapsulated as part of a distributed data broker will also be considered to support incentives and data sharing. Specifically this will result in integrating DLT (e.g. IoTA, Hyperledger) to create a permission-based decentralized network of entities that can provide reliable and traceable sharing of data relating to physical and digital processes in a secure and trusted manner across organizational boundaries and compute infrastructure. This component will encapsulating three pillars, firstly digital identity to verify the authenticity of any data object (i.e. trust in data source), secondly transactions that allows any permissioned network-connected object to participate (i.e. trust in ecosystem) and thirdly interactions, record events associated with data ensuring transparency and data provenance (i.e. trust in the actions/decisions).

3.3 Resource Orchestration andProvisioning

To enable the creation of value-added data-driven services through ecosystem collaboration using distributed learning techniques will be utilized. Building on current open-source technologies and communities (e.g. OpenMined), DISTiL will incorporate approaches and techniques that enable practitioners deploy and orchestrate advanced AI models across different computing tiers (i.e. edge, fog, cloud). Privacy and resource aware orchestration of data services across IIoT resources is also required. This focus is on the development of strategies that support the orchestration, monitoring and control of edge resources to support distributed learning within an industrial computing environment. Emphasis must be placed on resource efficiency and privacy preservation [9].

3.4 Use Case Scenario: Collaborative Predictive Maintenance

The maintenance of assets and systems is an integral part of almost every industry especially as our understanding and complexity of systems have advanced significantly in recent years. Maintenance approaches can come in many different guises from corrective maintenance, preventative maintenance, condition monitoring and predictive maintenance (PdM). Through digitalization, there is a drive towards fostering greater collaboration between the research community, machine learning engineers, data scientists, and domain experts to innovate new data-driven PdM. This collaboration can also take the form of providing more open data sets for practitioners to use in model research and development. However some challenges remain, while on one hand there is a reluctance to share data that could potentially reveal commercially sensitive information there is a need for more data to improve machine learning models that support PdM mechanisms. The DISTiL architecture can offers a solution for such a scenario.

Figure 2 provides an overview of the configuration for a PdM application, consider the same machine that is deployed across many different sites\organizations each generating its own local data sets relating to performance, operation and faults. A machine learning model to support the diagnosis and detection of faults has been developed by the machine supplier. This model is provided to the machine owners, to improve this model a federated learning [8] mechanism is implemented (more details of model training approach can be found in [10]) that allows for local model training and model aggregation to improve the model performance. As such organizations do not need to share their raw data sets, rather they only need to exchange model updates through the secure a DISTiL connector. Considering the three functional layers, the distributed data layer includes an interface to the machine/process data based on OPC UA, where a direct connection is not feasible intermediate data storage (e.g. OSI -PI) can be utilized. A local model training algorithm is deployed onsite and is used to train the machine learning model utilizing local data, the outcomes of this training is subsequently shared across the DISTiL network and aggregated (based on nominated aggregator) to an updated global model that is redistributed to all participants. In this way all participants get the benefit of shared model training using larger data set while maintaining control and privacy of their raw data. The connector will implement concepts such as those provided by IDS, data catalog, privacy enhancing technologies, data interconnects etc. The trust overlay considers Hyperledger Fabric[1] as the distributed ledger solution, this includes a number of Chaincode smart contracts that support identity management, certification generation, service

[1] https://www.hyperledger.org/use/fabric.

registration, end-point discovery and immutable recording of data interactions. Due to scalability and performance overhead, it is not envisaged to utilize Fabric layer to maintain all raw data, rather it will act as an intermediary to for access, authorization and policy enforcement between organizations operating within the DISTiL ecosystem. The resource orchestration and provisioning is based on machine learning task offloading based on available resources (at the edge and cloud). The use of trusted execution environments (TEE) is used to provide a secure enclave for computational task execution, these can be both on-site or remotely deployed and managed.

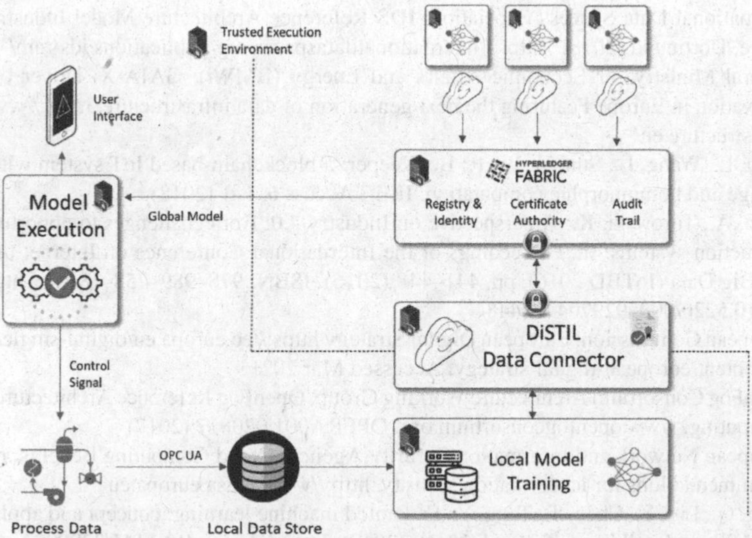

Fig. 2. DISTiL setup for collaborative PdM

Through the use of DISTiL for collaborative PdM, each participate can get access to an improved machine learning model that can be executed independently on-site. This can provide direct adaption to processes to address identified faults and\or provide feedback to maintenance staff to implement remedial action. DISTiL facilitates such a collaborative workflow by implementing secure data sharing and trust management approaches in the broader ecosystem.

4 Discussion and Next Steps

This paper provides an initial insight into the design of the DISTiL framework that aims to allow the manufacturing sector to shift towards new collaborative business models supported by innovation in digital technologies such as data spaces, Blockchain and distributed machine learning. Further exploration is required to provide a detailed specification of architectural patterns for collaborative workflows for a range of manufacturing use case scenarios. Next steps towards implementation includes the investigation of mechanisms to automate the auditing process for complex digital workflows and how information that supports trustworthiness assessments can be immutably recorded. The starting position is that DLT provides an opportunity to structure assets and provide self-executing services and mechanisms to incentivize data sharing, and the use of DLT as a platform for federated information sharing will be explored. A detailed examination of suitable ML techniques (e.g.TinyML, split learning) and edge resource provisioning that lend themselves applicable to distributed intelligence will be undertaken.

References

1. International Data Spaces Association: IDS Reference Architecture Model Industrial Data Space, Dortmund (2018). https://internationaldataspaces.org/publications/ids-ram/
2. Federal Ministry for Economic Affairs and Energy (BMWi): GAIA-X: Driver of digital innovation in Europe Featuring the next generation of data infrastructure. https://www.data-infrastructure.eu/
3. Zhou, L., Wang, L., Sun, Y., Lv, P.: BeeKeeper: a blockchain-based IoT system with secure storage and homomorphic computation. IEEE Access **6**, 1–1 (2018)
4. Khan, A., Turowski, K.: A perspective on Industry 4.0: from challenges to opportunities in production systems. In: Proceedings of the International Conference on Internet of Things and Big Data (IoTBD 2016), pp. 441–448 (2016). ISBN: 978–989–758–183–0. https://doi.org/10.5220/0005929704410448
5. European Commission: European Digital Strategy https://ec.europa.eu/digital-single-market/en/content/european-digital-strategy. Accessed Mar 2021
6. OpenFog Consortium Architecture Working Group, OpenFog Reference Architecture for Fog Computing. www.openfogconsortium.org. OPFRA001.020817 (2017)
7. European Network and Information Security Agency: Cloud Computing Benefits, risks and recommendations for in- formation security. http://www.enisa.europa.eu
8. Yang, Q., Liu, Y., Chen, T., Tong, Y.: Federated machine learning: concept and applications. ACM Trans. Intell. Syst. Technol. **10**(2), (2019). https://doi.org/10.1145/3298981
9. Boulemtafes, A., Derhab, A., Challal, Y.: A review of privacy-preserving techniques for deep learning. Neurocomputing **384**, 21–45 (2020)
10. Bharti, S., McGibney, A.: Privacy-aware resource sharing in cross-device federated model training for collaborative predictive maintenance. IEEE Access **9**, 120367–120379 (2021). https://doi.org/10.1109/ACCESS.2021.3108839

Using Model Selection and Reduction to Develop an Empirical Model to Predict Energy Consumption of a CNC Machine

Liam Morris[1,2,3](✉), Rose Clancy[1,2,3], Andriy Hryshchenko[3], Dominic O'Sullivan[1,2,3], and Ken Bruton[1,2,3]

[1] Department of Civil and Environmental Engineering, Intelligent Efficiency Research Group (IERG), University College Cork, Cork, Ireland
liam.morris@umail.ucc.ie
[2] MaREI Centre, Environmental Research Institute, University College Cork, Cork, Ireland
[3] School of Engineering, University College Cork, Cork, Ireland

Abstract. With an ever growing need to reduce energy consumption in the manufacturing industry, process users need to become more aware on how production impacts energy consumption. Computer numerically controlled (CNC) machining tools are a common manufacturing apparatus, and they are known to be energy inefficient. This paper describes the development of an empirical energy consumption model of a CNC with the aim of predicting energy consumption based on the number of parts processed by the machine. The model can then be deployed as part of a decision support (DS) platform, aiding process users to reduce consumption and minimise waste. In using the Calibrated Model Method, the data undergoes initial preparation followed by exploratory data analysis and subsequent model development via iteration. During this analysis, relationships between parameters are explored to find which have the most significant on energy consumption. A training set of 191 datapoints yielded a linear correlation coefficient of 0.95, between the power consumption and total units produced. RMSE, MAPE and MBE validation test yielded results of 0.198, 6.4% and 2.66% respectively.

Keywords: Empirical model · Calibrated model · CNC · Machining · Digital model · Linear regression · Energy consumption · Decision support platform

1 Introduction

In recent years, energy consumption has been an increasingly important consideration in the manufacturing industry, and with global energy demand estimated to increase by 45% from today's levels to 2030, all aspects of our energy system must be analysed [1]. With the industrial currently accounting for 41.9% of final electricity consumption [1], improving energy use in the industrial sector, can see substantial improvements in global energy demand and carbon emissions..

Traditionally, production is assessed by monitoring four main manufacturing attributes; cost, time, quality and flexibility [2]. While there is an increased awareness around energy consumption in the production industry [3], energy consumption

T. Margaria and B. Steffen (Eds.): ISoLA 2022, LNCS 13704, pp. 227–234, 2022.
https://doi.org/10.1007/978-3-031-19762-8_17

modelling for processes is far less common. Many studies look at particular processes in great detail or apply a bespoke prediction model to a certain process, however this makes it difficult to apply to other scenarios [4] and hence the outputs from this research is not easily replicable. Energy consumption data can be collected by various means, such as internal energy reading or by utilising external sensors and can be recorded, stored and used in varying formats, with little standardisation in terms of agreed schemas or naming conventions [5]. Because of this, general models are not very common to apply to different manufacturing settings so bespoke models are developed [5].

This paper was borne from research studies [6] focused on the development of an empirical energy consumption model of a CNC machine, which seeks to predict energy consumption based on only product throughput in the absence of other features to be rolled out as part of a decision support (DS) platform, aiding process users to reduce consumption and minimise waste.

2 Literature Review

The machining process is a fundamental manufacturing technique, where parts are shaped by the removal of unwanted material. Machining equipment are a high energy consumer within manufacturing and not very energy efficient, at less than 30% [7], due to the varying nature of the tools within the machines and the materials being used. Machining tools contain many motors and auxiliary devices, with varying energy consumptions. Various studies exist which attempt to further understand machining energy consumption. They also found that the power required to remove material has a small impact on the overall consumption, which means savings could stem from the overall cycle time [8]. Energy modelling can be a challenging task due to the complexity of machining tools [9]. This environment is often characterised by large variety in products in small batches, requiring real-time monitoring, dynamic scheduling and decision making, and adaptive capability [9].

When considering modelling approaches in manufacturing, many studies look at empirical modelling [9, 10] and Machine Learning (ML) [11, 12]. With machine learning however, one common constraint is the requirement of good, high-quality data to be fed into machine learning algorithms [13]. In the case of this study due to the lack of available sensors to develop models, ML performance would be impacted. Alternatively, empirical modelling is a data driven approach where the performance of the asset being modelled is translated into one or a set of algebraic equations [14]. These types of models are constructed with regards to prediction ability or model fit (data approximation), prognostic ability (forecasting) and model structure (agreement with theories and facts). They are becoming more and more common as the systems being modelled are becoming more complex and less structured [15]. [9] highlights that empirical models use actual production data to establish relationships between main variable and the energy consumption. [16] saw the development of an empirical modelling approach to predict energy consumption of a material removal process, with 90% accuracy. [7] sought to develop an empirical model of machining tools by building empirical models focusing on optimising process parameters to efficiently machine parts, thus reducing overall consumption. The model inputs on this study were identified as spindle motor power rating

(W), maximum spindle speed (rpm), maximum turning diameter and length (mm). From the literature examined, it was found that many CNC consumption models use many of these process tool parameters, as well as process throughput data to build models. In many cases, data to that level of detail can be difficult and very expensive to gather. From assessing the available data on the CNC analysed as part of this study and utilising model selection and reduction techniques, an effective modelling methodology was put forward and is introduced in the subsequent section. This approach could potentially be a more simplistic initial step for many CNC users looking to predict machine energy consumption without a myriad of in process sensor data.

3 Methodology

A common approach with empirical modelling in manufacturing is the use of the Response Surface Method (RSM) [7, 17]. The RSM works best between several explanatory variables and one response variable. Due to the presence of only one explanatory variable and one response variable, and limited available data in this study, the RSM output would be difficult to implement accurately. Thus, data calibration was studied. While calibrated approaches are not very common in manufacturing, there are studies where such approaches were utilised, such as [18]. The methodology selected to develop the model in this study is based on the Calibrated Model Method, a modelling methodology originally created to optimise the energy consumption of a building [19]. This approach inputs prepared data to an initial model and the model is iteratively calibrated with the data to improve predictability. While applications vary between building and machine modelling, the approaches do not. Both scenarios see a basic initial model developed, following iterative data improvements, this calibrates the model further to the eventual creation of an effective final model. This method is especially useful for when limited data is available and assessment sees modifications that can improve the final model.

With the selected methodology, three stages were defined to create the model. Firstly, in the Data Preparation stage, the data is gathered, formatted, and standardised for use in the energy model. The model requires two inputs, from energy data and production data. It is only after significant data preparation that both sets of data are ready for analysis. Both input files are indexed to be compatible with one another then merged for Data Analysis. In the case of time series data, ensuring data sets are sampled to the same time frame.

With data now prepared, the relationship between datapoints is examined in the Data Analysis stage. This includes data correlation, causation analysis and domain understanding. Utilising data visualisation, explanations for major outliers that could hinder model performance as well as other relationships can be assessed. Through iterative adjustments, relationships between datapoints are calculated to potentially generate assumptions, assess machine performance, and increase machine understanding. Each iteration on a model is documented in a version log, documenting what changes were made, any new assumptions, assumptions removed and validation scores.

Once Data Preparation and Data Analysis stages are complete, the data can then be modelled in the Data Modelling stage using datapoints with the highest correlation along with the most appropriate empirical modelling method (linear regression, multivariate regression etc.). The predicted results can then undergo validation using methods such as root mean squared error (RMSE), mean absolute percentage error (MAPE) and mean bias error (MBE). The with this model used as a tool for the decision support dashboard in development within the DENiM project, visualisations can provide process users insight on predicted performance.

4 Case Study

This methodology was applied to a DENiM research project pilot site, a medical device manufacturing process where a CNC machining lathe is used to machines raw blocks of material into the required shape. This model is to be used development as a component of a DS platform, aiding process users to reduce energy consumption and minimise waste in manufacturing.

The measured timeframe of the study was 12-h shifts periods. Key features of this CNC machine were determined an exhaustive literature review on CNC energy modelling and via subject matter expert workshops with key personnel. The workshop was held in consultation with process, automation and facilities engineers, production associates and members of the research team.

Production data (parts produced, parts scrapped) was readily available via an OSI PI network connection to the physical machine. Realtime power consumption at the time of development was not available however, thus power consumption was collected using a Fluke 1734 Energy Logger over five different production shift periods, recording energy consumption in kilo Watts every one minute. No other in process sensor data was available on this machine. Four of the five energy datasets were used as a training set while the fifth was retained as the testing set for model validation.

5 Model Development

5.1 Data Preparation

Figure 1 details the methodology as implemented in this study. Using the Python coding language, the input data first underwent data (production numbers and energy consumed) preparation ahead of the data analysis. The power training data, power testing data

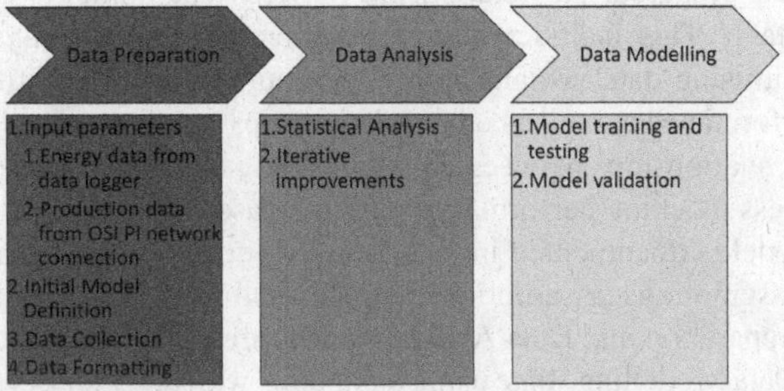

Fig. 1. Modelling steps overview.

and production data were used as inputs in this stage. Firstly, the power datasets were resampled from their original 1-min granularity to the 12-h production shifts, with the power data during the shifts summed. The production data from the CNC's shifts were then extracted to its own dataset. In this dataset, the total quantity of parts produced during the shift was calculated by summing the number of successful parts with the parts that were scrapped. Following this, both datasets were merged ahead of the next stage of the analysis (Table 1).

Table 1. Data analysis example

Date/Time	Power [kW]	Total units	Parts successful	Parts scrapped
2022-01-12 19:00:00	1781.665599	45	45	0
2022-01-13 07:00:00	1955.644445	59	58	1
2022-01-13 19:00:00	2005.026689	55	55	0
2022-01-14 07:00:00	2085.867077	63	63	0
2022-01-14 19:00:00	1206.358962	0	0	0

5.2 Data Analysis

With the prepared data, initial analysis included assessing the correlation between the power consumed per shift and the total units produced. Over iterative adjustments, it was identified that power consumption during the installation and removal mid shift caused inconsistencies, reducing model efficiency. These datapoints were then removed. After analysis, the dataset consisted of 191 points.

5.3 Data Modelling

From iterative improvements during analysis, the training data was used to create a linear regression model of the power consumption. Iterative changes made to the model included data manipulation, visualisation and interpretation. Examples of such changes included ensuring duplicate and non-numerical values were addressed, contextual outliers were understood and appropriate visualisation methods for process users. The training set of 191 datapoints yielded a high instance of correlation (0.95) between the power consumption and total units produced, which formed the input for the linear regression model. The data yielded a R^2 value of 0.904161 and a line of best fit with the equation Power $= 13.3362(\text{Total Units}) + 1199.93$. This model was then tested on a set of 41 datapoints.

6 Discussion

The adapted calibrated model method used to develop the empirical energy consumption model, provided an effective means to model energy consumption of a CNC when only

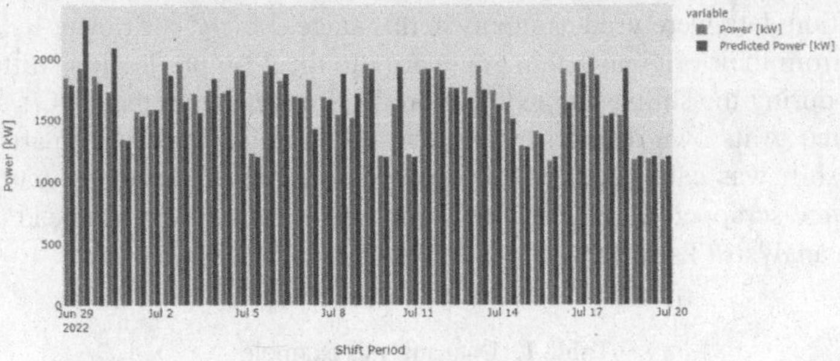

Fig. 2. Actual power consumption vs Predicted power consumption

energy consumption and product throughput data was available. With a training dataset of 191 points, the data was prepared and analysed.

This dataset identified a correlation of 0.95 between energy consumption and total parts produced, which were then inputted into a linear regression model. The model was tested on a 41-point dataset. Figure 2 shows the comparison between the actual and predicted energy consumption values of test data. Numerous validation methods were used to validate the energy consumption model's performance, namely normalised RMSE, MAPE and MBE. These validation methods yielded results of 0.198, 6.4% and 2.66% respectively. For the normalised RMSE, a value of less than 0.5 indicates a high level of predictability whereas for MAPE and MBE, a percentage score of close to zero indicates a high level of predictability. Overall, these values showed a high predictive capability for the model for future use on the CNC. For instance, if predicted energy is far less than actual energy consumed, process users would be made aware via the DS dashboard and the use of an FDD add on could potentially identify the reasons for machine underperformance leading to the high energy consumption.

The high correlation between energy consumption and product throughput indicated throughput was a very useful parameter for prediction. From the iterative analysis of the results, better correlations were established which ultimately made the model predictability more accurate. It was found that in preparing based on energy and production values, the data driven approach could be transferable across any similar CNC.

Future Work

The low number of 191 datapoints was to be expected owing to the lack of energy monitoring on the system. Following the use of temporary energy trackers, next steps would include the installation of energy meters to collect energy data on an ongoing basis and the additional data would be made available and used to train the model and improve accuracy. Initially, the parts from the machine were assumed to be of the same size and dimensions, with more data collected, size categorisation can be included in the model. From this, predictions can be tailored to the size of the parts being produced and allowing process users to identify parts which may drive higher energy consumption.

The collection of energy data could facilitate real time modelling of the CNC. The model will also be trialled on the 6 CNC machines from the same manufacturer to assess the model's applicability on the CNC machines, before rollout onto other CNCs and other machining assets, such as the saw and clean line.

With more data being gathered through the installation of the wireless energy sensors and being utilised to other machines, the calibrated approach can be applied in real time Thus, predicted consumption based on planned production throughput could see the model digitally integrated further into a Digital Twin.

Acknowledgments. The work detailed is part of the Digital intelligence for collaborative Energy management in Manufacturing (DENIM) project with funding from the European Union's Horizon 2020 research and innovation programme, under Grant Agreement N 958339.

References

1. IEA, Key World Energy Statistics 2021, Paris (2021). https://www.iea.org/reports/key-world-energy-statistics-2021/final-consumption. Accessed 26 Jul 2022
2. Salonitis, K., Ball, P.: Energy efficient manufacturing from machine tools to manufacturing systems. Procedia CIRP **7**, 634–639 (2013). https://doi.org/10.1016/j.procir.2013.06.045
3. Mulrennan, K., Donovan, J., D. Tormey, D., Macpherson, R.: A data science approach to modelling a manufacturing facility's electrical energy profile from plant production data. In: 2018 IEEE 5th International Conference on Data Science and Advanced Analytics (DSAA), pp. 387–391 (2018). https://doi.org/10.1109/DSAA.2018.00050
4. Cataldo, A., Scattolini, R., Tolio, T.: An energy consumption evaluation methodology for a manufacturing plant. CIRP J. Manuf. Sci. Technol. **11**, 53–61 (2015). https://doi.org/10.1016/j.cirpj.2015.08.001
5. Reimann, J., Wenzel, K., Friedemann, M., Putz, M.: Methodology and model for predicting energy consumption in manufacturing at multiple scales. Procedia Manuf. **21**, 694–701 (2018). https://doi.org/10.1016/j.promfg.2018.02.173
6. European Union H2020, DENiM: Digital intelligence for collaborative ENergy management in Manufacturing. https://denim-fof.eu/. Accessed 15 Aug 2022
7. Garg, G.K., Garg, S., Sangwan, K.S.: Development of an empirical model for optimization of machining parameters to minimize power consumption. IOP Conf. Ser. Mater. Sci. Eng. **346**, 12078 (2018). https://doi.org/10.1088/1757-899x/346/1/012078
8. Behrendt, T., Zein, A., Min, S.: Development of an energy consumption monitoring procedure for machine tools. CIRP Ann. **61**(1), 43–46 (2012). https://doi.org/10.1016/j.cirp.2012.03.103
9. Peng, T., Xu, X., Wang, L.: A novel energy demand modelling approach for CNC machining based on function blocks. J. Manuf. Syst. **33**(1), 196–208 (2014). https://doi.org/10.1016/j.jmsy.2013.12.004
10. Edem, I.F., Mativenga, P.T.: Modelling of energy demand from computer numerical control (CNC) toolpaths. J. Clean. Prod. **157**, 310–321 (2017). https://doi.org/10.1016/j.jclepro.2017.04.096
11. Kant, G., Sangwan, K.S.: Predictive modeling for power consumption in machining using artificial intelligence techniques. Procedia CIRP **26**, 403–407 (2015). https://doi.org/10.1016/j.procir.2014.07.072
12. Fard, R.H., Hosseini, S.: Machine Learning algorithms for prediction of energy consumption and IoT modeling in complex networks. Microprocess. Microsyst. **89**, 104423 (2022). https://doi.org/10.1016/j.micpro.2021.104423
13. Wuest, T., Weimer, D., Irgens, C., Thoben, K.-D.: Machine learning in manufacturing: advantages, challenges, and applications. Prod. Manuf. Res. **4**(1), 23–45 (2016). https://doi.org/10.1080/21693277.2016.1192517

14. Sun, P., et al.: Evaluation of applicability of empirical models of turbine performance to aircraft engine. Aerosp. Sci. Technol. **117**, 106953 (2021). https://doi.org/10.1016/j.ast.2021.106953
15. Militký, J.: 3 - Fundamentals of soft models in textiles. In: Majumdar, A. (ed.) Soft Computing in Textile Engineering. A volume in Woodhead Publishing Series in Textiles, pp. 45–102. Woodhead Publishing (2011)
16. Kara, S., Li, W.: Unit process energy consumption models for material removal processes. CIRP Ann. - Manuf. Technol. **60**(1), 37–40 (2011). https://doi.org/10.1016/j.cirp.2011.03.018
17. Altıntaş, R.S., Kahya, M., Ünver, H.Ö.: Modelling and optimization of energy consumption for feature based milling. Int. J. Adv. Manuf. Technol. **86**(9–12), 3345–3363 (2016). https://doi.org/10.1007/s00170-016-8441-7
18. Adeniji D., Schoop J., In-situ calibrated digital process Twin models for resource efficient manufacturing. J. Manuf. Sci. Eng. **144**, 4 (2021). doi: https://doi.org/10.1115/1.4052131
19. Raftery, P., Keane, M., O'Donnell, J.: Calibrating whole building energy models: an evidence-based methodology. Energy Build. **43**(9), 2356–2364 (2011). https://doi.org/10.1016/j.enbuild.2011.05.020

Crazy Nodes: Towards Ultimate Flexibility in Ubiquitous Big Data Stream Engineering, Visualisation, and Analytics, in Smart Factories

Mirco Soderi(✉) and John G. Breslin

National University of Ireland, Galway, Ireland
{mirco.soderi,john.breslin}@nuigalway.ie

Abstract. Smart Factories characterize as context-rich, fast-changing environments where heterogeneous hardware appliances are found beside of also heterogeneous software components deployed in (or directly interfacing with) IoT devices, as well as in on-premise mainframes, and on the Cloud. This inherent heterogeneity poses major challenges particularly when a high degree of resiliency is needed, and the ubiquitously deployed software components must be replaced or reconfigured at real-time to respond to the most diverse events, ranging from an out-of-range sensor detection, to a new order issued by a customer. In this work, a software framework is presented, which allows to deploy, (re)configure, run, and monitor the most diverse software across all the three layers of the Smart Factory (edge, fog, Cloud), from remote, via API calls, in a standardised uniform manner, relying on containerization technologies, and on a variety of software technologies, frameworks, and programming languages, including Node-RED, MQTT, Scala, Apache Spark, and Kafka. The most recent advances in the framework design, implementation, and demonstration, which led to the introduction of the so-called Crazy Nodes, are presented and motivated. A comprehensive proof-of-concept is given, where user interfaces and distributed systems are created from scratch via API calls to implement AI-based alerting systems, Big Data stream filtering and transformation, AI model training, storage, and usage for one-shot as well as stream predictions, and real-time Big Data visualization through line plots, histograms, and pie charts.

Keywords: Smart manufacturing · Resilient manufacturing · Cloud manufacturing · Artificial intelligence · AI · Distributed system · System of systems · Ubiquitous computing · Stream processing · Stream visualization · Micro-service · Application programming interface · API

This publication has emanated from research conducted with the financial support of Science Foundation Ireland under Grant Number SFI/16/RC/3918 (Confirm).

T. Margaria and B. Steffen (Eds.): ISoLA 2022, LNCS 13704, pp. 235–240, 2022.
https://doi.org/10.1007/978-3-031-19762-8_18

1 Introduction

1.1 Reconfigurable Manufacturing

Real-time (re)configurability is a key challenge in Smart Manufacturing [1]. The diversity of components is a significant obstacle for interoperability, and then for reconfigurability. On the other hand, a reconfigurable manufacturing allows among the others (i) a more sustainable and efficient manufacturing [2], by eliminating transportation; (ii) low-volume high-value production of customized or even personalised goods [3]; (iii) the alignment of production to demand [4]; (iv) a real-time fine tuning for optimizing energy consumption, mitigating the risk of damages, or increasing the safety of operators, based on sensor detections [5]. A real-world application to pharmaceuticals manufacturing is presented in [6]. Compared to other systems such as Apache AirFlow [7], our proposed framework allows to (i) tune/edit the workflow from remote while data is flowing; (ii) address low-to-high resource devices and the Cloud, uniformly; (iii) implement arbitrary flows; (iv) avail of thousands of ready-to-use modules; (v) implement reconfigurable user interfaces and data charts. However, since APIs are in our framework to instantiate arbitrary applications, the two systems can integrate.

1.2 Framework Overview

The main building blocks of the proposed software framework for the ubiquitous Big Data (stream) engineering, analytics, and visualization as a Service are listed as follows: (i) Network Factory; (ii) Transformation Library; (iii) Service and Crazy Nodes; (iv) AI Servers. The **Network Factory** is a Node-RED application available on the Docker Hub as msoderi/network-factory. It implements APIs that create, start, stop, upgrade, and delete, Docker bridges (fences) and a variety of specialized yet reconfigurable applications in Docker containers. It essentially turns any device equipped with Docker into a totally flexible, real-time remotely reconfigurable equipment. A **Transformation Library** is a containerized Node-RED application that consists in an extendable collection of reusable software modules meant to be loaded to the Service/Crazy Nodes via API calls, and there executed. **Service Nodes** [8], and **Crazy Nodes**, are also containerized Node-RED applications, and expose API calls for configuring input and output MQTT broker instances and topics, and the task to be executed. Depending on the specific module that is loaded into a Node, both input and output can be from/to MQTT brokers, or just one of those. **AI Servers** [9] are containerized Scala + Spark applications. They expose APIs for interfacing with Service and Crazy Nodes. AI Server nodes keep a configuration file for each interfacing Service and Crazy node, and include an extendable library of parallel/stream/AI-related tasks. AI servers also support the remote deployment and execution of Scala expression compiled on the fly when needed, without server restart. The framework is prone to **security issues**, which are mitigated through secure communication protocols, isolation (Docker bridges), and ACL nodes. A comprehensive example system is depicted in Fig. 1.

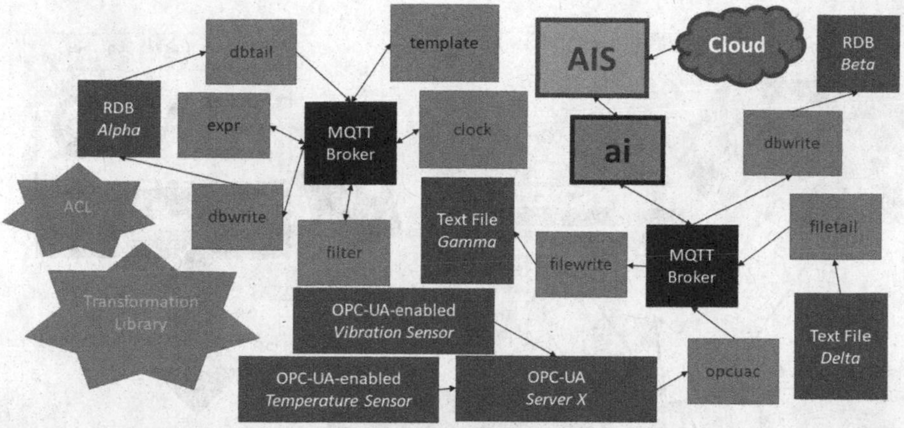

Fig. 1. An example distributed system that can be built through our proposed framework. Service/Crazy nodes are depicted each as an orange rectangle; some of them interface with IoT devices, databases, file systems... (blue labels), while others only interface with configured brokers (black labels), or with AI servers (bold large label). (Color figure online)

1.3 Paper Structure

The challenges that are posed by reconfigurable and resilient manufacturing, as well as its pivotal role in a wide range of use cases and applications, are outlined in Subsect. 1.1. An overview of the software framework is provided in Subsect. 1.2. Service and Crazy Nodes, and their interaction with AI Servers, are described in Sect. 2. A proof of concept is provided in Sect. 3. Conclusions are drawn in Sect. 4.

2 Service and Crazy Nodes

Service Nodes are containerized Node-RED applications. As soon as created through the Network Factory, they all look the same: they are disconnected from any data source, implement the identity function, and expose configuration APIs. Through appropriate calls, MQTT clients are created inside of Service Nodes, and configured to connect to input, output, and status MQTT brokers/topics. At creation time, Service Nodes are bound to a Transformation Library. Through appropriate calls, reusable software modules are copied from the Library to the Service Nodes, where they are then executed. In Fig. 2, the internals of a Service Node, and the ecosystem around it, are depicted. Transformation Library nodes are also created through the Network Factory. They natively include a variety of reusable modules for data input, RDB monitoring, data exchange over OPC-UA, data filtering, data transformation, and others. Service Nodes are not meant to perform Big Data processing, run parallel computations, or implement AI algorithms. Instead, they are suitable for edge computing, data preparing, and

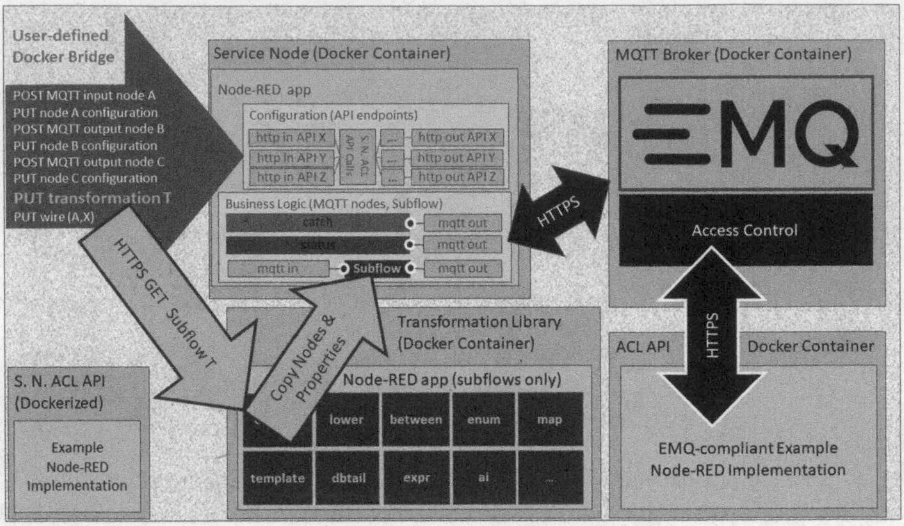

Fig. 2. The internals of a Service Node, and the ecosystem around of it. Instead, in Crazy Nodes, not only you can import/load/copy a task from the Transformation Library, but you can also freely modify the task that is executed inside of a specific node, from remote.

for implementing user interfaces, relying on the Node-RED dashboard module. The “ai” module, natively available in the Transformation Library, can be loaded to Service Nodes from remote to make them capable of interfacing with AI Servers through a variety of communication technologies. Being containerized, Service Nodes can be deployed and run everywhere a Docker Host is available, which makes them device-agnostic, and allows to deploy, configure, and run, heterogeneous software components in a uniform manner.

2.1 Crazy Nodes

Crazy Nodes are maximally reconfigurable Service Nodes. In a Service Node, the task that the node performs can only be one of those available in its associated Transformation Library, and the customization options are only those that the developer of the task has made available. Instead, in Crazy Nodes, in addition to importing reusable modules from the Transformation Library, it is possible to freely add, configure, link, and delete, specific parts in the task that the node executes. All changes have immediate effect and are operated through API calls, which makes Crazy Nodes suitable for (i) event-driven or sensor-driven fine tuning, (ii) incremental implementation, (iii) minor adjustments on the user interface, and remarkably, (iv) it opens to real-time software modifications in response to unforeseen events, which can be seen as the maximum achievable level of resiliency.

2.2 Towards the Cloud

The "ai" module must be loaded into a Service/Crazy Node to enable the interaction with an AI Server. The module implements: (i) configuration APIs, which call corresponding Server APIs for configuring the task that the Server must execute when input come from the Node; (ii) input API, which calls the corresponding Server API and triggers task execution; (iii) output and status APIs, which are asynchronously called by the Server to notify the Service/Crazy Node of status changes, and provide the result if applicable. For stream tasks, the Node only inputs control commands, while data are read/written from/to configured Kafka streams. The interaction is depicted in Fig. 3.

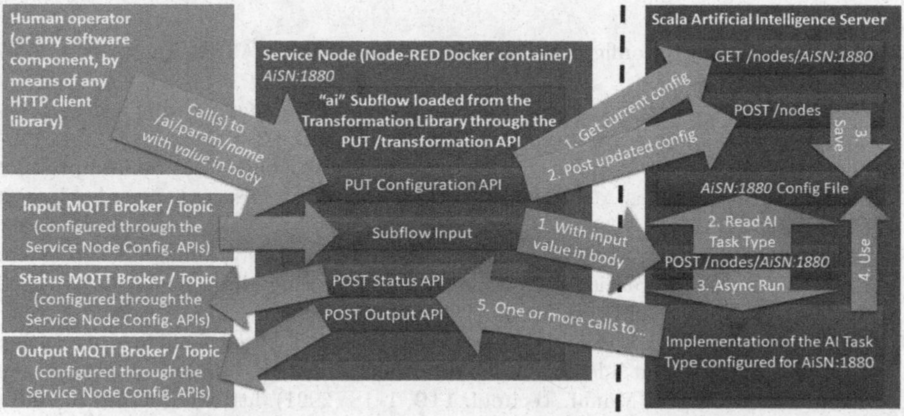

Fig. 3. How "ai" Service or Crazy Nodes interact with AI Servers

3 Proof of Concept

As a proof of concept, a former demo [10] has been extended, and API calls have been added for creating and connecting new user interfaces from scratch, without relying on any pre-existing module from the Transformation Library. The resulting proof of concept consists in a Postman collection including 1400+ API calls to build from scratch, configure, operate, destroy, distributed systems for (i) alerting applications, (ii) Big Data engineering, (iii) AI models training/storage/usage, and for (iv) real-time Big Data stream visualization [11]. A step-by-step demo presentation, the Postman export, the OpenAPI documentation, and all software artifacts are available in the GitHub repository[1].

[1] https://github.com/mircosoderi/State-of-the-art-Artifacts-for-Big-Data-Engineering-and-Analytics-as-a-Service.

4 Conclusions

In this work, a software framework for ubiquitous Big Data (stream) engineering, analytics, and visualization as a Service has been presented. In particular, containerized reconfigurable Node-RED applications named Crazy Nodes have been discussed. The improvements with respect to the former version of those applications, named Service Nodes, have been highlighted. A proof of concept has been proposed where new user interfaces have been constructed from scratch component by component from remote through API calls, and integrated in a pre-existing demo.

References

1. Koren, Y., et al.: Reconfigurable manufacturing systems. CIRP Ann. **48**(2), 527–540 (1999)
2. Bortolini, M., Galizia, F.G., Mora, C.: Reconfigurable manufacturing systems: literature review and research trend. J. Manuf. Syst. **49**, 93–106 (2018)
3. Zennaro, I., Finco, S., Battini, D., Persona, A.: Big size highly customised product manufacturing systems: a literature review and future research agenda. Int. J. Prod. Res. **57**(15–16), 5362–5385 (2019)
4. Lebovitz, R., Graban, M.: The journey toward demand driven manufacturing. In: Proceedings 2nd International Workshop on Engineering Management for Applied Technology. EMAT 2001, pp. 29–35 (2001). IEEE
5. Haghnegahdar, L., Joshi, S.S., Dahotre, N.B.: From IoT-based cloud manufacturing approach to intelligent additive manufacturing: industrial Internet of Things—an overview. Int. J. Adv. Manuf. Technol. **119**, 1–18 (2021). https://doi.org/10.1007/s00170-021-08436-x
6. Adamo, A., et al.: On-demand continuous-flow production of pharmaceuticals in a compact, reconfigurable system. Science **352**(6281), 61–67 (2016)
7. Singh, P.: Airflow. In: Learn PySpark, pp. 67–84. Apress, Berkeley, CA (2019). https://doi.org/10.1007/978-1-4842-4961-1_4
8. Soderi, M., Kamath, V., Morgan, J., Breslin, J.G.: Ubiquitous System Integration as a Service in Smart Factories. In: 2021 IEEE International Conference on Internet of Things and Intelligence Systems (IoTaIS), pp. 261–267 (2021). IEEE
9. Soderi, M., Kamath, V., Morgan, J., Breslin, J.G.: Advanced analytics as a Service in Smart Factories. In: 2022 IEEE 20th Jubilee World Symposium on Applied Machine Intelligence and Informatics (SAMI), pp. 000425–000430 (2022). IEEE
10. Soderi, M., Kamath, V., Breslin, J.G.: A demo of a software platform for ubiquitous big data engineering, visualization, and analytics, via reconfigurable micro-services, in smart factories. In: 2022 IEEE International Conference on Smart Computing (SMARTCOMP), pp. 1–3 (2022). IEEE
11. Soderi, M., Kamath, V., Breslin, J.G.: Toward an API-driven infinite cyber-screen for custom real-time display of big data streams. In: 2022 IEEE International Conference on Smart Computing (SMARTCOMP), pp. 153–155 (2022). IEEE

Formal Methods for DIStributed COmputing in Future RAILway Systems

Formal Methods for Distributed Control Systems of Future Railways

Alessandro Fantechi[1,2(✉)], Stefania Gnesi[2], and Anne E. Haxthausen[3]

[1] DINFO - Università degli Studi di Firenze, Via S. Marta 3, Florence, Italy
alessandro.fantechi@unifi.it

[2] Istituto di Scienza e Tecnologie dell'Informazione "A. Faedo" CNR, Via Moruzzi 1, Pisa, Italy
stefania.gnesi@isti.cnr.it

[3] DTU Compute, Technical University of Denmark, Lyngby, Denmark

1 Motivations and Goals

The adoption of formal methods in railway signalling has been the subject of specific tracks of past ISOLA conferences since a decade. The track on "Formal Methods for Intelligent Transportation Systems" held at ISOLA 2012 [3] was actually focused on railway applications, as a recognition on how much already the railway signalling sector had been a source of success stories about the adoption of formal methods. The "Formal Methods and Safety Certification: Challenges in the Railways Domain" track of ISOLA 2016 [2] was aimed at discussing advanced results and addressing the challenges posed by the increasing scale and complexity of railway systems. In 2019, a workshop colocated with the DisCoTec federated conference on distributed computing, DisCoRail ("Formal methods for DIStributed COmputing in future RAILway system") 2019, was set up with the aim of discussing how distributed computing was affecting the railway signalling domain, given that the new technologies being applied in this domain (with a main example represented by the wide deployment of ERTMS-ETCS systems on high speed lines as well as on freight corridors) were transforming railways in a very large geographic distributed computing system. It has soon appeared evident that the high expectations on safety, but also on availability and performance of future railway signalling systems, in presence of a high degree of distribution, could be addressed only by a systematic adoption of formal methods in their definition and development. This view has been shared by several projects within the Shift2Rail Joint Undertaking, that were also represented in the following edition of the DisCoRail workshop, that joined ISOLA in 2020/21 [4] (track on "Formal methods for DIStributed COmputing in future RAILway systems").

The DisCoRail 2019 workshop and the ISOLA DisCoRail track of 2021 have therefore discussed the intertwining of formal methods and distributed computing in the design and development of innovative train control systems, two dimensions naturally stemming from the two fundamental characteristics of this class of systems, namely that their functions are intrinsically distributed between

T. Margaria and B. Steffen (Eds.): ISoLA 2022, LNCS 13704, pp. 243–245, 2022.
https://doi.org/10.1007/978-3-031-19762-8_19

trains and wayside equipments, and that such functions are safety-critical, calling for rigorous proof of their safety.

Distribution of functionality enables distributing decisions as well. Currently, most of the crucial decisions needed to guarantee safety are however taken at centralised locations (such as the Radio Block Centre – RBC – in ETCS). Whether distributing vital decisions is indeed a matter of active research, especially considering that the related increasing importance of communication raises the need of uncertainty being taken into account: is the same safety level achievable by distributed decisions w.r.t. centralised ones? How formal methods can guarantee safety in such context? What about availability, interoperability, cybersecurity?

Moreover, the current research on autonomous driving for cars is inspiring a vision of autonomous trains in the next future. Autonomy requires even more distributed decisions based on local knowledge of the surrounding environment acquired also through AI-enabled sensors, e.g. employing artificial vision. Can formal methods be exploited to provide the necessary safety assurance for these systems?

Following the success of the previous DisCoRail editions, the track aims for a fruitful discussion on these topics between researchers and experts from industry and academia that have addressed these aspects in research and development projects.

Hence the aim of this track is to discuss (1) how distributed computing can change, and is actually changing, the domain of railway signaling and train control systems, and (2) how formal methods can help to address challenges arising from this change.

2 Contributions

The first three contributions analyse under different points of view the challenges posed by distribution and autonomy. The contribution [7] introduces those posed by advanced signalling systems in which AI will be a main enabling technology, discussing how formal methods research can address such challenges and outlining research problems that need to be further developed.

The paper [5] focuses on the effects that uncertainty on critical parameters (such as position or speed) can have on dependability of railway signalling systems, surveying various studies that have used state-based formal modelling of the system behaviour for a quantitative evaluation of such effects.

Certification of autonomous train operation systems using AI-based technology is discussed by [8], that considers existing standards and required modifications or extensions of existing standards.

The next two papers present instead specific solutions, also based on formal methods, to specific issues of future railway systems. Software Defined Networking (SDN) is proposed by [1] as a paradigm useful to dynamically reconfigure the network for an effective management of communication flows produced by moving trains. The paradigm is supported by a methodological framework based on model-driven engineering and formal methods.

The paper [6] proposes a pragmatic solution to guarantee security of a network of computers that supports the distribution of safety functions along a railway line.

The width of the issues addressed by the five contributions gives, we believe, a sufficient base for a deep discussion of the important challenges the research community has to address in the next years for what concerns future railway systems.

It is our opinion that, notwithstanding the limited space available, the contributions to the track succeed to give a glance of the state of the art and of the opportunities of the application of formal techniques to the distributed systems of systems represented by the future railway signalling systems.

References

1. Canonico, R., Flammini, F., Marrone, M., Vittorini, V., Nardone, N.: Automatic generation of domain-aware control plane logic for software defined railway communication networks. In: Margaria, T., Steffen, B. (eds.) ISoLA 2022. LNCS, vol. 13704, pp. 308–320. Springer, Cham (2022)
2. Fantechi, A., Ferrari, A., Gnesi, S.: Formal methods and safety certification: challenges in the railways domain. In: Margaria, T., Steffen, B. (eds.) ISoLA 2016. LNCS, vol. 9953, pp. 261–265. Springer, Cham (2016). https://doi.org/10.1007/978-3-319-47169-3_18
3. Fantechi, A., Flammini, F., Gnesi, S.: Formal methods for intelligent transportation systems. In: Margaria, T., Steffen, B. (eds.) ISoLA 2012. LNCS, vol. 7610, pp. 187–189. Springer, Heidelberg (2012). https://doi.org/10.1007/978-3-642-34032-1_19
4. Fantechi, A., Gnesi, S., Haxthausen, A.E.: Formal methods for distributed computing in future railway systems. In: Margaria, T., Steffen, B. (eds.) ISoLA 2020. LNCS, vol. 12478, pp. 389–392. Springer, Cham (2020). https://doi.org/10.1007/978-3-030-61467-6_24
5. Fantechi, A., Gori, G., Gnesi, S.: Future train control systems: challenges for dependability assessment. In: Margaria, T., Steffen, B. (eds.) ISoLA 2022. LNCS, vol. 13704, pp. 269–285. Springer, Cham (2022)
6. Lecomte, T.: Safe and secure architecture using diverse formal methods. In: Margaria, T., Steffen, B. (eds.) ISoLA 2022. LNCS, vol. 13704, pp. 321–333. Springer, Cham (2022)
7. Seisenberger, M. et al.: Safe and secure future AI-driven railway technologies: challenges for formal methods in railway. In: Margaria, T., Steffen, B. (eds.) ISoLA 2022. LNCS, vol. 13704, pp. 246–268. Springer, Cham (2022)
8. Peleska, J., Haxthausen, A.E., Lecomte, T.: Standardisation considerations for autonomous train control. In: Margaria, T., Steffen, B. (eds.) ISoLA 2022. LNCS, vol. 13704, pp. 286–307. Springer, Cham (2022)

Safe and Secure Future AI-Driven Railway Technologies: Challenges for Formal Methods in Railway

Monika Seisenberger[1(✉)], Maurice H. ter Beek[2], Xiuyi Fan[3], Alessio Ferrari[2], Anne E. Haxthausen[4], Phillip James[1], Andrew Lawrence[5], Bas Luttik[6], Jaco van de Pol[7], and Simon Wimmer[7]

[1] Swansea University, Swansea, UK
m.seisenberger@swansea.ac.uk
[2] ISTI–CNR, Pisa, Italy
[3] Nanyang Technological University, Singapore, Singapore
[4] Technical University of Denmark, Kongens Lyngby, Denmark
[5] Siemens Mobility Chippenham, Chippenham, UK
[6] Eindhoven University of Technology, Eindhoven, The Netherlands
[7] Aarhus University, Aarhus, Denmark

Abstract. In 2020, the EU launched its sustainable and smart mobility strategy, outlining how it plans to have a 90% reduction in transport emission by 2050. Central to achieving this goal will be the improvement of rail technology, with many new data-driven visionary systems being proposed. AI will be the enabling technology for many of those systems. However, safety and security guarantees will be key for wide-spread acceptance and uptake by Industry and Society. Therefore, suitable verification and validation techniques are needed.

In this article, we argue how formal methods research can contribute to the development of modern Railway systems—which may or may not make use of AI techniques—and present several research problems and techniques worth to be further considered.

1 Introduction

In 2020, the EU launched its sustainable and smart mobility strategy, outlining how it plans to have a 90% reduction in transport emission by 2050. This will be key to achieving the European Green deal of becoming carbon neutral by 2050[1]. Central for this reduction will be the improvement of rail technology, as rail is one of the greenest modes of transportation. To address this ambition and support the interoperability and efficiency in the rail domain, new visionary systems based on interdisciplinary approaches in Engineering and Computer Science are being proposed, for example, innovative signalling systems (including moving block technology), smart monitoring and maintenance, optimal scheduling, and

[1] https://ec.europa.eu/info/strategy/priorities-2019-2024/european-green-deal_en.

T. Margaria and B. Steffen (Eds.): ISoLA 2022, LNCS 13704, pp. 246–268, 2022.
https://doi.org/10.1007/978-3-031-19762-8_20

automated driving. Underpinning these new systems, data is recognized as a highly valuable asset. For instance, the UK's Rail Technical Strategy (10/2020) states: "Data will have fit for purpose governance, access arrangements, systems and technical skills. These building blocks underpin the progression of all the other functional priorities which each have their own specific data requirements and opportunities."[2] AI will be the enabling technology for such data driven systems. However, safety and security guarantees will be key for wide-spread acceptance and uptake by industry and society. Therefore, suitable verification and validation techniques are needed.

In the Railway Industry and in verification and validation research, there is a skills gap in terms of knowledge of AI principles, techniques, and practices. The Railway Industry is normally focused on developing software and systems with fully predictable, explainable and verifiable behaviour, while AI techniques are by nature adaptive, and open to different scenarios. More importantly, AI-based systems have explainability problems that collide with the idea of fully controllable and verifiable system behaviour. Therefore, the Railway Industry needs to exploit AI systems to deliver smart and green transport, whilst at the same time maintaining the highest standards in terms of safety and certification.

In the following, we propose several research questions and challenges to the formal methods community, to aid the development as well as the certification of safe and secure next generation rail systems, many of which will make of use of AI techniques. Currently, ERTMS/ETCS level 3[3] is in the process to replace the traditional discrete train separation mechanism (blocks protected by hardware installed along the tracks) by a continuous mechanism (moving block), and use radio communication for the exchange of position information between trains and track-side. Also, Automatic Train Operation (ATO) will, at the higher grades of automation, replace the human driver and require a continuous software-controlled interaction, not only of a train with the track-side system, but also of trains between each other. Future signalling systems will be an order of magnitude more complex than they are today, and formal modelling and verification technology will be essential to cope with that complexity. The three challenges presented in this article will relate directly or indirectly to this situation.

The first challenge concerns certification and the associated verification technology. Automation of the verification is required to address the massive scale and complexity of railway systems. This entails intricate symbolic and parallel verification algorithms. A major problem for certification is that the implementation of the verification tools themselves could contain errors. Needed is a theory to equip verification tools with certificate generation, thus enabling the answers of automated verification tools to be checked independently. Furthermore, there is a need to investigate how AI based systems can be certified as this is not in general possible on the basis of today's CENELEC standards [46–48].

---

[2] https://railtechnicalstrategy.co.uk/data-driven/.

[3] https://www.ertms.net/, https://www.era.europa.eu/activities/european-rail-traffic-management-system-ertms/.

The second challenge concerns the European Train Traffic Management System. ERTMS/ETCS level 3 is anticipated to be the main railway system in 10 years' time. By introducing true continuous (moving block) signalling, it allows for both capacity increases and lower energy consumption, with trains effectively and intelligently managed. However, it also introduces elements of a hybrid nature into sub-systems of ERTMS, with components working with both discrete- and continuous-valued data. Along with this, traditional modelling of both safety and security need to change to include this hybrid nature. ERTMS consists of many interconnected components that differ in nature. This provides modelling challenges in both terms of complete models of the system, but also in terms of understanding and modelling the safety and security requirements of the sub-systems, both individually and as a whole. In addition, such signalling projects are often large and involve various aspects of backward compatibility with older signalling systems (e.g., to deal with older rolling stock) which causes scalability issues for current techniques. Modelling and verifying hybrid systems of the size presented by ERTMS/ETCS level 3 is an open challenge for Computer Science. Needed is a complete model which includes the safety and security requirements it must uphold. This will also serve as a reference architecture for ERTMS/ETCS level 3 deployment projects and help with the faster roll-out.

The third challenge concerns the extension of formal methods to include the use of AI techniques. We will present in Sect. 4 how this can be achieved, and highlight some of the methods we plan to utilise, as well as the problems that need to be overcome. Our focus on AI integration aligns well with the planned successor of Shift2Rail, Europe's Rail Joint Undertaking (EU-Rail), which will specifically focus on digitalisation and automation. So far, there are very few research projects and white papers (cf., e.g., [2,24]) that look into the integration of AI into the Railway domain. Notable exceptions are the RAILS project (Roadmaps for A.I. Integration in the RaiL Sector)[4], which provided a first overview on available AI techniques, as well as application areas and work done in the Railway domain, and the TAURO project (Technologies for Autonomous Rail Operation)[5]. We aim to complement this research by focusing on the specific challenges for formal methods, from a methodological point of view and by means of specific case studies.

Finally, to complete the picture, we mention a few recent projects which address the usage of formal methods in various Railway areas and whose results should be beneficial for the proposed challenges. ASTRail (SAtellite-based Signaling and Automation SysTems on Railways along with Formal Method and Moving Block Validation)[6] studied how to enhance the ERTMS with satellite-based GNSS train positioning, moving block distancing, and automatic train driving by exploiting cutting-edge technologies from the automotive and avionics domains as well as suitably assessed formal methods. 4SECURail (FORmal Methods and CSIRT (Computer Security Incident Response Team) for the

[4] https://cordis.europa.eu/project/id/881782.
[5] https://cordis.europa.eu/project/id/101014984.
[6] http://www.astrail.eu.

Railway sector)[7] provided a demonstrator of state-of-the-art formal methods and tools with an evaluation of the cost/benefit ratio and learning curves for adopting the demonstrator in the railway environment. It also developed, tested, and validated a CSIRT model and prototype co-designed with the relevant rail stakeholders. Notable new projects on intelligent systems are IN2SMART2[8], which is concerned with smart maintenance of Railway assets, SMART2[9], which aims at an integrated automated system for obstacle and track intrusion detection, and PERFORMINGRAIL (PERformance-based Formal modelling and Optimal tRaffic Management for movING-block RAILway signalling)[10].

2 Certified Verification of Railway Designs

Railway signaling systems are complex and safety-critical, imposing high safety standards and strict certification requirements [51]. The need for extensive testing, verification, and certification imposes an unfortunate barrier to the quick adoption of innovative railway technologies, which are essential to provide interoperability between national systems and increase utilisation of the railways. Therefore, we propose to push automated verification techniques for their certification. The dynamic nature of moving blocks, communication between trains and infrastructure, and the need to anticipate malfunctioning hardware, lead to an explosion of interactions and case distinctions, which can hardly be managed manually. Consequently, to eliminate manual errors and provide the necessary scalability, the verification needs to be *automated*. Moreover, the verification process needs to interact with the overall railway engineering process, in particular certification by regulatory bodies. To cater for the needs of stakeholders in this process (e.g., non-verification engineers, regulators, auditors), verification needs to be *trustworthy* and *explainable* [59,105].

In the following, we will discuss the state-of-the-art and open challenges of verification technology regarding railway systems, and on the three axis of automation, trustworthiness, and explainability. We will also address the challenge of which standards to use for certifying train control (sub-)systems, specifically when they are based on AI technology.

2.1 Automated Verification

Automated verification of railway signalling poses a scientific challenge for several reasons, given next.

Complexity: As discussed above, the modern railway systems lead to highly complex designs (of software, hardware, systems). Here, based on our expertise, we focus primarily on the area of model checking for the automated verification of such designs. Model checking is a purely automatic method, which

[7] https://www.4securail.eu/.
[8] https://cordis.europa.eu/project/id/881574.
[9] https://cordis.europa.eu/project/id/881784.
[10] https://cordis.europa.eu/project/id/101015416.

decides if a given specification (model) satisfies a given requirement (property). Various model-checking algorithms, ranging from exhaustive (probabilistic) model checking [9] to statistical model checking [3], have been proposed. Model checking is based on discrete enumeration [37], while statistical model checking involves running a sufficient number of (probabilistic) simulations to obtain statistical evidence (with a predefined confidence level).

Parametricity: For an effective deployment of signalling systems, there is a need to verify standard components that can be combined and instantiated to particular situations (e.g., track layouts). However, parametric verification is in general an undecidable problem [6]. This means that some form of abstraction and manual intervention is necessary to achieve verification results of the required generality. Compositional verification techniques [80] can be employed to combine verified standard components.

Continuous reasoning: Obviously, railway systems need to operate in real-time! Moreover, innovations like moving blocks require reasoning about continuous variables, such as braking curves. Stochastic behaviour (like failure of hardware components) leads to other forms of continuous reasoning. These continuous extensions remain challenging, and sometimes even cross the border of computational decidability [65]. Moreover, in case of AI-based systems, some components might be machine-learned models. These are of an inherently probabilistic nature and can be considered to be black-box components around which one may need to build a safety shield for runtime enforcement of guarantees [94].

Model checking is essentially a smart enumeration method of the possible system behaviour. Typically, the properties are checked on-the-fly, during the enumeration. The major threat to model checking is the state space explosion, exhausting not only time resources, but also the memory of the computer. Statistical model checking scales better, since there is no need to explore the full state space and the required simulations can trivially be distributed and run in parallel, but contrary to model checking, exact results (with 100% confidence) cannot be achieved.

The field of model-checking algorithms has advanced tremendously over the last 25 years. Many improvements are based on symbolic reasoning algorithms, like abstraction, symmetry reduction, partial-order reduction, and the use of BDD, SAT, and SMT solvers. Other improvements deploy high-performance computing, like clusters of machines, multi-core hardware, or even many-core GPUs to off-load intensive verification tasks [73]. While model checking is a very active field of research with many open challenges we refrain from addressing them here. Instead, we consider issues more specific to the railway domain in the following.

2.2 Trustworthy and Certifiable Verification

Verification can be seen as an instance of *trust reduction*: when employing verification in the engineering process, trust in the safety of the resulting system will to a large extent be deduced from trust in the correctness of the model. Therefore, on the one hand, the model needs to be a suitable representation of the system and its environment. On the other hand, the results of the verification process need to be trustworthy. We focus on the latter issue, which poses three fundamental challenges:

1. Model-checking algorithms and implementations became so advanced and complicated that it is hard to guarantee that these verification tools themselves are free from bugs. Indeed, several cases of bugs in verification tools (and even verification theory [29,98]) have been reported in the literature. This is clearly a threat for the certification of safety-critical systems.
2. Model checkers often run in so-called "bug hunting" mode. This means that they are specialised in finding bugs. To save on computational resources (time, memory, energy), they use various search heuristics. These heuristics give up completeness of the search. Hence, not finding any bugs is no guarantee of correctness. In this sense, bug hunting with model checking is similar to advanced, automated testing, which is also inherently incomplete (as is statistical model checking).
3. Model checking provides an asymmetric method. In principle, the answer to a model-checking query is either yes or no (the model either satisfies the property or violates it). In the "no-case", the model checker typically returns a counterexample, which can be inspected, tested on the model or even on the real system, and used to debug the model or the property. However, in the "yes-case", no further evidence is provided[11]. This is very unfortunate for certification, not only in light of the previous limitations, but also since no information for the safety-case is provided, besides the fact that no bug has been found.

A simple way to ameliorate implementation errors (but not errors in the theory), would be to compare the outputs of multiple tools. To achieve highest levels of trustworthiness, one might proceed by formally verifying the model checker. This provides a rigorous mathematical proof, checked in an interactive theorem prover [96,102] (like Coq [23] or Isabelle/HOL [87]). This approach would ensure that the "yes-result" of the model checker is trustworthy. However, although possible in principle, verification of an advanced model checker would be a major undertaking. There is some progress in the formal verification of model-checking algorithms [88,92] and even code [21,26,30,45,104], but so far, this could only be applied to relatively simple algorithms and basic implementations. Consequently, the "verified model checkers" cannot match the efficiency of high-performance model checkers.

We propose *certified model checking*, which provides a sweet-spot here: In this approach, one uses high-performance, "unsafe" model checkers, but equips them with the potential to generate some form of certificates in the "yes-case". One builds a separate, independent certifier, which checks the certificates. Since checking certificates is much simpler than finding certificates, the certifier is a

[11] Note that this holds for safety properties, but for others the cases can be inverted.

relatively simple tool, which can be formally verified. If the formally verified certifier accepts the certificate generated by the model checker, then we achieve maximal confidence in the safety of the system-under-study. Hence, in certified model checking we combine maximal efficiency (high-performance model checkers) with maximal confidence (formally verified certifiers). The concept of certified model checking was conceived for the μ-calculus [86]. A proof of concept has been provided for SMT-based model checking [74] (where certificates are basically invariants) and more recently for liveness checking of finite-state systems [60] and timed automata [103] (where certificates consist of reachability invariants and topological ranking functions). In the latter case, the certifier was fully verified in the theorem prover Isabelle/HOL.

Certified model checking poses multiple challenges. The generated certificates should contain sufficient information to check the proof independently; yet be more concise than the full state space, and easier to check than to generate. Independent certificate checker need to be constructed, possibly based on an interactive theorem prover. The certificate checker should be simple and amenable for formal verification. This requires a formalisation of (part of) the meta-theory of the verification tools.

The certified model-checking method is in its infancy: It is an open question what certificates for complicated model-checking algorithms, like partial-order order or symmetry reduction, should look like. It is also unclear how to generate certificates from parallel implementations of on-the-fly model checkers. The formal verification of the certification theory and the certifiers remains a challenge for these novel applications.

Moreover, a *lack of standardization* in modelling formalisms makes it hard to define general-purpose model checking certificates and to provide checkers for them. This is also a particular concern regarding the verification of the certificate checkers, as a large part of the laborious formalisation process would need to be repeated for each modelling language. Naturally, a lack of standardization is equally challenging for collaboration with regulatory bodies.

Finally, the certified verification approach needs to be extended to AI-intensive systems. In particular, classifiers and schedules generated by game-based AI algorithms should be equipped with certificates, so their essential properties can be checked independently. Interestingly, several model checking techniques, originally designed to analyse systems, can be extended to synthesis tasks. Tools like Uppaal TIGA [19] and Uppaal Stratego [40] can solve real-timed games. PRISM-games [75] can solve stochastic games. The winning strategies generated by such algorithms can (in principle) be converted to safe (and optimal) controllers. The synthesis of safe and optimal driving strategies with Uppaal Stratego has recently been shown for ERTMS Level 3 moving block railway signalling [13]. However, certification of synthesis algorithms is still open. In particular, the generated controllers tend to be large and enumerate possibilities, rather than conditions on data. Recent work [8] proposed to use decision trees to represent winning strategies; this could be a useful approach to synthesise controllers that are not just correct and certifiable but also explainable.

2.3 Explainable Verification

While certifiable verification can significantly increase reliability of the verification process, it is a whole challenge in itself to transform the computed certificate into an understandable piece of evidence, which can contribute to the safety case for certification authorities. This explainable verification should be the ultimate goal of this line of research. Without aspiring to completeness, we identify some open challenges in explainable verification.

Documentation of Verification. In particular, this should contain the precise claim of what has been verified by the tools, including the modelling assumptions, the assumptions on the environment, and potential approximations and inaccuracies implied by the selected options in the verification tools.

Interactive Explainability. It could be fruitful to base explainable verification methods on counterfactual explanation techniques for AI [67]. Counterfactuals provide an understanding into AI models by identifying similar inputs with changes in decisive properties that lead to a different model outcome than the one under study. For instance, given a particular dangerous scenario, the verification tool should be able to generate an argument why this particular scenario cannot happen. Novel interactive approaches that allow in-depth investigation of these properties for verification models will be needed. This is important to increase the trust of domain experts and certification authorities in the verification technology.

Practicality. Application-oriented research is required to investigate if certified model checking can provide useful evidence for the safety-case of railway systems, so that it significantly speeds-up the (regulatory) certification process for novel railway technology. This requires a careful consideration of the current standards used for certification in railways.

2.4 Standardisation

Certification of autonomous train control systems with Grade of Automation GoA 4 (unattended train operation, neither the driver nor the staff are required) in open railway environments, is a challenge: while conventional train control sub-systems can be certified on the basis of today's CENELEC standards [46–48], this is not the case for all AI-based sub-systems. The certification of such AI-based systems will require extensions/modifications of the current CENELEC standards or additional use of other standards. Therefore, there is a need to investigate how that can be done. In [90], Peleska et al. have investigated how the ANSI/UL 4600 pre-standard for Evaluation of Autonomous Products [100] can be used as a supplement to the CENELEC standards to certify autonomous freight trains and metro trains based on AI technology.

3 Formal Modelling and Analysis for the Railway Domain

Historically, the application of formal methods in order to verify railway systems is well established within academia and although several success stories of formal development and verification of software for the railway domain have shown the potential advantages [51], these technologies are still not universally part of the usual toolboxes of railway signalling companies.

As early as 1995, formal methods were applied to verify interlockings [5, 16, 61, 63]. Since then, and indeed recently, newer approaches to interlocking verification have also been proposed, also at ISoLA, and have been shown to scale well to modern industrial systems [20, 22, 27, 32, 36, 44, 50, 52, 64, 66, 68–70, 79, 106]. In spite of this, such approaches still lack widespread use within the Rail industry often due to questions surrounding the usability and expertise required for applying formal methods [53, 54].

Railway infrastructure managers have started to use semi-formal modelling languages (e.g., UML and SysML) to specify requirements, but they often still have to delegate formal verification activities to academic partners. The culprit is that effectively using state-of-the-art formal verification technology requires a thorough academic background in formal methods. A formal method that can be used by railway engineers needs to facilitate modelling railway systems concisely at the right level of abstraction and it should be easily parametrisable with relevant data (e.g., a track layout). Also, it must allow for a straightforward specification of relevant safety and security properties, verification algorithms that scale for systems in the railway context, and provide insightful presentation of verification results.

In addition, in the next two decades, European railway infrastructure managers need to sustain an enormous growth in mobility by increasing the capacity of their networks at acceptable costs. Key to the capacity increase will be the introduction of innovative digital systems such as ERTMS level 3, which involves a radically new approach to train separation, and various forms of ATO. The smooth roll-out of such systems on the dense European railway networks is an enormous challenge. It is, e.g., unacceptable for a railway line to be unavailable for long periods, and it should be possible for the innovative system to coexist with the legacy system. Therefore, it is important to thoroughly prepare roll-out of new systems. Extensive use of formal modelling and analysis techniques in the development process will reduce the need for testing in the field.

3.1 Domain Specific Technology and Usability

Railway infrastructure managers have started to use (semi-)formal languages to model their systems. These models are typically very detailed and use concrete data. For an effective formal analysis, a domain-specific modelling language that supports the appropriate level of abstraction is essential. Furthermore, the modelling language should offer a means to model relevant continuous aspects of railway systems (e.g., braking curves). Safety and liveness properties must be formulated at the same level of abstraction. The latter is non-trivial in the context of the railway domain since normally railway engineers are not used to formulating safety requirements at the appropriate level of abstraction. It will be necessary to develop a property language that is, on the one hand, expressive enough to express relevant safety requirements, and on the other hand can be used by railway engineers. Formal verification in the railway sector has focussed on safety properties. The verification of liveness properties has not received much attention but is highly relevant in view of dependability of railway systems. For the verification of liveness properties, one typically needs to incorporate progress or fairness assumptions in the verification process. Verification technology for the domain-specific modelling language should be built on top of a state-of-the-art general-purpose verification engine.

Another concern that is limiting uptake is the need to model in such a way that requirements can be efficiently verified for all relevant track layouts. With virtual fixed or moving blocks, data-parameterised verification becomes more important because track layouts are dynamically configurable. Currently, formal verification by model checking must often be carried out for specific track layouts. There is a need to develop formal modelling and verification technology that can efficiently verify safety and liveness properties of a signalling system for a class of relevant track layouts. To this end, the modelling language should facilitate data parametrisation. Not all data are realistic and so any approach will need to investigate ways of efficiently expressing assumptions on the parametrisation domain (e.g., using probability distributions). These assumptions must then be considered in the verification activities. Finally, a core aspect of this verification process is that it must be usable by railway engineers, a non-trivial endeavour. For railway-specific modelling and verification technology it is a major concern that railway engineers without extensive formal methods expertise can use it to gain insights in their systems. To this end, the modelling language should be easy to use, and verification results should be visualised (e.g., by running a graphical simulation of a counterexample). Railway engineers verify their designs by considering how they behave with respect to various operational scenarios. Model-checking technology can be used to generate interesting operational scenarios as evidence for certain properties. The idea is to formulate meaningful properties to verify and obtain the operational scenarios as evidence.

3.2 Standardised Reference Architectures

To facilitate interoperability, European railway infrastructure managers and operators and railway supply industry pursue standardisation of command and control systems. The best-known example is ERTMS/ETCS, which aims to standardise train-trackside communication (GSM-R), the train control system (ETCS), and the train management layer (ERTMS). The standard is formulated mostly in natural language and is therefore inherently ambiguous, which hampers a smooth deployment. Another standardisation project is EULYNX[12]; it aims at standardising the interfaces between the components of signalling systems (interlockings

[12] https://eulynx.eu.

and field elements such as points, level crossings, light signals, etc.). In EULYNX the official standard is still formulated in natural language, but there is also an explicit aim to supplement standard with SysML models. The academic project FormaSig[13] develops verification and model-based testing technology by which these SysML models can be formally verified and used for model-based testing purposes [28]. Similar to EULYNX, railway operators have started OCORA in which a standardised modular architecture for on-board command and control equipment is developed. This effort too should be supported with formal methods.

Although parts of the ETCS standard have been formally modelled and analysed [10–12,14,20,25,34,35,91], it would be both challenging and highly desirable to develop a formal model of ETCS level 3. The ongoing development by railway infrastructure managers of an RCA (the reference Control Command and Signalling (CCS) architecture), a common reference architecture for railway command and control systems will be a convenient vehicle. This reference architecture consists of standardised components (e.g., interlocking and field elements with EULYNX-compliant interfaces), which will facilitate the deployment of innovative systems. Here, one particular challenge that is still open is to integrate ETCS level 3 with RCA by developing an integral model including all relevant components, in order to analyse the correctness of the interactions between those components and determine if the safety and security requirements are met. Of course this also requires a systematic analysis of both safety and security requirements for ETCS level 3.

3.3 Digital Railway Innovations

A number of upcoming digital railway innovations bring promises in terms of improved safety, capacity and resilience. With these adaptations to infrastructure come fresh challenges for formal modelling and verification in particular throughout the certification process of these systems.

A significant increase in capacity can be realised by going from blocks protected by train detection equipment to train separation based on more precise position information from the train. The introduction of such a new train separation system entails new challenges for the signalling system. For instance, it needs to be robust against radio connection problems between train and trackside and take into account inaccuracies in positioning information. But most importantly, for a significant period of time such a new system needs to coexist together with the old system. To deal with such issues, digital solutions are developed, and these are an order of magnitude more complex. An example is the Hybrid ERTMS/ETCS Level 3 concept, which tries to bring the flexibility of moving block train separation to a signalling system based on traditional trackside train detection [58]. The application of formal modelling and analysis techniques have proved to be beneficial for improving the specification of the concept and for coping with its complexity [7,10,15,31,38,41,57,62,81].

[13] https://fsa.win.tue.nl/formasig.

A further increase in capacity, energy consumption and reliability is expected to come from ATO. Railway infrastructure managers and operators are currently experimenting with a form of semi-automatic train operation. The automatic train operation system merely assists the driver with accelerating and decelerating efficiently, but the driver remains responsible for safe movement of the train. The next step is to integrate a form of ATO with ERTMS/ETCS. This integration serves as the perfect example of a complex hybrid system and thus modelling and verification challenges that exist for hybrid systems apply. In particular, this integration poses challenges in terms of the discrete and continuous nature of the system. Concretely, models need to be developed that focus on the interaction of the ATO system with the safety system, and that consider modelling the influence of braking curves. Following this, suitable abstractions that involve reasoning over continuous data need to be explored and verification processes that scale for such a setting developed.

4 Formal Methods for AI

Formal methods have become a well-established and widely applied technique for ensuring the correctness of fundamental components of safety-critical systems in the railway domain, in particular verification techniques based on model checking (cf. Sect. 2.1). However, while a survey on software engineering for AI-based systems considered 248 studies published during the past decade, of which more than two-thirds since 2018 [83], the application of formal methods to AI-based systems is still in its infancy. A recent paper by Wing [105] lists the following three key insights:

1. The set of trustworthiness properties for AI systems, in contrast to traditional computing systems, needs to be extended beyond reliability, security, privacy, and usability to include properties such as probabilistic accuracy under uncertainty, fairness, robustness, accountability, and explainability.
2. To help ensure their trustworthiness, AI systems can benefit from the scrutiny of formal methods.
3. AI systems raise the bar on formal methods for two key reasons: the inherent probabilistic nature of machine-learned models, and the critical role of data in training, testing, and deploying a machine-learned model.

We envision to improve this situation by developing verification techniques that provide explainability or guarantees for AI-based systems in the specific safety-critical domain of railway systems, because, as Bešinović et al. put it, "although AI is still in its very infancy for the railway sector, there is certain evidence showing that its potential should not be underestimated" [24]. To this aim, we will first need to identify the state of the art of formal methods techniques developed for and applied to systems with AI-based components in the specific setting of transport systems (railways, but also automotive [97,99]) and of safety certification. A key difference with respect to the traditional formal verification approach, i.e., verifying a correctness property specified in some logic over a system model, is the inherent probabilistic nature of the (machine-learned) model in case of AI-based systems. Based on our previous experiences, we intend to study how to deal with safety concerns in the presence of uncertainty, and how probabilistic (and statistical) model-checking techniques or correctness-by-construction techniques can be adapted to provide appropriate fail-safe guarantees for AI-based railway systems. Correctness-by-construction, in particular when considering also non-functional properties (X-by-construction), in combination with probability and runtime verification is being studied also at ISoLA [17,18]. The same holds for formal methods for AI [76].

4.1 Guaranteeing Safety Behaviour

The wide availability of AI technologies and the pace of their evolution makes it hard for industry, with its consolidated processes, to profit from the potential benefits offered by these techniques. This is particularly true for the railway domain, in which the safety culture is strong, thus reinforcing the attachment to traditional, well-established practices that have proven their relevance even for the development of software systems that are not safety-critical. While many railway systems are required to fulfil SIL-4 certification requirements, many others, most notably maintenance systems, could instead make full use of the benefit of AI and process or data mining techniques. At the same time, explainability always must be ensured, to guarantee that the system behaviour can be explained, also for legal reasons, in case a failure occurs. Additionally, correctness is desirable as it would be difficult for a human to intervene and rectify mistakes made by such a system. For example, if a train is incorrectly routed across a junction it may take some time before it can be routed back across the junction in the correct direction and this would have impact on other trains in the area.

A concrete example from industry concerns an AI scheduler. Modern railway control systems are equipped with automatic route setting and traffic management but it is not clear how well they perform, specifically in case of a divergence from operational norms (e.g., if a train breaks down). It is typically the task of a qualified human to ensure trains run according to schedule, and to intervene when problems occur. Initial implementations of an AI scheduler could provide the human with guidance is such cases, assisting the human signaller in an efficient fashion to return the railway to an operational state by rerouting trains around the problem. When assisted by such an AI component, it is natural to want solutions that are presented by the AI component to both be explained and justified, and to not lead to intervention from safety critical components (for example, by providing solutions that violate the rules of the governing interlocking). For the human in the loop case it is essential for the AI system to be explainable and produce a justification that can be manually checked prior to making a decision.

4.2 Learning Formal Models of Railway Behaviour

Formal behavioural models are the building blocks of automated verification techniques in the field of formal methods. Such models define how a system behaves as a result of interacting with its users and its environment. Traditionally, these models (e.g., variants of automata and state machines) are obtained starting from semi-formal models (e.g., UML and message sequence charts) developed during the initial development phase. However, it frequently occurs that such behavioural models are either unavailable or outdated and thus need to be reconstructed from implementations in order to enable formal analysis. In such cases, model learning is an automated technique that can produce such models. This is a popular research field and much progress has been made since Vaandrager noted that "even though model learning has been applied successfully in several domains, the field is still in its infancy" [101]. Recent examples include [4,39]. However, to the best of our knowledge, specific success stories in the railway domain are missing.

We envision the usage of data or process mining techniques to build digital twins of railway systems that can provide predictive (runtime) behaviour and ultimately enable real-time predictive monitoring and maintenance (cf. Sect. 4.3). Engineering digital twins is being studied also at ISoLA [55,56,82], including some initial, recent attempts in the railway domain [77]. This requires the use of a variety of techniques from formal methods, in particular probabilistic (and statistical) model checking to deal with the inherent probabilistic nature of the (machine-learned) model, game theory (for instance for controller synthesis), and automata or model learning, but also specific techniques from data or process mining [1]. Railway system models are characterised by the need to deal with real-time aspects and a degree of uncertainty. We will thus have to study how to perform data or process mining on the provided observation data, like execution traces (i.e., logs) of a railway system, and how to use this to learn a digital twin of the railway system. This digital twin is meant to be a formal model that can handle real-time and probabilistic or stochastic behaviour (e.g., conform to the timed stochastic models accepted by the Uppaal model checker).

4.3 AI for Monitoring and Maintenance

Current railway monitoring and maintenance systems are mostly rule-based and typically do not include AI-based components, which can be particularly useful, e.g., to predict possible failures and to plan specific maintenance actions [33,85]. AI systems, combined with existing rules provided by experts, can enable predictive maintenance, by identifying patterns of faults based on systems logs. Model learning for maintenance implies learning of the system model, and learning of a system's fault model, so that future faults can be predicted based on current system behaviour. The system's digital twin can also be used to forecast and simulate future long-term scenarios, thus helping to plan for maintenance actions in advance, i.e., before faults occur. Refactoring current rule-based maintenance systems with AI-based components poses numerous challenges. The effective exploitation of AI and process or data mining techniques requires the domain experts to annotate field data, such that the machine can learn from experts. Similarly, experts are needed to assess the correct behaviour and interpretation of possible failures of the AI-based maintenance system. Explainability of these systems becomes crucial, as well as correct communication of the behaviour's explanation to experts and other railway stakeholders. In the envisioned maintenance process, the behaviour of the onboard system can easily be reconstructed and visualised, and maintenance and improvement actions can be taken in a more flexible and effective way.

4.4 AI for Optimisation in Scheduling and Design

Whilst so far we addressed principal problems that need to be solved when using AI techniques, we now want to look at several specific applications in the railway domain. The first two applications concern problems for which currently no general optimal solutions exist, but where one can hope with the use of AI to achieve better solutions, i.e., solutions which are more efficient in terms of energy/time or which require less track-side equipment. For the solutions in this section it is, of course, essential that they are still safe and fulfil all safety requirements. Therefore it is anticipated that the solutions produced are not only very good, but that they also come with a guarantee or explanation. Overall, optimisations like, saving energy or requiring less track-side equipment contribute to the aim of reducing carbon. Also capacity improvements support the green deal (indirectly), as efficient and safe provision leads to a higher customer satisfaction and a higher uptake of railway use.

Our first application refers to scheduling which has frequently been considered as an optimisation problem in the past [42,71,72,84,89]. An AI Scheduler (cf. Sect. 4.1) could help to support and improve the decision making of a human signaller and optimising the flow of trains through the railway network.

A second standard application concerns the optimisation of railway design and layout. Railways are designed by engineers who create scheme plans with the topology of the railway and the layout of the equipment along the tracks. Published solutions for the automatic generation of signalling design seem not to consider optimisation at all. Desired would be an AI solution for the placement of the equipment that still fulfils all required constraints, such as number of balises in a given area, or a requested distance between balise groups, etc. Model checking/SMT solving can then be used to check the constraints and highlight counterexamples in a efficient way (where the visualisation of counterexamples in a domain specific area constitutes an interesting problem on its own.) Various AI techniques as well as Game theory and Explainable AI (XAI) can be used for the optimisation according to a given measure such as energy/material consumption.

5 Conclusion and Further Work

In this article, we discussed several challenges for Formal Methods in Railway linked to the areas of (1) Verification and Certification, (2) Modelling of ETCS related systems, and, (3) the use of AI in the railway domain. Their common aim is a robust development of complex railway technology that is reliable and efficient at the same time. Our specific focus in (1) and (3) was that any (new) techniques need to come with explanations/ guarantees in order to be accepted by the Railway engineers and the general public. Specifically, regarding the question of using AI techniques in Railway, further research is needed about which AI techniques we can apply and how to create explanations and guarantees. This is relatively straightforward in the case of applying, for instance, SMT-solving. Here, SMT-solving would provide counterexamples, and the gap to be closed concentrates on making these counterexamples (1) readable in the Railway context and (2) independently verifiable. Conversely, at the other end of the spectrum, if we want to apply machine-learning techniques for, e.g., classification, the situation is completely different: Explainable AI (XAI), with LIME [95] and SHAP [78] as prominent techniques, has become established for providing explanations, however recent work has demonstrated that different XAI techniques do not necessarily coincide on their results [43]. Problems like these prompt research towards a theory of faithful explanations [93] and the idea of Verifiable XAI [49]. More effort and case studies will be needed to develop these techniques and make them usable in the Railway context.

Acknowledgment. We would like to thank the anonymous referees for their constructive criticism and helpful comments.

References

1. van der Aalst, W.M.P.: Process Mining: Data Science in Action. Springer, Heidelberg (2016). https://doi.org/10.1007/978-3-662-49851-4
2. ADLINK Technology: Transforming the rail industry with artificial intelligence (2021). https://www.globalrailwayreview.com/whitepaper/127609/transforming-the-rail-industry-with-ai
3. Agha, G., Palmskog, K.: A survey of statistical model checking. ACM Trans. Model. Comput. Simul. **28**(1), 6:1-6:39 (2018). https://doi.org/10.1145/3158668
4. Aichernig, B.K., et al.: Learning a behavior model of hybrid systems through combining model-based testing and machine learning. In: Gaston, C., Kosmatov, N., Le Gall, P. (eds.) ICTSS 2019. LNCS, vol. 11812, pp. 3–21. Springer, Cham (2019). https://doi.org/10.1007/978-3-030-31280-0_1
5. Anselmi, A., et al.: An experience in formal verification of safety properties of a railway signalling control system. In: Rabe, G. (ed.) Proceedings of the 14th International Conference on Computer Safety, Reliability and Security (SAFECOMP 1995), pp. 474–488. Springer (1995). https://doi.org/10.1007/978-1-4471-3054-3_33
6. Apt, K.R., Kozen, D.: Limits for automatic verification of finite-state concurrent systems. Inf. Process. Lett. **22**(6), 307–309 (1986)
7. Arcaini, P., Kofroň, J., Ježek, P.: Validation of the Hybrid ERTMS/ETCS Level 3 using SPIN. Int. J. Softw. Tools Technol. Transfer **22**(3), 265–279 (2019). https://doi.org/10.1007/s10009-019-00539-x

8. Ashok, P., Jackermeier, M., Křetínský, J., Weinhuber, C., Weininger, M., Yadav, M.: dtControl 2.0: explainable strategy representation via decision tree learning steered by experts. In: TACAS 2021. LNCS, vol. 12652, pp. 326–345. Springer, Cham (2021). https://doi.org/10.1007/978-3-030-72013-1_17
9. Baier, C., Katoen, J.: Principles of Model Checking. MIT Press, Cambridge (2008)
10. Bartholomeus, M., Luttik, B., Willemse, T.: Modelling and analysing ERTMS hybrid level 3 with the mCRL2 toolset. In: Howar, F., Barnat, J. (eds.) FMICS 2018. LNCS, vol. 11119, pp. 98–114. Springer, Cham (2018). https://doi.org/10.1007/978-3-030-00244-2_7
11. Basile, D., ter Beek, M.H., Ciancia, V.: Statistical model checking of a moving block railway signalling scenario with UPPAAL SMC. In: Margaria, T., Steffen, B. (eds.) ISoLA 2018. LNCS, vol. 11245, pp. 372–391. Springer, Cham (2018). https://doi.org/10.1007/978-3-030-03421-4_24
12. Basile, D., ter Beek, M.H., Ferrari, A., Legay, A.: Modelling and analysing ERTMS L3 moving block railway signalling with Simulink and UPPAAL SMC. In: Larsen, K.G., Willemse, T. (eds.) FMICS 2019. LNCS, vol. 11687, pp. 1–21. Springer, Cham (2019). https://doi.org/10.1007/978-3-030-27008-7_1
13. Basile, D., ter Beek, M.H., Legay, A.: Strategy synthesis for autonomous driving in a moving block railway system with UPPAAL STRATEGO. In: Gotsman, A., Sokolova, A. (eds.) FORTE 2020. LNCS, vol. 12136, pp. 3–21. Springer, Cham (2020). https://doi.org/10.1007/978-3-030-50086-3_1
14. Basile, D., Fantechi, A., Rosadi, I.: Formal analysis of the UNISIG safety application intermediate sub-layer. In: Lluch Lafuente, A., Mavridou, A. (eds.) FMICS 2021. LNCS, vol. 12863, pp. 174–190. Springer, Cham (2021). https://doi.org/10.1007/978-3-030-85248-1_11
15. Basile, D., Fantechi, A., Rucher, L., Mandò, G.: Analysing an autonomous tramway positioning system with the UPPAAL statistical model checker. Formal Aspects Comput. **33**(6), 957–987 (2021). https://doi.org/10.1007/s00165-021-00556-1
16. Basten, T., Bol, R.N., Voorhoeve, M.: Simulating and analyzing railway interlockings in ExSpect. IEEE Parallel Distrib. Technol. Syst. Appl. **3**(3), 50–62 (1995). https://doi.org/10.1109/M-PDT.1995.414843
17. ter Beek, M.H., Cleophas, L., Legay, A., Schaefer, I., Watson, B.W.: X-by-Construction: correctness meets probability. In: Margaria, T., Steffen, B. (eds.) ISoLA 2020. LNCS, vol. 12476, pp. 211–215. Springer, Cham (2020). https://doi.org/10.1007/978-3-030-61362-4_11
18. ter Beek, M.H., Cleophas, L., Leucker, M., Schaefer, I.: X-by-Construction meets runtime verification. In: Margaria, T., Steffen, B. (eds.) ISoLA 2022. LNCS, vol. 13701, pp. 141–148. Springer, Cham (2022). https://doi.org/10.1007/978-3-031-19849-6_9
19. Behrmann, G., Cougnard, A., David, A., Fleury, E., Larsen, K.G., Lime, D.: UPPAAL-Tiga: time for playing games! In: Damm, W., Hermanns, H. (eds.) CAV 2007. LNCS, vol. 4590, pp. 121–125. Springer, Heidelberg (2007). https://doi.org/10.1007/978-3-540-73368-3_14
20. Berger, U., James, P., Lawrence, A., Roggenbach, M., Seisenberger, M.: Verification of the European Rail Traffic Management System in Real-Time Maude. Sci. Comput. Program. **154**, 61–88 (2018). https://doi.org/10.1016/j.scico.2017.10.011
21. Berger, U., Lawrence, A., Forsberg, F.N., Seisenberger, M.: Extracting verified decision procedures: DPLL and resolution. Log. Methods Comp. Sci. **11**(1), 1–18 (2015). https://doi.org/10.2168/LMCS-11(1:6)2015

22. Bernardeschi, C., Fantechi, A., Gnesi, S., Larosa, S., Mongardi, G., Romano, D.: A formal verification environment for railway signaling system design. Formal Methods Syst. Des. **12**(2), 139–161 (1998). https://doi.org/10.1023/A:1008645826258
23. Bertot, Y., Castéran, P.: Interactive Theorem Proving and Program Development - Coq'Art: The Calculus of Inductive Constructions. Texts in Theoretical Computer Science. An EATCS Series, Springer, Heidelberg (2004). https://doi.org/10.1007/978-3-662-07964-5
24. Bešinović, N., et al.: Artificial intelligence in railway transport: taxonomy, regulations and applications. IEEE Trans. Intell. Transp. Syst. **23**, 14011–14024 (2022). https://doi.org/10.1109/TITS.2021.3131637
25. Biagi, M., Carnevali, L., Paolieri, M., Vicario, E.: Performability evaluation of the ERTMS/ETCS - level 3. Transp. Res. C-Emer. **82**, 314–336 (2017). https://doi.org/10.1016/j.trc.2017.07.002
26. Blanchette, J.C., Fleury, M., Lammich, P., Weidenbach, C.: A verified SAT solver framework with learn, forget, restart, and incrementality. J. Autom. Reasoning **61**(1), 333–365 (2018). https://doi.org/10.1007/s10817-018-9455-7
27. Bouwman, M., Janssen, B., Luttik, B.: Formal modelling and verification of an interlocking using mCRL2. In: Larsen, K.G., Willemse, T. (eds.) FMICS 2019. LNCS, vol. 11687, pp. 22–39. Springer, Cham (2019). https://doi.org/10.1007/978-3-030-27008-7_2
28. Bouwman, M., van der Wal, D., Luttik, B., Stoelinga, M., Rensink, A.: A case in point: verification and testing of a EULYNX interface. Form. Asp. Comput. (2022). https://doi.org/10.1145/3528207
29. Bouyer, P., Laroussinie, F., Reynier, P.-A.: Diagonal constraints in timed automata: forward analysis of timed systems. In: Pettersson, P., Yi, W. (eds.) FORMATS 2005. LNCS, vol. 3829, pp. 112–126. Springer, Heidelberg (2005). https://doi.org/10.1007/11603009_10
30. Brunner, J., Lammich, P.: Formal verification of an executable LTL model checker with partial order reduction. J. Autom. Reason. **60**(1), 3–21 (2017). https://doi.org/10.1007/s10817-017-9418-4
31. Butler, M., Hoang, T.S., Raschke, A., Reichl, K.: Introduction to special section on the ABZ 2018 case study: Hybrid ERTMS/ETCS Level 3. Int. J. Softw. Tools Technol. Transfer **22**(3), 249–255 (2020). https://doi.org/10.1007/s10009-020-00562-3
32. Cappart, Q., Limbrée, C., Schaus, P., Quilbeuf, J., Traonouez, L., Legay, A.: Verification of interlocking systems using statistical model checking. In: Proceedings of the 18th International Symposium on High Assurance Systems Engineering (HASE 2017), pp. 61–68. IEEE (2017). https://doi.org/10.1109/HASE.2017.10
33. Carvalho, T.P., et al.: A systematic literature review of machine learning methods applied to predictive maintenance. Comput. Ind. Eng. **137**, 106024 (2019). https://doi.org/10.1016/j.cie.2019.106024
34. Chiappini, A., et al.: Formalization and validation of a subset of the European train control system. In: Proceedings of the 32nd International Conference on Software Engineering (ICSE 2010), pp. 109–118. ACM (2010). https://doi.org/10.1145/1810295.1810312
35. Cimatti, A., et al.: Formal verification and validation of ERTMS industrial railway train spacing system. In: Madhusudan, P., Seshia, S.A. (eds.) CAV 2012. LNCS, vol. 7358, pp. 378–393. Springer, Heidelberg (2012). https://doi.org/10.1007/978-3-642-31424-7_29

36. Cimatti, A., Giunchiglia, F., Mongardi, G., Romano, D., Torielli, F., Traverso, P.: Model checking safety critical software with SPIN: an application to a railway interlocking system. In: Ehrenberger, W. (ed.) SAFECOMP 1998. LNCS, vol. 1516, pp. 284–293. Springer, Heidelberg (1998). https://doi.org/10.1007/3-540-49646-7_22
37. Clarke, E.M., Henzinger, T.A., Veith, H., Bloem, R. (eds.): Handbook of Model Checking. Springer, Cham (2018). https://doi.org/10.1007/978-3-319-10575-8
38. Cunha, A., Macedo, N.: Validating the Hybrid ERTMS/ETCS level 3 concept with Electrum. Int. J. Softw. Tools Technol. Transfer **22**(3), 281–296 (2019). https://doi.org/10.1007/s10009-019-00540-4
39. Damasceno, C.D.N., Mousavi, M.R., Simao, A.S.: Learning by sampling: learning behavioral family models from software product lines. Empir. Softw. Eng. **26**(1), 1–46 (2021). https://doi.org/10.1007/s10664-020-09912-w
40. David, A., Jensen, P.G., Larsen, K.G., Mikučionis, M., Taankvist, J.H.: Uppaal Stratego. In: Baier, C., Tinelli, C. (eds.) TACAS 2015. LNCS, vol. 9035, pp. 206–211. Springer, Heidelberg (2015). https://doi.org/10.1007/978-3-662-46681-0_16
41. Dghaym, D., Dalvandi, M., Poppleton, M., Snook, C.: Formalising the hybrid ERTMS Level 3 specification in iUML-B and Event-B. Int. J. Softw. Tools Technol. Transfer **22**(3), 297–313 (2019). https://doi.org/10.1007/s10009-019-00548-w
42. Dillmann, S., Hähnle, R.: Automated planning of ETCS tracks. In: Collart-Dutilleul, S., Lecomte, T., Romanovsky, A. (eds.) RSSRail 2019. LNCS, vol. 11495, pp. 79–90. Springer, Cham (2019). https://doi.org/10.1007/978-3-030-18744-6_5
43. Duell, J., Fan, X., Burnett, B., Aarts, G., Zhou, S.M.: A comparison of explanations given by explainable artificial intelligence methods on analysing electronic health records. In: Proceedings of the 7th EMBS International Conference on Biomedical and Health Informatics (BHI 2021), pp. 1–4. IEEE (2021). https://doi.org/10.1109/BHI50953.2021.9508618
44. Eisner, C.: Using symbolic CTL model checking to verify the railway stations of Hoorn-Kersenboogerd and Heerhugowaard. Int. J. Softw. Tools Technol. Transf. **4**(1), 107–124 (2002). https://doi.org/10.1007/s100090100063
45. Esparza, J., Lammich, P., Neumann, R., Nipkow, T., Schimpf, A., Smaus, J.: A fully verified executable LTL model checker. Arch. Formal Proofs (2014). https://isa-afp.org/entries/CAVA_LTL_Modelchecker.html
46. European Committee for Electrotechnical Standardization: CENELEC EN 50128 – Railway applications - Communication, signalling and processing systems - Software for railway control and protection systems (2011)
47. European Committee for Electrotechnical Standardization: CENELEC EN 50126–1 – Railway applications - The specification and demonstration of reliability, availability, maintainability and safety (RAMS) - Part 1: Generic RAMS process (2017)
48. European Committee for Electrotechnical Standardization: CENELEC EN 50129 – Railway applications - Communication, signalling and processing systems - Safety related electronic systems for signalling (2018)
49. Fan, X.: Verifiable Explainable AI (2021)
50. Fantechi, A.: Distributing the challenge of model checking interlocking control tables. In: Margaria, T., Steffen, B. (eds.) ISoLA 2012. LNCS, vol. 7610, pp. 276–289. Springer, Heidelberg (2012). https://doi.org/10.1007/978-3-642-34032-1_26

51. Ferrari, A., ter Beek, M.H.: Formal methods in railways: a systematic mapping study. ACM Comput. Surv. (2022). https://doi.org/10.1145/3520480
52. Ferrari, A., Magnani, G., Grasso, D., Fantechi, A.: Model checking interlocking control tables. In: Schnieder, E., Tarnai, G. (eds.) Proceedings of the 8th Symposium on Formal Methods for Automation and Safety in Railway and Automotive Systems (FORMS/FORMAT 2010), pp. 107–115. Springer (2010). https://doi.org/10.1007/978-3-642-14261-1_11
53. Ferrari, A., Mazzanti, F., Basile, D., ter Beek, M.H.: Systematic evaluation and usability analysis of formal tools for railway system design. IEEE Trans. Softw. Eng. (2021). https://doi.org/10.1109/TSE.2021.3124677
54. Ferrari, A., Mazzanti, F., Basile, D., ter Beek, M.H., Fantechi, A.: Comparing formal tools for system design: a judgment study. In: Proceedings of the 42nd International Conference on Software Engineering (ICSE 2020), pp. 62–74. ACM (2020). https://doi.org/10.1145/3377811.3380373
55. Fitzgerald, J., Larsen, P.G., Margaria, T., Woodcock, J.: Engineering of digital twins for cyber-physical systems. In: Margaria, T., Steffen, B. (eds.) ISoLA 2020. LNCS, vol. 12479, pp. 49–53. Springer, Cham (2021). https://doi.org/10.1007/978-3-030-83723-5_4
56. Fitzgerald, J., Larsen, P.G., Margaria, T., Woodcock, J., Gomes, C.: Engineering of digital twins for cyber-physical systems. In: Margaria, T., Steffen, B. (eds.) ISoLA 2022. LNCS, vol. 13704, pp. 3–8. Springer, Cham (2022). https://doi.org/10.1007/978-3-031-19762-8_1
57. Tueno Fotso, S.J., Frappier, M., Laleau, R., Mammar, A.: Modeling the hybrid ERTMS/ETCS level 3 standard using a formal requirements engineering approach. Int. J. Softw. Tools Technol. Transfer **22**(3), 349–363 (2019). https://doi.org/10.1007/s10009-019-00542-2
58. Furness, N., van Houten, H., Arenas, L., Bartholomeus, M.: ERTMS level 3: the game-changer. IRSE News **232**, 2–9 (2017). https://www.irse.nl/resources/170314-ERTMS-L3-The-gamechanger-from-IRSE-News-Issue-232.pdf
59. Gossen, F., Margaria, T., Steffen, B.: Towards explainability in machine learning: the formal methods way. IT Prof. **22**(4), 8–12 (2020). https://doi.org/10.1109/MITP.2020.3005640
60. Griggio, A., Roveri, M., Tonetta, S.: Certifying proofs for SAT-based model checking. Formal Methods Syst. Des. **57**(2), 178–210 (2021). https://doi.org/10.1007/s10703-021-00369-1
61. Groote, J.F., Vlijmen, S.F.M., Koorn, J.W.C.: The safety guaranteeing system at station Hoorn-Kersenboogerd. In: Proceedings of the 10th Annual Conference on Computer Assurance Systems Integrity, Software Safety and Process Security (COMPASS 1995), pp. 57–68. IEEE (1995). https://doi.org/10.1109/CMPASS.1995.521887
62. Hansen, D., et al.: Validation and real-life demonstration of ETCS hybrid level 3 principles using a formal B model. Int. J. Softw. Tools Technol. Transfer **22**(3), 315–332 (2020). https://doi.org/10.1007/s10009-020-00551-6
63. Hartonas-Garmhausen, V., Kurfess, T.R., Clarke, E.M., Long, D.E.: Automatic verification of industrial designs. In: Proceedings of the Workshop on Industrial-Strength Formal Specification Techniques (WIFT 1995), pp. 88–96. IEEE Computer Society (1995). https://doi.org/10.1109/WIFT.1995.515481
64. Haxthausen, A.E., Kjær, A.A., Le Bliguet, M.: Formal development of a tool for automated modelling and verification of relay interlocking systems. In: Butler, M., Schulte, W. (eds.) FM 2011. LNCS, vol. 6664, pp. 118–132. Springer, Heidelberg (2011). https://doi.org/10.1007/978-3-642-21437-0_11

65. Henzinger, T.A., Kopke, P.W., Puri, A., Varaiya, P.: What's decidable about hybrid automata? J. Comput. Syst. Sci. **57**(1), 94–124 (1998). https://doi.org/10.1006/jcss.1998.1581
66. Hong, L.V., Haxthausen, A.E., Peleska, J.: Formal modelling and verification of interlocking systems featuring sequential release. Sci. Comput. Program. **133**, 91–115 (2017). https://doi.org/10.1016/j.scico.2016.05.010
67. Hvilshøj, F., Iosifidis, A., Assent, I.: ECINN: efficient counterfactuals from invertible neural networks. CoRR abs/2103.13701 (2021). https://doi.org/10.48550/arXiv.2103.13701
68. James, P., et al.: Verification of solid state interlocking programs. In: Counsell, S., Núñez, M. (eds.) SEFM 2013. LNCS, vol. 8368, pp. 253–268. Springer, Cham (2014). https://doi.org/10.1007/978-3-319-05032-4_19
69. James, P., Moller, F., Nguyen, H.N., Roggenbach, M., Schneider, S., Treharne, H.: Techniques for modelling and verifying railway interlockings. Int. J. Softw. Tools Technol. Transfer **16**(6), 685–711 (2014). https://doi.org/10.1007/s10009-014-0304-7
70. James, P., Moller, F., Nguyen, H.N., Roggenbach, M., Schneider, S., Treharne, H.: On modelling and verifying railway interlockings: tracking train lengths. Sci. Comput. Program. **96**, 315–336 (2014). https://doi.org/10.1016/j.scico.2014.04.005
71. James, P., et al.: Verification of scheme plans using CSP||B. In: Counsell, S., Núñez, M. (eds.) SEFM 2013. LNCS, vol. 8368, pp. 189–204. Springer, Cham (2014). https://doi.org/10.1007/978-3-319-05032-4_15
72. James, P., Roggenbach, M.: Encapsulating formal methods within domain specific languages: a solution for verifying railway scheme plans. Math. Comput. Sci. **8**(1), 11–38 (2014). https://doi.org/10.1007/s11786-014-0174-0
73. Kant, G., Laarman, A., Meijer, J., van de Pol, J., Blom, S., van Dijk, T.: LTSmin: high-performance language-independent model checking. In: Baier, C., Tinelli, C. (eds.) TACAS 2015. LNCS, vol. 9035, pp. 692–707. Springer, Heidelberg (2015). https://doi.org/10.1007/978-3-662-46681-0_61
74. Katz, G., Barrett, C.W., Tinelli, C., Reynolds, A., Hadarean, L.: Lazy proofs for DPLL(T)-based SMT solvers. In: Proceedings of the 16th Conference on Formal Methods in Computer-Aided Design (FMCAD 2016), pp. 93–100. IEEE (2016). https://doi.org/10.1109/FMCAD.2016.7886666
75. Kwiatkowska, M., Norman, G., Parker, D., Santos, G.: PRISM-games 3.0: stochastic game verification with concurrency, equilibria and time. In: Lahiri, S.K., Wang, C. (eds.) CAV 2020. LNCS, vol. 12225, pp. 475–487. Springer, Cham (2020). https://doi.org/10.1007/978-3-030-53291-8_25
76. Larsen, K., Legay, A., Nolte, G., Schlüter, M., Stoelinga, M., Steffen, B.: Formal methods meet machine learning (F3ML). In: Margaria, T., Steffen, B. (eds.) ISoLA 2022. LNCS, vol. 13703, pp. 393–405. Springer, Cham (2022). https://doi.org/10.1007/978-3-031-19759-8_24
77. Lecomte, T.: Digital modelling in the railways. In: Margaria, T., Steffen, B. (eds.) ISoLA 2020. LNCS, vol. 12479, pp. 124–139. Springer, Cham (2021). https://doi.org/10.1007/978-3-030-83723-5_9
78. Lundberg, S.M., Lee, S.: A unified approach to interpreting model predictions. In: Proceedings of the 31st Conference on Neural Information Processing Systems (NIPS 2017), pp. 4768–4777 (2017). https://proceedings.neurips.cc/paper/2017/hash/8a20a8621978632d76c43dfd28b67767-Abstract.html

79. Macedo, H.D., Fantechi, A., Haxthausen, A.E.: Compositional verification of multi-station interlocking systems. In: Margaria, T., Steffen, B. (eds.) ISoLA 2016. LNCS, vol. 9953, pp. 279–293. Springer, Cham (2016). https://doi.org/10.1007/978-3-319-47169-3_20
80. Macedo, H.D., Fantechi, A., Haxthausen, A.E.: Compositional model checking of interlocking systems for lines with multiple stations. In: Barrett, C., Davies, M., Kahsai, T. (eds.) NFM 2017. LNCS, vol. 10227, pp. 146–162. Springer, Cham (2017). https://doi.org/10.1007/978-3-319-57288-8_11
81. Mammar, A., Frappier, M., Tueno Fotso, S.J., Laleau, R.: A formal refinement-based analysis of the hybrid ERTMS/ETCS level 3 standard. Int. J. Softw. Tools Technol. Transfer **22**(3), 333–347 (2019). https://doi.org/10.1007/s10009-019-00543-1
82. Margaria, T., Schieweck, A.: Towards engineering digital twins by active behaviour mining. In: Olderog, E.-R., Steffen, B., Yi, W. (eds.) Model Checking, Synthesis, and Learning. LNCS, vol. 13030, pp. 138–163. Springer, Cham (2021). https://doi.org/10.1007/978-3-030-91384-7_8
83. Martínez-Fernández, S., et al.: Software engineering for AI-based systems: a survey. ACM Trans. Softw. Eng. Methodol. **31**(2), 37e:1-37e:59 (2022). https://doi.org/10.1145/3487043
84. Mazzanti, F., Spagnolo, G.O., Della Longa, S., Ferrari, A.: Deadlock avoidance in train scheduling: a model checking approach. In: Lang, F., Flammini, F. (eds.) FMICS 2014. LNCS, vol. 8718, pp. 109–123. Springer, Cham (2014). https://doi.org/10.1007/978-3-319-10702-8_8
85. Chenariyan Nakhaee, M., Hiemstra, D., Stoelinga, M., van Noort, M.: The recent applications of machine learning in rail track maintenance: a survey. In: Collart-Dutilleul, S., Lecomte, T., Romanovsky, A. (eds.) RSSRail 2019. LNCS, vol. 11495, pp. 91–105. Springer, Cham (2019). https://doi.org/10.1007/978-3-030-18744-6_6
86. Namjoshi, K.S.: Certifying model checkers. In: Berry, G., Comon, H., Finkel, A. (eds.) CAV 2001. LNCS, vol. 2102, pp. 2–13. Springer, Heidelberg (2001). https://doi.org/10.1007/3-540-44585-4_2
87. Nipkow, T., Wenzel, M., Paulson, L.C. (eds.): Isabelle/HOL. LNCS, vol. 2283. Springer, Heidelberg (2002). https://doi.org/10.1007/3-540-45949-9
88. Oortwijn, W., Huisman, M., Joosten, S.J.C., van de Pol, J.: automated verification of parallel nested DFS. In: TACAS 2020. LNCS, vol. 12078, pp. 247–265. Springer, Cham (2020). https://doi.org/10.1007/978-3-030-45190-5_14
89. Peham, T., Przigoda, J., Przigoda, N., Wille, R.: Optimal railway routing using virtual subsections. In: Collart-Dutilleul, S., Haxthausen, A.E., Lecomte, T. (eds.) RSSRail 2022. LNCS, vol. 13294, pp. 63–79. Springe, Cham (2022). https://doi.org/10.1007/978-3-031-05814-1_5
90. Peleska, J., Haxthausen, A.E., Lecomte, T.: Standardisation considerations for autonomous train control. In: Margaria, T., Steffen, B. (eds.) ISoLA 2022. LNCS, Springer (2022)
91. Platzer, A., Quesel, J.-D.: European train control system: a case study in formal verification. In: Breitman, K., Cavalcanti, A. (eds.) ICFEM 2009. LNCS, vol. 5885, pp. 246–265. Springer, Heidelberg (2009). https://doi.org/10.1007/978-3-642-10373-5_13
92. van de Pol, J.C.: Automated verification of nested DFS. In: Núñez, M., Güdemann, M. (eds.) FMICS 2015. LNCS, vol. 9128, pp. 181–197. Springer, Cham (2015). https://doi.org/10.1007/978-3-319-19458-5_12

93. Potyka, N., Yin, X., Toni, F.: Towards a theory of faithfulness: faithful explanations of differentiable classifiers over continuous data. CoRR abs/2205.09620 (2022). https://doi.org/10.48550/arXiv.2205.09620
94. Pranger, S., Könighofer, B., Posch, L., Bloem, R.: TEMPEST - synthesis tool for reactive systems and shields in probabilistic environments. In: Hou, Z., Ganesh, V. (eds.) ATVA 2021. LNCS, vol. 12971, pp. 222–228. Springer, Cham (2021). https://doi.org/10.1007/978-3-030-88885-5_15
95. Ribeiro, M.T., Singh, S., Guestrin, C.: "Why should I trust you?": explaining the predictions of any classifier. In: Proceedings of the Demonstrations Session of the 2016 Conference of the North American Chapter of the Association for Computational Linguistics: Human Language Technologies (NAACL HLT 2016), pp. 97–101 (2016). https://doi.org/10.18653/v1/n16-3020
96. Ringer, T., Palmskog, K., Sergey, I., Gligoric, M., Tatlock, Z.: QED at large: A survey of engineering of formally verified software. Found. Trends Program. Lang. **5**(2–3), 102–281 (2019). https://doi.org/10.1561/2500000045
97. Shafaei, S., Kugele, S., Osman, M.H., Knoll, A.: Uncertainty in machine learning: a safety perspective on autonomous driving. In: Gallina, B., Skavhaug, A., Schoitsch, E., Bitsch, F. (eds.) SAFECOMP 2018. LNCS, vol. 11094, pp. 458–464. Springer, Cham (2018). https://doi.org/10.1007/978-3-319-99229-7_39
98. Siegel, S.F.: What's wrong with on-the-fly partial order reduction. In: Dillig, I., Tasiran, S. (eds.) CAV 2019. LNCS, vol. 11562, pp. 478–495. Springer, Cham (2019). https://doi.org/10.1007/978-3-030-25543-5_27
99. Tuncali, C.E., Fainekos, G., Prokhorov, D.V., Ito, H., Kapinski, J.: Requirements-driven test generation for autonomous vehicles with machine learning components. IEEE Trans. Intell. Veh. **5**(2), 265–280 (2020). https://doi.org/10.1109/TIV.2019.2955903
100. Underwriters Laboratories Inc.: ANSI/UL 4600 Standard for Safety Evaluation of Autonomous Products (2022)
101. Vaandrager, F.W.: Model learning. Commun. ACM **60**(2), 86–95 (2017). https://doi.org/10.1145/2967606
102. Wiedijk, F. (ed.): The Seventeen Provers of the World. LNCS (LNAI), vol. 3600. Springer, Heidelberg (2006). https://doi.org/10.1007/11542384
103. Wimmer, S., Herbreteau, F., van de Pol, J.: Certifying emptiness of timed Büchi automata. In: Bertrand, N., Jansen, N. (eds.) FORMATS 2020. LNCS, vol. 12288, pp. 58–75. Springer, Cham (2020). https://doi.org/10.1007/978-3-030-57628-8_4
104. Wimmer, S., Lammich, P.: Verified model checking of timed automata. In: Beyer, D., Huisman, M. (eds.) TACAS 2018. LNCS, vol. 10805, pp. 61–78. Springer, Cham (2018). https://doi.org/10.1007/978-3-319-89960-2_4
105. Wing, J.M.: Trustworthy AI. Commun. ACM **64**(10), 64–71 (2021). https://doi.org/10.1145/3448248
106. Winter, K.: Optimising ordering strategies for symbolic model checking of railway interlockings. In: Margaria, T., Steffen, B. (eds.) ISoLA 2012. LNCS, vol. 7610, pp. 246–260. Springer, Heidelberg (2012). https://doi.org/10.1007/978-3-642-34032-1_24

Future Train Control Systems: Challenges for Dependability Assessment

Alessandro Fantechi[1](✉), Stefania Gnesi[2], and Gloria Gori[1]

[1] University of Florence, Via S. Marta 3, 50139 Florence, Italy
{alessandro.fantechi,golria.gori}@unifi.it
[2] ISTI-CNR, Via G. Moruzzi 1, 56127 Pisa, Italy
stefania.gnesi@isti.cnr.it

Abstract. The prospected advent of advanced train control systems, such as moving block and virtual coupling, raises the issue of the effects that uncertainty on critical parameters (such as position or speed) can have on dependability. Several approaches to the evaluation of such effects have been proposed, typically based on a state-based formal modelling of the system behaviour. We present a survey of such proposals.

Keywords: Train control systems · Dependability assessment · Uncertainty

1 Introduction

This century has seen several innovation proposals for railway transport, most of which ask for a significant advancement of train control systems. The increasing need to boost the volume of passenger and freight rail transport, while decreasing the cost, require running more trains on the existing tracks, asking for notable improvements of the operation principles of nowadays railways.

Buzzwords such as Moving Block, Virtual Coupling, Autonomous Trains, are frequently used in the visions of the railways of the future, although still quite far from the everyday life in the, rather conservative, railway domain.

The main reason for the conservativeness of the domain can be found in the safety concerns. Indeed, the advanced train control systems needed to realize the new functionalities, pose important challenges regarding safety guarantees.

One main paradigm shift that these new technologies require is to abandon the "absolute safety" that has often ruled the railway operation, in favour of a "probabilistic safety", that is anyway already foreseen in the safety guidelines issued for the development of signalling systems.

As reported in [15] one common problem of the proposed advanced train control systems is to guarantee safety in presence of some form of uncertainty on vital parameters, such as train positioning, train speed and acceleration, etc.

On the other hand, even though the same level of safety can be eventually guaranteed with respect to traditional systems, the actual adoption of the prospected

T. Margaria and B. Steffen (Eds.): ISoLA 2022, LNCS 13704, pp. 269–285, 2022.
https://doi.org/10.1007/978-3-031-19762-8_21

systems will be possible only if they can fully exhibit their dependability, expressed in terms of availability and performability, that is, in terms of service regularity and capacity.

An emerging trend of the latest decades is to address the evaluation of dependability by means of model-based quantitative evaluation of the dependability attributes that are of interest.

The aim of this paper is actually to survey the research efforts that are available in the literature that employ formal modelling to evaluate safety and/or some dependability attributes, such as availability and performability, under some form of (quantifiable) uncertainty over vital information produced by sensors or by the system itself.

The paper is organized as follows: in Sect. 2 the context and vision for future train systems is introduced, in Sect. 3 we give a short introduction to the formalisms adopted in the literature, in Sect. 4 a survey of the most recent literature contribution is provided and Sect. 5 closes the paper illustrating final considerations and future research challenges.

2 Context

2.1 Future Railway Systems

The increasingly wide deployment of ERTMS-ETCS systems witnesses the possible achievement of high safety standards by means of advanced ICT technologies.

ERTMS relies on the European Train Control System (ETCS), an Automatic Train Protection (ATP) system which continuously supervises the train, ensuring that the maximum safe speed and minimum safe distance are respected. ETCS is specified at four levels of operation, depending on the role of wayside equipment and on the way the information is transmitted to/from trains. Only the first two levels have been actually implemented to date.

The Level 3 of operation (ETCS-L3), currently still in development, improves upon Level 2 by removing the wayside equipment for detecting the occupancy of fixed-length tracks (fixed-block). Rather, the ETCS-L3 relies on the *moving block* principle, computing at run-time the maximum distance that a train is allowed to travel based on the knowledge of the position of the rear end of the foregoing train. In doing so, the headway between trains can be considerably reduced, improving the line capacity.

Although main line ETCS-L3 has been deployed only in experimental forms, moving block is currently implemented in automatic metros, as a feature of CBTC (Communication Based Train Control) [24]. CBTC systems for metro operations typically include Automatic Train Operation (ATO) systems, that are responsible for driving, but are still subject to a safety enforcing ATP system. ATO systems of this kind are increasingly considered for future main line implementation [1].

The availability of safe information about the position, speed, acceleration and deceleration of the preceding train, envisaged in ETCS Level 3 and in CBTC, has further inspired the idea of an innovative method of train formation, called

Virtual Coupling [17,40]. The concept is based on the idea of multiple trains (possibly, individual self propelling units) which run one behind the other without physical contact but at a smaller distance compared to that achievable with moving block. The strict real-time control of the dynamic parameters of the following train with respect to those of the preceding one allows the distance between trains to be minimized, therefore with consequent increased capacity. Increased flexibility is another goal, for example in the forwarding of different segments of a train to different destinations through "on-the-fly" composition and decomposition, without stopping the train. The cross-control between coupled trains has to be negotiated locally, with a train to train communication, since it requires a precision on the relative distance between the trains that cannot be supported by ETCS-like systems.

In a parallel with the automotive domain, and inheriting autonomous cars technology, another direction of innovation is to move more and more intelligence onboard trains, to let them take autonomous decisions, with little help of ground-based infrastructure [16]. However, the physics of train motion, that requires long stretches of free track to attain high speeds, poses several challenges to the adoption of autonomy in train control.

2.2 Uncertainty

In all the innovation directions sketched above, one key element is the availability of accurate information on position, speed, acceleration of trains, as well as a strict control of the timing at which such information is related. However, the need of accurate measures of position of trains and of their speed introduces the need of coping with *uncertainty* over such measures, quantified as an error interval around the measured quantity of interest.

Uncertainty in positioning is usually managed by allowing for a longer safety margin, by assuming a maximum uncertainty threshold: in railways, positioning of a reference (say, the head) of a train is one-dimensional, because it refers to a point on the line. Uncertainty makes position to stay within an interval, so safety margins have to be computed accordingly. Speed uncertainty can be handled similarly: if an error interval is known, integrating it over time gives a position uncertainty.

One cause of uncertainty of position information is given by the positioning mechanism itself. In fixed block systems, the position of a preceding train is given by the block that it currently occupies: it is not known where the train rear end actually is inside the block, and this is conservatively considered to be at the end of the block.

In the more sophisticated positioning systems required by moving block, uncertainty is typically associated to position and speed measurement, which may be affected by random or systematic errors.

Information on trains position and speed may also be provided by satellite positioning devices. These are widely used in avionic satellite navigation, and give, together with a position estimation, a so called *protection level.* The protection level is a statistical bound error computed to guarantee that the probability of the (unknown) real position error exceeding the protection level is smaller than or equal to a target value (called *integrity risk*). In other words, the interval (given by the protection level) around the estimated position does not contain the real position with probability less than the integrity risk. The target integrity risk can be computed in relation to the desired THR (Tolerable Hazard Rate), a measure of the accepted level of risk of collisions or derailments.

Delays in communication and the periodic, rather than continuous, nature of communications introduce another source of uncertainty: timestamps and time-out mechanisms are used in ETCS to prevent impact on safety of a missing or out-of-time MA reception, stopping the train when given uncertainty thresholds are passed.

Last but not least, we can foresee that autonomous driving of trains will be based, as their automotive counterpart, on an increasing usage of Artificial Intelligence (AI) techniques (e.g. for artificial vision systems), that pose a significant challenge to deterministic certification of safety [16]. The widespread adoption in automotive applications will favour the acceptance of machine learning engines, or similar techniques, as "proven in use" software, especially considering that trains move in a much more predictable environment than cars, hence favouring reliability of machine learning techniques. Anyway, the estimation of the probability of incorrect classification of an AI engine may constitute another source of quantified uncertainty.

2.3 Dependability Attributes

As indicated by the Shift2Rail JU [34], the primary objectives of introducing technological advances in train traffic control are not only related to an increase in the already very high safety standards of railways, but rather to preserve such standards while dramatically improving KPIs such as performability (often intended as adherence to expected timetables), availability of transport service and transport capacity, all attributes that in computer science terms could be tagged as *liveness properties*, that often conflict with safety objectives.

On the other hand, the large number of critical computing components and the complexity of distributed control algorithms increase the number of cases in which the failure of one component can bring to a fail-safe halt of a system, causing the partial or full unavailability of transport service.

This effect is worsened by the number of communication links employed in these systems: typically, the safety layers of the communication protocols adopted in these systems exploit the principle of *positive* control to allow movement of trains: a train cannot move if no explicit consensus or MA has been received. Any serious transmission error (that is, persistent over a given period of time) eventually leads to a fail-safe state. A careful evaluation of safety cannot therefore ignore an adequate analysis of availability attributes, in order to ensure an appropriate transport capacity, with the related operation cost effectiveness, through techniques of quantitative evaluation of these attributes [33].

3 Model-Based Evaluation of Dependability

In the domain of train control systems, if we look to approaches and techniques that address uncertainty, we are confronted with two main categories, with different final aim:

- "constructive" techniques: coming from control theory, typically consider uncertainty as a disturbance input to the control algorithm, and aim at maintaining at run time the stability of some critical parameter within a certain range. The range is determined a priori as a safe one for train control. An example of critical parameter is distance between the leader and the follower trains in a virtual coupling scheme. Techniques like Model Predictive Control are adopted to keep this distance within a predetermined range also in presence of limited disturbances due to the uncertainties of read parameters, e.g. inaccuracy of the position [44] or lost train-2-train messages [39]. The lower bound of the stability distance range is determined in this case by safety consideration, while the upper bound is determined so to guarantee the least capacity gain that is promised by the introduction of virtual coupling. This research stream has been pursued in several other research efforts, especially regarding virtual coupling: a complete account is not however in the scope of this paper.
- "deductive" techniques: quantitative analysis techniques have the aim to predict, off-line, specific dependability attributes (such as safety, availability, performability) in presence of uncertainty on critical information. Typically a dependability attribute is defined as the probability $P(t)$ of the system being in a certain state at time t; thresholds or upper/lower bounds to such prediction classify the system as safe or available, or are used to plan maintenance actions, depending on the attribute of interest.
  Quantitative analysis techniques allow to evaluate the $P(t)$ dependability attribute as a function of the uncertainty quantification by means of a state-based model of the behaviour of the system.
  Consider for example a train control system that should fulfill a safety requirement expressed by requiring that a collision between two controlled trains occurs less than once in 10^9 operation hours. Suppose that the train control system critically depends on the correct localization of one of the trains: knowing the uncertainty range of the computed position, a deductive quantitative evaluation allows for computing the probability of a collision due to wrong localization, as a function of such uncertainty. The resulting probability should be lower of the above threshold, in order to guarantee safety also in case of localization uncertainty.

However, the probabilistic estimation of dependability needs often to take into account the distributed structure and status of the system, and the occurrence of relevant events such as reception of messages or component failures. A state-based model can describe at best these dependencies. Attaching probabilities to events and states, allows then for a fine modelling of the evolution in time of dependability attributes as time varying probability distribution.

Model-based evaluation of dependability is therefore an important enabling technique to tackle the problems that we have introduced so far: a model of the behaviour of the system is first defined, and uncertainty is taken into account, in the form of probability of inaccuracy produced by uncertainty sources. An evaluation of the model allows in the end to estimate specific dependability attributes as a function of inaccuracy. Such evaluation can provide constraints over inaccuracy that keep dependability under control.

In this paper, we survey a selection of recent works that have adopted model-based quantitative analysis techniques according to the principles enunciated above in the railway domain, classifying them in terms of techniques used, problems addressed and kind of uncertainty considered. In the next section we briefly describe the quantitative analysis frameworks that have been used in the surveyed literature.

3.1 Proposed Modelling Frameworks

In the literature surveyed in Sect. 4 several modelling frameworks have been adopted, ranging from variants of Petri nets to Stochastic Activity Networks, from Probabilistic Timed Automata to Fault Trees, and several tools supporting their quantitative evaluation have been adopted. In the following, we give a short introduction for each adopted formalisms, mentioning the related support tools.

Petri Nets. A Petri net consists of places, transitions, and arcs [30]. Arcs run from a place to a transition or vice versa, but not between places nor between transitions. The places from which an arc runs to a transition are called the input places of the transition; the places to which arcs run from a transition are called the output places of the transition.

Graphically, places in a Petri net may contain a finite number of marks called tokens. Any distribution of tokens over the places will represent a configuration of the net called a marking. A transition of a Petri net may fire if it is enabled, i.e. there are sufficient tokens in all of its input places; when the transition fires, it consumes the required input tokens, and creates tokens in its output places. A firing is atomic, i.e. a single non-interruptible step.

Since firing is nondeterministic, and multiple tokens may be present anywhere in the net (even in the same place), Petri nets are well suited for modeling the concurrent behavior of distributed systems.

Stochastic Petri Nets. Stochastic Petri nets are an extension of Petri nets, where the transitions fire after a probabilistic delay determined by a random variable [6].

The analysis of SPN is based upon Markov theory; with respect to other popular fameworks exploiting Markov Theory, such as queueing networks, SPN have the ability to describe system behaviors like blocking, forking and synchronisation between distributed entities.

The π-Tool[1] was developed with the aim to establish a computer-supported, clear Petri net modeling of real systems with the implementation of a complete RAMS analysis. The tool provides a streamlined interface for creating comprehensive system models based on Petri nets. It allows a visualized simulation (token game), an analysis of the model and the identification of deadlocks, which are included in the model. All common stochastic distributions can be assigned to the transitions. With the help of simulation and the determination of the switching rates of the individual transitions, all values of the RAMS aspects can read off easily. For this π-tool uses various analysis methods, state-based or stochastic ones, to consider the system sufficiently reliable.

Another tool that supports analysis of Stochastic Petri Nets, as well as Coloured Petri Nets, is TimeNET, [45,46] which exploits different solution algorithms that can be used depending on the net class.

Stochastic Timed Petri Nets. The need for including timing variables in the models of various types of dynamic systems is apparent since these systems are real time in nature. When a Petri net contains a time variable, it becomes a Timed Petri Net [42].

The firing rules are defined differently depending on the way the Petri net is labeled with time variables. Stochastic timed Petri nets (STPN) are Petri nets in which stochastic firing times are associated with transitions. An STPN is essentially a high-level model that generates a stochastic process. STPN-based performance evaluation basically comprises modeling the given system by an STPN and automatically generating the stochastic process that governs the system behavior. This stochastic process is then analyzed using known techniques. STPN's are a graphical model and offer great convenience to a modeler in arriving at a credible, high-level model of a system.

The analysis of STPN is supported by the ORIS Tool [8,29], which efficiently implements the method of stochastic state classes, including regenerative transient, regenerative steady-state, and non-deterministic analyses.

Stochastic Colored Petri Nets. In a standard Petri net, tokens are indistinguishable. Because of this, Petri nets have the distinct disadvantage of producing very large and unstructured specifications for the systems being modeled. To tackle this issue, high-level Petri nets were developed to allow compact system representation. Colored Petri nets [25] and Predicate/Transition (Pr/T) nets [20] are among the most popular high-level Petri nets. A Colored Petri Net (CPN) has each token attached with a color, indicating the identity of the token. Moreover, each place and each transition has attached a set of colors. A transition can fire with respect to each of its colors. By firing a transition, tokens are removed from the input places and added to the output places in the same way as that in original Petri nets, except that a functional dependency is specified between the color of the transition firing and the colors of the involved tokens. The color

[1] https://www.iqst.de/en-pitool/.

attached to a token may be changed by a transition firing and it often represents a complex data-value. CPNs lead to compact net models by using of the concept of colors. CPN Tools [26] support analysis of CPNs, by simulation and state space exploration.

Stochastic Colored Petri Nets (SCPN) [19] combine the strength of GSPN (Generalised Stochastic Petri Nets) with a high-level programming language, making SCPN very powerful in modelling large, complex and dynamic systems in a compact way. Generalized Stochastic Petri Nets (GSPN) are an extension of Petri Nets incorporating two types of transitions: immediate transitions and timed transition. Immediate transitions correspond to transitions in classic Petri Nets and fire immediately if enabled. Timed transitions, by contrast, fire after an exponentially distributed time $t - \exp(\lambda)$.

Immediate transitions have priority over timed transitions. In case multiple immediate transitions are enabled, firing order is according to a specific firing policy.

Stochastic Activity Networks. Stochastic Activity Networks (SANs) are a convenient, graphical, high-level language for describing systems behavior. SANs are a stochastic generalization of Petri nets, defined for the modeling and analysis of distributed real-time systems. A SAN is composed of places, activities, input gates, and output gates. Places and activities have the same interpretation as places and transitions in Petri nets. Input gates control the enabling conditions of an activity and define the change of marking when an activity starts. Output gates define the change of marking upon completion of the activity. Activities can be of two types: instantaneous or timed. Instantaneous activities complete once the enabling conditions are satisfied. Timed activities take an amount of time to complete, following a temporal stochastic distribution function which can be, e.g., exponential or deterministic. Cases are associated to activities, and are used to represent probabilistic uncertainty about the action taken upon completion of the activity. Primitives of the SAN models are defined using C++ code.

The mostly used stochastic analysis tool for SANs are Möbius [11] that can be traced back much further, to its predecessors UltraSAN [12,31] and MetaSAN [32]. Möbius [11] offers a distributed discrete-event simulator, and, for Markovian models, explicit state-space generators and numerical solution algorithms.

Timed Automata and Statistical Model Checking. Timed automata are finite-state automata enhanced with real-time modelling through clock variables; their stochastic extension replaces non-determinism with probabilistic choice and time delays with probability distributions (uniform for bounded time and exponential for unbounded time). These automata may communicate via (broadcast) channels and shared variables. The resulting stochastic hybrid automata (SHA) form the input models of the statistical model checker UPPAAL SMC [13] on which it is possible to check (quantitative) properties over simulation runs. Statistical Model Checking (SMC) concerns running a sufficient number of (probabilistically distributed) simulations of a system model to obtain statistical evidence (with a predefined level of statistical confidence) of the quantitative properties to be checked. UPPAAL SMC is an extension of UPPAAL [21], a toolbox for the verification of real-time systems modelled by (extended) timed automata. The properties must be expressed in Weighted Metric Temporal Logic (WMTL) [9]. Statistical Model Checking may be traced back to hypothesis testing in the context of probabilistic bisimulation. Tools that support SMC are more recent: the first version of UPPAAL SMC was released in 2014.

Dynamic Fault Trees. Fault Tree Analysis (FTA) is one of the well-established and widely used methods for safety and reliability engineering of systems. Fault trees (FTs), in their classical static form, are directed acyclic graphs (DAG) with nodes defining a boolean relation (AND, OR, etc.) over the successor nodes. Nodes without successors are called basic (failure) events. Occurrences of basic events are governed by probability distributions. Similarly, a node fails if the failure condition over the children holds. The probability of failure of the top-level event can be computed by properly combining those of the basic events. FTs are however inadequate for modelling dynamic interactions between components and are unable to include temporal and statistical dependencies in the model. Dynamic Fault Trees (DFT) were introduced to enhance the modelling power of its static counterpart [10]. In DFT, the expressiveness of fault tree has been improved by introducing new dynamic gates. While the introduction of the dynamic gates helps to overcome many limitations of FTs and allows to analyse a wide-range of complex systems, it adds some overhead, e.g. the straightforward combinatorial approaches used for qualitative and quantitative analysis are no longer applicable to DFTs.

Several tools have been developed to model and analyse DFT [2], among which here we mention STORM [27], which performs probabilistic model checking by generating from the DFT a continuous-time Markov chain (CTMC) which captures its behavior of the DFT. The CTMC is analyzed with respect to reliability metrics.

4 Survey of Railway Case Studies

In the following survey of applications of model-based dependability techniques in the railway domain we start by the innovations that can be considered not far from deployment, by shifting gradually to the more visionary ones.

4.1 Performability Evaluation of the ERTMS/ETCS - Level 3

The pioneer paper [45] is considered the first to develop Stochastic Petri net models of communication behaviour of the ERTMS/ETCS L3 moving block system. Stochastic Petri nets are used to model and evaluate in a hierarchical way the failure and recovery behavior of the train-to-RBC communication link, and to model the exchange of location information and movement authority between train and RBC. The models evaluation, obtained through customized SPN resolution algorithms, supported by the TimeNET Tool [45,46] shows the significant influence of reliability of the underlying communication system on efficient train operation.

In [7], the authors develop the results of [45] by presenting a communication model with multiple concurrent non-exponential timers, computing an upper bound on the first-passage probability that a train is stopped due to a communication failure. The authors combine analytic evaluation of failures due to burst noise and connection losses with numerical solution of a non-Markovian model representing also failures due to handovers between radio stations. The analysis, supported by the ORIS tool, show that the periodic trains transit at handovers makes the behavior of the overall communication system recurrent over the period of message exchanges and the periodic arrivals at cell borders.

4.2 Safety Evaluation of Moving Block Systems by Statistical Model Checking

In [3] the full moving block specification for ETCS-L3 is formally described by Probabilistic Timed Automata. UPPAAL SMC is used to verify safety properties in presence of communication delays, and to verify whether the performability gain (1 min minimum headway) promised by moving block can be obtained in such setting.

Statistical Model checking is also used in [28] inside a more complex framework aimed at hazard and risk prediction in Communication Based Train Control based on train-to-train communication, also based on deep recurrent neural networks. An ad hoc algorithm based on SMC is used for estimating the probability of wrong Movement Authority calculation.

Finally, in [23], authors carry out an analysis of a Zone Controller (ZC) handover scenario, a typical operation function in Communication Based Train Control (CBTC) system. However, due to the nondeterministic communication between the onboard equipment and the ZC, the behavior of delay and timeout determines the complexity of probability evaluation. The authors propose a novel method based on Statistical Model Checking (SMC), which introduces a sequential operator to evaluate the probabilities of all scenarios in a CBTC system. In a CBTC system, different scenarios have different behaviors and probabilities. Therefore, in the ZC handover process, the trigger handover, crossing the demarcation point and logout switching scenarios are modeled by Network Priced Timed Automata (NPTA); the whole probability of successful ZC handover is evaluated as 0.99985, a high value that guarantees that the safety requirements of the CBTC system are satisfied.

4.3 Train-to-Train Communication Modeling

Due to high installation and maintenance costs of wayside equipment, moving more and more intelligence on board is considered as a promising direction, and this requires to develop adequate train-to-train communication means. Starting from his PhD Thesis [36], Haifeng Song has addressed, with colleagues in Braunschweig, modeling and analysis dependability attributes of innovative systems of this kind [37, 38]. In particular, an enhanced movement authority system is proposed, which combines advantages of the *train-centric communication* with current movement authority mechanisms. To obtain the necessary train distance interval data, the onboard equipment and a new train-to-train distance measurement system (TTDMS) are applied as normal and backup strategies, respectively. To assist the system development, Colored Petri nets are used to formalize and evaluate the system structure and its behavior. The system performance is assessed in detection range and accuracy by means of both mathematical simulation and practical measurements validation. In [39] availability and performance of a direct train-to-train communication system is studied, considering different parameters that can affect the performance of the communication system, such as bit error and transmission rates. The system availability and performance are evaluated by means of Stochastic Petri nets.

Train-to-train communication is also studied in [41] in the context of Virtual Coupling, as reported later in the section on this topic.

4.4 Modelling Uncertainty in Satellite Localisation

Satellite positioning has been recently considered as an enabling technique for moving block, since it potentially allows a train to know its position and speed at any time. A characteristic of this technology is that the position information given by a GNSS receiver comes already associated with an uncertainty measure, that shows the probability with which the real position is in an envelope centered on the computed position. Providing safety evidence for a system based on this technology necessarily requires hence to adopt quantitative safety evaluation.

In [22] the authors present a model-based approach, adapted for the evaluation of GNSS-based localisation systems in railway. Models are defined using probabilistic timed automata, to achieve a modular representation of trains dynamics in the context of GNSS-based localization. In particular, the representation of the position related errors, the mechanisms of balises detection and the dynamics of the trains movements are addressed. The safety and performance properties to be checked are formulated by means of temporal logics. The evaluation phase by UPPAAL-SMC yields both qualitative and quantitative results and allows for assessing the impact of various parameters and functional choices on both safety and performance.

4.5 Safety and Availability of Virtual Balises: The SISTER Project

Traditional solutions for tramway interlocking systems are based on physical sensors (balises) distributed along the infrastructure which detect passing of the trams and trigger different actions, like the communications with the ground infrastructure and the interlocking system. This approach is not easily scalable and maintainable, and it is costly. One of the aims of the SISTER project was the study of a possible substitution of track circuits by virtual track circuits supported by satellite positioning. The key idea is to trigger actions when the local position computed on board a tram corresponds to a virtual tag. However, the estimated position, even in absence of faults, is affected by errors, compared to the real one. Therefore, it is important to understand the impact of these new solutions on the traffic that can be supported by the tramway network.

In [5], the authors investigate this issue with the definition of a model of the envisaged solution, and its analysis using UPPAAL Statistical Model Checker. The analysis emphasises how the virtualisation of legacy track circuits and on-board satellite positioning equipment may give rise to new hazards, not present in the traditional system.

In [35] the same issue is faced with a stochastic modeling approach aiming to identify the parts of the tramway network that are more critical and sensible to the variation of the traffic conditions and to the setting of the key architectural parameters. The presented model is built using Stochastic Activity Networks and sensitivity analyses are run on the accuracy of the positioning, on the different SISTER parameters, and considering possible outages temporarily blocking the journey of a tram. This analysis allows to properly set and fine-tune the key architectural parameters, to understand the impact of the accuracy on the positioning, to understand the impact of the outages.

4.6 Virtual Coupling: Performability Evaluation

Virtual Coupling has raised the interest of several research groups active in model-based quantitative analysis.

In [14] the authors provide a proof of concept of Virtual coupling by introducing a specific operating mode within the ERTMS/ETCS standard specification, and by defining a coupling control algorithm accounting for time-varying delays affecting the communication links. To support the proof of concept with quantitative results in a case-study simulation scenario, the authors provide a numerical analysis exploiting a methodology used to study platooning in the automotive field.

[18] aims at providing an approach to investigate the potential of Virtual Coupling in railways by composing Stochastic Activity Networks model templates. to provide an approach to perform quantitative evaluation of capacity increase in reference to Virtual Coupling scenarios. The approach can be used to estimate system capacity over a modelled track portion, accounting for the scheduled service as well as possible failures. Due to its modularity, the approach can be extended towards the inclusion of safety model components. The contribution of this paper is a preliminary result of the PERFORMINGRAIL (PERformance-based Formal modelling and Optimal tRaffic Management for movING-block RAILway signalling) project funded by the European Shift2Rail Joint Undertaking.

The paper [41] presents a model-based approach for the evaluation of the communication system under virtual coupling operation. Namely, Stochastic Colored Petri Net (SCPN) models are developed to depict the exchanges of the various information needed under virtual coupling operation. The analysis scope is limited to function Supervising Train Separation Distance. Dependability evaluation is then performed by means of simulation; the impact of various communication parameters is examined while taking into account different operational scenarios. The obtained results allow the identification of the most impacting aspects on dependability analysis and provide valuable inputs to support the technological choices in terms of communication to implement virtual coupling.

In [44], the authors analyse the virtual coupling operation mode under train control system based on train-to-train communication, and compare it with a traditional train operation mode. A typical scenario of train virtual coupling is described by SysML, and the key properties of the function, such as boundedness and reachability, are validated by modeling with Colored Petri nets. In this paper, formal modeling and verification of typical scenarios in the train virtual coupling mode are carried out to ensure that the system meets safety, functionality and performance requirements.

4.7 Reliability and Maintenance Plans

Reliability engineering of railway infrastructure aims at understanding failure processes and improving the efficiency and effectiveness of investments and maintenance planning, so that a high quality of service is achieved. In particular, quantitative methods to analyze the service reliability associated with specific system designs are emerging as a promising research activity.

In [43] formal fault-tree modeling is proposed for providing a quantitative assessment of the railway infrastructure's service reliability in the design phase. While, individually, most subsystems required for route-setting and train control are well understood, the system reliability to globally provide its designated service capacity is less studied. To this end, a framework based on dynamic fault trees is proposed to analyze the possibilities of routing trains on paths provided by the interlocking system. The work focuses on the dependency of train paths on track-based assets such as switches and crossings, which are particularly prone to failures. By using probabilistic model checking to analyze and verify the reliability of feasible route sets for scheduled train lines, performance metrics for reliability analysis of the system as a whole as well as criticality analysis of individual (sub-)components become available. The fault trees obtained in the analysis of major stations contain up to 6 million states and are among the largest described in the literature. By allowing to pinpoint critical infrastructure components, the approach is suited to provide assistance in asset management to improve the effectiveness and efficiency of infrastructure investments, maintenance and monitoring systems.

4.8 Summary

Table 1 summarizes the findings in the cited literature. The *Goal* column shows the evaluation goal, where Av stands for Availability, R for Reliability, S for Safety, C for Capacity, P for some specific kind of Performability.

Table 1. Summary of the reviewed literature

Ref.	Y.	APPLICATION	FORM.	TOOL	UNCERTAINTY	Goal
[45]	2005	Comm. in ETCS L3	SPN, GSPN	TimeNET	Handover loss, packet loss	R
[7]	2017	ERTMS/ETCS-L3	STPN	ORIS	Burst noise, comm. losses	P
[3]	2022	ETMS/ETCS L3	PTA	UPPAAL SMC	Communication delays	S,P
[28]	2020	T2T comm. in CBTC	own tool	SMC	Wrong MA computation	S
[23]	2020	Zone controller	SMC	UPPAAL SMC	Communication delays	S
[37]	2017	T2T Dist. Meas. Sys.	CPN	CPNTools	Connection failures	S
[39]	2019	T2T communication	SPN	Pi-Tool	communication latency	Av,P
[22]	2021	satellite positioning	PTA	UPPAAL SMC	Positioning error	S, P
[5]	2021	sat. posit., tram	PTA	UPPAAL SMC	Positioning error	S
[35]	2021	sat. posit., tram	SAN	Moebius	Positioning error	Av
[14]	2020	Virtual Coupling	PN	Simulation	Communication delays	P
[18]	2021	Virtual Coupling	SAN	Moebius	Communication delays	C
[41]	2021	T2T communication	SCPN	TimeNET	Communication delays	Av
[44]	2020	Virtual Coupling	CPN	CPNTools	Communication delays	Av
[43]	2022	Infrastruct. Mainten.	DFT	STORM	Switch failures	R

Looking at the table, we can note a certain prevalence of Petri net based models and tools: the used tools are typically of academic origin, and although they may differ in the offered features and the evaluation algorithms employed, they are actually competing in the "market" of model-based dependability analysis.

We refer to [4] for a comparison of the modelling and analysis capabilities of two formalisms from the two classes and their associated support based tools, namely UPPAAL SMC and Moebius.

The existence of diverse, competing tools may serve the purpose of defining multiple modelling processes able to compare results obtained with different tools and formalisms, strengthening the results in case of concordance, and helping to detect modelling errors or biases otherwise. Due to the need of guaranteeing specific dependability targets in the domain of advanced railway signalling, multiple modelling can be an important element in the process.

5 Conclusions

The surveyed literature, far from being complete, is nevertheless representative of the main research activities in this area, and shows already that quantitative modeling of dependability of future train control systems is spreading more and more in the recent years in academic research, and is a promising enabling technique in support of the development of innovative and more performing train control systems. Support tools are still at a low Technical Readyness Level (TRL), although a few of them, such as UPPAAL and Moebius have a quite large adoption base. Industrial application of these techniques and tools is still limited, but will be in our opinion necessary for the successful adoption of the prospected future train control systems.

References

1. Amendola, A., et al.: Formal design and validation of an automatic train operation control system. In: Dutilleul, S.C., Haxthausen, A.E., Lecomte, T. (eds.) Proceedings of RSSRail 2022. LNCS, vol. 13294, pp. 169–178 (2022). https://doi.org/10.1007/978-3-031-05814-1_12
2. Aslansefat, K., Kabir, S., Gheraibia, Y., Papadopoulos, Y.: Dynamic fault tree analysis: state-of-the-art in modelling, analysis and tools, pp. 73–112, June 2020
3. Basile, D., ter Beek, M.H., Ferrari, A., Legay, A.: Exploring the ERTMS/ETCS full moving block specification: an experience with formal methods. Int. J. Softw. Tools Technol. Transfer **24**, 351–370 (2022)
4. Basile, D., ter Beek, M.H., Di Giandomenico, F., Fantechi, A., Gnesi, S., Spagnolo, G.O.: 30 years of simulation-based quantitative analysis tools: a comparison experiment between Möbius and Uppaal SMC. In: Margaria, T., Steffen, B. (eds.) ISoLA 2020. LNCS, vol. 12476, pp. 368–384. Springer, Cham (2020). https://doi.org/10.1007/978-3-030-61362-4_21
5. Basile, D., Fantechi, A., Rucher, L., Mandò, G.: Analysing an autonomous tramway positioning system with the Uppaal Statistical Model Checker. Formal Aspect. Comput. **33**(6), 957–987 (2021)
6. Bause, F., Kritzinger, P.S.: Stochastic Petri Nets - An Introduction to the Theory, 2nd edn. (2002)
7. Biagi, M., Carnevali, L., Paolieri, M., Vicario, E.: Performability evaluation of the ERTMS/ETCS - level 3. Transp. Res. Part C **82**, 314–336 (2017)
8. Bucci, G., Carnevali, L., Ridi, L., Vicario, E.: Oris: a tool for modeling, verification and evaluation of real-time systems. Int. J. Softw. Tools Technol. Transfer **12**(5), 391–403 (2010)
9. Bulychev, P., David, A., Larsen, K.G., Legay, A., Li, G., Poulsen, D.B.: Rewrite-based statistical model checking of WMTL. In: Qadeer, S., Tasiran, S. (eds.) Runtime Verification, pp. 260–275 (2013)
10. Cepin, M., Mavko, B.: A dynamic fault tree. Reliab. Eng. Syst. Saf. **75**(1), 83–91 (2002). https://doi.org/10.1016/S0951-8320(01)00121-1
11. Clark, G., et al.: The Möbius modeling tool. In: Proceedings of 9th International Workshop on Petri Nets and Performance Models, pp. 241–250 (2001)
12. Couvillion, J., et al.: Performability modeling with UltraSAN. IEEE Softw. **8**(5), 69–80 (1991)
13. David, A., Larsen, K.G., Legay, A., Mikučionis, M., Poulsen, D.B.: UPPAAL SMC tutorial. Int. J. Softw. Tools Technol. Transf. **17**(4), 397–415 (2015)
14. Di Meo, C., Di Vaio, M., Flammini, F., Nardone, R., Santini, S., Vittorini, V.: ERTMS/ETCS virtual coupling: proof of concept and numerical analysis. IEEE Trans. ITS **21**(6), 2545–2556 (2020)
15. Fantechi, A.: Connected or autonomous trains? In: Collart-Dutilleul, S., Lecomte, T., Romanovsky, A. (eds.) RSSRail 2019. LNCS, vol. 11495, pp. 3–19. Springer, Cham (2019). https://doi.org/10.1007/978-3-030-18744-6_1

16. Flammini, F., Donato, L.D., Fantechi, A., Vittorini, V.: A vision of intelligent train control. In: Dutilleul, S.C., Haxthausen, A.E., Lecomte, T. (eds.) Proceedings of RSSRail 2022. LNCS, vol. 13294, pp. 192–208. Springer, Cham (2022). https://doi.org/10.1007/978-3-031-05814-1_14
17. Flammini, F., Marrone, S., Nardone, R., Petrillo, A., Santini, S., Vittorini, V.: Towards railway virtual coupling. In: International Transportation Electrification Conference (ITEC) (2018)
18. Flammini, F., Marrone, S., Nardone, R., Vittorini, V.: Compositional modeling of railway virtual coupling with stochastic activity networks. Formal Aspects Comput. **33**(6), 989–1007 (2021). https://doi.org/10.1007/s00165-021-00560-5
19. Gehlot, V., Nigro, C.: Colored petri net model of the session initiation protocol (SIP). In: IECON 2010–36th Annual Conference on IEEE Industrial Electronics Society, pp. 2150–2155 (2010)
20. Genrich, H.J.: Predicate/transition nets. In: Brauer, W., Reisig, W., Rozenberg, G. (eds.) Petri Nets: Central Models and Their Properties, pp. 207–247 (1987)
21. Hendriks, M., et al.: UPPAAL 4.0. In: QEST 2006, pp. 125–126 (2006)
22. Himrane, O., Beugin, J., Ghazel, M.: Toward formal safety and performance evaluation of GNSS-based railway localisation function. IFAC-PapersOnLine **54**(2), 159–166 (2021)
23. Huang, J., Lv, J., Feng, Y., Luo, Z., Liu, H., Chai, M.: A novel method on probability evaluation of ZC handover scenario based on SMC. In: Qian, J., Liu, H., Cao, J., Zhou, D. (eds.) Robotics and Rehabilitation Intelligence, pp. 319–333 (2020)
24. IEEE: Vehicular technology society, 1474.1 - standard for communications - based train control (CBTC) - performance and functional requirements (2004)
25. Jensen, K.: Coloured petri nets. In: Brauer, W., Reisig, W., Rozenberg, G. (eds.) Petri Nets: Central Models and Their Properties, pp. 248–299 (1987)
26. Jensen, K., Kristensen, L.M., Wells, L.: Coloured Petri Nets and CPN tools for modelling and validation of concurrent systems. Int. J. Softw. Tools Technol. Transfer **9**(3), 213–254 (2007)
27. Katoen, J.: The probabilistic model checking landscape. In: Grohe, M., Koskinen, E., Shankar, N. (eds.) Proceedings of the 31st Annual ACM/IEEE Symposium on Logic in Computer Science, LICS 2016, New York, NY, USA, 5–8 July 2016, pp. 31–45 (2016). https://doi.org/10.1145/2933575.2934574
28. Liu, J., Zhang, Y., Han, J., He, J., Sun, J., Zhou, T.: Intelligent hazard-risk prediction model for train control systems. IEEE Trans. ITS **21**(11), 4693–4704 (2020)
29. Paolieri, M., Biagi, M., Carnevali, L., Vicario, E.: The ORIS tool: quantitative evaluation of Non-Markovian systems. IEEE Trans. Softw. Eng. **47**(6), 1211–1225 (2021)
30. Reisig, W.: Petri nets and algebraic specifications. Theor. Comput. Sci. **80**(1), 1–34 (1991). https://doi.org/10.1016/0304-3975(91)90203-E
31. Sanders, W., Obal, W., Qureshi, M., Widjanarko, F.: The UltraSAN modeling environment. Perform. Eval. **24**(1), 89–115 (1995). Performance Modeling Tools
32. Sanders, W., Meyer, J.: METASAN: a performability evaluation tool based on Stochastic Activity Networks, pp. 807–816, December 1986
33. Schulz, O., Peleska, J.: Reliability analysis of safety-related communication architectures. In: Schoitsch, E. (ed.) SAFECOMP 2010. LNCS, vol. 6351, pp. 1–14. Springer, Heidelberg (2010). https://doi.org/10.1007/978-3-642-15651-9_1
34. Shift2Rail Joint Undertaking: Multi-annual action plan, November 2015. http://ec.europa.eu/research/participants/data/ref/h2020/other/wp/jtis/h2020-maap-shift2rail_en.pdf

35. da Silva, L.D., Lollini, P., Mongelli, D., Bondavalli, A., Mandò, G.: A stochastic modeling approach for traffic analysis of a tramway system with virtual tags and local positioning. J. Braz. Comput. Soc. **27**(1), 2 (2021)
36. Song, H.: Development and analysis of a train-centric distance measurement system by means of Colored Petri Nets. Ph.D. thesis (2018)
37. Song, H., Liu, J., Schnieder, E.: Validation, verification and evaluation of a train to train distance measurement system by means of Colored Petri Nets. Reliab. Eng. Syst. Saf. **164**, 10–23 (2017)
38. Song, H., Schnieder, E.: Modeling of railway system maintenance and availability by means of colored Petri nets. EiN **20**(2), 236–243 (2018)
39. Song, H., Schnieder, E.: Availability and performance analysis of train-to-train data communication system. IEEE Trans. ITS **20**(7), 2786–2795 (2019)
40. UIC: Virtually coupled trains. http://www.railway-energy.org/static/Virtually_coupled_trains_86.php. Accessed 24 Feb 2019
41. Verma, S., Ghazel, M., Berbineau, M.: Model-based dependability evaluation of a wireless communication system in a virtually coupled train set. IFAC-PapersOnLine **54**(2), 179–186 (2021)
42. Wang, J.: Stochastic Timed Petri Nets and Stochastic Petri Nets, pp. 125–153 (1998)
43. Weik, N., Volk, M., Katoen, J.P., Nießen, N.: DFT modeling approach for operational risk assessment of railway infrastructure. Int. J. Softw. Tools Technol. Transfer **24**, 331–350 (2022)
44. Yong, Z., Sirui, Z.: Typical train virtual coupling scenario modeling and analysis of train control system based on vehicle-vehicle communication. In: 2020 IEEE 6th ICCSSE, pp. 143–148, July 2020
45. Zimmermann, A., Hommel, G.: Towards modeling and evaluation of ETCS real-time communication and operation. J. Syst. Softw. **77**(1), 47–54 (2005)
46. Zimmermann, A., Knoke, M., Huck, A., Hommel, G.: Towards version 4.0 of TimeNET, pp. 1–4, April 2006

Standardisation Considerations for Autonomous Train Control

Jan Peleska[1(✉)], Anne E. Haxthausen[2], and Thierry Lecomte[3]

[1] Department of Mathematics and Computer Science, University of Bremen, Bremen, Germany
peleska@uni-bremen.de

[2] DTU Compute, Technical University of Denmark, Kongens Lyngby, Denmark
aeha@dtu.dk

[3] CLEARSY, Aix en Provence, France
thierry.lecomte@clearsy.com

Abstract. In this paper, we review software-based technologies already known to be, or expected to become essential for autonomous train control systems with grade of automation GoA 4 (unattended train operation) in existing open railway environments. It is discussed which types of technology can be developed and certified already today on the basis of existing railway standards. Other essential technologies, however, require modifications or extensions of existing standards, in order to provide a certification basis for introducing these technologies into non-experimental "real-world" rail operation. Regarding these, we check the novel pre-standard ANSI/UL 4600 with respect to suitability as a certification basis for safety-critical autonomous train control functions based on methods from artificial intelligence. As a thought experiment, we propose a novel autonomous train controller design and perform an evaluation according to ANSI/UL 4600. This results in the insight that autonomous freight trains and metro trains using this design could be evaluated and certified on the basis of ANSI/UL 4600.

Keywords: Autonomous train control · Standards · Certification · Verification · Validation

1 Introduction

Motivation. Recently, the investigation of autonomous trains has received increasing attention, following the achievements of research and development for autonomous vehicles in the automotive domain. The business cases for autonomous train control are very attractive, in particular for autonomous rolling stock and metro trains [23].

However, several essential characteristics of autonomous transportation systems are not addressed in the standards serving today as the certification basis

J. Peleska—Partially funded by the German Ministry of Economics, Grant Agreement 20X1908E.

T. Margaria and B. Steffen (Eds.): ISoLA 2022, LNCS 13704, pp. 286–307, 2022.
https://doi.org/10.1007/978-3-031-19762-8_22

for train control systems. (1) For modules using machine learning, the *safety of the intended functionality* no longer just depends on correctness of a specification and its software implementation, but also on the completeness and unbiasedness of the training data used [12] (Flammini et al. [8] call this *"the opaque nature of underlying techniques and algorithms"*). (2) Agent behaviour based on belief databases and plans cannot be fully specified at type certification time, since the behaviour can change in a significant way later on, due to machine learning effects, updates of the belief database, and changes of plans during runtime [3]. (3) Laws, rules applying to the transportation domain, as well as ethical rules, that were delegated to the responsible humans (e.g. train engine drivers) in conventional transportation systems, are now under the responsibility of the autonomous system controllers. Therefore, the correct implementation of the applicable rule bases needs to be validated [7].

In this light, we analyse the pre-standard ANSI/UL 4600 [24] that addresses the safety assurance of autonomous systems at the system level. Together with several sub-ordinate layers of complementary standards, it has been approved by the US-American Department of Transportation for application to autonomous road vehicles.[1] While examples and checklists contained in this document focus on the automotive domain, the authors of the standard state that it should be applicable to *any* autonomous system, potentially with a preceding system-specific revision of the checklists therein [24, Sect. 1.2.1]. To the best of our knowledge, the ANSI/UL 4600 pre-standard is the first "fairly complete" document addressing system-level safety of autonomous vehicles, and its applicability to the railway domain has not yet been investigated.

Observe that driverless metro trains, people movers and similar rail transportation systems with *Grade of Automation GoA 4 (Unattended train operation, neither the driver nor the staff are required)* [8] have been operable for years[2], but in *segregated environments* [8]. In these environments, the track sections are protected from unauthorised access, and ubiquitous comprehensive automation technology is available, such as line transmission or radio communication for signalling, precise positioning information, as well as platform screen doors supporting safe boarding and deboarding of passengers between trains and platforms.

In contrast to this, we investigate the certifiability of autonomous train control systems with GoA 4 in *open railway environments*, where unauthorised access to track sections, absence of platform screen doors, and less advanced technology (e.g. visual signalling) have to be taken into account. This scenario is of high economic interest, and first prototype solutions have recently become available [19], but none of them has yet achieved GoA 4 with full type certification.

---

[1] https://www.youtube.com/watch?app=desktop&v=xCIjxiVO48Q&feature=youtu.be.

[2] The driverless Paris metro METEOR, for example, is operative since 1998 [2]. A list of automated train systems is available under https://en.wikipedia.org/wiki/List_of_automated_train_systems.

Flammini et al. [8] emphasise the distinction between automatic and autonomous systems. The latter should be *"... capable of taking autonomous decisions, learning from experience, and adapting to changes in the environment"*. The train protection systems considered in this paper exhibit a *"moderate"* degree of autonomy, as described below in Sect. 4: they react, for example, to the occurrence of obstacles and degradation of position information by slowing down the train's speed and decide to go back to normal velocity as soon as obstacles have been removed or precise positioning information is available. These reactions, however, are based on pre-defined deterministic behavioural models and do not depend on AI functionality or on-the-fly learning effects. Some data providers for the train protection system, as, for example, the obstacle detection module, use AI-based technology, such as image classification based on neural networks. We think that this moderation with respect to truly autonomous behaviour is essential for enabling certifiability for train operation in the current European railway infrastructure.

Main Contributions. We propose a novel design for an autonomous train control system architecture covering the functions *automatic train protection (ATP)* and *automatic train operation (ATO)*. This architecture is suitable for GoA 4 in an open environment. This operational environment is assumed to be heterogeneous, with diverse track-side equipment, as can be expected in Europe today. Furthermore, we assume the availability of controlled allocation and assignment of movement authorities, as is performed by today's interlocking systems (IXL, potentially supported by radio block centres (RBC)). Apart from the communication between train and RBC/IXL, no further "vehicle-to-infrastructure" communication channels are assumed. Moreover, the design does not require "vehicle-to-vehicle" communication, since this is not considered as standard in European railways today. As a further design restriction, we advocate the strict separation between conventional control subsystems, and novel, AI-based subsystems that are needed to enable autonomy. It turns out that the latter are only needed in the perception part of the so-called *autonomy pipeline*

$$\textit{sensing} \rightarrow \textit{perception} \rightarrow \textit{planning} \rightarrow \textit{prediction} \rightarrow \textit{control} \rightarrow \textit{actuation},$$

which is considered as the standard paradigm for building autonomous systems today [13]. Fail-safe perception results are achieved by means of a sensor→perceptor design with redundant, stochastically independent channels.

This deliberately conservative architecture serves as the setting for a thought experiment analysing whether such a GoA 4 system could (and should) be certified. The conventional subsystems can be certified on the basis of today's CENELEC standards [4–6]. For the AI-based portion of the design, however, the CENELEC standards cannot be applied. Instead, we use the ANSI/UL 4600 pre-standard [24] and investigate, whether this part can be certified according to this standard with a convincing safety case.

We demonstrate that this architecture for autonomous train control will be certifiable for freight trains and metro trains. In contrast to this, we deem the trustworthy safety assurance of autonomous high-speed passenger trains with GoA 4 to be infeasible today – regardless of the underlying ATP/ATO design. This assessment is justified by the fact that existing obstacle detection functions can only be executed to operate with sufficient reliability for trains with speed up to 120 km/h.

Related Work and Distinction from Other Approaches. The terminology in this paper is in line with terms and definitions introduced by Flammini et al. [8], where a wide range of existing and potential future technologies are discussed and classified.

It is important to point out that visions of autonomous train control far beyond the "fairly moderate" concepts considered in this paper exist. Trentesaux et al. [23] point out the attractiveness of business cases based on trains autonomously negotiating their way across a railway network in an open, uncontrolled (i.e. not fully secured) environment. To this end, they suggest a train control architecture whose behaviour is based on plans that are continuously adapted to increase safety and efficiency. A typical software implementation paradigm for this type of behaviour would be *belief-desire-intention (BDI) agents* [3]. Unsurprisingly, the authors come to the conclusion that the safety assurance and certification of such systems will be quite difficult. Indeed, we will point out below that exactly this type of train control is the one with the least prospects of becoming certifiable in the future.

Flammini et al. [8] discuss the certifiability issues of a variety of ATP/ATO concepts, including the "more futuristic" ones, in a more systematic manner. For all variants, the authors advocate a strict separation between automated ATP and ATO, because the former is safety critical and requires certification according to the highest safety integrity level SIL-4, while the latter could be certified according to a lower SIL, since ATP will ensure that the train will remain safe, even in presence of ATO malfunctions. This distinction between ATP and ATO has influenced the design decisions presented in Sect. 4.

It is interesting to note that the advantages of vehicle-to-vehicle communication deemed to be promising for future train control variants for various purposes [8,23] has already been investigated during 1990s, with the objective to abolish centralised interlocking systems [10]. For the architectural train control concept presented here, however, it is crucial that the safety of allocated train routes is performed by "conventional" IXLs/RBCs, so that these tasks are not contained in the trains' autonomy pipelines.

The paper presented here is inspired by the work of Koopman et al. discussing certification issues of road vehicles [14–16]. It will become clear in the remainder of this paper, however, that their results cannot be "translated in one-to-one fashion" for the railway domain.

The material presented here is complemented by a technical report containing behavioural specification models for some of the ATP/ATO aspects discussed in this paper [11, Appendix A].

Overview. In Sect. 2, the standards and pre-standards of interest in the context of this paper are briefly reviewed. In Sect. 3, we describe existing technology that is needed to realise autonomous train control systems. Up to now, most of these technologies have been used in proof-of-concept projects, so that conformance to standards and certification was not yet an issue. In Sect. 4, we present a new reference architecture for autonomous train control systems that we advocate, due to having fair chances of becoming certifiable in the near future. In Sect. 5, we perform an evaluation of certifiability according to ANSI/UL 4600 for the reference architecture introduced before. Lastly, Sect. 6 contains some concluding remarks.

2 Standardisation and Certification

In the railway domain, safety-critical track-side and on-board systems in Europe must be designed, verified and validated according to the CENELEC standards EN50126, EN50128, and EN50129, in order to pass type certification. None of these documents provides guidance for V&V of AI-based sub-functions involving machine learning, classification techniques, or agent-based autonomous planning and plan execution. Since, as outlined in Sect. 3, autonomous train control depends on such AI-based techniques, this automatically prevents the certification of autonomous train control systems on the basis of these standards alone.

To the best of our knowledge, the ANSI/UL 4600 pre-standard for the evaluation of autonomous products [24] is the first document that is sufficiently comprehensive to serve (in modified and extended form) as a certification basis for operational safety aspects of autonomous products in the automotive, railway, and aviation domains. The standard is structured into 17 sections and 4 annexes. Section 5 addresses the elaboration of safety cases and supporting arguments in general, and Sect. 6 covers general risk assessment. For the context of the paper presented here, Sect. 7 and Sect. 8 of the ANSI/UL 4600 standard are the most relevant parts.

The focus of Sect. 7 is on interaction between humans, animals and other systems and the autonomous system under evaluation (denoted as the *item* in the standard). While this section needs extensive cover for autonomous road vehicles in urban environments, its application is more restricted for the railway domain: here, the pre-planned interaction between humans and autonomous trains takes place in train stations on platforms, during boarding and deboarding. The safety of these situations is handled by the passenger transfer supervision subsystem discussed below. On the track, humans are expected on railway construction sites and level crossings, otherwise their occurrence is illegal. For both legal and illegal occurrences, the on-track interaction between humans and the train is handled by the obstacle detection subsystem described in Sect. 4.

Section 8 of the standard explicitly addresses the autonomy functions of a system, as well as auxiliary functions supporting autonomy. It explains how the impact of autonomy-related system functions on safety should be addressed by means of hazard analyses. For the non-negligible risks induced by these functions, it has to be explained how mitigating functions have been incorporated into the system design. The operational design domain with its different situations and changing environmental conditions needs to be specified, and it has to be shown how the hazards induced by each situation paired with environmental conditions are controlled by the safety mechanisms of the target system. To present hazards caused by autonomy functions, associated design decisions, and mitigations in a well-structured manner, the section is structured according to the autonomy pipeline introduced in Sect. 1.

The other sections of ANSI/UL 4600 cover the underlying software and systems engineering process and life cycle aspects, dependability, data, networking, V&V, testing, tool qualification, safety performance indicators, and assessment of conformance to the standard. These aspects are beyond the scope of this paper.

3 Technology

A number of technologies are required to implement autonomous train control on existing railway networks. The non-modification of existing infrastructure, in particular track-side signalling equipment, is sought in order to facilitate their deployment at lower cost.

We agree with the recommendations of the Federal Railroad Administration of the U.S. Department of Transportation [28] who envision a *sensor platform* combining several different technologies to identify *objects of interest (OOI)* (obstacles, landmarks enabling the improvement of position calculation, train stations, ...) and *conditions of interest (COI)* (*"track is free of obstacles up to location ..."*, *"the train location has distance n meters to its end of movement authority"*, ...). The perception of the immediate train environment is mandatory to ensure a correct navigation regarding signalling equipment, but also to avoid catastrophic collisions with obstacles (trains, objects, animals) by perceiving the scene up to its braking distance. The use of different types of sensing techniques and technologies (radar, laser, LiDAR, camera time-of-flight, camera IR) is necessary to obtain a functional capacity for a wide variety of environmental situations. By using different wavelengths or physical principles (or combination of), it is possible to avoid receiving incorrect information (from radar secondary lobe) or becoming completely blind under certain situations. Indeed, weather conditions (precipitation, snow, humidity, high light levels, mist, dust etc.) have a direct impact on the quality and accuracy of the perceived information, which can strongly alter the representation of the observed scene. For example, an occlusion (spot on an optic) could hide an obstacle; a low sun on the horizon in the axis of the rails could prevent the detection of a light due to sensor saturation.

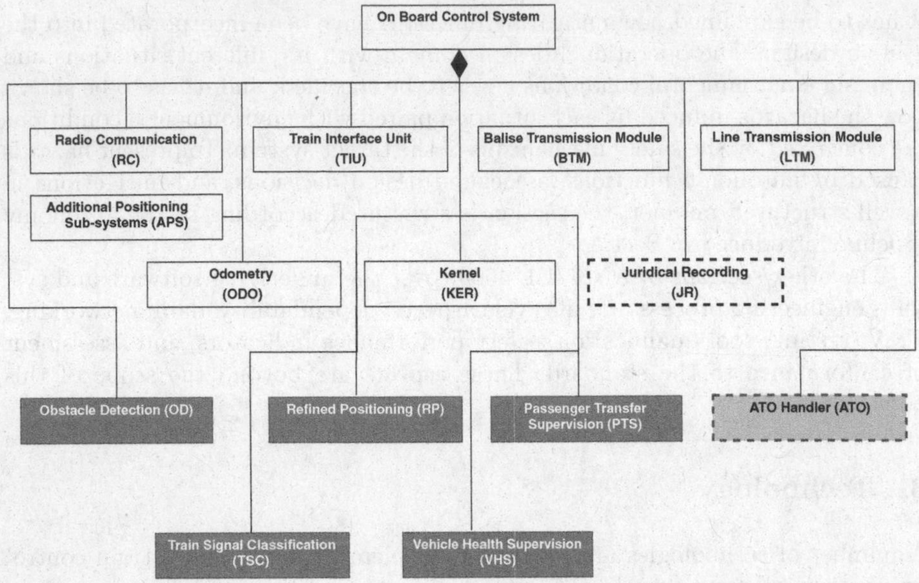

Fig. 1. Reference architecture of autonomous train to be considered for certification.

4 A Reference Architecture for Autonomous Train Controllers

Architecture – Functional Decomposition. In the subsequent paragraphs, we will investigate an autonomous on-board train controller, whose functional decomposition is shown in Fig. 1. The grey boxes are functions required for autonomous trains only. They cannot be certified on the basis of the CENELEC standards alone, because they rely on AI-based functionality.

The white boxes represent components already present in modern conventional on-board units supporting partially automated train control according to GoA 2[3], as suggested by the UNISIG recommendations for ETCS [25]. This structuring into conventional modules is re-used for the autonomous train architecture introduced here. Even existing GoA 2 module implementations could be re-used, but the kernel module has to be significantly extended, as described below. All "white-box modules" in Fig. 1 – even the kernel in its extended form – can be certified on the basis of the CENELEC standards, because no AI-based functionality is deployed on these modules.

In the detailed description below, it will turn out that the kernel in Fig. 1 realises the ATP functionality and the other solid-line boxes provide safety-relevant data to the kernel. Therefore, they need to be certified according to the highest safety integrity level SIL-4. The ATO handler, however, could be certified

[3] *Semi-automatic train operation.* ATO and ATP systems automatically manage train operations and protection while supervised by the driver [8].

according to lower integrity levels, because the automatic train operation is always supervised and restricted by the ATP functions. The same applies to juridical recording, since this has no impact on the train's dynamic behaviour. With this approach, the strict segregation between ATP and ATO advocated by Flammini et al. [8] has been realised.

Conventionally Certifiable On-Board Modules. The central module is the *kernel* which executes the essential ATP operations in various operational modes described below. All decisions about interventions of the normal train operation are taken in the kernel. Based on the status information provided by the other subsystems, the kernel controls the transitions between operational modes (Fig. 2 below). Interventions are executed by the kernel through access to the *train interface unit*, for activating or releasing the service brakes or emergency brakes. The decisions about interventions are taken by the kernel based on the information provided by peripheral modules: (1) The *odometry module* and *balise transmission module* provide information for extracting trustworthy values for the actual train positions. As known from modern high-speed trains, *additional positioning subsystems* provide satellite positioning information in combination with radar sensor information to improve the precision and the reliability of the estimated train location. (2) The *radio communication module* provides information about movement authority and admissible speed profiles, as sent to the train from interlocking systems via radio block centres. In the train-to-trackside transmission direction, the train communicates its actual position to radio block centre/interlocking system. (3) The *line transmission module* provides signal status information provided by trackside equipment for the train. (4) The *juridical recording module* stores safety-relevant kernel decisions and associated data.

Note that, depending on the availability of track-side equipment, not all the data providers listed above will be available. In the non-autonomous case, the missing information is compensated by the train engine driver who, for example, visually interprets signals if trackside line transmission equipment is unavailable. For the autonomous case, additional support modules as described below are required.

Operational Modes. The operational design domain and its associated hazard analyses regarding operational safety (this is further discussed in Sect. 5) induce different operational modes for the train protection component realised by the kernel, providing suitable hazard mitigations. These modes and the transitions between them are depicted in Fig. 2.

In the *autonomous normal operation (ANO)* mode, the train is fully functional and controlled with full autonomy within the range of its current position and the end of movement authority (MA) obtained from the interlocking system (IXL) via radio block controller (RBC). The ANO-(sub-)controller supervises the observation of movement authorities, ceiling speed and braking to target (e.g. the next train station or a level crossing). Its design and implementation

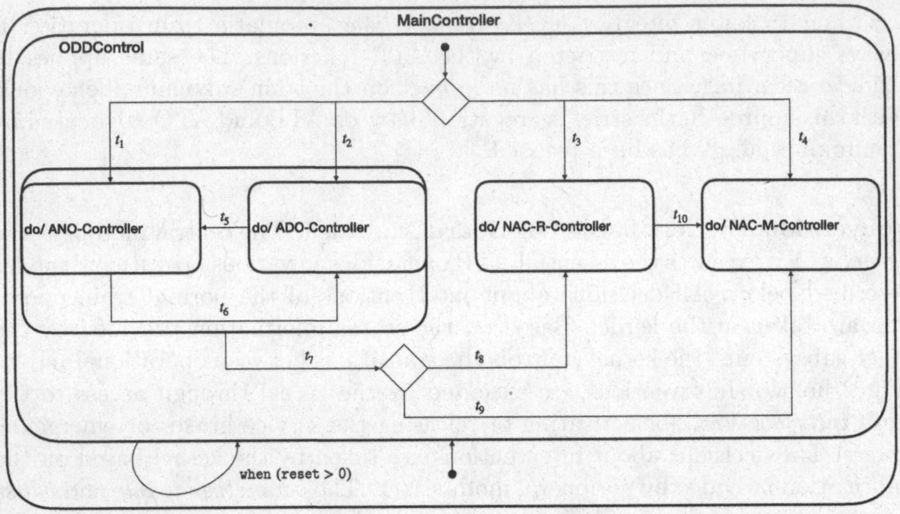

Fig. 2. Operational modes for train protection in autonomous trains.

is "conventional" in the sense that the complete functional behaviour is predetermined by formal models (e.g. state machines) available at type certification time. Indeed, the design of the ANO-controller can be based on that already used for (non-autonomous) ETCS trains today. The only difference is that the interface to the train engine driver is no longer used. Instead, acceleration and braking commands to be executed within the safety limits supervised by the ANO-controller are provided by the ATO-handler described below.

In *autonomous degraded operation (ADO)* mode, the train is still protected autonomously by the ADO-controller and operated by the ATO module, but with degraded performance (e.g., with lower speed). Mode ADO is entered from ANO, for example, if the available position information is not sufficiently precise, so that the train needs to be slowed down until trustworthy position information is available again (e.g. because the train passed a balise with precise location data). Also, the occurrence of an unexpected obstacle (e.g. animals on the track) leads to a transition to the ADO mode. It is possible to transit back from degraded mode to autonomous normal operation, if the sensor platform signals sufficiently precise location information (e.g. provided by a balise that has been passed) and absence of obstacles. Again, the ADO-controller can be modelled, validated and certified conventionally according to EN 50128 [4]. The difference to non-autonomous operation consists in the fact that the transition from ANO to ADO is triggered by events provided by the sensor and perceptor platform, since no train engine driver is available.

In case of a loss of vital autonomous sub-functions (see description of these functions below), the train enters one of the *non-autonomous control (NAC)* modes. In NAC-R, the train can still be remotely controlled by a human from some centralised facility. The operational safety of remotely controlled trains has been discussed by Tonk et al. [22]. If no remote control facility is available, the train enters mode NAC-M and has to be manually controlled by a train engine driver boarding the train.

Modules Supporting Autonomous Trains Operation. The *obstacle detection module (OD)* has the task to identify objects on the track, like persons, fallen trees, or cars illegally occupying a level crossing. Note that the absence of other trains on the track is already guaranteed by the IXL, so OD can focus on unexpected objects alone. OD uses a variety of sensors (cameras, LiDAR, radar, infrared etc.) [28] to determine whether obstacles are on the track ahead. In case an obstacle is detected, it would be required to estimate its distance from the train in order to decide (in the kernel) whether an activation of emergency brakes is required or if the service brakes suffice. A further essential functional feature is the distinction between obstacles on the train's track and obstacles of approaching trains on neighbouring tracks, where no braking intervention is necessary. Camera-based obstacle detection can be performed by conventional computer vision algorithms or by means of image classification techniques based on neural networks and machine learning [18,29]. None of the available technologies are sufficiently precise and reliable to be used alone for obstacle detection [28]. Instead, a redundant sensor combination based on several technologies is required, as described below. In any case, experimental evidence is only available for train speeds up to 120 km/h [18]; this induces our restriction to autonomous freight trains and metro trains. From the perspective of the autonomy pipeline described in Sect. 1, the obstacle detection module performs sensing and perception. It provides the *"obstacle present in distance d"* information to the kernel which operates on a state space aggregating all situational awareness data.

The *refined positioning module (RP)* provides additional train location information, with the objective to compensate for the train engine driver's awareness of the current location that is no longer available in the autonomous case. A typical use case for refined positioning information is the train's entry into a station, where it has to stop exactly at a halt sign. To achieve the positioning precision required for such situations, signposts and other landmarks with known map positions have to be evaluated. This requires image classification, typically based on trained neural networks [20]. Again, conventional image recognition based on templates for signs and landmarks to expect can be used [17] to allow for fusion of conventional and AI-based sub-sensors. The *train signal classification module (TSC)* is needed on tracks without line transmission facilities. Signals and other signs need to be recognised and classified. Summarising, the OD, RP, and TSC modules represent perception functions helping the kernel to update its situational awareness status. All three modules can be realised by means of sensor combination techniques involving both conventional image recognition methods and trained neural networks. These observations become important in the sample evaluation performed in Sect. 5.

The *passenger transfer supervision module (PTS)* is needed to ensure safe boarding and deboarding of passengers. It applies to the fully autonomous case of passenger trains being operated without any personnel and in absence of screen doors on the platform. This module requires sophisticated image classification techniques, for example, to distinguish between moving adults, children, and other moving objects (e.g. baggage carts on the platform). Again, PTS is a sensing and perception function providing the kernel with the *"passengers still boarding/deboarding at door ..."* and *"passengers or animals dangerously close to train"* information that shall prevent the train from starting to move and leave the station. Sensor combination with conventional technology could be provided by various sorts of light-sensors, in particular, safety light curtains[4].

The *vehicle health supervision module (VHS)* is needed to replace the train engine drivers' and the on-board personnel's awareness of changes in the vehicle health status. Indications for such a change can be detected by observing acoustic, electrical, and temperature values. The conclusion about the actual health status, however, strongly relies on the experience of the personnel involved. This knowledge needs to be transferred to the health supervision in the autonomous case [23]. Since the effect of human experience on the train's safety is very hard to assess, it is quite unclear how "sufficient performance" of module VHS should be specified, and how it should be evaluated. Therefore, we do not consider this component anymore in the sequel.

The handler for automated train operation *(ATO handler)* acts within the restrictions enforced by the ATP functionality. The kernel defines the actual operational level (ANO, ADO, NAC-R, NAC-M), and the ATO handler realises automated operation accordingly. In autonomous normal operation mode ANO, the ATO handler could, for example, optimise energy consumption by using AI-based strategies for efficient acceleration and braking [19]. After a trip situation leading to an emergency stop (this is controlled by the kernel, including the transition into autonomous degraded operation ADO), the ATO handler controls re-start of the train and negotiates with the IXL/RBC the location and time from where ANO can be resumed. The train movements involved are again within the limits of the actual movement authority provided by the IXL/RBC, so the essential safety assurance is provided by ATP. In the degraded mode NAC-R, the ATO handler performs the protocol for remotely controlled train operation. If remote control is unavailable, a switch to NAC-R is performed by the kernel, and the ATO handler becomes passive, since train operation is switched to manual.

Dual Channel Plus Voting Design Pattern. As a further design decision, we introduce a two-channel design pattern for the modules OD, TSC, RP, and PTS, as shown in Fig. 3. The objective of this design is to produce a fail-safe sensor→perceptor component, such that it can be assumed with high probability that *either the perception results transmitted to the kernel are correct, or the component will signal 'failure' to the kernel.* In the 'failure' case, the kernel will transit into one of the degraded modes ADO, NAC-R, NAC-M, depending on

[4] https://en.wikipedia.org/wiki/Light_curtain.

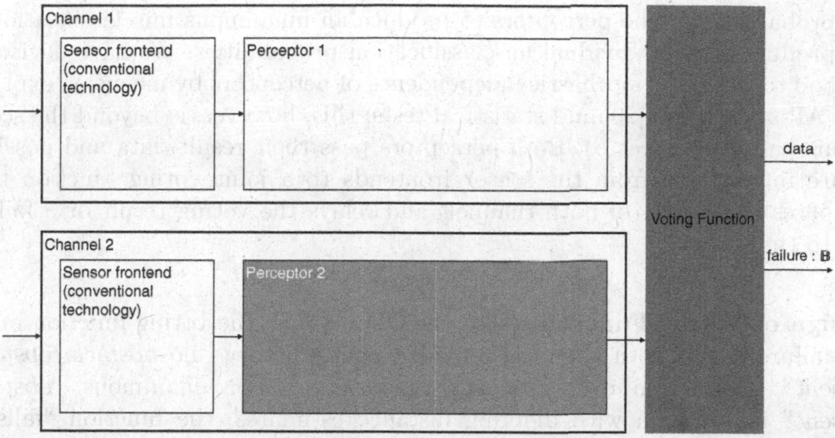

Fig. 3. Two-channel design pattern used for modules OD, TSC, RP, and PTS.

the seriousness of the fault. A *reliable* sensor→perceptor subsystem can then be constructed from three or more fail-safe components using complementary technologies (e.g. one component is based on radar technology, while the other uses cameras), so that a deterministic sensor fusion by means of m-out-of-n voting decisions can be made in the kernel.

Each channel of a fail-safe component has a sensor frontend (camera, radar etc.) for receiving environment information. The sensor frontends use redundant hardware, so that they can be assumed to be stochastically independent with respect to hardware faults. The remaining common cause faults for the sensors (like sand storms blinding all camera lenses) can be detected with high probability, because both sensor data degrade nearly simultaneously.

The sensor frontends pass their raw data to the perceptor submodules: each perceptor processes a sequence of sensor readings to obtain a classification result such as 'obstacle detected' or 'halt signal detected'. We require perceptors 1 and 2 to use 'orthogonal' technology, so that their classification results (e.g. 'obstacle present') are achieved in stochastically independent ways. For example, a pair of vision-based perceptors could be realised by neural networks with different layering structure and trained with different data sets. Alternatively, one perceptor could be based on trained neural networks, while the other uses conventional image recognition technology [18]. A third option is to combine two orthogonal sensor→perceptor technologies that are a priori independent, such as one channel based on camera vision, and another on radar.

Note that in this context, stochastic independence does not mean that the two perceptors are very likely to produce different classification results, but that they have obtained these results *for different reasons*. For example, one perceptor detects a vehicle standing on the track by recognising its wheels, while the other detects the same obstacle by recognising an aspect of the vehicle body (e.g. the radiator grill). This type of independence will allow us to conclude that the probability for the perceptors to produce an unanimous misclassification is the product of the individual misclassification probabilities. We have devised a method to verify the stochastic independence of perceptors by means of 'explainable AI' approaches [20] and statistical tests; this, however, is beyond the scope of this paper (see Sect. 6). Both perceptors pass their result data and possibly failure information from the sensor frontends to a joint voting function that compares the results of both channels and relays the voting result or a failure flag to the kernel.

Design of Voting Functions. For the OD module, the voting function raises the failure flag if both channels provided contradictory *"no obstacle/obstacle present"* information over a longer time period. For unanimous *"obstacle present"* information with differing distance estimates, the function "falls to the safe side" and relays the shorter distance to the kernel. Similar voters can be designed for RP, TSC, and PTS.

Table 1. Mapping of architectural components to SIL and autonomy pipeline.

	Sensing	Perception	Planning	Prediction	Control	Actuation
SIL-4	OD, TSC, RP, PTS, VHS	RC, ODO, APS, BTM, LTM	KER	KER	KER	TIU
SIL-4+AI		OD, TSC, RP, PTS, VHS				
Lower SIL+AI			ATO	ATO	ATO	

Mapping Modules to the Autonomy Pipeline. The architectural components discussed above can be mapped to the autonomy pipeline as shown in Table 1. The abbreviations used have been defined in Fig. 1. The table also shows the required safety integrity levels. These are derived from the existing CENELEC standards and their requirements regarding functional safety. The marker "+AI" in column 1 indicates that AI-based implementations are required for the respective components. For integrity level SIL-4, which is the main concern of this paper, AI-based methods are strictly confined to the perception part of the pipeline. As discussed above, the ATO module can be certified according to a lower SIL. It could contain both conventional sub-functions and AI-based functions. In the latter case (not discussed in this paper), the evaluation and certification would be performed according to ANSI/UL 4600.

5 A Sample Evaluation According to ANSI/UL 4600

Evaluation Procedure. In this section, Sect. 8 (*Autonomy Functions and Support*) of ANSI/UL 4600 is applied to analyse whether a safety case for the autonomous train control architecture described in Sect. 4 conforming to this standard could be constructed. The procedure required is as follows [24, 8.1]. (Step 1) Identify all hazards related to autonomy and specify suitable mitigations. (Step 2) Specify the autonomy-related implications on the operational design domain. (Step 3) Specify how each part of the autonomy pipeline contributes to the identified hazards and specify the mitigations designed to reduce the risks involved to an acceptable level.

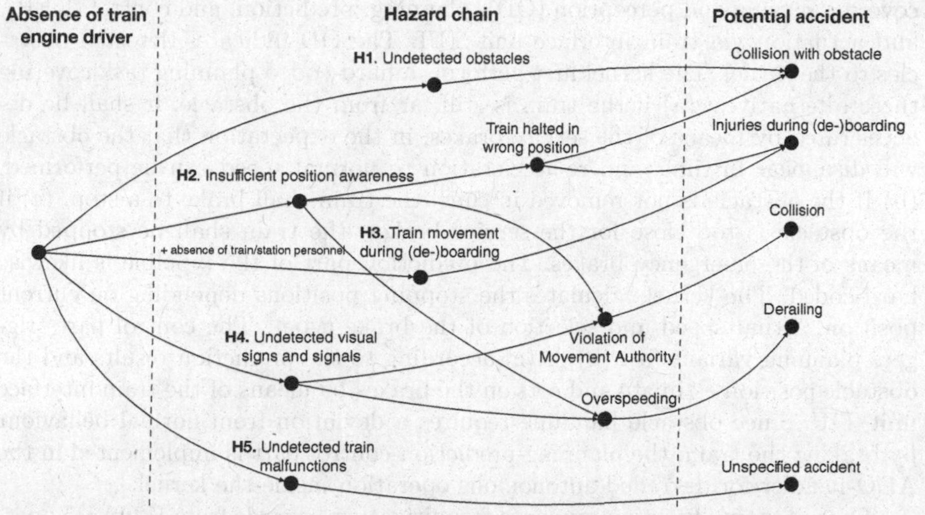

Fig. 4. Hazards caused by absence of train engine driver and personnel.

Step 1. Autonomy Functions, Related Hazards, and Mitigations. The absence of a train engine driver and other train service personnel induces the hazard chains shown in Fig. 4, together with the resulting potential accidents. In this diagram, the hazards from H1 to H5 have been identified as suitable for mitigation and thereby preventing each of the hazard chains from leading to an accident. The hazards marked from H1 to H5 are mitigated by the autonomic function pipelines listed in Table 2 as follows.

Table 2. Hazard mitigations to enable autonomy.

Id.	Hazard	Mitigations by pipeline
H1	Undetected obstacles	OD → KER → TIU
H2	Insufficient position awareness	{ODO,APS,BTM,RP} → KER → TIU
H3	Train movement during (de-)boarding	PTS → KER → TIU
H4	Undetected visual signs and signals	{LTM,TSC} → KER → TIU
H5	Undetected train malfunctions	VHS → KER → TIU

H1 (unidentified obstacles) is prevented by the pipeline OD → KER → TIU covering sensing and perception (OD), planning, prediction, and control (KER), and actuation via train interface unit TUI. The OD indicates detected obstacles to the kernel. The kernel first performs a hard-coded planning task covering three alternatives: (a) if the train is still far from the obstacle, it shall be de-accelerated by means of the service brakes, in the expectation that the obstacle will disappear in time, and re-acceleration to normal speed can be performed. (b) If the obstacle is not removed in time, the train shall brake to a stop. (c) if the obstacle is too close for the service brakes, the train shall be stopped by means of the emergency brakes. The prediction part of the pipeline is likewise hard-coded. The kernel calculates the stopping positions depending on current position, actual speed and selection of the brake type.[5] The control part triggers planning variant (a), (b) or (c) according to the prediction results and the obstacle position estimate and acts on the brakes by means of the train interface unit TIU. Since obstacle handling requires a deviation from normal behaviour by braking the train, the planning-prediction-control part is implemented in the ADO-handler for degraded autonomous operation inside the kernel.

The autonomy function pipelines for mitigating hazards from H2 to H5 operate in analogy to the pipeline mitigating H1.

These considerations show that the hazards are adequately mitigated, *provided that the associated mitigation pipelines from Table 2 fulfil their intended functionality* in the sense of ISO 21448 [12]. Therefore, each of the pipelines listed in Table 2 needs to be evaluated according to Sect. 8 (Autonomy Functions and Support) of the ANSI/UL 4600 standard, as described below.

Step 2. Operational Design Domain and Autonomy-Related Implications. The *operational design domain (ODD)* is defined in ANSI/UL 4600 as *"The set of environments and situations the item is to operate within."* [24, 4.2.30]. Safety cases conforming to this standard need to refer to the applicable ODD subdomains, when presenting safety arguments for autonomous system functions. Originally introduced for autonomous road vehicles [21], systematic

[5] This calculation is based on well-known braking models [27].

approaches to ODD elaboration in the railway domain exist [22]. For a comprehensive safety case, it has to be shown that system operation within the limits of the ODD and its subdomains is safe, and that transitions leaving the ODD are prevented or at least detected and associated with safe reactions (e.g. transitions to a safe state).

The attributes of an ODD are structured into three categories: (1) scenery, (2) environmental conditions, and (3) dynamic elements. In the context of this paper, one class of scenery attributes describes the railway network characteristics the train might visit or travel through: train stations, maintenance depots, tunnels, level crossings, "ordinary" track sections between stations. Note that it is not necessary to differentiate between network characteristics controlled by the interlocking, such as different kinds of flank protection or the availability of shunts in a given network location: since the safety of IXLs is demonstrated separately, and since our investigation is based on current IXL technology that can be certified by conventional means, these aspects can be abstracted away for the type of autonomous trains discussed here.

Regarding environmental conditions, weather and illumination conditions are critical for the sensors and perceptors enabling automated train protection. Moreover, the availability of supporting infrastructure (e.g. GPS, line transmission, balises) varies with the train's location in the railway network, and with exceptional conditions (e.g. unavailability of GPS).

Dynamic elements to be considered apart from the train itself are just illegally occurring obstacles, like vehicles or persons on closed level crossings or variants of obstacles on the track. There is no need to consider other trains, since their absence is controlled by the IXL.

Observe that large portions of the ODD can be created from existing knowledge compiled before to satisfy the reliability, availability, maintainability, and safety requirements for non-autonomous trains according to EN 50126 [5]. The new ODD aspects to be considered for the architecture advocated in this paper are related to the novel sensor and perceptor platform needed for OD, RP, PTS, TSC, and VHS.

As discussed next, the ODD induces V&V objectives that need to be fulfilled in order to guarantee that the train will operate safely under *all* scenarios, environmental conditions, and dynamic situations covered by the ODD. Note that for road vehicles, it is usually necessary to consider states outside the ODD (e.g. a car transported into uncharted terrain and started there), where safe fallback operation has to be verified. For the railway domain as considered here, the ODD is complete, since the IXL ensures that the train will only receive movement authorities to travel over admissible track sections of the European railway network.

Step 3. Evaluation of the Autonomy Pipeline. Each of the hazard mitigation pipelines listed in Table 2 needs to be evaluated according to ANSI/UL 4600, Sect. 8 to show that they really mitigate their associated hazards from H1 to H5 with acceptable performance under all conditions covered by the ODD. The pre-standard suggests to structure the evaluation according to the autonomy pipeline and address the specific operational safety aspects of every pipeline element separately.

Sensor Evaluation. Until today, cameras have been used on trains for obstacle detection and refinement of positioning information only in experiments. Evaluation results already obtained for cameras in autonomous road vehicles cannot easily be re-used, since the train sensor platform requires cameras detecting obstacles and landmarks in greater distances than cars. Also, adequate operation in presence of higher vibrations need to be considered. Experiments have shown, however, that raw image information of cameras can be provided with acceptable performance under the lighting and weather conditions specified in the ODD [18].

ANSI/UL 4600 requires a detailed evaluation of the sensor redundancy management. As described above, we exploit sensor redundancy to detect the (temporary) failure of the two-channel sensor→perceptor subsystem due to adverse weather conditions. Moreover, the sensor redundancy contributes to achieving stochastic independence between the two sensor→perceptor channels. Both redundancy objectives need to be validated separately at design level and in field tests. The ANSI/UL 4600 requirement to identify and mitigate risks associated with sensor performance degradation is fulfilled by the design proposed here in the following ways: (a) total (2-out-of-2) sensor failures are detected, communicated via voting unit to the kernel and lead to a switch into non-autonomous mode which is always accompanied by an emergency stop until manual train operation takes over. (b) 1-out-of-2 sensor failure is tolerated over a limited time period. If recovery cannot be achieved, a transition into non-autonomous mode becomes necessary, since the redundancy is needed to ensure the fail-safe property of the complete sensor→perceptor component. (c) Performance degradation in one sensor leads to discrepancies in the two perceptor channels. If the voter can "fall to the safe side" (e.g. by voting for 'HALT' if one TSC channel perceives 'HALT' while the other perceives 'GO'), the autonomous operation can continue. If no such safe results can be extracted from the differing channel data, a transition into non-autonomous mode is required.

Further sensor types (e.g. radar and GPS antennae) already exist on today's high-speed trains, and the certification credit obtained there can be re-used in the context of autonomous trains.

Perceptor Evaluation. The first evaluation goal consists in the demonstration that the perceptor's functional performance is acceptable. The main task to achieve this goal is to demonstrate that both the false negative rate and the false positive rate are acceptable. For the sensor→perceptor sub-pipelines mitigating hazards from H1 to H5, false negatives have the following meanings.

Id.	Definition of false negative
H1	indication 'no obstacle' though an obstacle is present
H2	indication 'no position error' though estimate is wrong
H3	indication 'no (de-)boarding passengers' though passengers are still present at doors or close to train
H4	indication 'no restrictive signal present' (e.g. HALT, speed restriction) though such a signal can be observed
H5	indication 'no malfunction' though malfunction is present

With these definitions, the false negative rates impair safety, while the false positive rates only impair availability. With the stochastic independence between the two perceptor channels and the voter principle to fall to the safe side, the false negative rates can be controlled.

For each perceptor, an ontology has to be created, capturing the events or states to be perceived (e.g. "obstacle on my track" or "obstacle on neighbouring track"). During the validation process, it has to be shown that the sensor data received is mapped by the perceptor to the correct ontology objects. The ontology needs to be sufficiently detailed to cover all relevant aspects of the ODD (e.g. "obstacle on my track in tunnel" and "obstacle on my track in open track section").

A considerable challenge consists in the justification of equivalence classes used during perceptor evaluation: since the number of different environment conditions and – in the case of obstacle detection – the number of different object shapes to detect is unbounded. As a consequence, feasible validation test suites require the specification of finite collections of equivalence classes, such that a small number of representatives from each class suffices to ensure that *every* class member is detected. The equivalence class identification is problematic, because human perception frequently uses different classes as a trained neural network would use [20]. We have elaborated a new method for equivalence class identification, but this is beyond the scope of this paper (see Sect. 6). In any case, the stochastic independence between channels, achieved through different perception methods applied, reduces the probability that both perceptor channels will produce the same false negatives, to be accepted by the voter.

For the perceptor channels based on neural networks and machine learning, it has to be shown that the training and evaluation data sets are sufficiently diverse, and that the correct classification results have been obtained "for the correct reasons" [20]. In the case of camera sensors and image classifier perceptors, this means that the image portion leading to a correct mapping into the ontology really represents the ontology element. Moreover, robustness, in particular, the absence of *brittleness* has to be shown for the trained neural network: small variations of images need to be mapped onto the same (or similar) ontology elements. Brittleness can occur as a result of overfitting during the training phase.

Evaluation of the "conventional" Sub-pipeline. We observe that the planning → prediction → control → actuation sub-pipeline does not depend on AI-techniques and is fully specified by formal models at type certification time. Consequently, no discrepancies between the safety of the specified functionality and that of the intended functionality are to be expected. Therefore, the evaluation of the kernel and train interface unit is performed as any conventional automated train protection system. The ODD helps to identify the relevant system-level tests to be performed, such as transitions between track sections with different equipment, or different weather conditions influencing the train's braking capabilities. These tests, however, are no different from those needed to establish operational safety of non-autonomous trains. Moreover, the functional safety model induces tests covering equipment failures (e.g. failures of the sensor→perceptor sub-pipeline) and the resulting changes between the operational modes described above.

6 Conclusion

We have presented a new architecture for autonomous train controllers in open environments with the normal infrastructure to be expected in European railways today. It has been demonstrated how this could be evaluated and certified on the basis of the existing CENELEC standards, in combination with the novel ANSI/UL 4600 pre-standard dedicated to the assurance of autonomous, potentially AI-based, transportation systems. As a main result, it has been shown that such an evaluation is feasible already today, and, consequently, such systems are certifiable in the case of freight trains and metro trains, but not in the case of high speed trains. This restriction is necessary because no reliable solutions for obstacle detection in high speed trains seem to be available today.

For a "real-world" certification, the qualitative results of this paper need to be supported by concrete risk figures. This is currently investigated, with the application of stochastic model checking on a world model covering the operational design domain, as well as the trains and their ATP mechanisms discussed here. Moreover, the automated synthesis of safety supervisors from ATP-submodels of the world model will be explored with a novel methodological approach by Gleirscher et al. [9], complementing existing results [1]. For calculating the probabilities of residual perceptor errors and for verifying stochastic independence between channels, we have developed a new method based on statistical tests, algorithms for the explanation of image classification results, and the construction of equivalence classes; the effectiveness of this method will be evaluated.

Acknowledgements. We would like to thank Mario Gleirscher for stimulating discussions of earlier releases of this paper. We are also grateful to the anonymous reviewers who provided very helpful suggestions leading to the revised version of this paper.

References

1. Basile, D., ter Beek, M.H., Legay, A.: Strategy synthesis for autonomous driving in a moving block railway system with UPPAAL STRATEGO. In: Gotsman, A., Sokolova, A. (eds.) Formal Techniques for Distributed Objects, Components, and Systems. LNCS, pp. 3–21. Springer, Cham (2020)

2. Behm, P., Benoit, P., Faivre, A., Meynadier, J.-M.: Météor: a successful application of B in a large project. In: Wing, J.M., Woodcock, J., Davies, J. (eds.) FM 1999. LNCS, vol. 1708, pp. 369–387. Springer, Heidelberg (1999). https://doi.org/10.1007/3-540-48119-2_22
3. Bordini, R.H., Hübner, J.F., Wooldridge, M.: Programming Multi-agent Systems in AgentSpeak Using Jason. Wiley, West Sussex (2007)
4. CENELEC: EN 50128: 2011 Railway applications - Communication, signalling and processing systems - Software for railway control and protection systems (2011)
5. CENELEC: EN 50126 Railway Applications - The Specification and Demonstration of Reliability, Availability, Maintainability and Safety (RAMS) - Part 1: Generic RAMS Process (2017)
6. CENELEC: Railway applications - Communication, signalling and processing systems - Safety related electronic systems for signalling (2018)
7. Fisher, M., Mascardi, V., Rozier, K.Y., Schlingloff, B.H., Winikoff, M., Yorke-Smith, N.: Towards a framework for certification of reliable autonomous systems. Auton. Agent. Multi-agent Syst. **35**(1), 8 (2020). https://doi.org/10.1007/s10458-020-09487-2
8. Flammini, F., Donato, L.D., Fantechi, A., Vittorini, V.: A vision of intelligent train control. In: Dutilleul, S.C., Haxthausen, A.E., Lecomte, T. (eds.) Reliability, Safety, and Security of Railway Systems. Modelling, Analysis, Verification, and Certification - 4th International Conference, RSSRail 2022, Paris, France, 1–2 June 2022, Proceedings. LNCS, vol. 13294, pp. 192–208. Springer, Cham (2022). https://doi.org/10.1007/978-3-031-05814-1_14
9. Gleirscher, M., Calinescu, R., Woodcock, J.: RISKSTRUCTURES: a design algebra for risk-aware machines. Formal Aspects Comput. **33**(4–5), 763–802 (2021). https://doi.org/10.1007/s00165-021-00545-4
10. Haxthausen, A.E., Peleska, J.: Formal development and verification of a distributed railway control system. IEEE Trans. Softw. Eng. **26**(8), 687–701 (2000)
11. Haxthausen, A.E., Lecomte, T., Peleska, J.: Standardisation considerations for autonomous train control - Technical Report. Technical report, Zenodo, February 2022. https://zenodo.org/record/6185229
12. ISO: ISO/DIS 21448: Road vehicles - Safety of the intended functionality. European Committee for Electronic Standardization (2021). iCS: 43.040.10, Draft International Standard
13. Kephart, J.O., Chess, D.M.: The vision of autonomic computing. Computer **36**(1), 41–50 (2003). https://doi.org/10.1109/MC.2003.1160055
14. Koopman, P., Kane, A., Black, J.: Credible autonomy safety argumentation. In: Proceedings of the 27th Safety-Critical Systems Symposium, February 2019. https://users.ece.cmu.edu/~koopman/pubs/Koopman19_SSS_CredibleSafetyArgumentation.pdf
15. Koopman, P., Wagner, M.: Toward a framework for highly automated vehicle safety validation. In: Proceedings of the 2018 SAE World Congress/SAE 2018-01-1071 (2018). https://users.ece.cmu.edu/~koopman/pubs/koopman18_av_safety_validation.pdf
16. Koopman, P., Wagner, M.D.: Autonomous vehicle safety: an interdisciplinary challenge. IEEE Intell. Transp. Syst. Mag. **9**(1), 90–96 (2017). https://doi.org/10.1109/MITS.2016.2583491
17. Marmo, R., Lombardi, L., Gagliardi, N.: Railway sign detection and classification. In: 2006 IEEE Intelligent Transportation Systems Conference, pp. 1358–1363 (2006)

18. Ristić-Durrant, D., Franke, M., Michels, K.: A review of vision-based on-board obstacle detection and distance estimation in railways. Sensors (Basel, Switzerland) **21**(10), 3452 (2021). https://www.ncbi.nlm.nih.gov/pmc/articles/PMC8156009/
19. Siemens Mobility GmbH: World premiere: DB and Siemens present the first automatic train, October 2021. https://press.siemens.com/global/en/pressrelease/world-premiere-db-and-siemens-present-first-self-driving-train, Press release
20. Sun, Y., Chockler, H., Huang, X., Kroening, D.: Explaining image classifiers using statistical fault localization. In: Vedaldi, A., Bischof, H., Brox, T., Frahm, J.-M. (eds.) ECCV 2020. LNCS, vol. 12373, pp. 391–406. Springer, Cham (2020). https://doi.org/10.1007/978-3-030-58604-1_24
21. The British Standards Institution (BSI), Centre for Connected & Autonomous Vehicles: PAS 1883:2020, Operational Design Domain (ODD) taxonomy for an automated driving system (ADS) - Specification, August 2022
22. Tonk, A., Boussif, A., Beugin, J., Collart-Dutilleul, S.: Towards a specified operational design domain for a safe remote driving of trains. In: ESREL 2021, 31st European Safety And Reliability Conference, p. 8p. Angers, France, September 2021. https://hal.archives-ouvertes.fr/hal-03328878, eSREL 2021, 31st European Safety And Reliability Conference, Angers, France, 19 September 2021–23 September 2021
23. Trentesaux, D., et al.: The autonomous train. In: 2018 13th Annual Conference on System of Systems Engineering (SoSE), pp. 514–520, June 2018
24. Underwriters Laboratories Inc.: ANSI/UL 4600-2020 Standard for Evaluation of Autonomous Products - First Edition. Underwriters Laboratories Inc., 333 Pfingsten Road, Northbrook, Illinois 60062-2096, 847.272.8800, April 2020
25. UNISIG: Basic System Description, Chapter 2, vol. Subset-026-2 of [26], February 2006. Issue 2.3.0
26. UNISIG (ed.): ERTMS/ETCS - Class 1 System Requirements Specification, vol. Subset-026, February 2006. Issue 2.3.0
27. UNISIG: ERTMS/ETCS System Requirements Specification, Chapter 3, Principles, Chapter 3, vol. Subset-026-3 of [26], February 2012. Issue 3.3.0
28. Withers, J., Stoehr, N.: Automated Train Operations (ATO) Safety and Sensor Development. Technical Report RR 20–21, U.S. Department of Transportation - Federal Railroad Administration, November 2020. https://railroads.dot.gov/elibrary/automated-train-operations-ato-safety-and-sensor-development
29. Zhang, Z., Wang, Y., Brand, J., Dahnoun, N.: Real-time obstacle detection based on stereo vision for automotive applications. In: 2012 5th European DSP Education and Research Conference (EDERC), pp. 281–285 (2012)

Automatic Generation of Domain-Aware Control Plane Logic for Software Defined Railway Communication Networks

Roberto Canonico[1], Francesco Flammini[2](✉), Stefano Marrone[3], Roberto Nardone[4], and Valeria Vittorini[1]

[1] University of Naples Federico II, Naples, Italy
{roberto.canonico,valeria.vittorini}@unina.it
[2] Mälardalen University, Eskilstuna, Sweden
francesco.flammini@mdu.se
[3] University of Campania "Luigi Vanvitelli", Caserta, Italy
stefano.marrone@unicampania.it
[4] University of Naples "Parthenope", Naples, Italy
roberto.nardone@uniparthenope.it

Abstract. The emergence of 5G technologies opens up new opportunities for railway communications. One of the foundational aspects of 5G architecture is its control-plane programmability, which can be achieved through Software Defined Networking (SDN). In railway scenarios, this can be used to dynamically reconfigure the network for a more effective and efficient management of communication flows produced by moving trains. The paper presents a framework for integrating modelling and analysis tools into a programmable control plane specifically tailored to railway communications. We introduce the concept of domain-awareness in the network control plane as an SDN-enabled feature that allows achieving application-specific advantages besides those purely expressed in terms of key performance indicators such as the quality of service. We propose a reference architecture in which domain-awareness in the control plane is obtained by considering information gathered by network devices and ad-hoc communication gateways that are able to detect relevant signalling events. In the architecture, the actual behaviour of the SDN controller is governed by applications that are able to react to specific triggers and re-configure network devices accordingly. We also provide a methodological framework based on model-driven engineering and formal methods, including dynamic state machines, for the automatic generation of SDN control plane logic.

Keywords: Railways · ERTMS/ETCS · FRMCS · NG2R · SDN · Control plane · QoS · Formal methods · MDE · DSTM

1 Introduction

In many railways, including high-speed lines, in Europe and all over the world, train-to-ground communication is based on the Global System for Mobile

T. Margaria and B. Steffen (Eds.): ISoLA 2022, LNCS 13704, pp. 308–320, 2022.
https://doi.org/10.1007/978-3-031-19762-8_23

Communications for Railways (GSM-R) technology, which was established between 1995 and 2000 as part of the European Rail Traffic Management System (ERTMS) standard. After more than twenty years of successful deployment, the GSM-R technology is showing some limitations and weaknesses. Hence, several initiatives have been launched over the past decade to prepare the ground for defining a new standard communication technology for ERTMS.

At the European level, the European Union Agency for Railways (ERA) has defined a roadmap for the definition and implementation of a new telecommunication standard for railways [20]. Another actor involved in this transition is the Future Railway Mobile Communications System (FRMCS) group, established by the International Union of Railways (UIC), and the Next Generation Radio for Rail (NG2R) working group of the European Telecommunications Standards Institute (ETSI). In 2020, UIC released the "FRMCS On-Board Architecture Functional Requirements Specification (FRS)". The currently ongoing European project 5GRAIL[1] aims at verifying the first set of FRMCS specifications and standards by developing and testing prototypes of the FRMCS ecosystem.

Today, it is widely agreed that the GSM-R successor will provide all-IP connectivity to end devices, including on-board units, and will be convergent, i.e., able to carry traffic generated by different applications [2]. Besides guaranteeing adequate Quality of Service (QoS) to train control traffic, which is crucial for safe and comfortable operation [19], a significant challenge for such a convergent infrastructure is represented by the ability to provide mobile broadband access to travellers [18]. Initially, most stakeholders believed that next generation communication systems for railways would be based on LTE-R, which is derived from fourth generation cellular standard Long Term Evolution (LTE), and its advanced version LTE-A [12]. With the advent of the fifth generation cellular architecture (i.e., 5G) for public telecommunication infrastructures, the adoption of 5G as the basis for future generation railways has been considered [9], in particular, to address the communications demands of travellers and security applications (e.g., video-surveillance) [21].

In the past few years, public 5G networks have been commercially deployed in several countries. The majority of them conform to the Non-Stand-Alone (NSA) 3GPP specifications, which basically allow the adoption of 5G New Radio (NR) base stations as extensions of the 4G EPC core network. This is an interim solution that is gradually overcome by new deployments conforming to the Standalone Architecture (SA). Only these new deployments will be able to fully benefit from the potential of 5G Core, whose design is based on new emerging networking paradigms, such as "softwarization" and virtualization of network functions. In particular, 5G Standalone deployments will be able to support ultra-reliable and low-latency communications (URLLC), a special type of communication that suits the stringent requirements of mission-critical applications. In the literature, it is widely agreed that a key enabler for URLLC services is control-plane programmability, which can be achieved through the adoption of Software Defined Networking (SDN) [1,7,15,22]. SDN allows a centralized

[1] https://5grail.eu.

control of network devices by physically separating control and data plane. In traditional networking, the control plane functionality is embedded in the device itself. With SDN, the control plane is located outside of network devices and is performed by a logically centralized SDN controller, i.e., a software running on a commodity server.

In general-purpose networking environments, the control plane logic implements generic communication "intents", typically expressed in terms of Quality-of-Service requirements and/or security policies. In our work, we move from the assumption that the control plane logic governing a railway communication infrastructure may be finely tuned to take into account the specific requirements and characteristics of the system. For instance, the train trajectories and timings may be considered as partially known in advance and this knowledge may be properly taken into account for resource management during handovers. This is, in essence, what we refer to as the "domain-aware control plane". In particular, in this paper we illustrate a methodological framework that is able to automatically generate the control plane logic of software defined railway communication networks. The framework integrates formal modelling, analysis tools and techniques into a programmable control plane specifically tailored to railway communication infrastructures. We introduce the concept of domain-awareness in the network control plane as an SDN-enabled feature that allows to achieve application-specific advantages besides those purely expressed in terms of network KPIs (Key Performance Indicators) such as QoS. To that aim, we propose a reference architecture in which domain-awareness in the control plane is obtained by taking into account information not only gathered by network devices but also coming from ad-hoc communication gateways that are able to detect relevant signalling events. In the proposed architecture, the actual behaviour of the SDN controller is governed by applications that are able to react to specific triggers of the communication and re-configure network devices accordingly. The flexibility and customizability of the network control plane is particularly suited to accommodate the communication requirements arising from new railway paradigms, such as moving block. Such an evaluation of the SDN potential in the railway context is in line with the growing interest of academy and industry in developing innovative solutions for future railway communications [17].

The remainder of this paper is organized as follows. Section 2 introduces ERTMS and its main constituents. Section 3 presents the reference SDN architecture integrated in ERTMS. Section 4 describes the approach for the automatic synthesis of control plan logic using model-checking approaches. Section 5 describes how the SDN control logic can be supported by formal models. Section 6 addresses current implementation of the prototype aimed at providing a proof-of-concept of the approach. Finally, Sect. 7 summarizes conclusions and future directions.

2 The European Rail Traffic Management System

The European Rail Traffic Management System (ERTMS) is the first international standard for train command-control and train-to-ground communication.

Initially defined and deployed in Europe to guarantee the interoperability of the European railway signalling systems, ERTMS has also been applied in many other countries all over the world. The ERTMS specifications include ETCS, i.e., the European Train Control System. ETCS provides two main features: in-cab signalling, i.e., information and commands for the train driver displayed in the cabin by a Driver Machine Interface (DMI), and Automatic Train Protection (ATP), i.e., the ability to activate warning signals and brakes to slow-down stop the train in case its speed exceeds the allowed speed profile. The ETCS reference architecture includes several subsystems: On-Board Unit (OBU); line-side, which is responsible for providing geographical position to the on-board subsystem; track-side, which is in charge of monitoring and controlling the movement of trains. The most important component of the track-side system is the Radio Block Centre (RBC). RBC is a computing system, whose aim is to ensure a safe inter-train distance on the track area under its supervision.

The ETCS control action is performed by an interaction between the RBC and the Euro Vital Computer (EVC), which is part of the OBU system. Such an interaction happens through a Communication Session established by means of the EURORADIO protocol and the GSM-R network. Figure 1 shows the interaction between RBC and EVC. RBC is also in charge of sending emergency stop messages and channel vitality messages that are needed by the EVC to react to situations when the communication channel is temporarily compromised due to unavailability, interferences, or other issues causing interruption or corruption in message stream. The RBC manages train movement using Movement Authorities (MAs). A train MA is a included in a specific message sent by RBC to EVC containing a data vector defining the maximum distance and allowed speed profiles associated to the track section ahead of the train. An MA includes the End of Authority (EoA), i.e. the stop location that the train is not authorized to pass until a new MA is issued. RBC issues MAs by combining: a) static information about the railway track layout and track elements, and b) dynamic information on train positions and track occupancy obtained from the trains and the interlocking system, respectively. A single RBC is in charge of continuously and concurrently controlling a number of connections with trains, depending on the characteristics of the GSM-R network. In large railways, traffic control is assigned to different cooperating RBCs. Each RBC is associated to an RBC track area. Hence, it may happen that, during a train's journey, its control is switched from one RBC to another; such a procedure is known as "RBC handover".

3 Software-Defined Communication Networks for Railways

A generic SDN architecture for future railways is depicted in Fig. 2, where we identify a Radio Access Network (RAN) and an SDN-enabled Core and Aggregation Network. Several recent works have proposed the use of the SDN paradigm in cellular networks, both in the core and in the radio-access parts of the infrastructure. A programmable control plane allows, in fact, a more flexible management of traffic flows and a more efficient handling of user mobility in these

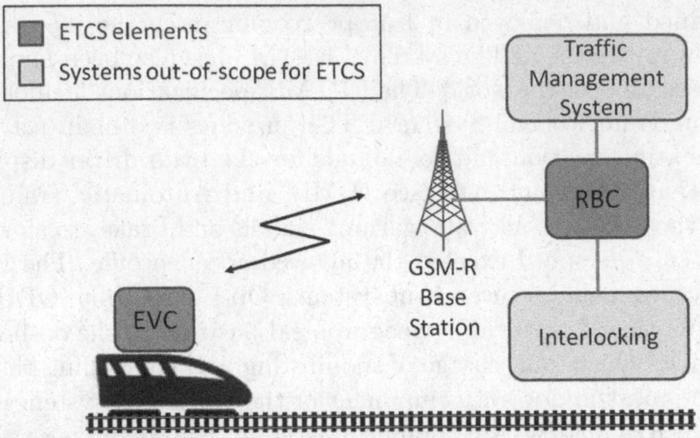

Fig. 1. Main ETCS components and their interconnections.

networks. The adoption of SDN in the mobile backhaul part of the railway communications infrastructure has been already proposed in the literature [11]. We consider the adoption of a programmable control plane in a railway network infrastructure as a valuable architectural innovation that opens-up new opportunities. We will briefly discuss such potential advantages in the following.

Differentiated End-to-End QoS for Vital and Non-vital Flows. By monitoring network conditions and by taking into account current ETCS signalling requirements in a given RBC area, a programmable SDN controller may provide differentiated QoS to the various network traffic flows (e.g., ETCS signalling, video-surveillance, passenger information, infotainment, etc.).

Flexible Resource Management. Network resources may be dynamically allocated to applications depending on the current network status. For instance, infotainment flows may be allocated a reduced bandwidth in congested areas. Furthermore, SDN may also be used to partition network resources among different tenants (i.e., network slicing).

Reactive Control Policies. Softwarization may be used to implement effective topology- and application-aware reconfiguration strategies after network failures (e.g., loss of nodes) and/or anomalous application-level events (e.g., loss of MA). In case a failure is detected, network may be progressively reconfigured to guarantee a fast recovery for vital services.

Proactive Control Policies. Softwarization may also be used to pre-configure network devices for efficiently managing large number of correlated traffic flows. For instance, when the railway communication network infrastructure is also used to provide Internet connectivity to passengers, a proactive management of handovers may lead to significative improvements of mobility management.

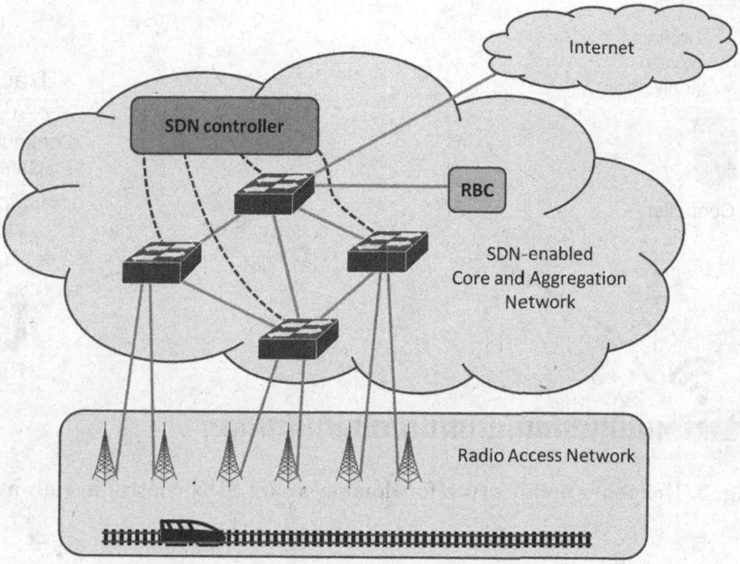

Fig. 2. SDN-enabled wireless backhaul for railways.

Advanced Network Services. A centralized control plane also enables new services, both for end-users (e.g., infotainment content caching) and the railway operator (e.g., traffic logs).

Figure 3 proposes a reference architecture for domain-aware SDN control applied to railways. Both the SDN Controller and the railway subsystems, i.e., on-board and track-side, are connected to the network by means of wired links, which are represented in the figure by continuous lines. Red lines represent communication flows established between the railway signalling endpoints, i.e., RBC and EVC. In this paper, we assume a one-to-one association between RBC and SDN controllers.

The control plane logic is governed by a customized application that interacts with the SDN controller through its northbound API. Such application can be modeled as a state machine that reacts to different events by instructing the SDN controller so that it can change the configuration of network switches; this is represented by dashed lines in Fig. 3. Some examples of relevant events are: (a) the occurrence of a specific network traffic condition (e.g., a link utilization exceeds a given threshold), (b) the detection of an emergency message sent by the RBC, or (c) a hardware failure in a network switch. To capture such events, a set of probes need to be set by the SDN controller. Some of these events could be obtained either directly from the SDN network switches, or by deploying specialized application-aware monitoring devices. This latter solution could leverage a Communication Gateway in charge of receiving unencrypted vital

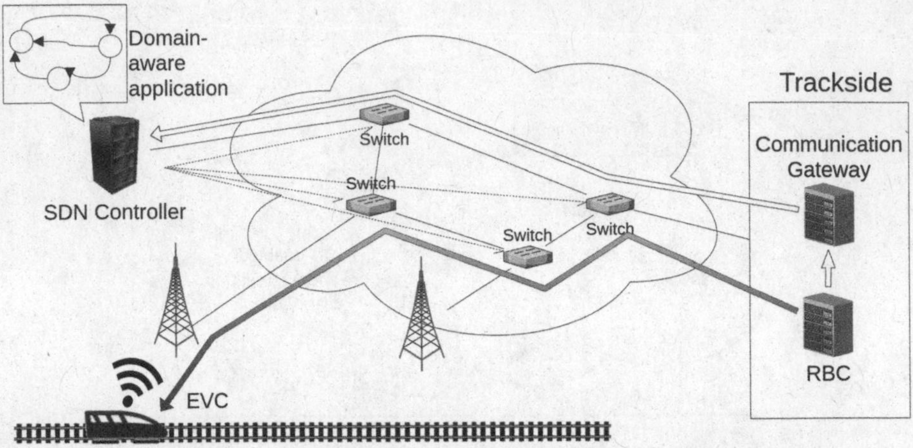

Fig. 3. Reference architecture for domain-aware SDN control in railways.

commands from the RBC, of extracting from them the relevant events, according to predefined probing rules, and of sending them to the SDN Controller; this is represented by the white arrow in Fig. 3.

4 Automatic Synthesis of Control Plane Logic

In order to perform an automatic synthesis of control plane logic in railway applications, it is necessary to investigate how to implement a network controller of a convergent SDN-based communication infrastructure that is able to automatically configure network devices by considering specific communication requirements of different traffic flows. Since signalling is essential for the proper operation of the entire railway, network control logic must be able to react to specific signalling events. To that aim, we propose a model-driven methodological framework based on three layers that leverages formal methods to automate network configuration. A global view of the framework is presented in Fig. 4.

In the specification layer, railway and network specialists provide the following inputs: (i) a model of network topology; (ii) a finite-state-machine representing the signalling protocol from which the relevant states of the signalling system and a related set of events can be deduced, and (iii) technological and application constraints. These information are used to generate sets of configuration rules and a state-machine modeling the behaviour of the SDN control plane. The configuration layer combines the state machine and the configuration rules to generate an application instructing the SDN controller through a controller-specific northbound API. The network layer is the physical communication network, whose control plane consists of the SDN controller and of the domain-aware application. A single set of configuration rules defines a bidirectional flow path on the network connecting two specific end points, namely RBC and EVC. To establish a given network path between the two end-points, proper

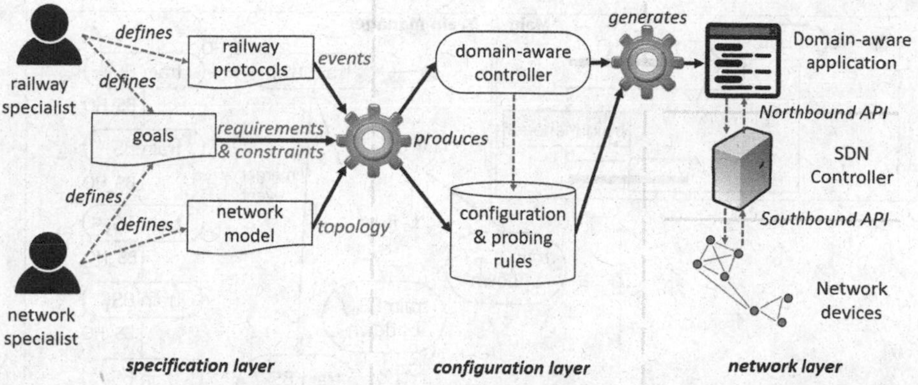

Fig. 4. Methodological framework to automate network configuration.

configuration rules need to be injected into each of the switches located along the path. In the following, we will refer to the switch connected to RBC as the root node, and the base station that provides wireless connectivity to the EVC located in the moving train as edge node. The problem of generating the flow paths between RBC and EVC is a constrained routing problem, where not only the network graph topology is considered, but also a number or variables and constraints must be taken into account in order to meet the requirements of a convergent communication infrastructure. To that aim, events must be identified that require a re-configuration of the network. We consider three classes of events that could trigger the activation of a new configuration:

1. Base station handover (i.e., the train moves from a base station to the next along the track);
2. Network and hardware failures;
3. Application-level relevant events (e.g., an emergency event).

We use model checking to automatically generate the configuration rules [6] and Dynamic State Machines (DSTM) [3] to model the network controller. DSTM is a recent extension of hierarchical state machines whose main advantage with respect to other state-based formalisms is that a DSTM machine can be parametric and dynamically instantiated. In this application, a DSTM machine models how the network must be configured to support the communication between RBC and a single train: a state models a specific network configuration at a specific time, while a transition models the occurrence of a network re-configuration, triggered by the events considered above (e.g., train movement, network device failures, application-level alarms, emergency conditions, etc.). Each instance of the DSTM model corresponds to a specific train under the supervision of the RBC. The configuration layer translates the DSTM model into executable code, which is then executed in the network layer. How this application is coupled to the SDN controller depends on the adopted SDN technology. The problem of

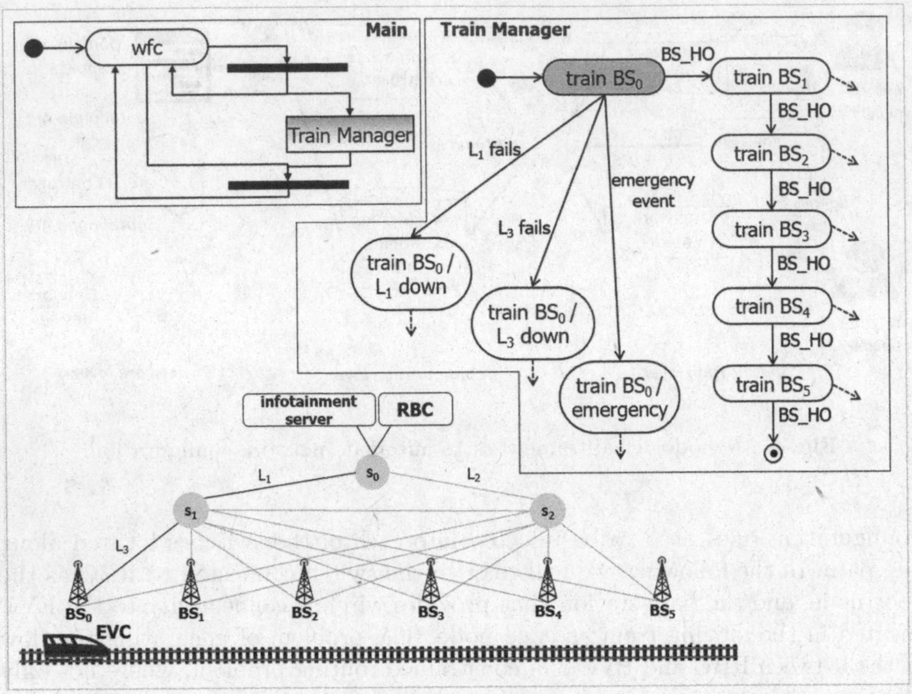

Fig. 5. SDN control plane logic using DSTM formal models.

making the controller able to detect and react to the expected events included into the network controller model may be only partially solved by current SDN implementations. How to expose the application-level semantics to the network controller is an open research challenge.

5 SDN Control Logic Supported by Formal Models

A basic control logic for exemplary purposes is depicted in Fig. 5. We consider a railway communication network consisting of 6 base stations covering the whole track, 3 switches and 16 links. We suppose that the network carries different communication flows: the so-called "vital" flow generated by signalling, and non-vital flows generated by the on-board infotainment services. The root node of both communication flows is the switch named s0. The DSTM model on top of Fig. 5 represents the network controller and specifies the control logic. The model consists of two machines: Main and Train Manager. The Main machine is in charge of detecting the connection requests from trains entering the RBC area. When a new train enters the area, a new instance of the Train Manager machine is created and executed by entering the "box" element of the language, i.e., the rectangle in the Main machine model. The Train Manager machine, on the top-right of Fig. 5, is a specific instance of the "box" element and models the control logic in terms of management of the communication flows for the specific train. Each state of such machine is associated to the configuration rules establishing the bidirectional communication paths for both vital and non-vital flows, in specific conditions. The states from RBC-BS0 to RBC-BS5 represent nominal communication conditions, in particular each state RBC-BSi models the specific network configuration allowing the considered flows between the root and the edge node BSi, when the train is on the track portion covered by the base station BSi. For each state RBC-BSi the controller model envisages the occurrence of possible events, such as device failures, which require the activation of a different network configuration. Figure 5 shows the part of the DSTM model related to the handling of a link failure event occurred when the train is connected to BS0. Furthermore, the detection of an emergency event at ETCS application protocol level leads to a different configuration supporting vital communication flows (i.e., signalling), while offering degraded service to non-vital flows.

6 Current Implementation

We used GraphML [5] to describe the network topology and device features, and Spin [13] as model checker to generate network configurations. The SDN-enabled railway network has been implemented by emulation. In the current prototype, the SDN control plane relies on OpenFlow [16]. The emulated network devices and end-system (RBC and EVC) are instantiated by means of the Mininet-Wifi emulator [10]. The SDN controller is Floodlight, a Java-based modular OpenFlow controller. Floodlight is used to proactively configure switches by receiving flow specifications from external entities, through a REST API. By executing a Python script, Mininet-WiFi instantiates the emulated nodes and runs real network programs in the emulated hosts. By using Mininet-WiFi, it is possible to reproduce node mobility and evaluate the impact on applications of variable network conditions (e.g. due to handovers) over time. Emulated end-systems are virtually connected to access point devices through emulated wireless links. Currently, Mininet-WiFi is only able to emulate IEEE 802.11-based wireless networks and not cellular networks; that was not an issue, since our interest was in the evaluation of the capability of the fixed part of the network to reconfigure its forwarding rules to follow train movements.

7 Conclusions and Future Directions

In the context of next generation communication networks applied to intelligent transportation systems, we discuss in this paper the advantages in applying the SDN paradigm to future railways. In fact, next generation smart-railways will be increasingly based on novel communication and networking paradigms, including the Internet of Things [14] requiring high performance and bandwidth due to the need for manipulating large amounts of data to support machine learning applications [4], high reliability and low latency to enable emerging signalling paradigms such as moving block and virtual coupling [8], as well as flexibility, dynamic context-awareness, adaptation, scalability, and support for advanced multimedia services.

In this paper, we introduced the concept of domain-awareness in the control plane of new generation communication networks used in railway applications, in order to achieve specific advantages besides those typically guaranteed by a plain SDN management (such as flexibility, fault-tolerance, and QoS). To that aim, we provided a reference architecture in which domain-awareness in the control plane is obtained by taking into account information gathered by network devices and by ad-hoc communication gateways that are able to detect relevant signalling events. In the proposed architecture, the actual behaviour of the SDN controller is governed by domain-aware applications to react to specific triggers and re-configure network devices accordingly. We also defined a methodological framework based on model-driven principles and formal methods aimed at automatically generating SDN control plan logic.

Future efforts will be aimed at refining the prototype to design experiments aimed at matching railway-specific requirements with the new communication and networking paradigms enabled by SDN technologies and their softwarization potential. Furthermore, with the stabilization of 3GPP standards for 5G networks, we also aim at improving the integration of our approach in 5G architectures, where separation of mission-critical control traffic and passengers' traffic can be achieved by exploiting the *network slicing* functionality envisioned by most recent releases of 5G standards and where the Core Network is organized around a collection of properly orchestrated Network Functions.

Acknowledgements. This research has received funding from the Shift2Rail Joint Undertaking under the European Union's Horizon 2020 research and innovation programme under grant agreement no. 101015416 PERFORMINGRAIL.

References

1. Agiwal, M., Roy, A., Saxena, N.: Next generation 5G wireless networks: a comprehensive survey. IEEE Commun. Surv. Tutorials **18**(3), 1617–1655 (2016)
2. Ai, B., et al.: Future railway services-oriented mobile communications network. IEEE Commun. Mag. **53**(10), 78–85 (2015)
3. Benerecetti, M., et al.: Dynamic state machines for modelling railway control systems. Sci. Comput. Program. **133**, 116–153 (2017)
4. Bešinović, N., et al.: Artificial intelligence in railway transport: taxonomy, regulations and applications. IEEE Trans. Intell. Transp. Syst. 1–14 (2021)
5. Brandes, U., Eiglsperger, M., Herman, I., Himsolt, M., Marshall, M.S.: GraphML progress report structural layer proposal. In: Mutzel, P., Jünger, M., Leipert, S. (eds.) GD 2001. LNCS, vol. 2265, pp. 501–512. Springer, Heidelberg (2002). https://doi.org/10.1007/3-540-45848-4_59
6. Canonico, R., Marrone, S., Nardone, R., Vittorini, V.: A framework to evaluate 5G networks for smart and fail-safe communications in ERTMS/ETCS. In: Fantechi, A., Lecomte, T., Romanovsky, A. (eds.) Reliability, Safety, and Security of Railway Systems. Modelling, Analysis, Verification, and Certification, vol. 10598, pp. 34–50. Springer, Cham (2017). https://doi.org/10.1007/978-3-319-68499-4_3

7. Chekired, D.A., Togou, M.A., Khoukhi, L., Ksentini, A.: 5G-slicing-enabled scalable SDN core network: toward an ultra-low latency of autonomous driving service. IEEE J. Sel. Areas Commun. **37**(8), 1769–1782 (2019)
8. Di Meo, C., Di Vaio, M., Flammini, F., Nardone, R., Santini, S., Vittorini, V.: ERTMS/ETCS virtual coupling: proof of concept and numerical analysis. IEEE Trans. Intell. Transp. Syst. **21**(6), 2545–2556 (2020)
9. ETSI Technical Committee Railway Telecommunications (RT): Future Rail Mobile Communication System (FRMCS) - Study on system architecture. Technical report. ETSI TR 103 459 V1.2.1 (2020-08), ETSI (2020)
10. Fontes, R., Afzal, S., Brito, S., Santos, M., Esteve Rothenberg, C.: Mininet-WiFi: emulating software-defined wireless networks. In: 2nd International Workshop on Management of SDN and NFV Systems, 2015(ManSDN/NFV 2015) (2015)
11. Gopalasingham, A., et al.: Software-defined mobile backhaul for future train to ground communication services. In: 2016 9th IFIP Wireless and Mobile Networking Conference (WMNC), p. 167 (2016)
12. He, R., et al.: High-speed railway communications: from GSM-R to LTE-R. IEEE Veh. Technol. Mag. **11**(3), 49–58 (2016)
13. Holzmann, G.: SPIN Model Checker, The: Primer and Reference Manual. Addison-Wesley Professional, Boston (2003)
14. Li, Q.Y., Zhong, Z.D., Liu, M., Fang, W.W.: Chapter 14 - smart railway based on the internet of things. In: Hsu, H.H., Chang, C.Y., Hsu, C.H. (eds.) Big Data Analytics for Sensor-Network Collected Intelligence, pp. 280–297. Intelligent Data-Centric Systems. Academic Press (2017)
15. Lin, Y.B., Huang, T.J., Tsai, S.C.: Enhancing 5G/IoT transport security through content permutation. IEEE Access **7**, 94293–94299 (2019)
16. McKeown, N., et al.: OpenFlow: enabling innovation in campus networks. SIGCOMM Comput. Commun. Rev. **38**(2), 69–74 (2008)
17. Moreno, J., Riera, J.M., Haro, L.D., Rodriguez, C.: A survey on future railway radio communications services: challenges and opportunities. IEEE Commun. Mag. **53**(10), 62–68 (2015)
18. Muller, M.K., Taranetz, M., Rupp, M.: Providing current and future cellular services to high speed trains. IEEE Commun. Mag. **53**(10), 96–101 (2015). https://doi.org/10.1109/MCOM.2015.7295469
19. Sniady, A., Soler, J.: LTE for railways: impact on performance of ETCS railway signaling. IEEE Veh. Technol. Mag. **9**(2), 69–77 (2014)
20. Van Liefferinge, M., Paties, L.: Preparing the future communication system for ERTMS. Eur. Railway Rev. **21**(1), 58–60 (2015)
21. Yan, L., Fang, X.: Reliability evaluation of 5G C/U-plane decoupled architecture for high-speed railway. EURASIP J. Wirel. Commun. Networking **2014**, 127 (2014)
22. Zaidi, Z., Friderikos, V., Yousaf, Z., Fletcher, S., Dohler, M., Aghvami, H.: Will SDN be part of 5G? IEEE Commun. Surv. Tutorials **20**(4), 3220–3258 (2018)

Safe and Secure Architecture Using Diverse Formal Methods

Thierry Lecomte(✉)

CLEARSY, 320 Avenue Archimède, Aix en Provence, France
thierry.lecomte@clearsy.com

Abstract. The distribution of safety functions along the tracks requires the networking of the ECUs (Electronic Control Unit is an embedded system that controls one or more electrical systems or subsystems) that support them, to facilitate their operation and maintenance. The latter enables logs to be sent, commands to be received and sent that will lead to a state change of one of the connected equipment, and the ECU application software to be updated. All these activities are naturally subject to targeted attacks aimed at reducing the availability of the equipment or disrupting its operational safety to the point of creating accidents. This article presents an innovative approach partitioning security and safety on two different computers. One computer connected to the network ensures security and is regularly updated according to known threats. The other computer ensures safety and communicates only through a secure filter. Each computer embeds technological elements that have been specified, implemented and proven with 2 different formal methods.

Keywords: Formal methods · Cybersecurity · Safety

1 Introduction

Railway signalling is a safety-critical system whose responsibility is to guarantee a safe and efficient operation of railway networks. The decentralised railway signalling systems have a potential to increase capacity, availability and reduce maintenance costs of railway networks. Given the safety-critical nature of railway signalling and the complexity of novel distributed signalling solutions, their safety should be guaranteed. With the forthcoming progressive distribution of the signalling functions (sensing, making decision, controlling) based on network connectivity, it is also mandatory to ensure their security as well. The two worlds, namely safety and security, are quite orthogonal as they require to resist to "probabilistic failures" on one hand and to specifically crafted attacks that would timely target the existing vulnerabilities on the other hand. Their requirements are sometimes contradictory, as safety critical systems are usually expected to last decades without modification once certified, while secure systems are supposed to evolve often to take into account uncovered vulnerabilities. The segregation between security and safety, enabling system updates at a different pace and in a decorrelated manner, has been at the centre of a technical

T. Margaria and B. Steffen (Eds.): ISoLA 2022, LNCS 13704, pp. 321–333, 2022.
https://doi.org/10.1007/978-3-031-19762-8_24

thinking, leading to a research project where safety and security aspects are developed on different computers and connected by a single secure link. This article intends to present the architecture being developed, based on existing, formally proven building blocks, and draw the picture of its future deployment modes for distributed computation.

This paper is structured in 7 parts. Section 2 introduces the terminology. Section 3 presents safety computation and computer. The CLEARSY Safety Platform, safety related building block, is exposed in Sect. 4. Section 5 presents the security requirements coming from various environments and standards. Section 6 sketches the technical architecture before concluding in Sect. 7.

2 Terminology

This section contains specific definitions, concepts, and abbreviations used throughout this paper.

ASIC refers to Application-specific integrated circuit. It is an integrated circuit chip which often include entire microprocessors, memory blocks, and other large building blocks.

CRC refers to Cyclic Redundancy Check. It is a checksum used for error detection.

Formal methods refers to mathematically rigorous techniques for the specification, development and verification of software and hardware systems. [8] identifies a collection of formal methods and tools that have been applied in railways.

Safety refers to the control of recognised hazards in order to achieve an acceptable level of risk.

Cybersecurity refers to the protection of digital systems and related networks from information disclosure, theft of or damage to their hardware, software, or electronic data, as well as from the disruption or misdirection of the services they provide.

HSM refers to Hardware Security Module. It is a device that safeguards and manages digital keys, performs encryption and decryption functions for digital signatures, strong authentication and other cryptographic functions.

OT refers to Operational Technology. It is the hardware and software that detects or causes a change, through the direct monitoring and/or control of industrial equipment, assets, processes and events. It is related to industrial control systems environment.

PKI refers to Public Key Infrastructure. It is a set of roles, policies, hardware, software and procedures needed to create, manage, distribute, use, store and revoke digital certificates and manage public-key encryption. It binds public keys with respective identities of entities. The binding is established through a process of registration and issuance of certificates at and by a certificate authority.

Softcore is a digital circuit that can be wholly implemented using logic synthesis on FPGA (programmable component). It allows to run and assess digital circuits (processors) without creating a costly ASIC[1] and with a slower execution speed.

TEE refers to Trusted Execution Environment. It is a secure area of a main processor. It guarantees code and data loaded inside to be protected with respect to confidentiality and integrity.

TPM refers to Trusted Platform Module. It is a secure cryptoprocessor, a dedicated microcontroller designed to secure hardware through integrated cryptographic keys, compliant to the TPM international standard.

3 Ensuring Safety

Safety computers control systems for which a catastrophic failure may lead to people being injured or killed. These computers have to be designed in conformance with domain-related standards. These standards provide guidance and recommendations, based on industry return of experience and current state-of-the-art. If they provide recommendations, they do not provide solutions - it is up to the designer to find a way to comply with the constraints. Following the standards is the easier way to get the system certified. However it is always possible not to follow the standards and to provide an original design, but in this case, the designer has to provide a demonstration that his design is safe, not only based on simulation, but rather on a reasoning [14]. In many cases, the certification is carried out by an individual who takes full responsibility in case of mistake and as such he is not tempted to stray from the standard.

For SIL3 and SIL4 functions, one processor is not enough to reach the expected safety/reliability - so a second processor is often used in combination with a voter. In case of diverging execution among the two processors, the system has to fall back to a safe mode [13] (also called restrictive mode) - usually the system simply stops its execution [6]. To improve availability, more than two processors are used, together with a voter, ensuring a continuous service even if one processor is failing. In [2], one processor is computing while a co-processor is checking memory and program counter coherency.

Common failure mode is one of the main aspect to take into account as it is considered unlikely to get the same failure happening on the multiple processors at the same time within the same conditions (if the common failure mode is possible, the voter cannot detect divergent execution and the safety is not ensured at all). It is not required that every part of a redundant system is developed differently from the others, with different components of different technology, different teams, different programming languages, different tools, etc. However the safety case have to demonstrate how it is not possible to meet common failure mode because of the development or verification cycle, compilation techniques, etc.

[1] The non-recurring engineering cost of an ASIC is in millions of euros while a FPGA board price is in hundreds or thousands euros.

A safety computer has to implement a number of technical features such as:

- a watchdog [12] to check liveness. The watchdog has to be hardware and not be re-programmable on the fly by software. Several watchdogs are typically used for low, medium and high latency actions.
- a memory checker to check coherency. In [9] each variable has two fields: a value (integer) and its corresponding signature (code[2]). When an arithmetic operation is performed or an assignment, both value and code are modified. If the code and the value do not correspond, a memory corruption is detected. Program counter corruption is also detected with so-called compensation tables: each function is initialized with a value, modified (masked) every time an instruction is executed. At the end of the function, the value calculated depends on the path (branches). The compensation table contains all possible values: if the calculated value does not belong to the compensation table, the program counter has been corrupted and the execution of the program has to stop.
- a voter for inputs correlation. Usually inputs are not safety related - they are just captured by a sensor and provided to the computer [11]. Inputs have to be cross-checked with data captured with another sensor, by the same sensor, but as seen from another processor. In case of analog data, different approaches may be used to reconcile input data and avoid system being switched off [5].
- the ability to communicate with other safety computers [10], involving several time-consuming verifications. The use of medium with protocol aimed at improving availability could jeopardize the safety [7].

In [3], the Vital Coded Processor is used in combination with the B formal method to respectively detect errors in the code production chain (compiling, linking, etc.) or resulting from hardware failures, and to detect design or coding errors.

4 The CLEARSY Safety Platform

The CLEARSY Safety Platform is a generic PLC able to perform command and control over inputs and outputs. For safety critical applications, the PLC has to be able to determine whether it is fully functional or not. In case of failure, the PLC should move to restrictive mode where all the outputs are deactivated. The stronger the risk of harming people in case of failure, the higher the Safety Integrity Level. For SIL3 and SIL4, the computations have to be performed by a minimum of two processors and checked with a voting system.

The CLEARSY Safety Platform is made of two parts: an IDE to develop the software and an electronic board to execute this software. From a safety point of view, the current architecture is valid for any kind of mono-core processor. Multi-core applications would require an hypervisor, a Memory Management Unit (MMU), and a micro-kernel able to guaranty memory isolation.

[2] One value is associated with a single code, but a code may be associated to several values.

The full development and execution process is described in Fig. 1 where CPU1 and CPU2 are PIC32 microcontrollers.

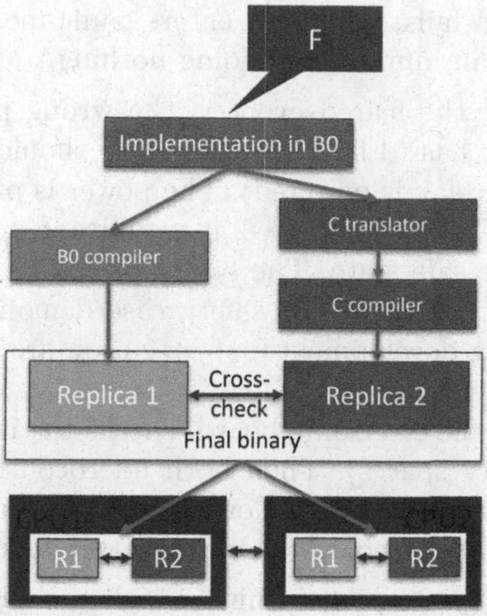

Fig. 1. Full path from function description to safe execution.

It strictly follows the B method which can be summarised as:

- specification model is written first from the natural language requirements (Function), then comes the implementation model, both using the same language (B).
- models are proved to be coherent and to be correct refinements.
- source code or binary is generated from implementation model:
  - Replica 1 (HEX file) is directly compiled from the implementation B model. The compiler has been developed in-house for supporting this technology.
  - Replica 2 (HEX file as well) is generated in two steps. First, Implementation models are translated to C, using the Atelier B C code generator. Then the C code is compiled with gcc.
- The two binaries are linked to a top-level sequencer and a safety library, both software developed in B by the CLEARSY Safety Platform IDE development team once for all, to constitute the final software.
- This software is then loaded on the flash memory of the two microcontrollers (bootload mode).
- When the board enters the execution mode or is reset, the content of the flash memory is copied in RAM for both microcontrollers which start executing it.

- For each microcontroller, the top-level sequencer enters a never-ending loop and
  - calls in sequence Replica 1 then Replica 2 for one iteration
  - calls the safety library in charge of performing verification.
  - If the verification fails, the board enters panic mode, deactivates its outputs and enters an infinite loop doing nothing.

For the safety case, the feared event is the wrong powering of one of the outputs i.e. this output has to be OFF (the relay should not be powered), but it is currently ON (the relay is powered). The power is provided by both microcontrollers, so if one of the two is reset, it would not power the relay and the board is in a restrictive safe state. The safety principles are distributed on the board and on the safety library. The safety case demonstrates that the verification performed during development and execution are sufficient to ensure the target safety integrity level.

The bootloader, on the electronic board, checks the integrity of the program (CRC, separate memory spaces). Then both microcontrollers start to execute the program. During execution, the following verifications are conducted. If any of these verification fails, the board enters the panic mode:

- internal verification (performed within a single microcontroller):
  - every cycle, Replica 1 and Replica 2 data memory spaces (variables) are compared within each microcontroller;
  - regularly, Replica 1 and Replica 2 program memory spaces are compared. This verification is performed "in the background" over thousands/millions cycles - to keep a reasonable cycle time.;
  - regularly, the identity between memory outputs states and physical output states is checked to detect if the board is unable to command the outputs.
- external verification (performed between both microcontrollers):
  - regularly (every 50 ms maximum), data memory spaces (variables) are compared between CPU1 and CPU2.

The safety is built on top of several principles:

- a B formal model of the function to develop, proved to be coherent, to correctly implement its specification, and to be programming error-free i.e. no division by zero, no overflow, no access to a table outside of its range;
- four instances of the same function running on two micro-controllers (two per micro-controller with different binaries obtained from diverse tool-chains) and the detection of any divergent behaviour among the four instances;
- the deferred cross-verification of the programs on-board the two microcontrollers;
- outputs require both CPU1 and CPU2 to be live and running as one provides energy and the other one the command;
- physical output states are regularly verified to comply with the software output states, to check the ability of the board to command its outputs;
- input signals are continuous (0 or 5V) and are made dynamic (addition of a frequency signal) in order not to consider short-circuit current as high level (permissive) logic.

5 Cybersecurity Requirements

Railway systems are becoming vulnerable to cyber attack due to the move away from bespoke stand-alone systems to open-platform, standardised equipment built using Commercial Off The Shelf (COTS) components, and increasing use of networked control and automation systems that can be accessed remotely via public and private networks. The connection of a safety computer to any network is not secure as this computer has been designed to resist to "probabilistic failures", not to specifically crafted attacks that would timely target the existing vulnerabilities. This connection eases the exploitation of the safety computer as it allows:

- **logs compilation and emission**, towards maintenance equipment or supervision system. This feature helps to gain an understanding of the internal of the device, but not to directly modify its behaviour.
- **commands receiving and sending**, when safety computers are used in combination. This feature is security critical as an attacker impersonating another device could modify the behaviour of the device.
- **safety-critical firmware update**. This feature is security critical as it allows an attacker to fully reprogram the device and to implement any dangerous behaviour.

None of the safety features implemented by the CLEARSY Safety Platform protect against such attacks. In particular, the main integrity check is based on CRC that is not considered as a cryptographic primitive[3]. Messages received can only be checked well-formed, but not issued from a valid emitter.

Moreover the embedding of cryptographic capabilities (algorithms, data storage) requires resources (computing, memory) that are not necessarily available onboard. Ciphering and deciphering, generating and managing keys, controlling correct protocol execution imply extra processing time that could prevent hard real-time compliance (in OT, availability is preferred over security).

The Technical Specification CLC/TS 50701 'Railway applications - Cybersecurity' has been issued in 2021 to provide requirements and recommendations to handle cybersecurity in a unified way for the railway sector. This specification takes into consideration relevant safety related aspects (EN 50126) and takes inspiration from different sources (IEC 62443-3-3, CSM-RA), adapting them to the railway context. It covers numerous key topics such as railway system overview, cybersecurity during a railway application life cycle, risk assessment, security design, cybersecurity assurance and system acceptance, vulnerability management and security patch management. In this paper, the focus is on the security design, without neglecting the other aspects which are all important.

OT security implies:

- **confidentiality** (keeping data secure): ensures that sensitive information are accessed only by an authorised person and kept away from those not authorised to possess them;

[3] They are not robust to collision attacks, meaning that somebody can take a given CRC and easily find a second input that matches it.

- **integrity** (keeping data clean): ensures that information are in a format that is true and correct to its original purposes.
- **availability** (keeping data accessible): ensures that information and resources are available to those who need them.

Usually security design implements these three principles with public key cryptography and specific hardware to constitute a Root of Trust, a source that can always be trusted within a cryptographic system and is critical for PKI. Hardware could rely on a TPM[4], a HSM[5] or any Secure Enclave module. In addition, an isolated execution environment (a TEE, such as ARM TrustZone) provides security features such as isolated execution, integrity of applications executing with the TEE, and confidentiality of their assets.

The security standards do not impose any particular architecture, so the detailed design may vary depending on the hardware platform (off-the-shelf component, softcore model running on a FPGA, tailored ASIC) and associated security features, on the software architecture (bare-metal or OS-based application), and selected communication protocols. Demonstration of compliance with security standards also depends: IEC 62443 covers the whole development cycle while Common Criteria-based CSPN[6] only requires a Security Target document, a user manual, and a third-party penetration testing.

Railways critical infrastructure have to demonstrate a strong resilience as the surface of attack (the network) is large (especially with communication-based safety systems), and the (usually nation-state) attackers have a high level of expertise and extensive resources. Equipment subject to cyber attacks have to resist to reverse engineering and physical attacks (side-channel, timing). They must also ensure a proper level of protection by taking into account discovered vulnerabilities and by regularly updating their software.

6 Resulting Architecture

6.1 Introduction

Designing an equipment combining safety and security on the same computer is difficult. Cybersecurity mechanisms [4] are difficult to reconcile with the real-time constraints of programmable controllers. Also Safety and security requirements are sometimes contradictory and lead to conflicts (a certified safety system is expected to not evolve any more while updates of a security system allow to protect against new attacks). Moreover the use of technologies not fully mastered

[4] A TPM contains a hardware random number generator, facilities for the secure generation of cryptographic keys for limited uses, a generator of unforgeable hash key summary of a configuration, and a data encryptor/decryptor.

[5] A HSM is similar to a TPM. HSMs are focused on performance and key storage space, where as TPMs are only designed to keep a few values and a single key in memory and don't put much effort into performance.

[6] Certification de Sécurité de Premier Niveau - https://www.ssi.gouv.fr/administra tion/produits-certifies/cspn/.

by the designer may leave unwanted access to the resources to be protected. This includes for example:

- the BadUSB exploit: USB flash drives, containing a programmable Intel 8051 microcontroller, can be reprogrammed, turning a USB flash drive into a malicious device.
- the UEFI vulnerabilities: as of February 2022, 23 vulnerabilities have been identified on the firmware (in one library of widely used framework). An attacker with privileged user access to the targeted system can exploit the vulnerabilities to install highly persistent malware. The attacker can bypass endpoint security solutions, Secure Boot, and virtualisation-based security. The active exploitation of all the discovered vulnerabilities can't be detected by firmware integrity monitoring systems due to limitations of the TPM.

6.2 Original Architecture

An original architecture Fig. 2 has been designed and is being implemented and assessed during the project CASES[7]. The CASES project was selected in the first call for projects "Development of critical innovative technologies" - launched by BPI France to co-finance R&D on innovative and critical technological bricks in cybersecurity. The project, entirely executed by CLEARSY, aims to build a safe and secure generic sovereign computer, enabling critical infrastructures to be controlled and commanded with the highest level of integrity. The project consists in the separation of the safety and the security on two different computers with a formally proven communication link in between.

The CASES ECU consists of two ECUs:

- a SIL4 level safety computer, the CLEARSY Safety Platform CS0 (see Sect. 4). This computer is based on 2 PIC32 microcontrollers, a secure bootloader (integrity) and a safety library to ensure safe operation even in case of malfunction. This ECU runs a monitoring/control application (reading the status of sensors, controlling outputs) - which can be a purely computational application if no inputs or outputs are monitored. The safety ECU can receive updates to the application (safety firmware) and send/receive commands from the outside.
- A security computer, which provides the (wired) interface between the safety computer and the outside world. This computer is based on a RISC-V type processor. A secure microkernel, ProvenCore[8], allows the isolation of the different services offered: updating of the safety firmware, reception and emission of commands, transmission of information (supervision). Communications are secured through a VPN and a TCP/TLS stack.

These 2 ECUs are each in the form of a daughter board to be plugged onto a motherboard providing power and secure inputs/outputs. The resulting ECU combines best practices in the areas of:

[7] https://www.clearsy.com/en/research-and-development/project-cases/.
[8] https://provenrun.com/products/provencore/.

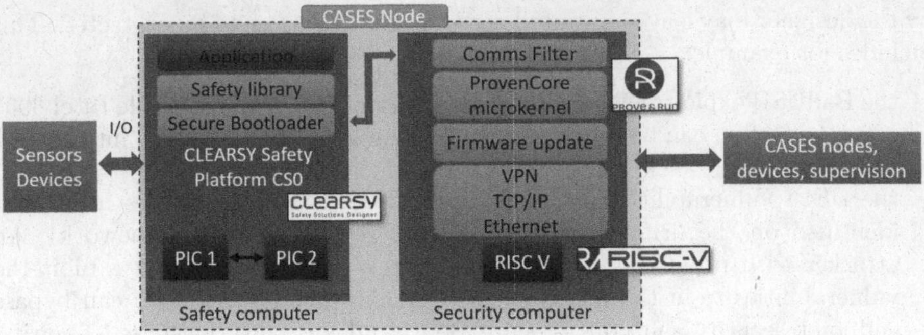

Fig. 2. Safe and secure architecture.

- safety: the CLEARSY Safety Platform computer is certified at SIL4 level by Bureau Veritas. SIL4 is the highest level defined by the EN50126 standard (railways);
- security: the microkernel ProvenCore is certified at EAL7 level by ANSSI[9] EAL7 is the highest level defined by the Common Criteria certification scheme.

6.3 Rationale

Both elements are formally developed and proved:

- the safety library and the vital part of the application are developed with B. Among the properties modelled are the correct verification of microcontroller structural elements like RAM and ALU, and the management of deadlines with watchdogs;
- the micro-kernel is developed in Smart language[10], using proprietary tools integrated to Eclipse. The main property of ProvenCore [1] is the isolation property. It ensures that the resources of a process cannot be observed and cannot be tampered by other processes, unless said process gave explicit authorisation.

The communication filter is the only link (serial interface) between the two ECUS. It is developed in B, to implement a grammar of messages defined once for all, including a number of integrity/security features like cryptographic hashes and message counter, based on shared secrets. Non complying messages are then discarded. Once the CLEARSY Safety Platform bootloader is able to handle this

[9] Agence Nationale de la Sécurité des Systèmes d'Information - https://www.ssi.gouv.fr/en/.

[10] Developed by Prove & Run, Smart lets one write both the implementation and the specifications, including the various properties, axioms, auxiliary lemmas, and so on. Smart is a strongly-typed polymorphic functional language with algebraic data-types (structures and variants).

communication, the security ECU may evolve without compromising the safety ECU certificate, as long as the communication protocol remains unchanged. The choice of a RISC-V based processor allows to go beyond EAL4 level. Digital circuits with security oriented features (like MMU or MPU) are often proprietary and their internals not available publicly for analysis, preventing them to reach Common Criteria highest security levels. With the Open Hardware movement, RISC-V offers the possibility to get access to these secure parts and to perform white box analysis. The communication with the outside (supervision/SCADA, other CASES ECUS, networked devices) relies on a PKI managed externally and on TLS to ensure confidentiality and authenticity.

6.4 Assessment

The use case identified is typical of the problem of decentralisation of decision-making in critical railway infrastructures. Decisions are to be taken as close as possible to the sensor and actuator, rather than having the information from the sensor/controller travel (tens of) kilometres via cables. This is (see Fig. 3) a turnout control system:

- Node 1: turnout
- Node 2: traffic light
- Remote PC: supervision, updating

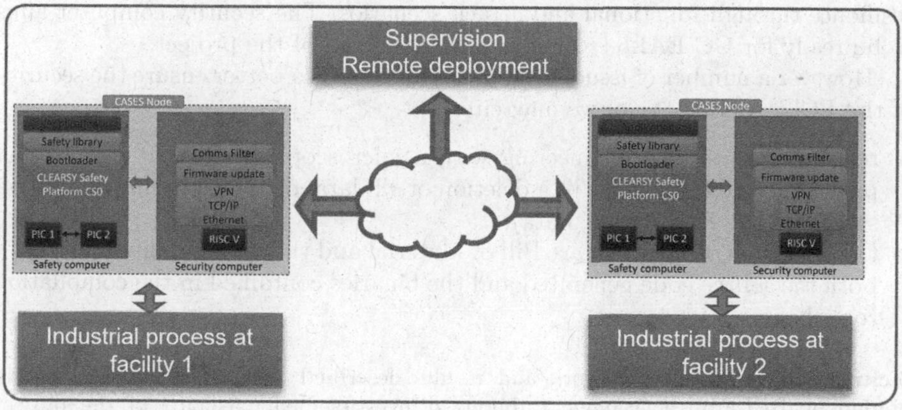

Fig. 3. Use case.

This demonstrator will allow the implementation of several functionalities necessary for the deployment of this technology:

- Communication (control) between 2 CASES nodes. Node 1 (switch) makes a decision based on a perceived state and information received. It tells node 2 to change its state in relation to the action to be taken on the actuator linked to node 1.)

- Communication (maintenance) between a CASES node and a supervision system. CASES nodes send maintenance information (status, statistics, etc.) synchronously or asynchronously.
- Communication (software update) between a supervisory system and a CASES node. A remote PC performs the update of the application software of the safety computer of the CASES nodes.

The development and assessment of the demonstrator is planned for 2022 and 2023. Results will be published when available.

7 Conclusion and Perspectives

This article does not directly address the distribution of railway signalling functions, but is more focused on the technical and regulatory constraints resulting from the operation of decentralised safety related devices connected to network. The architecture presented allows to address some of the regulatory constraints linked to safety and security design. From a functional point of view, the CASES ECU supports any algorithm and is not limited to the Boolean equations of PLC programming languages. It can be adapted to a wide variety of technical environments. The segregation between the safety and the security parts limits the surface of attack, while their interaction are verifiable. Two independent formal methods and related tooling are used to ensure respectively safety and security (isolation). A significant use-case is expected to demonstrate both usability and resilience through functional and attack scenarios. The security computer aims to be ready for CC EAL5+ certification at the end of the project.

However a number of issues need to be addressed to better ensure the security of the ECU. Among them, we may cite:

- resistance to reverse engineering with a microscopic mesh that detects any probe intrusion and leads to a deletion of all data, or the ciphering of all data stored on the ECU (code, data);
- the definition of the Software Bill of Material and the vulnerability analysis of both the source code generated and the binaries contained in the compilation tool-chains.

Acknowledgements. The work and results described in this article were partly funded by BPI-France (Banque Publique d'Investissement) as part of the project CASES (Calculateur Sûr et Sécuritaire) selected for the call "Stratégie Cyber 2021 - Développement de technologies innovantes critiques".

References

1. ProvenCore: Towards a Verified Isolation Micro-Kernel. Zenodo, January 2015. https://doi.org/10.5281/zenodo.47990
2. Baro, S.: A high availability vital computer for railway applications: architecture & safety principles. In: Embedded Real Time Software and Systems (ERTS2008), Toulouse, France, January 2008. https://hal.archives-ouvertes.fr/hal-02269811

3. Behm, P., Benoit, P., Faivre, A., Meynadier, J.-M.: Météor: a successful application of B in a large project. In: Wing, J.M., Woodcock, J., Davies, J. (eds.) FM 1999. LNCS, vol. 1708, pp. 369–387. Springer, Heidelberg (1999). https://doi.org/10.1007/3-540-48119-2_22
4. Bendovschi, A.: Cyber-attacks - trends, patterns and security countermeasures. Procedia Econ. Finance **28**, 24–31 (2015)
5. Cao, Y., Lu, H., Wen, T.: A safety computer system based on multi-sensor data processing. Sensors **19**, 818 (2019)
6. Cao, Y., Ma, L.C., Li, W.: Monitoring method of safety computer condition for railway signal system. Jiaotong Yunshu Gongcheng Xuebao/J. Traffic Transp. Eng. **13**, 107–112 (2013)
7. Essame, D., Arlat, J., Powell, D.: Padre: a protocol for asymmetric duplex redundancy, pp. 229–248, December 1999
8. Ferrari, A., et al.: Survey on formal methods and tools in railways: the ASTRail approach. In: Collart-Dutilleul, S., Lecomte, T., Romanovsky, A. (eds.) RSSRail 2019. LNCS, vol. 11495, pp. 226–241. Springer, Cham (2019). https://doi.org/10.1007/978-3-030-18744-6_15
9. Forin, P.: Vital coded microprocessor principles and application for various transit systems. IFAC Proc. Vol. **23**(2), 79–84 (1990). http://www.sciencedirect.com/science/article/pii/S1474667017526531, iFAC/IFIP/IFORS Symposium on Control, Computers, Communications in Transportation, Paris, France, 19–21 September
10. Gao, Y., Cao, Y., Sun, Y., Ma, L., Hong, C., Zhang, Y.: Analysis and verification of safety computer time constraints for train-to-train communications. Tongxin Xuebao/J. Commun. **39**, 82–90 (2018)
11. Ingibergsson, J., Kraft, D., Schultz, U.: Safety computer vision rules for improved sensor certification, April 2017
12. Kilmer, R., McCain, H., Juberts, M., Legowik, S.: Safety computer design and implementation, January 1985
13. Wang, H.F., Li, W.: Component-based safety computer of railway signal interlocking system, vol. 1, pp. 538–541, September 2008
14. Zheng, S., Cao, Y., Zhang, Y., Jing, H., Hu, H.: Design and verification of general train control system's safety computer, vol. 38, pp. 128–134+145, May 2014

Industrial Day

Formal Methods for a Digital Industry
Industrial Track at ISoLA 2022

Axel Hessenkämper[1], Falk Howar[2(✉)], Hardi Hungar[3], and Andreas Rausch[4]

[1] Schulz Systemtechnik GmbH, Visbek, Germany
falk.howar@tu-dortmund.de
[2] Dortmund University of Technology and Fraunhofer ISST, Dortmund, Germany
hardi.hungar@dlr.de
[3] German Aerospace Center, Braunschweig, Germany
[4] Clausthal University of Technology, Clausthal-Zellerfeld, Germany
andreas.rausch@tu-clausthal.de

Abstract. The industrial track at ISoLA 2022 provides a platform for presenting industrial perspectives on digitalization and for discussing trends and challenges in the ongoing digital transformation from the perspective of where and how formal methods can contribute to addressing the related technical and societal challenges. The track continues two special tracks at ISoLA conferences focused on the application of learning techniques in software engineering and software products [3], and industrial applications of formal methods in the context of Industry 4.0 [2,5].

1 Introduction

The infrastructure of the 21st century is defined by software. Software is the basis for almost every aspect of our daily lives and work: communication, banking, trade, production, transportation—to name only a few. This has led to a situation in which in many industrial and manufacturing companies with no particular background in software, software crept into processes and products—first slowly then with an ever increasing pace and scope, culminating in the mantra that "every company needs to become a software company".

From a technological perspective, the current situation is defined by a number of transformative innovations driven by advances in software technology and machine learning. In order to fully leverage the potential of this digital transformation, companies need strategies for the following three interdependent challenges:

- digital transformation of companies and business models,
- software engineering for/with AI (e.g., trained components), and
- rigorous software development for safety-critical systems.

What is missing today is a sound and holistic software engineering approach to these three challenges: The classical engineering process for safety critical applications starts with a (semi-)formal requirements specification, which is required

T. Margaria and B. Steffen (Eds.): ISoLA 2022, LNCS 13704, pp. 337–339, 2022.
https://doi.org/10.1007/978-3-031-19762-8_25

to be complete and correct. While this idealized process is typically not achievable, the requirements specification is later assumed as main input for test and verification. In the case of digital transformation, the finally successful business model is typically not known at the outset and software has to change continuously while exploring the space of opportunities. For the development of AI-based systems, in place of a requirements specification a huge data collection is used. This data collection is incomplete and may even contain a minimum percentage of incorrect data samples. In a sense, AI-based systems are machine-programmed using engineer-selected training data.

The industrial track provides a forum for contributions that focus on integrating business and technical perspectives, address industrial challenges in the software and data life-cycles or offer concepts, modeling formalisms, (formal) methods, tools, and quality metrics for every phase of the software life-cycle.

The industrial tracks aims at bringing together practitioners and researchers to explore the challenges and discuss progress made towards the goals sketched above—especially from a formal methods perspective.

2 Contributions

The track featured four contributions with accompanying papers. Contributions focused on software-enabled knowledge management and business engineering, open challenges in the realization of data spaces, modeling languages for industrial automation, and the application of formal analysis techniques in the domain of federated identity management systems.

2.1 Software-Enabled Business Engineering.

The paper *"Domain-Specificity: The Missing Key to Global Organization aLignment and Decision"* by Barbara Steffen and Steve Bosselmann [7] (in this volume) discusses how domain-specific languages can enhance the tool support for business modeling by enabling customized guidance of the various involved stakeholders.

2.2 Building Eco-Systems

The paper *"Evolving Data Space Technologies: Lessons Learned from an IDS Connector Reference Implementation"* by Julia Pampus, Brian-Frederik Jahnke, and Ronja Quensel [6] (in this volume) presents lessons learned from the design and implementation of a so-called "data space connector" that was used by multiple research projects. Data space connectors are envisioned to become the key technical enablers of inter-organizational data spaces.

The contribution *"Towards a methodology for formally analyzing federated identity management systems"* by Katerina Ksystra, Maria Dimarogkona, Nikolaos Triantafyllou, Petros Stefaneas, and Petros Kavassalis [4] (in this volume) compares multiple approaches, based on TLA+ and Maude, to formally analyzing federated identity management (FIM) systems.

2.3 Domain-Specific Languages for the Industry 4.0

The paper *"Model-driven edge analytics: a practical use case in Smart Manufacturing"* by Ivan Guevara, Hafiz Ahmad Awais Chaudhary, and Tiziana Margaria [1] (in this volume) presents a result from a case study in which a language workbench has been used to design a tailored domain-specific language for defining edge analytics pipelines involving EdgeX/FiWARE and eKuiper/IoT in the context of smart manufacturing.

References

1. Guevara, I., Chaudhary, H.A.A., Margaria, T.: Model-driven edge analytics: practical use cases in Smart Manufacturing. In: Margaria, T., Steffen, B. (eds.) ISoLA 2022. LNCS, vol. 13704, pp. 179–183 (2022)
2. Hessenkämper, A., Howar, F., Rausch, A.: Digital transformation trends: Industry 4.0, automation, and AI - industrial track at isola 2018. In Leveraging Applications of Formal Methods, Verification and Validation. Industrial Practice - 8th International Symposium, ISoLA 2018, Limassol, Cyprus, November 5–9, 2018, Proceedings, Part IV, pp. 469–471 (2018)
3. Howar, F., Meinke, K., Rausch, A.: Learning systems: machine-learning in software products and learning-based analysis of software systems. In: Margaria, T., Steffen, B. (eds.) ISoLA 2016. LNCS, vol. 9953, pp. 651–654. Springer, Cham (2016). https://doi.org/10.1007/978-3-319-47169-3_50
4. Ksystra, K., Dimarogkona, M., Triantafyllou, N., Stefaneas, P., Kavassalis, P.: Towards a methodology for formally analyzing federated identity management systems. In: Margaria, T., Steffen, B. (eds.) ISoLA 2022. LNCS, vol. 13704, pp. 382–405 (2022)
5. Margaria, T., Steffen, B. (eds.): Leveraging Applications of Formal Methods, Verification and Validation: Discussion, Dissemination, Applications - 7th International Symposium, ISoLA 2016, Imperial, Corfu, Greece, October 10–14, 2016, Proceedings, Part II. LNCS, vol. 9953 (2016)
6. Pampus, J., Jahnke, B.-F., Quensel, R.: Evolving Data Space Technologies: Lessons Learned from an IDS Connector Reference Implementation. In: Margaria, T., Steffen, B. (eds.) ISoLA 2022. LNCS, vol. 13704, pp. 366–381 (2022)
7. Steffen, B., Bosslemann, S.: Domain-specificity: The missing key to global organization aLignment and decision. In: Margaria, T., Steffen, B. (eds.) ISoLA 2022. LNCS, vol. 13704, pp. 340–365 (2022)

Domain-Specificity as Enabler for Global Organization aLignment and Decision

Barbara Steffen[1](✉) and Steve Boßelmann[2]

[1] University of Potsdam, Potsdam, Germany
barbarasteffen@gmx.net
[2] TU Dortmund University, Dortmund, Germany
steve.bosselmann@cs.tu-dortmund.de

Abstract. In this paper we illustrate the power of domain-specificity as a means to enhance the tool support for business modeling by enabling customized guidance of the various involved stakeholders as part of a holistic collaborative (innovation) process. The aim is to capture the enterprise/market characteristics of the considered scenario. We argue that it is the generality of current business modeling tools that prohibits adequate customization, and show how this weakness can be overcome via specialization: Using GOLD (Global Organization aLignment and Decision), our framework for the development of domain-specific (e.g., business modeling) tools, allows one to automatically generate tools from formalized domain models that do not only provide customized user support, but also align the contributions of the individual users along a globally consistent modeling process.

Keywords: Domain-specificity · Holisticity · GOLD Framework · Business model innovation · Business modeling · IT tool support

1 Introduction

Today, organizations face continuous change of their environments and industries. Due to globalization and digitalization the change cycles accelerated and became more disruptive [32]. To ensure their survival nevertheless, organizations need to react with desirable solutions at the right time and place [3,49]. Following BCG business model innovation is of particular importance: "[P]roduct and service innovation are essential, but business model innovation can deliver more lasting competitive advantage, particularly in disruptive times" [5].

However, due to today's complexity and uncertainty many business modeling facets and interdependencies are not sufficiently defined and understood. Thus, business modeling is confronted with vulnerable and ambiguous data/information/facts that complicate decision making and validation. Here, many organizations still have to rely solely on their internal expertise when e.g., designing new business models and anticipating the associated risks. While with time research added theories, models, methods, etc. this knowledge often is not readily

T. Margaria and B. Steffen (Eds.): ISoLA 2022, LNCS 13704, pp. 340–365, 2022.
https://doi.org/10.1007/978-3-031-19762-8_26

available and sufficiently concrete to be useful and adoptable by organizations [6]. To support practitioners in navigating this VUCA (vulnerable, uncertain, complex and ambiguous) context [2] further advances in today's *business modeling support* are needed to make research and insights usable in practice [6].

The State-of-the-Art of Business Modeling Support dominantly builds on the *Business Model Ontology* developed by Osterwalder in 2004 [23]. It set the basis for designing the *Business Model Canvas* (BMC) which established a de-facto standard modeling technique based on a structured template along nine essential components [26]. Since then canvases became a successful *user interface* offering standardized structure and visualizations to interdisciplinary teams. Compared to an empty-page approach, this level of support already decreased potential pitfalls of overlooking relevant aspects and eased communication.

Today, most models, methods and/or canvases are silo-ed approaches (cf. Fig. 2 and Fig. 4). Meanwhile a few projects have designed and developed support kits covering several models and methods supporting different phases and aspects of the projects'/products' lifecycle. Examples are the *Platform Innovation Kit* [27], *Data Sharing Toolkit* [11] and *Digital Innovation Kit* [12]. These kits offer newly designed refinements and/or extensions of the silo-ed approaches as pen and paper canvases to be used manually in the analog world. They address a narrowed down domain and offer complementary guidance via documents and videos.

To further ease (remote) collaboration the canvas templates are often copied to and filled out on other collaboration platforms like *Miro* [20] or in e.g., a *PowerPoint* [18] presentation shared via *Microsoft Teams* [19]. In addition, also dedicated IT tools exist. E.g., *Strategyzer* [44] an IT tool which was presented a few years after the introduction of the BMC can be regarded as a starting point for the advent of various IT-supported, canvas-based business modeling tools.

Roughly ten years after the advent of the first IT-supported tools, Szopinski et al. investigated the corresponding state of the art and derived a taxonomic classification of 24 prominent business modeling IT tools [45]. Their results reveal that the evaluated IT tools focus on adopting successful yet generic concepts of the analog world. They mainly enable users to paint the originally pen and paper-based graphical canvases that represent business models and other strategic notions in a web-based modeling tool. The main value added by these IT tools (see e.g., [9,44]) are collaborative aspects like remote collaboration and simultaneous, ubiquitous access that are facilitated by standard web technologies. Thus users are supported independently of their expertise and have to provide all the required (domain-) knowledge on their own (cf. Fig. 1, left-side):

Today's business modeling support is generic and easy to use, but lacks user guidance and is restricted to local problem scopes.

Dynamic Capability Theory emphasizes that organizations need to continuously *sense* their environment, *seize* the opportunities and *transform* their organizations to live up and adapt to the continuously changing challenges [50]. This *holistic* view on ensuring the survival of an organization requires the continuous adaptation of the domain knowledge over time. None of today's standardized

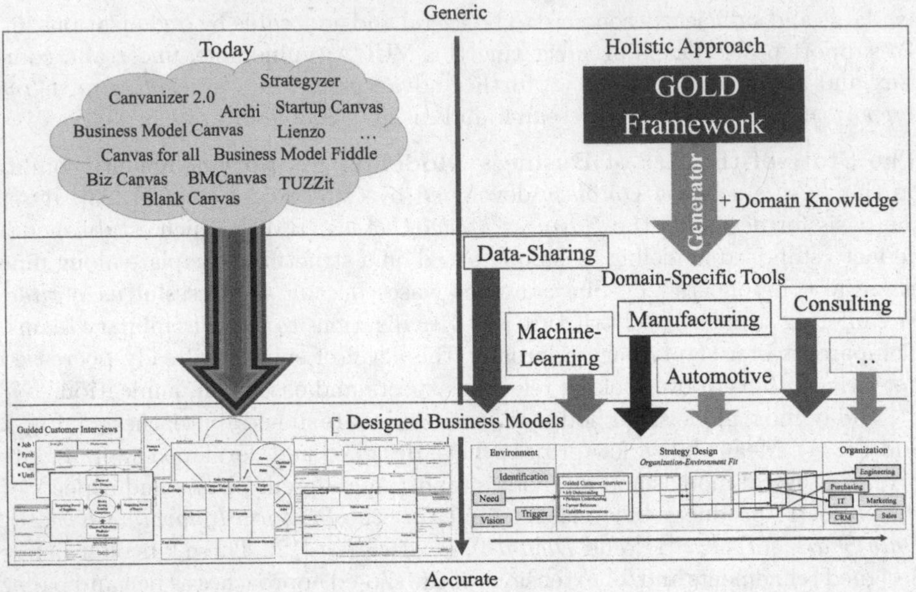

Fig. 1. Achieving accuracy: today's IT tools vs. GOLD's domain-specific tools

and generic approaches are even thought of to be prepared to help dealing with this dynamics: they all focus on the seizing stage only, where they offer silo-ed and generic business modeling support. They fail to ensure that the new business model fits the environment and do not foresee suitable and aligned implementation plans (cf. Fig. 2, bottom). Thus, organizations are left alone in their struggle to understand their specific circumstances and select, adopt and correctly apply a suitable mix of the offered support, e.g., canvases. To compensate for this they, e.g., hire consultants or attend dedicated workshops. While this support is useful it neither scales nor is it continuous.

There is no holistic, customized and adaptive guidance through the VUCA world (cf. Fig. 2, top).

Thorngate's Trade-Off reveals why current IT tools for business modeling are not ready to provide holistic and customized guidance. They aim at *generality*, to cover all scenarios, and *simplicity*, to ease adoption. However both, customization and holisticity, require a high level of *accuracy* and detail for their realization. Thorngate identified that achieving all three virtues is impossible and that theories and approaches can only achieve two of the three virtues [51]. As *simplicity* is a must for user acceptance, and *accuracy* is a must for customizable and holistic IT tools, generality has to be sacrificed.

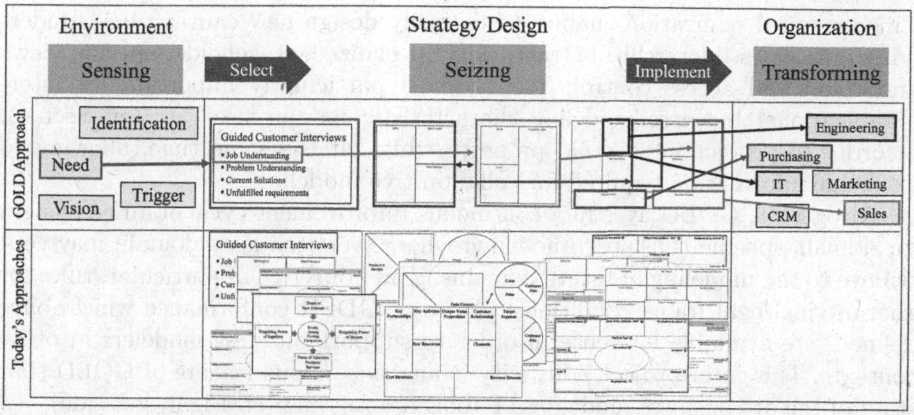

Fig. 2. Level of holisticity: today's approaches vs. the GOLD approach

This paper shows that the GOLD Approach [36] is able to overcome the shortcomings of today's IT tool support according to the hypothesis posed by Steffen et al. in 2021 [37]

> *Domain-Specific Languages can be regarded as enabler for tool-based automation in Business Engineering.*

GOLD achieves domain-specificity via a two phase modeling approach with a clear separation of concern (cf. Fig. 1, right-side):

1. Designing Domain-Specific Tools: This requires a *few* experts with domain and technical knowledge to formalize and model their domain expertise to generate domain-specific IT tools, and
2. Adopting the right Domain-Specific Tool: *Many* diverse stakeholders with limited technological and business modeling knowledge benefit from adopting the domain-specific tool offering customized and holistic guidance when collaboratively designing business models.

During business modeling, these two phase are iterated to stepwise refine both the domain specific tool and the actual business model.

The *domain-specificity* achieved by the first phase modeling provides a handle to systematically achieve continuous, customized and holistic tool support for business modeling (cf. Fig. 2, center) and corresponding *canvanization* [42]. Inter-canvas dependencies (see the colour code of Fig. 2) are modeled via business rules to ensure a holistic alignment along the refinement process. The GOLD Framework's refinement process even allows to guide the business model's implementation in a customized fashion, e.g., tailored to the different departments' roles and responsibilities. This improves the usability of the IT tools and eases their adoption incrementally.

Technologically, GOLD is based on the CINCO meta-tooling suite [22] that is designed for the development of domain-specific graphical modeling tools.

This technical realization enables us to easily design new canvas types, underlying ontologies, hierarchical structuring, specialized, stakeholder-specific views and role-based access control. The latter is particularly important for inter-organizational business modeling characteristic for our use case (cf. Sect. 4), in order to protect intellectual property while, at the same time, allowing to exchange information required for collaborative modeling.

Altogether, GOLD lives in a continuous improvement cycle of an ecosystem for domain-specific (business) modeling where every modeled domain may contribute to the modeling of future domains. This concerns, in particular, rules for guarantying legal frame conditions, like, e.g., GDPR conformance which, once defined, are available for reuse in order to support business modelers in other contexts. This inter-project holisticity is another unique feature of GOLD that state of the art business modeling IT tools are missing (cf. Fig. 1, left-side).

The modeling support varies significantly with increasing specificity. Figure 3 illustrates the full range from generic collaboration support where all input has to be given by the user as, e.g. provided, empty paper, PowerPoint presentations and/or Miro boards, up to IT tools where users are guided through a selection process, as is typical for, e.g., popular product/car configurators.

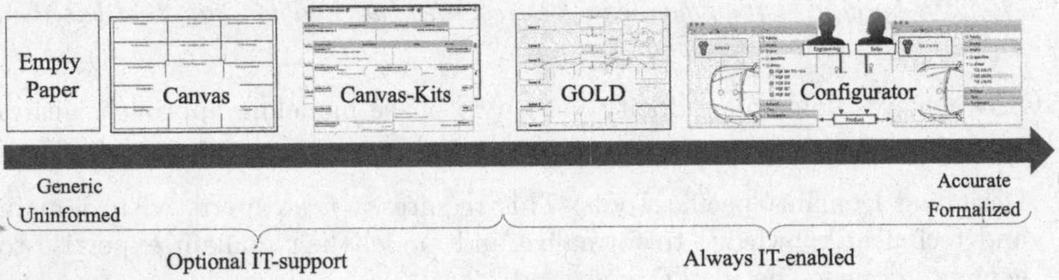

Fig. 3. Level of Support ordered by the availability of Pre-Defined Knowledge.

The various solutions located on a scale from unstructured and uninformed to fully structured and accurate offer completely different levels of guidance depending on the availability of pre-defined knowledge in the respective tool. The more explicit and accurate knowledge is available the greater is the guidance potential. E.g., the configuration with pre-defined components hardly requires any domain knowledge, letting users focus on their wishes and needs as all realization requirements are taken care of by the tool. The intention of domain-specific GOLD Tools is to provide a sweet spot with maximum guidance, but without restrictions that (unnecessarily) constrain the creativity.

In the following, Sect. 1 motivates the paper. Section 2 provides an overview of today's (IT-enabled) business modeling support, proposed research agenda and their gap. In Sect. 3 we introduce the GOLD Framework. Section 4 demonstrates the lever and benefits of the GOLD Framework with a use case. In Sect. 5 we conclude the paper.

2 Today's Approaches

This Section introduces today's approaches towards business modeling support, summarizes the current research agenda and analyses the gap between current and desired support.

2.1 Business Modeling Support as Boundary Objects

Globalization and digitalization lead to increased competitive pressures asking organizations to continuously adapt. Thus, organizations need to engage in and facilitate constant invention, creativity, and innovation requiring interdisciplinary collaboration. Unfortunately, collaboration across disciplines faces knowledge barriers, misunderstandings, and tensions due to the teams' semantic barriers [34]. Semantic barriers refer to misunderstandings despite collaborative intentions and knowledge sharing due to teams' differences in background, experiences, expertises, values, etc.

Boundary objects are an established concept to address the semantic barriers and intend to be "both plastic enough to adapt to local needs and the constraints of several parties employing them, yet robust enough to maintain a common identity across sites" ([33], p. 393). Common examples are artifacts, documents, concepts, repositories and prototypes [31,52].

This paper focuses on boundary objects for business modeling. Business models are defined as the blueprint of designing an organization's value creation, delivery and capture [48]. Here, Bouwman et al., view business model methods, frameworks or templates as 'boundary objects' that facilitate exchanging business model ideas between stakeholders [6]. Schwarz and Legner differentiate three types of boundary objects for business modeling support: conceptual models (e.g., canvases), methods (addressing concrete tasks during the implementation) and IT-support (e.g. digital tools) [31].

Conceptual Models refine identified key constructs of a selected problem scope. They are pre-defined templates establishing overview at one glance, a guiding structure and provide a shared language to facilitate and support the teams' discussions towards a shared mental model. Taxonomies are a common pre-design phase to "explicate and organize knowledge", e.g., identifying the relevant (meta-)dimensions and characteristics adopted by the conceptual models ([30], p. 1). One example is the taxonomy on design options for visual inquiry tools (also referred to as canvases) [21].

Canvases are a very popular conceptual model type due to the success of the Business Model Canvas [26]. It consists of nine components covering the most relevant aspects when designing a (new) business model. Other conceptual models are the Value Proposition Canvas [25], STOF model [7], Platform Alignment Canvas [40], Open Source Value Canvas [39] and Digital VALUE Canvas [35].

Methods are a more recent business modeling support addressing specific tasks when designing and implementing new business models [31]. Methods aim at showing "how to apply rather abstract [business model] approaches in practice, how to move from the existing [business model] to the desired one, how to implement [it] in an interorganizational setting [...]" [8]. Here, methods aim at supporting the transfer from theory to practice and ease the execution of business model design. Common examples are design issues and success factors [7], business model stress testing [15] and business model design innovation methodology [13].

IT-Tool Support. More than a decade after the need for computer-aided support from information systems research was formulated by Teece [48] and Osterwalder and Pigneur [24], we investigate the achievements by assessing recent studies on the current state of business modeling IT tools.

The taxonomy by Szopinski et al. provides an overview of 24 of today's IT tools and their technical features, especially focusing on the dimensions modeling, collaboration and technical realization. They tested and compared the IT tools by always adopting the respective Business Model Canvas support to design the exact same business model. As this exemplary application set the ground for the comparison the taxonomy mainly contains aspects that either focus on features of generic graphical modeling tools (elements, element connections, etc.) or web-based collaboration tools in general (chat, discussion board, member list, etc.).

The IT tools mostly adopt and support pre-existing analogous knowledge presented as taxonomies, models and methods almost 1:1 digitally, while focusing on visualization and supported (interdisciplinary) collaboration. Especially, canvases get software-enabled to support users in designing (new) business models. Here, the IT tools differ in the range of integrated canvases and templates. While the Strategyzer, e.g., emphasizes on the Business Model Canvas, the Value Proposition Canvas and some financial assessments [44], the Canvanizer 2.0 provides more than 40 pre-defined canvas templates and allows to design new and/or customized ones [9].

The fact that most of these criteria originate from Riemer et al., [28] - a paper evaluating process modeling tools - adds to our impression that they are merely generic in nature. They might be useful for the evaluation of collaborative modeling tools in general but not for the assessment of functionalities specifically designed to support business modeling. This is quite in contrast to what Osterwalder and Pigneur consider as the information systems research's role in *"contributing to increase understanding of the essence of business models and other strategic notions, and in improving their design"* ([24], p. 239).

2.2 Business Modeling Support: A Research Agenda

Figure 4 depicts today's mostly local and silo-ed support of business modeling. In the meantime also canvas-kits exist. While these paper and pen based kits suggest the use of several models and/or methods in a standardized and generic manner for dedicated purposes like digital platform design, e.g., the Platform Innovation Kit [27], even these do not integrate them into the users' context, e.g., customized guidance and/or pre-filled canvases with business model patterns.

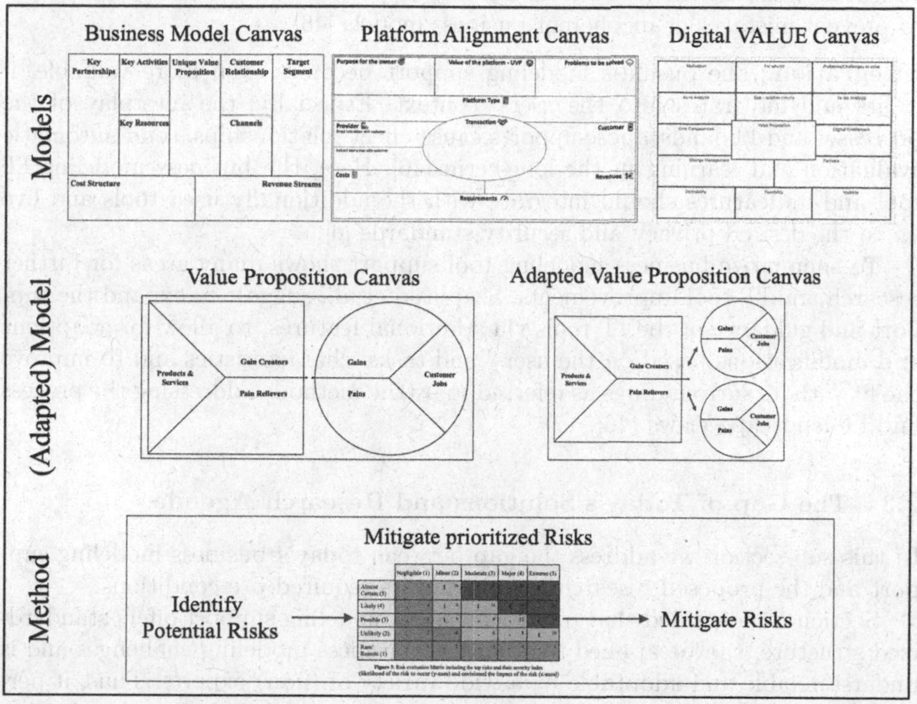

Fig. 4. Today's support: local and (mostly) silo-ed.

Given the status-quo of the IT-tool support several researchers proposed areas for further research and improvement. E.g., Szopinski et al., derived a quite extensive research agenda [46]. Generally, we identified the desire to design business modeling tools enhancing today's guidance, supporting the integration into the users' context and offer customization to fit the users' needs.

Customization. Currently the IT tools offer standardized structure and support. Thus, experts and non-experts face the same interface, options and support. This means that the IT tools suit some user profiles better than others. The currently generic and standardized approach also limits the guidance and correctness check support. Of course, generic rules like, e.g., "no empty fields" or "you seem to have used a synonym, please replace it" are possible, however they provide little guidance for business modeling. Ideally the IT tools should be *customized* to better fit the users' and tasks' characteristics [46].

Guidance. The IT tools offer very limited guidance if at all lacking guaranteed user-friendliness and simplicity [6]. As a consequence, non-experts, e.g., struggle due to missing information, explanations, examples, and business model patterns [1]. Also additional guidance with regard to deriving consensus and educated-decisions via fitting feedback and suggestions would be a great enabler to prevent mistakes or incoherent business models [46].

Integration. The business modeling support becomes even more valuable, if it fits and integrates into the users' context. Especially, the interplay of the processes and IT landscapes supports cause-effect relationships, semi-automatic evaluation and learning in the long-term [46]. Here, the business modeling IT tool and its features should integrate with the additionally used tools and live up to the desired privacy and security standards [6].

To summarize business modeling tool support shows many areas for further research and IT tool improvements. Szopinski et al., suggest to expand the support and guidance of the IT tools via additional features, to allow for adaptions and modifications based on the users' and tasks' characteristics and to improve the fit with its surroundings as referred to by the methods addressing the process and IT landscape views [46].

2.3 The Gap of Today's Solutions and Research Agenda

In this sub-section we address the gap between today's business modeling support and the proposed research agenda and its required pre-conditions.

Section 2.1 identified that today's business modeling support offers standardized structure, can be applied to almost all business modeling challenges and is understandable and adoptable by a wide variety of (non) experts. Thus, it perfected to be simultaneously *generic* and *simple* explaining their wide adoption and success.

In Sect. 2.2 the research agenda revealed three goals for improvement: *customization*, *guidance* and *integration*. In addition, we also propose *holistic* understanding.

Holisticity covers several facets: complete phenomena (e.g., organizations including their complexities and interdependencies), entire processes (e.g., trigger to implementation) and all of that over time (learning from the past, creating something new and sustainable in the present and planning and preparing for the future). It aims at moving from silo-ed support towards multi-perspective and multi-step support (see Fig. 5).

In recent work we designed methodological approaches comprised of and connecting different models proposing multi-perspective and multi-step analyses providing customized guidance to practitioners [41]. The aim is to derive multi-step guidance addressing the specific challenges at hand. Two examples of multi-perspective approaches are *Towards Platform Risk Mitigation* [38] and *Towards Mitigating Sustainability Risks* [29]. These are also shown exemplary as middle and bottom examples in Fig. 5.

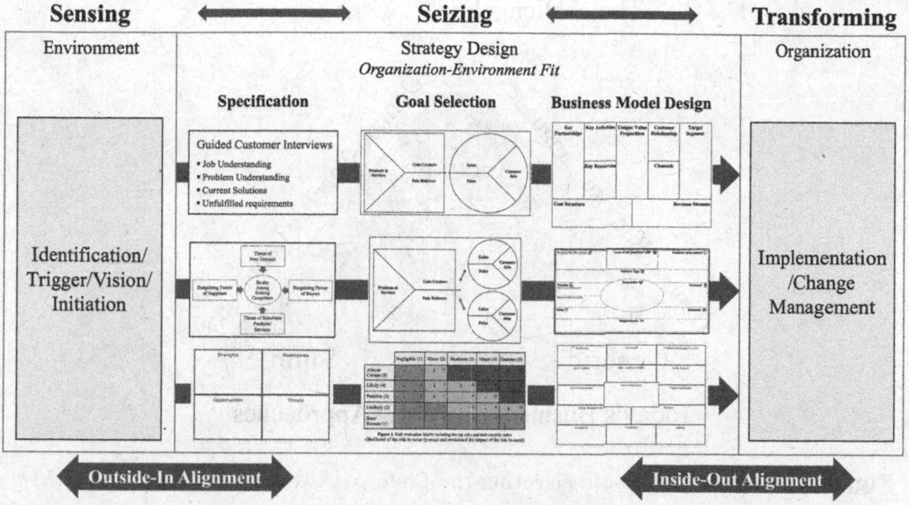

Fig. 5. Model- and method-driven support embedded as holistic processes.

Teece et al. designed the *Dynamic Capability Theory* embedding business model design into a three-stage process [47,50]: sensing the environment ("*why* is a new business model needed?"), seizing the opportunity via new business models ("*what* to offer?") and transforming by implementing the business model ("*how* to (successfully) implement it?") (cf. Fig. 5). Here, business models act as alignment piece for achieving the organization-environment fit.

Combining the need for (more) holistic support with customization, guidance and integration as detailed in Sect. 2.2 asks for a new era of IT tools leveraging the digital potential. However, today's generic and simple approaches cannot enable any of these four goals which all require *accuracy* fitting the target user context. Here, accuracy refers to refinements sufficient to be correctly interpreted even by IT tools.

Adopting Thorngate's trade-off *"It is impossible for a theory of social behaviour to be simultaneously general, simple [...], and accurate"* [51] meaning that to add accuracy one of the other two virtues currently embraced needs to be replaced. Figure 6 shows the optimal solutions for each of the three possible pairings: Today's business modeling approaches excel at generic and simple solutions while general purpose languages as are common in computer science offer generality and accuracy. These languages are complex and thus not usable by non-computer scientists. Thus, in our case *domain-specificity* is the keyword. Domain-specific languages are customized to one specific domain and its requirements enabling accuracy and simplicity to provide the desired features while maintaining usability.

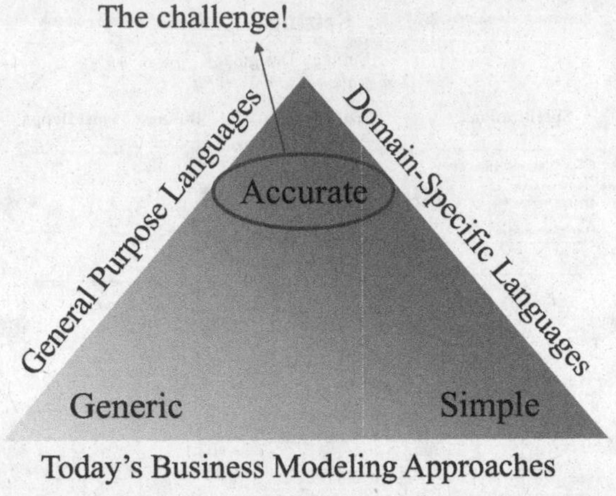

Fig. 6. Thorngate's trade-off: selecting the preferred two virtues based on [37,51].

Building domain-specific IT tools is a well-developed research field in computer science. Thus, from the IT-perspective building such a domain-specific tool is not a challenge as long as the domain is sufficiently formalized. Accordingly, for our GOLD Framework it is sufficient to formalize the explicit and tacit (business modeling) knowledge to generate corresponding domain-specific tools. Unfortunately, today's approaches to business modeling do not provide this kind of accuracy. Thus the main challenge is to establish formalization processes that make the business knowledge sufficiently transparent and tangible for the IT experts to design the domain-specific IT tools enabling holistic customization, guidance and integration. Here, the business and information systems communities can learn a lot from computer science concerning the potential of syntactic, semantic and pragmatic accuracy.

2.4 Towards Holistic Business Modeling

As a provisional conclusion, we consider today's solutions as rather generic. They might support brainstorming at the ideas stage pretty well but lack support for more sophisticated applications. Not only has this assessment been confirmed by studies in recent literature but it also appears evident that the identified research agenda with regards to tool support does not focus on the necessary leverage of existing modeling capabilities for exploiting the specifics of business modeling and other strategic notions in a thorough and consistent manner.

We are convinced that such support can only be achieved with specific IT tools customized towards the respective target domain taking the purposes of the modeling languages as well as the mind-sets of the involved stakeholders into account. Hence, the overall goal is not to build one tool that fits all generic requirements but to establish a full workshop of utility tools for rapid crafting of accurate and customized solutions. Building reliable (business modeling) solutions fast requires profound knowledge in specifying modeling languages as well as technology that supports rapid generation of complete modeling environments from these specifications. We benefit from many years of expertise in language design incorporated into the CINCO Framework when using it for generating tailored GOLD Tools for specific use cases that leverage the conceptual ideas and requirements formulated for the GOLD Framework. This way, we not only support the generic modeling tasks like the other available tools but we also can meet the more sophisticated and advanced requirements emerging from the high demands on support for holistic business modeling solutions.

In turn, we argue that the lack of support for holistic business modeling in today's solutions is not caused by the lack of expertise or tool support for generating powerful and comprehensive modeling environments. We are confident that, from an IT perspective, everything is in place. In contrast, we see a strong need for concretizing and formalizing fundamental rules for refining and combining different types of models and components as well as for complex relationships and mutual dependencies in terms of, in particular, multi-model approaches. The GOLD Framework is designed to deliver domain-specific solutions for holistic business modeling, independent of the complexity of the requirements.

3 The GOLD Framework and Tool

Based on the arguments and findings above, we revisit the GOLD Framework and discuss existing and envisioned features of the GOLD Tool. As the full feature set has already been discussed in [36] along with tangible examples, here we mention briefly those features that are particularly useful to tailor specific solutions towards different use cases and application domains in order to create a simplicity-driven yet powerful and accurate modeling environment that provides the best guidance for users in creating holistic business models. Hence, we highlight those features that distinguish GOLD from existing generic solutions.

3.1 Tailored Modeling Environment

The GOLD Framework has been designed from the ground up to meet the demanding needs of a holistic business modeling approach. It sets out to deal with the heterogeneous landscape spanning business models and similar strategic notions by integrating well-defined types of models and components and interlinking them in a consistent manner. Thereby, we provide contingencies for all in terms of different dimensions of specialization.

Domain-Specific aspects comprise the prevailing terminology as well as constraints and regulations from a particular field or the identified domain. Think of technical or special terms used in a particular business as well as a set of ground rules associated with the respective surroundings. In this context, sophisticated guidance by means of tool support means taking all these aspects into account and validating the generated model against identified boundary conditions.

Purpose-Specific aspects address the goal and task orientation of a particular modeling approach. Providing an appropriate tool set to choose from may very well depend on which concrete goals and tasks have to be supported. The better the tool set is adapted to specific tasks the better the overall guidance and support. All-purpose tools might be universally usable but less useful for a different specific task.

Mindset-Specific aspects address the knowledge, skills and expertise of the respective individual. Additionally, different stakeholders involved may have different views, opinions and beliefs on a range of issues. Addressing different views and perspectives is key for an effective tool to provide guidance, support knowledge sharing and increase the overall user experience.

This tailoring towards specific needs has two goals: *Accuracy* in model design and *simplicity* for the users involved. Although simplicity has been identified as a driver for agile innovation in general [17] as well as for the creation of tools for business model design in particular [4], it is only vaguely understood and receives little formal attention [14]. Simplicity cannot be regarded as a universal feature as it depends on the mindset, experience and knowledge of the respective user. Hence, simplicity requires tailored solutions.

These considerations do not mean that the GOLD Tool ships with a complete set of possible variants and options from all thinkable target domains, purposes and mindsets. Instead, in order to cover domain-/purpose-/mindset-specific aspects, we are prepared for tailoring the modeling environment towards specific requirements and constraints stemming, for example, from a particular application domain. This may either result in a specific product line or lead to the integration of various types of models, components and properties into the same tool and let users pick suitable subsets that are particularly useful for the respective use case. However, we explicitly do not want to provide yet another generic business modeling tool. Instead, we strive for accuracy by means of being as specific as possible and only as generic as necessary (cf. Fig. 6). We believe that this approach is best suited to provide comprehensive guidance in a simplicity-driven manner.

3.2 Model Types and Customization

In order to achieve a customized modeling environment the GOLD Framework facilitates tailoring available model types and component types to domain-/purpose-/mindset-specific requirements and needs. This does not only mean selecting and integrating various types of business models and similar strategic notions but also allowing for their customization. The latter may reach from changing the model design in terms of, for example, available fields or categories in common canvas-based notions, to customization down to specific properties of model components. In general, the basic customization comes down to which types of models and components are available as well as what properties these models and components have. The latter permits the definition of various characteristics over different instances of one and the same type of model or model component.

3.3 Consistent Interlinking

The GOLD Framework natively supports the interlinking of models. This is realized by means of providing model components whose primary task is to represent another model. As the latter, again, may contain such proxy elements, the modeling environment natively supports hierarchical refinement. This facilitates pushing details or further descriptions into sub-models or even distributing separate aspects across multiple sub-models for one and the same model element. By repeating these steps for the elements in these sub-models an ongoing hierarchical refinement can be achieved. However, each of these sub-models may again be of different types depending on which one is the most suitable to express the respective aspects of interest.

From an opposite perspective, the logical separation of specific aspects by means of interlinked model elements and sub-models of different types allows for re-use on the model level. Furthermore, the approach naturally facilitates the creation of separate standalone yet self-contained models to become part of an ever-growing collection constituting a library of building blocks. If shared, these building blocks may even be re-used across different modeling projects and may thereby spread common knowledge and foster consistency even across project boundaries. Altogether, the users of the GOLD Tool can continuously extend the modeling environment with re-usable components in a dynamic yet intuitive manner.

3.4 Component Taxonomies

Just like for model types, the selection of suitable component types depends on the actual domain, the purpose of the models to be created as well as on the mindset of the involved users. The outcome may significantly differ according to whether the modeling environment is tailored towards specific user groups, like analysts or consultants, towards specific industries, like automotive or clothing, or even towards single departments, teams or individuals within a specific organization. The GOLD Framework facilitates the creation and integration of domain-/purpose-/mindset-specific taxonomies of model components. Typically, based on the concepts and terminology from the target domain, users can define entities and arrange them in taxonomy models to apply hierarchical classification based on certain criteria. This way, in contrast to today's generic business modeling approaches based on painting notepads and putting unrelated words on them, the GOLD Framework encourages a more structured approach using a well-defined library of components. This allows re-using these components across various models by means of selecting a component from the library and add it to the respective model. Each of these added components holds a reference to the very same element in the component library. This way, consistency can be achieved. The various components across different models can never be out-of-sync as they all reference the component library as the single source of truth.

Changing information or properties of a particular component in the library would have immediate effect on all related components throughout the models.

As already discussed in [36] the creation of such taxonomies may happen in a preceding customization step or on-the-go during modeling, either manually or automatically by, for example, making use of knowledge discovery techniques. However, the result is a custom library of "building blocks" which holds the available model components and delivers formalized information by means of the components' characterization that paves the way for model validation as well as modeling guidance.

3.5 Model Validation and Modeling Guidance

In general, using components based on well-known terms and concepts, e.g. from the target domain, significantly improves the expressiveness and meaning of the created models and simplifies the whole model creation process. The modeling environment can guide this creation process by providing a well-defined set of components for the user to choose from. Additionally, different component types may even have specific graphical presentations in the diagram.

Just like the task of building a meaningful library of building blocks also model validation largely depends on well-defined component types. In contrast to generic approaches, where the model validation can only tell *that* an element is missing, in presence of a suitable classification it can communicate *which* type of element is missing. Furthermore, the components' properties can be taken into account to even validate the usage and combination of specific component variants. Altogether, it means switching from mere syntactical checks to validating semantics, i.e. what the models and the comprised components with their respective characteristics actually mean.

Model validation and modeling guidance are closely connected topics. When model validation checks various syntactical rules and formal constraints to discover potential defects and violations it follows clear formal instructions on what is allowed and what is not. Thereby, such constraints can be automatically verified at the model level in order to provide the modeler with feedback or enforced by construction to make it completely impossible to construct violating models [43]. The very same instructions as used to check syntactical rules can be used to provide guidance not only by means of communicating the identified defects and rule violations but also by making proposals for fixing them and improving the models. The more concrete and specific these recommendations are, the more likely it is that users adopt them to reach their design goals. Hence, the quality of guidance increases with the domain-/purpose-/mindset-specificity of the modeling languages in terms of both syntax and semantics. However, the challenging task in building valuable guidance and model validation is not a technical one. From a tooling perspective, it is clear *how* to implement it but today the theory of business modeling and other strategic notions only vaguely define *what* the semantics actually are.

The GOLD Tool is envisioned to validate whatever syntactic specifications are defined for specific model types. Such syntax rules may restrict which types of model components can be used, how they are arranged and whether they can be associated with each other by means of different types of connections between them. In context of the GOLD Tool, syntax validation is built in by design because it is developed with the *CINCO SCCE Meta Tooling Framework* [22] that facilitates the definition of graphical modeling languages and generates the respective model editors, including validation routines for the specified syntax. This also includes type and consistency checks for interconnected models, in particular in terms of sub-model integration for hierarchical refinement.

Beyond that, arbitrary validation routines can be defined in the course of the tool creation process for dynamically checking whatever semantic rules need to be ensured for the model structure. These checks may take the types of models and components as well as their properties into account. They may also rely on the characterizations of model components as defined in component taxonomies (cf. Sect. 3.4). Altogether, model validation not only ensures the correct use of models, components and their properties but also enforces consistency, especially across different interconnected models.

3.6 Aggregation and Views

When it comes to managing a heterogeneous landscape of interlinked models and components, data aggregation is key for understanding complex contents and relationships. In the context of modeling languages, aggregation means collecting and processing vast information spread across models and their components to prepare combined datasets and clear presentations for an easier overview that supports well-informed decision-making. In the GOLD Framework, such aggregation can be applied on different parts of the modeling landscape.

- On a global level, the modeling environment can collect and present data regarding the usage of different types of models as well as associated characteristics and model properties.
- For each single model, relevant information about integrated sub-models can be collected recursively and presented in an aggregated manner.
- Just like for models themselves, the characteristics and properties of their components can be collected, processed, aggregated and presented in a clear and concise manner.
- Apart from the actual models and their components, aggregation may as well be applied on model validation results to efficiently highlight errors or insufficiencies at convenient places.

The presentation of aggregated data is not limited to text or numerical values. As the GOLD Tool is comprising mainly graphical modeling languages we can make use of various kinds of catchy indicators for the visualization of such aggregated values. This way, even small differences in similar values can be spotted at first glance.

As already discussed in [36], we plan to integrate the support for different views into the GOLD Framework to address different stakeholders involved with different skills, knowledge, roles and responsibilities.

3.7 Collaboration

In contrast to the discussed characteristics of model structures, available components and their properties, collaboration means exchanging ideas and information *about* models, model components or even whole modeling projects. Furthermore, collaborative modeling also means being able to work on shared artefacts (models, projects, etc.) simultaneously, independent of the type or structure of those artefacts. However, these aspects can be considered orthogonal to those directly addressing the modeling languages with regards to model structures and component characteristics. As an example, allowing collaborative modeling by means of enabling different users to work on the same model at the same time has little to do with the modeling language in the first place but is a matter of platform capabilities and the features provided by the respective editor.

Our approach to collaborative business modeling involves migrating the GOLD Tool from a classical desktop application to modern web technologies. For this, we make use of the CINCO CLOUD project (originating from [54]) that is currently in active development. It eases the creation of domain-specific collaborative online modeling environments [53] and, in particular, allows using any CINCO product directly in the web browser. Hence, as the GOLD Tool is a CINCO product, we will be able to migrate to the web by the push of a button. The required collaboration features will then be provided by means of platform services offered by CINCO CLOUD, which aims at realizing aligned, purpose-driven cooperation [54]. This out-of-the box includes features like real-time collaborative editing, user and role management, project management and task sharing. Furthermore, the GOLD Tool will benefit from the increasing number of features eventually built into CINCO CLOUD, like version control, issue management, discussion boards and many more.

4 Exemplary Application of the GOLD Framework

This Section demonstrates the benefits of the GOLD Framework's lever to design holistic and customized business modeling IT tools. GOLD has been developed to allow (business modeling) domain-experts to define and implement a holistic and customized support for tackling the envisioned users' challenges. This Section introduces one use case implemented as domain-specific instantiation. The use case's business model design gets embedded into the three-stage approach of the dynamic capability theory (cf. the basis of the holistic structure of Fig. 2 and Fig. 5). Adopting this theory ensures that business models address a specific purpose and get implemented following a suitable plan.

Designing Multilateral Data-Sharing Collaborations

Today, data and data-driven business models are hot topics [16]. For years software-driven organizations like Google, Amazon, Apple and Uber have demonstrated the lever of data for generating value and new business models. Now also more traditional industries like automotive or manufacturing aim at making use of their (existing) data, data of their supply chain partners, and of other ecosystems. As the potential value increases with the access to more data and/or more diverse data sources, the Collaborative Condition Monitoring (CCM) project group of the Plattform Industrie 4.0 project works on concepts, pre-conditions and enablers for multilateral data-sharing [10]. To enable data-sharing and the design of multilateral data-sharing collaborations beyond the typical bilateral settings, the CCM team developed a domain-specific, hierarchical, canvas-based guidance structure to, in particular, address the vital economic, legal and technical interoperability (cf. Fig. 7). Following this domain-specific structure supports the design of multilateral collaborations for data sharing to deal with the following three challenges:

- designing new **inter-organizational** collaborations,
- **pre-evaluating** the organizations' fit for collaboration before investing time and resources, and
- **aligning** the organizations with their unique sets of interests, needs, competences and resources, while maintaining **data sovereignty**, i.e., without disclosing their intellectual property.

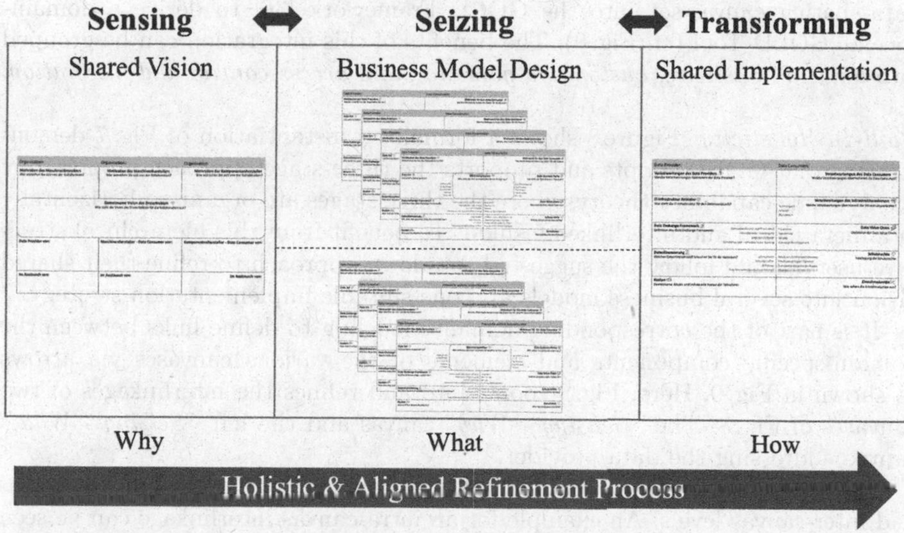

Fig. 7. Towards the holistic design of multilateral data-sharing collaborations.

The domain-specific canvas support consists of four interlinked canvas types (cf. Fig. 7). Each of the three stages gets addressed via one canvas type except for stage two - *seizing* - which gets addressed by two different canvas types better matching the different profiles of the data producers and data consumers. While in both the *sensing* and *transforming* stages one canvas gets filled out by all envisioned collaborators together the *seizing* stage asks each envisioned collaborator to define a viable and attractive business model by herself to ensure that each organization benefits from the collaboration (also presented in cf. Fig. 7 by the number of canvases at each stage). Thus, together the four canvas types are designed to cover, refine and align the design of new collaborations following the dynamic capability theory to:

- define one shared vision and the available resources (cf. sensing), to
- enable each partner to design attractive business models (cf. seizing) and to
- aggregate the legal and technical requirements of the partners to derive one shared data exchange infrastructure fulfilling the diverse demands (cf. transforming).

The overall goal is to answer the following three questions by/for each partner individually to increase transparency and tangibility easing the collaboration, alignment and execution or to reveal misfits early ensuring to *fail fast*:

- Does the offered data fit the demanded data?,
- Do all collaborators benefit "sufficiently"?,
- Can the partners agree on a suitable implementation strategy?

In the following, we demonstrate the advantages of integrating the multilateral data-sharing canvas-set into the GOLD Framework [36] to derive a domain-specific GOLD Tool (cf. Fig. 8). The benefits of this integration can be grouped into *built-in holisticity*, *customized guidance*, and *access control and integration.*

Built-In Holisticity: Figure 8 shows a formalized instantiation of Fig. 7 demonstrating that GOLD adopts and supports the three-stage approach proposed by the dynamic capability theory, where the three stages are organized horizontally in a hierarchical and interlinked fashion. To benefit from this hierarchical structure users should follow the suggested top-down approach to refine their shared vision into several business models and one suitable implementation strategy.

It is part of the corresponding domain modeling to define links between the domain-specific components and elements of the various canvases via arrows as shown in Fig. 9. Here, Fig. 9 zooms into and refines the interlinkages of two canvases of Fig. 8: The *"Sensing - Why"* canvas and the left *"Seizing - What"* canvas addressing the data provider.

In particular, GOLD enables to link and connect components on the intra- and inter-canvas levels: An example for an intra-canvas interlinkage can be seen in the top canvas of Fig. 9. Here, the element *Shared Vision* is e.g., dependent and thus interlinked with the elements *Motivation DP* and *Motivation DC* referring to the pre-defined motivation of the data provider(s) and data consumer(s). The inter-canvas level connection can, e.g., be seen in Fig. 9 between the element *Offered Data* of the upper canvas and the elements *Specification Offered*

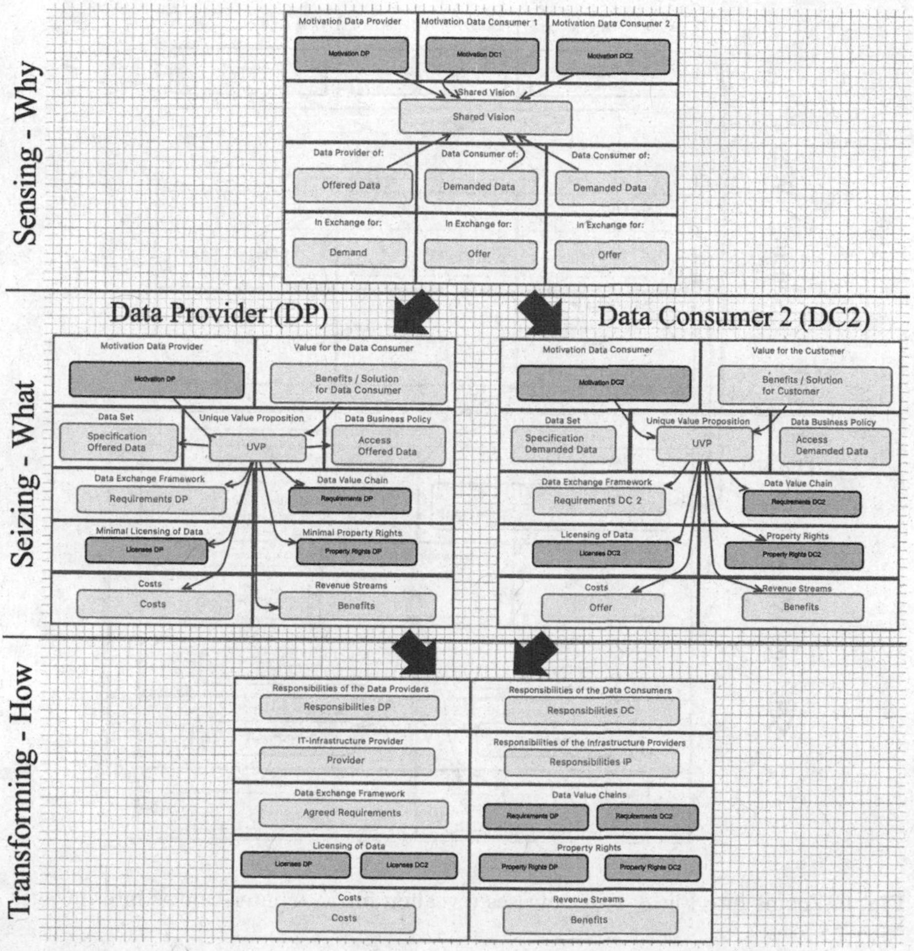

Fig. 8. Domain-specific GOLD tool integration for holistic and customized guidance.

Data and *Access Offered Data* of the lower canvas. These interlinkages and connections ensure that users consider the elements of the previously filled out canvases/components to achieve alignment.

Please note that new refinements and findings could also lead to updates bottom-up on the aggregated levels. For example if the collaborators agree on specific license options and rules for dealing with the property rights of the different collaborators on the *"Transforming - How"* level, it is important that also the information and plans on the *"Seizing - What"* level get updated to check whether the envisioned business models are still possible given the agreed upon changes of the conditions on the *"Transforming - How"* level (cf. Fig. 8).

These interlinkages ensure the up-to-dateness of all components by making changes visible and suggesting to revisit interlinked components/elements to

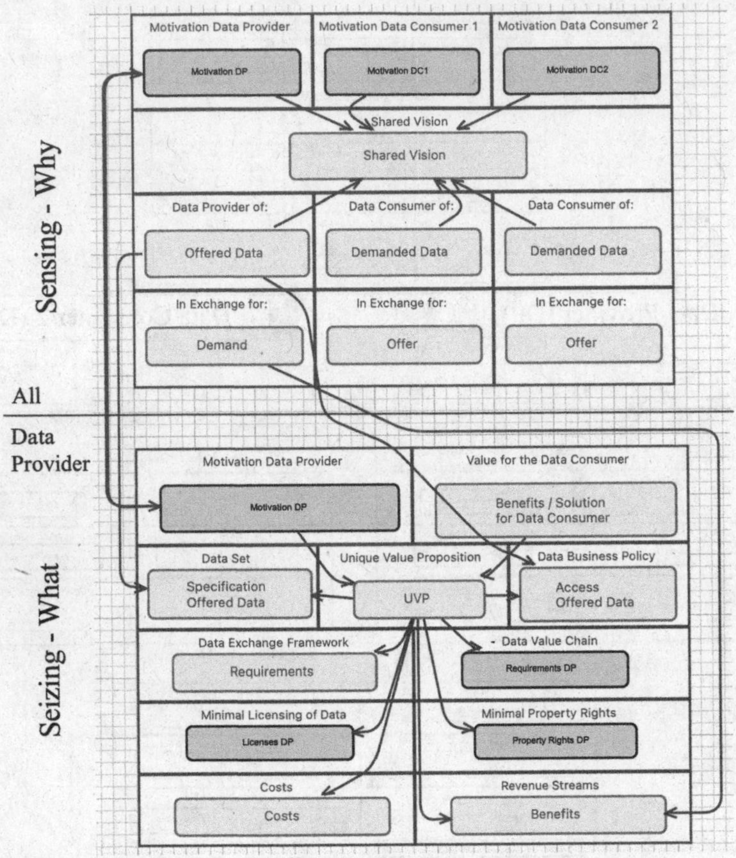

Fig. 9. Zooms-into Fig. 8: two canvases revealing intra- & inter-canvas interlinkages.

re-check their correctness. See e.g., the components Licensing of Data, Data Value Chains and Property Rights on the *"Transforming - How"* level where the individual elements of the *"Seizing - What"* level get aggregated allowing to discuss contradictions and define acceptable conditions (cf. Fig. 8).

Additionally, in contrast to grey boxes, blue boxes refer to another model on a lower hierarchical level. Here, all blue boxes with an identical name reference the same sub-canvas. E.g., in Fig. 8, *Motivation DP* exists twice, once on the *"Sensing - Why"* level and once on the *"Seizing - What"* level of Fig. 9. These two blue boxes are connected via a bi-directional arrow underlining that changes made on the sub-canvas of *Motivation DP* shown in Fig. 10 count automatically for both.

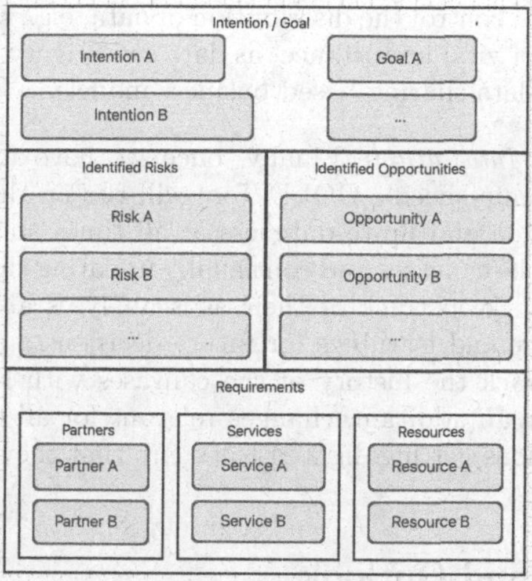

Fig. 10. Cross-referenced sub-canvas: *Motivation Data Provider (DP)*.

Whenever elements become more complex or should be analyzed more carefully also currently grey boxes only detailing the information written on them can turn blue by transforming them into a link to a new hierarchical sub-canvas. Here, taxonomies and ontologies define the reference points and establish a single source of truth structuring elements at different hierarchy levels, canvases, components, etc.

Customized Guidance: Domain-specificity is a powerful customization concept which, in particular, supports user guidance during business modeling in a collaborative fashion. Three kinds of GOLD-based guidance can be distinguished.

- **Domain-Specific Guidance.** Formalized knowledge in terms of (business) knowledge may be used, e.g., to ensure that at least one data-provider canvas and one data-consumer canvas get filled out (ensuring that data is offered and demanded), that at least three canvases get filled out (fulfilling the precondition of *multilateral* data-sharing), or that certain fields are required and must therefore be filled out, e.g., ensuring that the requirements of all collaborators get considered on the how-level. Moreover, based on adequate domain models, GOLD may also structurally support that only admissible elements are possible, e.g., that the elements have the right format, or more restrictively, that they need to be taken from a predefined set.
- **Process-Driven Guidance.** Collaborative business modeling comes with natural bottlenecks, e.g., that progress is prohibited by a missing entry. In this case GOLD may send reminders to the responsible organization/person.
- **User Profile-Oriented Guidance.** Individual users can be individually guided based on their roles, rights, and competences. This increases the efficiency by allowing experts to, e.g., fast track the entries, but, at the same

time, also allows to control the distribution of data, e.g., to secure intellectual property. This is of vital importance, as data sovereignty is one of the central requirements for data sharing-based business models.

Access Control and Integration: Finally, once we have migrated to CINCO Cloud [54], each domain-specific GOLD Tool will run on the web allowing synchronized collaboration and up-to-dateness at all times and at all places. This also eases revisiting the canvases and continually updating the information. Here, the collaborators can keep track of their as-is analyses also allowing them to derive new knowledge and learnings for future decisions and projects. Further, the tool allows to track the history of the canvases with regard to who made which changes when. In addition, changes relevant for all collaborators asking for new joined decisions get highlighted to ensure that they get revisited in the next meeting.

5 Conclusion and Outlook

In this paper we have illustrated the power of domain-specificity as lever to enhance the tool support for business modeling. Domain-specificity enables customized guidance of diverse stakeholders as part of a holistic collaborative modeling process. This guidance is particularly important when dealing with complex scenarios like multilateral collaborations for data sharing where the needs of various involved stakeholders have to be aligned. Such an alignment requires a holistic approach to design one global vision which gets refined by individual and diverse business models which then get realized via one global implementation strategy. To achieve this it is success critical to enable and guide the hierarchical and stakeholder-specific refinement from vision to implementation.

We have argued that using GOLD, our framework for the development of domain-specific (e.g., business modeling) IT tools, allows to build IT tools from formalized domain models that do not only provide customized user support, but also achieve the required alignment of the contributions of the individual users along a globally consistent and hierarchical modeling process.

In fact, the GOLD Framework is designed to automatically generate domain-specific IT tools that are customized to the specific needs, strengths and weaknesses of particular industries, organizations or technologies as soon as a sufficient formalization of domain-specific knowledge, e.g., in terms of ontologies and business rules, is provided.

Thus, to develop the desired domain-specific IT tools only requires that the corresponding domain-experts learn to sufficiently formalize their currently rather tacit knowledge. This is particularly difficult in domains that primarily focus on human interaction and that are not used to express their explicit and tacit knowledge at the required level of accuracy for generating suitable IT tool support [37]. This does not mean, however, that reaching the required level of formalization is impossible in these domains, as one can achieve this level in a guided specification refinement process that successively increases the accuracy and thereby the potential support of the accordingly generated, domain-specific tool.

To live up to the latest requirements of accessibility and interdisciplinary collaboration, we are currently migrating the GOLD technology to the web utilizing CINCO CLOUD [54]. It is planned to make the web-based version of GOLD available to early adopters like consultants for innovation projects. Their feedback will be vital to improve GOLD's domain modeling functionality and to evaluate the impact of the provided domain-specific modeling support.

References

1. Athanasopoulou, A., De Reuver, M.: How do business model tools facilitate business model exploration? Evidence from action research. Electron. Markets **30**(3), 495–508 (2020)
2. Bennett, N., Lemoine, G.J.: What a difference a word makes: understanding threats to performance in a VUCA world. Bus. Horiz. **57**(3), 311–317 (2014)
3. Bocken, N.M., Geradts, T.H.: Barriers and drivers to sustainable business model innovation: organization design and dynamic capabilities. Long Range Plan. **53**(4), 101950 (2020)
4. Boßelmann, S.: Simplicity in application development for business model design. In: Herzwurm, G., Margaria, T. (eds.) ICSOB 2013. LNBIP, vol. 150, pp. 225–226. Springer, Heidelberg (2013). https://doi.org/10.1007/978-3-642-39336-5_24
5. BostonConsultingGroup: Business model innovation. https://www.bcg.com/de-de/capabilities/innovation-strategy-delivery/business-model-innovation. Accessed 15 Aug 2022
6. Bouwman, H., De Reuver, M., Heikkilä, M., Fielt, E.: Business model tooling: where research and practice meet. Electron. Mark. **30**(3), 413–419 (2020)
7. Bouwman, H., Faber, E., Fielt, E., Haaker, T., Reuver, M.D.: Stof model: critical design issues and critical success factors. In: Bouwman, H., De Vos, H., Haaker, T. (eds.) Mobile Service Innovation and Business Models, pp. 71–88. Springer, Heidelberg (2008). https://doi.org/10.1007/978-3-540-79238-3_3
8. Bouwman, H., et al.: Business models tooling and a research agenda, July 2012
9. Canvanizer. https://canvanizer.com. Accessed 15 Aug 2022
10. CCM Project Group of the Plattform Industrie 4.0: Multilateral data sharing in industry: Concept using "Collaborative Condition Monitoring" as a basis for new business models (2022). https://www.plattform-i40.de/IP/Redaktion/EN/Downloads/Publikation/Multilateral_Data_Sharing.pdf?__blob=publicationFile&v=2. Accessed 25 Aug 2022
11. DataSharingToolkit. https://www.nesta.org.uk/toolkit/data-sharing-toolkit/. Accessed 1 Sept 2022
12. DigitalInnovationKit. https://j2c.de/de/formats/digital-innovation-kit/. Accessed 1 Sept 2022
13. Doll, J., Eisert, U.: Business model development & innovation: a strategic approach to business transformation. Bus. Transf. J. **11**, 7–15 (2014)
14. Floyd, B.D., Boßelmann, S.: Itsy-simplicity research in information and communication technology. Computer **46**(11), 26–32 (2013)
15. Haaker, T., Bouwman, H., Janssen, W., de Reuver, M.: Business model stress testing: a practical approach to test the robustness of a business model. Futures **89**, 14–25 (2017)

16. IEDS: Incentives and Economics of Data Sharing: Fields of action of cross-company data exchange and status quo of the German economy (2022). https://ieds-projekt.de/wp-content/uploads/2022/08/IEDS-Whitepaper_Englisch.pdf. Accessed 19 Aug 2022
17. Margaria, T., Steffen, B.: Simplicity as a driver for agile innovation. Computer **43**(6), 90–92 (2010)
18. Microsoft. https://www.microsoft.com/microsoft-365/powerpoint. Accessed 1 Sept 2022
19. Microsoft. https://www.microsoft.com/microsoft-teams/group-chat-software. Accessed 1 Sept 2022
20. miro. https://miro.com/. Accessed 1 Sept 2022
21. Möller, F., Steffen, B.: License to VIT - a design taxonomy for visual inquiry tools. In: Proceedings of the 55th Hawaii International Conference on System Sciences (2022)
22. Naujokat, S., Lybecait, M., Kopetzki, D., Steffen, B.: CINCO: a simplicity-driven approach to full generation of domain-specific graphical modeling tools. Int. J. Softw. Tools Technol. Transfer **20**(3), 327–354 (2018)
23. Osterwalder, A.: The business model ontology a proposition in a design science approach. Ph.D. thesis, Université de Lausanne, Faculté des hautes études commerciales (2004)
24. Osterwalder, A., Pigneur, Y.: Designing business models and similar strategic objects: the contribution of is. J. Assoc. Inf. Syst. **14**(5), 3 (2012)
25. Osterwalder, A., Pigneur, Y., Bernarda, G., Smith, A.: Value proposition design: How to create products and services customers want. John Wiley & Sons (2015)
26. Osterwalder, A., Pigneur, Y., Oliveira, M.A.Y., Ferreira, J.J.P.: Business model generation: a handbook for visionaries, game changers and challengers. Afr. J. Bus. Manage. **5**(7), 22–30 (2011)
27. PlatformInnovationKit. https://platforminnovationkit.com. Accessed 1 Sept 2022
28. Riemer, K., Holler, J., Indulska, M.: Collaborative process modelling-tool analysis and design implications. In: ECIS (2011)
29. Ryan, S., Steffen, B.: Towards multi-perspective consulting in times of disruption. In: 2022 IEEE 46th Annual Computers, Software, and Applications Conference (COMPSAC). IEEE (2022)
30. Schoormann, T., Möller, F., Szopinski, D.: Exploring purposes of using taxonomies. In: International Conference on Wirtschaftsinformatik (2022)
31. Schwarz, J.S., Legner, C.: Business model tools at the boundary: exploring communities of practice and knowledge boundaries in business model innovation. Electron. Mark. **30**(3), 421–445 (2020)
32. Scuotto, V., Nespoli, C., Palladino, R., Safraou, I.: Building dynamic capabilities for international marketing knowledge management. International Marketing Review (2021)
33. Star, S.L., Griesemer, J.R.: Institutional ecology, translations' and boundary objects: amateurs and professionals in berkeley's museum of vertebrate zoology, 1907–39. Soc. Stud. Sci. **19**(3), 387–420 (1989)
34. Steffen, B.: Inter- & intradepartmental knowledge management barriers when offering single unit solutions. Student Undergraduate Res. E-journal! **2** (2016)
35. Steffen, B.: Asking Why: Towards Conscious Decision-making in Times of VUCA. Electron. Communi. EASST (to appear, 2022)

36. Steffen, B., Boßelmann, S.: GOLD: global organization alignment and decision - towards the hierarchical integration of heterogeneous business models. In: Margaria, T., Steffen, B. (eds.) ISoLA 2018. LNCS, vol. 11247, pp. 504–527. Springer, Cham (2018). https://doi.org/10.1007/978-3-030-03427-6_37
37. Steffen, B., Howar, F., Tegeler, T., Steffen, B.: Agile business engineering: from transformation towards continuousinnovation. In: International Symposium on Leveraging Applications of Formal Methods, pp. 77–94. Springer (2021)
38. Steffen, B., Moeller, F.: Linking multi-perspectives to enable educated decision making in digital platform design. In: 2022 IEEE 46th Annual Computers, Software, and Applications Conference (COMPSAC). IEEE (2022)
39. Steffen, B., Möller, F.: Analyzing and evaluating today's power of open source: The open source value canvas. In: International Conference on Wirtschaftsinformatik (2022)
40. Steffen, B., Möller, F., Nowak, L.: Transformer(s) of the logistics industry - enabling logistics companies to excel with digital platforms. In: Proceedings of the 55th Hawaii International Conference on System Sciences (2022)
41. Steffen, B., Möller, F., Rotgang, A., Ryan, S., Margaria, T.: Towards living canvases. In: Margaria, T., Steffen, B. (eds.) ISoLA 2021. LNCS, vol. 13036, pp. 95–116. Springer, Cham (2021). https://doi.org/10.1007/978-3-030-89159-6_7
42. Steffen, B., Braun von Reinersdorff, A., Rasche, C.: IT-based Decision Support for Value-Based Healthcare in times of VUCA, Disorder and Disruption (to appear)
43. Steffen, B., Naujokat, S.: Archimedean points: the essence for mastering change. LNCS Trans. Found. Mastering Change (FoMaC) **1**(1), 22–46 (2016)
44. Strategyzer. https://www.strategyzer.com/app. Accessed 15 Aug 2022
45. Szopinski, D., Schoormann, T., John, T., Knackstedt, R., Kundisch, D.: How software can support innovating business models: a taxonomy of functions of business model development tools. In: AMCIS (2017)
46. Szopinski, D., Schoormann, T., John, T., Knackstedt, R., Kundisch, D.: Software tools for business model innovation: current state and future challenges. Electron. Mark. **30**(3), 469–494 (2020)
47. Teece, D.J.: Explicating dynamic capabilities: the nature and microfoundations of (sustainable) enterprise performance. Strateg. Manag. J. **28**(13), 1319–1350 (2007)
48. Teece, D.J.: Business models, business strategy and innovation. Long Range Plan. **43**(2–3), 172–194 (2010)
49. Teece, D.J., Petricevic, O.: Capability-based theories of multinational enterprise growth. In: The Oxford Handbook of International Business Strategy, p. 56 (2021)
50. Teece, D.J., Pisano, G., Shuen, A.: Dynamic capabilities and strategic management. Strateg. Manag. J. **18**(7), 509–533 (1997)
51. Thorngate, W.: "In General" vs. "It Depends": some comments of the gergenschlenker debate. Personality Soc. Psychol. Bull. **2**(4), 404–410 (1976)
52. Wenger, E.: Communities of practice: Learning, meaning, and identity. Cambridge University Press (1999)
53. Zweihoff, P., Naujokat, S., Steffen, B.: Pyro: generating domain-specific collaborative online modeling environments. In: Proceedings of the 22nd International Conference on Fundamental Approaches to Software Engineering (FASE 2019) (2019)
54. Zweihoff, P., Tegeler, T., Schürmann, J., Bainczyk, A., Steffen, B.: Aligned, purpose-driven cooperation: the future way of system development. In: Margaria, T., Steffen, B. (eds.) ISoLA 2021. LNCS, vol. 13036, pp. 426–449. Springer, Cham (2021). https://doi.org/10.1007/978-3-030-89159-6_27

Evolving Data Space Technologies: Lessons Learned from an IDS Connector Reference Implementation

Julia Pampus(✉), Brian-Frederik Jahnke, and Ronja Quensel

Fraunhofer Institute for Software and Systems Engineering, Emil-Figge-Straße 91, 44227 Dortmund, Germany
{julia.pampus,brian-frederik.jahnke,ronja.quensel}@isst.fraunhofer.de

Abstract. The establishment of sovereign data spaces is a cutting-edge topic in industrial data sharing scenarios. For instance, organizations like the International Data Spaces (IDS) Association and the Gaia-X European Association for Data and Cloud design standards for sovereign data exchanges and involved governance structures. As an implementation of these standards, data space technologies are of central importance for ensuring secure and sovereign processes and thus establishing trust between data space participants. In this paper, we present our approach, an IDS Connector reference implementation, to integrate data sharing and processing systems into data spaces by providing identity and data management, secure communication protocols, easy-to-use digital contract administration, and prototypical data usage control enforcement. After presenting the software architecture and design, we outline the successful application in selected use cases and derive lessons learned for further developments of data space technologies.

Keywords: Data space technologies · Data sovereignty · International Data Spaces · IDS Connector · Data sharing · Usage control

1 Introduction

Ideas and approaches focusing on the management and economic value of data assets have been of great importance since the early 80s. Recent work in research and industry demonstrates that data as economic goods and a strategic resource is becoming increasingly relevant and can be seen as an "essential feature of digitization and data economy" [28] (p.1). Thereby, innovations from data are mainly created by combining and analysing heterogeneous data (in terms of their format, preparation, value) from different sources [38]. However, as a prerequisite for such processing, data first needs to be collected and aggregated. This is why corresponding research fields are primarily dealing with issues related to the topic of data sharing and, in this course, with the establishment of data spaces.

In this context, the advantages of joint data processing are often obscured by the business stakeholders' major fear of particularly malicious actions and data

T. Margaria and B. Steffen (Eds.): ISoLA 2022, LNCS 13704, pp. 366–381, 2022.
https://doi.org/10.1007/978-3-031-19762-8_27

misuse by, e.g., competing companies [37]. As a result, the importance of data sovereignty meaning the "capability of being entirely self-determined with regard to [...] data" [40] (p.71) grows. The *data provider*, typically the data owner, that wants to share their data within a data space takes an active role by defining the purpose of the data usage [32]. In return, a *data consumer* that wants to use and process accessed data must ensure the compliance with any predefined regulations (hereinafter referred to as *usage policies*).

Allowing data transfers in a controlled manner and under mutual governance rules is a central benefit of building common data spaces. By doing so, it is particularly important and at the same time challenging to design software components that are able to establish and implement trust between data sharing stakeholders [27]. By focusing on standardized communication and transfer processes, the Dataspace Connector, as a software artifact following the specifications of the IDS [39], addresses previously named challenges and technically ensures a confidential and secure handling of data.

The remainder of this paper is structured as follows: As a basis, Sect. 2 introduces existing data space standards, particularly the IDS. Section 3 describes our approach of a sovereign data space technology, covering architecture and implementation. Afterwards, Sect. 4 presents the development of this approach and its application in selected use cases. From this, Sect. 5 addresses gained experiences and derives learnings for future work and developments of sovereign data space technologies. In Sect. 6, similar implementations and approaches are described and evaluated. Finally, the conclusion in Sect. 7 summarizes the contents of this paper and outlines future work.

2 Background

The aforementioned governance rules and technical specifications are facilitated, for instance, by evolving data space standards like Gaia-X and the IDS. Both projects focus on solving data sharing problems in industrial contexts. In doing so, they build on existing standards, like the Data Catalog Vocabulary [53] or the Open Digital Rights Language [52], and leverage well-known cloud technologies. With its Reference Architecture Model (RAM) [31], the IDS, formerly Industrial Data Space, describe business processes and key components of a sovereign data space to create "secure, trusted, and semantically interoperable" [3] (p.1) data processes between different stakeholders. In the context of this, detailed specifications and concepts state how the deployed components authenticate, integrate, and communicate [30]. To ensure interoperability, various working groups focus on the specification of a common ontology, the IDS Information Model [33], and the definition of legal and technical participants of a data space [2].

One of the central components in this context is the *IDS Connector*. This enables participants to share or consume data respecting sovereignty concepts by its integration with existing data providing, processing, or maintaining systems. To publish a data offer, data is enriched with metadata and, as part of this, usage policies that specify how data may be accessed, processed, or distributed (all the way from the data source to the data sink). These usage policies are negotiated as part of digital contracts and are enforced on a technical level by any service along the data value chain. For this purpose, the IDS Connector can intercept data flows, prohibit data accesses, or even modify data in transit. In doing so, it allows for decentralized peer-to-peer data transfers and serves as a gateway to an IDS ecosystem for proprietary systems, encapsulating their capabilities and APIs [25,35]. In summary, an IDS Connector takes care of the following tasks: sharing data offers, negotiating usage policies within contracts, transferring data, making data flows observable, and enforcing usage policies to ensure data sovereignty. While doing so, it communicates with other central IDS services that address the main disciplines of a data space: identity, catalog, vocabulary, service, and logging.

Supplementing and improving the fundamental ideas of the IDS, projects around and members of Gaia-X aim for building a distributed data infrastructure in Europe. Next to adopting previously mentioned concepts for sovereign data exchanges, they concentrate on standardizing fully decentralized data space technologies that can be deployed on any cloud infrastructure [6,7].

3 Approach

As previously stated, novel data space standards introduce multiple new concepts to participating organizations, in particular the importance of sovereign data handling and the relevance of usage control. The **Dataspace Connector (DSC)** is a software artifact that addresses the technical manifestations of these concepts in industrial data sharing scenarios. Since, in the DSC's design phase, the IDS provided new approaches of combining both the ideas of data spaces and sovereignty, these were considered as part of the functional requirements. Thereby, the focus is not on redefining data security, but rather on using established technologies and standards, as the security requirements for industrial automation and control systems (DIN EN IEC 62443-4-2 [9]), and incorporating them with the concepts of data sovereignty. Hence, the DSC follows best practices for software engineering [26,34,50] and is written in Java using the Spring Framework [51] with PostgreSQL [49] as metadata storage.

3.1 Architecture

The DSC is designed as a stateless REST server composed of multiple APIs. It interacts with other data space services (authentication, cataloging, logging) and follows the standards for defining requirements for a security gateway focusing on the exchange of industrial data and services (DIN SPEC 27070 [10]). Similar to a data space that is divided into different disciplines (see Sect. 2), the DSC, as an IDS Base Connector reference implementation, focuses on conforming responsibilities: identity, cataloging, discovery, contract, transfer, service.

As depicted in Fig. 1, the DSC integrates into an IT environment with monitoring, data consuming (processing), and/or data providing systems. In doing

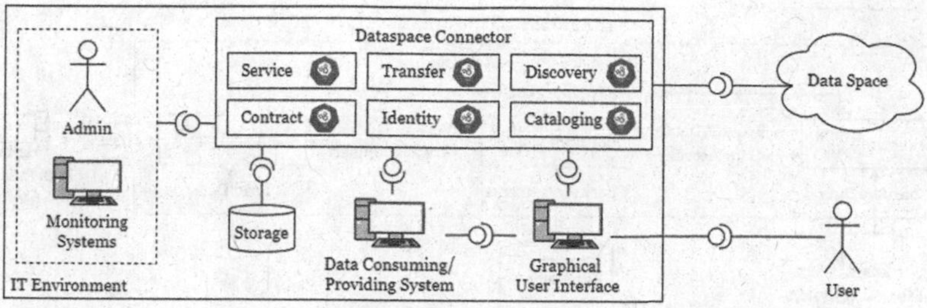

Fig. 1. Systems and users interacting with the DSC as a data flow orchestrator.

so, it adopts multiple roles: First, it acts as an adapter and proxy by forwarding data requests while ensuring sovereign data handling. In addition, it acts as a data storage that persists metadata and administers data sources and/or raw data. Finally, the DSC is a logical component that incorporates additional data space-specific elements (authentication, discovery, usage control) into common data transfers. Details are explained in the following.

- **Identity:** During communication with other data space components, the DSC must identify itself and its owning company. This is done by using X.509 certificates and involving a trusted third-party (OAuth [41] server) into communication processes. Thus, all interactions can be uniquely assigned, and, on this basis, data access control can be enforced. As a backend service that integrates into existing IT landscapes, the DSC does not offer user management itself, but could easily be connected to any external identity and access management systems, e.g., via Spring Security.
- **Cataloging:** As stated in Sect. 2, a core task of an IDS Connector is the management of data offers. For this, the DSC provides a REST API that allows to enrich data with information about its context (*metadata*), e.g., a title or license. Nesting multiple metadata entities increases the amount of available information: Data can be grouped as *resources* and *catalogs*. Each group may contain data that is exposed via different *representations*. Each representation describes and links to an *artifact* that in turn points to the actual shared data asset (e.g., a file or a data stream) and encapsulates specific attributes (e.g., byte size, access information). Additionally, linked *contracts* and *rules* add enforceable usage policies to available data offers. After creation, these data offers can be exposed for discovery.
- **Discovery:** Being part of a data space means exchanging data and information. To make data offers discoverable, the DSC serves an API for (un)registering them at a cataloging service. In doing so, the metadata stored inside the DSC (following the previously described semantics) is translated to the data space ontology, e.g., the IDS Information Model [33], on the fly. This separation and the way of abstracting the used communication protocol (IDS Multipart [30]) allows to exchange versions or technologies dynamically and, thus, to integrate into different data spaces (using a domain-specific

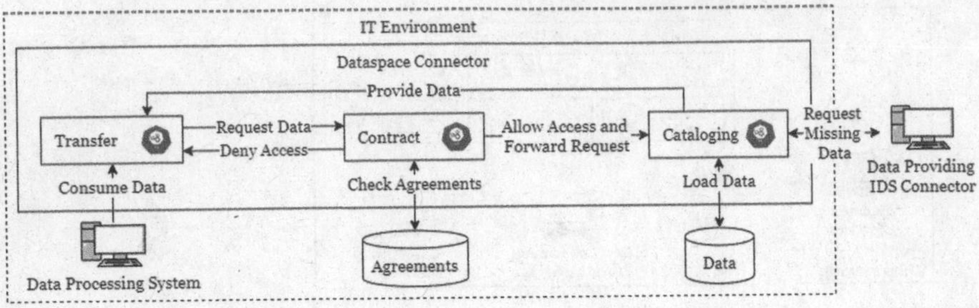

Fig. 2. Interaction example for the data transfer API.

Information Model) easily. The provided API helps to identify other data space participants as well as browse published data offers and attached contracts.

- **Contract:** As introduced in Sects. 1 and 2, data sovereignty is enabled by clearly defining *who* is allowed to access data and *how* it should be used in a first step. For this, contract agreements, based on contract offers that are part of the data offers, are negotiated before access to the data is granted. This mandatory process is called *contract negotiation* and, in this approach, follows the definition of the IDS RAM [31]. Initiating a contract negotiation requires the identifier of the data offer the data consumer is interested in and the usage policies it agrees to in turn for gaining access to it. Next, the DSC will start a communication with the offering data connector. In case of a rejection, a new contract request must be provided. If the offering participant agrees, the DSC will automatically start communication sequences to add and persist the metadata and data as managed data. This includes the final contract agreement. In the course of *policy enforcement*, the DSC will continuously scan managed agreements ensuring compliance with policies and take further actions if necessary (e.g., required data removal).
- **Transfer:** To ensure access and usage control enforcement as defined by the negotiated contract agreements, the DSC exposes a dedicated API that allows managed data to be consumed via HTTP(S). As depicted in Fig. 2, on each data request, the DSC will check for existing agreements and evaluate their content. If any agreement, that matches the requested data and requesting participant, allows the access, the data is returned without obstruction. If the evaluation prohibits the access, the DSC will reject the request. For customization of data flows (on the data provider and consumer sides), the DSC offers an API to setup workflows using Apache Camel [48] and integrate data applications that are downloaded as Docker [11] images.
- **Service:** The integration of sovereign data handling needs to fit into the IT environment of the utilizing organization/company (data space participant). For this reason, the DSC can be deployed in multiple environments ranging from baremetal (without virtualization) over containerized to cloud environments. To fully utilize and integrate with IT environments, the DSC offers a Service API. This exposes health and status information as well as control endpoints for automating the DSC to the environment it integrates with.

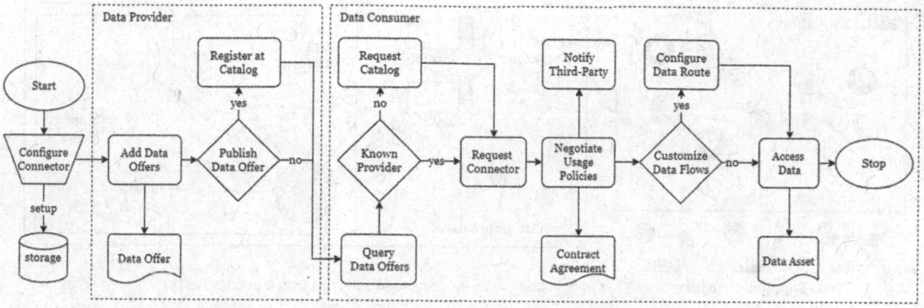

Fig. 3. Process of providing and consuming data with the DSC.

3.2 Integration

The interfaces to the data space follow the specifications of the IDS [30], while all other interfaces that can be accessed by data consuming/providing systems, graphical user interfaces, or human users (i.a., administrators) (see Fig. 1) are based on established standards such as HTTP 1.1 [15] and JSON [8].

The usage of well-known frameworks and programming languages allows for an easy integration, and the stateless design allows for a scalable deployment. By using Java, as previously mentioned, the DSC can be run baremetal, in a container, and in the cloud. Thus, it can be used in projects across a wide range of domains and can help to perform simple data flows in various deployment scenarios, in compliance with the concepts of sovereign data handling.

As Sect. 3.1 outlined the provided functionalities, Fig. 3 visualizes the interactions in order to participate in a data space via a running DSC. In the presented process, a data space participant that could be a single human being or a whole organization first acts as a data provider (left-hand side) and then as a data consumer (right-hand side): At the beginning, the DSC is configured and adapted to the data space by integrating the interfaces of the central data space components and assigning an issued identity for participation. Next, as a data providing service, the DSC is filled with information (metadata) about the data that should be shared. This will be provided as a data offer either via the component's IDS self-description or published at a central cataloging system. In the same way, the DSC can be used to search the data space as a data consumer. Once a suitable offer has been found, a data space participant can trigger its DSC to negotiate an appropriate contract and to download the data, while policy enforcement is ensured. As additional functionality, the DSC can continuously exchange information with a central third-party to log data requests and usages, and data flows can be enriched, e.g., by data processing applications.

4 Evaluation

The DSC is published as open-source software on GitHub [22] (further maintained in a Git fork [23]), licensed under the Apache 2.0 License [47]. Its development

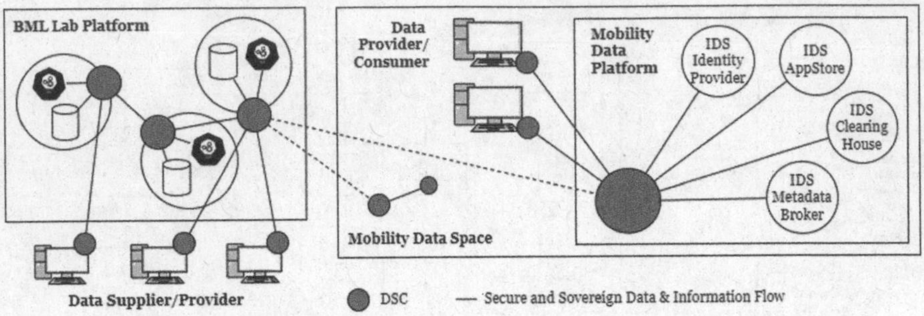

Fig. 4. Representative illustration of the DSC's integration in selected use cases.

process adapted the *Extreme Programming* software development method [4], whose focus is primarily on developing an approach in small iterations and with an extensive involvement of the user and customer group. In our case, this group (hereinafter referred to as *focus groups*) included, i.a., project managers, software developers, and DevOps from partners of various industry and research projects who were involved in the application of the DSC in their use cases.

These use cases served as a starting point. As examples, we want to outline two manifestations of a data space in which the DSC can enable data sovereignty: In Fig. 4, the visualization on the left-hand side depicts the application of data sovereignty in a laboratory platform. For instance, the Bauhaus.MobilityLab (BML) unifies the domains of logistics, energy, and mobility. Within the scope of this project, a new lab platform allows companies, as customers, to aggregate and process data and to test, evaluate, and further develop AI services in real world scenarios. For this purpose, the citizens of a district of Erfurt, Germany, volunteer as participants in a living lab. The DSC is used to implement data sovereignty for data exchanges within the lab platform or between different data suppliers or lab customers. Following the specifications of the IDS, this ensures the interoperability with other IDS ecosystems [24], as the Energy Data Space [5] or the Mobility Data Space (MDS).

The representation on the right-hand side shows how the concepts of data sovereignty can be applied in data marketplaces. For instance, the MDS focuses on establishing a secure and trustworthy data space in the mobility domain. In cooperation with various companies/organizations from this industry, different use cases are set up in which partners exchange, e.g., mobility or weather data, e.g., to optimize smart parking or traffic forecasting. Following the setup presented in Fig. 1, data transfers are realized by using DSCs. As shown in Fig. 4, according to the decentralized architecture of the IDS, the MDS also provides a data platform serving central IDS components, such as the Identity Provider and a Metadata Broker (cataloging system) [12].

A summary of the essential steps of the development process is shown in Fig. 5. As illustrated, after collecting the requirements within the *Exploration Phase*, these were prioritized and development efforts were estimated in the

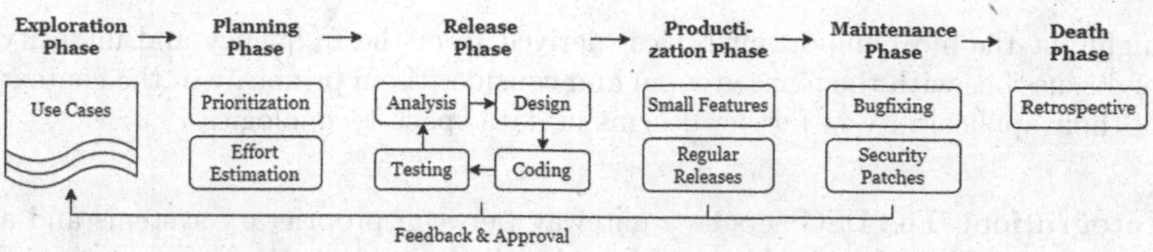

Fig. 5. Development process adapting the extreme programming life cycle in [1].

Planning Phase. As a next step, the *Release Phase* included various development cycles, which in turn followed a waterfall model: analysis, design, implementation (coding), and testing [4]. New features were developed in multiple iterations and with continuous integration and testing. The latter included unit tests, integration tests, and end-to-end tests, as well as experimental deployments by the project partners, e.g., in the MDS or BML. For the design phase, especially the communication with the IDS community and upcoming data space initiatives was of major importance to advance and comply with evolving standards.

During the *Productization Phase* and *Maintenance Phase*, small releases were published on a regular basis and bugfixes and security patches were provided. The DSC was continuously tested and evaluated by the focus groups so that decisions could be quickly confirmed or requirements refined. This was especially helpful due to the simultaneous application of our approach in numerous projects. The *Death Phase* shown in Fig. 5 marks the date of this publication. The results of the retrospective and feedback sessions are discussed next.

5 Lessons Learned

In summary, the development process that was outlined in the previous section was very agile and close to the actual industrial contexts where data space technologies finally are being used. The continuous communication (bi-weekly Q&A sessions, project jour fixes, hands-on sessions) with the focus groups (see Sect. 4) allowed to gain experience and identify problems. From those, in collaboration with IDSA working groups, feedback for further work and the refinement of the IDS as a data space standard has been provided. However, our experiences are not limited to this project, nor are they limited to the IDS Connector as such. From a combination of requirements, retrospectives, and the successful or unsuccessful application of formal specifications, we draw the following lessons learned that can provide benefits to the development of sovereign data space technologies in general. These lessons learned are divided into the openly communicated expectations of the focus groups and our general observations.

5.1 Expectations

Most of the formal functional and non-functional requirements for data space technologies can be described with common best practices in software development, which have already been mentioned in Sect. 3. In the following, we highlight the most important topics (derived from the frequency and intensity of discussions with the focus groups) and consider them primarily in the context of their applicability in further designs of data space technologies.

Integration. The DSC acts as a gateway between proprietary systems and a data space. The related additional functionalities, such as the incorporation of metadata and the connection of data sources, must be applied within existing IT landscapes and without causing changes to external systems. The implementation of data space technologies has thus to identify deployment environments and communication protocols that are broadly supported. Experience from the previously mentioned use cases has shown that the choice of referring to HTTP 1.1 and JSON for all APIs of the DSC was appropriate for an easy integration. For instance, the Silicon Economy Logistics Ecosystem, with its aim to build up a platform economy for the logistics sector [42], developed an IDS Integration Toolbox [45] that simplifies the integration of IDS components, such as the DSC. Even though this already encapsulates complex data space standards, some interactions can be aggregated and further abstracted according to the needs. This reduces the development effort for integration tools to a minimum.

Extensibility. As the development of data space standards integrating the concept of data sovereignty is young and fast-moving, any data space component must be easily extensible to communicate with upcoming and evolving technologies. This extensibility is not limited to the communication within the data space but also includes requirements such as connecting to other systems that provide, consume, or process data. As the communication with the focus groups has shown, workflows and processes for consuming and producing data, as well as system management, can vary significantly in any new use case. Therefore, a sovereign data space component needs to be a platform for validating and executing user-defined processes and workflows. In this course, it has to be designed in a way that it can be easily customized, resulting in a lightweight core and clearly defined interfaces for extensibility. Using a modular architecture allows for exchanging needed capabilities in order to provide a seamless integration and easy adaptation to changing requirements.

Nevertheless, there is a risk of providing too much extensibility as integrating software approaches are more beneficial than one software monolith that adapts to an arbitrary number of use cases. As an example, data space technologies that are designed for cloud deployments may not suit IoT systems at the same time.

Stability. For the scalability of a data space and systems to constantly integrate and still be able to communicate with each other, compatibility and interoperability are required first and foremost. As described in Sect. 2, the IDS aim to fulfil these requirements by standardizing interfaces and communication protocols. The application within projects like the MDS showed that the required stability of existing data space technologies (following the IDS standard) is not yet in place. Despite complex and reliable processes, especially in terms of changes, both IDS reference architecture and technical specifications, currently, are more likely to be considered as living documents. The root cause is primarily a slow top-down development process and the late incorporation of technical implementations and real-world requirements by industrial stakeholders. The multitude of adaptations that are required at this stage, such as the detailed elaboration of existing specifications, causes challenges to especially the compatibility and interoperability, and results in breaking changes on a technical level.

By providing stable interaction interfaces, not all changes need to be propagated to the user interacting with a data space component like the DSC, or to any systems connecting with it. Moreover, stable interfaces allow for cross version compatibility between different components. This allows data space participants to focus on their use cases and prevents artificial version lock-in that could obstruct adoption of data sovereignty concepts.

Usability. By entering data spaces, an organization encounters challenges, e.g., about how to interact with other participants adhering to the paradigm of data sovereignty. Any data space component needs to increase the usability by self-documenting and providing as much information as possible to the user about the current context, functionalities, and changes applied to the system. By serving detailed and well-prepared context information, the user may utilize the component easily and without any profound knowledge about data sovereignty. This has been particularly clear in the previously mentioned projects.

Deriving from this, data space technologies should further be considered from a user-centric perspective. The DSC and other IDS components are designed as backend services that primarily address the technical aspects of data sovereignty by focusing on machine-to-machine interaction according to appropriate standards. The provided interfaces are intended to simplify the automation and integration of the system into existing deployments, and to abstract complex processes. However, the current data space concepts lack human-to-machine interaction with regards to sovereignty aspects. The components and their graphical user interfaces are currently not designed to be operated by a non-technical person without domain knowledge. However, data sovereignty should not only be addressed at a technical level but should also involve the human user. Here, the challenge is to design processes transparently and to create trust so that the user can comprehend and understand information and data flows. With solving this, there will be a better comprehension of data space concepts like the IDS.

Sovereignty. The exchange with the user group of the DSC showed that especially the technical integration of data sovereignty aspects is still in an early stage. Many companies already address security issues and apply strict guidelines in their daily business. How data security is differentiated from sovereignty is often not entirely clear. As shown in Sect. 4, many use cases focus primarily on data transfers between IDS Connectors and focus on access policies. Thereby, the value and application of usage policies, and therefore usage control, is mostly disregarded and not considered in the short-term. It is also apparent that many companies do not solely trust technologies such as the DSC, but rather make consortium agreements in data space projects that determine the data exchanges from a legal point of view. In this context, the technical possibilities of data space components are merely a nice-to-have.

5.2 Observations

In addition to the clearly communicated requirements of the focus groups, we made some general observations regarding the development and utilization of data space technologies that should be considered in future works and discussions. These are explained below.

There is a Need for a Common Understanding of Data Spaces. Although there is a lot of literature about data spaces and ecosystems (cited in Sects. 1 and 2), it appeared that people have a different understanding of used terms like *policy* or *contract*, e.g., due to various levels of expertise or personal experiences. What characterizes a data space on a business and technical level? How does one data space differentiate from another one? How can data spaces interact with each other? A major concern in this regard is the lack of clear role and rights concepts and the alignment of legal contracts, access policies, and the delimitation of both terms from their usage in the context of data spaces. Due to this, the DSC currently does not implement any role concepts, nor does it support the integration into more than one data space at runtime. To build up a data space and establish a common understanding, fundamental role concepts and used terms need to be defined and agreed on at an early stage.

Usage Control Enforcement is the Biggest Challenge for the Technical Realization of Data Sovereignty. Usage control extends access control by providing the ability "to continuously monitor and control the usage of resources such as files or services" [43] (p.289). This way, the data owner/provider cannot only restrict access to their data but control its usage. However, the implementation of this is conceptually as well as technically difficult, especially in cloud environments. The DSC currently focuses on implementing policies that provide or restrict the access to data (connector-, time-, or security-level-restricted). As it comes with a default database integration, data can even be deleted after a specified time interval. The usage control capabilities of the DSC likely cover the basic needs of users, yet one fundamental question came up frequently: How to ensure that data does not leave the controlled system environment or is copied, especially within complex cloud deployment scenarios or third-party data processing? This results in necessary future research and work, especially regarding the importance of usage control in sovereign data spaces.

Open Source is a Chance for the Evolution of Data Space Technology. Essentially, open-source software development is an opportunity for companies to bring together various skill sets and to collaboratively work on a topic and drive innovation. The concepts and core ideas behind open source are reflected especially in the context of data spaces and data sovereignty: establishing a high level of transparency and trust both in an open-source project and in a sovereign data space [46]. Thus, as shown by the application of the DSC (see Sect. 4) and the increasing interest and engagement of potential users via GitHub, the collaborative development of software in this domain helps to build data spaces in which organizations can participate by using jointly developed software. This in turn results in increased trust in the used technology.

6 Related Work

In the design phase of the approach presented in Sect. 3, only few implementations of sovereign data space technologies were available – most of them in the context of IDS. In general, the open-source software movement for data space technologies was not that advanced and, i.a., nowadays often presented and referenced IDS Connectors like the ones from TNO [36] and Engineering [14] were not publicly available. For instance, the Trusted Connector [16], as an IDS Connector reference implementation, focuses on IoT systems. Due to the high level of security, the Trusted Connector requires the use of hardware anchors and cannot communicate with components that do not implement a specific IDS communication protocol that integrates remote attestation [44]. In addition, missing persistence capabilities and REST interfaces do not allow for an easy integration and out-of-the-box usage. The Clearing House [17] builds on the Trusted Connector while focusing solely on information logging by leveraging blockchain technologies. The Enterprise Integration (EI) Connector [19], which is no longer being developed, excelled in implementing the IDS Information Model natively. Its usage was restricted to locally stored files and the connection of a graph database. A special version of the EIC is the Metadata Broker [20] that completely focuses on cataloging capabilities and the management of metadata. Usage control is not supported by either component.

A comparison of chosen criteria (availability of code, integrated technologies, deployment options, supported protocols, level of security, implemented usage control) shows that the DSC combines more requirements than any approach at that time: (1) It is available open-source. (2) It connects to easily exchangeable relational databases. (3) It can be executed in various deployment environments. (4) It implements interfaces that follow established standards and best practices. (5) By supporting two IDS protocols (IDS Multipart and IDSCPv2 [30]) and implementing all mandatory communication processes (authorization, discovery, contract negotiation, logging), the DSC is compatible with many of the mentioned technologies: Trusted Connector, EI Connector, TNO Connector, TRUsted Engineering Connector, Metadata Broker, Clearing House, and the meanwhile existing IDS AppStore (combination of IDS Connector and Docker registry) [18]. (6) With the use of IDSCPv2 and remote attestation, the DSC, just like the Trusted Connector, can be run with an increased level of security. (7) By natively integrating Apache Camel, data flows (routes) can be customized and intercepting usage control frameworks, such as LUCON [43] or MyData [21], can be easily integrated to extend the provided usage control enforcement.

Being labelled as *IDS-ready* [29] and recently being used in a variety of industrial and research projects, as outlined in Sect. 4, demonstrates the need for technology that enables data sovereignty in industrial contexts, and shows that the DSC provides major functionalities to be leveraged as a sovereign data space component.

7 Conclusion

At the beginning of this paper, we introduced the relevance of data spaces and data sovereignty. As an approach addressing these topics, the concepts of IDS were briefly presented. To address the technical manifestations of data sovereignty in industrial data sharing scenarios, we developed a data space connector following the specifications of the IDS. Next, we highlighted the successful adoption of our approach in different projects as proof-of-concept. During the development of the DSC, we initiated discussions with various focus groups from industry and research and achieved acceptance in the community that critically deals with the implementation of data space technologies. To conclude, we derived lessons learned that can be considered for further designs and developments of data space technologies, not only in the context of IDS or Gaia-X.

Based on its successful adoption, the DSC is further evolved in the Eclipse Dataspace Connector (EDC) project that was founded in summer 2021. The EDC, as open-source software, aims at providing a highly scalable, modular, and extensible framework for sovereign data exchanges. By adopting the essential concepts and learnings of the DSC, it addresses advanced data sharing challenges, such as identity management and interoperability across multiple jurisdictions and data sovereignty in cloud-native environments [13].

References

1. Abrahamsson, P., Salo, O., Ronkainen, J., Warsta, J.: Agile software development methods: review and analysis. Proc. Espoo **2002**, 3–107 (2002)
2. Ahmadian, A.S., Jürjens, J., Strüber, D.: Extending model-based privacy analysis for the industrial data space by exploiting privacy level agreements. In: Proceedings of the 33rd Annual ACM Symposium on Applied Computing, pp. 1142–1149. ACM, New York (2018). https://doi.org/10.1145/3167132.3167256
3. Bader, S., et al.: The international data spaces information model – an ontology for sovereign exchange of digital content. In: Pan, J.Z., Tamma, V., d'Amato, C., Janowicz, K., Fu, B., Polleres, A., Seneviratne, O., Kagal, L. (eds.) ISWC 2020. LNCS, vol. 12507, pp. 176–192. Springer, Cham (2020). https://doi.org/10.1007/978-3-030-62466-8_12
4. Beck, K.: Embracing change with extreme programming. Computer **32**(10), 70–77 (1999)
5. Berkhout, V., Frey, C., Hertweck, P., Nestle, D., Wickert, M.: Energy Data Space, pp. 329–341. Springer (2022). https://doi.org/10.1007/978-3-030-93975-5_20
6. Biegel, ., et al.: GAIA-X: Driver of digital innovation in Europe. Federal Ministry for Economic Affairs and Energy, Public Relations Division (2020). www.bmwi.de
7. Braud, A., Fromentoux, G., Radier, B., Le Grand, O.: The Road to European Digital Sovereignty with Gaia-X and IDSA. IEEE Network **35**(2), 4–5 (2021). https://doi.org/10.1109/MNET.2021.9387709

8. Bray, T.: The JavaScript Object Notation (JSON) Data Interchange Format, RFC 8259, December 2017. https://doi.org/10.17487/RFC8259, Accessed 23 Feb 2022
9. Security for industrial automation and control systems - Part 4–2: Technical security requirements for IACS components (Dec 2019)
10. Requirements and reference architecture of a security gateway for the exchange of industry data and services. (March 2020)
11. Docker Inc.: Develop faster. Run anywhere., https://www.docker.com/, (Accessed: 04.09.2022)
12. Drees, H., Kubitza, D.O., Lipp, J., Pretzsch, S., Schlueter Langdon, C.: Mobility Data Space - First Implementation and Business Opportunities (2021)
13. Eclipse Foundation: Eclipse Dataspace Connector (2021–2022). https://github.com/eclipse-dataspaceconnector/DataSpaceConnector. Accessed 10 Jan 2022
14. Engineering Ingegneria Informatica S.p.A.: TRUE (TRUsted Engineering) Connector (2022). https://github.com/Engineering-Research-and-Development/true-connector. Accessed 21 Feb 2022
15. Fielding, R., Reschke, J.: Hypertext Transfer Protocol (HTTP/1.1): Semantics and Content, RFC 7231, June 2014. https://doi.org/10.17487/RFC7231. Accessed 23 Feb 2022
16. Fraunhofer AISEC: Trusted Connector (2016–2022). https://github.com/International-Data-Spaces-Association/trusted-connector. Accessed 21 Feb 2022
17. Fraunhofer AISEC: IDS Clearing House (2021–2022). https://github.com/International-Data-Spaces-Association/ids-clearing-house-service. Accessed 21 Feb 2022
18. Fraunhofer FIT: IDS AppStore (2021–2022). https://github.com/International-Data-Spaces-Association/IDS-AppStore. Accessed 04 Sept 2022
19. Fraunhofer IAIS: Enterprise Integration Connector (2020–2021). https://github.com/International-Data-Spaces-Association/IDS-Enterprise-Integration-Connector. Accessed 21 Feb 2022
20. Fraunhofer IAIS: IDS Metadata Broker (2020–2022). https://github.com/International-Data-Spaces-Association/metadata-broker-open-core. Accessed 21 Feb 2022
21. Fraunhofer IESE: MY DATA Control Technologies (2022). https://www.mydata-control.de/, Accessed 10 Jan 2022
22. Fraunhofer ISST: Dataspace Connector (2020–2022). https://github.com/FraunhoferISST/DataspaceConnector. Accessed 10.June 2022
23. Fraunhofer ISST and sovity GmbH: Dataspace Connector (2020–2022). https://github.com/International-Data-Spaces-Association/DataspaceConnector. Accessed 10 June 2022
24. Frey, C., Hertweck, P., Richter, L., Warweg, O.: Bauhaus. MobilityLab: A Living Lab for the Development and Evaluation of AI-Assisted Services. Smart Cities **5**(1), 133–145 (2022). https://doi.org/10.3390/smartcities5010009
25. Gallay, Olivier and Korpela, Kari and Tapio, Niemi and Nurminen, Jukka K.: A peer-to-peer platform for decentralized logistics. In: Proceedings of the Hamburg International Conference of Logistics (HICL). pp. 10 31. epubli (2017). https://doi.org/10.15480/882.1473
26. Gamma, E., Helm, R., Johnson, R., Johnson, R.E., Vlissides, J., et al.: Design patterns: elements of reusable object-oriented software. Pearson Deutschland GmbH (1995)
27. Gelhaar, J., Otto, B.: Challenges in the emergence of data ecosystems. In: Proceedings of the 24th Pacific Asia Conference on Information Systems: Information Systems (IS) for the Future, PACIS 2020, June 2020

28. Hosseinzadeh, A., Eitel, A., Jung, C.: A systematic approach toward extracting technically enforceable policies from data usage control requirements. In: Proceedings of the 6th International Conference on Information Systems Security and Privacy, pp. 397–405. SCITEPRESS - Science and Technology Publications (2020). https://doi.org/10.5220/0008936003970405
29. International Data Spaces e.V.: IDS-ready: Open-Source-Software "Dataspace Connector" Enables Sovereign Data Exchange (2020). https://internationaldataspaces.org/ids-ready-open-source-software-dataspace-connector-enables-sovereign-data-exchange/. Accessed 10 June 2022
30. International Data Spaces e.V.: IDS-G (2022). https://github.com/International-Data-Spaces-Association/IDS-G. Accessed 20 Feb 2022
31. International Data Spaces e.V.: IDS Reference Architecture Model (2022). https://github.com/International-Data-Spaces-Association/IDS-RAM_4_0. Accessed 21 June 2022
32. Jarke, M., Otto, B., Ram, S.: Data sovereignty and data space ecosystems. Bus. Inf. Syst. Eng. **61**(5), 549–550 (2019). https://doi.org/10.1007/s12599-019-00614-2
33. Mader, C., Pullmann, J., Petersen, N., Lohmann, S., Lange-Bever, C.: Fraunhofer IAIS and Fraunhofer FIT: International Data Spaces Information Model (2021). https://international-data-spaces-association.github.io/InformationModel/docs/index.html. Accessed 20 Feb 2022
34. Martin, R.C.: Clean code: a handbook of agile software craftsmanship. Pearson Education (2009)
35. Nast, M., et al.: Towards an International Data Spaces Connector for the Internet of Things. In: 2020 16th IEEE International Conference on Factory Communication Systems (WFCS), pp. 1–4 (2020). https://doi.org/10.1109/WFCS47810.2020.9114503
36. Nederlandse Organisatie voor Toegepast Natuurwetenschappelijk Onderzoek (TNO): TNO Security Gateway (2022). https://tno-tsg.github.io/. Accessed 10 June 2022
37. Opriel, S., Möller, F.O., Burkhardt, U., Otto, B.: Requirements for Usage Control based Exchange of Sensitive Data in Automotive Supply Chains. In: Proceedings of the 54th Hawaii International Conference on System Sciences, p. 431 (2021). https://doi.org/10.24251/HICSS.2021.051
38. Otto, B., Burmann, A.: Europäische Dateninfrastrukturen. Informatik Spektrum **44**(4), 283–291 (2021). https://doi.org/10.1007/s00287-021-01386-4
39. Otto, B., Jürjens, J., Schon, J., Auer, S., Menz, N., Wenzel, S., Cirullies, J.: Industrial Data Space - Digitale Souveränität über Daten. White Paper, Fraunhofer-Gesellschaft zur Förderung der angewandten Forschung eV, München (2016)
40. Otto, B., et al.: Reference Architecture Model for the Industrial Data Space. Fraunhofer-Gesellschaft, Munich 88 (2017)
41. Parecki, Aaron: OAuth 2.0. https://oauth.net/2/. Accessed 04 Sept 2022
42. Qarawlus, H., Hellmeier, M., Pieperbeck, J., Quensel, R., Biehs, S., Peschke, M.: Sovereign data exchange in cloud-connected IoT using international data spaces. In: 2021 IEEE Cloud Summit (Cloud Summit), pp. 13–18 (2021). https://doi.org/10.1109/IEEECloudSummit52029.2021.00010
43. Schütte, J., Brost, G.S.: LUCON: data flow control for message-based IoT systems. In: 2018 17th IEEE International Conference On Trust, Security And Privacy In Computing And Communications/12th IEEE International Conference On Big Data Science And Engineering (TrustCom/BigDataSE), pp. 289–299. IEEE (2018). https://doi.org/10.1109/TrustCom/BigDataSE.2018.00052

44. Schütte, J., Brost, G.S., Wessel, S.: Der Trusted Connector im Industrial Data Space. Fraunhofer-Publication of Fraunhofer Institute for Applied and Integrated Security, Garching (2018). http://arxiv.org/abs/1804.09442
45. Silicon Economy: IDS Integration Toolbox (2020–2022). https://www.silicon-economy.com/project/ids-integration-toolbox/. Accessed 03 Sept 2022
46. Ten Hompel, M., Schmidt, M.: Silicon Economy: Logistics as the Natural Data Ecosystem. Designing Data Spaces, p. 263 (2022)
47. The Apache Software Foundation: Apache License, Version 2.0 (2004). https://www.apache.org/licenses/LICENSE-2.0. Accessed 24 Feb 2022
48. The Apache Software Foundation: Apache Camel (2004–2022). https://camel.apache.org/. Accessed 19 Jan 2022
49. The PostgreSQL Global Development Group: PostgreSQL (1996–2022). https://www.postgresql.org/. Accessed 24 Feb 2022
50. Ullenboom, C.: Java ist auch eine Insel, vol. 1475. Galileo Press (2004)
51. VMware Inc.: Spring Framework (2022). https://spring.io/projects/spring-framework. Accessed 24 Feb 2022
52. World Wide Web Consortium (W3C): ODRL Information Model 2.2 (2018). https://www.w3.org/TR/odrl-model/. Accessed 09 Apr 2022
53. World Wide Web Consortium (W3C): Data Catalog Vocabulary (DCAT) - Version 2 (2020). https://www.w3.org/TR/vocab-dcat-2/. Accessed 09 Apr 2022

Towards a Methodology for Formally Analyzing Federated Identity Management Systems

Katerina Ksystra[1(✉)], Maria Dimarogkona[2], Nikolaos Triantafyllou[1], Petros Stefaneas[2], and Petros Kavassalis[1]

[1] i4m Lab (Information Management Lab), University of Aegean, Mytilene, Greece
katerinaksystra@aegean.gr

[2] λ-Form (Formal Methods Research Group), National Technical University of Athens, Athens, Greece

Abstract. The aim of this paper is to develop an appropriate methodology for formally analyzing federated identity management (FIM) systems. For this purpose, two different formal frameworks are considered; the first uses TLA+, a specification language for modeling complex industrial systems, whereas the second uses the Maude language, a more research-oriented approach. Using these frameworks, we first model an API Connector, developed in the context of an EU eIDAS project to facilitate the integration of Service Providers with the eIDAS Network. On the basis of the produced specifications we verify the aforementioned API Connector by model-checking an important security property. Finally, the two approaches are compared in terms of efficiency and accessibility based on a set of carefully selected criteria.

Keywords: Identity management systems · Federated identity · Formal methods · Temporal logic of actions · Rewriting logic · TLA+ · Maude · eIDAS

1 Introduction

Federated identity management (FIM) refers to an architecture for connecting authoritative identity resources (Identity and Attributes Providers) with Relying Parties (Service Providers) within the trust framework of a voluntary association.

FIM systems provide "third party" user authentication and authorization to the members of the federation. As a result, the federation's end-users utilize their authorization credentials, issued from one or more Identity/Attribute Providers, to gain automatic access to online services offered by any Service Provider in the federation [1,2]. Today there is an increasing need for the use of federated identity networks both in the private and in the public sector, such as cloud computing platforms, private organizations, and global markets. Prominent examples of identity federations are the network operated by the academic and research

T. Margaria and B. Steffen (Eds.): ISoLA 2022, LNCS 13704, pp. 382–405, 2022.
https://doi.org/10.1007/978-3-031-19762-8_28

institutions (eduGAIN) [3], the EU/EEA countries (eIDAS Network) [4], or the private partnerships enabled by the use of commercial software, such as Oracle Identity Federation [5]. One of the challenges when implementing such complex systems is the proper interoperation of the different system components. For federation to optimally work, users' identity information should be shared between the federation entities entrusted with authentication. But not all components of a federation conform to the same security standards, especially components that usually exist to translate core federation standards such as SAML to common enterprises technologies (JWT, OIDC etc.) which may exhibit critical vulnerabilities. As trust and security are top concerns in these environments, it is not surprising that industries like IBM have invested in the development of techniques to eliminate the security risks of FIM systems, the biggest of which seems to be user's identity theft. In order to avoid potential flaws that could endanger the security of federated identity networks, we need to have a precise description of their architecture, especially of the periphery parts (i.e. federation-edge). Formal methods can help to protect FIM systems, especially the "Service Provider" type of entities, from attacks capable of compromising the security of protocols used at the edge of the federation. To this end, in order to enhance the formal and rigorous analysis of FIM systems, we present two alternative formal approaches;

- One that expresses an FIM system as a rewrite logic theory, written in Maude,
- Another that expresses the same FIM system as a temporal logic of actions specification, written in TLA+.

Both approaches allow us to formally reason about the specified system, and automatically verify the desired security properties, using model checking techniques.

The rest of this paper is organized as follows: in Sect. 1.1, we briefly present related work and discuss differences with our approach. Section 2 describes the theoretical foundations of the two approaches. In Sect. 3, we present the proposed frameworks which formally express the actions of FIM systems as rewrite rules and temporal actions (in Maude and TLA+, respectively). In Sect. 4, we apply those frameworks in a case study. In Sect. 5 we compare the two approaches and report on the lessons learnt. Finally, Sect. 5 concludes the paper and discusses future research.

1.1 Related Work

Research has revealed critical logic flaws in commercial web SSO systems like Microsoft Passport, OpenID and SAML, as well as vulnerabilities in detection flaw [7,8]. Following these findings several solutions have been proposed, spanning from alternative federated identity architectures [9], to more secure FIM protocols like BBAE [10]. The same has been done for cloud environments like OpenID and OAuth [11,23]. Aiming at enabling secure online business collaboration, IBM has developed Tivoli, a federated access management solution that provides web and federated SSO to end users across multiple applications [13].

To develop this commercial software IBM invested on extended research, including the security analysis and proofs of existing browser-based FIM protocols like SAML [8]. The federated identity architecture of the European eID system has also been analysed and evaluated in terms of performance and scalability [2]. Nevertheless, most of the early security analyses were informal, except from the development of a generic framework for security proofs of browser-based protocols supported by IBM, which uses state machines and state machine diagrams [14]. This formal framework was used to model the WS-Federation Passive Requestor Interop profile - an important FIM protocol -, and prove that it provides authenticity and secure channel establishment in a realistic trust scenario. According to the authors this constitutes the first rigorous security proof for a browser-based identity federation protocol.

Formal approaches are gaining in popularity and more companies offer and/or use formal methods [15], but it remains an open question which of the existing relevant tools are best suited for the task of formally analysing FIM systems. In the analysis of the InfoCard protocol in [16], for example, Wuang et al. use AVISPA [17], a push-button integrated tool for the Automated Validation of Internet Security Protocols and Applications. AVISPA provides - among others - a role-based (and TLA-based) specification language for security protocols, properties, channels, and intruder models, called HLPSL; and a model-checker called OFMC, which employs several symbolic techniques for the exploration of the state space in a demand-driven way. Our work supports this line of development, namely, the formal analysis and verification of FIM protocols and implementations, as the best way to tackle the critical security issues involved in federated identity.

Our approach differs from the ones already mentioned in the following points: TLA+, one of the tools we chose to experiment with, is a mathematical language for describing the abstraction of state machines, and Maude is based on rewriting logic and membership equational logic. Most importantly, both tools produce executable specifications unlike [14], and have a much more general field of application than AVISPA [17]. Finally, in Maude the agreement of mathematical and operational semantics is proven by the existence of the relevant isomorphism [18]; this makes automated verification using Maude a well-founded approach.

2 Preliminaries

2.1 Federated Identity Management Systems

Federated identity management refers to the agreements, standards, and technologies that enable the portability of identities, attributes, and entitlements across multiple enterprises and numerous applications, supporting thousands - or even millions - of users. The sharing of digital identities allows users to access applications and resources across multiple domains, managed by different organizations, by authenticating only once. The cooperating organizations form a federation based on agreed-upon standards and mutual levels of trust.

A generic FIM system architecture includes users, identities, identity providers, and service providers. In this setting, an identity is defined for each user - which is further associated with a set of attributes - and a means is established by which the user can verify his identity.

In most federated identity management schemes, the user stores his credentials in the identity provider. Then, when logging into a service he does not need to provide credentials to the service provider; the service provider trusts the identity provider to validate the user's credentials (the identity provider acquires attribute information through dialog and protocol exchanges with users and administrators). Consequently, the user only has to provide credentials directly to the identity provider. This is how single-sign-on (SSO), the ability of a user to access all network resources after a single authentication, is implemented.

One of the biggest advantages of FIM systems is that they allow companies to share applications without having to adopt the same authentication technologies, directory services, and security. Furthermore, SSO authentication minimizes costs, as it simplifies the authentication process, and increases security, as it lowers the risks associated with authenticating identity information multiple times. FIM systems also improve privacy compliance by effectively controlling user access to information sharing. Finally, it leads to a significant enhancement of the end-user experience by eliminating the need for managing a large number of accounts and passwords. However, FIM systems can exhibit security and trust vulnerabilities because of their many components and their complex interaction.

2.2 Specification Languages

Maude is a declarative programming and specification language based on rewriting logic, a computational logic that can naturally deal with state and concurrent computations. It was developed by José Meseguer and his research team in SRI International [19], and has been influenced by Goguen's OBJ3 language[1]. More details about Maude and its syntax can be found in the Annex (Sect. A.1).

In Maude distributed systems are modelled as rewrite theories, and the relevant requirements are formalized using linear temporal logic. Data types are defined algebraically by equations (which amounts to defining functions in a functional programming language), while the dynamic behaviour is defined by rewrite rules, which describe how a part of the system's state can change in one step. In other words a Maude program is a logical theory, and a Maude computation is a logical deduction using the axioms specified in the theory/program. Thus, similar to TLA+, a system is represented as a set of behaviours described by an initial condition and a set of rewrite rules playing the role of state transitions of the system.

TLA+ is a specification language based on temporal logic of actions (TLA), a variation of linear temporal logic[2] developed by Leslie Lamport [24]. TLA adds

[1] OBJ3 is a version of OBJ based on order-sorted rewriting.

[2] Linear temporal logic (LTL) was first proposed by Pnueli [20] as a tool for the specification, formal analysis, and verification of reactive and concurrent programs

the concept of actions to temporal logic, providing ways to formalize the actions used in concurrent systems. More details about TLA+ and its syntax can be found in the Annex (Sect. A.2).

3 Proposed Frameworks

In this section we describe two formal approaches for specifying federated identity management systems: Rewriting Logic and Temporal Logic of Actions (TLA). An older version of the above general approach (based on the formalism of equational logic) has been presented in [6].

The key **entities** of a federated identity management system are the identity provider, the user and the service provider[3], as shown in Fig. 1. The **objects** of such a system are the user's attributes, a "security" token and the user's credentials. Finally the main **actions** of the system are the user's authentication, and the actions of sending and receiving the authentication attributes.

3.1 Specifying FIM Systems Using Rewriting Logic

Rewriting logic specifications are created using:

- Observable values which are pairs of (parameterized) names and values [*Obs*];

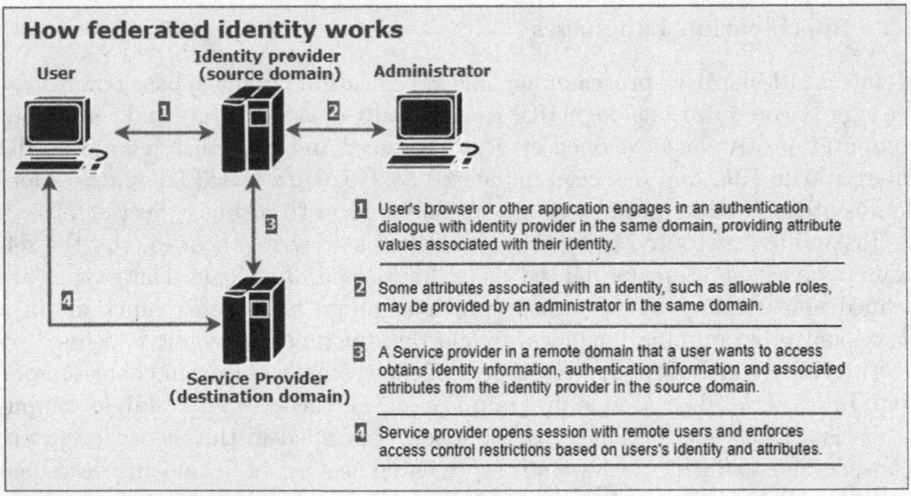

Fig. 1. Federated identity management system key components.

and systems, and is currently the most popular and widely used temporal logic in computer science. LTL is especially useful for expressing safety, liveness, fairness, and precedence properties of infinite computations in reactive systems [21].

[3] https://www.networkworld.com/article/2285444/understanding-federated-identity.html.

- States which are expressed as collections (soups) of observable values [*State*];
- State transitions which are described by rewrite rules [*Trans Obs* < *State*].

A federated identity management system can be expressed in terms of rewriting logic, if we map the **actions** of the system into (conditional) rewrite rules. In order to describe the effects of the actions, we use observable values.

Since some actions correspond to the exchange of user's attributes, in order to describe them we need an observable value *Attributes* that stores the authentication attributes, and another observable value *Response* that stores the response containing the received user attributes.

op Attributes[_]:_ : *User Attributes* -> *Obs*.
op Response:_: *Attributes* -> *Obs*.

The **entities** and the **objects** of the system are expressed as modules with appropriately defined operators and equations.

Definition 1. *Assume the state space Y and the following set of Actions of a federated identity management system; Ai,* $i = 1 \leq i \leq n$. *We define the following set of observable values (O) and transitions (T):*

- $O = O' \cup \mathit{Attributes} \cup \mathit{Response}$
- $T = \{Ai \,|\, 1 \leq i \leq n\}$

In the above definition, O' denotes additional observable values that may be used for the definition of generic actions and their side effects. Transitions are the actions of the system. These can be generic actions with external changes, *Ai*: $Y\ D \rightarrow Y$ (where $D = D1, \ldots, Dn$ are datatypes that may be needed for the definition of the actions of a specific FIM system), or some of the predefined actions of the system, *sendAttributes*: $Y\ U\ A \rightarrow Y$ (send a set of Attributes A of User U) and *receiveAttributes*: $Y\ A \rightarrow Y$ (receive a set of Attributes A).

The actions of the federated system are defined as transitions through the following steps;

1. If *Ai* is the action of sending a set of authentication attributes its effect on the *Attributes* observable value is defined as;

   $crl\ [sendAttributes] : sendAttributes(u, a)\ (Attributes : a1)\ (Response : r1)$
   $\Rightarrow sendAttributes(u, a)\ (Attributes : a)\ (Response : r1)\ if\ Ci(d1, \ldots, dn)$.
2. If *Ai* is the action of receiving the authentication attributes its effect on the observable value *Response* is defined as,

   $crl\ [receiveAttributes] : receiveAttributes(a)\ (Attributes : a1)\ (Response : r1)$
   $\Rightarrow receiveAttributes(a)\ (Attributes : a1)\ (Response : r1 \cup a)\ if\ Ci(d1, \ldots, dn)$.

3. If Ai is a generic action, we define;

$$crl\ [Ai] : Ai(d1, \ldots, dn)\ (oi : vi)\ D \Rightarrow Ai(d1, \ldots, dn)\ (oi : vj)\ D.$$

In the above definitions inside the brackets [] we declare the label of the transition rule. The keyword *crl* is used because the rewrite rule is conditional. $a1$ and $r1$ denote arbitrary values of the observable values *Attributes* and *Response* in the previous state, respectively. Also, $D = D1, \ldots, Dn$ denotes arbitrary data types that may needed for the definition of the transition (that depends on the specified system). Finally, *oi* are extra observable values that may be needed for the definition of the rules and vi, vj are variables of appropriate sorts. In step 4 for example, we state that the observable value will become vj if the condition of the rule is true, as this is the effect of the generic action Ai.

3.2 Specifying FIM Systems Using TLA

A federated identity management system can be expressed in terms of temporal logic of actions, if we map the **actions** of the FIM system to TLA actions. The effects of the actions are described using appropriate variables. The basic variables are called *Attributes* and *Response*, and have the same meaning as before.

The **entities** and the **objects** of the system are defined as constants using appropriate functions. For expressing the functionalities of a FIM system we need a function that takes as input a user and returns his attributes, and another function that given a set of attributes returns the corresponding user, as shown below:

$getAttributes[u \in userset] == Attributes[CHOOSE\ i \in 1..Len(User) : User[i] = u]$
$getUser[att \in attset] == User[CHOOSE\ i \in 1..Len(Attributes) : Attributes[i] = att]$

Definition 2. *Assume the following set of Actions of a federated identity management system;* Ai , $i = 1 \leq i \leq n$. *We define the following set of the variables (V) and TLA actions (A):*

- $V = V' \cup Attributes \cup Response$
- $A = \{Ai \mid 1 \leq i \leq n\}$

In this definition, *Attributes* and *Response* are the predefined variables that store the user's attributes and contain the received user attributes, while V' denotes additional variables that may be used for the definition of generic actions and their side effects. The set of TLA actions A are the actions Ai of the FIM system.

The actions of the FIM system are defined as temporal actions through the following steps;

1. If Ai is the action of sending a set of authentication attributes, it is defined as;

   $sendAttributes(a, u, d1, ..., dn) == \text{IF } Ci(d1, ..., dn) = true$
   $\text{THEN } Attributes' = a$
   $\text{ELSE } Attributes' = Attributes$
   $\text{UNCHANGED } << Response >>$

   Where a denotes the set of attributes of user u, $Ci(d1, ..., dn)$ is the condition of the action, and $d1, \ldots, dn$ are other datatypes that may be needed for the definition of the action.
2. If Ai is the action of receiving the authentication attributes it is defined as;

   $receiveAttributes(a, d1, ..., dn) == \text{IF } Ci(d1, ..., dn) = true$
   $\text{THEN } Response' = a$
   $\text{ELSE } Response' = Response$
   $\text{UNCHANGED } << Attributes >>$
3. If Ai is a generic action, we define;

   $Ai(u, d1, ..., dn) == \text{IF } Ci(d1, ..., dn) = true$
   $\text{THEN } vi' = ni$
   $\text{ELSE } vi' = vi$

In more details; Step 1 states that the action $sendAttributes(a, u, d1, ..., dn)$ is applied successfully if the condition $Ci(d1, ..., dn)$ of the action holds, and as a result the variable Attributes takes the value a while the variable Response remains unchanged (otherwise, i.e. if the condition does not hold, the variable Attributes remains unchanged). In step 2 it is stated that when the action $receiveAttributes(a, d1, ..., dn)$ is applied, the variable Response stores the value a (while the variable Attributes remains unchanged). Finally, step 3 states that when we have the application of a generic action, we describe its effects using additional variables vi, which define how their values change when the action is applied successfully.

4 Case Study: eIDAS LEPS API Connector

4.1 System Description

eIDAS Network provides a pan-European infrastructure to connect national IdPs and eID schemes based on SAML 2.0[4]. Online Service Providers who are part of this infrastructure can transparently use a trusted federated environment for cross-border user authentication, based on technical specifications which have emerged through STORK 2.0 pilots experience, and from requirements laid down in the eIDAS Implementing Act.

[4] https://ec.europa.eu/digital-building-blocks/wikis/display/DIGITAL/eID.

LEPS project [46] introduced the concept of a stand-alone API Connector that can be easily deployed within SP's premises and interoperate with existing applications and operations modes, thus making integration with a (proxy-based) eIDAS Node a standardized and lean process. The eIDAS ISS 2.0 API Connector aims to allow the SPs to retrieve eIDAS authentication values as part of a federation, resulting in the simplification of the SP deployment process within the eIDAS network.

These values contain personal private data of the person that requests authorization and thus it is important not to be forged or exposed to third parties. In addition, the adoption by the SPs requires stable and secure API connectors.

The protocol defined by the LEPS API Connector[5], is shown in Fig. 2, and can be defined as follows:

1. The user visits SP page.
2. The user's login request is redirected to ISS, this is a browser redirection. The required redirection parameters are session identifier generated by the SP, the id of the SP on ISS and the user's country of origin.
3. ISS retrieves the list of eIDAS attributes requested by the SP based on received SP id, this is done via a backchannel API call to the SP.
4. The ISS generates a suitable eIDAS SAML request and sends it to connected eIDAS node.
   (a) User Authenticates
   (b) ISS receives list of eIDAS attributes from eIDAS node
5. ISS sends list of received eIDAS attributes to the SP. This is done via a backchannel API call. The parameters of this call include the original session identifier and the received attributes as a JSON. The SP responds with an acknowledgment
6. The ISS redirects the browser to the SP success or fail page, depending on the response from the previous step (with the session id as the redirection parameter)

Additional goals of the LEPS Interconnection Supporting Service protocol are:

1. Privacy for the users: the protocol must guarantee the privacy of the user identification attributes.
2. Security for the Service Providers: The protocol must guarantee the authenticity and integrity of the received user attributes.
3. Safety for the Service Providers: The protocol must ensure that the user identified is the one actual using the service.

4.2 Formal Analysis Using Maude

Specification. A state in rewriting logic is described as a collection (soups) of observable values. In order to specify the LEPS API connector as a rewrite transition system using Definition 1, we use the following observable values.

[5] For more details about the LEPS ISS 2.0 API Connector Architecture we refer the reader to [28].

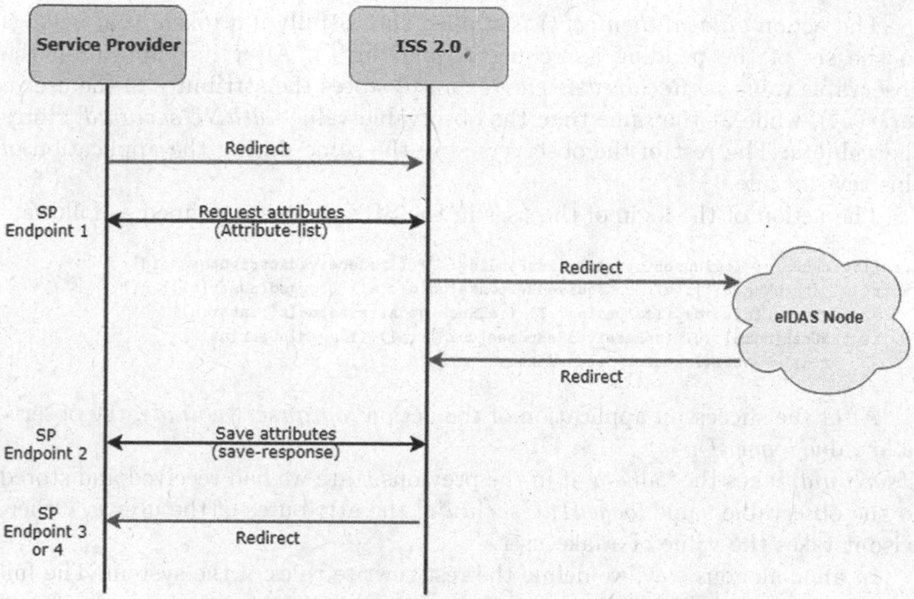

Fig. 2. LEPS ISS 2.0 API Connector Architecture.

```
op issPending:_ : TS -> Obs .
op issReceivedAttributes[_]:_ : Token Attributes -> Obs .
op spReceivedResponse[_]:_ : Token Attributes -> Obs .
op authNUser[_]:_ : Token User -> Obs .
op loggedInUser[_]:_ : Token User -> Obs .
```

Thus, an arbitrary state of the system is defined as: `(issPending: T) (issReceivedAttributes [uuid1]: a1) (authNUser[t1]: u1) (spReceivedResponse[uuid1]: a1) (loggedInUser[t1]: u1)`.

Where TS is the sort denoting a Set of Tokens, and T, $uuid1$, $a1$ and $u1$ are predefined variables representing arbitrary values of the corresponding sorts.

The transitions of the system are the actions of the FIM system:

```
op startsession : Token -> Trans .
op eidasauthent : User Token -> Trans .
op issResponse : Attributes Sender Token -> Trans .
op loginuser : User Token -> Trans .
```

The action of the authentication of a user, for example, can be described by the following rewrite rule:

```
crl [eidasauthent] : eidasauthent(u,t) (issPending: T) (issReceivedAttributes[uuid1]:
a1) (authNUser[uuid1]: u1) (spReceivedResponse[uuid1]: a1) (loggedInUser[uuid1]: u1)
   => eidasauthent(u,t) (issPending: T) (issReceivedAttributes[uuid]: attr(u))
   (authNUser[uuid]: u) (spReceivedResponse[uuid1]: a1) (loggedInUser[uuid1]: u1)
      if (uuid in T) .
```

The action *eidasauthent*(u, t) is applied successfully if a token *uuid* belongs to the set of the pending iss requests (uuid in T). After its application the observable value *issReceivedAttributes*[*uuid*] stores the attributes of the user u (*attr*(u)), while at the same time the observable value *authNUser*[*uuid*] stores the value u. The rest of the observers stay the same during the application of this rewrite rule.

The action of the login of the user in the SP's service is defined as follows:

```
rl [loginuser] : loginuser(u,uuid) (issPending: T) (issReceivedAttributes[uuid]:
attr(u)) (authNUser[t]: u) (spReceivedResponse[uuid]: a1) (loggedInUser[t1]: u1)
   => loginuser(u,uuid) (issPending: T) (issReceivedAttributes[t]: attr(u))
   (authNUser[uuid]: u) (spReceivedResponse[uuid]: a1) (loggedInUser[uuid]:
       if a1 == attr(fakeuser) then fakeuser else u fi) .
```

After the successful application of the action *loginuser*$(u, uuid)$, the observable value *loggedIn*
User[*uuid*] takes the value u, if in the previous state we had received and stored in the observable value *loggedInUser*[*uuid*] the attributes of the user u. Otherwise it takes the value of a fake user.

In an analogous way, we define the rest rewrite rules of the system. The full specification of the FIM system as a rewrite transition system can be found at [29].

Verification Support. For the verification of the FIM system, we use Maude's model checking tools to establish whether or not the desired security properties hold. We will explain the methodology using the current case study.

For the LEPS API Connector, a desired invariant security property is presented below:

SP 1 The response received by SP should denote the actual user identified via eIDAS.

This property expresses the main purpose of the system and its security goals and thus it is important for the FIM system. To prove such a property, we first define the initial state of the system:

```
eq init = (issPending: emptyTS) (issReceivedAttributes[uuid0]: null)(authNUser
[uuid0]: nil) (spReceivedResponse[uuid0]: null) (loggedInUser[uuid0]: nil) .
```

Initially the set of pending iss requests is empty, the iss received attributes and sp received response are empty as well, and there is no authenticated or logged in user in the system.

Then we use the search predicate of Maude ($\Longrightarrow$) asking to find a state reachable from the initial state of the system, in which the safety property does not hold. If the predicate does not return any such state it means that it could not find a counterexample and we can proceed with verifying the property with other stronger proving techniques such as theorem proving. In the case where Maude returns a state in which the property is violated, we have found a counterexample and we should revisit our specification and maybe redesign our system. Finally, if Maude has found a counterexample we can use the command show path id, to see the exact path of rewrite rules causing the property violation.

Returning to our case study, we ask Maude to find a state starting from the initial state of the FIM system in which the sp received response is different from the iss received attributes. This is expressed in the following way:

```
search in SYSTEM-INIT : init =>*
    (issPending: T) (issReceivedAttributes[uuid2]: attr(u)) (authNUser[uuid2]: u)
    (spReceivedResponse[uuid2]: a2) (loggedInUser[uuid2]: u1)
        such that a2 =/= attr(u) .
```

In this case Maude finds a **counterexample**:

```
Solution 1 (state 4)
states: 5  rewrites: 24 in -25734788537461ms cpu (0ms real) (~ rewrites/second)
uuid2 --> uuid2
T --> emptyTS
u --> u
att1 --> a
att2 --> fake
u1 --> fakeuser
```

By using the command *show path 4* Maude returns detailed feedback about the state path that leads to the security violation of the system (Table 1):

Table 1. LEPS API connector security violation.

System's state	State description
State 0	Initial state
State 1 = startsession(uuid2)	User initiates a session with ISS for eIDAS authentication
State 2 = eidasauthent(u, uuid2)	User u authenticates through eIDAS under ISS session uuid2
State 3 = issResponse(att1, iss, uuid2)	ISS sends attributes att1 to SP for session uuid2
State 4 = issResponse(att2, intruder, uuid2)	Adversary sends attributes att2 to SP for session uuid2
State 5 = loginuser(u, uuid2)	ISS redirects user browser to the SP with token uuid2
Counterexample: State 4	

This means that the above violation can occur after the execution of the following steps:

1. The Service Provider starts an ISS 2.0 session to authenticate a user (by generating the appropriate session id and redirecting the browser of the user)

2. The Adversary (or fake user) gains access to session id. This can happen because the user's front channel communications are not secure (either by an Adversary performing MiTM attack or actual user is malicious)
3. The user authenticates through eIDAS.
   The next steps may change order depending on SP implementation:
4. ISS 2.0 sends the received eIDAS identification attributes to the SP using the session id
5. Next, the Adversary sends fake attributes to the SP back end using the spoofed session id (in a sense impersonates ISS 2.0 to the SP, i.e. there exists an authenticity breach in the protocol). Depending on the SP business logic it will:
   (a) either store the first received set of attributes (in which case the adversary will try to send the fake attributes to the SP backend before the ISS)
   (b) or it will store the last set of attributes received for a session id.
6. ISS 2.0 redirects to SP success page with the session id as a redirection parameter
7. Finally, the SP following these steps has given access to a user with fake attributes received from step 5 (This consists the Integrity breach of the system)

Therefore, it is clear that there is a security hole in the FIM system and that it should be redesigned to avoid such security attacks. The full proof can be found at [29].

4.3 Formal Analysis Using TLA+

Specification. In order to specify the LEPS API connector in TLA+ we define the following constants and variables (according to Definition 2):

```
CONSTANT User, Token, Attributes, Sender

VARIABLES  issPending,
            issRcvdAttributes,
            spRcvdResponse,
            loggedInUser,
            authNUser
```

The initial state of the system is defined as follows:

```
Init == /\ issPending = {}
        /\ issRcvdAttributes = {}
        /\ spRcvdResponse =  {}
        /\ loggedInUser =  {}
        /\ authNUser = {}
```

As we can see in the initial state all the variables are empty.

The temporal actions of the system are the actions of the FIM system. For example, the action of sending the attributes of the user back to the SP is defined as follows:

```
issResponse(sender, uuid) ==  /\ (uuid \in issPending)
                              /\ \E r \in authNUser: r.sid = uuid
                              /\ ~(\E r \in spRcvdResponse: r.sid = uuid)
                              /\ IF sender = "ISS"
                                 THEN spRcvdResponse' = spRcvdResponse \cup
                                 {[sid |-> uuid, att |-> getAttributes
                                 [(CHOOSE r \in authNUser: r.sid = uuid).user]]}
                                ELSE spRcvdResponse' = spRcvdResponse \cup
                                {[sid |-> uuid, att |-> "a"]}
                                /\ issPending' = issPending \ {uuid}
                                /\ UNCHANGED <<issRcvdAttributes, loggedInUser,
                                authNUser>>
```

This action is applied successfully if the token *uuid* belongs to the set of iss pending requests. After the application of the action, and if the sender of the attributes is the ISS, the variable *spRcvdResponse* stores the attributes of the user that had previously been authenticated. Otherwise, it stores the attributes of a fake user. Also the token *uuid* is removed from the set of pending requests. The rest of the variables remain unchanged.

In an analogous way, we define the rest actions of the system. The full specification of the FIM system in TLA+ can be found at [29].

Verification Support. The security property of the FIM system (SP1) is formally defined in TLA+ as follows:

```
SP1 ==  \A att \in attset, uuid \in Token:
          IF \E r \in spRcvdResponse: r.sid = uuid
           THEN att = (CHOOSE r1 \in spRcvdResponse: r1.sid = uuid).att =>
                getUser[att] = (CHOOSE r2 \in authNUser: r2.sid = uuid).user
           ELSE TRUE
```

In order to prove such properties using TLC model checker we first define the model of the system. In our case we specify the following values for the declared constants:

```
Attributes <- <<"u1","u2","u3">>
Token <- {t1, t2, t3}
Sender <- {"ISS","AD"}
User <- <<"u1","u2","u3">>
```

Then we check if the invariant SP1 holds for every reachable state of the system. For the above model, TLC informs us that the invariant SP1 is violated.

In the error trace we see that the actions that lead to the state where the property does not hold are the following: $startSession(t1)$, $eidasAuth(u1, t1)$, $issResponse(iss, t1)$ and $issResponse(adv, t1)$.

In this state the variables of the system have the following values:

```
/\ authNUser = {[sid |-> t1, user |-> "u1"]}
/\ issPending = {}
/\ issRcvdAttributes = {[sid |-> t1, att |-> "a1"]}
/\ loggedInUser = {}
/\ spRcvdResponse = {[sid |-> t1, att |-> "a"]}
```

As we can observe the value of the variable *issRcvdAttributes* is different from the value of the variable *spRcvdResponse* and thus the property is violated for the reasons explained above. The full proof can be found at [29].

5 Discussion

In choosing the criteria on the basis of which the two approaches will be compared, first we need to take into account the basic characteristics of FIM systems, and the degree to which each language can express them. In particular, FIM systems are concurrent, distributed, non-deterministic, and complex (multi-component). These characteristics can be expressed in the form of the following evaluative criteria:

- Support for concurrency
- Support for distribution[6]
- Support for non-determinism
- Support for composition

Both languages satisfy the above (FIM) domain-specific criteria, and this is one of the reasons why they were chosen to begin with [27,30]; the other reason is that they are representatives of two basic families of formal methods used for the specification and verification of safety-critical systems.

Apart from this, the two methodologies should also be evaluated in terms of their technical characteristics, the support they offer to the various development phases, their usability, and how appropriate they are for modelling industrial FIM applications [32].

Table 2. Comparison of TLA+ and Maude based on modeling criteria.

Modeling criteria	TLA+	Maude
Support for modelling of time and performance properties	x	x
Expressibility of various special (domain-specific) concepts	x	x

Regarding the above modeling criteria, in TLA+ time must be defined explicitly, typically following Lamport's idea that time is just another "variable". Furthermore, according to [39], TLA+ does not allow analyzing system performance

[6] i.e. being able to model a distributed system.

and time. On the other hand, Maude provides support for both the modeling of real-time systems and their timed/metric temporal logic model checking through the Real-Time Maude tool [40]. But Maude does not provide much support for probabilistic systems, although they can be modeled "by hand" by specifying the probability distributions and the samplings explicitly. Then the PVeStA [41] or MultiVesta [42] tool could be used to statistically analyze these systems (Table 2).

Table 3. Comparison of TLA+ and Maude based on supported development phases.

Supported development phases	TLA+	Maude
Specification	x	x
Verification	x	x
Detailed feedback when a property is violated		x

While both languages are flexible enough when it comes to specifying FIM systems - both languages can specify (domain-specific) concepts, by allowing the user to define his own datatypes and can express rich concepts, because of their modular structure - an important drawback in the case of TLA+ is the way it treats types. In particular, while Maude expresses them - as well as their relations - in the form of sort declarations within the respective modules, in TLA+ types are not declared; instead the user has to perform type checking himself.

For the verification of the system's properties, TLA+ and Maude support both model checking and theorem proving techniques. This allows for the extension of the proposed methodologies to include stronger verification tools. Note however that in Maude the agreement of mathematical and operational semantics is proven by the existence of the relevant isomorphism [19]; this makes automated verification using Maude a well-founded approach.

Finally, when it comes to the feedback returned when a property is violated, Maude ranks higher than TLA+, based on our experience. While TLA+ gives a counterexample consisting in the sequence of states leading to the violation, in Maude - by using the show path command - the user gets a detailed account of the sequence of the applied rewrite rules. This is important in the case of industrial applications, as "industry is mostly interested in tools that find bugs rather than tools that prove correctness" [44] and counterexamples are a means of debugging [45] (Table 3).

Table 4. Comparison of TLA+ and Maude based on technical criteria.

Technical criteria	TLA+	Maude
Interoperability with other methods and/or other tools	x	x
Integration of methodology and tools with the usual development methods and tools (IDEs)	x	x

Even though we haven't explored the interoperability of TLA+ and Maude with other methods and/or tools, there are several attempts to combine them with other frameworks [34,35] as well as with each other [36]. Especially Maude, due to its reflective logical framework of rewriting logic, can be used to combine different logical formalisms [37].

Each specification language comes with a set of development tools integrated in an eclipse-based IDE; the TLA toolbox can be used to write and edit specifications, and run the TLC model checker, or the TLA+ proof system. The Maude system, on the other hand, is embedded into the eclipse environment via two plugins, the Maude Deamon and the Maude simple GUI (comprising a text editor and the Maude console view to control the Maude execution). Based on our experience, the TLA+ IDE is easier to use; in particular, using the Maude IDE we encountered some tedious problems, especially with the function of the Maude console view (Table 4).

Table 5. Comparison of TLA+ and Maude based on usability criteria.

Usability criteria	TLA+	Maude
Learning curve	x	
Available (online) documentation	x	
General understandability		x

Maude has a steeper learning curve than TLA+, based on our experience. TLA+ requires two-to-three weeks of practicing with the language, until someone is capable of applying it to a medium scale project. This is achieved mainly by the use of PlusCal and the available documentation. On the other hand, learning Maude is a more time-consuming process, since the user has to get familiarized with the semantics of the logics behind it. TLA+, is easier to learn and understand due its underlying "ordinary logics" [43].

Available online documentation is better in the case of TLA+, which except from a detailed webpage and the respective manual, also provides a series of easy to follow video courses. Maude also provides a detailed wiki page and manual, but has a limited number of online resources.

When it comes to general understandability (which refers to the specified model), our experience showed that Maude specifications can be understood more easily by non-experts. This is due to the fact that Maude supports equational logic, which is closer to everyday reasoning. However, L. Lamport has developed another formal specification language called PlusCal which resembles C and transpiles to TLA+, making specifications easier for programmers to understand. Nevertheless, PlusCal is designed to be used as an entry point to modelling, since it cannot express more complex specifications [47]. We should mention here that both languages support visualization/animation of the system's model [35,38] (Table 5).

Table 6. Comparison of TLA+ and Maude based on industrial applicability criteria.

Industrial applicability	TLA+	Maude
Scalability	x	x
Amount of (industrial) experience	x	x
Availability and licensing of method and tools	x	x

Although we have not examined how well the two languages scale in larger problems - this is left to be explored as future work -, both can and have been used in modeling complex real-life systems [23,39]. In the first approach, Real-Time Maude is used for analysing a novel safety pattern for medical devices. The authors demonstrate practicality and applicability of their pattern by instantiating it to a pacemaker specification, and they then validate this pattern by verifying the safety invariant in the pacemaker instantiation. In the second approach, Amazon engineers use TLA+ to prevent serious but subtle bugs from reaching production. The drawback that the Amazon engineers found with TLA+ is that it did not allow analyzing system performance and time.

As regards the amount of industrial experience, although formal methods are not yet widely adopted by the industry, both languages have been used in significant individual projects (TLA+ in formalizing Amazon Web Services, and Maude in NASA). However, due to the proliferation of safety-critical AI systems such as smart contracts and cryptocurrencies, and the security attacks they have suffered, many industrial companies have begun considering the use of formal methods to ensure the reliability of their software products [15].

Finally, both languages are open source, and free to download and use (Table 6).

Concluding, based on the experience gained throughout our research, we believe that Maude - and therefore the rewriting based proposed methodology - is more promising for the specification and verification of FIM systems.

6 Conclusion and Future Work

In this paper, we have presented two alternative approaches for the formal analysis of FIM systems, based on rewriting logic and the temporal logic of actions. Both produce executable specifications, which can then be used for the automated verification of security properties via model checking techniques. The process of formally analysing FIM systems deepened our understanding of their behavior and, thus, we believe such approaches can significantly increase the reliability of their design.

The proposed approaches were used to create two different formal models of the LEPS API Connector, and to model-check an important security property. In both cases, we discovered that the original protocol failed to satisfy the desired property, which means that the system needs to be redesigned.

To address the security violation of the FIM system we propose to "Salt and Hash" the session identifier of the ISS 2.0 response back to the SP. The SP and the ISS 2.0 admin can agree on a salt/secret during the configuration of the ISS 2.0 (same as configuring endpoints). With this change the protocol of the API Connector remains the same except from one step, i.e. instead of simply sending a JSON containing the attributes received from eIDAS and the session identifier, the ISS 2.0 sends the attributes to the SP's backend, the session identifier (uuid) and the salted hash of these values together (using MACSHA256). This way the SP can verify the authenticity of the sent information by simply calculating the same hash (since the salt is secret, it can be certain that the attributes are indeed sent from the ISS 2.0).

The redesigned API Connector was further used in the context of other projects (SEAL [48] and GRIDS [49]).

As a next step, we plan to use the rewriting logic based approach, as it is expected to be more effective for the analysis and verification of FIM systems, in more complex case studies and tackle the important issue of scalability. Our intent is to specify a composite system and see how effectively our approach can support composition/decomposition, and the expression of global system properties of correctness.

We also plan to apply the presented approach beyond FIM systems, to decentralised protocols for identity management (usually referred to as Self Sovereign Identity Management [50]). This new approach to identity management offers increase privacy protection for the user [51]. However, the protocols involved are significantly more complex due to their decentralized architecture. As a result this field could significantly benefit from the application of formal reasoning to ensure their security.

A ANNEX

A.1 Maude: Basic Syntax and Notation

In Maude, operators are functions taking zero or more arguments of some sort and returning a term of a specific sort [22]. Sorts are declared as *sort* $\langle Sort \rangle$, or *sorts* $\langle Sort\text{-}1 \rangle \ \ldots \ \langle Sort\text{-}n \rangle$ Subsorts can also be defined as *subsort* $\langle Sort\text{-}1 \rangle \ \ldots \ \langle Sort\text{-}2 \rangle$. Variables are constrained to range over a particular sort and are declared as *var* $\langle VarName \rangle : \langle Sort \rangle$. Operators are declared as *op* $\langle OpName \rangle : \langle Sort\text{-}1 \rangle \ \ldots \ \langle Sort\text{-}n \rangle \rightarrow \langle Sort \rangle$, while a constant is defined by an operator having no domain *op* $\langle OpName \rangle : \rightarrow \langle Sort \rangle$. The ground terms of our system are defined by function symbols. Ground terms denote the data values, and are build up by the data constructors which are declared as *op* $\langle OpName \rangle : \langle Sort\text{-}1 \rangle \ \ldots \ \langle Sort\text{-}n \rangle \rightarrow \langle Sort \rangle$ [*ctor*]. Equations define the declared functions and have the form *eq* $\langle Term\text{-}1 \rangle = \langle Term\text{-}2 \rangle$. A term is either a constant, or a variable, or the application of an operator to a list of argument terms. Data types as natural numbers, and Boolean values are defined as many-sorted equational specifications which consist in: a set of sorts, a set of function symbols (operators), and a set of equations defining the functions. Rewrite rules are declared as $rl\ [\langle label\rangle]\ :\ \langle Term\text{-}1\rangle\ \Rightarrow\ \langle Term\text{-}2\rangle$. If a rule is conditional it has the form $crl\ [\langle label\rangle]\ :\ \langle Term\text{-}1\rangle \Rightarrow \langle Term\text{-}2\rangle\ if\ \langle Cond\text{-}1\rangle \wedge \cdots \wedge \langle Cond\text{-}n\rangle$.

A Maude specification is organized as a collection of modules, each of which constitutes a rewrite theory comprising a term language, equations, and rewrite rules[7]. A module is declared as $[mod\ \ldots\ endmod]$, except if it does not contain rewrite rules, in which case it is called functional, and is declared as $[fmod\ \ldots\ endfm]$[8]. Thus functional modules are included as a special case in system modules. To build a new module on the basis of an old one we write *protecting* $\langle MODULE\text{-}NAME\rangle$.

The overall system has the form of a module - usually named $SYSTEM$ - build upon a number of other modules, whose rewrite rules are meant to define its concurrent evolution. States can be expressed as tuples of values $\langle a_1, a_2, b_1, b_2\rangle$, or as collections of observable values $(o_1[p_1] : a_1)\ (o_1[p_2] : a_2)\ (o_2[p_1] : b_1)\ (o_2[p_2] : b_2)$, where observable values are pairs of (parameterized) names and values. The initial state is usually defined in a separate module called $SYSTEM\text{-}INIT$ as an equation: $init\ =\ \langle initialstate\rangle$. When Maude executes, it rewrites terms according to the given specifications. Rules are applied at "random", and if an equation might be applied to a term, it will always be applied before a rewrite rule. The command search performs a breadth-first search to check whether a given state pattern can be reached from the initial state and has the form $search\ [n, m]\ in\ \langle ModId\rangle\ :\ \langle Term\text{-}1\rangle \Longrightarrow \langle Term\text{-}2\rangle$. Where n and m state the number of desired solutions and the maximum depth of the search respectively, $ModId$ is the module where the search is performed, and $\langle Term\text{-}1\rangle$, $\langle Term\text{-}2\rangle$ the terms we wish to match. Whenever there exists a match from the left-hand-side argument to the right-hand-side argument the predicate $\Longrightarrow$ evaluates to true. After the creation of the system's specification using the appropriate notation and syntax, we can employ Maude's built-in search command to model-check the desired system properties.

A.2 TLA+: Basic Syntax and Notation

In TLA+ functions are closer in nature to hashes, or dictionaries, except that you can choose to programmatically determine the value from the key. More specifically, functions can be defined in two ways: either as $Function == [s \in S \mapsto eq]$, or as $Function[s \in S] == eq$, where eq can be any equation. An ordered n-tuple, declared as $\langle e_1, \ldots, e_n\rangle$, is a function with domain $1, \ldots, n$ that maps i to e_i. Records in TLA+ are functions (that is, hashes) specified as $[key \mapsto value]$, and we query them using either ["key"], or key. Note that instead of

[7] Note that the distinction between equations and rewrite rules is only semantic. They are both executed as rewrite rules by rewrite engines, following the simple, uniform and parallelizable match-and-apply principle of term rewriting.

[8] a module's set of equations must be confluent and terminating. This is not automatically checked by Maude, but there are separate termination and confluency checkers.

key $|\rightarrow$ *value*, we can also write *key* : *set*, in which case instead of a record we get the set of all records having, for each given key, a value in the set.

Variables are of two types: rigid variables and flexible variables. Rigid variables are the well-known variables of predicate logic, which are here called constants (like the bound variables introduced by the constant operators). Flexible variables are simply called variables.

Non-constant operators include action and temporal operators. An action is a Boolean formula that may contain primed and unprimed variables. In an action an unprimed instance of a variable denotes its value in the current state, and a primed instance denotes its value in the next state. For action reasoning x and x' can be considered to be completely unrelated variables. The action operators can be defined in terms of primed variables, i.e. p' equals p with every variable x replaced by its primed version x', $[A]_e$ equals $A \vee (e' = e)$, $< A >_e$ equals $A \wedge (e' \neq e)$, and $UNCHANGED$ equals $e' = e$. Finally, some of the temporal operators are $\Box F$ (F is always true), $\Diamond F$ (F is eventually true), and $F \leadsto G$ (F leads to G).

A TLA+ specification is organized as a collection of modules, each of which comprises a sequence of statements, where a statement is a declaration, definition, assumption, or theorem. A declaration statement adds to the module the declarations of constant and variable symbols, and has the form $CONSTANT\ Name1$, $Name2$, $Name3$ and $VARIABLES\ Name1$, $Name2$, $Name3$. A declared symbol is a "free parameter" of the module. A definition always defines a symbol to equal an expression containing only declared symbols, bound variables that are different from any symbols typed by the user, and built-in operators of TLA+. Symbols can also be defined to equal operators that take arguments. A module can contain assumptions of the form ASSUME exp, where exp stands for an expression which can contain symbols declared or defined anywhere in the module. A module can also contain theorems of the form $THEOREM\ P$, which assert that P can be proven using the module's definitions and assumptions. Finally, one builds large hierarchical specifications by building a new module on the basis of old modules. One way of doing this is by using the $EXTENDS$ statement at the beginning of the module i.e. $EXTENDS\ ModuleName$, which amounts to adding the declarations and definitions from an existing module to the current one.

In TLA+ an execution - or behaviour - of a system is modelled as a sequence of states, where an event is represented by a pair of consecutive states (a step). The overall system is represented as the set of behaviours describing all of its possible executions. Such a set is described in TLA+ by an initial condition specifying the possible starting states, and a next-state relation, specifying the possible steps. In other words, each possible system behaviour must begin with a state satisfying the initial condition and its every step must satisfy the next-state relation. Note that the next-state relation which consists of a finite number of next-state actions, specifies what steps may happen; it does not specify what steps, if any, must happen. Thus, the necessary steps for the verification of a system using TLC (a model-checker and simulator of executable TLA+ specifications) are the following: first the system's specification is written using the language's specific notation and syntax. Then a model is created, for which we specify the initial condition, the next relation, and the values[9] of declared constants. Finally, after we have checked the type-correctness invariant (usually named *TypeOK*), we can proceed to check the invariance of further conditions[10] (formulas which are required to be true in every reachable state), or the validity of desired properties (temporal formulas required to be true in every possible behaviour). Note that the execution time and space grow exponentially with the size of the model.

References

1. Chadwick, D.W., Inman, G.: Attribute Aggregation in Federated Identity Management. IEEE Computer Society (2009). https://ieeexplore.ieee.org/document/5070036/references#references
2. Carretero, J., et al.: Federated Identity Architecture of the European eID System (2018). https://ieeexplore.ieee.org/abstract/document/8543142
3. EduGain. https://edugain.org/
4. eIDAS Netowrk. https://ec.europa.eu/cefdigital/wiki/pages/viewpage.action?pageId=82773030
5. Fusion Middleware Administrator's Guide for Oracle Identity Federation. https://docs.oracle.com/en/middleware/
6. LEPS. D7.2 - Cost-benefit assessment of CEF eID uptake by private sector. Petros Kavassalis (2018). http://www.leps-project.eu/node/359
7. Ghazizadeh, E., Manan, J.A., Zamani, M., Pashang, A.: A survey of security issues for cloud computing. J. Netw. Comput. Appl. **71, C**, 11–29 (2016)
8. Groß, T.: Security analysis of the SAML single sign-on browser/artifact profile. In: Proceedings ACSAC 2003 (19th Annual Computer Security Applications Conference)
9. Rodriguez, U.F., Laurent-Maknavicius, M., Incera-Dieguez, J.: Federated identity architectures. In: Proceedings MCIS 2006 (Mediterranean Conference of Information Systems)
10. Pfitzmann, B., Waidner, M.: Federated identity-management protocols. In: Proceedings of the 11th International Conferenc on Security, pp. 153–174 (2003)
11. You, J.H., Jun, M.S.: A mechanism to prevent RP phishing in OpenID system. In: Proceedings of 9th International Conference on Computer and Information Science (2010)
12. Sun, S.T.: Simple but not secure: an empirical security analysis of OAuth 2.0-based single sign-on systems. In: Proceedings of ACM Conference on Computer and Communications (2012)
13. IBM Tivoli Federated Identity Manager Data Sheet. [8] J. Carretero. Federated Identity Architecture of the European eID System. IEEE Access (2018)
14. Groß, T., Pfitzmann, B., Sadeghi, A.: Proving a WS-federation passive requestor profile with a browser model. In: Proceedings of SWS 2004 (Workshop on Secure Web Service), pp. 77–86

[9] In TLA+ every value is a set.

[10] Typical safety properties like mutual exclusion and deadlock freedom are actually invariants.

15. Formal Methods Europe (FME) industry oriented website. https://fme-industry.github.io/
16. Wuang, J., Hongxin, H.U., Bo, Z., Fei, Y., Huanguo, Z., Qianhong, W.U.: Formal analysis of information card federated identity-management protocol. Chinese J. Electron. **22**(1), 83–88 (2013)
17. Avispa. http://www.avispa-project.org/
18. Clavel, M., et al.: All About Maude - a High-performance Logical Framework: How to Specify, Program and Verify Systems in Rewriting Logic
19. Olveczky, P.C.: Designing Reliable Distributed Systems. Springer, London (2017). https://doi.org/10.1007/978-1-4471-6687-0
20. Pnueli, A.: The temporal logic of programs. In: Proceedings of the 18th Annual Symposium on Foundations of Computer Science (SFCS 1977), pp. 46–57. IEEE Computer Society, Washington, DC (1977)
21. Manna, Z., Pnueli, A.: The Temporal Logic of Reactive and Concurrent Systems. Springer, Heidelberg (1992). https://doi.org/10.1007/978-1-4612-0931-7
22. Meseguer, J., et al.: Maude Manual Version 2.7.1 (2016)
23. Sun, M., Meseguer, J., Sha, L.: A formal pattern architecture for safe medical systems. In: Ölveczky, P.C. (ed.) WRLA 2010. LNCS, vol. 6381, pp. 157–173. Springer, Heidelberg (2010). https://doi.org/10.1007/978-3-642-16310-4_11
24. Lamport, L.: Specifying Systems (2002)
25. Lamport, L.: The Operators of TLA+. SRC Technical Note (1997)
26. Lamport, L.: Specifying Concurrent Systems with TLA+ (2000)
27. Riesco, A., Verdejo, A.: Distributed applications implemented in Maude with parameterized skeletons. In: Bonsangue, M.M., Johnsen, E.B. (eds.) FMOODS 2007. LNCS, vol. 4468, pp. 91–106. Springer, Heidelberg (2007). https://doi.org/10.1007/978-3-540-72952-5_6
28. LEPS. D4.2 - eIDAS Interconnection Supporting Service. Petros Kavassalis (2018). http://www.leps-project.eu/node/347
29. λ-ForM Formal Methods Research Group. http://fsvg.math.ntua.gr/
30. Lamport, L.: The TLA+ Home Page. https://lamport.azurewebsites.net/tla/tla.html
31. Applications of Maude. http://maude.cs.illinois.edu/w/index.php/Applications
32. How to Evaluate the Suitability of a Formal Method for Industrial Deployment? A Survey Technical Report, SCCH-TR-1603 - 2016
33. Riesco, A.: An integration of CafeOBJ into full Maude. In: Escobar, S. (ed.) WRLA 2014. LNCS, vol. 8663, pp. 230–246. Springer, Cham (2014). https://doi.org/10.1007/978-3-319-12904-4_13
34. Hansen, D., Leuschell, M.: Translating B to TLA+ for validation with TLC. Sci. Comput. Program. **131**, 40–55 (2016)
35. Mason, I.A., Talcott, C.L.: IOP: the interoperability platform and IMaude: an interactive extension of Maude. Electron. Notes Theoret. Comput. Sci. **117**, 315–333 (2005)
36. Aoumer, N., Barkaoui, K., Saake, G.: Towards MAUDE-TLA based foundation for complex concurrent systems specification and certification. In: Proceedings of the 5th International Conference on Information Technology: New Generations, pp. 1305–1307 (2008)
37. Clavel, M., Meseguer, J.: Reflection and strategies in rewriting logic. Electron. Notes Theoret. Comput. Sci. **4**, 126–148 (1996)
38. ProB animator for TLA+. https://www3.hhu.de/stups/prob/index.php/TLA

39. Newcombe, C., Rath, T., Zhang, F., Munteanu, B., Brooker, M., Deardeuff, M.: How Amazon web services uses formal methods. Commun. ACM **58**(4), 66–73 (2015)
40. Olveczky, P.C., Meseguer, J.: Real-Time Maude: a tool for simulating and analyzing real-time and hybrid systems. Electron. Notes Theoret. Comput. Sci. **36**, 361–382 (2000)
41. Parallel Statistical Model Checking and Quantitative Analysis Tool. http://maude.cs.uiuc.edu/tools/pvesta/
42. MultiVeStA: Distributed Statistical Model Checking for Discrete Event Simulators. https://sysma.imtlucca.it/tools/toolmultivesta/
43. Zhang, H., Merz, S., Gu, M.: Specifying and verifying PLC systems with TLA+: a case study. Comput. Math. Appl. **60**(3), 695–705 (2010)
44. Barjaktarovic M.: The state-of-the-art in formal methods. Technical report/Wilkes University and WetStone Technologies (1998). http://www.cs.utexas.edu/users/csed/formal-methods/docs/StateFM.pdf. Accessed 20 May 2019
45. Clarke, J.E.M., et al.: Formal methods: state of the art and future directions. ACM Comput. Surv. **28**(4), 626–643 (1996)
46. Leveraging eID in the Private Sector. LEPS EU-funded project website. http://www.leps-project.eu/
47. Lamport, L.: The PlusCal Algorithm Language (2009)
48. Student and Citizen Identities Linked. SEAL EU-funded project website. https://project-seal.eu/about
49. Increasing trust with eID for developing business. GRIDS EU-funded project website. https://www.grids-cef.eu/
50. Satybaldy, A., Nowostawski, M., Ellingsen, J.: Self-sovereign identity systems. In: Friedewald, M., Önen, M., Lievens, E., Krenn, S., Fricker, S. (eds.) Privacy and Identity 2019. IAICT, vol. 576, pp. 447–461. Springer, Cham (2020). https://doi.org/10.1007/978-3-030-42504-3_28
51. Naik, N., Jenkins, P.: Governing principles of self-sovereign identity applied to blockchain enabled privacy preserving identity management systems. In: 2020 IEEE International Symposium on Systems Engineering (ISSE), pp. 1–6 (2020)

Model-Driven Edge Analytics: Practical Use Cases in Smart Manufacturing

Ivan Guevara[1,3](✉), Hafiz Ahmad Awais Chaudhary[1,3], and Tiziana Margaria[1,2,3]

[1] CSIS, University of Limerick, Limerick, Ireland
{ivan.guevara,ahmad.chaudhary,tiziana.margaria}@ul.ie
[2] Lero - The SFI Software Research Centre, Limerick, Ireland
[3] Confirm - Centre for Smart Manufacturing, Castletroy, Ireland

Abstract. In the Internet of Things (IoT) era, devices and systems generate enormous amounts of real-time data, and demand real-time analytics in an uninterrupted manner. The typical solution, a cloud-centred architecture providing an analytics service, cannot guarantee real-time responsiveness because of unpredictable workloads and network congestion. Recently, edge computing has been proposed as a solution to reduce latency in critical systems. For computation processing and analytics on edge, the challenges include handling the heterogeneity of devices and data, and achieving processing on the edge in order to reduce the amount of data transmitted over the network.

In this paper, we show how low-code, model-driven approaches benefit a Digital Platform for Edge analytics. The first solution uses EdgeX, an IIoT framework for supporting heterogeneous architectures with the eKuiper rule-based engine. The engine schedules fully automatically tasks that retrieve data from the Edge, as the infrastructure near the data is generated, allowing us to create a continuous flow of information. The second solution uses FiWARE, an IIoT framework used in industry, using IoT agents to accomplish a pipeline for edge analytics. In our architecture, based on the DIME LC/NC Integrated Modelling Environment, both integrations of EdgeX/eKuyper and FiWARE happen by adding an External Native DSL to this Digital Platform. The DSL comprises a family of reusable Service-Independent Building blocks (SIBs), which are the essential modelling entities and (service) execution capabilities in the architecture's modelling layer. They provide users with capabilities to connect, control and organise devices and components, and develop custom workflows in a simple drag and drop manner.

Keywords: Smart manufacturing · Internet of Things · Edge analytics · Model-Driven development · XMDD · DIME · Low-code/No-code

1 Introduction

The key challenges in the adoption of advanced knowledge, information management and AI systems in smart manufacturing ecosystems [7,9,28] center on close

T. Margaria and B. Steffen (Eds.): ISoLA 2022, LNCS 13704, pp. 406–421, 2022.
https://doi.org/10.1007/978-3-031-19762-8_29

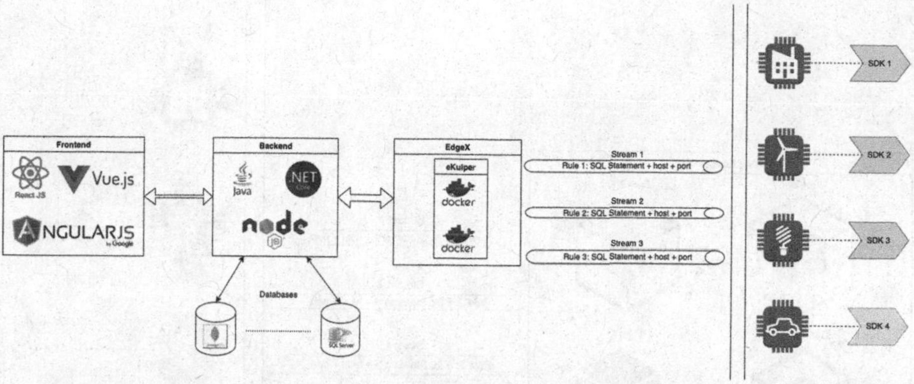

Fig. 1. Conventional approach for developing an edge analytics pipeline

collaboration between industries and research centres and sustainable manufacturing and products. These problems require the orchestration of the different actuators involved, dealing with heterogeneous protocols, different types of architectures and latency in edge devices. Such requirements pose great challenges to the stakeholders, due to the inherent complexity of the systems themselves, the possibility of boilerplate or legacy code needing to be understood and amended, and people lacking necessary skills that are nevertheless required to fully build a system with the desired characteristics. Therefore, solving the underlying data integration problem needs to be simplified. We adopt two open-source frameworks to address this heterogeneity and the corresponding integration problem. FiWARE [27] is an open-source platform supported by the European Union to develop and deploy IoT applications. The main idea behind FiWARE is to support collaboration and establish an open, free architecture that allow companies to develop their products in this context. On the other hand, EdgeX Foundry is a scalable and flexible software framework that facilitates the interoperability between devices and applications at the IoT Edge level. It acts as a middleware between the cloud and enterprise applications on one side, and the devices and "things" on the other side, providing a uniform way to define communication pipelines [8].

The traditional approach shown in Fig. 1 presents a significant complexity during the development cycle: to complete an entire application, one has to define and manage at the code level a frontend, backend, databases, setting up IoT frameworks and the IoT devices, and finally creating the workflows to interact with the Edge. In this approach, users deal with:

1. having to produce code by hand, that could be possibly be prone to errors,
2. a steep learning curve to fully understand the procedures involved, and
3. a large number of state-of-the-art technology skills, where is difficult to find specially trained people.

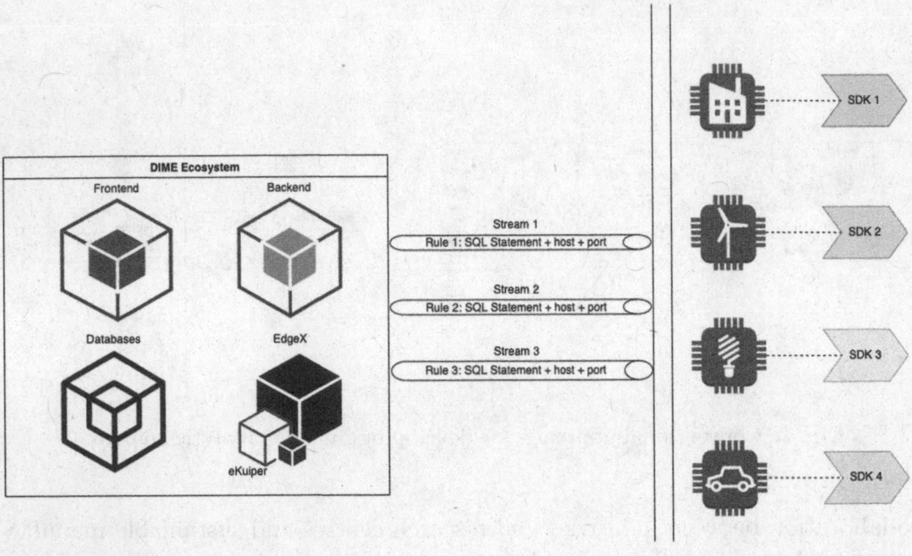

Fig. 2. MDD approach for developing the edge analytics pipeline using EdgeX/eKuiper in DIME

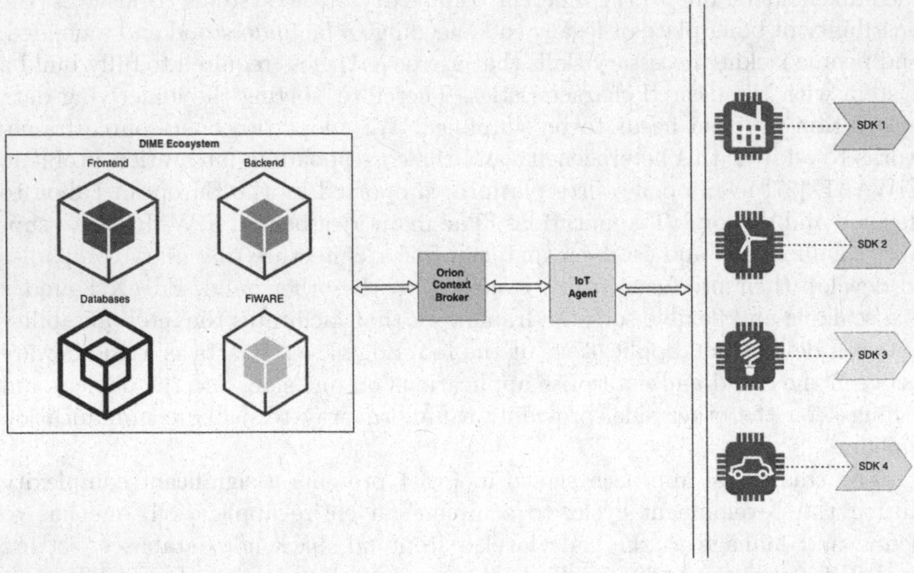

Fig. 3. FiWARE Architecture using the Context Broker and the IoT Agent in DIME

In contrast, building the same system application using models brings advantages over the conventional direct code approach. As shown in Fig. 2 and Fig. 3 this model-centred approach provides a more straightforward way to build the system: adequate models provide the low-code solutions. They enable a rapid and efficient development of applications involving IoT, EdgeX/FiWARE and eKuiper/IoT Agents using the DIME Domain-oriented Integrated Modelling Environment [1]. DIME empowers prototype-driven application development following the One Thing Approach [18] and enables an Extreme Model-Driven Design collaboration between domain experts and programmers [19]. Our low-code solution integrates both platforms by means of the DIME extension through an External Native DSL for eKuiper (see Fig. 2) and the FiWARE IoT Agent (see Fig. 3). This way, the rich facilities provided by the EdgeX/FiWARE framework become part of the DIME ecosystem, recreating in the context of the Digital Platform, a m2m communication in a low-code fashion way. Either way, users can build and deploy a cohesive platform without having to deal with complex cross-platform integrations. We take advantage of DIME's flexible capability to extend its behaviour by adding a new palette of external native SIBs, implemented using Java code. Once the code is available, we define our convenient SIB-level API to interact with the Edge.

Considering the three challenges posed by a traditional code-based adoption, there is no need to deal with complex logic functionality or to understand boilerplate code (1), as in our architecture we rely on reusable Service Independent Building blocks (SIBs), executable and reusable modelling components previously defined and implemented by experts, and the application development amounts to composing the entire workflow process using such provided SIBs, and then generating the code automatically from that workflow and the SIBs that occur in it. This also lowers the learning curve (2), as the user of our system does not need to master the technical details nor implementation of the platform, and thus we also avoid the shortage of trained experts (3).

The rest of the paper is organized as follows: Sect. 2 covers related work in the application domain as well as some examples of our technology of choice. Section 3 explains in detail our API and DSL setup, the architecture developed to support the functionalities enabled and the corresponding integration work. Section 4 describes a use case that uses the developed DSL, and Sect. 5 reports our conclusions.

2 Related Work

2.1 Literature Review

Related work in the context of Model-Driven design with a focus in Smart Manufacturing evidences the importance of low-code approaches. Cadavid et al. [3] state the goal is "to be able to reuse processes definitions, by having readily available manufacturing actions that can be chained together to form compound processes". The authors utilise Eclipse Papyrus [14], an open-source Model-Based Engineering tool that uses different representation schemas (such as UML 2.5.0, SysML 1.1 and 1.4, etc.) to create a high-level representation of the system. It also contains a framework called Moka [10], that enables executing models using an animation and simulation framework. It leverages the usage of models to fully setup a working workflow "representing a gain of time and effort as it provides a starting point of existing processes". Trenzer et al. [30] provide a model-driven approach for developing data collection architectures. The authors consider these model-driven solutions as "capable of significantly lower manual implementation efforts" and leverage the usage of Eclipse Modeling Framework (EMF) [26]. EMF is a framework and code generation facility for building tools based on a structured data model. It provides support to produce a set of Java classes for the model, along with a set of adapter classes that enable viewing and command-based editing of the model, and a basic editor[1] to build the architecture itself, making the development more straightforward. The framework developed by the authors still is not being considered for productive environments, as there is no automatic link and synchronization between the graphical representation and the model instances, which represents a clear impediment when deploying an application. Vogel-Heuser et al. [31] propose a Model-Based System Engineering (MBSE) approach based on the systems modeling language SysML [12] that "enables an optimized deployment of a production system's automation software to automation hardware resources". The system might leverage itself from implementations such as SystemC [20] used for functional and timing verification and code synthesis (hardware and software). SystemC allows design and verification at the system level, allowing to test and verify any kind of architectural decision at a high level. Thramboulidis et al. [29] utilizes a Model Integrated Mechatronics (MIM) in the context of a cyber-physical system, where MIM belongs to the MDE paradigm for the development of Manufacturing Ecosystems. These ecosystems are defined as a composition of other mechatronics components, such as mechanics, electronics and software with the objective to do specific tasks. The authors define a meta-model with UML [13] notation and leverage from tools such as SysML and RDF [2]. The process goes through a "translation process" in order to get the specification of then tasks and act in consequence.

2.2 Own Previous Work

Previous state-of-the-art solutions developed with DIME, show the potential of this approach in simplifying the integration of heterogeneous components and application development. In the smart manufacturing context, in terms of integration of heterogeneous domains and technologies. Margaria et al. [16] show a remote control of a UR3 robot through a web-based application connecting to an IP address. Operations through domain-specific languages (DSLs) are added to DIME for the UR3, then used in the workflow of the Web application to control the robotic arm. Margaria et al. [17] show how to extract the digital twin of this composite system (robot and controller). Chaudhary et al. [6] show use cases for integration of the platform to support R and REST services. R is a programming language for statistical computing and graphical visualization of the outcomes. It provides statistical capabilities (linear, nonlinear, statistical

[1] https://www.eclipse.org/modeling/emf/ - accessed 4th Sept. 2022.

tests, time series analysis, classification etc.), one of its strengths is the ease to produce well-designed publication-quality plots with mathematical symbols and formulas [22]. Representational State Transfer (REST), in the other hand, is an architectural style for service-oriented computing, very popular as a simple way of exposing service interfaces, especially in comparison with earlier protocols such as the complex and heavyweight SOAP/WS-* and similar RPC-inspired protocols [21]. Guevara et al. [11] includes a preliminar work in eKuiper as well, where sets the foundations of SIBs to leverage the MDD approach for Edge Analytics in the context of a Smart Manufacturing case.

The integration of FiWARE and eKuiper in DIME presented in this paper is a contribution to the construction of the Digital Thread Platform described in Margaria et al. [15], that aims to include heterogeneous technologies within a DIME-based low-code platform for application development in order to facilitate a seamless and rapid development of end-to-end applications that include functionalities stemming from different domains. Currently, the platform also includes a persistence layer with MongoDB and ElephantSQL, analytics in R and using cloud-based services (AWS), IoT capabilities using MQTT directly and through EdgeX, and the already mentioned robotics and REST capabilities.

3 Methodology

For both integrations, we introduce virtualization through the Service-Independent Building blocks (SIBs) mechanism of DIME. SIBs are high-level abstractions that hide their implementation details, and lift the technical vocabulary used in the system design and implementation to the domain specific language of the domain experts. This reduces the technical complexity of definition, design, and implementation of use cases, focussing the design on the specific step of the problem. Domain-specific collections of SIBs that integrate external tools or platforms are called here External Native DSLs (domain specific languages). This significantly speeds up the development of larger components and applications.

We sketch next the integration process (Sect. 3.1), then delve into EdgeX (Sect. 3.2) and FiWARE (Sect. 3.3) the analytics on the Edge (Sect. 3.4), and through eKuiper (Sect. 3.5).

3.1 The Integration Process

To achieve a proper integration of external resources and capabilities, application and DSL designers need to tackle together the following steps:

1. definition of the use case,
2. define the SIBs palette,
3. if the SIBs are missing, define functions and methods
4. define the application logic inside the SIB
5. test functionality,
6. use the SIB in the application domain

As in the traditional software development lifecycle, once the use case is defined (Step 1), we define in general terms the SIBs needed in our system (Step 2). A SIB declaration (Step 3) has a very user-friendly syntax, as shown in Fig. 4 (left) to upload device profile into system. A SIB declaration consists essentially of its signature, which is easy to read and produce: it has the same structure and elements as a function/method declaration. It starts with the SIB name, then it specifies the full path to the Java package where the class is located (the functionality itself) and the name of the method to call it. Then it lists the input parameters and the outgoing branches, i.e., the different continuation paths the function can take, they are mostly failure/success, but in general there can be many outgoing branches) and the (optional) outputs associated with each branch.

```
sib upload_device_profile: info.scce.dime.app.demo.Native#read_device_data
  file_path : text
  -> success
  file_handler : file
  -> failure
  exception : text
```

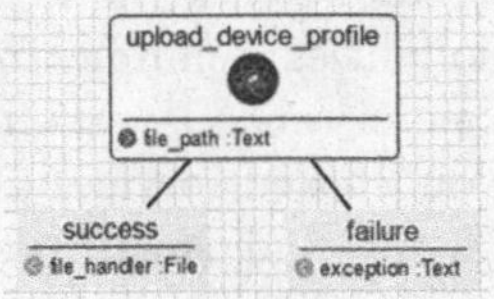

Fig. 4. Syntax and representation of a SIB within DIME

Once the SIB is properly declared, in Step 4 we define the functions and methods that implement it in Java code. A Java SIB body takes advantages of all the services and functionality provided by the Eclipse IDE and the OpenJDK 11, which include performance improvements and functional programming approaches that are useful for improving syntactic sugar. Alternatively, a complex SIB can itself be implemented by a process (Step 4 too) and contain business logic and other SIBs.

In Step 5, once a SIB has both a declaration and an implementation, it is thoroughly tested in order to make sure it fulfils the expected behaviour. We recommend using unit testing and integration tests for the expected use and the most common kinds of incorrect use: trying to emulate a typical use case it will be expected to work with is effective to find potential issues and resolve them.

Finally, in Step 6 the functionality is ready to be used into the DIME development environment (loading the SIB, or the palette to which it belongs), and then used in applications by dragging and dropping its symbol from the list of SIBs available in our platform.

3.2 Architectural Components in EdgeX

The EdgeX Foundry framework facilitates this interaction with simpler data structures to get the information from the IoT devices. The architecture is basically composed by four main services: 1) Device Services 2) Core Services 3) Supporting Services. 4) Application Services. The first layer are the connectors which interacts with the IoT devices (sensors, actuators, sensors + actuators) to get data from/to them. The second layer, Core Services, contains the information about what devices are connected, the type of data going through and how to connect with them. The third layer, Supporting Services, contains eKuiper (the rule engine framework), and other frameworks for logging, scheduling and data cleaning. Finally, the fourth layer, the Application Services which extracts, process and send data from EdgeX to any endpoint of choice[2]

3.3 Architectural Components in FiWARE

FiWARE as previously mentioned, is another open source platform to deploy Internet of Things applications. FiWARE uses Docker containers and the architecture consists of two main components: 1) the Orion Context Broker and 2) the IoT Agent. The Contex Broker allows us to manage the entire lifecycle of context information, including updates, queries, registrations and subscriptions. The information consists of entities (i.e., objects we want to track) and their attributes (i.e., the properties of the objects). Orion implements an NGSIv2 server to manage information and availability, and it also provides creational capabilities to include elements and manage them through updates and queries. NGSI is a standard by the ETSI (European Telecommunications Standards Institute) to improve the communication framework with these types of devices. The IoT Agent acts as a bridge between the IoT devices and the Context Broker which maintains the state for each of them. The IoT Agent takes care of the requests from IoT devices and the petitions created from the user in an uniform way, also taking into consideration the security for each actuator/sensor[3].

3.4 Computing on the Edge and Data Analytics

Edge Analytics could be defined as "receive and interpret data from Edge computing". Specifically, based on the information collected from the sensors, we establish a decision-making process and take actions based on those decisions. Edge Analytics can span several levels of complexity, from a simple SQL query to retrieve a few rows of data to complex heterogeneous machine learning systems to leverage a PdM system (predictive maintenance). There are currently two main approaches to accomplish Edge analytics:

1. run the analytics service in each device/sensor, or
2. deliver data from sensors to an analytics service in the cloud.

According to Shi et al. [23], the first option has an advantage over the second one for three main reasons:

1. Computing tasks in the cloud are efficient, but it faces a bottleneck in the speed of data, i.e., the bandwidth to transport the data towards the network.

[2] https://www.edgexfoundry.org/software/platform/#ApplicationServices - accessed 7th Sept. 2022.

[3] http://www.fiware.org - accessed the 7th of September.

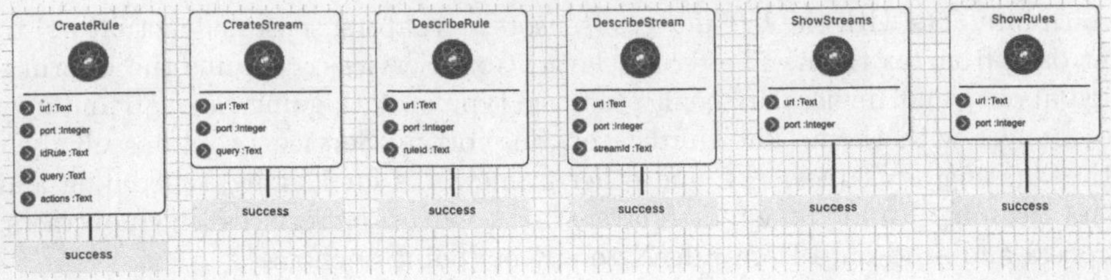

Fig. 5. SIB Library created to abstract and virtualize the logic building blocks from the EdgeX eKuiper Rule Engine

2. Everything is becoming part of the Edge IoT environment, leading to a massive production of data for which the conventional cloud computing approach is not efficient enough.
3. Security: as the edge devices are becoming data consumers, it makes sense to process data in edge devices (e.g., mobile phones) instead of uploading raw data to cloud services for subsequent processing.

3.5 Towards Model-Driven Edge Analytics with IoT Agents and eKuiper

Our providing a model-driven approach for edge analytics using two main tools, 1) EdgeX and 2) FiWARE, builds upon previous work already done with DIME and EdgeX [4,5], where we retrieved data from IoT devices using REST API. Both EdgeX and FiWARE technologies provide many functionalities to handle data from the Edge. However, they still rely on complex code that an adopter needs to understand. Due to the complexity of the system itself, it also lacks the simplicity of an easy setup of the environment. In the specific context of the Digital Thread Platform realised with DIME, its XMDD paradigm gives us several benefits. The integration via SIBs, as per steps 2 to 6 described in Sect. 3.1, leads to the DSLs of Figs. 5 and 11, which show the SIBs created to automate the set-up and use workflow.

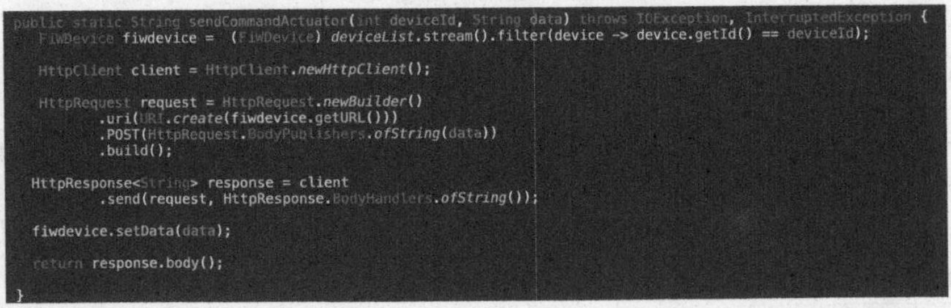

```
public static String sendCommandActuator(int deviceId, String data) throws IOException, InterruptedException {
    FiWDevice fiwdevice =  (FiWDevice) deviceList.stream().filter(device -> device.getId() == deviceId);

    HttpClient client = HttpClient.newHttpClient();

    HttpRequest request = HttpRequest.newBuilder()
            .uri(URI.create(fiwdevice.getURL()))
            .POST(HttpRequest.BodyPublishers.ofString(data))
            .build();

   HttpResponse<String> response = client
            .send(request, HttpResponse.BodyHandlers.ofString());

   fiwdevice.setData(data);

   return response.body();
}
```

Fig. 6. Code using the traditional approach (part 1)

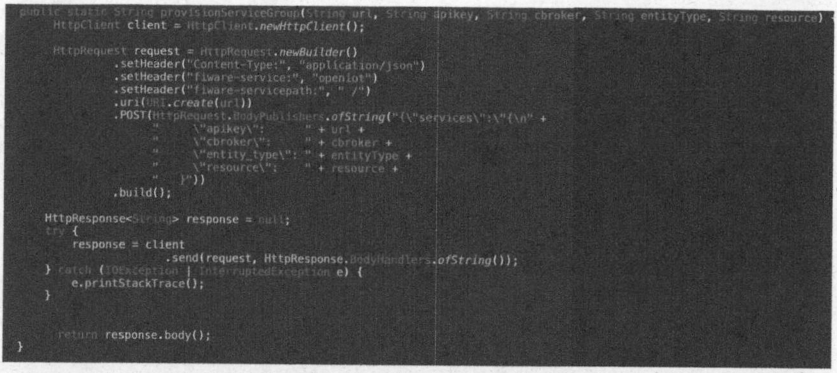

```
public static String provisionServiceGroup(String url, String apikey, String cbroker, String entityType, String resource) {
    HttpClient client = HttpClient.newHttpClient();

    HttpRequest request = HttpRequest.newBuilder()
            .setHeader("Content-Type:", "application/json")
            .setHeader("fiware-service:", "openiot")
            .setHeader("fiware-servicepath:", " /")
            .uri(URI.create(url))
            .POST(HttpRequest.BodyPublishers.ofString("{\"services\":\"{\n" +
                "     \"apikey\":       " + url +
                "     \"cbroker\":      " + cbroker +
                "     \"entity_type\": " + entityType +
                "     \"resource\":     " + resource +
                "   }"))
            .build();

   HttpResponse<String> response = null;
   try {
       response = client
               .send(request, HttpResponse.BodyHandlers.ofString());
   } catch (IOException | InterruptedException e) {
       e.printStackTrace();
   }


    return response.body();
}
```

Fig. 7. Code using the traditional approach (part 2)

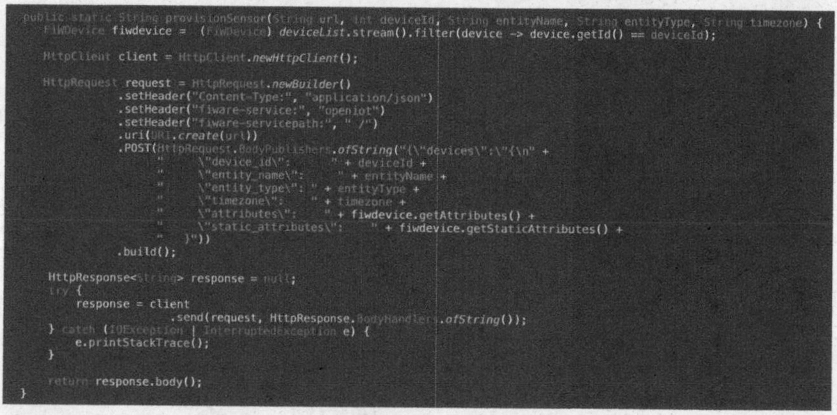

```
public static String provisionSensor(String url, int deviceId, String entityName, String entityType, String timezone) {
   FiWDevice fiwdevice =  (FiWDevice) deviceList.stream().filter(device -> device.getId() == deviceId);

   HttpClient client = HttpClient.newHttpClient();

   HttpRequest request = HttpRequest.newBuilder()
            .setHeader("Content-Type:", "application/json")
            .setHeader("fiware-service:", "openiot")
            .setHeader("fiware-servicepath:", " /")
            .uri(URI.create(url))
            .POST(HttpRequest.BodyPublishers.ofString("{\"devices\":\"{\n" +
                "     \"device_id\":       " + deviceId +
                "     \"entity_name\":      " + entityName +
                "     \"entity_type\": " + entityType +
                "     \"timezone\":     " + timezone +
                "     \"attributes\":     " + fiwdevice.getAttributes() +
                "     \"static_attributes\":      " + fiwdevice.getStaticAttributes() +
                "   }"))
            .build();

   HttpResponse<String> response = null;
   try {
       response = client
               .send(request, HttpResponse.BodyHandlers.ofString());
   } catch (IOException | InterruptedException e) {
       e.printStackTrace();
   }

   return response.body();
}
```

Fig. 8. Code using the traditional approach (part 3)

As we can see in Fig. 6, Fig. 7 and Fig. 8, the traditional code-level approach requires an average of 15 LOC per functionality. The code concerns the management of: 1) REST API requests and 2) Stream Java API, therefore requiring to be versed also in 3) functional programming, 4) exceptions, and 5) Java HttpRequest API. In a quick comparison with the DIME solution shown in Fig. 9, the workflow solution is more straightforward to setup and execute over the system. Despite the fact we still need to define the technical properties, this model level is more manageable and easier to understand than the traditional code-based approach.

4 Results and Discussion

4.1 EdgeX and eKuiper Integrations

The DIME version of the Edge Analytics application system, using EdgeX and eKuiper, has the simple setup workflow shown in Fig. 10 and a simpler way to

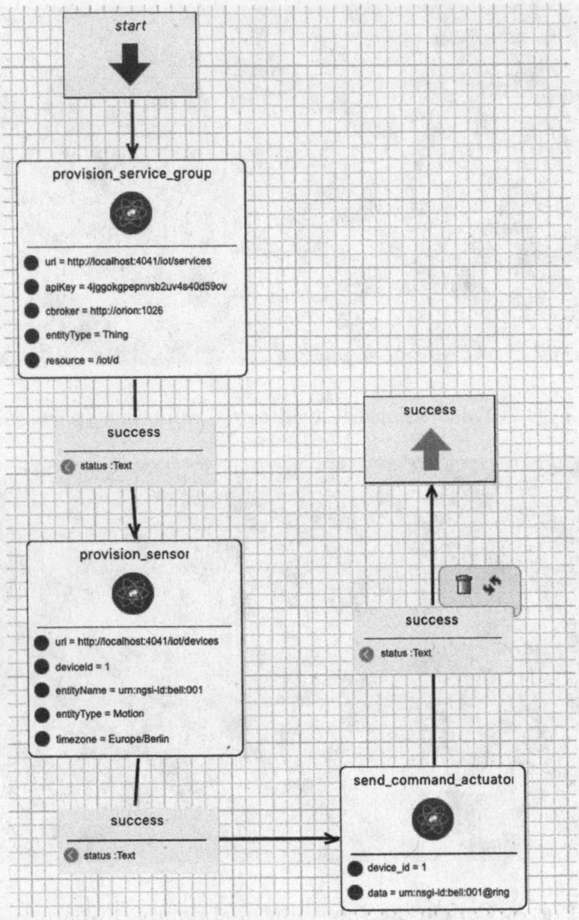

Fig. 9. DIME workflow to support interaction with FiWARE

connect the different functionalities and tasks, such as create a device or start a rule to perform analytics on the edge. Also, here we rely on the model-driven approach: defining the different properties of each SIB and connecting them along the control flow and data flow puts the focus on the problem instead of in the implementation details:

1. we create a given Device (with an internal reference to it),
2. start it,
3. create a stream to communicate,
4. create a rule,
5. show the available rules,
6. and finally the available streams.

In spite of its simplicity, this application is complete and serves as template for adoption and blueprint for further evolution. The definitions of the SIBs

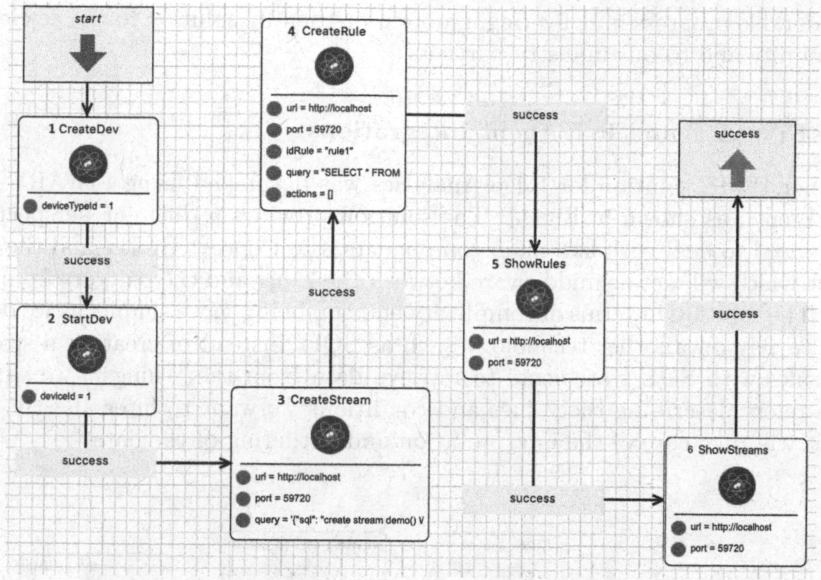

Fig. 10. DIME workflow for the set-up and use of eKuiper rule-based analytics

happen through their declaration: it is easy to understand and change by any person with no technical knowledge of software development, as the SIBs declarations and use are very intuitive to follow. Due to the formal nature of these models, they are also a vehicle to formal verification and in perspective automated synthesis techniques, e.g., along the lines of Steffen et al. [24].

There is still much more functionality to be addressed in both platforms. The DSLs integrations will happen organically over time, following the requirements of the additional use cases. We expect the additions to be carried out mostly by adopters of the Digital Thread platform, and not by ourselves. Our concern here is to show the simplicity and elegance of this set up in DIME, as a combination of SIB DSL and workflows. In parallel we are working on refining and testing this approach on productive environments.

We rely for the rule definition language on SQL queries (this is the original eKuiper language of choice) and on the expertise of those who define them, as well as their understanding for structuring a JSON object. With the DIME approach one could consider a further abstraction layer that frees the user form the need to know SQL and JSON, through another DSL that lifts those functionalities to a more intuitive language/schema followed by transformation to SQL/JSON. This is similar to the approach taken in [25] for the DSL-driven integration of highly parameterized HTTP services and REST services as a hierarchy of DSLs at different levels of abstraction and virtualization.

We intend to tackle these still pending issues in the future, in order to make the model-driven programming environment more appealing to expert users who are not programmers. So far, we consider our contribution to constitute a considerable progress in delivering a more user-friendly solution to the academic community and to our industry partners.

4.2 FiWARE and IoT Agent Integrations

Another DIME solution for Edge Analytics was developed using FiWARE and IoT Agents, as shown in Fig. 11. The solution provides a different perspective, as we need to deal with two main components, the Context Broker and the IoT Agent which will act as middleware between the Edge and the requests from the user. The solution in terms of complexity ends up being more simple, as we don't need to rely on another technology such as SQL. Instead of creating a stream and rules with SQL statements to retrieve data from the "things", we simply use a query describing the values and conditions we want to filter and the IoT Agent will take care of the interpretation and gathering of the data.

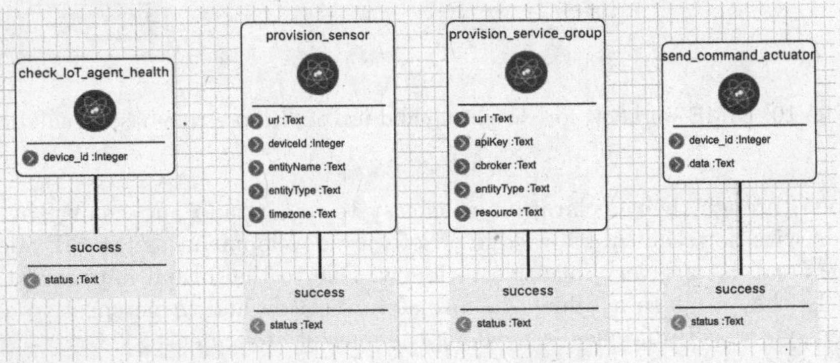

Fig. 11. SIB Library created for interaction with FiWARE

5 Conclusion

This paper establishes a major step towards an edge analytics low-code solution for Smart Manufacturing environments. This happens in the context of the Digital Thread Platform for smart advanced manufacturing currently under development, and through the adoption and extension of the DIME no-code/low-code platform. This technology choice privileges domain-specific abstractions that empower people with non-technical or non-programming expertise to create, deploy and run fully functional analytics solutions, virtualizing the underlying technologies, and thus making them opaque to the application designers that reuse the SIBs as pre-defined, pre-tested building blocks. We showed this on the basis of the eKuiper Rule Engine, that is part of the EdgeX ecosystem and IoT Agents as part of the FiWARE ecosystem, The effect is to democratise the development cycle and tackle down the high learning curve that is otherwise required in order to manage all these layers of knowledge. We believe this move can have a significant impact on the ability of manufacturing experts to use advanced analytics and, more in general, integration and interoperability platforms that they would not be able to program, manage and evolve with the current need of heterogeneous coding and architectural expertise.

The platform still needs some refinement (testing in productive environments and improvement of user experience), but we have a fairly complete palette of Service-Independent Building blocks (SIBs) to encapsulate the behaviour of each step and provide a high-level abstraction to the users. All they need to do is understand the SIBs and their parameters, and then orchestrate them in an appropriate way using our Digital Thread platform. Our case study targets the usage of the EdgeX Foundry framework and its advanced services like the eKuiper Rule Based engine for analytics, and FiWARE with the Context Broker and the IoT Agents, leverages a more straightforward way to use it, having to deal much less with configuration files and boiler-plate code.

Acknowledgements. This work was supported by the Science Foundation Ireland grants 13/RC/2094 (Lero, the Irish Software Research Centre) and 16/RC/ 3918 (Confirm, the Smart Manufacturing Research Centre).

References

1. Boßelmann, S., et al.: DIME: a programming-less modeling environment for web applications. In: Margaria, T., Steffen, B. (eds.) ISoLA 2016. LNCS, vol. 9953, pp. 809–832. Springer, Cham (2016). https://doi.org/10.1007/978-3-319-47169-3_60
2. Bray, T.: What Is RDF (1998). https://www.xml.com/pub/a/2001/01/24/rdf1.html. Accessed 4 Sept 2022
3. Cadavid, J., Alférez, M., Gérard, S., Tessier, P.: Conceiving the model-driven smart factory. In: Proceedings of the 2015 ICSSP 2015, pp. 72–76 (2015)
4. Chaudhary, H.A.A., et al.: Model-driven engineering in digital thread platforms: a practical use case and future challenges. In: Margaria, T., Steffen, B. (eds.) ISoLA 2022. LNCS, vol. 13704, pp. 195–207. Springer, Cham (2022)
5. Chaudhary, H.A.A., Guevara, I., John, J., Singh, A., Margaria, T., Pesch, D.: Low-code internet of things application development for edge analytics. In: IFIP International Internet of Things Conference. Springer (2022)
6. Chaudhary, H.A.A., Margaria, T.: Integrating external services in DIME. In: Margaria, T., Steffen, B. (eds.) ISoLA 2021. LNCS, vol. 13036, pp. 41–54. Springer, Cham (2021). https://doi.org/10.1007/978-3-030-89159-6_3
7. Dingli, D.J., et al.: The manufacturing industry-coping with challenges. Technical report (2012)
8. EdgeX Foundry: The preferred edge IoT plug and play ecosystem - eabled open source software platform. https://www.edgexfoundry.org/. Accessed May 2022
9. Ee Shiang, L., Nagaraj, S.: Impediments to innovation: evidence from Malaysian manufacturing firms. Asia Pac. Bus. Rev. **17**(02), 209–223 (2011)
10. Guermazi, S., Tatibouet, J., Cuccuru, A., Dhouib, S., Gérard, S., Seidewitz, E.: Executable modeling with fUML and Alf in Papyrus: tooling and experiments. Strategies **11**, 12 (2015)

11. Guevara, I., Chaudhary, H.A.A., Margaria, T.: A low-code proposal for a rule-based engine integration in a digital thread platform context. In: International Manufacturing Conference IMC 38 (2022)
12. Holt, J., Perry, S.: SysML for systems engineering, vol. 7. IET (2008)
13. Jacobson, I., Booch, G., Rumbaugh, J.: The unified modeling language. University Video Communications (1996)
14. Lanusse, A., et al.: Papyrus UML: an open source toolset for MDA. In: Proceedings of the Fifth ECMDA-FA 2009, pp. 1–4. Citeseer (2009)
15. Margaria, T., Chaudhary, H.A.A., Guevara, I., Ryan, S., Schieweck, A.: The interoperability challenge: building a model-driven digital thread platform for CPS. In: Margaria, T., Steffen, B. (eds.) ISoLA 2021. LNCS, vol. 13036, pp. 393–413. Springer, Cham (2021). https://doi.org/10.1007/978-3-030-89159-6_25
16. Margaria, T., Schieweck, A.: The digital thread in Industry 4.0. In: Ahrendt, W., Tapia Tarifa, S.L. (eds.) IFM 2019. LNCS, vol. 11918, pp. 3–24. Springer, Cham (2019). https://doi.org/10.1007/978-3-030-34968-4_1
17. Margaria, T., Schieweck, A.: Towards engineering digital twins by active behaviour mining. In: Olderog, E.-R., Steffen, B., Yi, W. (eds.) Model Checking, Synthesis, and Learning. LNCS, vol. 13030, pp. 138–163. Springer, Cham (2021). https://doi.org/10.1007/978-3-030-91384-7_8
18. Margaria, T., Steffen, B.: Business process modeling in the jABC: the one-thing approach. In: Handbook of Research on Business Process Modeling, pp. 1–26. IGI Global (2009)
19. Margaria, T., Steffen, B.: eXtreme model-driven development (XMDD) technologies as a hands-on approach to software development without coding. In: Tatnall, A. (ed.) Encyclopedia of Education and Information Technologies, pp. 732–750. Springer, Cham (2020). https://doi.org/10.1007/978-3-319-60013-0_208-1
20. Panda, P.R.: SystemC: a modeling platform supporting multiple design abstractions. In: Proceedings of the 14th International Symposium on Systems Synthesis, pp. 75–80 (2001)
21. Pautasso, C., Wilde, E., Alarcon, R.: REST: Advanced Research Topics and Practical Applications. Springer, New York (2013). https://doi.org/10.1007/978-1-4614-9299-3
22. R: The R project for statistical computing. https://www.r-project.org/. Accessed May 2022
23. Shi, W., Cao, J., Zhang, Q., Li, Y., Xu, L.: Edge computing: vision and challenges. IEEE Internet Things J. **3**(5), 637–646 (2016)
24. Steffen, B., Margaria, T., Claßen, A., et al.: Heterogeneous analysis and verification for distributed systems. In: Software-Concepts and Tools, vol. 17, pp. 13–25. Springer (1996)
25. Steffen, B.: DSL-driven integration of http services in dime. BSc thesis, Fakultät für Informatik. TU Dortmund, Germany (2022)
26. Steinberg, D., Budinsky, F., Merks, E., Paternostro, M.: EMF: Eclipse Modeling Framework. Pearson Education, London (2008)
27. FIWARE Team: FiWARE (2022). https://www.fiware.org/. Accessed 5 Sept 2022
28. Thomas, A.J., Byard, P., Evans, R.: Identifying the UK's manufacturing challenges as a benchmark for future growth. J. Manuf. Technol. Manage. (2012)
29. Thramboulidis, K., Kontou, I., Vachtsevanou, D.C.: Towards an IoT-based framework for evolvable assembly systems. IFAC-PapersOnLine **51**(11), 182–187 (2018)
30. Trunzer, E., Vogel-Heuser, B., Chen, J.K., Kohnle, M.: Model-driven approach for realization of data collection architectures for cyber-physical systems of systems to lower manual implementation efforts. Sensors **21**(3), 745 (2021)

31. Vogel-Heuser, B., Wildermann, S., Teich, J.: Towards the co-evolution of industrial products and its production systems by combining models from development and hardware/software deployment in cyber-physical systems. Prod. Eng. Res. Devel. **11**(6), 687–694 (2017). https://doi.org/10.1007/s11740-017-0765-0

Author Index

Ali, Shaukat 9
Arcaini, Paolo 9

Bate, Iain 37
Bharti, Sourabh 219
Bogomolov, Sergiy 139
Boldo, Michele 184
Bombieri, Nicola 184
Boßelmann, Steve 340
Breslin, John G. 235
Bruton, Ken 227
Buhagiar, Aaron John 22

Cameron, David 71
Canonico, Roberto 308
Centomo, Stefano 184
Chaudhary, Hafiz Ahmad Awais 195, 406
Clancy, Rose 227

Dai, Xiaotian 37
De Marchi, Mirco 184
Demrozi, Florenc 184
Dimarogkona, Maria 382

Eisenberg, Martin 54

Fan, Xiuyi 246
Fantechi, Alessandro 243, 269
Ferrari, Alessio 246
Fitzgerald, John 3, 139
Flammini, Francesco 308
Freitas, Leo 22

Ghosal, Amrita 195
Gnesi, Stefania 243, 269
Gomes, Cláudio 3, 89, 159
Gori, Gloria 269
Gorm Larsen, Peter 3
Guevara, Ivan 195, 406

Hallerstede, Stefan 159
Hatledal, Lars Ivar 110
Haxthausen, Anne E. 243, 246, 286
Hessenkämper, Axel 337
Howar, Falk 337
Hryshchenko, Andriy 227
Hungar, Hardi 337

Ishikawa, Fuyuki 9

Jahnke, Brian-Frederik 366
James, Phillip 246
John, Jobish 195
Johnsen, Einar Broch 71

Kamburjan, Eduard 71
Kanazawa, Motoyasu 110
Kavassalis, Petros 382
Klungre, Vidar Norstein 71
Ksystra, Katerina 382
Kulik, Tomas 159
Kuruppuarachchi, Pasindu 208

Larsen, Peter Gorm 22, 159
Lawrence, Andrew 246
Lecomte, Thierry 286, 321
Lehner, Daniel 54
Lekić, Aleksandra 126
Lesage, Benjamin 37
Li, Guoyuan 110
Liu, Le 126
Luttik, Bas 246

Macedo, Hugo Daniel 159
Margaria, Tiziana 3, 179, 195, 406
Marrone, Stefano 308
McGibney, Alan 179, 208, 219
Morris, Liam 227

Nardone, Roberto 308

O'Sullivan, Dominic 227

Pampus, Julia 366
Peleska, Jan 286
Pesch, Dirk 179, 195
Popov, Marjan 126
Pravadelli, Graziano 184

Quaglia, Davide 184
Quensel, Ronja 366

Rausch, Andreas 337
Rea, Susan 208

Schlatte, Rudolf 71
Scott III, William E. 22
Seisenberger, Monika 246
Sindelar, Radek 54
Singh, Amandeep 195
Skulstad, Robert 110
Soderi, Mirco 235
Soudjani, Sadegh 139
Stankaitis, Paulius 139
Stefaneas, Petros 382
Steffen, Barbara 340

Tarifa, S. Lizeth Tapia 71
ter Beek, Maurice H. 246
Triantafyllou, Nikolaos 382
Turetta, Cristian 184

van de Pol, Jaco 246
Vittorini, Valeria 308

Wang, Tongtong 110
Wimmer, Manuel 54
Wimmer, Simon 246
Woodcock, Jim 3, 89
Wright, Thomas 89

Yue, Tao 9

Zhang, Houxiang 110
Zhao, Shuai 37

Printed in the United States
by Baker & Taylor Publisher Services

Printed in the United States
by Baker & Taylor Publisher Services